Praise for

Programming Microsoft Visual C# 2005: The Language

"How deep do you want to go? Most books only skim the surface of many topics, but Donis Marshall's book will take you as deep as you want to go in every topic. I'm excited to see that Donis is sharing his vast knowledge and I hope to see future books from him."

—Glenn Johnson; Author of *Microsoft ASP.NET Step by Step* (Microsoft Press)

"Donis Marshall is easily the best C# and C++ trainer in the business. His deep practical knowledge combined with a talent for knowledge transfer is legendary. Given that, this book is a crucial resource for any developer serious about going deeper into C#."

—John Alexander; Director, Visionpace, Microsoft Regional Director, Kansas City

"Donis Marshall's book does not just give the reader a roadmap to C#; it delivers the keys to being a better .NET developer. Donis' expert knowledge of the many topics gets the reader to think about programming C# from multiple levels. If you develop in C#, this book should be the cornerstone of your collection."

—John Bruno; Systems Consultant, NCCI Holdings, Inc.

"This book covers C#, the internal workings of the .NET Framework, much better than any other book on the market because Donis has such a vast amount of knowledge on this subject. I'm excited to see that Donis is sharing this knowledge and I hope to see more books from him in the future."

—Amy Vargo; Technical Account Manager, Microsoft Corporation

"Donis Marshall really has written the 'core reference' book. His practical experience and deep understanding of .NET are revealed on every page."

—Richard Hundhausen; Microsoft Regional Director, MVP for Visual Developer–Visual Studio Team System

Microsoft®

Programming Microsoft® Visual C#® 2005: The Language

Donis Marshall

PUBLISHED BY
Microsoft Press
A Division of Microsoft Corporation
One Microsoft Way
Redmond, Washington 98052-6399

Library of Congress Control Number 2005934153

Printed and bound in the United States of America.

3 4 5 6 7 8 9   QWT   0 9 8 7 6

Distributed in Canada by H.B. Fenn and Company Ltd.

A CIP catalogue record for this book is available from the British Library.

Microsoft Press books are available through booksellers and distributors worldwide. For further information about international editions, contact your local Microsoft Corporation office or contact Microsoft Press International directly at fax (425) 936-7329. Visit our Web site at www.microsoft.com/mspress. Send comments to mspinput@microsoft.com.

Acquisitions Editor: Ben Ryan
Project Editor: Valerie Woolley
Technical Editor: James D. Rogers
Copy Editor: Nancy Sixsmith
Indexer: Tony Ross and Lee Ross

Body Part No. X11-50074

This book is dedicated to my father, Herbert Marshall. He was a nuclear engineer, an artist, a confidant, a doting husband to my mother, and most of all a compassionate person. He was a giant amongst men and touched innumerable lives. His three sons, including myself, miss him every day.

Contents at a Glance

Table of Contents

Acknowledgments

Programming Microsoft Visual C# 2005: The Language was completed with the collaboration of several people. I am credited on the cover, but the contribution of others is no less important. I want to especially acknowledge the contributions of Valerie Woolley, Ben Ryan, and Jim Rogers. If possible, they would also receive cover credit. Valerie was the project manager and provided support, encouragement, patience, and the occasional nudge when necessary. Ben, who was the acquisitions editor, had unyielding confidence in my ability, which is greatly appreciated. Jim Rogers was the technical editor and diligently reviewed hundreds of pages of manuscript and code. He helped assure the superb quality of the book.

I also want to thank John Bruno, who is an exceptional engineer, for reviewing and commenting on each chapter, which was very helpful.

Writing a book is an all-consuming project. Unfortunately, much of this burden is carried by friends and loved ones. I appreciate the patience and support of my mother, Lynn, and of my friends Herb, Jr., Chuck, and Patty, along with a long list of other friends who were treated shabbily during this project. Thanks for your understanding.

Finally, I want to acknowledge my children: Jason, Kristen, and Adam. They make every day special. They are my motivation. A special acknowledgment is reserved for Jason. During most of this project, Jason was stationed in Iraq as a Marine. He recently returned home safely. We are proud of you.

Introduction

Microsoft Visual C# 2005 includes several enhancements to earlier versions of the language. If you want to learn the new features of the language, *Programming Microsoft Visual C# 2005: The Language* offers detailed explanations of each improvement. One of the most awaited additions to the .NET environment is generics. Other additions include anonymous methods, static classes, and new classes that affect garbage collection. This book introduces these new features, provides context, and displays sample code.

Enhancements are not limited to the language. The Microsoft Visual Studio IDE has also been enhanced in Visual Studio 2005. Microsoft continues to expand upon the impressive assortment of rapid application development (RAD) tools that are available. The Exception Assistant, code snippets, and visualizers are some of the more notable advancements, where the emphasis is on providing helpful information that markedly increases developer productivity. This book details these and other improvements to previous versions of Visual Studio.

A larger portion of the lifetime of an application is spent in maintenance and debugging. Efficient and effective debugging tools and techniques can facilitate a more robust application, which reduces the need to debug. You can also resolve problems more quickly when they inevitably occur. A managed application has a managed veneer and an unmanaged underpinning. Debugging requires an understanding of both realms where a managed application exists: managed and unmanaged. From a debugging context, Chapter 12 examines both realms of a managed application and helps developers understand how to effectively debug a managed application.

Who Is This Book For?

Programming Microsoft Visual C# 2005: The Language is for developers who want a comprehensive explanation of Visual C# 2005 or want to explore a specific aspect of the language. It is a composite of chapters sequenced to provide a rational and complete review of the language. Each chapter is also reviewable as an independent unit that encapsulates a specific topic.

This book targets both professional and casual developers. Practical, in-depth explanations are offered for even the most ardent developers. Sample code is provided as a complement to the content. For casual developers, code is often the clearest explanation of in-depth concepts. Actually, even for professional developers, sample code is often invaluable. For this reason, this book contains reams of code examples.

Organization of This Book

Programming Microsoft Visual C# 2005: The Language is organized into five parts.

The first part, "Core Language," introduces the basic concepts of the language. Chapter 1 contains a general overview of the language. Chapter 2 introduces types, which include classes and value types. Chapter 3 explains inheritance in C# and the related keywords, such as *virtual*, *override*, *sealed*, and *abstract*.

The second part, "Core Skills," covers the core skills required to create a C# application. Chapter 4 reviews Visual Studio 2005, which is the central tool in developing a managed application. Chapter 5 explains arrays and collections. It is hard to imagine a competent C# application that does not employ arrays or collections. Chapter 6 introduces generics, which is a new feature of .NET Framework 2.0. Chapter 7 pertains to iterators and the capability to enumerate collection-related classes.

The third part, "More C# Language," focuses on additional language features. Chapter 8 details managed function pointers, which are represented by delegates and events in managed code. Chapter 9 explains structured exception handling in the run time and within the C# language.

The fourth part, "Debugging," is an all-inclusive explanation of debugging managed code. The first two chapters in this section provide an internal view of an assembly, which is critical for anyone debugging a managed application: Chapter 10 introduces metadata and reflection; Chapter 11 is an overview of Microsoft intermediate language (MSIL) programming. Chapter 12 discusses debugging with Visual Studio, which is the preferred debugging environment for most developers. Finally, Chapter 13 discusses advanced debugging using the MDbg, Windbg, and SOS debugger extensions.

The final part is "Advanced Concepts." Chapter 14 covers managed memory and garbage collection in the managed environment. Chapter 15 explains unsafe code and direct pointer manipulation. This chapter also discusses calling functions that are in unmanaged (native) libraries.

System Requirements

You'll need the following hardware and software to build and run the code samples for this book:

- Microsoft Windows XP with Service Pack 2, Microsoft Windows Server 2003 with Service Pack 1, or Microsoft Windows 2000 with Service Pack 4

- Microsoft Visual Studio 2005 Standard Edition or Microsoft Visual Studio 2005 Professional Edition

- 600 MHz Pentium or compatible processor (1 GHz Pentium recommended)

- 192 MB RAM (256 MB or more recommended)

- Video (800 × 600 or higher resolution) monitor with at least 256 colors (1024 × 768 High Color 16-bit recommended)

- 2 GB available space on installation drive; 1 GB available space on system drive. With MSDN, the hard disk requirements are 2.8 GB and 1 GB, respectively.

- CD-ROM or DVD-ROM drive

- Microsoft Mouse or compatible pointing device

Technology Updates

As technologies related to this book are updated, links to additional information will be added to the Microsoft Press Technology Updates Web page. Visit this page periodically for updates on Visual Studio 2005 and other technologies:

http://www.microsoft.com/mspress/updates/

Code Samples

All the code samples discussed in this book can be downloaded from the book's companion content Web page at the following address:

http://www.microsoft.com/mspress/companion/0-7356-2181-0/

Support for This Book

Every effort has been made to ensure the accuracy of this book and the companion content. As corrections or changes are collected, they will be added to a Microsoft Knowledge Base article. To view the list of known corrections for this book, visit the following article:

http://support.microsoft.com/kb/905044

Microsoft Press provides support for books and companion content at the following Web site:

http://www.microsoft.com/learning/support/books/

Questions and Comments

If you have comments, questions, or ideas regarding the book or the companion content, or questions that are not answered by visiting the previous sites, please send them to Microsoft Press via e-mail to

mspinput@microsoft.com

Or via postal mail to

Microsoft Press

Attn: *Developer Series* Editor

One Microsoft Way

Redmond, WA 98052-6399

Please note that Microsoft software product support is not offered through the preceding addresses.

Part I
Core Language

In this part:

Chapter 1

Introduction to Visual C# Programming

Microsoft Visual C# 2005 is an object-oriented programming language used to develop applications targeting the .NET environment. Programming languages are not unlike natural languages such as Spanish, Latin, French, Chinese, or English—human languages that are written or spoken. Each natural language includes rules that describe proper syntax and structure; we use these rules to convey cohesive thoughts and ideas. A natural language also evolves over time, sometimes from or within a genus of other languages. Programming languages share many of these attributes and also include rules for proper syntax and structure and often evolve from other languages.

Acquiring proficiency in a programming language is similar to obtaining a high level of competency in a natural language. Having acquired a level of competency in FORTRAN, Turkish, English, COBOL, Spanish, German, C, and other languages (not necessarily in that order), I speak from experience. Languages are languages. When you're learning a human language, your goals are literacy and being able to have a conversation. If, as a student of French, you can sit in a Parisian café and read the menu while discussing current events with the locals, your language skills are a *fait accompli*. The goal of this chapter is the same: for you to become conversational in C#.

Learning a language typically begins with core elements of language. In English, these elements include consonants, vowels, nouns, verbs, adjectives, phrases, and sentences. They represent the building blocks of the language; you cannot read, write, or speak English without a fundamental understanding of these language components. The key elements of C# are symbols and tokens, keywords, expressions, statements, functions, and classes. Effective C# programming requires, of course, a fundamental understanding of these elements, which this chapter will provide.

As you know, a sentence in English is more than random words terminated with a period. Likewise, in C#, a programming statement is more than a collection of random clauses. The following English sentence and C# statement are both nonsensical:

Programming fun is C#.

```
for(i<5;int i=0;++i)
```

In both cases, the correct elements are present, but the structure is incorrect. Using either a human language or a programming language to convey cohesive ideas, concepts, tasks, or instructions requires organizing the words and other elements of the language correctly. In the English language, syntax (the rules of a language) indicates where a linking verb is placed in relation to the noun object. By comparison, C# syntax orders the clauses of a *for* statement. According to C# syntax, the previous *for* statement should be structured like this: *for(int i=0;i<5;++i)*. Understanding the underlying language syntax is equally important for natural and programming languages. This chapter will also provide the basic syntax of the C# language.

Mandarin Chinese is a tonal language, whereas English is a stress language. Learning Chinese is more than simply assimilating new words and sentence structures. You must also learn tones because the meaning of a Chinese word can change based on tone. Speaking Chinese with English enunciation would be confusing and amusing at best. Similarly, C# is an object-oriented language, not a procedural language (more on this difference later). C#, C++, Java, SmallTalk, Eiffel, and other object-oriented languages are only as effective as your appreciation of object-oriented concepts and programming techniques. I recommend a basic knowledge of object-oriented analysis and design concepts as a complement to the newly acquired C# skills this book will give you.

Finally, languages do not emerge spontaneously. Natural languages have been evolving for nearly 150,000 years, and knowing the heritage of and the influences on a language can be informative and helpful. For example, English, French, German, Yiddish, and related languages are heavily influenced by their Latin language heritage. As such, they have common words, syntax, and structures that are characteristic of the Latin metalanguage. The origin of C# does not date back centuries, but an understanding of its evolution is invaluable.

Language Origin

From the time when the first natural language appeared, hundreds of thousands of languages have emerged. Many of these languages are now extinct, leaving about six thousand languages that are currently spoken. Some of these languages are similar and grouped by classification.

Other languages are quite distinct, such as Kora, which incorporates a series of click sounds and is spoken by bushmen in Africa.

A list of programming languages is modest when compared with the catalogue of natural languages. Beginning in the 1940s with Plankalkül, more than 1,000 programming languages have been documented. Like natural languages, the variety and diversity of these languages is impressive: the succinctness of assembler, the verbosity of COBOL, and the efficiency of C. For a comprehensive list of programming languages, visit this link: *http://oop.rosweb.ru/ Other/*.

The motivations that inspire the creation of languages are diverse: FORTRAN was created for scientific analysis, COBOL for building business applications, RPG for report genera-tion, and so on. Some languages serve as refinements of earlier languages. CPL combined the best ingredients of several languages, including ALGOL, FORTRAN, and COBOL. C# is an independently developed, object-oriented language and a member of the C family of languages. It shares similar syntax and some concepts with other C-family languages; more important, however, C# has few if any vestiges of procedural programming, in which the basic programming element is the procedure (that is, a named sequence of statements, such as a routine, subroutine, or function). Unfortunately, C++ inherited many of the artifacts of procedural programming from C. C#, however, was designed to be a purely object-oriented language.

ALGOL is arguably the most influential programming language in history. The language was introduced in 1958 but became popular when ALGOL-60 was released in 1960. ALGOL quickly became the dominant language in Europe during the 1960s. Its impact on future languages such as Pascal, C, and Java is undeniable—these languages' grammatical syntax borrows heavily from ALGOL. I've programmed professionally in ALGOL, assembler, COBOL, FORTRAN, C, C++, C#, Basic (in various renditions), Forth, JavaScript, HTML, XML, MISL, and many more—and ALGOL remains my favorite language. The major design goals of ALGOL were portability, a formal grammar, and support for algorithms. ALGOL-68 extended the language, but the additions increased complexity and furthered abstraction from hardware. This abstraction prevented developers from easily accessing devices and the lower tiers of the operating environment. Soon, languages were introduced that were less complex and not as abstracted from the architecture. One of these new languages was C.

The journey from ALGOL to C began with CPL. CPL, a derivative of ALGOL-60, was devel-oped at the Computer Lab of Cambridge University. CPL was created in 1963 by David Barron, Christopher Strachey, and Martin Richards. Although CPL is not as abstracted as ALGOL, it did maintain one characteristic of ALGOL: complexity. Martin Richards intro-duced Basic CPL (BCPL) in 1967 as a lean version of CPL. Ken Thompson of Bell Labs drafted B in 1970 as the successor to BCPL. B was lighter, faster, and more appropriate for systems programming. C was developed by Dennis Ritchie, also of Bell Labs, in 1972. C returned some of the abstraction removed from B while keeping that language simple and quick. Although initially consigned to the UNIX operation system and systems programming, C is a general-purpose language and has been used for a diverse assortment of applications across a variety of platforms and operating systems.

FORTAN, ALGOL, and COBOL dominated the procedural programming landscape in the 1960s. On a separate track, Simula was created between 1962 and 1965 by Ole-Johan Dahl and Kristen Nygaard at the Norwegian Computing Center. Simula is notable for being the first object-oriented programming (OOP) language. It was designed for simulation, but evolved into a general-purpose language. Simula introduced the important OOP concepts of classes, inheritance, and dynamic binding.

Combining aspects of C and Simula, Bjarne Stroustrup introduced C with Classes in 1979 as an enhancement of the C programming language. Later, under Stroustrup's stewardship, C++ was created as a direct descendant of C with Classes and was publicly recognized in 1983. C++ rapidly became the premier object-oriented programming language and introduced structured exception handling, templates, and much more.

C# premiered at the Professional Developers Conference (PDC) held in Orlando, Florida, in 2000. The primary architects of C# were Anders Hejlsberg, Scott Wiltamuth, Peter Sollichy, Eric Gunnerson, and Peter Golde. C# was designed to be a fully object-oriented language focusing on developing components in a distributed environment and was launched as part of a larger initiative by Microsoft called Microsoft .NET. Underscoring the importance of .NET to Microsoft, Bill Gates was the keynote speaker at the PDC that year. I attended the PDC in 2000 and was both intrigued and motivated by the introduction of .NET and C#. .NET is emblematic of a philosophical change at Microsoft and an embracing of the standards community.

Both .NET, as defined by the Common Language Infrastructure (CLI), and C# were submitted to two international standards organizations: ECMA and ISO/IEC. Also, .NET and .NET languages, described in the Common Language Specification (CLS), continue the trend toward truly portable code. You can write an application in one environment and run it anywhere else. Simultaneously, a new version of Microsoft Visual Studio was announced: Visual Studio .NET. Visual Studio .NET provides rapid application development tools for developing a wide variety of .NET applications.

More Info   For information on the various standards for C# and .NET, follow these links. The current ECMA standards for the C# Language Specification:http://www.ecma-international.org/publications/standards/Ecma-334.htm. The current ECMA standards for the Common Language Infrastructure: http://www.ecma-international.org/publications/standards/Ecma-335.htm. The current ISO/IEC standards for the C# Language Specification: http://www.iso.org/iso/en/CatalogueDetailPage.CatalogueDetail?CSNUMBER=36768&ICS1=35&ICS2=60&ICS3=. The current ISO/IEC standards for the CLI: http://www.iso.org/iso/en/CatalogueDetailPage.CatalogueDetail?CSNUMBER=36769&scopelist=.

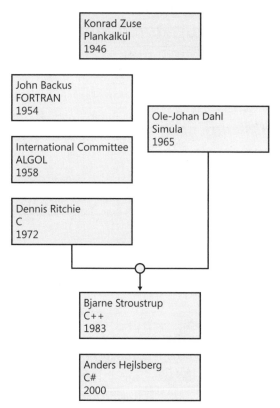

Figure 1-1   Evolution of programming languages from inception to C#

C# Core Language Features

Natural and programming languages consist of both simple and complex structures. The complex structures can be decomposed into simple elements. When learning a new natural language, you probably wouldn't start with a review of sentence structure. Instead, you probably would begin with an exploration of nouns, verbs, and the simpler components of the language. For C#, the simpler components are symbols, tokens, white space, punctuators, comments, preprocessor statements, and other elements. This is an excellent place to start when learning C#.

Symbols and Tokens

Symbols and tokens are the basic constituents of the C# language. Sentences are composed of spaces, tabs, and characters. Similarly, C# statements consist of symbols and tokens. Indeed, statements cannot be articulated without an understanding of these basic elements. Table 1-1 provides a list of the C# tokens.

Table 1-1   C# Symbols and Tokens

Description	Symbols or Tokens
White space	*Space*
Tab	*Horizontal_tab, Vertical_tab*
Punctuator	. , : ;
Line terminator	*carriage_returns*
Comment	// /* */ /// /**
Preprocessor directive	#
Block	{}
Generics	< >
Nullable Type	?
Character	*Unicode_character*
Escape character	\code
Numeric Suffix	f d m u l ul lu
Operator	+, -, >, <, *, ??, ( ) and so on

White Space

White space is defined as a space, horizontal tab, vertical tab, or form feed character. White space characters can be combined; where one character is required, two or more contiguous characters of white space can be substituted. Where white space is permitted, one or more instances of white space are allowed.

Tabs

Tabs—horizontal and vertical—are white space characters. Refer to the preceding explanation of white space.

Punctuators

Punctuators separate and delimit elements of the C# language. Punctuators include the semi-colon (;), dot (.), colon (:), and comma (,), which are discussed in this section.

Semicolon punctuator   In a natural language, sentences consist of phrases and clauses and are units of cohesive expression. Sentences are terminated with a period (.). Statements consist of one or more expressions and are the commands of the C# programming language. Statements are terminated by a semicolon (;). C# is a free-form language in which a statement can span multiple lines of source code and start in any position. Conversely, multiple statements can be combined on a single source code line, assuming that each statement is delimited by a semicolon. This statement is not particularly good style, but it is syntactically correct:

```
int variablea=
        variableb +
            variablec;
```

Dot punctuator   Dot syntax connotes membership. The dot character (.) binds a target to a member, in which the target can be a namespace, type, structure, enumeration, interface, or object. This assumes the member is accessible. Membership is sometimes nested and therefore described with multiple dots.

Dot punctuator:

Target..Member

This is an example of the dot punctuator:

```
System.Windows.Forms.MessageBox.Show("A nice day!")
```

Colon punctuator   The colon punctuator is used primarily to delimit a label, to describe inheritance, to indicate the implementation of an interface, to set a generic constraint, and as part of the conditional operator. (The conditional operator, the only ternary operator in C#, is reviewed later in this chapter. Inheritance and generic constraints are discussed in later chapters.) Labels are tags where program execution can be transferred. A label is terminated with a colon punctuator. The scope of a label is limited to the containing block and any nested block. Jump to a label with the *goto* statement.

Label punctuator:

label_identifier: statement

A statement must follow a label, even if it's an empty statement.

Comma punctuator   The comma punctuator delimits array indexes, function parameters, types of an inheritance list, statement clauses, and most other lists of C# language elements. The comma punctuator is separating statement clauses in the following code:

```
for(int iBottom=1, iTop=10; iBottom < iTop; ++iBottom, --iTop) {
        Console.WriteLine("{0}x{1} {2}", iBottom, iTop, iBottom*iTop);
}
```

A statement clause is similar to a sentence phrase or clause, which are also sometimes delimited by commas. A statement clause is a substatement in which multiple statement clauses can be substituted for a single statement. Not all statements are replaceable with statement clauses—check the documentation of the statement to be sure.

Line Terminators

Line terminators separate lines of source code. A carriage-return, line-feed, line-separator, and paragraph-separator are the line terminators of C#. Where one line terminator is inserted, two or more are acceptable. Line terminators can be inserted anywhere white space is allowed. The following code is syntactically incorrect:

```
int variablea=var
        iableb+variablec;
```

As an identifier, *variablea* cannot contain spaces. Thus, line terminators are also disallowed.

Comments

C# supports four styles of comments: single-line, delimited, single-line documentation, and delimited documentation comments. Comments cannot be nested. Although comments are not mandated, liberal comments are considered good programming style. Self-documenting code and comments in your source code aid in later maintenance. Be kind to the maintenance program—comment! In *Code Complete, Second Edition*, (Microsoft Press, 2004), Steve McConnell gives valuable best practices on programming, including how to properly document your source code.

Single-line comments: //   Single-line comments start at the symbol and end at the line terminator:

```
Console.WriteLine(objGreeting.French);  // Display Hello (French)
```

Delimited comments: /* and */   Delimited comments, also called multiline or block comments, are bracketed by the /* and */ symbols. Delimited comments can span multiple lines of source code:

```
/*
        Class Program: Programmer Donis Marshall
*/
class Program {
    static int Main(string[] args) {
        Greeting objGreeting = new Greeting();// Display Hello (French)
        Console.WriteLine(objGreeting.French);
        return 0;
    }
}
```

Single-line documentation comments: ///   Use documentation comments to apply a consistent format to source code comments. Documentation comments precede types, members, parameters, delegates, enums, and structs; they do not precede namespaces. Documentation comments use XML tags to classify comments. These comments are exportable to an XML file using the documentation generator. The resulting file is called the documentation file, which can be bound to a Visual Studio project to augment the information presented in IntelliSense and the Object Browser.

Single-line documentation comments are automated in the Visual Studio IDE, which makes them more popular than delimited documentation comments. Visual Studio IDE has Smart Comment Editing that inserts the comment framework after immediately inputting the /// symbol.

The following code snippet shows the previous code after preceding the *Main* method with a single-line documentation comment ///. From there, Smart Comment Editing completed the remainder of the comment framework, including adding comments and XML tags for the method parameter and return. You only need to add specific comments.

```
/// <summary>
///
/// </summary>
class Program {
/// <summary>
///
/// </summary>
/// <param name="args"></param>
/// <returns></returns>
   static int Main(string[] args) {
        Greeting objGreeting = new Greeting();
        Console.WriteLine(objGreeting.French
        return 0;
    }
}
```

Here are the documentation comments with added details:

```
/// <summary>
/// Starter class for Simple HelloWorld
/// </summary>
class Program {
   /// <summary>
   /// Program Entry Point
   /// </summary>
   /// <param name="args">Command Line Parameters</param>
   /// <returns>zero</returns>
   static int Main(string[] args) {
        Greeting objGreeting = new Greeting();
        Console.WriteLine(objGreeting.French);
        return 0;
    }
}
```

The C# compiler is a documentation generator. The /doc compiler option instructs the compiler to generate the documentation file. Alternatively, you can request that the documentation file be generated in the Visual Studio IDE. Select the Properties menu item from the Project menu. From the Properties window, switch to the Build options. In the Build pane (see Figure 1-2), you can activate and enter the name of the XML documentation file.

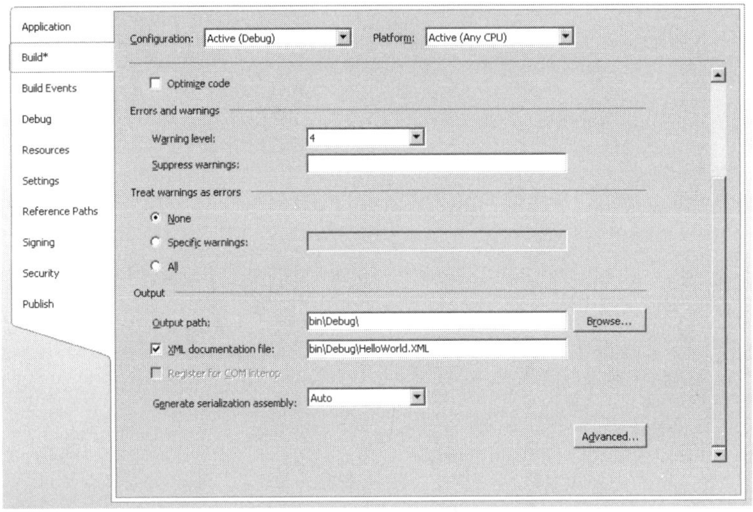

Figure 1-2 The Build pane of the Project Settings window

Delimited documentation tags Delimited documentation tags can be used instead of the single-line version. Smart Comment Editing is not available with delimited documentation tags. Documentation symbols, XML tags, and comments must be entered manually, which is the primary impediment to using delimited documentation tags. Here is an example of delimited documentation tags:

```
/**<summary>
Starter class for Simple HelloWorld</summary>
*/
```

This is the documentation file generated by the C# compiler from the preceding source code:

```
<?xml version="1.0" ?>
<doc>
<assembly>
    <name>HelloWorld</name>
</assembly>
<members>
    <member name="T:HelloWorld.Program">
        <summary>Starter class for Simple HelloWorld</summary>
    </member>
    <member name="M:HelloWorld.Program.Main(System.String[])">
        <summary />
        <param name="args" />
        <returns />
    </member>
</members>
</doc>
```

The documentation generator assigns IDs to element names. T is the prefix for a type, whereas M is a prefix for a method. Here's a listing of IDs:

E	Event
F	Field
M	Method
N	Namespace
P	Property
T	Type
!	Error

Preprocessor Directives

Use preprocessor directives to define symbols, include source code, exclude source code, name sections of source code, and set warning and error conditions. The variety of preprocessor directives is limited when compared with C++, and many of the C++ preprocessor directives are not available in C#. There is not a separate preprocessor for preprocessor statements. Preprocessor statements are processed by the normal C# compiler. The term "preproccesor" is used for historical connotations only.

Preprocessor directive:

#command expression

This is a list of preprocessor commands available in C#:

#define	*#undef*	*#if*
#else	*#elif*	*#endif*
#line	*#error*	*#warning*
#region	*#endregion*	*#pragma*

The preprocessor symbol and subsequent command are optionally separated with a space, but must be on the same line. For this reason, preprocessor commands can be followed only with a single line comment.

Declarative preprocessor directives   The declarative preprocessor directives are *#define* and *#undef*, which define and undefine a preprocessor symbol, respectively. Defined symbols are implicitly true, whereas undefined symbols are false. Declarative symbols must be defined in each compilation unit where the symbol is referenced. Undeclared symbols default to undefined and false. The *#define* and *#undef* directives must precede any source code. Redundant *#define* and *#undef* directives are trivial and have no affect.

Declarative preprocessor directives:

#define identifier

#undef identifier

Conditional preprocessor directives   Conditional preprocessor directives are the *#if*, *#else*, *#elif*, and *#endif* directives, which exclude or include subsequent source code. A conditional preprocessor directives begins with *#if* and ends with *#endif*. The intervening conditional preprocessing directives, *#else* and *#elif*, are optional.

Conditional preprocessor directives:

#if boolean_expression

#elif boolean_expression

#else

#endif

The *boolean_expression* of the *#if* and *#elif* directive is a combination of preprocessor symbols and normal Boolean operators. If the *boolean_expression* is true, the source code immediately after the *#if* or *#elif* directive is included in the compilation. If the *boolean_expression* is false, the source code is hidden. The *#else* directive can be combined with an *#if* or *#elif* directive. If the *boolean_expression* of *#if* or *#elif* is false, the code following the *#else* is included in the compilation. When true, the source code after the *#else* is hidden. Here's sample code with preprocess symbols and related directives:

```
#define DEBUGGING

using System;

namespace Donis.CSharpBook {
    class Starter{
#if DEBUGGING
        static void OutputLocals() {
            Console.WriteLine("debugging...");
        }
#endif
        static void Main() {
#if DEBUGGING
            OutputLocals();
#endif
        }
    }
}
```

Finally, the *#elif* directive essentially nests *#if* conditional preprocessor directives:

```
#if expression
    source_code
#elif expression
    source_code
#else
    source_code
#endif
```

Diagnostic directives   Diagnostic directives include the *#error*, *#warning*, and *#pragma* directives. The *#error* and *#warning* directives display error and warning messages, correspondingly. The diagnostic messages are displayed in the Error List window of the Visual Studio IDE. Similar to standard compilation errors, an *#error* directive prevents the program from compiling; a *#warning* directive does not prevent the program from successfully compiling. Use conditional directives to conditionally apply diagnostic directives.

Diagnostic directives:

```
#error error_message
#warning error_message
```

The *error_message* is of string type and is optional.

The *#pragma* directive enables or disables standard compilation warnings.

Pragma directives:

```
#pragma warning disable warning_list
#pragma warning restore warning_list
```

The *warning_list* contains one or more warnings delimited with commas. The status of a warning included in the *warning_list* remains unchanged until the end of the compilation unit unless altered in a later *#error* directive.

This *#pragma* directive disables the 219 warning, which is the "variable is assigned but its value is never used" warning:

```
#pragma warning disable 219
    class Starter{
        static void Main() {
         int variablea=10;
         }
    }
```

Region directives   Region directives mark sections of source code. The *#region* directive starts a region, whereas the *#endregion* directive ends the region. Region directives can be nested. The Visual Studio IDE outlines the source code using region tags. In Visual Studio, you can collapse or expand regions of source code.

Region directives:

```
#region identity
source_code
#endregion
```

Line directives   Line directives modify the line number reported in subsequent compiler errors and warnings. There are three versions of the line directive.

Line directives:

```
#line line_number source_filename
#line default
#line hidden
```

The first *#line* directive shown renumbers the source code from the location of the directive until the end of the compilation unit is reached or overridden by another *#line* directive. In the following code, the *#line* directive resets the current line to 25:

```
#line 25
static void Main() {
    Console.WriteLine("#line application");
    int variablea=10;   // 219 warning
}
```

The second type of *#line* directive resets or undoes any previous *#line* directive. The line number is reset to the natural line number.

The third *#line* directive is only tangentially related to the line number. This directive does not affect the line number; it hides source code from the debugger. Excluding another *#line* hidden directive, the source code is hidden until the next *#line* directive is encountered.

Blocks

Blocks define the scope of a type, where type is a class, struct, or enum. Additionally, members of the type are listed inside the block.

Block:

```
type typename{  // block
}
```

Blocks are used as compound statements. Paragraphs join related sentences that convey an extended thought or concept. A statement block combines related statements as a single entity. In this context, a statement block is a compound statement and can contain one or more statements. Each statement of the statement block is delimited by a semicolon. In most circumstances in which a single statement is allowed, a statement block can be substituted. Statement blocks are prevalent as method bodies but are used with conditional and iterative statements.

The *if* statement in the following code, which is a conditional statement, controls a single statement. The *Console.WriteLine* is controlled by the *if* statement that precedes it, so a statement block is not required.

```
static void Main() {
    int variablea=5, variableb=10;
    if(((variablea*variableb)%2)==0)
        Console.WriteLine("the sum is even");
}
```

In the modified code, the *if* statement controls multiple statements, and a statement block is needed. Some would suggest, and I agree, that always using statement blocks with conditional statements is a good practice. This prevents a possible future omission when additional statements are added to the realm of the conditional statement:

```
static void Main() {
    int variablea=5, variableb=10;
    if(((variablea*variableb)%2)==0) {
        Console.WriteLine("{0} {1}", variablea,
            variableb);
        Console.WriteLine("the sum is even");
    }
}
```

Generic Types

Generic types are templated types. A type is an abstraction of identity: a car class is an abstraction of a type of car, an employee class is an abstraction of an employee, and a generic type is an abstraction of the specifics of a type.

The *NodeInt* class partially implements and is an abstraction of a node within a linked list of integers:

```
class NodeInt {
    public NodeInt(int f_Value, NodeInt f_Previous) {
        m_Value=f_Value;
        m_Previous=f_Previous;
    }

    // Remaining methods

    private int m_Value;
    private NodeInt m_Previous;
}
```

The *Node* class is further abstracted when compared with the *NodeInt* class. The integer specifics of the *NodeInt* class have been removed. This resulting type could be a link list of any type:

```
class Node<T> {
    public Node(T f_Value, Node<T> f_Previous) {
```

```
        m_Value=f_Value;
        m_Previous=f_Previous;
    }

    // Remaining methods

    private T m_Value;
    private Node<T> m_Previous;
}
```

The generics symbol bounds the type parameters, which is *T* in the preceding program.

There is much more about generics later in the book.

Nullable Types

Nullable types are value types that can be assigned a null value. Nullable types provide a consistent mechanism for determining whether a value type is empty (null).

Nullable type:

```
valuetype? identifier;
```

Nullable types are discussed in detail later in this chapter.

Characters

C# source files contain Unicode characters, which are the most innate of symbols. (Every element, keyword, operator, or identifier in the source file is a composite of Unicode characters.)

Numeric Suffixes

Numeric suffixes cast a literal value to a related type. Literal integer values can have the L, U, UL, and LU suffixes appended to them; literal real values can have the F, D, and M suffixes added. The suffixes are case insensitive. Table 1-2 describes each suffix.

Table 1-2   Description of Suffixes

Description	Type	Suffix
Unsigned integer or unsigned long	uint or long	u
Long or unsigned long	long or ulong	l
Unsigned long	ulong	ul
Float	float	f
Double	double	d
Money	decimal	m

When casting a real type using the M suffix, rounding might be required. If so, banker's rounding is used, which rounds to the nearest possible value. If midway between two values, the even number is returned. Gaussian rounding, albeit harder to pronounce, is another name for banker's rounding.

Here is an example:

```
int variable=10u;
```

The next statement causes a compile error. You cannot append a real suffix to an integral literal value because they are not related types.

```
long variable = 456f;
```

Escape Characters

The escape character provides an alternate means of encoding Unicode characters, especially special characters that are not available on a standard keyboard. Escape sequences can be used as characters within identifiers and elsewhere.

Unicode escape sequences must have four hexadecimal digits and are therefore limited to a single character.

Escape sequence:

```
\uhexadecimal digit1 digit2 digit3 digit4
```

Hexadecimal escape sequences define one or more Unicode characters and contain one or more digits.

Hexadecimal sequence:

```
\xhexadecimal digit1 digit2 digitn
```

Table 1-3 shows a list of the predefined escape sequences in C#.

Table 1-3   Predefined Escape Sequences

Simple Escape	Sequence
Single quote	\'
Double quote	\"
Backlash	\\
Null	\0
Alert	\a
Backspace	\b
Form feed	\f
New line	\n
Carriage return	\r
Horizontal tab	\t

Table 1-3   Predefined Escape Sequences

Simple Escape	Sequence
Unicode character	\u
Vertical tab	\v
Hexadecimal character(s)	\x

This is an unconventional version of the traditional Hello World program:

```
class HelloWorld {
    static void Main() {
        Console.Write("\u0048\u0065\u006C\u006C\u006f\n");
        Console.Write("\x77\x6F\x72\x6c\x64\x21\b");
    }
}
```

Verbatim Characters

The verbatim character prevents the translation of a string or identifier, where it is treated "as-is." To create a verbatim string or identifier, prefix it with the verbatim character.

A verbatim string is a string literal prefixed with the verbatim character. The characters of the verbatim string, including escape sequences, are not translated. The exception is the quote escape character, which is translated even in a verbatim string. Unlike a normal string, verbatim strings can contain physical line feeds.

Here is a sample verbatim string:

```
class Verbatim{
    static void Main() {
    string fileLocation=@"c:\datafile.txt";
    Console.WriteLine("File is located at {0}",
            fileLocation);
      }
}
```

A verbatim identifier is an identifier prefixed with the verbatim character that prevents the identifier from being parsed as a keyword. Although this is of limited usefulness, porting source code from another language—in which the keywords are different—is a circumstance in which verbatim identifiers might be helpful. Otherwise, it is a best practice not to use this language feature because verbatim identifiers make your code less readable and harder to maintain.

This is a partial translation of French to English:

L'espoir is a waking dream.

Can you decipher this sentence? Unless you are fluent in French, the partial translation is inef-fectual at best. The original sentence was "L'espoir est un rêve de réveil." The following is an equally unskillful translation, although technically acceptable:

```
public class ExampleClass {
    public static void Function() {
        int @for = 12;
        MessageBox.Show(@for.ToString());
    }
}
```

In the preceding code, the *for* statement is being used as a variable name. Although technically acceptable, it is confusing at best. The *for* statement is common in C# and many other pro-gramming languages. For this reason, most developers would view the *for* as a statement regardless of the usage, which will inevitably lead to confusion.

Operators

Operators are used in expressions and always return a value. There are three categories of operators: unary, binary, and ternary. The following sections describe most of the operators in C#.

Unary operators   Table 1-4 is a list of unary operators.

- Unary operators have a single parameter.
- Prefix operators are evaluated before the encompassing expression.
- Postfix operators are evaluated after the encompassing expression.

Table 1-4   Unary Operators

Operator	Symbol	Sample
Unary Plus	+	*variable=+5; 5*
Unary minus	−	*variable=−(−10); 10*
Boolean Negation	!	*variable=!true; false*
Bitwise 1's complement	~	*variable=~((uint)1); 4294967294*
Prefix Increment	++	*++ variable; 11*
Prefix Decrement	−−	*−− variable; 10*
Postfix Increment	++	*variable ++; 11*
Postfix Decrement	−−	*variable −−; 10*
Cast Operator	( )	*variable =(int) 123.45; 123*
Function Operator	( )	*FunctionCall(parameter); return value*
Array Index Operator	[ ]	*arrayname[iIndex]; nth element*
Global Namespace Qualifier	::	

Binary operators   This section lists and discusses the use of binary operators.

- Binary operators have two operands: a left and right operand.

- Integer division truncates the floating point portion of the result.

- Bitwise Shift Left (*value* << *bitcount*).

- Bitwise Shift Right (*value* >> *bitcount*).

Table 1-5 details the binary operators.

Table 1-5   Binary Operators

Operator	Symbol	Sample	Result
Assignment	=	*variable=10;*	10
Binary Plus	+	*variable=variable + 5;*	15
Binary Minus	–	*variable=variable – 10;*	5
Multiplication	*	*variable=variable * 5;*	25
Division	/	*variable=variable / 5;*	5
Modulus	%	*variable=variable % 3;*	2
Logical And	&	*variable=5 & 3;*	1
Logical Or	|	*variable=5 | 3;*	7
Bitwise XOR	^	*variable=5 ^ 3;*	6
Bitwise Shift Left	<<	*variable=5 << 3;*	40
Bitwise Shift Right	>>	*variable=5 >> 1;*	2
Null Coalescing	??	*variableb=variablea??5*	2

Compound operators   Compound operators combine an assignment and another operator. If the expanded expression is '*variablea=variablea operator value*', the compound operator is '*variable operator= value*'.

```
variable=variable+5;
```

The preceding compound operation is equivalent to this:

```
variable+=5;
```

Compound operations are a shortcut and are never required in lieu of the expanded operation. Table 1-6 lists the compound operators.

Table 1-6   List of Compound Operators

Operator	Symbol	Sample
Addition Assignment	+=	*variable+=5;*
Subtraction Assignment	–=	*variable–=10;*
Multiplication Assignment	*=	*variable*=5;*
Division Assignment	/=	*variable/=5;*

Table 1-6   List of Compound Operators

Operator	Symbol	Sample
Modulus Assignment	%=	*variable%=3;*
And Assignment	&=	*variable&=3;*
Or Assignment	|=	*variable|=3;*
XOR Assignment	^=	*variable^= 3;*
Left-Shift Assignment	<<=	*variable<<=3;*
Right-Shift Assignment	>>=	*variable>>=1*

Boolean operators   Boolean expressions evaluate to true or false. The integer values of nonzero and zero cannot be substituted for a Boolean true or false.

There are two versions of the logical And and Or operators. The *&&* and *||* operators support short-circuiting, whereas *&* and *|* do not. What is short-circuiting? If the result of the expression can be determined with the left side, the right side is not evaluated. Without disciplined coding practices, short-circuiting might cause unexpected side effects.

This is an example of possible short-circuiting:

```
if(FunctionA() && FunctionB()) {

}
```

In the preceding code, assuming that *FunctionA* returns false, the entire expression evaluates to false. Therefore, the expression short-circuits and *FunctionB* is not invoked.

Table 1-7 shows the Boolean operators.

Table 1-7   List of Boolean Operators

Operator	Symbol
Equals	==
Not Equal	!=
Less Than	<
Greater Than	>
And (Short Circuiting)	&&
Or (Short Circuiting)	||
And	&
Or	|
Less Than or Equal	<=
Greater Than or Equal	>=
Logical XOR	^

Ternary operators   The conditional operator is the sole ternary operator in C# and is an abbreviated *if else* statement.

Conditional operator:

```
boolean_expression?truth_statement:false_statement
```

This is the conditional operator in source code:

```
variable>5?Console.WriteLine(">5"):Console.WriteLine("<= 5");
```

Pointer operators   Pointer operators are available in unsafe mode and support conventional pointers. The unsafe compiler option builds a program in unsafe mode. Alternatively, in Visual Studio IDE, set the Allow Unsafe Mode option on the Build Page of Project Settings. Table 1-8 includes the pointer operators.

Table 1-8   List of Pointer Operators

Operator	Symbol	Description
Asterisk Operator[1]	*	Declare a pointer
Asterisk Operator[2]	*	Dereference a pointer
Ampersand Operator	&	Obtain an address
Arrow Operator	->	Dereference a pointer and member access

Here is some sample code using pointers:

```
static void Main(string[] args)
{
   unsafe {
        int variable = 10;
        int* pVariable = &variable;
        Console.WriteLine("Value at address is {0}.",
             *pVariable);
   }
}
```

The above code must be compiled with the unsafe compiler option on. A more extensive review of pointers is presented later in the book.

Identifiers

An identifier is the name of a C# entity, which includes type, method, property, field, and other names. Identifiers can contain Unicode characters, escape character sequences, and underscores. A verbatim identifier is prefixed with the verbatim character (as discussed earlier in this chapter).

Keywords

One of the strengths of C# is that the language offers relatively few keywords. C# keywords represent the verbs, nouns, and adjectives of the language. The nouns of C# are instances of classes, structs, interfaces, delegates, and namespaces. Verbs infer an action. The *goto*, *for*, *while*, and similar keywords have that role in C#. The adjectives, including the *public*, *private*, *protected*, and *static* keywords, are modifiers of the C# nouns.

Table 1-9 is an overview of the C# keywords. Extended explanations of each keyword are provided in context at the appropriate location in the book.

Table 1-9   Overview of C# Keywords with Explanations

Keyword	Syntax	Explanation
abstract[1]	abstract class *identifier*	The class *identifier* cannot be instantiated.
abstract[2]	abstract *return identifier*	The method *identifier* is not implemented in the current class.
as	*identifier* as *type*	Casts object *identifier* to a related *type* or null.
base	base.*identifier*	Accesses the member *identifier* of the base class.
break	Break	Exits current loop or switch statement.
case	case *label*	Switch statements jumps to a matching case *label*.
catch	catch(*filter*)	Filters exceptions thrown from a try block.
checked[1]	checked(*expression*)	Exception is raised if *expression* overflows.
checked[2]	checked { *statement_block* }	Exception is raised if any expression within statement block overflows.
class	class *identity*	Defines a new class named *identity*.
const	const *type identity*	Declares a constant variable or member named *identity*. Constant instances cannot be modified at run time.
continue	Continue	Jumps to the end of a loop and starts a new iteration.
default	default	The default label to jump to in a switch statement.
delegate	delegate *return method*	Defines a type that holds function pointers.

Table 1-9 Overview of C# Keywords with Explanations

Keyword	Syntax	Explanation
do	do { *statement_block* } while(*expression*)	Defines a *do* loop with the iterative test at the end.
else	else { *statement_block* }	The *else* statement is matched to the nearest *if* statement and provides the false *statement_block*.
enum	enum *enumname*	Defines an enumeration type.
event	event *delegate_identifier identifier*	Defines an event named *identifier* of the *delegate_identifier* type.
explicit	explicit operator *conversiontype*	Using the user-defined conversion operator requires an explicit cast.
extern	extern *return method*	A method implemented externally.
false	false	A Boolean value.
finally	finally {*statement_block* }	Paired with a try block. Clean up or must exit code placed in finally *statement_block*.
fixed	fixed(*declaration*)	Fixes a pointer in memory and prevents relocation of variable by the garbage collector.
for	for(*initializers;boolean_expression;iterators*)	*For* loop that iterates until *boolean_expression* is false.
foreach	foreach(*element* in *enumerable_collection*)	Iterate *elements* in an *enumerable_collection*.
get	get	Accessor method of property member.
goto[1]	goto *identifier*	Jumps to a label named *identifier*.
goto[2]	goto case *identifier*	Jumps to an *identifier* label inside a *switch* statement.
goto[3]	goto default	Jumps to a default case inside a switch *statement*.
implicit	implicit operator *conversiontype*	When needed, a user-defined conversion operator casts implicitly. An explicit cast is not required.
in	foreach(*element* in *enumerable_collection*)	Iterate *elements* in an *enumerable_collection*.
interface	interface *identifier*	Defines an interface named *identifier*.
internal	internal *identifier*	*Identifier* is a type or method and accessible only within the current assembly.
is	*object* is *type*	Expression evaluates to true if *object* is related to *typename*; otherwise, evaluates to false.

Table 1-9   Overview of C# Keywords with Explanations

Keyword	Syntax	Explanation
lock	lock(*object*) {*statement_block*}	*Statement_blocks* locked with the same object are protected by a shared critical section.
namespace	namespace *identifier*	Creates a namespace called *identifier*.
new[1]	new *identifier*(*constructor*)	Allocates memory for a class *identifier* on a managed heap and returns a reference to the object.
new[2]	new *return method*	*Method* hides the same method in the base class.
null	null	Sets unused references and nullable value types to null.
object	object	Object is an alias for *System.Object*, which is the base class to all .NET objects (value or reference type).
operator	operator *operator_name*	Implements a user-defined *operator_name* in the current type.
readonly	readonly *type identifier*	*Identifier* is a field name and can be initialized at declaration or in a constructor only.
ref	ref *type parameter*	The actual *parameter* is passed into the method and can be modified. *Parameter* must be initialized before function invocation.
return	return *object*	Returns an *object* from a method. Methods that return void can have an empty "return;".
sealed	sealed *identifier*	*Identifier* is a class name and is not inheritable.
set	set	Assignment method of property member.
sizeof	sizeof(*valuename*)	*Sizeof* returns the size of a value type; supported only in unsafe mode.
stackalloc	stackalloc *type* [*expression*]	Allocates an array of *type* on the stack; supported only in unsafe mode. *Expression* determines the size of the array.
static	static *return method*	*Method* is class-bound and not associated with a specific instance.
struct	struct *identity*	Defines a structure named *identity*.

Table 1-9   Overview of C# Keywords with Explanations

Keyword	Syntax	Explanation
switch	switch(expression) { *statement_block* }	Control is transferred to either the matching switch label, if any, or to the default case in the *statement_block*.
this	This	The *this* object is a reference to the current object.
throw	throw *object*	Throws a user-defined exception. *Object* should be derived from *System.Exception*.
true	True	*True* is a Boolean value.
try	try { *statement_block* }	*Try* guards for exceptions in the *statement_block*.
typeof	typeof(*object*)	Returns the type of the *object*.
unchecked[1]	unchecked(*expression*)	*Expression* is truncated if overflowed.
unchecked[2]	unchecked { *statement_block* }	If an expression within statement block is overflowed, the expression is truncated.
unsafe[1]	unsafe class *identifier*	Class *identifier* can have unsafe code such as pointers.
unsafe[2]	unsafe *return method*	The *method* can contain unsafe code such as pointers.
using[1]	using *identifier*	*Identifier* is a namespace. The *using* keyword makes the namespace implicit.
using[2]	using(identifier) block	*IDisposable.Dispose*, which is the explicit destructor, is called on *identifier* when block is exited.
virtual	virtual *method*	Virtual makes the *method* overridable in a derived class.
void[1]	void *method*	A void return means that the *method* does not return a value. The *method* can omit a return statement or have an empty return.
void[2]	void *identifier*	*Identifier* is a pointer name. A void pointer is a conventional and typeless pointer; supported only in unsafe mode.
volatile	volatile *fieldname*	Accesses to a volatile *fieldname* are immediate, which is useful in a multithreaded environment.

Table 1-9   Overview of C# Keywords with Explanations

Keyword	Syntax	Explanation
where	class *classname*<*parameters*> where *constraint*	The where clause sets constraints on the *classname*. It must be a generic class.
while	while(*boolean_expression*) { *statement_block* }	The *statement_block* of the while loop is repeated until the *boolean_expression* is false.
yield	yield *iterator_value*	In the enumerator pattern, the *yield* keyword adds values to be enumerated.

Primitives

Intrinsic data types, commonly called primitives, are predefined in C#. Primitives historically found in C-base languages, including int, long, and many others, inure to C#. The intrinsic types are declared as C# keywords but are alias for types in the .NET Framework Class Library. Except for the string type, the primitives are value types and allocated on the stack as structures. The string type is a class and allocated on the managed heap.

As indicated, primitives in C# (see Table 1-10) are value types but are nonetheless objects with a published interface. For numeric types, the *min* property, *max* property, and *Parse* methods of the public interface are particularly useful. The *min* and *max* property are invaluable for bounds checking, whereas the *Parse* method converts the string to the primitive.

Table 1-10   Primitives in C#

Type	Primitive	Description	Range
bool	System.Boolean	Boolean	true or false
byte	System.Byte	8-bit integer	0 to 255
char	System.Char	16-bit Unicode character	/u0000 to /uffff
decimal	System.Decimal	128-bit decimal	$\pm 1.0 \times 10^{-28}$ to $\pm 7.9 \times 10^{28}$, with 28 to 29 digits of precision
double	System.Double	64-bit floating point	−1.79769313486232e308 to 1.79769313486232e308
float	System.Single	32-bit floating point	$\pm 1.5 \times 10^{-45}$ to $\pm 3.4 \times 10^{38}$, with 7 digits of precision
int	System.Int32	32-bit unsigned integer	−2,147,483,648 to 2,147,483,647
long	System.Int64	64-bit integer	−9,223,372,036,854,775,808 to 9,223,372,036,854,775,807
sbyte	System.SByte	8-bit integer	−128 to 127
short	System.Int16	16-bit integer	−32,768 to 32,767

Table 1-10   Primitives in C#

Type	Primitive	Description	Range
string	System.String	not applicable	String is an immutable variable length string.
uint	System.UInt32	32-bit unsigned integer	0 to 4,294,967,295
ulong	System.UInt64	64-bit unsigned integer	0 to 18,446,744,073,709,551,615
ushort	System.UInt16	16-bit unsigned integer	0 to 65,535

Sample C# Program

In deference to Martin Richards, the founder of the BCPL language and author of the first "Hello, World!" program, I present a "Hello, World!" program. Actually, I offer an enhanced version that displays "Hello, World" in English, Italian, or Spanish. The program is a console application. For simplicity, no error checking is performed. C# is case sensitive.

Here is my version of the HelloWorld program:

```
using System;

namespace HelloNamespace {

    class Greetings{
    public static void DisplayEnglish() {
          Console.WriteLine("Hello, world!");
    }
    public static void DisplayItalian() {
          Console.WriteLine("Ciao, mondo!");
    }
    public static void DisplaySpanish() {
          Console.WriteLine("Hola, imundo!");
      }
    }

    delegate void delGreeting();

    class HelloWorld {
        static void Main(string [] args) {

    int iChoice=int.Parse(args[0]);
    delGreeting [] arrayofGreetings={
          new delGreeting(Greetings.DisplayEnglish),
          new delGreeting(Greetings.DisplayItalian),
          new delGreeting(Greetings.DisplaySpanish)};

    arrayofGreetings[iChoice-1]();
      }
    }
}
```

Csc.exe is the C# compiler. The following csc command compiles the hello.cs source file to create the executable hello.exe, which is a .NET assembly:

```
csc hello.cs
```

As a .NET assembly, the Hello.exe contains metadata and MISL code but not native binary.

Run the Hello application from the command line. Enter the program name and the language (1 for English, 2 for Italian, or 3 for Spanish). For example, the following command line displays "Ciao, mondo" ("Hello, world" in Italian).

```
Hello 2
```

The source code of the Hello application has the features common to most .NET applications: a *using* statement, a namespace, types, access modifiers, methods, and data.

The *HelloNamespace* namespace contains the *Greetings* and *HelloWorld* types. The *Greetings* class has three static methods, and each method displays "Hello, World" in a different language. Static methods are invoked on the type (*classname.member*), not an instance of that type. The static methods of the *Greetings* type are also public and therefore visible inside and outside the class.

Delegates define a type of function pointer. The *delGreeting* delegate is a container for functions pointers that point to functions that return void and have no parameters. This is not so coincidentally the function signature of the methods in the *Greetings* type.

The entry point of this and any other C# application is the *Main* method. Command-line parameters are passed as the *args* parameter, which is a string array. In the Hello program, the first element of the *args* array is a number indicating the language of choice, as inputted by the user. The Hello application converts that element to an integer. Next, the program defines an array of function pointers, which is initialized with function pointers to methods of the *Greetings* class. This statement invokes a function pointer to display the chosen Hello message:

```
arrayofGreetings[iChoice-1]()
```

The variable *iChoice* is an index into the delegate array. It is decremented to account for the fact that arrays in C# are zero-based.

The remainder of the chapter discusses the important features of the Hello and any other C# application, except for types that will be reviewed in the next chapter.

Namespaces

Namespaces provide hierarchical clarity and organization of types and other members. A container of hundreds of classes, the .NET Framework Class Library (FCL) is an example of effective use of namespaces. The Framework Class Library would sacrifice clarity if planned as a single namespace with a flat hierarchy. Instead, the Framework Class Library organizes its members into numerous namespaces. *System*, which is the root namespace of the FCL, contains the classes ubiquitous to .NET, such as the *Console* class. Types related to data services are grouped in the *System.Data* namespace. Data services are further delineated in the *System.Data.SqlClient* namespace, which contains types specific to Microsoft SQL. The remaining types are organized similarly in other namespaces.

A namespace identifier must be unique within the namespace declaration space, which contains the current namespace but not a nested namespace. A nested namespace is considered a member of the containing namespace. Use the dot punctuator (.) to access members of the namespace.

A namespace at file scope, not nested within another namespace, is considered part of the compilation unit and included in the global namespace. A compilation unit is a source code file. A program partitioned into several source files has multiple compilation units—one compilation unit for each source file. Any namespace, including the global namespace, can span multiple compilation units. For example, all types defined at file scope are included into a single global namespace that spans separate source files.

The following code has two compilation units and three namespaces. Because of identical identifiers sharing the same scope, errors occur when the program is compiled.

```
// file1.cs

public class ClassA {
}

public class ClassB {
}

namespace NamespaceZ {
   public class ClassC {
   }
}

// file2.cs

public class ClassB {
}

namespace NamespaceY {
   public class ClassA {
   }
}

namespace NamespaceZ {

   public class ClassC {
   }

   public class ClassD {
   }
}
```

Compile the code into a library:

```
csc /t:library file1.cs file2.cs
```

In the preceding code, the global namespace has four members. *NamespaceY* and *NamespaceZ* are members. The classes *ClassA* and *ClassB* are also members of the global namespaces. The members span the File1.cs and File2.cs compilation units, which both contribute to the global namespace.

ClassB and *ClassC* are ambiguous. *ClassB* is ambiguous because it is defined twice in the global namespace, once in each compilation unit. *ClassC* is defined in the *NamespaceZ* namespace in both compilation units. Because *NamespaceZ* is one cohesive namespace, *ClassC* is also ambiguous.

The relationship between compilation units, the global namespace, and nonglobal namespaces are illustrated in the Figure 1-3.

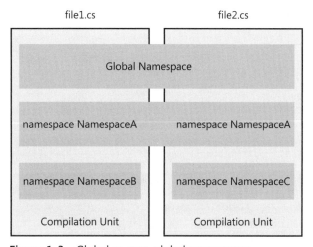

Figure 1-3   Global vs. non-global namespaces

The *using* directive makes a namespace implicit. You can access members of the named namespace directly without the fully qualified name. Do you refer to members of your family by their fully qualified names or just their first names? Unless your mother is the queen, you probably refer to everyone directly by simply using their first names, for the sake of convenience. The *using* directive means that you can treat members of a namespace like family members.

The using directive must precede any members in the namespace where it is defined. The following code defines the namespace member *ClassA*. The fully qualified name is *NamespaceZ.NamespaceY.ClassA*. Imagine having to type that several times in a program!

```
using System;

namespace NamespaceZ {
```

```
namespace NamespaceY {
    class ClassA {
        public static void FunctionM() {
            Console.WriteLine("FunctionM");
        }
    }
}

namespace Application {
    class Starter {
        public static void Main() {
            NamespaceZ.NamespaceY.ClassA.FunctionM();
        }
    }
}
```

The following using directive makes *NamespaceZ.NamespaceY* implicit. Now you can directly access *ClassA*.

```
namespace Application {
    using NamespaceZ.NamespaceY;
    class Starter {
        public static void Main() {
            ClassA.FunctionM();
        }
    }
}
```

Ambiguities can occur when separate namespaces with identically named members are made implicit. When this occurs, the affected members can be assessed only with their fully qualified names.

The using directive can also define an alias for a namespace or type. Aliases are typically created to resolve ambiguity or as a convenience. The scope of the alias is the declaration space where it is declared. The alias must be unique within that declaration space. In this source code, an alias is created for the fully qualified name of *ClassA*:

```
namespace Application {
    using A=NamespaceZ.NamespaceY.ClassA;
    class Starter {
        public static void Main() {
            A.FunctionM();
        }
    }
}
```

In this code, *A* is a nickname for *NamespaceZ.NamespaceY.ClassA* and can be used synonymously.

Using directive statements are not cumulative and are evaluated independently.

Main Entry Point

Main is the entry point method for a C# application and a member function of a class or struct (the entry point method is where the C# application starts executing). There are four valid signatures of *Main* being used as the entry point method:

```
static void Main() {
    // main block
}

static int Main() {
    // main block
}

static void Main(string [] args) {
    // main block
}

static int Main(string [] args) {
    //
}
```

Notice that the entry point method must be static.

A class or struct can contain only one valid entry point method. The accessibility of the *Main* entry point method is irrelevant to the invocation of that method. Even a private *Main* method is reachable as an entry point method.

Entry point methods can pass command line arguments into an application as a string array. Arrays in .NET derive from *System.Array*. You can use the properties and methods of *System.Array* to examine the command line arguments, including the *Length* field to determine the count of arguments. The command arguments start at element zero of the string array. When no arguments are passed, the *arg* parameter is non-null but the array count is zero.

The return of an entry point method is cached internally for interprocess communication. If the application is part of a system and spawned to complete a specific task, the return could represent a status code or the result of the task. The default exit code of an application is zero. The exit code of a process is stored in the Process Environment Block (PEB) and readable through the *GetExitCodeProcess* API.

What if the entry point is ambiguous?

```
using System;

namespace Application{
    class StarterA{
        static void Main() {

        }
    }
```

```
class StarterB{
    static void Main() {

    }
  }
}
```

The preceding code has two valid entry points, which is inherently ambiguous. The main compiler is available to select between multiple entry points. This command successfully compiles the program: *csc/main:Application.StarterB main.cs.*

Local Variables

Local variables are objects declared in a statement block. Local variables can be declared anywhere in the block, but must be defined before use. Local variables can be either value or reference types. A value type is allocated storage on the stack, whereas reference types have memory allocated on the managed heap. The storage for value types is released deterministically at the end of a statement block. Reference types are allocated with the new keyword and removed nondeterministically by the Garbage Collector, which is a component of the Common Language Runtime (CLR).

Variables can be declared with or without the assignment operator and they can be declared without being initialized. That is not a good practice, however. Use the assignment operator to declare and initialize a variable. Variables can be declared in a single declaration statement individually or by daisy-chaining the variable names:

```
int variablea=5, variableb, variablec=10;
```

The scope and visibility of a local variable is the statement block, where it is declared, and any nested statement blocks. This is called the variable declaration space, in which local variables must be uniquely identified.

A variable that is not to be modified at run time should be *const*. (*Const* variables must be initialized at compile time and cannot be changed later at run time.)

In the following code, several local variables are defined. The storage for *variablea, variableb, variablec,* and *variabled* are released at the end of the function block. However, the lifetime of *variablee,* a local variable, is managed by the Garbage Collector. Setting *variablee* to null is a hint to the Garbage Collector that the object is no longer required, and that it should hasten cleanup:

```
void Function() {
    int variablea=0;
    int variableb=1,variablec, variabled=4;
    const double PI=3.1415;
    UserDefined variablee=new UserDefined();
```

```
    // function code

    variablee=null;
    }
```

Nullable Types

In the previous code, a reference type is set to null. Assigning a null to an object indicates that it is unused. This is consistent for all reference types. Can you similarly flag an integer as unused? Nulls are not assignable to primitive value types. (It would cause a compiler error.)

```
int variablea=null;
```

Setting an integer to −1 is a possible solution, assuming that this value is outside the set of expected values. However, this is a proprietary solution; it requires explicit documenting and is not very extensible. A consistent solution is required for all integers and indeed for all value types.

Nullable types are a consistent solution for determining whether a value object is empty. Declare a nullable type by adding the ? type modifier in a value type declaration. Here is an example:

```
double? variable1=null;
```

The object *variable1* is a nullable type and the underlying type is double. A nullable type extends the interface of the underlying type with the *HasValue* and *Value* properties. Both properties are public and read-only. *HasValue* is a Boolean property, whereas the type of *Value* is the same as the underlying type. If the nullable type is assigned a non-null value, *HasValue* is true and the *Value* property is accessible. Otherwise, *HasValue* is false, and an exception is raised if the *Value* property is accessed. The acceptable range of values for a nullable type includes the null value and the extents of the underlying type.

Set the default value of a nullable type with the null coalescing operator. The operator is ??. The default value must be the same type as the underlying type. The default value is returned if the nullable type is null—otherwise empty. This code sets the default value for *variablea* to zero. Otherwise, *variable2* is assigned the value of *variable1*:

```
double variable2=variable1??0;
```

This code demonstrates nullable types:

```
static void Main() {
    int? variablea=null;
    Console.WriteLine(variablea.HasValue); // false
    int variableb=variablea??5;
    Console.WriteLine(variableb);  // 5
}
```

Expressions

Expressions evaluate one or more operators. Most expressions and the operators therein return a value. Operators have operands: Unary operators have a right-side operand, whereas binary operators have a left-side and right-side operand. Although expression statements should assign the result of an expression, expression statements consisting of function invocation, increment, decrement, and new operators are exempted from this requirement.

With the exception of the assignment operator, operands of an expression are evaluated from left to right. Expressions can contain multiple operators; operators are evaluated in order of precedence. Use parentheses to change the precedence or simply clarify the default precedence.

Table 1-11 lists the order of precedence.

Table 1-11   Order of Precedence for Expressions

Precedence	Operator
1	array '[ ]', checked , function '( )', member operator '.', new, postfix decrement , postfix increment, typeof, and unchecked operators
2	unary addition '+', casting '( )', one complement '~', not '!', prefix decrement, prefix increment, unary subtraction '–'operators
3	division '/', and modulus '%', multiplication '*' operators
4	binary addition '+' and binary subtraction '–' operators
5	left-shift '<<' and right-shift '>>' operators
6	as, is, less than '<', less than or equal to '<=', greater than '>', greater than or equal to '>=' operators
7	equals '==' and not equal '!=' operators
8	Logical And '&' operator
9	Logical XOR '^' operator
10	Logical Or '|' operator
11	Conditional And '&&' operator
12	Conditional Or '||' operator
13	Conditional '?:' operator
14	Assignment '=', compound '*=, /=, %=, +=, –=, <<=, >>=, &=, ^=, and |=', and null coalescing '??' operator

Selection Statements

A selection statement evaluates an expression to determine what code is executed next. Based on the expression, a selection statement transfers control to either the next or some other statement.

An *if* statement evaluates a Boolean expression. If the expression is true, control is transferred to the next *statement_block*. If the expression is false, execution is transferred to the first statement after the *statement_block*.

Here's an example of an *if* statement:

```
if(boolean_expression) {statement_block}
```

When combined with an *else* condition, the *if* statement has *true_statement_block* and *false_statement_block*. The *false_statement_block* immediately follows the *else* statement. When the *boolean_expression* is true, you are transferred to the *true_statement_block*. If it is false, control is transferred to the *false_statement_block*. If nested, the *else* statement belongs to the nearest *if* statement, and each *else* statement must have a matching *if* statement.

Here is the syntax:

```
if(boolean_expression)
     true_statement;
else
     false_statement;
```

An alternative to nested *if* and *else* statements is the *else if* clause, which is particularly useful in evaluating choices. The *else if* statement can also be combined with an *else* statement.

The syntax appears here:

```
if(boolean_expression¹)
     true_statement;
else if(boolean_expression²)
     true_statement²;
else if(boolean_expressionⁿ)
     true_statementⁿ;
else
     false_statement;
```

The following code is typical:

```
static void Main() {
    Console.WriteLine("Enter command:");
    string menuChoice=(Console.ReadLine()).ToLower();

    if(menuChoice=="a")
        Console.WriteLine("Doing Task A");
    else if(menuChoice=="b")
        Console.WriteLine("Doing Task B");
    else if(menuChoice=="c")
        Console.WriteLine("Doing Task C");
    else
        Console.WriteLine("Bad choice");
}
```

A *switch* statement, which is a better solution to the preceding code, jumps to the switch label that matches a switch expression. The switch expression must resolve to an integral, char, enum, or string type. The switch label is a constant or literal and must have the same underlying type as the switch expression.

Switch statement:

```
switch(switch_expression)
{
    case switch_label1:
        switch_statement1;
    case case_labeln:
        switch_statementn;
    default:
        default_statement;
}
```

A *switch* statement has a switch expression that is followed by a switch block, which should contain one or more *case* statements. A *case* statement identifies a switch label. After the switch expression is evaluated, control is transferred to the matching switch label. A matching label has the same value as the switch expression. Each switch label must be unique. If switch label matches the switch expression, control is transferred to the default label or to the first statement after the *switch* statement if a default label is not provided.

Unlike C and C++, cascading between *case* statements is not allowed—you cannot "crash the party" of another *case* statement. A *break*, *goto*, *return*, or *throw* are some of the ways to preclude falling into the next case. There is one exception to this rule, however: You can fall through cases that have no statements.

This is an alternative to the *if* code presented earlier:

```
static void Main() {
    Console.WriteLine("Enter command:");
    string resp=(Console.ReadLine()).ToLower();
    switch(resp) {
        case "a":
            Console.WriteLine("Doing Task A");
            break;
        case "b":
            Console.WriteLine("Doing Task B");
            break;
        case "c":
            Console.WriteLine("Doing Task C");
            break;
        default:
            Console.WriteLine("Bad choice");
            break;
    }
}
```

Any object, value, or reference type that is convertible to an integral, char, enum, or string type is acceptable as the *switch_expression*, which is demonstrated in the following code. It must be a one-step conversion to one of the acceptable types.

```csharp
class Employee {
    public Employee(string f_Emplid) {
        m_Emplid=f_Emplid;
    }

    static public implicit operator string(Employee f_this) {
        return f_this.m_Emplid;
    }

    private string m_Emplid;
}

class Starter {
    static void Main() {
        Employee newempl=new Employee("1234");
        switch(newempl) {
            case "1234":
                Console.WriteLine("Employee 1234");
                return;
            case "5678":
                Console.WriteLine("Employee 5678");
                return;
            default:
                Console.WriteLine("Invalid employee");
                return;
        }
    }
}
```

Iterative Statements

C# has the full repertoire of C-style iterative statements plus the *foreach* statement. Iterative statements repeat *statement_blocks* until a condition has been satisfied.

The *for* statement is designed for structured iteration when a proper iterator is available. The *for* statement contains three clauses. First is the *initializer_clause* in which the loop iterators are declared. The scope of an iterator is the *for* statement and *statement_block*. Second is the *boolean_expression* that must evaluate to a Boolean type. The expression normally compares the iterator to an end value. Third, the *iterator_expression* is executed at each iteration and is usually responsible for updating iterator values. Each clause is optional and delimited with a semicolon. The *statement_block* is repeated until the *boolean_expression* is false.

The *statement_block* is repeated zero or more times. If the *boolean_expression* is initially false, the *statement_block* is executed zero times.

This is a *for* statement:

```
for(initializer_clause;boolean_expression;iterator_expression) { statement_block }
```

This is a rather mundane *for* loop:

```
static void Main() {
    for(int iCounter=0;iCounter<10;++iCounter) {
        Console.Write(iCounter);
    }
}
```

Both the *initializer_clause* and *iterator_expression* can contain multiple statements delimited by commas. This allows additional flexibility and complexity than shown previously. Here is an example:

```
static void Main() {
    for(int iBottom=1, iTop=10; iBottom < iTop; ++iBottom, --iTop) {
        Console.WriteLine("{0}x{1} {2}", iBottom, iTop, iBottom*iTop);
    }
}
```

The *while* statement, which is an iterative statement, is more free-form than the *for* statement. The *statement_block* of the *while* statement is executed while the *boolean_expression* is true. The *statement_block* is executed zero or more times. If the *boolean_expression* is initially false, the *statement_block* is executed zero times.

Typically, the *statement_block* is responsible for altering an iterator or something else whereupon the *boolean_expression* evaluates to false, which ends the loop. Care should be taken to avoid unattended infinite loops.

This is an example of a *while* statement:

```
while(boolean_expression) { statement_block }
```

This is source code for selecting a choice rewritten with a *while* statement:

```
static void Main() {
    string resp;
    Console.WriteLine("Enter command ('x' to end):");
    while((resp=(Console.ReadLine()).ToLower()) != "x") {
        switch(resp) {
            case "a":
                Console.WriteLine("Doing Task A");
                break;
            case "b":
                Console.WriteLine("Doing Task B");
                break;
            default:
                Console.WriteLine("Bad choice");
```

```
            break;
        }
    }
}
```

A *do* statement is a loop with the *boolean_expression* after the *statement_block*. This is the reverse of the *while* statement. The impact is that the *statement_block* of the *do* statement is repeated one or more times. The niche for the *do* statement is when the *statement_block* needs to execute once before the *boolean_expression*. The iteration of the *statement_block* continues while the *boolean_expression* is true.

This is a *do* statement:

```
do { statement_block } while(conditional_statement)
```

Here is sample code of the *do* statement:

```
static void Main() {
    string resp;
    do {
        Console.WriteLine("Menu\n\n1 - Task A");
        Console.WriteLine("2 - Task B");
        Console.WriteLine("E - E(xit)");
        resp=(Console.ReadLine()).ToLower();
    }
    while(resp!="e");
}
```

The *foreach* statement is a convenient mechanism for automatically iterating elements of a collection. The alternative is manually iterating a collection with the requested enumerator object. The *foreach* statement is unquestionably simpler. Collections implement the *IEnumerable* interface.

This is the syntax of the *foreach* statement:

```
foreach(type identifier in collection) { statement_block }
```

The *foreach* statement iterates the elements of the *collection*. As each element is enumerated, the *identifier* is assigned the new element, and the *statement_block* is repeated. The scope of the *identifier* is the *foreach* statement and *statement_block*. When the *collection* is fully iterated, the iteration stops, and the *statement_block* no longer repeats.

The *identifier* is a class, struct, or interface. The *identifier* type should be related to the type of elements extracted from the *collection*. In addition, the *identifier* is read-only. Even using the *identifier* in a context that implies change, such as passing the *identifier* as a ref function parameter, is an error.

The *foreach* statement confirms that the enumerator or elements of the *collection* are disposable objects. If so, the *foreach* statement calls the *Dispose* method on the applicable objects. Disposable objects implement the *IDisposable* interface.

This code iterates an array of numbers:

```
static void Main() {
    string [] numbers={ "uno", "dos", "tres",
        "quatro", "cinco"};
    foreach(string number in numbers) {
    Console.WriteLine(number);
    }
 }
```

The *break* statement prematurely exits the containing switch or iterative statement and transfers control to the statement after the *statement_block*. For switch statements, the break prevents fall through between *switch_labels*. For an iterative statement, the break stops the iteration unconditionally and exits the loop. Control is transferred to the statement following the iterative loop. If the switch or iterative *statement_block* is nested, only the immediately *statement_block* is exited.

The *continue* statement transfers control to the end of a *statement_block* where execution continues. The *boolean_expression* of the iterative statement then determines whether the iteration continues, and the *statement_block* is repeated. This is sample code of the *break* statement:

```
static void Main() {
    string resp;
    while(true) {
        Console.WriteLine("Menu\n\n1 - Task A");
        Console.WriteLine("2 - Task B");
        Console.WriteLine("E - E(xit)");
        resp=(Console.ReadLine()).ToLower();
        if(resp=="e") {
            break;
        }
    }
}
```

Classes

This chapter introduced the fundamental ingredients of any C# program. The next chapter expands upon classes, which is the most important of those ingredients. It is hard to envision a functional or nontrivial C# program without at least one class. Classes are the nouns of the C# language, and it is certainly difficult to write a great story without any nouns. It is doubly difficult to write a C# program without classes.

Chapter 2

Types

Types are the places, persons, and things of an application. As part of the object design, scenarios are often drafted as a "day in the life" of a problem domain. The scenarios are mined for nouns, which become potential future classes. Object-oriented programs model real-world problems, in which types represent identities from your problem domain. An employee in a personnel program, a general ledger entry in an accounting package, and geometric shapes in a paint application are examples of types. Types include reference types, value types, and unsafe pointers. The topic of unsafe pointers is included in Chapter 14, "Memory Management."

A *reference type* refers to an object created on the managed heap, and the lifetime of the resulting object is controlled by garbage collection services provided by the Common Language Runtime (CLR). The reference holds the location of an object created on the managed heap. Reference types derive from *System.Object* implicitly and are created with the new keyword. The archetypal reference type is a class. Other reference types are interfaces, arrays, and delegates.

Value types are lightweight components that are placed on the stack. Value types directly contain their value. Value types are customarily created statically. For custom initialization, a value type can be constituted using the new statement. This does not fabricate a value type on the managed heap. It still resides on the stack. Value types derive from *System.ValueType*, which is derived from *System.Object*. *System.ValueType* defines a value type by rewriting most of the semantics of *System.Object*. Primitives such as *int*, *float*, *char*, and *bool* are archetypal value types. As a primitive, a string is a hybrid. Strictly speaking, strings are reference types. However, strings have some of the characteristics of a value type. Structures and enumerations complete the list of value types.

Classes and structures are the primary focus of this chapter. A class or structure is a blueprint for creating components of similar behavior and attributes. A class instance is called an object, whereas an instance of a structure is a value. An *Employee* class would describe the common attributes and behavior an employee. A *Fraction* structure would calculate fractions. Each instance of an *Employee* or a *Fraction* shares common behavior with their siblings but has a distinct state. Within a classification of objects, the *GetHashCode* method returns a unique value that distinguishes a specific component from any other sibling.

View classes and structures as independent contractors. They should be isolated and self-sufficient. Types collaborate through a published interface and hide extraneous details. Classes and structures should be fully abstracted. This avoids dependencies between components, which leads to error-prone and harder-to-maintain software.

Enumerations, also described in this chapter, represent a discrete set of constant values. The months of the year are ideal for enumeration. There are a discrete number of months: 12. Months can logically be assigned constant values from 1 to 12. Liberal use of enumerations can make code safer and more readable.

Classes

Classes are the irreplaceable ingredient of any .NET assembly. First, all executable code must be contained in a type, usually a class. Global functions and variables are not permitted in C#, preventing problematic dependences caused by disparate references to global entities. Second, classes published in the .NET Framework Class Library provide important services that are integral to any .NET application.

Classes are described in a class declaration. A class declaration consists of a class header and body. The class header includes attributes, modifiers, the class keyword, the class name, and the base class list. The class body encapsulates the members of the class, which are the data members and member functions. Here is the syntax of a class declaration:

attributes accessibility modifiers **class** *classname* : *baselist* { *class body* };

Attributes further describe the class. If a class is a noun, attributes are the adjectives. For example, the *Serializable* attribute identifies a class that can be serialized to storage. There is an assortment of predefined attributes. You can also define custom attributes. Attributes are optional, and there are no defaults. Further details on attributes are contained in Chapter 11, "Metadata and Reflections."

Accessibility is the visibility of the class. Public classes are visible in the current assembly and assemblies referencing that assembly. Internal classes are visible solely in the containing assembly. The default accessibility of a class is internal. Nested classes have additional accessibility options, which are described later in this chapter.

Modifiers refine the declaration of a class. For example, the *abstract* keyword prevents instances of the class from being created. Modifiers are optional, and there is no default. Table 2-1 elucidates the modifiers.

Table 2-1   Class Modifier Table

Modifier	Description
Abstract	Class is abstract; future instances of the class cannot be created.
Sealed	Class cannot be inherited and refined in a derived class.
static	Class contains only static members.
Unsafe	Class can contain unsafe constructs, such as a pointer; requires the unsafe compiler option.

A class can inherit the members of a single base class. Multiple inheritance is not supported in the Common Language Specification of .NET. However, a class can inherit and implement multiple interfaces. The *baselist* lists the class inherited and any interfaces to be implemented. By default, classes inherit the *System.Object* type. Inheritance and *System.Object* are expanded upon in Chapter 3, "Inheritance."

The class body encompasses the members of the class that entail the behavior and state of a class. The member functions are the behavior, whereas data members are the state. As a design goal, classes should expose an interface composed of the public functions of the class. The state of the class should be abstracted and described through the behavior of the class. You manage the state of an object through its public interface.

Classes do not require members. All members can be inherited. In addition, an empty class can function as a valuable marker or cookie at run time when ascertaining Run-time Type Information (RTTI).

The semicolon at the end of the class is optional.

XInt is a class and a thin wrapper for an integer:

```
internal sealed class XInt {
.....public int iField=0;
}
```

The *XInt* class has internal accessibility and visibility in the current assembly, but is not visible to an external assembly. The sealed modifier means that the class cannot be refined through inheritance.

The following code uses the *new* statement to create an instance of a class:

```
.....public void Func() {
.........XInt obj=new XInt();
.........obj.iField=5;
.....}
```

Class Members

Classes are composed of members: member functions and data members. Use the dot syntax to access members. The dot binds an instance member to an object or a static member to a class. In the following code, *Fred.name* accesses the name field of the *Fred* object:

```
using System;

namespace Donis.CSharpBook{
    public class Employee{
        public string name;
    }
    public class Personnel{
        static void Main(){
            Employee Jim=new Employee();
            Fred.name="Wilson, Jim";
        }
    }
}
```

Table 2-2 describes the list of potential class members.

Table 2-2   Type Members

Member	Description
Classes	Nested classes
Constants	Invariable data members
Constructor	Specialized methods that initializes a component or class for static constructors
Delegate	Type-safe containers of one or more function pointers
Destructor	Specialized method that performs cleanup of object resources upon garbage collection
Events	Callbacks to methods provided by a subscriber
Fields	Data members
Indexer	Specialized property that indexes the current object
Interfaces	Nested interface
Method	Reusable code sequence
Operators	Operator member functions that override implicit operator behavior
Properties	Get and set functions presented as a field
Structures	Nested structure within a class

When a member is declared, attributes can be applied and accessibility defined. Members are further described with attributes. Accessibility sets the visibility as class member.

Member Accessibility

Members defined in a class are scoped to that class. However, the visibility of the member is defined by accessibility keywords. The most common accessibility is public and private. Public members are visible inside and outside of the class. The visibility of private members is restricted to the containing class. Private is the default accessibility of a class member. Table 2-3 details the accessibility keywords:

Table 2-3   Accessibility

Accessibility	Description
internal	Visible in containing assembly
internal protected	Visible in containing assembly or descendants of the current class
private	Visible inside current class
protected	Visible inside current class and any descendants
public	Visible in containing assembly and assemblies referencing that assembly

Member Attributes

Attributes are usually the first element of the member declaration and further describe a member and extend the metadata. The *Obsolete* attribute exemplifies an attribute and marks a function as deprecated. Attributes are optional. By default, a member has no attributes.

Member Modifiers

Modifiers refine the definition of the applicable member. Modifiers are optional and there are no defaults. Some modifiers are reserved for classification of members. For example, the *override* modifier is applicable to member functions, not data members. Table 2-4 lists the available modifiers.

Table 2-4   Modifiers

Modifier	Description
abstract	A member function has no implementation and is described through inheritance.
Extern	Implemented in a foreign dynamic-link library (DLL).
New	Hides a similar member or members in the base class.
Override	Indicates that a function in a derived class overrides a virtual method in the base class.
Readonly	Read-only fields are initialized at declaration or in a constructor.
Sealed	The member function cannot be further refined through inheritance.
Static	Member belongs to a class and not an instance.
Virtual	Virtual functions are overridable in a derived class.
Volatile	Volatile fields are modifiable by the environment, a separate thread, or hardware.

Instance and Static Members

Members belong either to an instance of a class or to the class itself. Members bound to a class are considered static. Except for constants, class members default to instance members and are bound to an object via the *this* object. Constant members are implicitly static. Static members are classwise and have no implied *this* context. Not all members can be static or instance members; destructors and operator member functions are representative of this. Destructors cannot be static, whereas operator member functions cannot be instance members.

Instance members are qualified by the object name. Here is the syntax of a fully qualified instance member:

objectname.instancemember

Static members are prefixed with this class name:

classname.staticmember

The lifetime of static members is closely linked to the lifetime of the application. Instance members are inexorably linked to an instance and are accessible from the point of instantiation. Access to instance members ceases when the instance variable is removed. Therefore, the lifetime of an instance member is a subset of the lifetime of an application. Static members are essentially always available, whereas instance members are not. Static members are similar to global functions and variables but have the benefit of encapsulation. Static members can be private.

Your design analysis should determine which members are instance versus static members. For example, in a personnel application for small businesses, there is an *Employee* class. The employee number is an instance member of the class. Each employee is assigned a unique identifier. However, the company name member is static because all employees work for the same company. The company name does not belong to a single employee, but to the classification.

Static class   A static class is a class that contains static members and no instance members. Because static classes have no instance data, a static class cannot be instantiated. This is a static class:

```
public static class ZClass {
    public static void MethodA() {}
    public static void MethodB() {}
}
```

this Object

The *this* reference refers to the current object. Instance members functions are passed a *this* reference as the first and hidden parameter of the function. In an instance function, the *this* reference is automatically applied to other instance members. This assures that within an instance member function, you implicitly refer to members of the same object. In this code, *GetEmployeeInfo* is an instance member function referring to other instance members (the *this* reference is implied):

```
public void GetEmployeeInfo(){
    PrintEmployeeName();
    PrintEmployeeAddress();
    PrintEmployeeId();
}
```

Here is the same code, except that the *this* pointer is explicit (the behavior of the function is the same):

```
public void GetEmployeeInfo(){
    this.PrintEmployeeName();
    this.PrintEmployeeAddress();
    this.PrintEmployeeId();
}
```

In the preceding code, the *this* reference was not required. The *this* reference is sometimes required as a function return or parameter. In addition, the *this* reference can improve code readability and provide IntelliSense for class members when editing the code in Microsoft Visual Studio.

Static member functions are not passed a *this* reference as a hidden parameter. For this reason, a static member cannot directly access nonstatic members of the class. For example, you cannot call an instance method from a static member function. Static members are essentially limited to accessing other static members. Instance members have access to both instance and static members of the class.

The *this* reference is a read-only reference. As part of error handling, setting a *this* reference to null would sometimes be beneficial. Alas, it is not allowed.

Data and Function Members

Members are broadly grouped into data and function members. This chapter reviews constants, fields, and nested types, which are data members. Methods, constructors, destructors, and properties are member functions (and are covered in this chapter). The remaining members, such as events and delegates, are discussed in Chapter 8, "Delegates and Events."

Data members are typically private to enforce encapsulation and the principles of data hiding and abstraction. Abstraction abstracts the details of a class and restricts collaboration to the public interface. The developer responsible for the class obtains implementation independence and has the freedom to modify the implementation when required as long as the interface is unchanged. The interface is immutable—like a contract between the class and any client. As a best practice, data members should be private and described fully through the public interface. The class interface consists of the public member functions. Do not make every member function public; internal functionality should remain private.

Except for constructors and destructors, members should not have the same name as the containing class. As a policy, class names should differ from the surrounding namespace.

Constants

Constants are data members. They are initialized at compile time using a constant expression and cannot be modified at run time. Constants have a type designation and must be used within the context of that type. This makes a constant type-safe. Constants are usually a primitive type, such as *integer* or *double*. A constant can be a more complex type. However, classes and structures are initialized at run time, which is prohibited with a constant. Therefore, constant class and structures must be assigned null, which limits their usefulness. Following is the syntax of a constant member:

const syntax:

accessibility modifier const *constname=initialization*;

The only modifier available is *new*, which hides inherited members of the same name. Constants are tacitly static. Do not use the static keyword explicitly. The initialization is accomplished with a constant expression. You can declare and initialize several constants simultaneously.

The following code presents various permutations of how to declare and initialize a constant data member:

```
public class ZClass {
    public const int fielda=5, fieldb=15;
    public const int fieldc=fieldd+10;  // Error

    public static int fieldd=15;
}
```

The assignment to *fieldc* causes a compile error. The *fieldd* member is a nonconstant member variable and is evaluated at run time. Thus, *fieldd* cannot be used in a constant expression, as shown in the preceding code. Constant expressions are limited to literals and constant types.

Fields

As a data member, fields are the most prevalent. Instance fields hold state information for a specific object. The state information is copied into the managed memory created for the object. Static fields are data owned by the class. A single instance of static data is created for the class. It is not replicated for each instance of the class. Fields can be reference or value types. Here is the syntax for declaring a field:

accessibility modifier type *fieldname=initialization*;

Fields support the full assortment of accessibility. Valid modifiers for a field include *new*, *static*, *read-only*, and *volatile*. Initialization is optional but recommended. Uninitialized fields are assigned a default value of zero or null. Alternatively, fields can be initialized in constructor functions. Like constants, fields of the same type are declarable individually or in aggregate in the initialization list.

Initialization is performed in the textual order in which the fields appear in the class, which is top-down. This process is demonstrated in the following code:

```
using System;

namespace Donis.CSharpBook{
    internal class ZClass {
        public int iField1=FuncA();
        public int iField2=FuncC();
        public int iField3=FuncB();

        public static int FuncA() {
            Console.WriteLine("ZClass.FuncA");
            return 0;
        }

        public static int FuncB() {
            Console.WriteLine("ZClass.FuncB");
            return 1;
        }

        public static int FuncC() {
            Console.WriteLine("ZClass.FuncC");
            return 2;
        }
    }

    public class Starter{
        public static void Main(){
        ZClass obj=new ZClass();
        }
    }
}
```

Running this code confirms that *FuncA*, *FuncC*, and *FuncB* are called in sequence the textual order of the initialization. Avoid writing code dependent on the initialization sequence—writing code that way makes the program harder to maintain without clear documentation.

Private fields exposed through accessor functions, a *get* and *set* method, are *read-write*. Eliminate the *get* or *set* method to make the field *read-only* or *write-only*, respectively. However, this relies on programmer discipline. The *read-only* keyword is safer.

A *read-only* field is enforced by the run time. These fields are different from constants. Although constants can be initialized only at compile time, *read-only* fields can also be initialized in a constructor. Alternatively, *read-only* fields can be initialized with nonconstant expressions. These are subtle but important nuances and provide considerable more flexibility to a *read-only* field. In addition, *read-only* fields can be instance or static members, whereas constant are only static.

This code highlights *read-only* fields:

```
public class ZClass {
    public ZClass() { // constructor
        fieldc=10;
    }

    public static int fielda=5;
    public readonly int fieldb=fielda+10;
    public int fieldc;
};
```

Volatile Fields

Because of the intricacy of program execution, writes and reads to a field might not be immediate. This latency can cause problems, particularly in a multithreaded application. Reads and writes to volatile fields are essentially immediate. Volatile makes automatic what locks do programmatically. Locks are explained in Chapter 9, "Threading."

Member Functions

Member functions contain the behavior of the class. Methods, properties, and indexers are the member functions. Methods are straightforward functions that accept parameters as input and return the result of an operation. Properties are accessor methods, a *get* and *set* method, masked as a field. An indexer is a specialized property. Indexers apply *get* and *set* methods to the *this* reference, which refers to the current object. The discussion of indexers is deferred to Chapter 6, "Arrays and Collections."

Function Code

Functions encapsulate a sequence of code and define the behavior of the class. A function is not necessarily executed in sequential order and sometimes contains iterative and conditional transfer control statements. Return statements provide an orderly exit to a function. Void functions can simply fall through the end of the function. The compiler extrapolates the code paths of a function and uncovers any unreachable code, which is subsequently flagged by the compiler. All paths must conclude with an orderly exit. The following code includes both unreachable code and a code path without an orderly exit:

```
public static int Main(){
    if(true) {
        Console.WriteLine("true");
    }
```

```
    else {
        Console.WriteLine("false");
    }
}
```

The *if* statement is always true. Therefore, the *else* code is unreachable. Main returns *int*. However, the method has no return. For these reasons, the application generates the following errors when compiled:

```
unreachable.cs(10,17): warning CS0162: Unreachable code detected
unreachable.cs(5,27): error CS0161: ' Donis.CSharpBook.Starter.Main()': not all code paths
return a value
```

Keep functions relatively short. Extended functions are modestly harder to debug and test. A class comprised of several functions is preferable to class of a few convoluted functions. Remoted components are the exception: A narrower interface is preferred to minimize client calls and optimize network traffic. Comparatively, local invocations are relatively quick and efficient.

Methods own a code sequence, local variables, and parameters. The local variables and parameters represent the private state of the method.

Local Variables

Local variables and parameters represent the private state of the function. Local variables are reference or value types. Declare a local variable anywhere in a method. However, a local variable must be defined before use. Optionally, initialize local variables at declaration. There are competing philosophies as to when to declare local variables: Some developers prefer to declare local variables at the beginning of a method or block, where they are readily identifiable; other developers like to declare and initialize local variables immediately prior to use. They feel that local variables are more maintainable when situated near the affected code. Local variables are not assigned a default value prior to initialization. For this reason, using an unassigned local variable in an expression causes a compile error. This is the syntax of a local variable:

modifier type variablename=initialization;

The *const* modifier is the only modifier that is applicable. Variables that are *const* must be initialized at compile time.

The scope of a local variable or function parameter is the entire function. Therefore, local variables and function parameters must have unique names. Local variables of the same type can be declared individually or in aggregate.

Scope Local variables are declared at the top level or in a nested block within the method. Although the scope of a local variable is the entire function, the visibility of a local variable starts where the local variable is declared. Visibility ends when the block that the local variable is declared is exited. Local variables are visible in descendant blocks, but not ascendant blocks. Because local variables maintain scope throughout a function, names of local variable cannot be reused—even in a nested block. Figure 2-1 illustrates the relationship between scope and visibility of local variables.

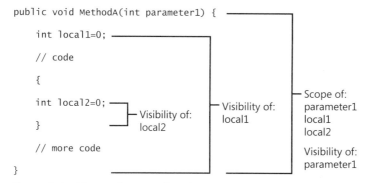

```
public void MethodA(int parameter1) {

    int local1=0;

    // code

    {

    int local2=0;

    }

    // more code

}
```

Visibility of: local2

Visibility of: local1

Scope of:
parameter1
local1
local2

Visibility of:
parameter1

Figure 2-1   Figure diagramming the scope and visibility of a local variable

Local variables of a value type are removed from the stack when a function is exited. Local references are also removed from the stack at that time, whereas the objects they referred to become candidates for garbage collection. This assumes that no other references to the object exist at that time. If other outstanding references exist, the object associated with the reference remains uncollectible. When a reference is no longer needed, assign null to the reference. This is a hint to the garbage collector that the related object is no longer needed.

Local variables are private to the current function. Functions cannot access private data of another function. Identically named local variables in different functions are distinct and separate entities, which are stored at different memory addresses. To share data between functions, declare a field.

Methods

Methods are the most common function member. Methods accept parameters as input, perform an operation, and return the result of the operation. Both parameters and the return result are optional. Methods are described through the method header, and implemented in the method body. Here is the syntax of a method:

Method syntax:

attributes accessibility modifiers returntype methodname(parameter list) { method body };

Any attribute that targets a method can prefix the method. The accessibility of methods included in the class interface is public. Methods not included in the interface are typically protected or private. Methods can be assigned the *sealed, abstract, new,* and other modifiers, as explained in Chapter 3. The return is the result of the method. Methods that return nothing stipulate a void *returntype*. The parameter list, which consists of zero or more parameters, is the input of the method. The method body contains the statements of the method.

Method Return   Execution of a function starts at the beginning and ends at a return. The *return* keyword provides the result of function or an error code. A value or reference type can be returned from a method as defined by the return type. Functions can contain multiple returns, each on a separate code path. More than one return along a single code path results in unreachable code, which causes compiler warnings.

Functions with a void return type can be exited explicitly or implicitly. An empty return statement explicitly exits a function of a void return type. For an implicit exit, execution is allowed to exit the function without a return statement. At the end of the function block, the function simply exits. Implicit returns are reserved for functions that return void. A function can have multiple explicit returns but only one implicit return. The end of a function must be reached for an implicit return, whereas an explicit return can exit the function prematurely. In the following code, *Main* has both an explicit and implicit exit:

```
static void Main(string [] arg){
    if(arg.Length>0) {
        // do something
        return;
    }

    // implicit return
}
```

A function that returns void cannot be used in an assignment. This type of method evaluates to nothing and is thereby not assignable. This prevents a function that returns void from being used as a left- or right-value of an assignment. Other functions are usable in assignments and more generally in expressions. A function evaluates to the *return* value. When a reference type is returned, a function is available as a left- or right-value of an assignment. Functions that return a value type are restricted to right-values of an assignment. The following code demonstrates the use of methods in expressions:

```
public class ZClass {
    public int MethodA() {
        return 5;
    }

    public void MethodB() {
        return;
    }

    public int MethodC(){
        int value1=10;
        value1=5+MethodA()+value1;  // Valid
        MethodB();                  // Valid
        value1=MethodB();           // Invalid
        return value1;
    }
}
```

At the calling site, the return of a function is temporarily copied to the stack. The return is discarded after that statement. To preserve the return, assign the method return to something. Returns are *copy by value*. When returning a value type, a copy of the result is returned. For reference types, a copy of the reference is returned. This creates an alias to an object in the calling function. Look at the following code:

```
using System;

namespace Donis.CSharpBook{

    public class XInt {
        public int iField=0;
    }

    public class Starter{

        public static XInt MethodA() {
            XInt inner=new XInt();
            inner.iField=5;
            return inner;
        }

        public static void Main(){
            XInt outer=MethodA();
            Console.WriteLine(outer.iField);
        }
    }
}
```

In the preceding code, *MethodA* creates an instance of *XInt*, which is subsequently returned from the method. The scope of the reference called *inner*, which is a local variable, is *MethodA*. After the return, *outer* is an alias and refers to the *inner* object, which prevents the object from becoming a candidate for garbage collection, even thought the *inner* reference is no longer valid.

A method returns a single item. What if you want to return multiple values? The solution is to return a structure containing a data member for each value. Structures are lightweight and appropriate for copying by value on the stack.

Function parameters   Functions have zero or more parameters, where an empty function call operator indicates zero parameters. Parameter lists can be fixed or variable length. Use the *param* keyword to construct a variable length parameter list, which is discussed in Chapter 6. Parameters default to pass by value. When the parameter is a value type, changes to the parameter are discarded when the method is exited and the value is removed from the stack. In the following code, changes made in the function are discarded when the function returns:

```
using System;

namespace Donis.CSharpBook{
    public class Starter{
```

```
        public static void MethodA(int parameter) {
            parameter=parameter+5;
        }    //  change discarded

        public static void Main(){
            int local=2;
            MethodA(local);
            Console.WriteLine(local); // 2 outputted
        }
    }
}
```

As a parameter, reference types are also passed by value. A copy of the reference, which is the location of the object, is passed by value. Therefore, the function now has an alias to the actual object, which can be used to change the object. Those changes will persist when the function exits.

This code revises the preceding code. An integer wrapper class is passed as a parameter instead of an integer value. Changes made to the object in *MethodA* are not discarded later.

```
using System;

namespace Donis.CSharpBook{

    public class XInt {
        public int iField=2;
    }

    public class Starter{

        public static void MethodA(XInt alias) {
            alias.iField+=5;
        }

        public static void Main(){
            XInt obj=new XInt();
            MethodA(obj);
            Console.WriteLine(obj.iField);  // 7
        }
    }
}
```

Pass a parameter *by reference* using the *ref* modifier. The location of the parameter is passed into the function. The *ref* attribute must be applied to the parameter in the function signature and at the call site. The function now possesses the location of the actual parameter and can change the parameter directly. The following code has been updated to include the *ref* modifier. Unlike the first revision of this code, changes made in *MethodA* are not discarded.

```
using System;

namespace Donis.CSharpBook{
    public class Starter{
```

```
        public static void MethodA(ref int parameter) {
            parameter=parameter+5;
        }

        public static void Main(){
            int var=2;
            MethodA(ref var);
            Console.WriteLine(var); // 7
        }
    }
}
```

What happens when a reference type is passed *by reference*? The function receives the location of the reference. Because a reference contains a location to an object, the location of the location is passed into the function. In the following code, a reference type is passed *by value*, which creates an alias. Because the reference is passed by value, changes to the alias are discarded when the function exits.

```
using System;

namespace Donis.CSharpBook{

    public class XInt {
        public int iField=2;
    }

    public class Starter{

        public static void MethodA(XInt alias) {
            XInt inner=new XInt();
            inner.iField=5;
            alias=inner;
        }  // reference change lost

        public static void Main(){
            XInt obj=new XInt();
            MethodA(obj);
            Console.WriteLine(obj.iField);  // 2
        }
    }
}
```

Next, the code is slightly modified to include the *ref* attribute. The assignment in *MethodA* is not discarded when the method exits. Therefore, *obj* is updated to reference the object created in the method.

```
using System;

namespace Donis.CSharpBook{

    public class XInt {
        public int iField=2;
    }
```

```
public class Starter{

    public static void MethodA(ref XInt alias) {
        XInt inner=new XInt();
        inner.iField=5;
        alias=inner;
    }

    public static void Main(){
        XInt obj=new XInt();
        MethodA(ref obj);
        Console.WriteLine(obj.iField);   // 5
    }
}
}
```

Local variables must be initialized before use. The following code is in error. The *obj* reference is unassigned but initialized in the method. However, the compiler is unaware of this and presents an error for using an unassigned variable. The *out* parameter is a hint to the compiler that the parameter is being set in the function, which prevents the compiler error. The *out* parameter is not required to be initialized before the method call. These parameters are often used to return multiple values from a function.

```
using System;

namespace Donis.CSharpBook{

    public class XInt {
        public int iField=5;
    }

    public class Starter{

        public static void MethodA(ref XInt alias) {
            XInt inner=new XInt();
            alias=inner;
        }

        public static void Main(){
            XInt obj;
            MethodA(ref obj); // Error
        }
    }
}
```

In the following code, the parameter modifier is changed to *out*. The program compiles and runs successfully when the attribute is changed to *out*:

```
using System;

namespace Donis.CSharpBook{

    class XInt {
```

```
        public int iField=5;
    }

    class Starter{

        public static void MethodA(out XInt alias) {
            XInt inner=new XInt();
            alias=inner;
        }

        public static void Main(){
            XInt obj;
            MethodA(out obj);
            Console.WriteLine(obj.iField);   // 5
        }
    }
}
```

Function Overloading

Function overloading permits multiple implementations of the same function in a class, which promotes a consistent interface for related behavior. The *SetName* method would be overloaded in the *Employee* class to accept variations of an employee name. Overloaded methods share the same name but have unique signatures. Parameter attributes, such as *out*, are considered part of the signature. (The signature is the function header minus the return type.) Because they are excluded from the signature, functions cannot be overloaded on the basis of a different return type. The number of parameters or the type of parameters must be different. With the exception of constructors, you cannot overload a function based on whether a member is a static or instance member.

The process of selecting a function from a set of overloaded methods is called *function resolution*, which occurs at the call site. The closest match to a specific function is called as determined by the number of parameters and the types of parameters given at function invocation. Sometimes a function call matches more than one function in the overloaded set. When function resolution returns two or more methods, the call is considered ambiguous, and an error occurs. Conversely, if no method is returned, an error is also manifested.

This sample code overloads the *SetName* method:

```
using System;

namespace Donis.CSharpBook{

    public class Employee {

        public string name;

        public void SetName(string last) {
            name=last;
        }
```

```
        public void SetName(string first, string last) {
            name=first+" "+last;
        }

        public void SetName(string saluation, string first, string last) {
            name=saluation+" "+first+" "+last;
        }

    }

    public class Personnel {
        public static void Main(){
            Employee obj=new Employee();
            obj.SetName("Bob", "Jones");

        }
    }
}
```

Functions with variable-length parameter lists can be included in the set of overloaded functions. The function is first evaluated with a fixed-length parameter list. If function resolution does not yield a match, the function is evaluated with variable-length parameters.

Constructors

A constructor is a specialized function for initializing the state of an object. Constructors have the same name of the class. The main purpose of a constructor is to initialize the fields and guarantee that object is in a known state for the lifetime of the object. Constructors are invoked with the new operator. Here is the syntax of a constructor:

Constructor syntax:

accessibility modifier typename(parameterlist)

The accessibility of a constructor determines where new instances of the reference type can be created. For example, a public constructor allows an object to be created in the current assembly and a referencing assembly. A private constructor prevents an instance from being created outside the class. *extern* is the only modifier for constructors.

The parameter list of constructors has zero or more parameters.

This is the constructor for the *Employee* class:

```
using System;

namespace Donis.CSharpBook{

    public class Employee {

        public Employee(params string []_name) {
            switch(_name.Length) {
```

```
                case 1:
                    name=_name[0];
                    break;
                case 2:
                    name=_name[0]+" "+_name[1];
                    break;
                default:
                    // Error handler
                    break;
            }

        }

        public void GetName() {
            Console.WriteLine(name);
        }

        private string name="";
    }

    public class Personnel{

        public static void Main(){
            Employee bob=new Employee("Bob", "Wilson");
            bob.GetName();
        }
    }
}
```

Classes with no constructors are given a default constructor, which is a parameterless constructor. Default constructors assign default values to fields. An empty new statement invokes a default constructor. You can replace a default constructor with a custom parameterless constructor. The following new statement calls the default constructor of a class:

```
Employee empl=new Employee();
```

Constructors can be overloaded. The function resolution of overloaded constructors is determined by the parameters of the new statement. This *Employee* class has overloaded constructors:

```
using System;

namespace Donis.CSharpBook{

    public class Employee {

        public Employee(string _name) {
            name=_name;
        }

        public Employee(string _first, string _last) {
            name=_first+" "+_last;
        }
```

```
            private string name="";
        }

        public class Personnel {
            public static void Main(){
                Employee bob=new Employee("Jim", "Wilson");   // 2 arg c'tor
            }
        }
    }
```

In the preceding code, this would cause a compile error:

```
Employee jim=new Employee();
```

This is the error message:

```
overloading.cs(20,26): error CS1501: No overload for method 'Employee' takes '0' arguments
```

Why? Although the statement is syntactically correct, the *Employee* class has lost the default constructor. Adding a custom constructor to a class removes the default constructor. If desired, also add a custom parameterless constructor to preserve that behavior.

A constructor can call another constructor using the *this* reference, which is useful for reducing redundant code. A constructor cannot call another constructor in the method body. Instead, constructors call other constructors using the colon syntax, which is affixed to the constructor header. This syntax can be used only with constructors and not available with normal member functions. In this code, all constructors delegate to the one argument constructor:

```
class Employee {

    public Employee()
        : this(""){
    }

    public Employee(string _name) {
        name=_name;
    }

    public Employee(string _first, string _last)
        : this(_first+" "+_last){
    }

    public void GetName() {
        Console.WriteLine(name);
    }

    private string name="";
}
```

Constructors can also be static. Create a static constructor to initialize static fields. The static constructor is invoked before the class is accessed in any manner. There are limitations to static constructors, as follows:

- Static constructors cannot be called explicitly.

- Accessibility defaults to static, which cannot be set explicitly.

- Static constructors are parameterless.

- Static constructors cannot be overloaded.

- Static constructors are not inheritable.

- The return type cannot set explicitly. Constructors always return void.

As mentioned, static constructors are called before a static member or an instance of the classes is accessed. Static constructors are not called explicitly with the new statement. In the following code, *ZClass* has a static constructor. The static constructor is stubbed to output a message. In *Main*, the time is displayed, execution is paused for about five seconds, and then the *ZClass* is accessed. *ZClass.GetField* is called to access the class and trigger the static constructor. The static constructor is called immediately before the access, which displays the time. It is about five seconds later.

```
using System;
using System.Threading;

namespace Donis.CSharpBook{

    public class ZClass{

        static private int fielda;
        static ZClass() {
            Console.WriteLine(DateTime.Now.ToLongTimeString());
             fielda=42;
        }

        static public void GetField() {
            Console.WriteLine(fielda);
        }
    }

    public class Starter{
        public static void Main(){
            Console.WriteLine(DateTime.Now.ToLongTimeString());
            Thread.Sleep(5000);
            ZClass.GetField();
        }
    }
}
```

Singleton   Singletons provide an excellent example of private and static constructors. A singleton is an object that appears once in the problem domain. Singletons are limited to one instance, but that instance is required. This requirement is enforced in the implementation of the singleton. A complete explanation of the singleton pattern is found at *http://www.microsoft.com/patterns*.

The singleton presented in this chapter has two constructors. The private constructor means that an instance cannot be created outside the class. That would require calling the constructor publicly. However, an instance can be created inside the class. The single instance of the class is exposed as a static member, which is initialized in the static constructor. The instance members of the class are accessible through the static instance. Because the static constructor is called automatically, one instance—the singleton—always exists.

A chess game is played with a single board—no more or less. This is the singleton for a chess board:

```
using System;

namespace Donis.CSharpBook{

    public class Chessboard {
        private Chessboard() {
        }

        static Chessboard() {
            board=new Chessboard();
            board.start=DateTime.Now.ToShortTimeString();
        }

        public static Chessboard board=null;
        public string player1;
        public string player2;
        public string start;
    }

    public class Game{
        public static void Main(){
            Chessboard game=Chessboard.board;
            game.player1="Sally";
            game.player2="Bob";
            Console.WriteLine("{0} played {1} at {2}",
                game.player1, game.player2,
        game.start);
        }
    }
}
```

In *Main*, *game* is an alias for the *ChessBoard.board* singleton. The local variable is not another instance of *Chessboard*. The alias is simply a convenience. I preferred *game.player1* to *ChessBoard.board.player1*.

Destructors

An application can clean up unmanaged resources of an object in the destructor method. Destructors are not directly callable and called by the run time prior to garbage collection removing the object from the managed heap. Garbage collection is nondeterministic. A destructor is invoked at an undetermined moment in the future. Like a constructor, the destructor has the same as the class, except a destructor is prefixed with a tilde (~). The destructor is called by the *Finalize* method, which is inherited from *System.Object*. In C#, the *Finalize* method cannot be used directly. You must use a destructor for the cleanup of object resources. For deterministic garbage collection, inherit the *IDisposable* interface and implement *IDisposable.Dispose*. Call dispose to relinquish managed or unmanaged resources associated with the object. Implementing a disposable pattern is one of the topics found in Chapter 16.

Destructors differ from other methods in the following ways:

- Destructors cannot be overloaded.
- Destructors are parameterless.
- Destructors are not inherited.
- Accessibility cannot be applied to destructors.
- Extern is the sole destructor modifier.
- The return type cannot be set explicitly. Destructors return void.

Here is the syntax of a destructor.

Destructor syntax:

modifier ~typename()

Destructors have performance and efficiency implications. Understand the ramifications of destructors before inserting a destructor in a class. These topics are also covered in Chapter 16.

The *WriteToFile* class is a wrapper for a *StreamWriter* object. The constructor initializes the internal object. The *Dispose* method closes the file resource. The destructor delegates to the *Dispose* method. The *Main* method tests the class.

```
using System;
using System.IO;

namespace Donis.CSharpBook{

    public class WriteToFile: IDisposable {
```

```
    public WriteToFile(string _file, string _text) {
        file=new StreamWriter(_file, true);
        text=_text;
    }

    public void WriteText() {
        file.WriteLine(text);
    }

    public void Dispose() {
        file.Close();
    }

    ~WriteToFile() {
        Dispose();
    }

    private StreamWriter file;
    private string text;
}

public class Writer{
    public static void Main(){
        WriteToFile sample=new WriteToFile("sample.txt", "My text file");
        sample.WriteText();
        sample.Dispose();
    }
}
}
```

Properties

Properties are *get* and *set* methods exposed as properties. Public fields do not adhere to encapsulation. Private fields are good policy where the fields are exposed through accessor methods. A property combines the convenience of a public field and the safety of access methods. For clients of the public interface of a class, properties are indistinguishable from fields. The client appears to have direct access to the state of the class or object. There several benefits of properties:

- Properties are safer than public fields. Use the *set* method to validate the data.

- Properties can be computed, which adds flexibility. Fields represent a data store and never a calculation.

- Lazy initialization can be used with properties. Some data is expensive to obtain. A large dataset is an ideal example. Deferring that cost until necessary is a benefit.

- Write- and read-only properties are supported. Public fields are fully accessible.

- Properties are valid members of an interface. As part of the interface contract, a class can be required to publish a property. Interfaces do not include fields.

A property is a *get* and *set* method. Neither method is called directly. Depending on the context of the property, the correct method is called implicitly. As a left-value of an assignment, the *set* method of the property is called. When used as a right-value, the *get* method of the property is called. When a property is the target of an assignment, the *set* method of the property is invoked. The *get* method is called if a property is used within an expression. Here is the syntax of a property:

Property syntax:

accessibility modifier type propertyname { attributes get *{getbody} attributes* set *{setbody} }*

The *accessibility* and any modifier included in the property header apply to both the *get* and *set* method. However, the *set* or *get* method can override the defaults of the property. *Type* is the underlying type of the property. Neither the *get* nor *set* method has a return type or parameter list. Both are inferred. The *get* method returns the property type and has no parameters. The *set* method returns void and has a single parameter, which is the same type of the property. In the *set* method, the *value* keyword represents the implied parameter.

In this code, the *Person* class has an age property:

```
using System;

namespace Donis.CSharpBook{

    public class Person {
        private int prop_age;
        public int age {
            set {
                // perform validation
                prop_age=value;
            }
            get {
                return prop_age;
            }
        }
    }

    class People{

        public static void Main(){
            Person bob=new Person();
            bob.age=30; // Calls set method
            Console.WriteLine(bob.age);  // Call gets method
        }
    }
}
```

Properties have no inherent data storage. If desired, the data storage must be declared in the class. Computed properties might not require data storage. As a guideline, the property is public, whereas the data store is private. There is considerable flexibility available. The data store of a property could consist of several private fields. Conversely, multiple properties can share the same data store. This is demonstrated in the following code, where the *fullname*, *firstname*, and *lastname* property share the *prop_name* data store:

```csharp
using System;

namespace Donis.CSharpBook{

    public class Employee {

        private string prop_name;
        public string name {
            get {
                return prop_name;
            }
            set {
                prop_name=value;
            }
        }

        public string first {
            get {
                return (prop_name.Split(' '))[0];
            }
            set {
                string lastname=name.Split(' ')[1];
                prop_name=value+" "+lastname;
            }
        }
        public string last {
            get {
                return (prop_name.Split(' '))[1];
            }
            set {
                string firstname=name.Split(' ')[0];
                prop_name=firstname+" "+value;
            }
        }
    }

    public class Personnel{
        public static void Main(){
            Employee bob=new Employee();
            bob.name="Lisa Miller";
            bob.first="Frank";
            Console.WriteLine(bob.name);  // Jane Wilson
            Console.WriteLine(bob.last);  // Wilson
        }
    }
}
```

Read-only and write-only properties   Read-only properties offer only the *get* method and omit the *set* method. Birth date is an ideal read-only property. Conversely, write-only properties have a *set* only, which is common with a password property:

```
public class SensitiveForm{
    private string prop_password;
    public string password {
        set {
            prop_password=value;
        }
    }
}
```

Error handling   Validating the state of an object is important to avoid the "garbage-in/garbage out" syndrome. An object or class is only as useful as the quality of the data it contains. Validation can be performed in the *set* method of a property. What is the appropriate action if the validation fails? You cannot return an error code from a *set* method. There are two options. First (and preferably), raise an application exception. Second, if the property type is a reference or nullable type, set the property to null. For the *person* class, an age greater than 130 is probably an error. The estimated maximum age of a person is 120. In case someone is especially hearty, an age greater than 130 is flagged as invalid. Here are both approaches to handling an error condition in a property:

```
private int prop_age;
public int age {
    set {
        if(value<0 || value>120) {
            throw new ApplicationException("Not valid age!");
        }
        prop_age=value;
    }
    get {
        return prop_age;
    }
}

public class Person {
    private int? prop_age;
    public int? age {
        set {
            if(value<0 || value>120) {
                prop_age=null;
                            return;
            }
            prop_age=value;
        }
        get {
            return prop_age;
        }
    }
}
```

Nested Types

Nested types are classes and structures declared inside a class. Nested classes are advantageous when modeling systems of interconnecting components. This is an example of a nested class:

```
public class Outer {

    public void FuncA() {
    }

    public class Inner {

        static public void FuncB() {
            Console.WriteLine("Outer.Inner.FuncB()");
        }
    }
}
```

Nested types can be public, private, or other accessibility. A full complement of modifiers is available. In addition, the new modifier is available to nested types, which hides a nested class of the base class.

Use the dot syntax to access members of the nested class. This code calls a static method of the *inner* class:

```
Outer.Inner.FuncB();
```

You can build an instance of the *nested* class, which is an inner reference. If public, references to the *nested* class can be created inside or outside the *outer* class. A nested class that is private can be instantiated only in the *outer* class. The *this* object of the inner reference includes members of the *inner* class alone. Instance members of the *outer* class are not accessible from the *this* object of the inner reference. Pass a reference of the outer component into the constructor of the inner component. The back reference is then available to access the instance members of the outer component from within the inner component. The static members of the *outer* class, regardless of accessibility, are available in the *inner* class.

The *Automobile* class models a car engine, which is a system. An automobile system contains alternators, ignition, steering system, and other systems. This is an abbreviated version of the *Automobile* class:

```
using System;

namespace Donis.CSharpBook{

    public class Automobile {
```

```
        public Automobile() {
            starter=new StarterMotor(this);
        }

        public void Start() {
            starter.Ignition();
        }

        private bool prop_started=false;
        public bool started {
            get {
                return prop_started;
            }
        }

        private class StarterMotor {
            public StarterMotor(Automobile _auto) {
                auto=_auto;
            }

            public void Ignition() {
                auto.prop_started=true;
            }
            Automobile auto;
        }

        private StarterMotor starter;
    }

    public class Starter{
        public static void Main(){
            Automobile car=new Automobile();
            car.Start();
            if(car.started) {
                Console.WriteLine("Car started");
            }
        }
    }
}
```

Partial Classes

A *partial* class can span multiple source files. When compiled, the *partial* class is reassembled in the assembly. Each source file has a complete class declaration and body. The class declaration is preceded with the *partial* keyword. The class body in each source file includes only the members that the *partial* class is contributing to the overall type. Code generators will benefit from *partial* classes. Rely on the code generator or wizard to generate the core code. The developer can then extend the code without disturbing the base code. Teams of developers collaborating on an application also benefit from *partial* classes. The class can be parceled based on responsibility. The developer works in separate source files, which isolate changes and focus a developer on code relevant to their responsibility.

Consistency is the key to partial types:

- Each partial type is preceded with the *partial* keyword.
- The partial types must have the same accessibility.
- If any part is sealed, the entire class is sealed.
- If any part is abstract, the entire class is abstract.
- Inheritance at any partial type applies to the entire class.

Here is the example of a class separated into partial types:

```
// partial1.cs

using System;

namespace Donis.CSharpBook{

    public partial class ZClass {

        public void CoreMethodA() {
            Console.WriteLine("ZClass.CoreA");
        }
    }

    public class Starter{
        public static void Main(){
            ZClass obj=new ZClass();
            obj.CoreMethodA();
            obj.ExtendedMethodA();
        }
    }
}

// partial2.cs

using System;

namespace Donis.CSharpBook{

    public partial class ZClass {

        public void ExtendedMethodA() {
            Console.WriteLine("ZClass.ExtendedA");
        }
    }
}
```

Figure 2-2 shows the *ZClass* combined in the assembly, which demonstrates that the partial classes are merged.

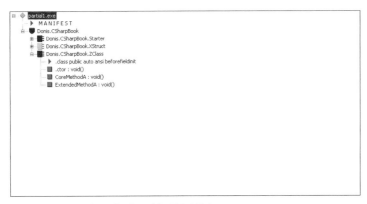

Figure 2-2   *ZClass* depicted in ILDASM

Structures

Structures are lightweight classes. Similar to classes, structures have behaviors and attributes. As a value type, structures directly contain their value and are stored on the stack. Because structures reside on the stack, keep them small. Do not cache large objects on the stack. The implementation of structures in C# enforces the policy of using a structure as a lightweight class. The following list details the differences between structures and classes:

- Structures are sealed and cannot be inherited.

- Structures cannot inherit classes and other structures.

- Structure implicitly inherits from *System.ValueType*.

- The default constructor of a structure cannot be replaced by a custom constructor.

- Custom constructors of a structure must fully initialize the value of the structure.

- Structures do not have destructors.

- Field initialization is not allowed. Const members of a structure can be initialized.

Structure syntax:

attributes accessibility **struct** *structname: interfacelist { structbody };*

There are several attributes that target structures. Structures support the same accessibility of a class. Structures implicitly inherit *System.ValueType* and cannot explicitly inherit another type. However, structures can implement interfaces. *Interfacelist* is a list of interfaces the structure implements. The *structbody* encompasses the member functions and data members of the structure.

The default constructor of a structure initializes each field to a default value. You cannot replace the default constructor of a structure. Unlike a class, adding custom constructors to a structure does not remove the default constructor. Invoke a custom constructor with the new operator. The new operator will not place the structure on the managed heap. It is a call to the parameterized constructor of a structure. Structures are commonly declared without the new operator. In that circumstance, the default constructor is called.

Fraction is a structure that models naturally a fraction. *Fraction* has two double members. It is small and ideal for a structure.

```
using System;

namespace Donis.CSharpBook{

    public struct Fraction {

        public Fraction(double _divisor, double _dividend) {
            divisor=_divisor;
            dividend=_dividend;
        }

        public double quotient {
            get {
                return divisor/dividend;
            }
        }

        private double divisor;
        private double dividend;

    }

    public class Calculate{
        public static void Main(){
            Fraction number=new Fraction(4,5);
            Console.WriteLine("{0}", number.quotient);
        }
    }
}
```

Enumeration

An enumeration is a set of discrete and related values. Enumerations expand into a type, whereas the members of the enumeration are defined as constant. The default underlying type of an enumeration is integer. An enumeration is never required; integer variables can be used instead. However, enumerations are safer, more extensible, and enhance readability. The *Months.GetMonth* method outputs the name of a month. The method relies on integer values.

```
public class Months {
    static public void GetMonth(int iMonth) {
        switch(iMonth) {
            case 1:
                Console.WriteLine("January");
                break;
```

```
            case 2:
                Console.WriteLine("Febuary");
                break;
            case 3:
                Console.WriteLine("March");
                break;
            // and so on...
            default:
                Console.WriteLine("Invalid Month");
                break;
        }
    }
}
```

Here is the *Months* class rewritten to use an enumeration:

```
public enum Month {
    January=1,
    February,
    March
  }
  public class Months{
  public static void GetMonth(Month m) {
        Console.WriteLine(m.ToString());
    }
  }
```

Which version of *Months* is simpler and more readable?

Here is the syntax of an enumeration:

accessibility enum *enumname*: *basetype* {*memberlist*};

Enumerations support public and other accessibility. The default underlying type is integer. The *basetype* element changes the underlying type. This can be any integral type, except the character type. For the *Month* enumeration, changing the underlying from integer to byte is more efficient. The *memberlist* includes all the constants of the enumeration. By default, the constant members are numbered in textual order from zero to n-1. Each member can be assigned a specific value. Here is the updated enumeration called *Month*:

```
public enum Month: byte {
    January=1,
    February,
    March
}
```

When assigning values to enumeration members, sequential ordering is not required. In addition, duplicate values are allowed. Some members can be set without initializing others. The value of the preceding member is incremented and assigned to any unassigned member.

ZEnum is a mixture of explicitly and implicitly initialized members. Optional values are listed in the comments.

```
public enum ZEnum{
    item1=6,
    item2=3,
    item3,      // 4
    item4,      // 5
    item5=8,
    item6       // 9
}
```

Enumerations are derived from the *System.ValueType* method, which offers important services for enumeration types. Table 2-5 lists some of those services.

Table 2-5   Important *System.Enum* Methods

Method Name	Description
static string GetName(Type enumtype, object value)	Returns the string representation of a specific item of the enumeration.
static string[] GetNames(Type enumtype)	Returns a string array containing the string representation of every item of the specified enumeration.
static Array GetValues(Type enumtype)	Returns an array of the underlying type. The array contains the numerical representation of each value of the enumeration.
static Type GetUnderlyingType(Type enumType)	Returns the underlying type of the enumeration.

Bitwise Enumeration

Bitwise enumeration is for mutually inclusive flags. Each member of the enumeration is assigned a unique bitwise value. Apply the *flags* attribute to an enumeration to specify bitwise enumeration.

Combine bitwise flags using the *or* operator (|). Confirm the existence of a flag with the bitwise *and* operator (&).

The following code demonstrates the *flags* attribute of an enumeration:

```
using System;

namespace Donis.CSharpBook{

    [Flags] public enum Contribution {
        Pension=0x01,
        ProfitSharing=0x02,
        CreditBureau=0x04,
        SavingsPlan=0x08,
```

```
        All=Pension|ProfitSharing|CreditBureau|SavingsPlan
    }

    public class Employee {
        private Contribution prop_contributions;
        public Contribution contributions {
            get {
                return prop_contributions;
            }
            set {
                prop_contributions=value;
            }
        }
    }

    public class Starter{
        public static void Main(){
            Employee bob=new Employee();
            bob.contributions=Contribution.ProfitSharing|
                Contribution.CreditBureau;
            if((bob.contributions&Contribution.ProfitSharing)
                == Contribution.ProfitSharing) {
                Console.WriteLine("Bob enrolled in profit sharing");
            }
        }
    }
}
```

Identity versus Equivalence

Reference and value types support different memory models. References refer to objects created on the managed heap, whereas value types are created on the stack. Equivalence and identity complement the memory model. Equivalence is the value or state of an instance. Related instances that have the same value are equivalent. Identity is the location of an object.

Equivalent values are related types that contain the same value. In the following code, integers *locala* and *localc* are equivalent. However, the variables are not identical because they are stored at different locations on the stack. The variables *locala* and *localb* are neither equivalent no identical. They have differenet values and are stored at different locations on the stack:

```
int locala=5;
int localb=10;
int localc=5;
```

Assigning a value type copies the value. The target and source are equivalent after this assignment, but not identical:

```
locala=localb;  // locala and localb are equivalent.
```

For reference types, there is synchronicity of equivalence and identity. Related references containing the same value are equivalent and identical. Assigning a reference creates an alias, which can create unplanned side affects. For this reason, be careful when assigning references. The following code has some unplanned side effects:

```
using System;

namespace Donis.CSharpBook{

    public class XInt {
        public int iField=0;
    }

    public class Starter{
        public static void Main(){
            XInt obj1=new XInt();
            obj1.iField=5;
            XInt obj2=new XInt();
            obj2.iField=10;

            // Alias created and second instance lost
            obj2=obj1;
            obj1.iField=15; // side affect
            Console.WriteLine("{0}", obj2.iField); // 15
        }
    }
}
```

Class Refinement

Classes can be refined through inheritance, which is code reuse. The common members of related classes can be extracted and placed in a base class. Child classes inherit and refine a base class. A personnel application might have *SalariedEmployee*, *HourlyEmployee*, and *CommissionedEmployee* classes that inherit the *Employee* class. The *Employee* class holds the common members of all *Employee*-derived classes. Each derived class adds members to refine the base class. Optionally, derived classes can override members of the base class. Sealed classes cannot be inherited. Inheritance and polymorphism are closely related. Polymorphism calls the correct method at run time from a base reference to a derived object, and it can add considerable efficiencies to an application.

Inheritance and polymorphism and other strategies to refine class usage are reviewed in Chapter 3.

Chapter 3
Inheritance

Classes are often related to other classes. The two popular methods of relating classes are *containment*, also known as composition, and *inheritance*. Containment is a "has a" relationship, where a class contains or embeds another class. For example, a timestamp contains time. Inheritance is based on the "is a" relationship, in which one class is a type of another class. For example, an hourly employee is a kind of employee.

Inheritance involves a *base type* and a *derived type*, where a derived type is a kind of base type. Derived types inherit the members of the base type. In essence, they are derived from the base type.

A base type represents a generalization, whereas a derived type represents a specialty. Specialties are derivatives of generalizations. A personnel program might contain different types of employees. Hourly, salaried, commissioned, temporary, and retired are possible types of employees. Each is a kind of employee and distinct from any other employee specialization. For example, an hourly employee is different from a salaried employee. Employee is a generalization of all employees and is therefore a base class. Conversely, *HourlyEmployee*, *SalariedEmployee*, *CommissionedEmployee*, *TemporaryEmployee*, and *RetiredEmployee* are specializations and are therefore derived classes.

Derived types refine base types. A base type holds the common members of the generalization. Derived classes inherit those members and add specialty members. These members refine the base class in the context of the derived class. The *Employee* class, which is a base class, defines the *FullName* and *EmplID* members. Every employee has a name and employee number. As such, those members belong in the base type. The *SalariedEmployee* class adds members for the salary and number of pay periods. This is unique to the salaried employee specialization. The *HourlyEmployee* class has additional fields for the hourly rate and the number of hours worked. Both *SalariedEmployee* and *HourlyEmployee* classes refine the *Employee* class with these extra members.

Inheritance provides hierarchical clarity. The employee and derived types form a hierarchy. Without this clarity, you face a greater challenge in programming an application. Classes are analogous to marbles in a bin. A large bin holds hundreds of marbles. The bin is an indiscriminate jumble of marbles. From this jumble, you might try to find the one marble that is a clearie and has gray and white stripes. You could be looking for awhile, as shown in Figure 3-1. The marbles could be organized into separate bins for regular, boulder, and steelie marbles. Regular marbles are further segmented into cat's eyes and clearies, which are placed in smaller subcontainers. With this additional organization, finding the clearie with gray and white stripes is easier. (See Figure 3-2.)

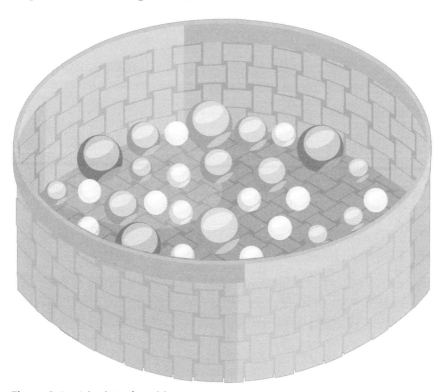

Figure 3-1   A basket of marbles

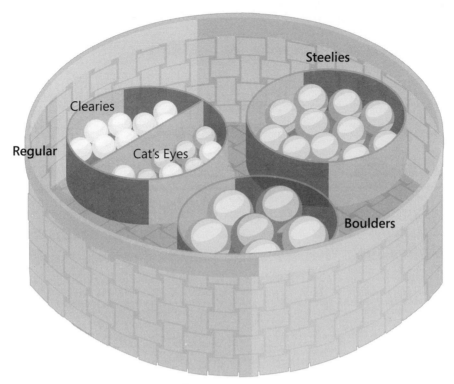

Figure 3-2   Organized baskets of marbles

As part of the design phase, scenarios are often employed. The nouns in the scenarios are candidates for classes. Figure 3-3 shows the nouns found in a scenario for a Personnel application. There is no order or hierarchy. You should look for relationships. The "is a" or "is a kind of" phrases are excellent for identifying inheritance and discerning the base to derived class relationships. When the classes are organized by relationships, clarity blooms, as shown in Figure 3-4.

Class hierarchy in moderation is helpful. However, excessive hierarchy is as cumbersome as no hierarchy at all. An overly vertical hierarchy is as incoherent as a flat hierarchy. There are also performance penalties for extended class hierarchies. The best practice in C++ was to limit class hierarchies to six levels or fewer. For example, the copious layers of classes in Microsoft Foundation Classes (MFC) contributed to the complexity of the product. Wading through the extensive class hierarchy of the MFC is sometimes a tedious task. In addition, understanding the members of a class is harder when dozens of other classes seed that class with methods, properties, fields, and so on. Hierarchical clarity is lost, which affects your productivity. The Active Template Library (ATL) is on the opposite end of the spectrum and has a flatter model. It is trivial to navigate the ATL hierarchy, which is appreciated.

Figure 3-3   Nouns from the Personnel scenario

Inheritance also promotes code reuse. Without inheritance, common members would be implemented repeatedly—once in each derived type. Modifications would require updating several classes. This is a recipe for problems and is neither efficient nor versionable. Inheritance has a cascade effect, which is better. A member is implemented once in a base class, and the implementation cascades to all derived classes. Changes to a base member ripple to all descendants. Insert base members at the highest relevant point in the hierarchy. This creates the widest cascade and efficient utilization of the member. Inserting a member too low in the hierarchy forces related types to separately implement that member.

Reference types can inherit classes and interfaces. Inheriting a class exemplifies code reuse. The derived class inherits the members—including the code—of the base class. Conversely, an interface has no code. It is a contract. Types that implement the interface contract to implement every member of the interface, whereas the interface contracts to be immutable. This is important because changes to the interface would break any type derived from that interface. Value types and primitives are not inheritable; they are sealed. For example, you cannot inherit an int.

Value types cannot inherit other value types or classes. The exception is the *System.ValueType* class. Value types implicitly inherit the *System.ValueType* class. A struct can inherit interfaces.

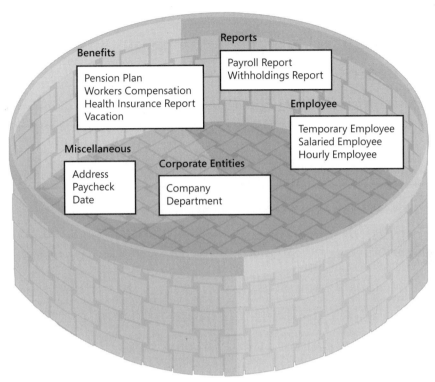

Figure 3-4   Nouns grouped by relationships

Terminology is important. Accurate terminology enhances a conversation, whereas incorrect or unclear terminology muddles the discussion. Object-oriented analysis and design introduced a plethora of new terms, some of which are identical or similar. Some terms are intended for design, whereas others are for the implementation phase. However, this distinction is often lost. Table 3-1 shows a list of terms similar to base and derived types. In this chapter, the *base/derived* and *parent/child* terms are used interchangeably.

Table 3-1   Inheritance Terminology

Inheritable Class	Inheriting Class
Superclass	Subclass
Parent	Child
Ascendant	Descendant
Base	Derived

Inheritance is not a mechanism to simply drop members into a class. From a design perspective, those members should belong in that class. For example, a timestamp has the properties of time and a stamp. A timestamp is a kind of stamp and has a time piece. However, a timestamp is not a kind of time. A *TimeStamp* class should inherit from the *Stamp* class but not the *Time* class. The "has a" relationship between the timestamp and time infers containment. Embedding a *Time* class in the *TimeStamp* class is the preferable implementation.

Inheritance Example

Before introducing the specifics of inheritance, an example that includes all the prerequisite elements of inheritance might be helpful. In the code, *XParent* is the base class. *XChild* is the derived class and inherits the *XParent* class. *XChild* inherits a method, property, and field from the base class. *XChild* extends *XParent* by adding a method and field to this assemblage. *XChild* has five members: three from the base and two from itself. In this manner, *XChild* is a specialty type and refines *XParent*. In *Main*, instances of the *XParent* and *XChild* classes are created. Base methods are called on the *XParent* instance. Both base and derived methods are called on the *XChild* instance.

```
using System;

namespace Donis.CSharpBook{
    public class Starter{
        public static void Main(){

            XParent parent=new XParent();
            parent.MethodA();
            XChild child=new XChild();
            child.MethodA();
            child.MethodB();
            child.FieldA=10;
            Console.WriteLine(child.FieldA);
        }

        public class XParent {
            public void MethodA() {
                Console.WriteLine("XParent.MethodA called from {0}.",
                    this.GetType().ToString());
            }

            private int propFieldA;

            public int FieldA {
                get {
                    return propFieldA;
                }
                set {
                    propFieldA=value;
                }
            }

        }

        public class XChild: XParent {
            public int MethodB() {
                Console.WriteLine("XChild.MethodB called from {0}.",
```

```
                    this.GetType().ToString());
                return fieldb;
            }

            private int fieldb=5;
        }
    }
}
}
```

Cross-Language Inheritance

Inheritance is language-agnostic. Managed languages can inherit classes written in another managed language. For library developers, this expands the universe of potential clients. Developers no longer need to maintain language-specific versions of a library or create complex workarounds. Just as important, a family of developers is not excluded from using a certain library. Another benefit of cross-language inheritance is collaboration. Team members collaborating on a software system can develop in the language of their choice. The entire team is not compelled to select a single source language.

Managed languages compile to Microsoft intermediate language (MSIL) code. The Common Language Runtime (CLR) does not perceive a Microsoft Visual Basic .NET class inheriting from a C# class. It views one MSIL class inheriting from another MSIL class. Language independence is easier to achieve when specific languages dissolve into a shared common language at compilation.

Cross-language inheritance fractures without compliance to the Common Language Specification (CLS)—at least relative to the base or derived class. Language-specific and noncompliant artifacts must be wrung from classes when cross-language inheritance is planned or expected. For example, the following class, although perfectly okay in C#, is unworkable in Visual Basic .NET. Visual Basic .NET is case insensitive, making *MethodA* in the following code ambiguous:

```
public class XBase {
    public void MethodA() {
    }
    public void methoda() {
    }
}
```

The following code is an example of successful cross-language inheritance. The base class is written in C#, whereas the derived class is Visual Basic .NET.

```
' VB Code: which includes derived class.

Imports System
Imports Donis.CSharpBook

Namespace Donis.CSharpBook
    Public Class Starter
```

```
            Public Shared Sub Main
                Dim child as New XChild
                child.MethodA()
                child.MethodB()
            End Sub
        End Class

        Public Class XChild
            Inherits XParent

            Public Sub MethodB
                Console.WriteLine("XChild.MethodB called from {0}.", _
                    Me.GetType().ToString())
            End Sub
        End Class
End Namespace
// C# Code: which includes base class

using System;

namespace Donis.CSharpBook{
    public class XParent {
        public void MethodA() {
            Console.WriteLine("XParent.MethodA called from {0}.",
                this.GetType().ToString());
        }

        private int propFieldA;

        public int FieldA {
            get {
                    return propFieldA;
            }
            set {
                    propFieldA=value;
            }
        }
    }
}
```

System.Object

System.Object is the ubiquitous base type. All managed types inherit from *System.Object*, either directly or indirectly. *System.Object* encompasses the baseline behavior accorded to all managed types. Reference types without an explicit base class inherit *System.Object* implicitly. Reference types that inherit another type explicitly still inherit *System.Object*, but indirectly. You can inherit *System.Object* explicitly. However, that is somewhat redundant and, therefore, is not often done. Value types inherit from *System.ValueType*, which then inherits *System.Object*. *System.ValueType* overrides *System.Object* members to implement the semantics of a value type.

The members of the *System.Object* class are explained in Table 3-2.

Table 3-2   *System.Object* Methods

Method Name	Description
Constructor	public Object()
	This is the default constructor of the *System.Object*. It is called whenever an instance of an object is created. The *object* keyword is an alias for the *System.Object* type.
Equals	public virtual bool Equals(object obj)
	public static bool Equals(object obj1, object obj2)
	Equals returns *true* if the value of two objects is equal. For reference types, this is an object comparison, which compares identity. For value types, this method compares state, which is an equivalency test. Override this method to perform a more appropriate equality comparison of a derived type.
Finalize	protected override *void Finalize()*.
	This method is called when an instance is garbage collected. This method cleans up unmanaged resources associated with an instance. In C#, the destructor is called from the *Finalize* method. Destructors and finalization are discussed in Chapter 14, "Memory Management."
GetHashCode	public virtual int *GetHashCode()*
	This method returns a hash code of an instance. The default hash code is not guaranteed to be unique or have even distribution. You can override this method to return a meaningful hash code for a derived type or provide better distribution.
GetType	public Type *GetType()*
	This method returns a Type reference, which can be used to inspect the structure of an instance. A Type reference is often the first ingredient in Reflection. Reference is discussed in Chapter 10, "Metadata and Reflections."
MemberwiseClone	protected object *MemberwiseClone()*
	This method creates and returns a new instance of the current object. It performs a shallow copy. For this reason, reference members of the original and cloned object point to the same objects. This method is protected and cannot be overridden in the derived type.
ReferenceEquals	public static bool *ReferenceEquals*(object obj1, obj2)
	This method returns true if the identity, not the state, of two objects is the same.
ToString	public virtual string *ToString()*
	This method returns a string representation of the current instance. The default return is the fully qualified name of the type for the current instance. *ToString* is frequently overridden to return more pertinent information.

Object.Equals Method

For reference types, the *Object.Equals* method compares identity. References are equal when pointing to the same object. References that point to different objects but have the same state are not equal. You can override the *Equals* method to perform a value comparison. For value types, the *Equals* method is already overridden to compare values.

In *Applied Microsoft .NET Framework Programming* (Microsoft Press, 2001), author Jeffrey Richter mentions four tenets of the *Equals* method: reflexivity, symmetry, transitivity, and consistency.

- **Reflexive** An object is always equal to itself. The obj1.Equal (obj1) call should always return *true*.

- **Symmetric** If obj1.Equals(obj2) is *true*, then obj2.Equals(obj1) must also be *true*.

- **Transitive** If obj1.Equals(obj2) and obj2.Equals(obj3) are both *true*, then obj3.Equals(obj1) is *true*.

- **Consistent** If obj1.Equals(obj2) is *true*, then obj1 and obj2 should always be equal. This assumes that the state of neither object has changed.

The *Employee* class is a base class. The *HourlyEmployee*, *CommissionedEmployee*, and *SalariedEmployee* classes derive from the *Employee* class and represent specific types of employees. This is the override of the *Equals* method in the *Employee* class:

```
public static bool operator==(Employee obj1, Employee obj2) {
    return obj1.Equals(obj2);
}

public static bool operator!=(Employee obj1, Employee obj2) {
    return !obj1.Equals(obj2);
}

public override bool Equals(object obj) {
    Employee _obj=obj as Employee;

    if(obj==null) {
        return false;
    }
    return this.GetHashCode()==_obj.GetHashCode();
}
```

The preceding code also includes overloads of the operators == and !=. The default implementation of these operators will not call the overridden *Equals* method. This can cause inconsistencies, where the comparison operators behave differently from the *Equals* method. For this reason, both operators have been overloaded.

When overriding the *Equals* method, you should also override the *GetHashCode* method. If not, a compiler warning occurs. Objects that are equal should have the same hash code. Therefore, equality can be based on comparing hash codes. In the *Equals* method, call *GetHashCode* to retrieve and compare hash codes.

Object.GetHashCode Method

GetHashCode returns a hash code as a 32-bit integer. Override this method when a reference type is used as a key in a collection. As indicated in the previous section, the *Equals* and *GetHashCode* methods should be implemented in tandem.

The fields associated with a hash code should be immutable. If the fields are not immutable, when the fields change, the hash code is also modified. This could necessitate updating the key in a collection. If not, the original key is stale. Stale keys in a collection can cause problems. For this reason, hash codes should not be transient, and the related fields should not change.

The following code shows the *GetHashCode* method for the *Employee* class. The *EmplID* field used for the hash is read-only. After the *Employee* instance is created, *EmplID* cannot be modified. It is immutable. There are a variety of algorithms for creating efficient and distributed hash codes—some quite complex. For simplicity, this implementation of *GetHashCode* simply returns the *EmplID* property:

```
public override int GetHashCode() {
    return EmplID;
}
```

Hash codes are recyclable. When a reference is garbage collected, the hash code is returned to the available pool. The hash code is then assignable to a future instance. For this reason, you should remove dead objects from any collections.

Object.GetType Method

The *GetType* method returns a *Type* instance, which describes the current object. Type objects are useful in interrogating the composition of an associated object. Members, such as *GetMethods* and *GetFields*, return the underlying architecture of a type. This process is called Reflection.

The following code demonstrates Reflection. The public methods of *System.Object* are enumerated and displayed. As expected, the methods of Table 3-3 are shown. This excludes the *Object.MemberwiseClone* method, which is not a public method.

```
using System;
using System.Collections;
using System.Reflection;

namespace Donis.CSharpBook{

    public class Starter{
        public static void Main(){
            Object obj=new Object();
            Type t=obj.GetType();
            foreach(MethodInfo m in t.GetMethods()) {
                Console.WriteLine(m.Name);
            }
        }
    }
}
```

Object.ToString Method

The *ToString* method returns a string representation of an instance. The default return is the fully qualified name of the type. Value types override *ToString* to return the value of the instance. The following code displays the default string representation of a value and a reference type:

```
int locala=10;
Console.WriteLine(locala.ToString());  // 10
Object obj=new Object();
Console.WriteLine(obj.ToString());     // System.Object
```

In the *Employee* class, *ToString* is overridden to return the name of the employee:

```
public override string ToString() {
   return FullName;
}
```

Object.MemberwiseClone Method

MemberwiseClone returns a new instance of an object. A shallow copy is performed. An object is cloned by performing a bitwise copy of each member. If a member is a value type, the values are copied and there is no side effect. For a member that is a reference type, the reference—not the object—is copied. The result is that the reference members of both objects point to the same memory, as shown in Figure 3-5. When this occurs, any changes in the original object will affect the cloned object, and vice versa.

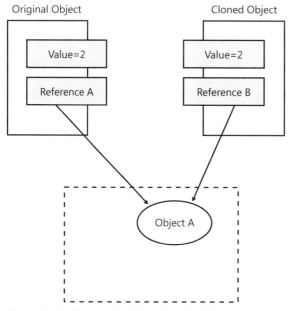

Figure 3-5   The result of *MemberwiseClone*

MemberwiseClone is protected and cannot be overridden. The method is typically called from a derived class when implementing the *ICloneable* interface. The *ICloneable* interface defines an interface for cloning objects. The only member is the *ICloneable.Clone* method.

The following code shows the implementation of the *ICloneable.Clone* method in the *Employee* class. As expected, the code delegates to the *MemberwiseClone* method. In the *Employee* class, *emplName* is a member and a reference type. In *Main*, *obj2* is a clone of *obj1*. The hash of both objects is displayed. This confirms the separate identities of each object. Nonetheless, changes to the employee name affect both objects, which is a nasty side effect. Both objects point to the same name in memory.

```
public class Starter{
    public static void Main(){
        Employee obj1=new Employee(5678);
        Employee obj2=(Employee) obj1.Clone();
        obj1.Last="Marshall";
        obj2.First="Donis";
         Console.WriteLine("Obj1 HC "+
            obj1.GetHashCode().ToString());
        Console.WriteLine(obj1.EmplID+": "+obj1.FullName);
        // 5678: Donis Marshall
        Console.WriteLine("Obj2 HC "+
            obj2.GetHashCode().ToString());
        Console.WriteLine(obj2.EmplID+": "+obj2.FullName);
        // 5678: Donis Marshall
    }
}


class Employee: ICloneable {

    public Employee(int id) {
        if((id<1000) || (id>9999)) {
            throw new Exception(
                "Invalid Employee ID");
        }

        propID=id;
    }

    public object Clone() {
        return MemberwiseClone();
    }
//  end of partial listing...
```

Object.ReferenceEquals Method

The *ReferenceEquals* method compares identity. If the objects are the same, *ReferenceEquals* returns *true*. Otherwise, *false* is returned. *ReferenceEquals* is not virtual and cannot be overridden in the derived class. The following code compares an original object and a cloned object.

The objects have the same state but different identities. Because the identities are distinct, the *ReferenceEquals* method returns *false*.

```
Employee obj1=new Employee(5678);
Employee obj2=(Employee) obj1.Clone();
if(Employee.ReferenceEquals(obj1, obj2)) {
    Console.WriteLine("objects identical");
}
else {
    Console.WriteLine("objects not identical");
}
}
```

Employee Class

This is the complete listing of the *Employee* class, including the overridden methods of the *System.Object* class:

```
using System;
using System.Collections;

namespace Donis.CSharpBook{

    public class Starter{
        public static void Main(){
            Employee obj1=new Employee(5678);
            Employee obj2=new Employee(5678);
            if(obj1==obj2) {
                Console.WriteLine("equals");
            }
            else {
                Console.WriteLine("not equals");
            }
        }
    }

    class Employee {

        public Employee(int id) {
            if((id<1000) || (id>9999)) {
                throw new Exception(
                    "Invalid Employee ID");
            }

            propID=id;
        }

        public static bool operator==(Employee obj1, Employee obj2) {
            return obj1.Equals(obj2);
        }

        public static bool operator!=(Employee obj1, Employee obj2) {
            return !obj1.Equals(obj2);
```

```
        }

        public override bool Equals(object obj) {
            Employee _obj=obj as Employee;

            if(obj==null) {
                return false;
            }
            return this.GetHashCode()==_obj.GetHashCode();
        }

        public override int GetHashCode() {
            return EmplID;
        }

        public string FullName {
            get {
                return propFirst+" "+
                    propLast;
            }
        }

        private string propFirst;
        public string First {
            get {
                return propFirst;
            }
            set {
                propFirst=value;
            }
        }

        private string propLast;
        public string Last {
            get {
                return propLast;
            }
            set {
                propLast=value;
            }
        }

        private readonly int propID;
        public int EmplID {
            get {
                return propID;
            }
        }

        public override string ToString() {
            return FullName;
        }
    }

}
```

Implementing Inheritance

Inheritance requires a base class and a derived class, where the derived class inherits from the base class. The members of the base class are inherited into the derived type. Derived classes can override and extend the interface inherited from the base type.

This is the syntax for inheritance syntax:

class *derivedclass*: *baseclass*, *interface*^{1}, *interface*^{2}, *interface*^{n} {
    derived body
}

In the class header, the colon stipulates inheritance and prefixes the base list. The base list is a comma-delimited list that includes at most one base class and any number of interfaces. Classes are limited to inheriting a single class. However, a class can inherit multiple interfaces. C++ developers are probably familiar with multiple inheritance. C++ allows multiple inheritance of classes. Excluding multiple inheritance was an important design decision for C#. Personally, I endorse that decision. First, multiple inheritance is not used that often. Second, multiple inheritance often causes more problems than are resolved. Third, multiple inheritance allows for the increased probability of ambiguousness of members.

A base type must have the same or greater accessibility than the derived type. A compiler error occurs in the following code. The accessibility of the base class is narrower than the derived class, which is an error.

```
internal class ZClass {
}
public class YClass: ZClass {
}
```

.NET supports only public inheritance. C++ supported public, protected, and private inheritance. Despite this flexibility in C++, practically all inheritance was public inheritance. Most C++ developers were not familiar with or ever used any other kind of inheritance. Thus, protected and private inheritance will probably not be missed.

Access Modifiers

Access modifiers set the visibility of members to the outside world and the derived type. Table 3-3 describes member accessibility.

Table 3-3   Member Accessibility

Member Access Modifier	Outside World	Derived Class
public	Yes	Yes
private	No	No
protected	No	Yes
internal	Yes (this assembly)	Yes (this assembly)
internal protected	Yes (this assembly)	Yes

Are private members of the base class inherited? Private members are indeed inherited but are not visible to the derived type and are not directly accessible in the derived class. These members are accessible through the public and protected functions of the base class. Therefore, a derived type has two realms of private variables. One realm includes private members that are defined in a derived class. These members are visible in the derived type. The other realm includes inherited private members, which are not visible to the derived type.

Overriding

A derived class can override behaviors in the base class, which allows a derived type to substitute different implementations where appropriate. The *Pay* method of the *Employee* class is overridden in *CommissionedEmployee* to include commissions in each paycheck. In the *SalariedEmployee* class, the *Pay* method is overridden to calculate pay by prorating annual income. Methods, properties, and indexers can be overridden. Fields and static members of the base cannot be overridden in the derived class. However, derived types can hide fields and static members of the base class.

When is a child class allowed to override the parent? Most parents hope that their children inherit their sterling behavior. However, the behavior of the parent is merely a suggestion to the child. Children are often inclined to override the behaviors of the parents. The parent is hopeless in preventing this substitution. In many object-oriented languages, that is the model. Child or derived classes can override the behavior of the parent or base class. The derived class might override a behavior inappropriately and destabilize the base class. This is called the fragile base class problem: a problem that is acute with class libraries where a child class is more likely to inherit a type and unknowingly or incorrectly override a base member. The model is different in C#. By default, functions cannot be overridden. Parent classes must tacitly approve the overriding of a method. In addition, the child class must acknowledge its intent to override the method. This prevents the child from unknowingly overriding a member of the base class.

Virtual and Override Keywords

The *virtual* keyword indicates that a member can be overridden in a child class. It can be applied to methods, properties, indexers, and events. In the derived class, the *override* keyword indicates the intention to override a virtual member of the base class. The *virtual* and *override* keywords complement each other. The *virtual* keyword propagates to descendants. A virtual method is overridable in a derived class and descendants.

Overriding is not an all-or-nothing condition. Using the *base* keyword, the public and protected members of the base class are accessible in the derived type. The syntax is base.*member.* You cannot skip levels with the *base* keyword. For example, you cannot access a member in a grandfather class. The base.base.*member* syntax is illegal. In the following code, the *SalariedEmployee.Pay* method calls the *Employee.Pay* method to display an employee name on a paycheck:

```
public class Employee: ICloneable {

    public Employee() {
    }

    public Employee(int id) {
        if((id<1000) || (id>9999)) {
            throw new Exception(
                "Invalid Employee ID");
        }

        propID=id;
    }

    public virtual void Pay() {
        Console.WriteLine("Employee: "+FullName);
    }

    // partial listing
}

public class SalariedEmployee: Employee {

    public override void Pay() {
        base.Pay();
        Console.WriteLine("Pay is: {0,6:c}",
            propSalary/(decimal)propPeriods);
    }

    // partial listing

}
```

Overload versus Override

Override and overload are different concepts. When a member of a base class is overridden, the signature of the base and the signature of the derived member are the same. Overloading requires different signatures. In a derived class, a function can be overloaded, overridden, or both. When a member is overridden with a different signature, a compiler warning occurs in the derived type. This prevents an accidental overload, where method overriding was intended. This is shown in the following code, where *MethodA* is overloaded in the *YClass* class but not overridden. In *Main*, both the base and the derived implementation are called.

```
using System;

namespace Donis.CSharpBook{

    public class Starter{
```

```
        public static void Main(){
            YClass obj=new YClass();
            obj.MethodA();
            obj.MethodA(10);
        }
    }


    public class ZClass {
        public virtual void MethodA() {
            Console.WriteLine("ZClass.MethodA");
        }
    }

    public class YClass: ZClass
    {
        public override void MethodA(int a) {
            Console.WriteLine("YClass.MethodA");
        }

    }
}
```

Overriding Events

For completeness, the following is sample code for overriding an event. Events are discussed in Chapter 8, "Delegates and Events."

```
public class ZClass {

    public virtual void MethodA() {
    }

    public delegate void MyDel();
    public virtual event MyDel MyEvent {
        add{
        }
        remove{
        }
    }
}

public class YClass: ZClass {

    public override event MyDel MyEvent{
        add{
            // different implementation
        }
        remove{
            // different implementation
        }
    }
}
```

New Modifier

The new modifier hides a member of the base class. New is the default modifier when a member is replicated in a derived type. However, unless the *new* keyword is stated explicitly, a compiler warning is presented to prevent the inadvertent hiding of a member of the base class. Explicit use of the *new* keyword prevents the warning. A virtual member and overridden member are related, which is important to polymorphism. The derived member and hidden member are, however, unrelated.

NET supports hide-by-signature and hide-by-name techniques. C# only supports hide-by-signature, where a single member is hidden using the new modifier. Hide-by-name hides the entire interface of a member, which may entail several functions. This option is available in Visual Basic .NET.

In the following code, *ZClass* is the base class and contains *MethodA* and *MethodB* members. Both are virtual methods, and *MethodB* calls *MethodA*.

```
public virtual void MethodB() {
    MethodA();
}
```

YClass is a derived class and inherits from *ZClass*. *MethodA* is overridden in the derived type, but *MethodB* is not overridden. Therefore, two versions of *MethodA* exist: a base version and a derived version. When *YClass.MethodB* is called, which version of *MethodA* is invoked in the method? Because *MethodA* is virtual, the most derived method is called. *YClass.MethodA* is invoked. With a virtual method, the compiler prefers the most derived method.

Here is the code:

```
using System;

namespace Donis.CSharpBook{

    public class Starter{
        public static void Main(){
            YClass obj=new YClass();
            obj.MethodB();  // YClass.MethodA
        }
    }


    public class ZClass {
        public virtual void MethodA() {
            Console.WriteLine("ZClass.MethodA");
        }

        public virtual void MethodB() {
            MethodA();
        }
    }
```

```
public class YClass: ZClass
{
    public override void MethodA() {
        Console.WriteLine("YClass.MethodA");
    }
}
}
```

The following code is almost identical to the previous code. However, *ZClass.MethodA* is not overridden in the derived class. Instead, *YClass* hides the base class implementation of *MethodA* with the new modifier. *ZClass.MethodA* and *YClass.MethodA* are now unrelated. Therefore, the compiler will not delegate to *YClass.MethodA* for an implementation inherited from the parent. For this reason, *YClass.MethodB* calls *ZClass.MethodA*. This prevents functions inherited from the base class in calling unrelated functions, which could cause the fragile base class problem.

```
using System;

namespace Donis.CSharpBook{

    public class Starter{
        public static void Main(){
            YClass obj=new YClass();
            obj.MethodB();  // ZClass.MethodA
        }
    }

    class ZClass {
        public virtual void MethodA() {
            Console.WriteLine("ZClass.MethodA");
        }

        public virtual void MethodB() {
            MethodA();
        }
    }

    class YClass: ZClass
    {
        public new void MethodA() {
            Console.WriteLine("YClass.MethodA");
        }
    }
}
```

Interestingly, although the new modifier hides the base class member, you can still access the base class implementation with the *base* keyword. This is demonstrated in the following code:

```
public class ZClass {

    public virtual void MethodA() {
        Console.WriteLine("ZClass.MethodA");
    }
}
```

```
public class YClass: ZClass
{
    public new void MethodA() {
        base.MethodA();
        Console.WriteLine("YClass.MethodA");
    }

}
```

Virtual methods are overridable in all descendants. The new modifier ends the propagation of this characteristic. The new modifier changes virtual methods to nonvirtual. The method cannot be overridden in further descendants. A function can be declared as both new and virtual. In that circumstance, the function hides the base method and is overridable to descendants.

The following code demonstrates that a member with the new modifier cannot be overridden:

```
public class ZClass {
    public virtual void MethodA() {
    }

    public virtual void MethodB() {
    }
}

public class YClass: ZClass
{
    public new virtual void MethodA() {
    }                 ⌐ = override

    public new void MethodB() {
    }

}

public class XClass: YClass
{
    public override void MethodA() {
    }

    /*   ERROR

    public override void MethodB() {
    }
    */
}
```

Base fields and static members cannot be overridden in a derived class. However, both can be hidden with the new modifier. Hiding field and static members can cause confusion. When you use this feature, I recommend thorough supporting documentation in your code.

In the following code, ZClass has a static method and field. Their purpose is to count ZClass instances. YClass inherits ZClass and hides the two static members of the base type. The new members count the instances of the *YClass*. Therefore, there are simultaneous counts—the base class and derived class counters. In *Main*, multiple instances of the *ZClass* and *YClass* are created. Both counters are then displayed.

```csharp
using System;

namespace Donis.CSharpBook{

    public class Starter{
        public static void Main(){
            ZClass obj1=new ZClass();
            YClass obj2=new YClass();
            YClass obj3=new YClass();
            ZClass.DisplayCounter();
            YClass.DisplayCounter();
        }
    }


    public class ZClass {
        public ZClass() {
            ++count;
        }

        public static int count=0;
        public static void DisplayCounter() {
            Console.WriteLine("ZClass.Count:");
            Console.WriteLine(count);
        }

/*      ERROR - static methods cannot be virtual

        public static virtual void DisplayCounter() {
            Console.WriteLine("ZClass count:");
            Console.WriteLine(count);
        }
*/

    }

    public class YClass: ZClass
    {
        public YClass() {
            ++count;
        }

        private new static int count=0;

        public new static void DisplayCounter() {
            Console.WriteLine("YClass count:");
            Console.WriteLine(count);
        }
    }
}
```

Abstract

Abstract classes are concepts. Object-oriented applications model the real world, which is replete with concepts. For developers of a graphics program, a geometric shape is a concept. Have you even seen a geometric shape? No. Rather, you have seen types of geometric shapes, such as triangles, ellipses, rectangles, and lines. *Geometric shape* is a description of a category— a kind of shape. Conversely, a rectangle is tangible: A television, a box, and this book are actual rectangles.

The *Employee* class is an abstract class. Why? In the personnel domain, employee is a categorization of employees. Each employee is specifically an hourly, salary, or commissioned employee. How an employee is paid is determined by the type of employee. Payroll calculations are conducted into the derived type, such as *HourlyEmployee*. The *Employee* base type is a container of general information such as the employee name. However, without pay specifics, the *Employee* class is incomplete. Most employees value getting paid. For that reason, *Employee* is a concept and abstract.

The *abstract* keyword makes a class abstract. Abstract classes exist extensively for inheritance. You cannot create an instance of an abstract class. Nonabstract classes are concrete classes. You can create an instance of a concrete class. Static classes, value types, and interfaces do not support the abstract modifier.

In the next example, *Employee* is the base class and is abstract. *HourlyEmployee* is the derived class and is concrete.

```
public class Starter{
    public static void Main(){
        Employee obj1=new Employee();                // Not valid
        HourlyEmployee obj2=new HourlyEmployee();   // Valid
    }
}

public abstract class Employee { // abstract
}

public class HourlyEmployee: Employee {  // concrete
}
```

Members can also be abstract. Methods, properties, indexers, and event members can be abstract. However, static members cannot be abstract. In addition, classes with abstract members must also be abstract. An abstract member has a signature but no function body. Virtual is implied with abstract functions. Abstract members must be implemented in the derived type.

In the real world, a parent can ask a child to do something with or without instructions. The parent can provide instruction to the child to complete the request. Alternatively, a parent might provide no directions. The child must accomplish the task. However, the parent does not care about the details of the implementation. An abstract function is an example of the latter. Abstract methods are a means of assuring that derived types implement required methods. The derived type inherits no implementation (instructions) from the base type. Derived types must override all abstract functions. If not, the derived type is incomplete and in error.

In the following code, *Employee* mandates that derived types implement the *CalculatePay* method. Because the class has an abstract method, the *Employee* class is also abstract:

```
public abstract class Employee {
    public virtual void Pay() {
    }

    public abstract void CalculatePay();
}

public class HourlyEmployee: Employee {
    public override void Pay() {
        CalculatePay();
    }

    public override void CalculatePay() {
    }
}
```

For completeness, here is an example of an abstract property:

```
public abstract class ZClass {
    public abstract int PropA {
        get;
        set;
    }
}

public class YClass: ZClass {
    public override int PropA {
        get {
            return 0;
        }
        set {
        }
    }
}
```

Sealed

Sealed classes are the reverse of abstract classes. Abstract types must be inherited. You cannot create an instance of an abstract type. Conversely, sealed types cannot be inherited and are concrete. Sealed classes cannot be refined by a derived type. Sealed classes are terminating nodes in the class hierarchy.

The sealed modifier can also be applied to instance methods, properties, events, and indexers. It cannot be applied to static members. Sealed members are allowed in sealed and nonsealed classes. A sealed member must override a virtual or implied virtual member, such as an abstract member. However, a sealed member itself cannot be overridden. It is sealed. The sealed modifier must be combined with the override modifier. Although sealed members cannot be overridden, a sealed member in a base class can be hidden in a derived type with the new modifier. As a bonus, the CLR can perform optimizations on sealed members.

The following code demonstrates both a sealed class and a sealed member. In this example, the *HourlyEmployee* class cannot be further refined. In addition, the *HourlyEmployee.Pay* method cannot be overridden.

```
public abstract class Employee {
    public virtual void Pay() {
    }

    public abstract void CalculatePay();
}

public sealed class HourlyEmployee: Employee {
    public sealed override void Pay() {
        CalculatePay();
    }

    public override void CalculatePay() {
    }
}
```

Constructors and Destructors

Constructors and destructors are not inherited. However, both the bases and derived components of an object require initialization. The base component of an object is responsible for initializing base members, whereas the derived component is responsible for initializing derived members. Constructors of both the derived and base components are called for this reason. Because constructors are not inheritable, derived types must implement local constructors to initialize derived members.

During the instantiation of a derived type, the default or parameterless instance constructor of the based type is called by default. If the base class does not have a default constructor, a compile error occurs unless the derived class calls a constructor in the base class that has a parameter. In the following code, *ZClass* does not have a default constructor and will not compile:

```
public class ZClass {
    public ZClass(int param) {
    }
}

public class YClass: ZClass {
}
```

Constructors in a derived class can explicitly call constructors in the base class. This is particularly useful for calling parameterized constructors in the base class. Base class constructors are called from the derived class using a constructor initializer list. The initializer list can only be affixed to instance constructors in the derived type. The derived constructor is responsible for initializing the derived type and possibly calling the base class constructor.

This is the constructor initializer syntax:

accessibility modifier typename(parameterlist[1]) : base(parameterlist[2])

{constructorbody}

The constructor initializer list follows the derived constructor name and colon. The *base* keyword refers to the base class constructor. The *parameterlist[2]* determines which base class constructor is called. Parameters of the derived constructor can be used in the parameter list of the base class constructor.

In the following example, the *YClass* constructor explicitly calls the one-argument constructor of the base class:

```
public class ZClass {
public ZClass(int param) {
    }
}

public class YClass: ZClass {
public YClass(int param) : base(param) {
    }
}
```

Instances of a derived type are created inside out. The base element is created first, and then the derived elements. In support of this model, the constructors are walked bottom-up. This facilitates passing parameters from derived constructors to base constructors. After the parameters are passed up the class hierarchy, the constructors are executed top-down, beginning with the constructor in the root class.

The following code confirms that constructor initializers are called bottom-up but the constructors are invoked top-down starting with the constructor in the base class:

```
using System;

namespace Donis.CSharpBook{

    public class Starter{
        public static void Main(){
            XClass obj=new XClass();
        }
    }


    public class ZClass {
        public ZClass(int param) {
            Console.WriteLine("ZClass constructor");
        }
    }
```

```
public class YClass: ZClass {
    public YClass(int param) : base(YClass.MethodA()) {
        Console.WriteLine("YClass constructor");
    }

    public static int MethodA() {
        Console.WriteLine("YClass constructor initializer");
        return 0;
    }
}

public class XClass: YClass {
    public XClass() : base(XClass.MethodA()) {
        Console.WriteLine("XClass constructor");
    }

    public static new int MethodA() {
        Console.WriteLine("XClass constructor initializer");
        return 0;
    }
}
}
```

This is the output from the code, which confirms the sequencing of base constructor initializers and the actual invocation of constructors:

```
C:\>insideout
XClass constructor initializer
YClass constructor initializer
ZClass constructor
YClass constructor
XClass constructor
```

Objects are not fully created until the constructor has finished completely. Therefore, the *this* reference of the derived type cannot be used as a parameter in the base class constructor initializer list:

```
public class ZClass {
  public ZClass(YClass obj) {
  }
}

public class YClass: ZClass {
  public YClass() : base(this) {  // Illegal
  }
}
```

Destructors are called in reverse order of constructors. Derived objects are destroyed outside-in, where the most-derived component is destroyed first. Correspondingly, destructors are called bottom-up. Because destructors are parameterless, there is no information to pass between them. In C#, base class destructors are called automatically. Do not attempt to call the base class destructor explicitly.

The following code has three classes—each with a destructor—which form a class hierarchy. At the end of the program, the destructors are called bottom-up, which confirms the sequencing of destructors.

```
using System;

namespace Donis.CSharpBook{

    public class Starter{
        public static void Main(){
            XClass obj=new XClass();
        }
    }

    public class ZClass {
        ~ZClass() {
            Console.WriteLine("ZClass destructor");
        }
    }

    public class YClass: ZClass {
        ~YClass() {
            Console.WriteLine("YClass destructor");
        }
    }

    public class XClass: YClass {
        ~XClass() {
            Console.WriteLine("XClass destructor");
        }
    }
}
```

This is the output from the program:

```
C:\>destructors
XClass destructor
YClass destructor
ZClass destructor
```

Interfaces

An interface is a contract and defines the requisite behavior of generalization of types. For example, vehicle behavior includes ignition on, ignition off, turn left, turn right, accelerate, and decelerate. A car, truck, bus, and motorcycle are included in the vehicle category. As such, they must encapsulate baseline behavior representative of all vehicles. The vehicle interface defines that baseline. Specific vehicle types implement that baseline behavior differently than others. A car accelerates differently from a motorcycle. A motorcycle turns differently from a bus. An interface mandates a set of behaviors, but not the implementation. The derived type is free to implement the interface in an appropriate manner. Interfaces must be inherited. You cannot create an instance of an interface.

Any class or structure that inherits an interface commits to implementing the members of that interface. An interface is an array of related functions that must be implemented in a derived type. Members of an interface are implicitly public and abstract.

An interface is similar to an abstract class. Both types must be inherited. You cannot create an instance of either. Abstract members require implementation in the derived type. Interface members require implementation in a derived type. Although abstract and interface members are similar, there are several differences:

- An abstract class can contain some implementation. Interfaces have no implementation.
- Abstract classes can inherit other classes and interfaces. Interfaces can only inherit other interfaces.
- Abstract classes can contain fields. Interfaces cannot have state.
- Abstract classes have constructors and destructors. Interfaces have neither.
- Interfaces can be inherited by structures. Abstract classes are not inheritable by structures.
- Interfaces support multiple inheritance. Abstract classes support single inheritance.

When choosing between defining an interface versus an abstract class that has all abstract members, select the interface. With an interface, you can still inherit other types. Furthermore, interfaces are clearer. The *ZClass* in the following code is simply not as clear as a comparable interface:

```
public abstract class ZClass {
    abstract public void MethodA (int a);
    abstract public void MethodB (int a);
    abstract public void MethodC (int a);
    abstract public void MethodD (int a);
}

public interface IZ {
    void MethodA (int a);
    void MethodB (int a);
    void MethodC (int a);
    void MethodD (int a);
}
```

This is the syntax of an interface:

attributes accessibility modifiers interface *interfacename :baselist*
    {*interface body* }

An interface can begin with an attribute. Use attributes to further describe an interface, such as the *ObsoleteAttribute*. For accessibility, independent interfaces can be public or internal. Nested interfaces can also be protected or private. Interfaces can be nested in classes and structs, but not in other interfaces. Interfaces support the unsafe modifier. For nested interfaces, the new modifier is also applicable. *Baselist* is a list of zero or more interfaces that this interface inherits. The interface body contains the members of the interface, which consists of methods, properties, indexers, and events. As mentioned, interface members are implicitly public and abstract.

Interfaces can inherit from other interfaces. The inherited members are added to the members of the current interface. The inherited interface essentially extends the current interface. A type inheriting the interface must implement the aggregate interface, which includes the members of the current interface and members that interface inherited from other interfaces. If a member appears in both the current interface and an inherited interface, there is no ambiguity. An identical member in a current interface hides the same member in an inherited interface. However, a compiler warning is generated. Add the new modifier to the member in the current interface to avoid the warning.

In the following code, *IZ* and *IY* are interfaces. The *IY* interface inherits *IZ*. *MethodB* is a member of both interfaces. For that reason, *IY.MethodB* hides *IZ.MethodB* with the new modifier. Types implementing the *IY* have to implement the *MethodA*, *MethodB*, and *MethodC* methods. These are members of both interfaces.

```
public interface IZ {
    void MethodB();
    void MethodC();
}

public interface IY: IZ{
    void MethodA();
    new void MethodB();
}
```

A type can inherit multiple interfaces. The type must implement the members of each interface that is inherited. Those interfaces may have identical members. For example, assume that *IZ* and *IY* interfaces contain a *MethodA* method. The single implementation in the derived type satisfies the requirements for both *IZ.MethodA* and *IY.MethodA*. Therefore, the same method in multiple interfaces is not ambiguous. The implementation in the type consolidates all requirements for the interface member.

Implementing Interfaces

Members of an interface are implicitly public. The implementation in the type must also be public.

In the following code, the *Car* class inherits the *IVehicle* interface. As required, the members of the *IVehicle* interface are implemented in the *Car* class.

```
public interface IVehicle {
    void IgnitionOn();
    void IgnitionOff();
    void TurnLeft();
```

```
        void TurnRight();
}

public class Car: IVehicle{

    public void IgnitionOn(){
    }

    public void IgnitionOff(){
    }

    public virtual void TurnLeft() {
    }

    public virtual void TurnRight(){
    }
}
```

A class that inherits multiple interfaces probably falls into multiple categorizations. An amphibious vehicle is a combination of a vehicle and a boat. In the following code, the *Amphibious* class inherits both the *IVehicle* and *IBoat* interfaces. The members of both interfaces are implemented in the *Amphibious* class. As discussed, duplicate interface members are implemented only once.

```
using System;

namespace Donis.CSharpBook {

    public interface IVehicle {
        void IgnitionOn();
        void IgnitionOff();
        void TurnLeft();
        void TurnRight();
    }

    public interface IBoat {
        void IgnitionOn();
        void IgnitionOff();
        void TurnLeft();
        void TurnRight();
        void FishFinder();
        void Rudder();
    }


    public class Amphibious: IVehicle, IBoat {
        public void IgnitionOn(){
        }
        public void IgnitionOff(){
        }
        public void TurnLeft() {
        }
        public void TurnRight() {
        }
```

```
            public void FishFinder() {
            }
            public void Rudder(){
            }
        }
    }
```

Explicit Interface Member Implementation

You can associate the implementation of an interface member with a specific interface. This is called *explicit interface member implementation*. Explicit interface member implementation binds an interface member to a particular interface, which requires prefixing the member with the interface name. Members implemented in this manner are not accessible through the derived type. For this reason, the accessibility modifier is omitted from explicitly implemented interface member. These members are available only via an interface cast. The modifiers abstract, virtual, override, or static are also not allowed.

In the following code, the *ZClass* inherits the *IA* interface. The *IA.MethodA* is an explicitly implemented interface member, whereas *IA.MethodB* is implemented regularly. Because it is explicitly implemented, *MethodA* is prefixed with the interface name. Because the implementation of *MethodA* is hidden, it cannot be called from a *ZClass* instance type. However, you can cast the instance to the underlying interface, which is interface *IA*. The method can then be called on that interface.

```
public class Starter{
    public static void Main(){
        ZClass obj=new ZClass();
        obj.MethodA(); // Error
        obj.MethodB();
        IA i=obj;
        i.MethodA();
    }
}

public interface IA {
    void MethodA();
    void MethodB();
}

public class ZClass: IA {

    void IA.MethodA() {
        Console.WriteLine("IA.MethodA");
    }

    public void MethodB() {
        Console.WriteLine("IA.MethodB");
    }
}
```

Explicit interface implementation is most helpful when duplicate members require separate implementations. Members inherited from multiple interfaces might require separate implementation. Normally, they are consolidated with a single implementation. Another possibility is duplicate members between the interface and derived type. You can implement duplicate members separately with explicit interface implementation. Explicit interface implementation provides separate implementation without ambiguity.

The following code is for the amphibious vehicle. Steering a boat is different from steering a car. Therefore, *TurnLeft* and *TurnRight* are explicitly implemented for the *IBoat* interface. *TurnLeft* and *TurnRight* are also implemented explicitly for the *IVehicle* interface. To assign defaults, *Amphibious* delegates to *IVehicle.TurnLeft* and *IVehicle.TurnRight* from identical functions in the class.

```
using System;

namespace Donis.CSharpBook {

    public class Starter{
        public static void Main(){

            Amphibious marinevehicle=new
                    Amphibious();
            marinevehicle.IgnitionOn();
            marinevehicle.TurnLeft();
            IBoat boatmaneuvers=marinevehicle;
            boatmaneuvers.TurnLeft();
            marinevehicle.IgnitionOff();
        }
    }

    public interface IVehicle {
        void IgnitionOn();
        void IgnitionOff();
        void TurnLeft();
        void TurnRight();
    }

    public interface IBoat {
        void IgnitionOn();
        void IgnitionOff();
        void TurnLeft();
        void TurnRight();
        void FishFinder();
        void Rudder();
    }


    public class Amphibious: IVehicle, IBoat {

        public void IgnitionOn(){
            Console.WriteLine("Ignition on.");
        }
```

```
    public void IgnitionOff(){
        Console.WriteLine("Ignition off.");
    }

    public void TurnLeft() {
        IVehicle vehicle=this;
        vehicle.TurnLeft();
    }

    public void TurnRight() {
        IVehicle vehicle=this;
        vehicle.TurnRight();
    }

    void IVehicle.TurnLeft() {
        Console.WriteLine("Turn vehicle left.");
    }

    void IVehicle.TurnRight() {
        Console.WriteLine("Turn vehicle right.");
    }

    void IBoat.TurnLeft() {
        Console.WriteLine("Turn boat left.");
    }

    void IBoat.TurnRight() {
        Console.WriteLine("Turn boat right.");
    }

    public void FishFinder() {
        Console.WriteLine("Fish finder in use.");
    }

    public void Rudder(){
        Console.WriteLine("Adjust rudder.");         }
    }
}
```

Another reason to use explicit interface implementation is to hide some portion of a class or struct. The explicitly implemented members are hidden from clients of the class. You must cast the type to the interface to access the hidden interface members.

In the following code, the *Car* class inherits and implements the *IVehicle* and *IEngine* interface. The two interfaces have no overlapping members. A driver doesn't usually interface with the engine directly. That is usually left to the mechanic. Therefore, the *IEngine* interface is hidden in the *Car* class.

```
using System;

namespace Donis.CSharpBook{

    public class Starter{
        public static void Main(){
            Car auto=new Car();
```

```
        auto.IgnitionOn();
        auto.IgnitionOff();

        //  Access engine.

        IEngine e=auto.AccessEngine();

        //  Inspect engine.
    }
}

public interface IVehicle {
    void IgnitionOn();
    void IgnitionOff();
    void TurnLeft();
    void TurnRight();
}

public interface IEngine {
    void Alternator();
    void Ignition();
    void Transmission();
}

public class Car: IVehicle, IEngine{

    public void IgnitionOn(){
        Console.WriteLine("Ignition on.");
        AccessEngine().Ignition();
    }

    public void IgnitionOff(){
        Console.WriteLine("Ignition off.");
    }

    public void TurnLeft() {
        Console.WriteLine("Turn left.");
    }

    public void TurnRight(){
        Console.WriteLine("Turn right.");
    }

    public IEngine AccessEngine() {
        return this;
    }

    void IEngine.Alternator(){
        Console.WriteLine("Alternator.");
    }

    void IEngine.Ignition() {
        Console.WriteLine("Ignition");
    }

    void IEngine.Transmission(){
```

```
            Console.WriteLine("Transmission");
        }
    }
}
```

Reimplementation of Interfaces

A child class can reimplement an interface that was implemented in a base class. In the following code, *ZClass* inherits interface *IZ*. *YClass* inherits *ZClass* and reimplements the *IZ* interface. This interface reimplementation in the derived class hides the implementation of the base class. Unless the new modifier is specified, warnings will occur in the derived class.

```
public interface IZ {
    void MethodA();
    void MethodB();
}

public class ZClass: IZ {
    public void MethodA(){
    }
    public void MethodB(){
    }
}

public class YClass: ZClass, IZ {
    public new void MethodA(){
    }
    public new void MethodB(){
    }
}
```

Polymorphism

Polymorphism is one of the major goals of inheritance. With polymorphism, related types can be treated in a generic manner. In a graphics program, instead of calling separate algorithms or operations for rectangle, ellipse, and triangle shapes, you leverage their commonality and call a generic algorithm or operation. This is more extensible and maintainable than handling each type of geometric shape differently.

The following program draws rectangles, ellipses, and triangles:

```
using System;

namespace Donis.CSharpBook{

    public class Starter{
        public static void Main(){
            Rectangle shape1=new Rectangle();
            Rectangle shape2=new Rectangle();
            Ellipse shape3=new Ellipse();

            shape1.Draw();
```

```
            shape2.Draw();
            shape3.Draw();
        }
    }

    public abstract class Geoshape {
        public Geoshape() {
            ++count;
            ID=count;
        }

        private static int count=0;
        protected int ID=0;

        public virtual void Draw() {
        }
    }

    public class Rectangle: Geoshape {
        public override void Draw() {
            Console.WriteLine("Drawing Shape {0} : rectangle",
                ID.ToString());
        }
    }

    public class Triangle: Geoshape {
        public override void Draw() {
            Console.WriteLine("Drawing Shape {0} : triangle",
                ID.ToString());
        }
    }

    public class Ellipse: Geoshape {
        public override void Draw() {
            Console.WriteLine("Drawing Shape {0} : ellipse",
                ID.ToString());
        }
    }

}
```

The two primary advantages to polymorphism are late binding and extensibility:

■   Late binding is when a specific function call is decided at run time. Early binding sets the function call at compile time, which is not always feasible. For example, in a competent graphics program, users decide the objects to draw at run time. The previous program does not accommodate this. The same objects are drawn every time.

■   Extensible code adapts easily to future changes. In the preceding code, the *Draw* method is called separately for each kind of geometric type. A rectangle is drawn differently from an ellipse. As the program evolves into the future, more geometric shapes are likely to be added. It could eventually support 50 types of shapes. An extensible process for drawing a variety of shapes is needed. Do you want to call *Draw* 50 different times—once for each type of shape?

Polymorphism starts with a base class reference to an instance of a derived type. Assign an instance of a derived type to a base class reference. When a virtual function is called on the base class reference, the compiler automatically delegates to the overridden method in the derived instance. Virtual and overridden methods have a special relationship. Virtual methods delegate to overridden methods when possible. *BaseReference.VirtualMethod* delegates to different implementations depending on the derived object assigned to the base class reference.

In the following code, *Geoshape* is the base class reference, and *Draw* is the virtual method. At run time, two derived instances are created and assigned to the base class reference. *Geoshape* references *shape[0]* and *shape[1]* are assigned an *Ellipse* and *Rectangle* object, respectively. The *Draw* method is invoked on the *Geoshape* base class reference. At that time, the compiler delegates to the *Draw* methods overridden in the derived types (*base.virtualfunc-> derived. overriddenfunc*). Therefore, a virtual function has different behavior depending on the kind of object assigned to the reference.

```
Geoshape [] shapes={ new Ellipse(),
                     new Rectangle() };

shapes[0].Draw();   // Geoshape.Draw()->Ellipse.Draw()
shapes[1].Draw();   // Geoshape.Draw()->Rectangle.Draw()
```

In the following code, the *DrawShape* method draws a geometric shape. Can you predict which *type.Draw* is called? The method has one parameter, which is the *Geoshape* base class. This is a reference to a base class. When a *Rectangle* instance is passed as a parameter, it is a derived instance to a base reference. This is one of the requirements of polymorphism. The base reference points to *Rectangle* instance, which means *Rectangle.Draw* is called. When the *Triangle* instance is passed as a parameter, *Triangle.Draw* is called. Therefore, one statement, *shape.Draw*, calls different implementations for related types. The *shape.Draw* statement is extensible.

```
public static void Main(){
    DrawShape(new Ellipse());
    DrawShape(new Rectangle());
}

public static void DrawShape(Geoshape shape) {
    shape.Draw();  // which Draw is called?
}
```

Polymorphism requires three things:

- Related classes
- Common method
- Different behavior

The following code demonstrates polymorphism. There are related types: *Triangle*, *Ellipse*, and *Rectangle*. The common method is *Draw*. Each *Draw* method is implemented differently in the derived class. At the command line, clients indicate which shapes to draw. This command draws a rectangle, ellipse, triangle, and another rectangle. Therefore, the decision about what to draw is deferred to run time:

```
shapes r e t r
```

The program defines a collection of base references. At compile time, we know that clients will draw shapes but we don't know the specific shape. Therefore, a collection of *Geoshape* base class references is defined, which is a generalization of all shape types. Plus, polymorphism begins with base references to derived instances. In the first loop, derived instances are created and added to the collection of base class references. In the second loop, the array of *Geoshape* base class references is iterated. *Rectangle.Draw*, *Ellipse.Draw*, or *Triangle.Draw* is called based on the type of derived object assigned to the base reference. Therefore, each call to the *Geoshape.Draw* could initiate a different operation. This is the polymorphic behavior.

```csharp
using System;
using System.Collections.Generic;

namespace Donis.CSharpBook{

    public class Starter{
        public static void Main(string [] shapeArray){
            List<Geoshape> shapes=new List<Geoshape>();
            Geoshape obj=null;
            foreach(string shape in shapeArray) {
                if(shape.ToUpper()=="R") {
                    obj=new Rectangle();
                }
                else if(shape.ToUpper()=="E") {
                    obj=new Ellipse();
                }
                else if(shape.ToUpper()=="T") {
                    obj=new Triangle();
                }
                else {
                    continue;
                }
                shapes.Add(obj);
            }

            foreach(Geoshape shape in shapes) {
                shape.Draw();  // polymorphic behavior
            }
        }
    }

    public abstract class Geoshape {
        public Geoshape() {
            ++count;
            ID=count;
        }
```

```
        private static int count=0;
        protected int ID=0;

        public abstract void Draw() {
        }
    }

    public class Rectangle: Geoshape {
        public override void Draw() {
            Console.WriteLine("Drawing Shape {0} : rectangle",
                ID.ToString());
        }
    }

    public class Triangle: Geoshape {
        public override void Draw() {
            Console.WriteLine("Drawing Shape {0} : triangle",
                ID.ToString());
        }
    }

    public class Ellipse: Geoshape {
        public override void Draw() {
            Console.WriteLine("Drawing Shape {0} : ellipse",
                ID.ToString());
        }
    }

}
```

Geoshape is an abstraction and not concrete. You cannot draw a generic geometric shape. For that reason, in the *Geoshape* class, the *Draw* method should also be abstract. There is an added benefit of an abstract *Draw* in the base class. Derived types are forced to implement a specific *Draw* method. They are not inheriting the *Draw* method of the base class, which does nothing:

```
public abstract void Draw();
```

Interface Polymorphism

Interface polymorphism employs base interfaces instead of base classes. The result is the same. Because it has some implementation, the *Geoshape* class cannot be entirely replaced with an interface. However, the *Draw* abstract method can be lifted from the class and placed in an *IDraw* interface:

```
using System;
using System.Collections.Generic;

namespace Donis.CSharpBook{

    public class Starter{
        public static void Main(string [] shapeArray){
            List<Geoshape> shapes=new List<Geoshape>();
            Geoshape obj=null;
            // partial listing
```

```
                    foreach(IDraw shape in shapes) {
                        shape.Draw();
                    }
                }
            }

    public interface IDraw {
        void Draw();
    }

    public abstract class Geoshape: IDraw {
        public Geoshape() {
            ++count;
            ID=count;
        }

        private static int count=0;
        protected int ID=0;

        public abstract void Draw();
    }
// partial listing
```

New Modifier and Polymorphism

The new modifier interrupts normal polymorphism and can cause unexpected results. Unlike an overridden member, the compiler will not delegate from a virtual member to a member that has the new modifier. They are considered unrelated.

The following code demonstrates the potential problem. *ZClass.MethodA* method is virtual and polymorphic. *YClass.MethodA* overrides *ZClass.MethodA*. *XClass* derives from *YClass*. In the *XClass*, the new modifier defines an unrelated *MethodA*. *XClass.MethodA* is also marked a virtual. *WClass.MethodA* overrides *XClass.MethodA*. *ZClass.MethodA* and *YClass.MethodA* define a group of related methods. *XClass.MethodA* and *WClass.MethodA* define a second group. In *Main*, several related objects are instantiated. The derived instances are cached in an array of *ZClass* references, which is an array of base class references. In the loop, *MethodA* is called through the derived objects.

```
using System;

namespace Donis.CSharpBook{

    public class Starter{
        public static void Main(){
            ZClass [] zArray={
                new ZClass(),
                new YClass(),
                new XClass(),
                new WClass(),
                new YClass(),
                new ZClass() };
            foreach(ZClass obj in zArray) {
```

```
                obj.MethodA();  // polymorphic behavior
            }
        }
    }

    public class ZClass {
        public virtual void MethodA(){
            Console.WriteLine("ZClass.MethodA");
        }
    }

    public class YClass: ZClass {
        public override void MethodA(){
            Console.WriteLine("YClass.MethodA");
        }
    }

    public class XClass: YClass {
        public new virtual void MethodA(){
            Console.WriteLine("XClass.MethodA");
        }
    }


    public class WClass: XClass {
        public override void MethodA(){
            Console.WriteLine("WClass.MethodA");
        }
    }
}
```

The following code shows the result of running the application. Notice that *XClass.MethodA* and *WClass.MethodA* are not called. The new modifier on the *XClass.MethodA* method interrupts the polymorphic hierarchy.

```
C:\ >newapp
ZClass.MethodA
YClass.MethodA
YClass.MethodA
YClass.MethodA
YClass.MethodA
ZClass.MethodA
```

Casting

Casting a derived object to a base type is always safe. As shown in the previous section, this is the common cast for polymorphism and is legitimate in all circumstances. Derived types extend base types. Because derived types encompass everything about the base type, a derived-to-base-type cast is guaranteed to be safe. You can even cast a derived instance to an abstract base class. This was demonstrated earlier. Casting from a derived object to a base reference provides a base view of the instance. You are limited to members of the base type.

The refinements of the derived type are not visible through a base reference to a derived instance, although the derived class implementation of an abstract base class method will be visible. After the cast, the base reference is an alias to the original derived object.

Casting a value type to a base interface has different semantics. The result of casting a reference type to an interface is an alias. However, when casting a value type to an interface, a separate entity is created. Interfaces are reference types. Boxing always occurs when casting a value type to a reference type. This includes casting a value type to an interface. Boxing creates a copy of the value type, which is placed on the managed heap. The original and copy are unrelated. Changes to one will not affect the other.

In the following code, the *ZStruct* structure implements the *IAdd* interface. Structures are value types. The *IAdd.Increment* method increments a counter. In *Main*, a *ZStruct* local variable is cast to an *IAdd* interface, which is legitimate. Boxing happens, and a copy of the *ZStruct* is placed on the managed heap. Changes to one will not affect the other. When the counts are displayed, the variables have different counts that confirm their separate identities.

```
using System;

namespace Donis.CSharpBook{

    public class Starter{
        public static void Main(){
            XStruct val=new XStruct();
            val.Increment();
            IAdd obj=val;
            val.Increment();
            Console.WriteLine("Val: {0}",
                val.Count);
            Console.WriteLine("Obj: {0}",
                obj.Count);

        }
    }

    public interface IAdd {
    void Increment();
        int Count {
            get;
        }
    }

    public struct XStruct: IAdd {

    public void Increment() {
            ++propCount;
        }

        private int propCount;
        public int Count {
            get {
                return propCount;
```

```
          }
        }
      }
    }
```

A base class or interface can be used as a function parameter or return value. In this circumstance, you can substitute any related type for the function parameter or return value. There are three major reasons to use a base class or interface as a parameter or return value:

- It generalizes a function call or return. The function parameter or return can be used with different types.

- A specific parameter or return type may not be known at compile time. A base reference supports late binding, where the type is selected at run time.

- Returning a base class or interface restricts access to an object. This is especially useful for class libraries that want to hide internal implementation.

The following code is an example of a class library—albeit a rather small library. The library contains a single class, which is the *ZClass*. It is marked as internal and visible solely within the class library. *IExposed* defines the public face of the *ZClass* type and clients of the library. *LibraryClass.Method* returns a *ZClass* instance through the *IExposed* public interface. This prevents clients from accessing the other methods of the *ZClass*. Those methods are internal and reserved for use in the class library.

```
using System;
namespace Donis.CSharpBook{

    public class LibraryClass{
        public IExposed GetSomething() {
            ZClass obj=new ZClass();
            // do something
            obj.InternalA();
            obj.InternalB();
            obj.MethodA();
            return obj;
        }
    }

    public interface IExposed {
        void MethodA();
        void MethodB();
    }

    internal class ZClass: IExposed {
        public void MethodA() {
        }

        public void MethodB() {
        }

        public void InternalA() {
        }
```

```
        public void InternalB() {
        }
    }
}
```

As shown several times in this chapter, casting a derived object to a base reference is safe. However, you cannot implicitly cast a base object to a derived reference. The derived type might have members not defined in the base type. Therefore, the derived reference might access members not available to the base object. For this reason, the cast is unsafe. An explicit cast can force the compiler to accept the unsafe cast of a base object to a derived reference. Because the cast remains unsafe, an exception is raised at run time at the cast. You have simply deferred the problem from compile time to run time.

This code raises an exception at run time because of an invalid cast:

```
using System;

namespace Donis.CSharpBook{

    public class Starter{
        public static void Main(){
            ZClass obj=new ZClass();

            // Fails at compile time
            // YClass alias=obj;

            // Fails at run time
            YClass alias=(YClass) obj;

            obj.MethodA();
            obj.MethodB();
        }
    }

    public class ZClass {
    public virtual void MethodA() {
        }
    public virtual void MethodB() {
        }
    }

    public class YClass: ZClass {
    public override void MethodA() {
        }
    }
}
```

Inheritance Operators

The *is* and *as* operators are convenient tools for testing the pedigree of an instance. These operators confirm the presence of a class or interface somewhere in the hierarchy of an instance. This confirmation is useful for promoting type-safe function calls. You can also develop algorithms that vary based on class types, for example, to display extra menu items for managers.

This is the syntax of the *is* operator:

bool *result*=*expression* is *type*;

The *is* operator returns *true* if the expression type and target type are related. If the expression type and target type are unrelated, *false* is returned.

The following code displays a menu. If employee is a manager, additional menu items are displayed. The *is* operator confirms that the employee is a manager.

```
using System;

namespace Donis.CSharpBook{

    public class Starter{
        public static void Main(){
            Manager person=new Manager("Accounting");
            Console.WriteLine("[Menu]\n");
            Console.WriteLine("Task 1");
            Console.WriteLine("Task 2");
            if(person is IManager) {
                IManager mgr=person;
                Console.WriteLine("\n[{0} Menu]\n",
                    mgr.Department);
                Console.WriteLine("Task 3");
            }
        }
    }

    public interface IManager {
        string Department {
            get;
        }
    }

    public class Employee {
    }

    public class SalariedEmployee: Employee {
    }

    public class Manager: SalariedEmployee, IManager {

        public Manager(string dept) {
            propDepartment=dept;
        }

        private string propDepartment;
        public string Department {
```

```
            get {
                return propDepartment;
            }
        }
    }
}
```

This is the syntax of the *as* operator:

typeinstance=expression as *type*

The *as* operator evaluates an expression in the context of the target type. If the expression type and target type are related, an instance of the target type is returned. If the expression type and target type are unrelated, null is returned.

Here is the previous code rewritten with the *as* operator (this is a partial listing):

```
using System;

namespace Donis.CSharpBook{

    public class Starter{
        public static void Main(){
            Manager person=new Manager("Accounting");
            Console.WriteLine("[Menu]\n");
            Console.WriteLine("Task 1");
            Console.WriteLine("Task 2");
            IManager mgr=person as IManager;
            if(mgr != null) {
                Console.WriteLine("\n[{0} Menu]\n",
                    mgr.Department);
                Console.WriteLine("Task 3");
            }
        }
    }
}

// Partial listing
```

Attribute Inheritance

By default, custom attributes are not inheritable. The *AttributeUsage* attribute can make an attribute inheritable. For the *AttributeUsage* attribute, set the *Inherited* option to *true* to enable inheritance.

Inheriting classes with attributes sometimes can cause interesting behavior. In the following code, *ZClass* is the base class, and *YClass* is the derived class. Both classes are adorned with the *PrincipalPermission* attribute, which identifies the users or roles that can call functions in a particular class. In the example, the *ZClass* function can be called by managers; *YClass* function calls are limited to accountants. The *YClass* inherits *MethodA* from the *ZClass*. Who can call *YClass.MethodA*? Because *MethodA* is not overridden in the derived class, *YClass* is relying on the implementation of *MethodA* in the base class, which includes any applicable attributes. Therefore, only managers can call the *YClass.MethodA*, whereas *YClass.MethodB* is available to accountants and not managers, as demonstrated in the following code:

```
using System;
using System.Security;
using System.Security.Permissions;
using System.Security.Principal;
using System.Threading;

namespace Donis.CSharpBook{
    public class Starter{
        public static void Main(){
            GenericIdentity g=new GenericIdentity("Person1");
            GenericPrincipal p=new GenericPrincipal(g,
                new string [] {"Manager"});
            Thread.CurrentPrincipal=p;
            ZClass.MethodA();
            YClass.MethodA();
//          YClass.MethodB();     // Security exception.
        }
    }

    [PrincipalPermission(SecurityAction.Demand,
        Role="Manager")]
    public class ZClass {

        static public void MethodA() {
            Console.WriteLine("ZClass.MethodA");
        }
    }

    [PrincipalPermission(SecurityAction.Demand,
        Role="Accountant")]
    public class YClass: ZClass {

        static public void MethodB() {
            Console.WriteLine("ZClass.MethodB");
        }
    }
}
```

Visual Studio .NET 2005

The next chapter introduces Visual Studio .NET 2005, including an overview and walk-through. Visual Studio is an integrated development environment for developing managed code in a variety of languages. It is an environment for creating secure, robust, and scalable applications. In addition, Visual Studio hosts a variety of rapid application development tools that facilitate the quick and painless development of managed applications.

Visual Studio .NET 2005 includes several enhancements. Improved editing capabilities have been added, such as Code Expansion and Auto IntelliSense. Code snippets have also been improved. Refactoring is an exciting new feature and the friend of every developer. New build alternatives such as MSBuild are available for professional developers. Microsoft has also added a pantheon of new project and template types, such as Smart Devices, to Visual Studio. These new Visual Studio 2005 options provide developers with additional choices for managed development.

Part II
Core Skills

Introduction to Visual Studio 2005

Microsoft Visual Studio 2005 is the centerpiece of a suite of products for developing, debugging, and deploying managed applications from Microsoft. Visual Studio 2005 is the latest evolution of Visual Studio and includes several enhancements that improve developer productivity, effectiveness, and collaboration. Code snippets, class diagrams, IDE Navigator, MSBuild, and ClickOnce are some of the noteworthy additions to Visual Studio. Visual Class 2005 also has several new debugging features, which are discussed in Chapter 12, "Debugging with Visual Studio 2005." Tools for developers collaborating on software systems have been enriched with introduction of Visual Studio Team System. *Working with Microsoft Visual Studio 2005 Team System* from Microsoft Press and authored by Richard Hundhausen is a great resource on Visual 2005 Team System. Visual Studio 2005 is a worthy successor to a strong legacy of Visual Studio products.

Visual Studio 2005 has additional build and deployment options. The Microsoft Build Engine (MSBuild) is a new build environment, which is integrated into Visual Studio 2005, but also available separately. MSBuild projects are XML files that choreograph the build process of an application. ClickOnce Deployment deploys a desktop application from a centralized server and has several benefits when compared with traditional Windows Installer technology, such as self-updating. It is the perfect merger of desktop and Web technology, which provides hands-free distribution of desktop applications. Finally, Windows Installer technology remains available and is improved with the introduction of Microsoft Installer 2.0.

Visual Studio 2005 is more online-enabled than before. Developers can easily participate in the developer community, submit questions to Microsoft, and visit a variety of online resources. In addition, Help is now online-enabled.

With the exception of debugging, this chapter demonstrates many of the new features of Visual Studio 2005.

Integrated Development Environment

Visual Studio 2005 is an integrated development environment (IDE) for developing and maintaining managed, native, and mixed-mode applications. A variety of project templates are available to create a diverse assortment of applications. There are templates for Microsoft Windows Forms, Console, ASP.NET Web Site, ASP.NET Web Service, SmartPhone2003, Windows CE 5.0, and other types of applications. There are templates that target specific devices, including mobile devices. In addition, developers can choose the language of their choice, including C#, Microsoft Visual Basic .NET, and Managed C++.

The Visual Studio 2005 IDE has many rapid application development (RAD) tools. The Visual Studio Code Editor, Microsoft IntelliSense, Solution Explorer, Class View, Object Browser, and the class diagram are essential components of the user interface and contribute to improved developer productivity, accuracy, and efficiency. Many of the tools have been updated, such as IntelliSense and the Object Browser. Other tools, including the class diagram, are new.

Start Page

Start Page is the gateway screen into Visual Studio. For many developers, the Start Page is the first window presented in Visual Studio. The Start Page, shown in Figure 4-1, is completely redesigned in Visual Studio 2005. Visual Studio normally starts with the Start Page. If the page is not visible, open the Start Page from the View Menu. Select the Other Windows submenu and then the Start Page menu command.

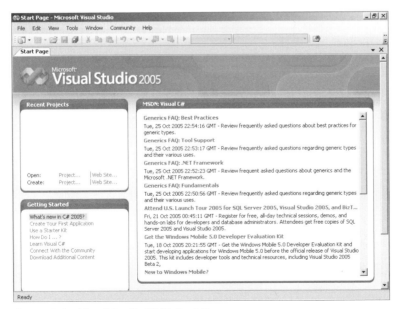

Figure 4-1 Visual Studio 2005 Start Page

The redesigned Start Page has four panes:

- **Recent Projects**   This pane lists the recently opened projects. Select an item in the project list to open that project. The Open and Create buttons at the bottom of this pane open or create a new project.

- **MSDN: Visual C#**   This pane contains links to recent news on Visual Studio and C#. Each topic is previewed. Click the related link to view the complete article.

- **Getting Started**   This pane contains helpful links for new Visual Studio developers.

- **Visual Studio Headlines**   This pane allows developers to submit feedback directly to Microsoft.

Community Integration

The Visual Studio community is an important resource for both novice and experienced developers of managed and unmanaged code. The availability of the aggregate knowledge of developers is of great benefit to everyone. Visual Studio 2005 has a menu dedicated to the developer community. The Community menu provides convenient access to the developer community, which makes participation easier. The Community menu offers the following command choices:

- **Ask a Question**   This command redirects developers to the Microsoft Community Forum, where questions are posted to Microsoft. You can also view previous posts and responses.

- **Check Question Status**   This command redirects developers to the Microsoft Community Forum, where the status of previous posts can be checked.

- **Send Feedback**   This command redirects developers to the MSDN Product Feedback Center.

- **Developer Center**   This command redirects developers to the Microsoft Visual C# Development Center, where C#-related topics are discussed.

- **Codezone Community**   This command redirects users to the Microsoft Codezone page, which features a Web site each month that makes substantial technological contributions to the developer community. It also lists number of online communities.

- **Partner Products Catalog**   This command redirects users to the Microsoft Visual Studio Industry Partner program. You can search for a particular Microsoft partner, product, or solution from this page.

- **Community Search**   This command searches online for downloadable project templates, code snippets, macros, and other helpful resources.

Creating Projects

Developing an application in Visual Studio typically starts with the creation of a project. Projects are the basic organization component of Visual Studio, in which files, resources, reference, and other constituents of an application are grouped. Related projects are sometimes grouped into solutions, which can contain projects of different types and languages. For example, during the development cycle, it is common to group applications and related libraries in the same solution. The option to add a new project to an open solution or creating the project in a new solution has changed. Figure 4-2 shows the New Project dialog box. Toward the bottom of the dialog box is a drop-down list box containing the choices Create New Solution and Add To Solution. This option is not available unless a solution is already open. If desired, select the Create Directory For Solution option box to create a separate directory for the solution.

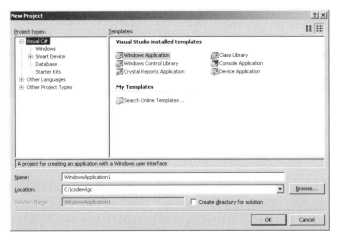

Figure 4-2   New Project dialog box

Solution Explorer

You can configure both solutions and projects from the Solution Explorer window. If not visible, display the Solution Explorer window from the View menu. Solution Explorer is shown in Figure 4-3. In this example, the solution is Airline Seats, which has two projects: Airline Seats and Person. Developers can change the properties of a solution or any project. From Solution Explorer, open the shortcut menu on the solution or project icon and then select the Properties menu item. In the Project properties, configure the application settings, configure the build environment, configure debug settings, resources, define default application settings, view or add references to the project, publish the ClickOnce manifests, or sign assemblies. The user interface of Project properties has changed and been renamed as the Project Designer window, shown in Figure 4-4.

In the Solution Explorer window, the *AssemblyInfo.cs* file has been moved to the Properties folder. The *AssemblyInfo.cs* file contains assembly attributes that define assembly level metadata, such as the version number and culture.

The location of Solution Explorer and some other Visual Studio windows default to a docking window. In Visual Studio 2005, these windows can be tabbed or set to auto hide, which is an improvement. Figure 4-5 shows Solution Explorer in a tabbed window. Display the shortcut menu on the window header to change the alignment to Tabbed Document.

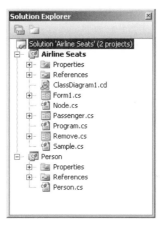

Figure 4-3 Solution Explorer window

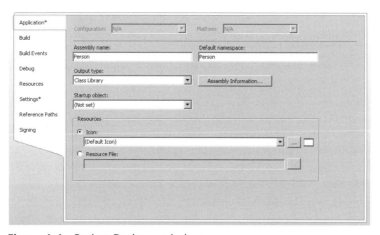

Figure 4-4 Project Designer window

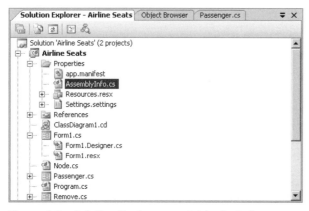

Figure 4-5 Solution Explorer as a tabbed window

Project Types

In Visual Studio 2005, a wide assortment of projects are available. Common projects, such as a Windows Application and Class Library, are still available. However, new project types have also been introduced. Table 4-1 lists the standard project types available.

Table 4-1   Project Types

Template Name	Description
Windows Application	Create a Windows Forms desktop application using this template.
Class Library	Create a managed dynamic-link library (DLL) using this template.
Windows Control Library	Create custom controls for Windows Forms applications using this template.
Web Control Library	Create custom Web server controls for ASP.NET applications using this template.
Console Application	Create a console application using this template.
Windows Service	Create a Windows Service application, which is a daemon process that can run across logon sessions, using this template.
Empty Project	Create a custom project, which is devoid of the normal files, with this template. The developer is responsible for building the project from essentially nothing.
Crystal Reports Application	Create a Windows Forms application that contains a Crystal Report using this template.

Web applications are no longer included with the standard templates detailed in Table 4-1. Web applications are created from the File menu. Select the New submenu and the Web Site menu command. The New Web Site dialog box appears, displaying Web application templates. Table 4-2 lists the available Web templates.

Table 4-2   Web Project Types

Template	Description
ASP.NET Web Site	Create an ASP.NET Web application using this template.
ASP.NET Web Service	Create an ASP.NET Web Service using this template.
Personal Web Site Starter Kit	Create an ASP.NET 2.0 starter Web site, including an initial home page, using this template.
Empty Web Site	Create a custom Web project, which is devoid of the normal files, using this template. The developer is responsible for building the Web site from essentially nothing.
ASP.NET Crystal Reports Web Site	Create a new Web site that includes a sample Crystal Report using this template.

Visual Studio 2005 also includes a variety of special-purpose project templates. Some of these templates are detailed in Table 4-3.

Table 4-3   **Special-Purpose Project Templates**

Template	Description
Smart Device Project Type	This project type includes the Pocket PC 2003, Smartphone 2003, and Windows CE 5.0 category of templates, which target mobile and embedded devices.
SQL Server Project	Create a database project targeting a Microsoft SQL Server 2005 database using this template. In this project, developers can create a variety of classes for database constructs, such as stored procedures.
Starter Kit Project Types	This project type includes the Screen Saver Starter Kit and Movie Collection Starter Kit templates. The Screen Saver Starter Kit is a sample screen saver that displays new articles from Really Simple Syndication (RSS) feeds. The Movie Collection Starter Kit is a sample application that demonstrates various programming techniques, including SQL programming.
Setup And Development Project Type	This type includes the Setup, Web Setup, Merge Module, Setup Wizard, CAB, and Smart Device CAB project templates. These are templates for creating setup and deployment applications and files.
Extensibility	Extensibility templates include the Visual Studio Add-In and Shared Add-In templates. These are templates for creating add-ins, which are managed DLLs that run within the context of Visual Studio.

Adding References

Developers add application references to projects to access foreign types contained in those applications. The Add Reference dialog box in Visual Studio 2005 has some new windows. To add a reference from the Project menu, choose the Add Reference menu command. Add Web Reference adds a reference to a Web service application. References can also be added from Solution Explorer. Open a shortcut menu on the Reference folder. From the menu, choose the Add Reference or Add Web Reference menu command. The Add Reference command now has five windows. References can be added from any of the windows.

- The .NET window lists system libraries of the Common Language Runtime (CLR) and .NET Framework Class Library.

- The COM window lists registered COM servers, which contain unmanaged code.

- The Projects window lists references to other projects in the current solution.

- The Browse Window allows developers to browse for references.

- The Recent window lists recent references that have been added to this solution.

Data Menu

In Visual Studio 2005, the Data menu has been added to the menu system. From this menu, developers can add a new data source to the project or show available data sources. When adding new data sources, you are presented with the Data Source Configuration Wizard, shown in Figure 4-6.

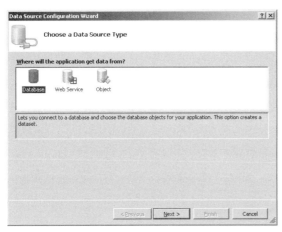

Figure 4-6   Data Source Configuration Wizard

The Data Source Configuration Wizard works with three types of data sources:

■ A Database data source is a connection to a database, which returns a dataset to the application. A dataset is a disconnected client-side representation of data at the data source.

■ A Web Service data source retrieves data from a Web service. This option adds a Web reference to the specified Web service application.

■ An Object data source retrieves data from a managed object.

Managing Windows in Visual Studio

Visual Studio offers an array of windows for a variety of purposes. The potential windows include Code Editor windows, a variety of toolboxes, Server Explorer, Solution Explorer, Property windows, and much more. Most of these windows are movable, but can also be docked. In Visual Studio, it has been easy to misplace windows or muddle the interface while attempting to dock a window. Visual Studio 2005 provides visual clues to aid in moving and docking windows, including a guide diamond with docking arrows to help dock windows correctly.

Switching between project files and windows is also improved. Visual Studio 2005 has the IDE Navigator to help toggle between open files and windows. Pressing Ctrl+Tab opens the IDE Navigator. Once there, you can navigate between open files and windows. This IDE Navigator dialog box is shown in Figure 4-7. When the window is open, use Ctrl+arrow keys or Ctrl+Tab to navigate the items in the window.

Figure 4-7   IDE Navigator

AutoRecover

AutoRecover is another feature that is added to Visual Studio 2005. This option periodically saves a project and prevents the loss of data when Visual Studio is exited abnormally. Figure 4-8 shows the AutoRecover window of the Options dialog box. Open this window from the Tools menu and Options menu command. AutoRecover is found in the Environment settings. In the AutoRecover window, set the frequency of auto saves and the length of time backups are retained.

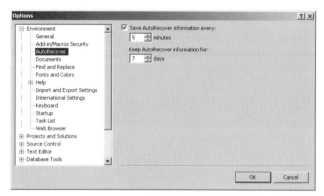

Figure 4-8   AutoRecover window

When re-entering Visual Studio after an abnormal termination, the Microsoft Visual Studio Recovered Files dialog box automatically displays. (See Figure 4-9.) In the dialog box, confirm the files to recover.

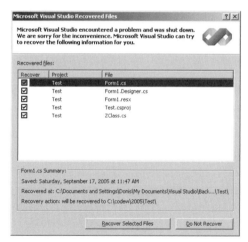

Figure 4-9   Microsoft Visual Studio Recovered Files dialog box

Class Hierarchies

Visual Studio 2005 offers several visual tools that depict class hierarchies. These tools also depict individual types, such as classes, structures, and interfaces. This includes showing relationships between types, including inheritance. The Class View and Object Browser have been updated with new features. The class diagram is new and adds a capable object-modeling tool to Visual Studio 2005.

Class View Window

The Class View window provides a visual representation of the types included in projects of the current solution. Expand the project and then expand class nodes to display the class hierarchy. Each item in the class hierarchy has a shortcut menu with helpful commands. For example, the shortcut menu can display classes in a class diagram. The Class View window can now show classes in referenced applications. Open the Project References folder to find references and view their classes. Figure 4-10 shows the Class View window, including the Project Reference folder. If the Class View window is closed, open it from the View menu.

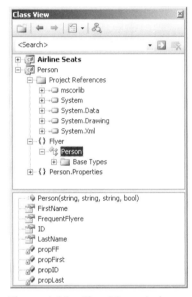

Figure 4-10   Class View window

The Class View window has two panes: The top pane contains the hierarchy, whereas the bottom pane displays the details of whatever item is selected in the class hierarchy. Across the top of the class view window are four icons: New Folder, Forward, Back, and Class View Settings. Beneath the icons is the search combo box, which is used to search the hierarchy for a symbol. This is especially helpful for extensive class hierarchies. Type the search text and press Enter to initiate a search. All symbols—such as classes, methods, fields, and properties, which contain some part of the search text—are returned in the Class View window.

Object Browser

The Object Browser is an alternative to the Class View window. The Object Browser displays the class hierarchy of the current project, referenced applications, and system libraries. If the

Object Browser is not visible, open it from the View menu. Figure 4-11 shows the Object Browser window.

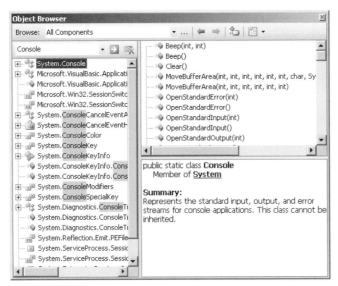

Figure 4-11   Object Browser window

The Object Browser window contains three panes. The left pane contains the class hierarchy. The two right panes list the members and a description of the selected type, respectively. The Object Browser toolbar has the Browser Scope, Edit Custom Component Set, Back, Forward, Add Reference, and Object Browser Settings buttons. The Browser Scope button filters the class hierarchy. You can display classes from the current solution, custom component set, .NET Framework, or all classes. Browse a class in a foreign assembly using the Edit Custom Component Set button. The Add Reference button adds a reference to the project for the application of the selected type. Above the class hierarchy is a combo box for searching. Use the search box to find specific types in the class hierarchy.

Class Diagram

Visual Studio 2005 introduces the class diagram. Class diagrams are created by the Class Designer, which is an internal component of Visual Studio 2005. Developers can model object-oriented applications using class diagrams. This tool will assuredly continue to evolve in the future and is destined to be a developer favorite. For me, it has already become one of the most frequently used tools in Visual Studio. Class diagrams present a visual representation of a type and type hierarchy. It's important to note that class diagrams are not static. Developers can add new types, create new relationships, insert members, delete members, and much more. The class diagram is synchronized with the source code of the application. Changes to types modeled in the class diagram are immediately reflected in code. Conversely, changes in the source code immediately appear in a relevant class diagram. Therefore, the application and diagram consistently remain in sync. Updated design documents are one of the seminal benefits of the class diagram. Where do design documents vanish to after the project implementation has begun? This is a common problem that plagues developers of object-oriented applications. For many applications, original design documents are not available or have not been updated as the software evolved. Often, design documents quickly become stale and sometimes vanish shortly after the implementation phase. Class diagrams help update these important documents, including changes to the original design. Conversely, class diagrams can be saved as images preserving a snapshot of the design. With the class design, the design and implementation phase is truly iterative, which translates into better-developed applications. It also makes maintaining applications exponentially easier.

Class diagrams provide a high-level perspective of an application, which is beneficial throughout the life cycle of the application. This is particularly useful with complex systems that entail hundreds of classes and dozens of relationships. Reviewing code in this circumstance is a tedious, time-consuming process. It also does not transfer the clarity of understanding that only a synoptic view of an application affords. Class diagrams present a general overview, in which introspection is available as needed. This information is particularly invaluable to programmers maintaining an application. The class diagram represents a new starting point for anyone who has to maintain a product with Visual Studio.

The entire class hierarchy can be presented in the class diagram. However, developers control how much information is presented in the class diagram. You can view one class, a dozen types, or everything in the class diagram. It depends on developer discretion. In addition, multiple class diagrams can be added to group-related types or simply to reduce the amount of information presented in any particular diagram. In the diagram, you can view all types: classes, structures, and interfaces. Relationships between types, such as inheritance and association, are also available.

In Visual Studio 2005, there are several ways to create a class diagram. One way is to select the Add New Item command on the Project menu. From the Add New Item dialog box, choose Class Diagram. In the edit box, name the class diagram. (Class diagram files are automatically given the *.cd* file extension.) You can also open a new class diagram from the Solution Explorer or Class View window. In Solution Explorer, open a shortcut menu for the project name or source file and then choose View Class Diagram. This creates a new class diagram that contains all the classes found in the project or source file. In Class View, open a shortcut menu for the project name or class and choose View Class Diagram.

Class diagrams have a surface. There are several ways to add existing or new types to this surface, as listed here. Types added to the class diagram surface are represented by shapes.

- Drag a type from the Class View window or the Object Browser to the class diagram surface.

- Drag a file from Solution Explorer to the class diagram surface.

- Add a new type from the Class Designer toolbox.

Figure 4-12 shows a class diagram with a single class on the surface. The single class is contained in a shape. Shapes have a header and a details pane. Click once on the class label in the shape header to change the name of the class. Double-click the class label to view the related source code. There is also an expand button or collapse button. The expand button is the double-down arrow and shows the details of the type. The collapse button is the double-up arrow and hides the details of the type. The expand and collapse buttons toggle, depending on whether the details are expanded or collapsed.

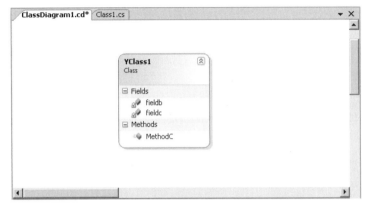

Figure 4-12   Class diagram that contains a single class

Types can be removed from a class diagram. Select the shape for the type and open the shortcut menu from the class header. Choose Remove From Diagram. The type is removed from the diagram, but remains in the program. The Delete Code option is not the same. This option not only removes the class from the class diagram but also deletes it from the project. An easier method of removing a class from the diagram is simply to select the type and then press Delete.

The class detail shows the members of the class. Members are grouped by type, where fields, methods, properties, and other member types are grouped. Each group can be collapsed or expanded. From the shortcut menu, members can be refactored, deleted, copied, pasted, and more. Members can also be viewed and maintained in the Class Details window, as shown in Figure 4-13. If the Class Details window is not visible, display it from the shortcut menu of any shape in the class diagram.

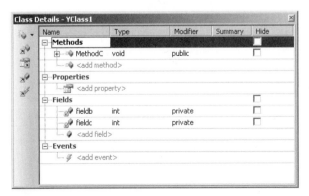

Figure 4-13   Class Details window

In the Class Details window, you can view, change, or add new members to the class. You can change the name, type, or accessibility of a type. The Hide option hides or displays a member in the class diagram. The shortcut menu of the class header has the Show All Members command, which shows all members, including any hidden members.

The Class Details toolbox has four buttons. The New Member button adds a Method, Property, Field, Event, Constructor, Destructor or constant to a class. The Navigate To Methods button selects that method category in the Class Details window. This is helpful for large classes with dozens of members. The final three buttons navigate to properties, fields, and events, respectively.

Class Diagram Toolbox

Class diagrams have a specific toolbox, as shown in Figure 4-14. The top buttons of the toolbox add new types to the application and the class diagram. You can add a new class, enumeration, interface, abstract class, structure, and delegate. Double-clicking the associated button adds the new type to the application, which is then displayed in the class diagram. Alternatively, you can drag the related button from the toolbox onto the class diagram surface to add the new type. The New Type dialog box is displayed when a new type is added. (See Figure 4-15.) The type name, accessibility, and file name can be entered into the dialog box.

Figure 4-14   Class Diagram toolbox

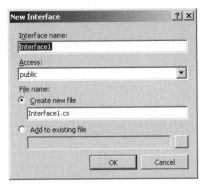

Figure 4-15   Add New Interface Dialog box

After the buttons for adding new types, the inheritance and association buttons appear next on the toolbox. The inheritance button creates an inheritance line, which links a base class and a derived class. The association button creates an association line that defines the relationship between an embedded class and the owning class. The comment button is the last item on the toolbox and adds comments to the class diagram.

Inheritance

Inheritance is visualized in the class diagram. Inheritance lines depict the base-to-derived-type relationship. Implicit inheritance of *System.Object* and *System.ValueType* are not shown in the class diagram. Figure 4-16 shows class inheritance in the class diagram. In the figure, *XClass1* inherits the *ZClass* class. The inheritance line is the arrow that starts at the base class and ends at the derived class. Delete the inheritance line to remove the inheritance relationship. Alternatively, you can remove the inheritance line from the shortcut menu. Open a shortcut menu on the inheritance line and then select Delete Code.

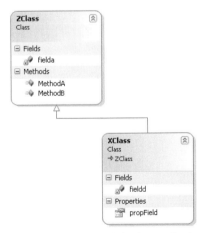

Figure 4-16   Class inheritance in the class diagram

You can define new base and derived classes in the class diagram. Select the inheritance line in the toolbox. Drag the inheritance line from the base class to the derived class. This assumes that both the base and derived classes are already on the class diagram. If the base class is not on the class diagram, drag the class from the Class View window onto the derived class shape in the class diagram. This both creates the inheritance relationship and adds the derived class to the class diagram.

Interface inheritance and class inheritance are similarly shown in the class diagram. Add interface inheritance to a type using the inheritance line. To fully implement the interface, the class diagram adds stubs for each member of the interface in the derived type. In the Code Editor, developers can replace the stubs with the appropriate implementation. Interface inheritance is not depicted as an inheritance line. Instead, interface inheritance is displayed as a lollipop atop the derived type. This is displayed in Figure 4-17, in which the *ZClass* class inherits the IA interface. You can change how the interface is implemented using the shortcut menu of the interface label. This includes whether to implement the interface implicitly or explicitly.

Figure 4-17   Interface inheritance in the class diagram

Relationship lines, which are the inheritance and association lines, can be rerouted. Simply click the line and drag the mouse to reroute. Lines can be rerouted multiple times. Figure 4-18 shows a rerouted inheritance line. Dragging the endpoints of the line repositions the relationship line on the class shape. The mouse cursor looks like a cross when positioned over the endpoint of a relationship line. The shortcut menu of a relationship line can hide, reroute, delete, or display the properties of the relationship.

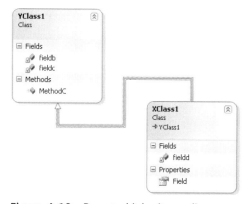

Figure 4-18   Rerouted inheritance line

Class diagrams can find the base or derived class of a type. Open the shortcut menu on the class shape header. The Show Base Class command finds the base class of the type in the class diagram. If not already present, the base class is added to the class diagram. The Show Derived Classes command selects the derived type.

Association

Association lines define a "has-a" relationship, in which a class owns another class. The class is embedded as a property. Figure 4-19 shows an association relationship in the class diagram. In the figure, the *XClass* class owns the *YClass* class, which is embedded as a property. The association line looks slightly different from the inheritance line.

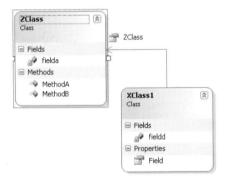

Figure 4-19   Association relationship

Select the association line in the class diagram toolbox to create a new relationship. Both classes and interfaces can be embedded. Drag the association line from the owning type to the embedded type. A property is created in the owning class for the embedded class. You can then switch to the Code Editor and implement the property, which should return an instance of the embedded type. When the association line is visible, the embedded member is not shown in the class details pane of the shape. If desired, you can show the embedded member and hide the association line. Open the shortcut menu of the association line and select the Show As Property command. To reverse that decision, open the shortcut menu and select Show As Association.

Class Diagram Walkthrough

This walkthrough demonstrates the class diagram—particularly creating new types and relationships.

1. Create a new class library. In Visual Studio 2005, from the File menu, choose the New submenu to create a new project. You can also accomplish this by clicking New Project on the Standard toolbar. The Class Library template is selected from a C# project. The project is named Personnel.

2. Add a class diagram to the project. Open the Project menu and select the Add New Item menu item. From the Add New Item dialog box, add a class diagram. The class diagram is named Employee.

3. Add a new interface using the class diagram toolbox. Name the interface **IEmployee**. Other defaults are accepted.

4. Add a new abstract class using the class diagram toolbox. Name the class **Employee**.

5. Add another class using the class diagram toolbox. Name this class **HourlyEmployee**.

6. Add a new struct using the class diagram toolbox. Name the struct **Name**. Structs are depicted in the class diagram as rectangles with square corners.

From the Class Details window, add three members to the *IEmployee* interface. (See Figure 4-20.) The *EmployeeInfo* method returns a string. The *Age* property is an integer and gets and sets the age of an employee. Finally, the *Fullname* property is of the *Name* type and gets the *Employee* name.

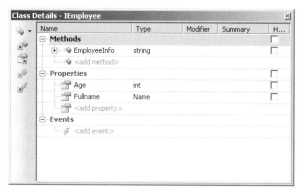

Figure 4-20 IEmployee interface details

The *Employee* class should inherit and implement the *IEmployee* interface. Select the inheritance line in the class diagram toolbox. Drag the inheritance line from the *Employee* class to the *IEmployee* interface. The interface members now appear in the class details of the *Employee* class. In addition, *Employee* is given the stubbed implementations of the interface members:

```
public abstract class Employee : IEmployee
{
    #region IEmployee Members

    public int Age
    {
        get
        {
            throw new Exception(
                "The method or operation is not implemented.");
        }
        set
        {
```

```
        throw new Exception(
            "The method or operation is not implemented.");
    }
}

// Partial listing
```

Derived types of the *Employee* class must have a calculate pay operation. Add an abstract *CalculatePay* method to the *Employee* class. The method returns a decimal. In the header of the *Employee* class, open a shortcut menu. Select the Add submenu and the Method menu command. Name the new method **CalculatePay**. In the Class Details window, set decimal as the return type. The method should be abstract. Open the shortcut menu for the *CalculatePay* method and change the Inheritance Modifier to abstract. A message box is displayed asking you to confirm this decision. Click Yes.

The *HourlyEmployee* class should inherit the *Employee* class. This relationship is created with the inheritance line. Drag the inheritance line from the *HourlyEmployee* class to the *Employee* class.

Finally, add a *Pay* method to the *HourlyEmployee* class. The *Pay* method has a single parameter, which is the hours worked. In the Class Details window, expand the row for the *Pay* method to expose the Add Parameter item. Select the Add Parameter row and enter **Hours** as the parameter name. Change the type to decimal. To complete the class, add a *HourlyRate* property to the class. It is a decimal type.

The *Name* struct has two string properties: *FirstName* and *LastName*. Both properties can be added in the Class Details window.

The final class diagram for the Personnel application is shown in Figure 4-21.

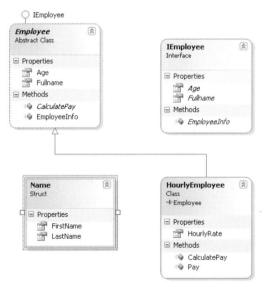

Figure 4-21   Class diagram of the Personnel library

This is code created per the class diagram. The functions are stubbed. Implementing the stubbed methods is the only remaining step:

```
public interface IEmployee
{
    int Age
    {
        get;
        set;
    }

    Name Fullname
    {
        get;
        set;
    }

    string EmployeeInfo();
}

public struct Name
{
    public string FirstName
    {
        get
        {
            throw new System.NotImplementedException();
        }
        set
        {
        }
    }

    public string LastName
    {
        get
        {
            throw new System.NotImplementedException();
        }
        set
        {
        }
    }
}

public abstract class Employee : IEmployee
{
    #region IEmployee Members

    public int Age
    {
        get
        {
            throw new Exception(
                "The method or operation is not implemented.");
```

```
        }
        set
        {
            throw new Exception(
                "The method or operation is not implemented.");
        }
    }

    public Name Fullname
    {
        get
        {
            throw new Exception(
                "The method or operation is not implemented.");
        }
        set
        {
            throw new Exception(
                "The method or operation is not implemented.");
        }
    }

    public string EmployeeInfo()
    {
        throw new Exception(
            "The method or operation is not implemented.");
    }

    #endregion

    public abstract decimal CalculatePay();
}

public class HourlyEmployee : Employee
{
    public decimal HourlyRate
    {
        get
        {
            throw new System.NotImplementedException();
        }
        set
        {
        }
    }

    public override decimal CalculatePay()
    {
        throw new Exception(
            "The method or operation is not implemented.");
    }

    public void Pay(decimal Hours)
    {
        throw new System.NotImplementedException();
    }
}
```

Error List Window

The Error List window is new to Visual Studio 2005. It displays edit and compile errors, warnings, and general messages. Unique icons are assigned to each type of message. For example, error messages are decorated with a red circle that contains an x. If there are compile errors, compiling a program automatically displays the Error List window. (See Figure 4-22.) You can also display the Error List window from the View menu.

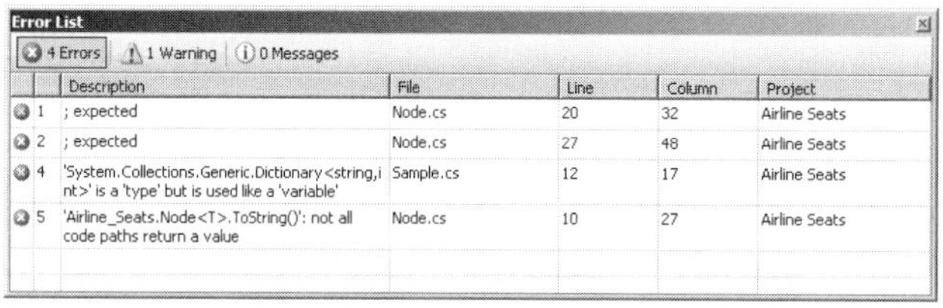

Error List

	Description	File	Line	Column	Project
1	; expected	Node.cs	20	32	Airline Seats
2	; expected	Node.cs	27	48	Airline Seats
4	'System.Collections.Generic.Dictionary<string,i nt>' is a 'type' but is used like a 'variable'	Sample.cs	12	17	Airline Seats
5	'Airline_Seats.Node<T>.ToString()': not all code paths return a value	Node.cs	10	27	Airline Seats

Figure 4-22   Error List window

The Error List window displays different categories of messages. The Error, Warning, and General buttons hide or show a particular category of messages. The Error List buttons also indicate the number of messages in each category. For each error, the error number, description, and location are shown. Double-clicking an error message in the error list will jump to the related source code. In addition, you can use the column headers to sort the error list. Column headers can be dragged to change column order.

Code Editor

In Visual Studio 2005, the Code Editor has been enhanced. Developers can add, format, and edit code with the Code Editor. Code is often organized by file, region, and color. Some of the improvements to the Code Editor include better IntelliSense, code snippets, smart tags, and additional formatting options.

IntelliSense

IntelliSense helps developers enter code correctly and efficiently. It minimizes the keystrokes required to enter code while improving developer accuracy. IntelliSense is available in both the Code Editor and the immediate mode command window. IntelliSense is actually a group of related features that includes the completion list, parameter information, quick info, and complete word.

IntelliSense is a dynamic drop-down list called the completion list and appears as developers type new commands or words. The completion list automatically appears after a space separator or dot for a member is typed. You can also force a completion list at a dot or the Ctrl+spacebar shortcut key. The completion list contains items for namespaces, types, type members, language keywords, and code snippets. As text is entered, the first matching item in the list is selected. As more text is entered, the match is refined. When the desired item is selected, press Tab to insert. Assuming that the IntelliSense For Most Recently Used Members option is enabled, recently used items that match the input text are selected first. Function overloads are not shown in the completion list. For example, there are 19 overloads of the *Console.WriteLine* method. However, *WriteLine* appears in the member list just once. The overload versions of a function, if any, are displayed with the IntelliSense for parameter info.

Parameter Info, a form of IntelliSense, displays the parameters of a function, including the overloaded versions of the function, which have different signatures. Use the arrows to cycle through the available overloads (shown in Figure 4-23). Parameter Info is prompted at the open parentheses of a function. Within function parentheses, the Ctrl+Shift+spacebar keystroke prompts Parameter Info.

```
Console.WriteLine (|
▲ 1 of 19 ▼   void Console.WriteLine ()
Writes the current line terminator to the standard output stream.
```

Figure 4-23   Parameter info for Console.WriteLine

IntelliSense in Visual Studio 2005 auto detects generics types and arguments. (See Figure 4-24.) A generic dictionary is defined that has string keys and integer values. When creating a new instance of the generic type, IntelliSense filters the completion list. The completion list automatically highlights the correct generic, key, and value types.

Figure 4-24   IntelliSense for a generic type

There are other circumstances in which IntelliSense filters the completion list:

- Interfaces
- Base classes
- Attributes
- *As* and *is* operators
- Catch clauses

Add using   Have you ever attempted to use a type without the proper *using* statement? It requires stopping, determining the correct namespace, and then explicitly entering the namespace before the type or adding a using statement. The Add Using feature of IntelliSense avoids the distraction of resolving unbound types. This is yet another way IntelliSense improves developer productivity.

When an unbound type is entered, a smart tag, which appears as a narrow red box, is placed beneath the last character. The smart tag is shown when the cursor is in or immediately adjacent to the unbound type. From the smart tag menu, you have two choices: Either insert the *using* statement or prefix the unbound type with the required namespace. Figure 4-25 shows the smart tag menu. Alternatively, open a shortcut menu on the unbound type, choose the Resolve submenu, and then choose from the two menu choices.

Figure 4-25   Add Using smart tag menu

Surround With

Visual Studio allows developers to surround code with an item on the completion list. You can surround a block of code with a region. A block of statements can be surrounded with a *for* loop. The Surround With feature surrounds selected text with something from the completion list. First select the text to be surrounded. Open a shortcut menu on the selected text and choose the Surround With command. The Surround With command will display the completion list. Select the item that should surround the text.

Font and Color Formatting

Visual Studio has always allowed developers to customize the color scheme of the user interface. Visual Studio 2005 .NET extends custom formatting to user types, user keywords, and other information. This is done in the Options dialog box, which is opened from the Tools menu. In the dialog box, switch to the Environment window and select Fonts and Colors. Figure 4-26 shows the Fonts and Colors window.

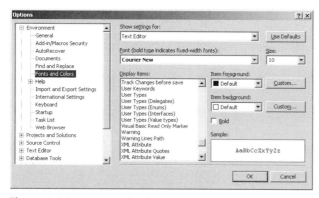

Figure 4-26   Fonts and Colors window

Source Code Formatting

Visual Studio 2005 provides developers additional control over code formatting. Developers control code indentation, new line spacing, code spacing, and the wrapping of blocks. This is done in the Options dialog box on the Tools menu. In the dialog box, open the Formatting window in the Text Editor section under the C# node. (See Figure 4-27.) Except for the General node, the bottom-right pane is the code preview area, in which options can be reviewed before accepting.

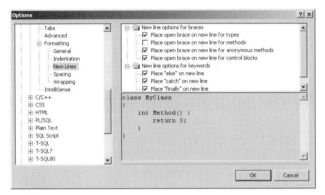

Figure 4-27   Source Formatting window

Change Tracking

Change tracking distinguishes saved from unsaved code. Visual Studio 2005 colorizes the far left pane to indicate the status of code. Saved code is highlighted in green. Unsaved code is marked in yellow. Original code, which is code unchanged since the source file was opened, is not highlighted. This is demonstrated in Figure 4-28.

```
using System;
using System.Collections.Generic;
using System.Text;

namespace Airline_Seats
{
    class Sample
    {
        public void MethodA()
        {
            Dictionary<string, int> lookup =
                Dictionary<string, int>();
            // changed but not saved
        }
    }
}
```

Figure 4-28   Change tracking of code

Profile

Almost every aspect of the Visual Studio 2005 user interface is customizable. Some developers spend considerable time creating the ideal look and feel. They might want to preserve these settings to reapply when necessary. User interface settings are saved in a profile, which includes window and text settings. The profile is particularly useful when reinstalling Visual Studio because the user interface settings are lost at that time. The profile is a convenient tool for reasserting preferred user preferences. The profile is helpful when you want to configure the Visual Studio user interface similarly on different machines. Developers can share profiles with other developers to identically configure their machines. This is helpful when developers are working together on a project.

Profiles can be exported or imported in the Import And Export Settings Wizard dialog box on the Tools menu. In the dialog box, you can import, export, or reapply the defaults of the user interface. (See Figure 4-29.) Exporting the user interface settings creates a profile, whereas importing reads a profile that is applied to the user interface. The Import And Export Settings Wizard dialog box guides the user through the process.

Figure 4-29   Import And Export Settings Wizard dialog box

Code Snippets

Developers are connoisseurs of code and tend to collect useful code in a variety of places. While other people collect coins, books, or PEZ dispensers, developers collect code snippets. Why? Developers do not like typing. There is some irony considering how much typing is involved in programming. If you want to improve developer productivity, reduce the amount of typing. This also reduces the number of typos and resulting compiler errors, which require an inordinate amount of developer attention. Code reuse is another reason why developers collect code. Even unique applications are largely composed of small but common code snippets. These are the same code elements enlisted in almost every program: loops, classes, exception handling, and so on. Developers traditionally cut and paste code to prevent repetitive typing. However, this has considerable limitations, including limited persistence. There should be a more viable solution.

That solution is code snippets, introduced in Visual Studio 2005, which are capsules of reusable source code. A code snippet is an alias for code. Insert a code snippet to insert the aliased code into the source file at the cursor or selection. Code snippets improve developer efficiency and accuracy.

There are multiple sources for snippets. Visual Studio 2005 has a set of default snippets for common tasks, such as the *for*, *try*, and *while* snippets. Snippets are available online to be downloaded, and developers can create custom snippets.

There are three kinds of snippets, described as follows:

- **Expansion**   An Expansion snippet inserts code at the cursor.
- **Surround With**   A Surround With snippet envelops selected code.
- **Refactoring**   A Refactoring snippet is used with refactoring.

Snippet types are not mutually exclusive. For example, the while snippet is both an Expansion and Surround With template.

Copy and Paste

Of course, copying and pasting code remains available. The main disadvantages are that the Clipboard is a shared resource—the contents of the Clipboard can be altered by another application. Clipboard data is not retained across logon sessions. Visual Studio lets developers copy source code directly to the toolbox. The code is then preserved on the toolbox for future placement. This is not as elegant as a snippet but sometimes quicker and more convenient— especially when a custom snippet is required. Code placed on the toolbox is preserved between Visual Studio and logon sessions. Unlike the Clipboard, the toolbox is not a shared resource and is available only to Visual Studio.

There are two methodologies for placing code on the toolbox. Select the code and copy to the Clipboard. Next click on the toolbox and paste the code. You can also drag the code onto the toolbox. A button is then created on the toolbox for the code. Multiple passages of code can be added to the toolbox. Moving the mouse over a code button in the toolbox displays the saved code. Click a code button to insert the code at the cursor. As a best practice, create a separate tab on the toolbox to group code. Intermingling code with nonrelated buttons can be confusing. A toolbox populated with source code is shown in Figure 4-30. A tab called Code was added to the toolbox to group the source code.

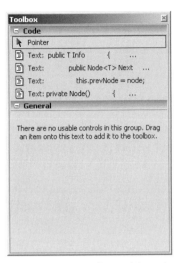

Figure 4-30 Toolbox with code

Insert a Code Snippet

There are several ways to insert code snippets into source code. IntelliSense is probably the simplest method. Code snippets appear in the completion list as a torn page. Use a complete word to select the code snippet and then press Tab to insert. Alternatively, double-click the snippet in the completion list.

Use the following techniques to select and insert code snippets. Inserting a snippet is called code expansion.

- Insert a code snippet using IntelliSense. The completion list includes snippets.

- Insert a code snippet from a menu using the Insert Snippet menu command. Insert Snippet is also available from the shortcut menu in the Code Editor. You will be prompted to insert the name of the snippet. Find the Insert Snippet menu command on the Edit menu and the IntelliSense submenu. The resulting completion list includes only code snippets. This is called the snippet picker.

- Ctrl+K and then Ctrl+X is the keyboard shortcut for the Insert Snippet menu command.

- Insert a code snippet using Auto IntelliSense. Position the cursor where the snippet should be inserted, type the name of snippet, and then press Tab twice.

Some code snippets are templates and contain editable fields. After inserting the code snippet, a developer customizes the template by assigning values to each field. The first field is selected automatically when the code snippet is inserted. Other fields in the code template are color-highlighted. There can be multiple instances of a field in the same code snippet. For example, there are several instances of the *i* field in the code snippet of the *for* keyword. The first instance of a field is color-highlighted and editable. Remaining instances are notated with a dotted border. Tab moves to the next field, whereas Shift-Tab moves to the previous file. You can double-click to select a field. Fields with tooltips display the tip when the field is selected. Figure 4-31 shows the code snippet of the *for* keyword. It has the '*i*' and *length* fields. Figure 4-32 presents the snippet with the fields customized.

```
for (int i = 0; i < length; i++)
{

}
```

Figure 4-31   Code snippet of the for keyword

```
for (int count = 0; count < 5; count++)
{

}
```

Figure 4-32   Customized code snippet

When using a Surround With template, select the target code first and then insert the snippet. The snippet will surround the code. For example, the following code increments a counter:

```
int count = 0;
Console.WriteLine(++count);
if (count == 10)
{
    break;
}
```

This is the result of selecting the code and inserting the code snippet for the *while* keyword:

```
while (true)
{
    int count = 0;
    Console.WriteLine(++count);
    if (count == 10)
    {
        break;
    }
}
```

Default Snippets

Visual Studio 2005 has default snippets for tasks that are routine for developers. The default is a mixture of expansion and surround with code snippets. Default snippets appear in the IntelliSense completion list and the code snippet picker. Table 4-4 lists some of the default code snippets.

Table 4-4   Default Code Snippets

Code Snippet Name	Description
#if	This code snippet surrounds code with *#if* and *#endif* directive.
#region	This code snippet surrounds code with a *#region* and *#endregion* directive.
~	This code snippet inserts a destructor.

Table 4-4   Default Code Snippets *(Continued)*

Code Snippet Name	Description
attribute	This code snippet inserts a declaration for a customized attribute, which is a class derived from *System.Attribute*.
checked	This code snippet surrounds code with a checked block.
class	This code snippet inserts a class declaration.
ctor	This code snippet inserts a constructor.
cw	This code snippet inserts a *Console.WriteLine* statement.
do	This code snippet surrounds code with a *do while* block.
else	This code snippet inserts an *else* block.
enum	This code snippet inserts an *enum* declaration.
equals	This code snippet overrides the *Equals* method inherited from the *System.Object* type.
exception	This code snippet inserts the declaration of an application exception, which is derived from *System.Exception*.
for	This code snippet surrounds code with a *for* loop.
foreach	This code snippet surrounds code with a *foreach* loop.
forr	This code snippet surrounds code with a *decrementing for* loop.
if	This code snippet surrounds code with an *if* block.
indexer	This code snippet inserts an indexer function.
interface	This code snippet inserts an interface declaration.
iterator	This code snippet inserts an iterator.
interindex	This code snippet inserts a named iterator and indexer.
invoke	This code snippet inserts and invokes an event.
lock	This code snippet surrounds code with a lock block.
mbox	This code snippet inserts the *MessageBox.Show* statement.
namespace	This code snippet surrounds code with a namespace.
prop	This code snippet inserts a property and backing field.
propg	This code snippet inserts a read-only property. Read-only properties have only a *get* method.
sim	This code snippet inserts an entry point method that is static and returns an integer.
struct	This code snippet inserts a *struct* declaration.
svm	This code snippet inserts an entry point method that is static and returns void.
switch	This code snippet inserts a *switch* statement.
try	This code snippet inserts a *try-catch* block.
tryf	This code snippet inserts a *try-finally* block.
unchecked	This code snippet surrounds code with an unchecked block.
unsafe	This code snippet inserts an *unsafe* block.
using	This code snippet surrounds code with a *using* block.
while	This code snippet surrounds code with a *while* loop.

Code Snippets Manager

Use the Code Snippets Manager to manage snippets, including adding, removing, importing, and searching for snippets.

The Code Snippets Manager is available on the Tools menu. (See Figure 4-33.) The folders shown in the Code Snippets Manager are snippet directories. Open a folder to view individual snippets. For each snippet, the follow information is provided:

- Description of the code snippet

- Alias or shortcut of the code snippet

- Snippet type

- Author of the snippet

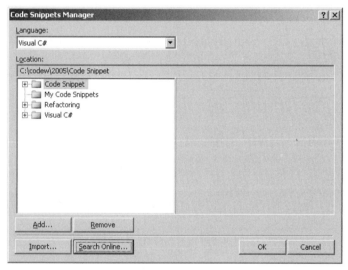

Figure 4-33 Code Snippets Manager

The Add button in the dialog box adds another directory to the list of code snippet directories. A code snippets directory contains code snippet files, which are XML files with the *.snippet* suffix. For C#, the default snippets directories are My Code Snippets, Refactoring, and Visual C#. The Remove button removes a snippet directory from the list. The Import button imports a code snippet file. Use the Search Online button to browse for code snippets. This button opens a general search window, in which developers can search for the code snippets. When you find the code snippet you're searching for, you can download it to the local machine.

Downloading snippets found online can pose security problems. A snippet is not guaranteed to have innocuous XML. In addition, the snippet might hide malicious scripts. The *Help URL* element defined in the snippet might stealthily launch a script. Also, code snippets can silently add references. Malicious calls are then possible to functions in the reference. Long snippets can hide potentially harmful code. Be careful when downloading code snippets with database access, code-access security, role-base security, or validation code. As a best practice, carefully review the source code of code snippets that are downloaded before using in an application.

Creating Snippets

You can create custom code snippets to encapsulate reusable code not found in a default snippet, which allows you to maintain private libraries of reusable code. Different industries might benefit from specialized code snippets. For example, a developer of medical software may have a need for medical code snippets. Developers of legal software could benefit from legal code snippets. I am confident that vendors will publish industry-specific code snippets in the future.

Custom code snippets are created in XML files. Microsoft publishes an XML schema for code snippets. Code snippet files should have the *.snippet* extension. When the schema is set, Visual Studio 2005 offers IntelliSense on the XML elements and attributes, which helps considerably in creating properly formed code snippet files. You can group custom snippets in directories. Add these directories to the Code Snippets Manager to make using the custom snippets more convenient.

The XML schema for code snippets defines the structure of a code snippets file. For a complete explanation of the schema, visit the Code Snippet Schema Reference at *http://msdn2 .microsoft.com/en-us/library/ms171418(en-us,vs.80).aspx*. Some parts of the schema are discussed in the next few pages.

CodeSnippets and CodeSnippet Elements

The *CodeSnippets* element is the root element of the code snippet file. The *xlmns* attribute names the code snippet schema:

```
<CodeSnippets xmlns="http://schemas.microsoft.com/VisualStudio/2005/CodeSnippet">
  <CodeSnippet Format="1.0.0">
```

An individual code snippet is described inside *CodeSnippet* elements:

```
<CodeSnippet>
  <!-- Insert code snippet here. -->
</CodeSnippet>
```

Header Element

The *Header* element has child elements, which together provide the basic information about the code snippet. The title, author, description, shortcut, and snippet type are some of the details that can be provided. The title is the name of the code snippet as it appears in the Code Snippet Picker, whereas the shortcut name appears in the IntelliSense completion list. The description of the snippet found in the Code Snippets Manager is read from this element.

This is the *Header* element for an example snippet for *StringBuilder* types:

```
<Header>
  <Title>StringBuilder</Title>
  <Shortcut>sb</Shortcut>
  <Description>Creates a new String Builder</Description>
  <Author>Donis Marshall</Author>
</Header>
```

Snippet, References, and Imports Elements

The *Snippet* element encapsulates the actual code of the code snippet. *References* and *Imports* are child elements of the *Snippet* element. The *References* element identifies references required for the code snippet. Within the *References* element, there are *Reference* child elements for each individual reference. The *Imports* element names implicit namespaces. Within the *Imports* element, there are *Import* child elements that identify each namespace to import. Importing a namespace allows implicit access of members in a namespace without explicitly mentioning that namespace. An *Import* element is identical to the *using namespace* statement of C#.

This is an example of the *References* and *Import* elements. The *System.Text* namespace contains the *StringBuilder* type:

```
<Snippet>
  <References>
    <Reference>
      <Assembly>System.Text.Dll</Assembly>
    </Reference>
  </References>
  <Imports>
    <Import>
      <Namespace>System.Text</Namespace>
    </Import>
  </Imports>
```

Declarations, Literal, and Object Elements

The *Declarations* element describes the fields used in the code snippet. It is also a child element of the *Snippet* element. There are literal and object fields. The *Literal* element declares a literal field, which is a field that is fully contained in the code snippet. This would include string and numeric literals. The *Object* element also declares a field, which is a field defined outside the snippet. This usually describes a type.

The *Literal* and *Object* elements can contain *ID*, *Default*, *Tooltip*, *Type*, and *Function* child elements:

- The *ID* element is the name of the field.
- The *Default* element is the default value of the field.
- The *Tooltip* element is the tooltip of the field.

- The *Type* element sets the type of the field.

- The *Function* element names a function. This is a function to call whenever the field is selected.

This is the *Declarations* element of the *StringBuilder* code snippet:

```
<Declarations>
  <Literal>
    <ID>Name</ID>
    <Default>mytext</Default>
    <ToolTip>Name of new StringBuilder</ToolTip>
  </Literal>
  <Literal>
    <ID>Size</ID>
    <ToolTip>Capacity of String</ToolTip>
  </Literal>
</Declarations>
```

Code and <![CDATA]> Elements

The *Code* element contains individual lines of code. It also selects the language of the code snippet. *Code* is a child element of the *Snippet* element. The target language is set in the *Language* attribute. Valid languages are CSharp, VB, VJSHARP, and XML.

Each line of code is placed in a *<![CDATA]>* element. The code must be written in the syntax of the chosen language.

CDATA syntax:

```
<![CDATA[snippetcode]]>
```

In snippet code, fields are bounded with dollar signs (*$field$*). This is the snippet code for the *StringBuilder* snippet:

```
<Code Language="CSharp">
  <![CDATA[StringBuilder $Name$=]]>
  <![CDATA[    new StringBuilder($Size$);]]>
</Code>
```

String Builder Code Snippet

The following code is the complete listing of the sample code snippet, which creates a new *StringBuilder* type. The *StringBuilder* type is found in the *System.Text.Dll* library and the *System.Text* namespace. Fields are defined for the name and size of the *StringBuilder* type.

```
<?xml version="1.0" encoding="utf-8"?>
<CodeSnippets xmlns="http://schemas.microsoft.com/VisualStudio/2005/CodeSnippet">
  <CodeSnippet Format="1.0.0">
    <Header>
      <Title>StringBuilder</Title>
      <Shortcut>sb</Shortcut>
      <Description>Creates a new String Builder</Description>
      <Author>Donis Marshall</Author>
```

```
    </Header>
    <Snippet>
      <References>
        <Reference>
          <Assembly>System.Text.Dll</Assembly>
        </Reference>
      </References>
      <Imports>
        <Import>
          <Namespace>System.Text</Namespace>
        </Import>
      </Imports>
      <Declarations>
        <Literal>
          <ID>Name</ID>
          <Default>mytext</Default>
          <ToolTip>Name of new StringBuilder</ToolTip>
        </Literal>
        <Literal>
          <ID>Size</ID>
          <ToolTip>Capacity of String</ToolTip>
        </Literal>
      </Declarations>
      <Code Language="CSharp">
        <![CDATA[StringBuilder $Name$=]]>
        <![CDATA[new StringBuilder($Size$);]]>
      </Code>
    </Snippet>
  </CodeSnippet>
</CodeSnippets>
```

Create a Code Snippet Walkthrough

The section provides a walkthrough for creating a code snippet. Before creating a snippet, it is best to write and test the code. Convert the code into a code snippet only after a successful code compilation. Custom code snippets should be placed in dedicated directories reserved for custom snippets. Make sure that the directory is eventually added as a code snippet directory using the Code Snippets Manager.

This walkthrough creates a code snippet that reflects the methods of a type. This code tests the proposed snippet:

```
// Snippet starts
Type t = typeof(Object);
string typename = t.Name;
string typenamespace = t.Namespace;
MethodInfo [] methods = t.GetMethods();
// Snippet ends
Console.WriteLine("Type Name:"+typename);
Console.WriteLine("Namespace Name:"+typenamespace);
foreach (MethodInfo method in methods)
{
    Console.WriteLine(method.Name);
}
```

These are the steps for creating the preceding snippet:

1. Create an XML file in Visual Studio. The filename of the code snippet is *reflectmethod.snippet*.

2. All snippet files begin with the *CodeSnippets*, *CodeSnippet*, and *Header* elements, which name the file schema and describe the basic attributes of the code snippet:

```xml
<?xml version="1.0" encoding="utf-8"?>
<CodeSnippets xmlns="http://schemas.microsoft.com/VisualStudio/2005/CodeSnippet">
  <CodeSnippet Format="1.0.0">
    <Header>
      <Title>ReflectMethod</Title>
      <Shortcut>rm</Shortcut>
      <Description>Reflects methods of a type.</Description>
      <Author>Donis Marshall</Author>
    </Header>
  </CodeSnippet>
</CodeSnippets>
```

3. Reflection requires the *Reflection* namespace. Import the *System.Reflection* namespace with an *Import* element, which is defined within the *Imports* element. The *System.Reflection* namespace is declared in the *System.DLL*, which is automatically referenced from managed code. For that reason, a *Reference* element is not needed.

```xml
<Snippet>
  <Imports>
    <Import>
      <Namespace>System.Text</Namespace>
    </Import>
  </Imports>
</Snippet>
```

4. The code snippet has four fields, which name the type, type instance, namespace, and *MethodInfo* array. The type instance is an object field. The other fields are literals and contained within the code snippet. Defaults for the fields are gleaned from the code used to test the code snippet. Fields are defined within the *Declarations* element with literal and object elements:

```xml
<Declarations>
  <Literal>
    <ID>Instance</ID>
    <Default>t</Default>
    <ToolTip>Name of instance.</ToolTip>
  </Literal>
  <Literal>
    <ID>TypeName</ID>
    <Default>typename</Default>
    <ToolTip>Name of type.</ToolTip>
  </Literal>
  <Literal>
    <ID>TypeNamespace</ID>
    <Default>typenamespace</Default>
    <ToolTip>Namespace of type.</ToolTip>
  </Literal>
  <Literal>
```

```
    <ID>Methods</ID>
    <Default>Methods</Default>
    <ToolTip>Type methods</ToolTip>
  </Literal>
  <Object>
    <ID>Type</ID>
    <Default>Object</Default>
    <ToolTip>object type</ToolTip>
    <Type>System.Object</Type>
  </Object>
</Declarations>
```

5. Paste the code for the snippet into *<![CDATA]>* elements, which are placed within the *Code* element. Add extra line feeds to separate lines of source code. After pasting the code, substitute the field names into the code:

```
<Code Language="CSharp">
  <![CDATA[Type $Instance$ = typeof($Type$);
  ]]>
  <![CDATA[string $TypeName$ = $Instance$.Name;
  ]]>
  <![CDATA[string $TypeNamespace$ = $Instance$.Namespace;
  ]]>
  <![CDATA[MethodInfo [] $Methods$ = $Instance$.GetMethods();
  ]]>
</Code>
```

6. Save the file for the code snippet in the directory reserved for custom code snippets.

7. Test the snippet in Visual Studio 2005. Open a source file and insert the code snippet using the code snippet picker. Figure 4-34 shows the snippet.

```
Type t = typeof(Object);
string typename = t.Name;
string typenamespace = t.Namespace;
MethodInfo[] Methods = t.GetMethods();
```

Figure 4-34   Reflect Method snippet

Refactoring

Refactoring helps developers re-engineer their code and removes much of the tedium of maintaining an application. Considerable time is spent re-engineering during the lifetime of an application. This sometimes starts as early as the development phase and accelerates as the application matures. This includes—but is not limited to—renaming variables, moving methods, changing method signatures, and redesigning classes. The objective is to improve the application. The process is tedious. Finding and changing a variable in a software system that spans dozens of source files can be challenging. Another example is changing the signature of a commonly used method. Method calls throughout the application must be located and corrected. These changes are made to improve an application. However, if executed poorly, these changes have the opposite effect. Worst-case scenario: Maintenance might introduce bugs into otherwise pristine applications. Visual Studio 2005 introduces refactoring as a tool to help developers re-engineer code quickly and accurately. Refactoring is a multifaceted tool. It

assists in the renaming of variables, changing of method signatures, extrapolating of interfaces, converting fields to properties, and much more.

A Refactoring menu is available in the Visual Studio 2005 user interface that shows the refactoring operations. Table 4-5 list the various refactoring operations. The refactoring menu is
also available in the Code Editor using a shortcut menu.

Table 4-5   Refactoring Operations

Operations	Description
Rename	The Rename operation renames a symbol, such as a variable or method name, throughout an application.
Extract Method	The Extract Method operation creates a new method that encapsulates the selected code.
Encapsulate Field	The Encapsulate Field operation creates a property that abstracts the selected field.
Extract Interface	The Extract Interface operation extracts an interface from a type.
Promote Local Variables To Parameters	The Promote Local Variables To Parameters operation promotes a local variable to a parameter of the current method.
Remove Parameters	The Remove Parameters operation removes a parameter from the parameter list of a function. Call sites for the function are updated to reflect the removed parameter.
Reorder Parameters	The Reorder Parameters operation reorders the parameters of a function. Call sites for the function are updated for the new sequence of parameters.

The Preview Changes dialog box is invaluable because it provides you with an opportunity to
preview refactoring changes before applying them. Figure 4-35 displays the Preview Changes
dialog box.

Figure 4-35   Preview Changes dialog box

Refactoring can span multiple projects in the same solution, which occurs with project-to-project references. A project-to-project reference is a reference in which both the referencing and referenced assemblies are built in projects of the same solution. The Projects window in the Add Reference dialog box inserts a project-to-project reference.

Refactoring Walkthrough

This walkthrough demonstrates some of the features of refactoring, including the renaming of variables and extracting of interfaces. The walkthrough refactors the Airline Seats application. This application manages the first class and coach standby lists of an airline flight. This is the user interface (shown in Figure 4-36) presented to flyers on overhead monitors at the airport gate.

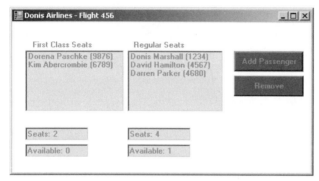

Figure 4-36   Airline Seats application

The following steps outline the walkthrough.

1. The application defines a *Node* class, which is a generic collection class in the *node.cs* file. The value of the node is returned from the *Info* property. The property should be renamed *Value*, which is probably more intuitive. Select the Info name in the source file. From the shortcut menu, choose the Refactor submenu and the Rename menu command.

2. The Rename dialog box appears. The selected text is displayed with its location. Three option buttons are presented. The Preview Reference Changes option requests a preview window before the changes are applied. This option is selected by default. The Search In Comments option searches comments for the renamed text. The Search In String option extends the search to literals, such as string literals. Change the text to *Value* and proceed with the renaming operation. (See Figure 4-37.)

3. The Preview Changes–Rename dialog box appears. (See Figure 4-38.) You can review the pending changes in this window. Specific changes can be selected or unselected. When acceptable, click Apply, and the specified changes are enacted. If necessary, you can undo refactoring changes using the Undo (Ctrl+Z) feature of Visual Studio.

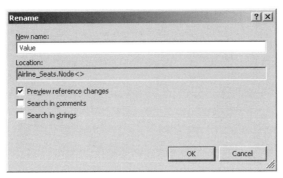

Figure 4-37   Rename dialog box

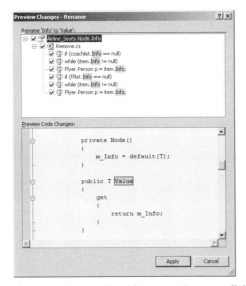

Figure 4-38   Preview Changes—Rename dialog box

4. The capability to extrapolate interfaces from classes is another great feature of refactoring. Manually extracting interfaces from types is a time-consuming process for developers. The Airline Seats application has a *Person* class that represents the flyer. In the future, other types of people may be added to the application. For that reason, the *Person* interface is extrapolated for future use. Position the cursor within the class and open the shortcut menu. From the Refactor menu, select the Extract interface menu command. The Extract Interface dialog box appears, as shown in Figure 4-39. Enter the interface name and file name. A list of potential members is presented. You can select which members to include in the interface. As a convenience, Select All and Deselect All buttons are provided.

5. The *Passenger* class, which is a form, has two public fields. A tenet of object-oriented programming is that fields should be private. Exposing fields as public properties is more secure.

```
public Node<Flyer.Person> coachlist=null;
public Node<Flyer.Person> fflist= null;
```

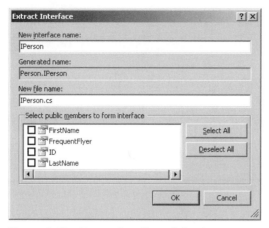

Figure 4-39   Extract Interface dialog box

6. Select the first field. From the shortcut menu, select the Refactoring menu and Encapsulate Field menu command. The Encapsulate Field dialog box appears. (See Figure 4-40.) Enter the property name and accept.

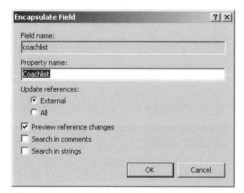

Figure 4-40   Encapsulate Field dialog box

7. After accepting the Encapsulate Field dialog box, the Preview Reference Changes dialog box appears. This dialog box shows the potential changes. You can accept or reject individual changes.

8. Repeat steps 6 and 7 to convert the second field to a property. Despite the numerous changes in various parts of the application, you can now compile and run the program successfully.

This is the interface created from the Extract Interface refactoring operation. It is saved to a separate file. In the file, change the namespace containing the interface appropriately. For the sample application, the namespace is changed to *Flyer*.

```
interface IPerson
{
    string FirstName { get; }
```

```
    bool FrequentFlyer { get; }
    string ID { get; }
    string LastName { get; }
}
```

Refactoring also updated the *Person* class to inherit the *IPerson* interface:

```
public class Person : IPerson
{
    // partial listing
}
```

This is one property created from refactoring a field:

```
private Node<Flyer.Person> coachlist = null;

public Node<Flyer.Person> Coachlist
{
    get { return coachlist; }
    set { coachlist = value; }
}
```

Building and Deployment

The Microsoft Build Engine (MSBuild) is a new build environment. The build process is orchestrated in an XML-based project file. MSBuild replaces traditional *.mak* files. The project file describes the build process, build configuration, and input and output files.

Visual Studio 2005 supports conventional deployment based on Windows Installer technology. With Windows Installer technology, an application is packaged in a Setup.exe file and then deployed to the local machine or a public share. The Setup.exe program installs the application on the local machine. ClickOnce deployment is introduced in Visual Studio 2005 as an alternate deployment strategy. ClickOnce deploys an application from a central location and combines a desktop application with Web-based delivery system.

MSBuild

MSBuild does not require Visual Studio. This is ideal for lab environments in which Visual Studio is not installed. Individual builds are organized in project files. Build project files are XML files and have a *.proj* extension. As an XML file, the build project is platform-independent and extensible. For a complete explanation of MSBuild, consult the MSBuild Reference at the Microsoft Developer Network (MSDN) at *http://winfx.msdn.microsoft.com/library/ default.asp?url=/library/en-us/dv_fxgenref/html/093395e1-70da-4f74-b34d-046c5e2b32e8.asp.*

Build projects consist of items, properties, and tasks, as described in the following sections.

Items

Items are the input of the build process. Items are created as child elements of the *ItemGroup* element. Items sharing the same name are considered a collection. Item collections are addressable in the build project as @(*ItemCollectionName*). Item collections are primarily used as parameters in build tasks.

For example, the *Compile* element is a standard item. It defines the source files that are included or excluded from the build. The *Include* attribute specifies a file to be included in the build. The *Exclude* attribute, naturally, excludes files. The following code defines a *Compile* collection, which includes two items:

```
<ItemGroup>
  <Compile Include="source1.cs"/>
  <Compile Include="source3.cs" Exclude="source2.cs"/>
</ItemGroup>
```

Properties

Properties are configuration data used during the build process. Properties represent individual values and cannot be grouped into collections. Properties are defined as child elements of the *PropertyGroup* element. Refer to properties in the project using the $(*property*) syntax:

```
<PropertyGroup>
  <ApplicationVersion>1.2.3.4</ApplicationVersion>
</PropertyGroup>
```

There are several reserved properties in the MSBuild environment. Table 4-6 lists the reserved properties.

Table 4-6   Reserved Properties

Property	Description
MSBuildProjectDirectory	This property is the absolute path to the MSBuild project file.
MSBuildProjectFile	This property is the name and extension of the MSBuild project file.
MSBuildProjectExtension	This is the file extension of the MSBuild project file. It should include the . prefix.
MSBuildProjectFullPath	This property is the fully qualified name of the MSBuild project file.
MSBuildProjectName	This property is the name of the MSBuild project file without the extension.
MSBuildBinPath	This property is the path to the MSBuild binaries.
MSBuildProjectDefaultTargets	This property is the list of targets specified in the project element of the MSBuild project file.
MSBuildExtensionsPath	This property is the supplemental directory for custom target files, which is found under the Program Files directory.

Tasks

Tasks are the build operations of the MSBuild project and child elements of the *Target* element. Tasks can accept parameters, which are the attributes of the *Task* element. Item collections and properties are valid parameters to tasks. Create multiple targets to batch groups of build operations. The MSBuild tool can invoke different targets. For example, you can create targets for release versus debug builds.

Tasks are written in a managed language and are available to any MSBuild project. Developers can author specialty tasks in managed code. Build tasks are classes that implement the *ITask* interface.

Table 4-7 list the defaults tasks available in the MSBuild environment.

Table 4-7   Default Tasks

Task	Description
AL	This task invokes the Assembly Linker (AL) tool.
AspNetCompiler	This task invokes *aspnet_compiler.exe*, which precompiles ASP.NET applications.
AssignCulture	This task creates an item for a culture.
Copy	This task copies files to a specified directory.
CreateItem	This task copies items between collections.
CreateProperty	This task copies properties.
Csc	This task invokes *csc.exe*, which is the C# compiler.
Delete	This task deletes files.
Exec	This task executes an application or command.
FindUnderPath	This task determines which items are found within a specified directory and its subdirectories.
GenerateApplicationManifest	This task creates an application manifest or native manifest for a ClickOnce application.
GenerateBootstrapper	This task locates, downloads, and installs an application.
GenerateDeploymentManifest	This task creates a deployment manifest for a ClickOnce application.
GenerateResource	This task creates *.resources* files from *.txt* and *.resx* files.
GetAssemblyIdentity	This task returns assembly metadata and stores the results in an item collection.
GetFrameworkPath	This task obtains the path of the .NET Framework assemblies.
GetFrameworkSDKPath	This task obtains the path of the .NET Framework SDK.
LC	This task converts a *.licx* to a *.license* file.
Makedir	This task makes a directory.
MSBuild	This task builds an MSBuild project from another build project.
ReadLinesFromFile	This task reads MSBuild items from a file.

Table 4-7   Default Tasks *(Continued)*

Task	Description
RegisterAssembly	This task reads the metadata of an assembly and registers the assembly as a COM server, which allows COM clients to access the assembly.
RemoveDir	This task deletes a directory.
ResolveAssemblyReference	This task determines which assemblies depend on another assembly.
ResolveComReference	This task resolves the location of type library (TLB) files.
ResolveKeySource	This task determines the strong name of a key source.
Sgen	This task is a wrapper for the XML Serialization Generator Tool (*sgen.exe*).
SignFile	This task signs a file with a certificate.
Touch	This task sets the access and modification time of a file.
UnregisterAssembly	This task unregisters an assembly from the registry. Afterward, the assembly is no longer available to COM clients.
Vbc	This task invokes *vbc.exe*, which is the Visual Basic .NET compiler.
VcBuild	This task wraps *vcbuild.exe*, which builds a Visual C++ project.
WriteLinesToFiles	This task writes the paths of the specified items to a file.

Project File

A project file is a generalized skeleton of an MSBuild project. An MSBuild project can have any number of tasks, item collections, and properties. This is entirely dependent on the requirements of the actual project.

```
<?xml version="1.0" encoding="utf-8"?>
<!-- MSBuild Schema -->
<Project xmlns="http://schemas.microsoft.com/developer/msbuild/2003">
  <ItemGroup>
    <!-- Item Collection -->
  </ItemGroup>
  <Target Name="Task1">
    <!-- Task(s) -->
  </Target>
  <PropertyGroup>
    <!-- Properties -->
  </PropertyGroup>
  <ItemGroup>
    <!-- Item Collection -->
  </ItemGroup>
  <Target Name="Task2">
    <!-- Task(s) -->
  </Target>
</Project>
```

This is the syntax of the MSBuild command line:

```
Msbuild switches projectfile
```

MSBuild command-line switches are listed in Table 4-8.

Table 4-8   **MSBuild Switches**

Task	Description
/help	This switch displays help information on the MSBuild command. */?* and */h* are also help switches.
/noconsolelogger	This switch disabled the default console logger. Events should not be logged to the console window.
/nologo	This switch suppresses the startup banner and copyright information.
/version	This switch displays the version of the MSBuild tool.
@file	This switch reads command-line instructions from a batch file.
/noautoresponse	This switch disables the automatic include of the MSBuild.rsp file.
/target:targetnames	This switch identifies the targets to execute. The targets are delimited by commas or semicolons.
/property:name=value	This switch sets the value of a property. Multiple properties are delimited by commas or semicolons.
/logger:logger	This switch logs MSBuild events to a logger.
/consoleloggerparameters: parameters	This switch sets the parameters of the console logger.
/verbosity:level	This switch sets the amount of information written to the event log. The levels are as follows: ■ *q*—quiet ■ *m*—minimal ■ *n*—normal ■ *d*—detailed ■ *diag*—diagnostic
/validate:schema	This switch validates the project file. If no schema is provided, the default schema is used to perform the validation.

MSBuild Walkthrough

This section provides a walkthrough of a normal MSBuild project. The project contains two tasks: The first task compiles an assembly from the available source files, and the second task creates a DLL from a source file. The project then compiles the remaining sources files. This requires a reference to the DLL. The walkthrough MSBuild project is documented with steps. Here is the project, followed by a description of each step:

```
<?xml version="1.0" encoding="utf-8"?>
<!-- Step One-->
```

```
<Project xmlns="http://schemas.microsoft.com/developer/msbuild/2003">
  <!-- Step Two -->
  <ItemGroup>
    <Compile Include="source1.cs"/>
    <Compile Include="source2.cs"/>
  </ItemGroup>
  <!-- Step Three -->
  <PropertyGroup>
    <DebugType>none</DebugType>
  </PropertyGroup>
  <PropertyGroup>
    <AssemblyName>sample.exe</AssemblyName>
  </PropertyGroup>
  <!-- Step Four -->
  <Target Name="Application1">
    <Csc Sources="*.cs" OutputAssembly="$(AssemblyName)"
        DebugType="$(DebugType)"/>
  </Target>
  <!-- Step Five-->
  <Target Name="Application2">
    <Csc Sources="source3.cs" TargetType="library"/>
    <Csc Sources="@(compile)" References="source3.dll"
        OutputAssembly="$(AssemblyName)" DebugType="$(DebugType)"/>
  </Target>
</Project>
```

- Step 1 establishes the schema for the MSBuild schema.

- Step 2 creates an item collection for the *Compile* element. The source files *source1.cs* and *source2.cs* are named in the collection.

- Step 3 sets the defaults for the *DebugType* and *AssemblyName* properties.

- Step 4 creates target *Application1*, which has a single task. The task compiles the source files in the current directory. It uses both the *AssemblyName* and *DebugType* properties.

- Step 5 creates target *Application2*, which contains two tasks: The first task compiles *source3.cs* and places the results in a library assembly; the second task compiles the item collection and references the library assembly.

This MSBuild command line reads the *sample.proj* project file. The output is the *donis.exe* assembly. The *debugtype* property is assigned *full*, whereas the *assemblyname* property is assigned *donis.exe*. This overwrites the default values of those properties. Finally, MSBuild invokes the *Application1* target:

```
C:\>msbuild /p:debugtype=full,assemblyname=donis.exe
    sample.proj /target:application1
```

The following MSBuild command executes the tasks of the *Application2* target:

```
C:\ >msbuild /p:debugtype=full,assemblyname=donis.exe
    sample.proj /target:application2
```

Click Once Deployment

With ClickOnce deployment, developers browse to Window applications published on an ASP.NET Web server. Setup and deployment of desktop and non-Web applications have recently become increasingly complex. In addition, installation must be repeated for updates and future versions of the product. There is also the productivity problem of having to physically install the product on multiple machines. Conversely, deployment of Web applications is hands-free. You simply browse to the application using the proper URL. No installation required. Web applications are also self-updating. Users automatically obtain the latest version of the Web application whenever the Web site is browsed. Productivity is improved because per-machine installations are avoided. The benefits of a Web distribution extend to ClickOnce deployment.

ClickOnce deployment is nonintrusive. Windows Installer technology is intrusive as the application is installed to the local machine. ClickOnce deployment downloads an application into the download cache, in which there is limited impact to the local machine. There are security considerations because these applications execute in the download cache with potentially limited security privileges. These security considerations must be addressed in the application or on the local machine. Because the deployment is hands-free, user experience is improved.

ClickOnce applications are self-updating, which is particularly useful for applications that require frequent updates. Deploying applications that require frequent updates within the Windows Installer technology model was a time-consuming process. ClickOnce applications are deployed once and updated online automatically. Updates require online connectivity.

Another benefit includes the security privileges required to perform an installation. Windows Installer technology sometimes required administrative permissions, but ClickOnce deployment does not require administrative permissions to deploy the application.

ClickOnce deployment publishes an application at a Web site on an ASP.NET server. The client machine must support the .NET Framework. This is more likely in an intranet deployment, in which the desktops are controlled. It is also feasible in an extranet environment, in which requirements can be published and a reasonable level of compliance can be expected. ClickOnce applications can be deployed in a traditional manner, but require online connectivity for self-updating.

ClickOnce deployment has two modes of deployment. The online-only mode executes the application from the Web, which requires the client to be connected to the server computer whenever the application is executed. The full installation mode executes the installation on the client computer. This is similar to a traditional installation from an .msi or .cab file. Updates still require online connectivity.

ClickOnce deployment uses an application manifest (which is an XML file) to define dependent assemblies, files, and security permissions required for the application. ClickOnce deployment also uses a deployment manifest. This manifest contains deployment configuration information, such as the current version, the location of required files, deployment mode, and update policies.

Create application and deployment manifests with the Manifest Generation and Editing (MageUI) tool, which is distributed in the .NET Framework. To create a new application manifest, choose the File menu and then choose the New submenu. From the submenu, select Application Manifest The Name window of the application manifest appears first. This window contains the general information on the deployment. The Airline Seats application is published as a ClickOnce application. Figure 4-41 shows a view of the Name window in the MageUI tool for the Airline Seats application.

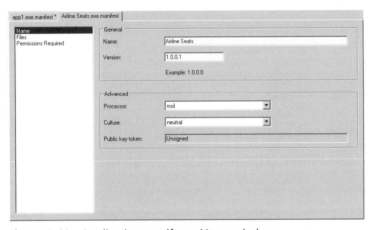

Figure 4-41   Application manifest—Name window

The Files window lists the files included in the deployment. (See Figure 4-42.)

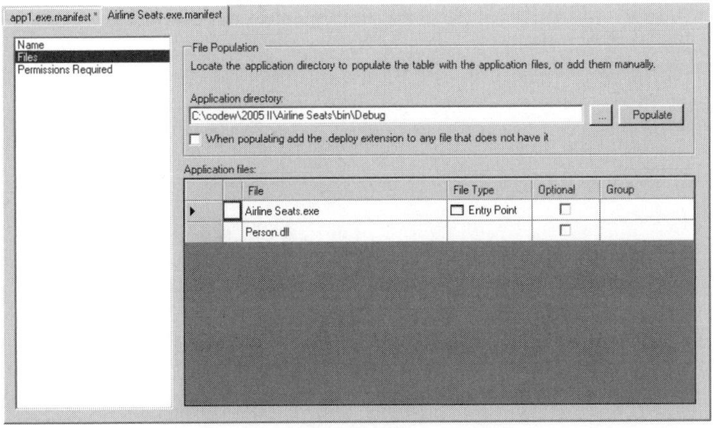

Figure 4-42   Application manifest—Files window

The Permissions Required window sets the security required to execute the deployed application.(See Figure 4-43.)

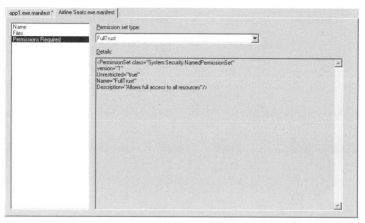

Figure 4-43 Application manifest—Permissions Required window

You can also open the deployment manifest using the MageUI tool. The Names windows for both the deployment and application manifests are the same. For the deployment manifest, the two most important windows are the Deployment and Update Options windows.

The Deployment Options window sets the ClickOnce deployment mode and the URL of the published application. (See Figure 4-44.)

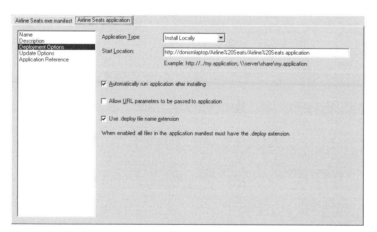

Figure 4-44 Deployment manifest—Deployment Options window

The Update Options window configures how updates are managed for an application deployed with ClickOnce technology. Figure 4-45 shows the Update Options window.

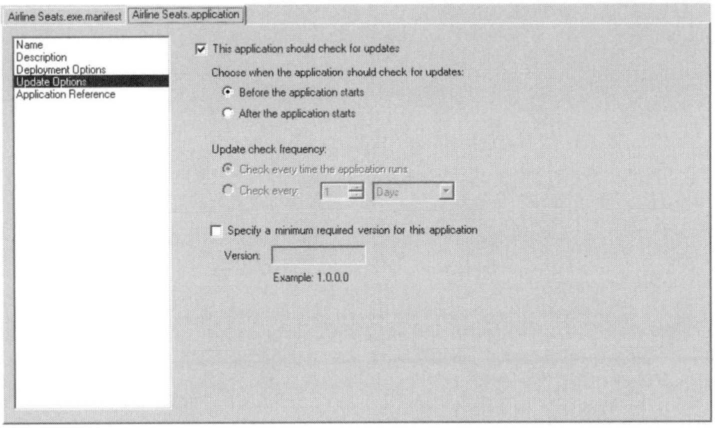

Figure 4-45   Deployment manifest—Update Options window

Publish a ClickOnce Application

Fortunately, ClickOnce deployment is automated in Visual Studio 2005. This includes the creation of both manifest files and Web server configuration. In Visual Studio 2005, developers use the Publish Wizard to set up an application for ClickOnce deployment. Open the project shortcut menu and choose Publish to launch the Publish Wizard.

The Publish Wizard has several steps. The first step provides the URL in which the application is published. Figure 4-46 shows the first window of the Publish Wizard.

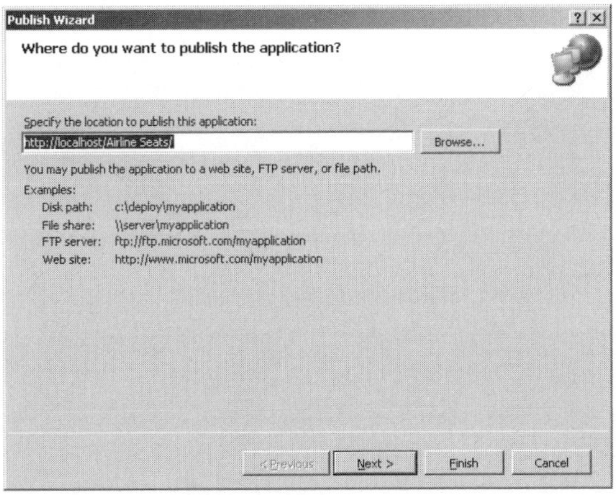

Figure 4-46   Publish Wizard—step 1

Step 2 of the Publish Wizard sets the online connectivity requirements of the deployed application. (See Figure 4-47.)

Step 3 (shown in Figure 4-48) is the confirmation window, in which a developer can review the ClickOnce settings and confirm the deployment.

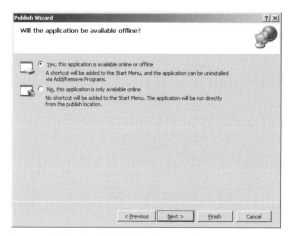

Figure 4-47 Publish Wizard—step 2

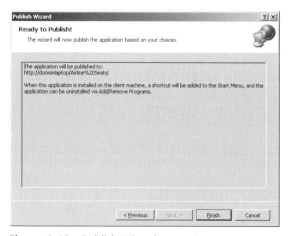

Figure 4-48 Publish Wizard—step 3

Arrays and Collections

The next chapter reviews arrays and collections. Arrays are collections of related types, and they are the only native collection. C# supports one- and multidimensional arrays. Jagged arrays are also supported, which are arrays of arrays. *System.Array* is the underlying type of all arrays, which defines the baseline behavior of all arrays. You learn a lot about arrays in examining the *System.Array* class. For example, the *Array.SyncRoot* property is used to synchronize access to an array. Arrays implement a myriad of interfaces, such as *ICloneable*, *ICollection*, and *IEnumerable*. The next chapter discusses the merits of each of these interfaces.

More sophisticated collections are sometimes needed. The .NET Framework offers *ArrayList*, *Queue*, *Stack*, *HashTable*, and other useful collections. Specialty collections are also available, including *BitVector32*, *HybridDictionary*, and *NameValueCollection*.

Chapter 5
Arrays and Collections

An *array* is a collection of related instances, either value or reference types. Arrays possess an immutable structure, in which the number of dimensions and size of the array are fixed at instantiation. C# supports single-dimensional, multidimensional, and jagged arrays. Single-dimensional arrays, sometimes called *vectors*, consist of a single row. Multidimensional arrays are rectangular and consist of rows and columns. A jagged array also consists of rows and columns, but is irregularly shaped.

Arrays are represented in most programming languages. Most developers have some familiarity with the concept of arrays. Arrays are employed in a variety of ways. A personnel program would contain an array of employees. Graphic programs might have one array for each type of geometric object, such as ellipses, rectangles, or triangles. An accounting and scheduling application for automobile repair likely would have an array of automobile repair tickets. The Space Shuttle program would have an array of astronauts.

Arrays are intrinsic to the language. Other collections, such as *Stack*, *Queue*, and *Hashtable*, are not native to the language. As such, ease of use is one of the benefits of arrays. Another benefit is familiarity. Arrays are available and functionally similar in almost every programming language. Few developers have not worked with arrays.

An array is a container, which is an abstraction of a data structure. As a container, an array holds data items called *elements*. Elements of an array are always related, such as an array of apples or an array of oranges. An array might consist of *SalariedEmployee*, *HourlyEmployee*, and *CommissionedEmployee* instances. However, an array of apples and employees is probably invalid because those objects are probably unrelated. In addition, an array is a data structure that is a composite of elements that reside in contiguous memory.

Arrays are reference types, and the memory for the array is allocated on the managed heap. Even an array of value types is allocated on the managed heap and not on the stack. An array of 30 integer values would have the same number of 32-bit slots allocated in contiguous memory for the array elements. With arrays of reference types, the objects are not stored in contiguous memory; the references are stored in contiguous memory. However, the objects themselves are stored in noncontiguous memory, which is pointed to by the reference. Figure 5-1 shows the difference in memory allocation between arrays of reference versus value types.

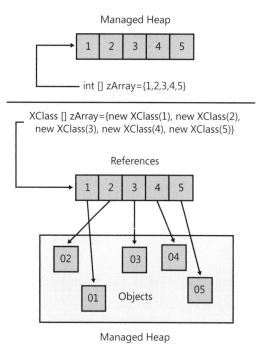

Figure 5-1   Array of reference types versus value types

Elements are relative to the beginning of the array and are identified with indexes, which are either integer or long types. Indexes are also commonly called indices or subscripts, and placed inside the indexing operator ([ ]). Arrays are zero-based where the index is actually an offset. Array indexes are offsets from the beginning of the array to a particular element. Therefore, the first element is at the start of the array, which is an offset of zero. For an array of five elements, a proper index is from zero to four. Therefore, the last element of the array is at index $n-1$. This is a common cause of fencepost errors. Fencepost errors occur when referring to array elements with indexes outside the bounds of an array. If an array has five elements, accessing element six is a fencepost error.

As mentioned, arrays are immutable. This means that an array is statically sized, and the dimensions cannot be changed at run time. The *System.Array.Resize* method, which is a generic method, seemingly resizes an array. However, appearances can be deceiving. *Array.Resize* creates an entirely new array that is the new size. The new array is initialized with the elements of the source array. Afterward, the original array is discarded.

Single-dimensional arrays are indigenous to the run time. There are specific MSIL instructions for vectors, including *newarr, ldelem, ldlen,* and *stelem.* There are no built-in instructions for multidimensional arrays. This direct manipulation of single-dimensional arrays makes them more efficient. In addition, some of the members of the *System.Array* type, which is the underlying type for all arrays, cannot be applied to multidimensional arrays. Conversely, all the methods and properties of the *System.Array* type are applicable to single-dimensional arrays.

The *System.Array* type is the underpinning of all arrays. It is an abstraction of an array. Instances of arrays are instances of the *System.Array* type. Thus, arrays are implicitly reference types. Arrays can access many of the instance methods and properties of the *System.Array* type. *System.Array* is a combination of original methods and the implementation of a series of interfaces. Table 5-1 lists the interfaces that *System.Array* implements.

Table 5-1   Interfaces Implemented at System.Array

Interface	Description
ICloneable	This interface defines a method to clone an instance of an array.
ICollection	This interface defines methods to count the number of elements of an array and for thread synchronization.
IEnumerable	This interface defines a method that enumerates the elements of a collection.
IList	The interface defines methods to access an index-based collection. Some members of this interface are not publicly implemented.

Create arrays as local variables or fields. Use arrays also as method parameters and return types. The rationale of using an array as a local variable, field, method parameter, or return type is the same as any type. Arrays are passable into or out of a method as a parameter. The semantics of an array parameter are the same as any parameter. Because an array is a reference type, it is passed by reference. Therefore, the content of the array can be changed in the called method. Parameter modifiers, such as the ref modifier, are assignable to array parameters.

Arrays

Following is the syntax for declaring a one-dimensional array. A vector has a single index. When declaring an array, the indexing operator on the right-hand side sets the size of the array.

$$type \; [] \; arrayname^1;$$

$$typea \; [] \; arrayname^2 = new \; typeb[n];$$

$$typea \; [] \; arrayname^3 = new \; typeb[n] \; \{ilist\};$$

$$typea[] \; arrayname^4 = new \; typeb[] \; \{ilist\};$$

$$typea[] \; arrayname^5 = \{ilist\};$$

The first syntax declares a reference to an array that is not initialized. You can later initialize the array reference using the right hand side (RHS) syntax of declaring an array. This is sample code of the first syntax of declaring an array. It declares an integer array named *zArray*. The array is then assigned an array of 10 integers that initializes the references. However, the array elements of 10 integers are not initialized. Array elements default to zero or null: zero for value types and null for reference type elements. In this code, the array elements are set to zeroes:

```
int [] zArray;
zArray=new int[10];
```

The second syntax declares and initializes a reference to an array. The array reference is assigned a reference to the new instance. An array of a value types must be initialized to an array of the same value type. Otherwise, *typea* and *typeb* must be identical. Even if *typea* and *typeb* are convertible, the declaration is not allowed. Bytes are convertible to integers. However, an array of bytes is not convertible to an array of integers. The size of the array is *n*. The elements are indexed from zero to *n – 1*.

This is sample code of the second syntax:

```
byte aValue=10;
int bValue= aValue;        // convertible
int [] zArray=new byte[5];  // not convertible
int [] yArray=new int[5];   // convertible
```

Unlike value types, an array of reference types can be initialized to an array of the same or derived types. In the declaration, *typeb* must be the same or a derivation of *typea*, which is demonstrated in the following code:

```
public class Starter{
    public static void Main(){
        XBase [] obj=new XDerived[5]; // base     <- derived
        XDerived [] obj2=new XBase[5]; // derived <- base [invalid]
    }
}

public class XDerived: XBase {
}

public class XBase {
}
```

The third syntax declares, initializes, and assigns values to the array elements. The initialization list (*ilist*) contains the initial value for the elements of the array, where the values are comma-delimited. The number of values in the list should match the number of elements in the array exactly—no more and no less.

This is an example of the third syntax for declaring an array:

```
int [] zArray=new int[3] {1,2,3}; // valid
int [] yArray=new int[3] {1,2};   // invalid
ZClass [] xArray=new ZClass[3] {   // valid
    new ZClass(5), new ZClass(10),
    new ZClass(15) };
```

The fourth syntax also declares, initializes, and assigns values to array elements. However, in this circumstance, the initialization list sets the number of elements. The array size is not stipulated in this syntax. The compiler counts the number of items in the initialization list to set the length of the array.

This is an example of the fourth syntax:

```
int [] zArray=new int[] {1,2,3,4,5};  // 5 elements
```

The fifth syntax is an abbreviation of the fourth syntax, where the array type and number of elements are inferred from the initialization list.

This is an example of the fifth syntax:

```
int [] yArray={1,2,3,4,5};
```

As in a local variable or field definition, multiple declarations can be combined:

```
public class ZClass{
    private int [] first={1,2,3},
                   second={4,5,6},
                   third={7,8,9};

    // Remainder of class...
}
```

Array Elements

Indexing operators refer to elements of an array. With an index, the indexing operator returns a specific element of the array. When an indexing operator is used on the left hand side (LHS), the element value is changed. On the RHS, the indexing operator returns the value of the element.

The following *for* loop lists the elements of an array. The element and indexing operator appear as an *l*-value to total the array. It is used as an *r*-value to display each element:

```
int [] zArray={1,2,3,4,5};
int total=0;
for(int count=0;count<zArray.Length;++count) {
    total+=zArray[count];                // l-value
    int number=zArray[count];            // r-value
    Console.WriteLine(number);
}
Console.WriteLine("\nThe total is {0}.",
    total);
```

Multidimensional Arrays

You are not limited to one-dimensional arrays. Multidimensional arrays are rectangular arrays and have multiple dimensions and indices. Two-dimensional arrays, which consist of rows and columns, are the most prevalent kind of multidimensional array. Each row contains the same number of columns, thus making the array rectangular. From a geometric perspective, the x-axis consists of rows and the y-axis consists of columns. Multidimensional arrays are stored in row-major order and are processed in row-major order.

The total number of elements in a multidimensional array is the product of the indices. For example, an array of 5 rows and 6 columns has 30 elements. The *Array.Length* property returns the total number of elements in the array. The *Array.GetLength* method returns the number of elements per index. The indices are numbered from zero. For a two-dimensional array, row is the zero dimension, whereas column is the one dimension. *GetLength(0)* would then return the number of rows in the multidimensional array.

This is the syntax to declare a two-dimensional array. Notice the indexing operator. Row and column indexes in the indexing operator are delimited with a comma.

> *type* [,] *arrayname*[1];
>
> *typea* [,] *arrayname*[2]=new *typeb*[r,c];
>
> *typea* [,] *arrayname*[3]=new *typeb*[r,c] {*ilist*};
>
> *typea*[,] *arrayname*[4]=new *typeb*[,] {*ilist*};
>
> *typea*[,] *arrayname*[5]={*ilist*};

The following code shows various declarations of multidimensional arrays. The initialization list of a multidimensional array includes nested initialization lists for each row. If an array has two rows, the initialization list includes two nested initialization lists. This is the syntax of a nested initialization list:

{ {*nlist*}, {*nlist*}, {*nlist*} ...}

The following code shows the various declaration syntaxes, including nested initialization lists:

```
int [,] array1;              // syntax 1
array1=new int[1,2];
int [,] array2=new int[2,3];  // syntax 2
int [,] array3=new int[2,3] {  // syntax 3
    {1,2,3}, {4,5,6} };
int [,] array4=new int[,] {    // syntax 4
    {1,2,3}, {4,5,6} };
int [,] array5= {             // syntax 5
    {1,2,3}, {4,5,6} };
```

To access an element of a multidimensional array, specify a row and column index in the indexing operator. It can be used on the LHS and RHS to set or get the value of an element, respectively. The following code calculates the total of the elements. This requires enumerating all the elements of a multidimensional array.

```
int [,] zArray=new int[2,3] {
    {1,2,3}, {4,5,6} };
int total=0;
```

```
for(int row=0;row<zArray.GetLength(0);++row) {
    for(int col=0;col<zArray.GetLength(1);++col) {
        total+=zArray[row, col];              // LHS
        int number=zArray[row, col];          // RHS
        Console.WriteLine(number);
    }
}
Console.WriteLine("\nThe total is {0}.",
    total);
```

We have been focusing on two-dimensional arrays. However, arrays can have more than two dimensions. In fact, there is no limit to the number of dimensions. Three- and four-dimensional arrays are less common than two-dimensional arrays, but are seen nonetheless. More dimensions are rarely enunciated. Most developers find multidimensional arrays beyond two indices mind-numbing to manage and manipulate. Additional dimensions require added comma-delimited indexes when the array is, declared, defined, and used.

This is an example of a four-dimensional array:

```
int [,,,] array=new int[1,2,3,2]
    {{{{1,2}, {1,2},{1,2}},{{1,2},{1,2},{1,2}}}};
```

How is the preceding code interpreted? A multidimensional array can be viewed as a hierar-chical array that consists of layers. Each layer represents a different level of array nesting. The previous example defines a single-dimensional array, which aggregates two nested arrays. The nested arrays each contain three other arrays. Each of these lower nested arrays contains two elements.

This is a diagram of the array hierarchy:

{   1   }; // layer 1

{{   1   },{   2   }}; // layer 2

{{{ 1 },{ 2 },{ 3 }},{{{ 1 },{ 2 },{ 3 }}; // layer 3

{{{{1,2}, {1,2},{1,2}} , {{1,2},{1,2},{1,2}}}}; // layer 4

The following code demonstrates a practical use of a multidimensional array. The program maintains the grades of students. Each student attends two classes. Each class has a class name and grade. Object elements are defined to make the array generic. Strings, integers, reference types, or anything else can be placed in an object array. Everything is derived from *System.Object* in managed code. The downside is boxing and unboxing of grades, which are value types.

```
using System;

namespace Donis.CSharpBook{
    public class Starter{
        public static void Main(){
```

```
string [] names={"Bob", "Ted", "Alice"};
object [,,] grades=new object[3,2,2]
    {{{"Algebra",85},  { "English",75}},
     {{"Algebra",95},  { "History",70}},
     {{"Biology",100}, { "English",92}}};

for(int iName=0;iName<names.Length;++iName) {
    Console.WriteLine("\n{0}\n", names[iName]);
    for(int iCourse=0;iCourse<2;++iCourse) {
        Console.WriteLine("{0} {1}",
            grades[iName, iCourse, 0],
            grades[iName, iCourse, 1]);
    }
}
    }
  }
}
```

Jagged Arrays

The most frequently found definition of a jagged array is an array of arrays. More specifically, a jagged array is an array of vectors. Although other arrays are rectangular, a jagged array, as the name implies, is jagged as each vector in the array can be of different length. With jagged arrays, first define the number of rows or vectors in the jagged array. Second, declare the number of elements in each row.

The syntax for declaring a jagged array is similar to a multidimensional array. Instead of a single bracket ([r,c]), jagged arrays have two brackets ([r][]). When declaring a jagged array, the number of columns is not specified and is omitted. The number of elements in each row is set individually. This is the syntax of a jagged array:

> *type* [][] *arrayname*[1];
>
> *typea* [][] *arrayname*[2]=new *typeb*[r][];
>
> *typea* [][] *arrayname*[3]=new *typeb*[r][] {*ilist*};
>
> *typea*[][] *arrayname*[4]=new *typeb*[][] {*ilist*};
>
> *typea*[][] *arrayname*[5]={*ilist*};

This is sample code for declaring a jagged array:

```
int [][] zArray;                        // syntax 1
int [][] yArray=new int[3][];           // syntax 2
int [][] xArray=new int[3][]            // syntax 3
    {new int [] {1,2,3},
     new int[] {1,2},
     new int[] {1,2,3,4}};
int [][] wArray=new int[][][{            // syntax 4
    new int [] {1,2,3},
    new int[] {1,2},
```

```
              new int[] {1,2,3,4}};
      int [][] wArray={                    // syntax 5
          new int [] {1,2,3},
          new int[] {1,2},
          new int[] {1,2,3,4}};
```

The rows of the jagged array are initialized to one-dimensional arrays. Because the rows are assigned distinct arrays, the length of each row may vary. Therefore, a jagged array is essentially an array of vectors:

```
jarray[row]=new type[elements];
```

Here is sample code that employs a jagged array. Each row of the jagged array has an increasing number of elements. The first nested loop creates and initializes each row of the jagged array. At the end, the values of each row are totaled and displayed.

```
using System;

namespace Donis.CSharpBook{
    public class Starter{
        public static void Main(){
            int [][] jagged=new int [7][];
            int count=0;
            for(int row=0;row<jagged.GetLength(0);++row) {
                Console.Write("\nRow {0}:", row);
                jagged[row]=new int[row+1];
                for(int index=0; index<row+1; ++index) {
                    ++count;
                    jagged[row][index]=count;
                    Console.Write(" {0}", count);
                }
            }
            Console.WriteLine("\n\nTotals");
            for(int row=0;row<jagged.GetLength(0);++row) {
                int total=0;
                for(int index=0; index<jagged[row].GetLength(0);
                        ++index) {
                    total+=jagged[row][index];
                }
                Console.Write("\nRow {0}: {1}",
                    row, total);
            }

        }
    }
}
```

Vectors and multidimensional arrays are both collections. As such, arrays implement a combination of an array and some collection-specific interfaces, which are encapsulated in the *System.Array* type. *System.Array* implements the *ICollection*, *IEnumerable*, *IList*, and *ICloneable* interfaces. *System.Array* also implements array-specific behaviors, such as the *Array.GetLength* method.

System.Array

The *System.Array* type houses the fundamental methods and properties that are essential to an array. This includes sorting, reversing, element count, synchronization, and much more. Table 5-2 lists the methods of the *System.Array* type. Many of the methods are static, which is noted in the syntax. In addition, some methods are for single-dimensional arrays and are not usable with multidimensional arrays. This fact is noted in the method description in Table 5-2.

Table 5-2   *System.Array* Members

Description	Syntax
AsReadOnly This is a generic method that returns a read-only wrapper for an array.	```static ReadOnlyCollection<T> AsReadOnly<T>(T[] sourceArray)```
BinarySearch This method conducts a binary search for a specific value in a sorted one-dimensional array.	```static int BinarySearch(Array sourceArray, object searchValue)```
There are several overloads for this method. The two more common overloads are shown.	```static int BinarySearch<T>(T[] sourceArray, T value)```
Clear This method sets a range of elements to zero, null, or false.	```static void Clear(Array sourceArray, int index, int length)```
Clone This method clones the current array.	```sealed object Clone()```
ConstrainedCopy This method copies a range of elements from the source array into a destination array. You set the source index and destination index, where the copy is started in both arrays.	```static void ConstrainedCopy{ Array sourceArray, int sourceIndex Array destinationArray, int destinationIndex, int length)```
ConvertAll This is a generic method that converts the type of an array.	```static <destinationType> ConvertAll<sourceType, destinationType>(sourceType sourceArray, Converter<sourceType, destinationType> converter)```
Copy This method copies elements from the source array to the destination array. The specified number of elements is copied.	```static void Copy(Array sourceArray, Array destinationArray, int length)```
There are four overloads to this method. The two more common overloads are listed.	```static void Copy(Array sourceArray, int sourceIndex, Array destinationArray, int destinationIndex, int length)```

Table 5-2 *System.Array* Members (Continued)

Description	Syntax

CopyTo
 	
This method copies the current one-dimensional array to the destination array starting at the specified index.
	`void CopyTo(Array destinationArray,`
	`    int index)`
	`void CopyTo(Array destinationArray,`
	`    long index)`

CreateInstance
 	
This method creates an instance of an array at run time.
 	
This method has several overloads. One-dimensional and two-dimensional versions of the method are listed.
	`static Array CreateInstance(`
	`    Type arrayType,`
	`    int length)`
	
	`static Array CreateInstance(`
	`    Type arrayType,`
	`    int rows,`
	`    int cols)`

Exists
 	
This is a generic method that confirms that an element matches the conditions set in the predicate function.
	`static bool Exist<T> {`
	`    T [] sourceArray,`
	`    Predicate<T> match)`

Find
 	
This is a generic method that finds the first element that matches the conditions set in the predicate function.
	`static T Find<T>(`
	`    T[] sourceArray,`
	`    Predicate<T> match)`

FindAll
 	
This is a generic method that returns all the elements that match the conditions set in the predicate function.
	`static T[] FindAll<T>(`
	`    T[] sourceArray,`
	`    Predicate<T> match)`

FindIndex
 	
This is a generic method that returns the index to the first element that matches the conditions set in the predicate function.
	`static int FindIndex<T>(`
	`    T[] sourceArray,`
	`    Predicate<T> match)`
	
	`static int FindIndex<T>(`
	`    T[] sourceArray,`
	`    int startingIndex,`
	`    Predicate<T> match)`
	
	`static int FindIndex(`
	`    T[] sourceArray,`
	`    int startingIndex,`
	`    int count,`
	`    Predicate<T> match)`

FindLast
 	
This is a generic method that returns the last element that matches the conditions set in the predicate function.
	`static T FindLast<T>{`
	`    T[] sourceArray,`
	`    Predicate<T> match)`

FindLastIndex
 	
This is a generic method that returns the index to the last element that matches the conditions set in the predicate function.
	`static int FindLastIndex(T[] sourceArray,`
	`    Predicate<T> match)`
	
	`static int FindLastIndex(T[] sourceArray,`
	`    int startingIndex,`
	`    Predicate<T> match)`
	
	`static int FindLastIndex(T[] sourceArray,`
	`    int startingIndex,`
	`    int count,`
	`    Predicate<T> match)`

Table 5-2   *System.Array* Members (Continued)

Description	Syntax

ForEach
 	
This is a generic method that performs an action on each element of the array, where action refers to a function.
	`public static void ForEach<T>(`
	`    T[] array,`
	`    Action<T> action)`

GetEnumerator This method returns an enumerator that implements the enumerator pattern for collections. You can enumerate the elements of the array with the enumerator object.	`sealed IEnumerator GetEnumerator()`
GetLength This method returns the number of elements for a dimension of an array.	`int GetLength(int dimension)`
GetLongLength This method returns the number of elements as a 64-bit integer for a dimension of an array.	`long GetLongLength(int dimension)`
GetLowerBound This method returns the lower bound of a dimension, which is usually zero.	`int GetLowerBound(int dimension)`
GetUpperBound This method returns the upper bound of a dimension.	`int GetUpperBound(int dimension)`

GetValue
 	
This method returns the value of an element at the specified index.
 	
This method has several overloads. A one-dimensional version and a multidimensional version of the method are shown here.
	`object GetValue(int index)`
	
	`object GetValue(params int[] indices)`

IndexOf
 	
This method returns the index of the first element in a one-dimensional array that has the specified value.
 	
This method has several overloads. A generic and a nongeneric version of the method are listed.
	`static int IndexOf(Array sourceArray,`
	`    object find)`
	
	Generic version:
	
	`static int IndexOf<T>(T[] sourceArray,`
	`    T value)`

Initialize This method initializes every element of the array. The default constructor of each element is called.	`void Initialize()`

LastIndexOf
 	
This method returns the index of the last element that matches the specified value in a one-dimensional array.
 	
This method has several overloads. A generic version and a nongeneric version are listed.
	`static int LastIndexOf(Array sourceArray,`
	`    object value)`
	
	Generic version:
	
	`static int LastIndexOf<T>(T[] sourceArray,`
	`    T value)`

Table 5-2 *System.Array* Members (Continued)

Description	Syntax

Resize
 	
This is a generic method that changes the size of a one-dimensional array.
	```static void Resize<T>(```
	   ```ref T[] sourceArray,```
	   ```int newSize)```

Reverse
 	
This method reverses the order of elements in a one-dimensional array.
	```static void Reverse(Array sourceArray)```
	
	```static void Reverse(Array sourceArray,```
	   ```int index, int length)```

SetValue
 	
This method sets the value of a specific element of the current one-dimensional array.
 	
This method has several overloads. Two of the overloads are listed.
	```void SetValue(object value, int index)```
	
	```void SetValue(object value,```
	   ```params int[] indices)```

Sort
 	
This method sorts the elements of a one-dimensional array.
 	
This method has several overloads. A nongeneric version and a generic version of the method are listed.
	```static void Sort(Array sourceArray)```
	
	```static void Sort<T>(```
	   ```T[] sourceArray)```

TrueForAll
 	
This is a generic method that returns *true* if all elements of an array match the conditions set in the predicate function.
	```static bool TrueForAll<T>(```
	   ```T[] array,```
	   ```Predicate<T> match)```

The following sections offer sample code and additional descriptions for some of the *System.Array* methods.

Array.AsReadOnly Method

The following code creates and initializes an integer array. The second element of the array is then modified, which demonstrates the read-write capability of the collection. *Array .AsReadOnly* is called to wrap the array in a read-only collection. The *ReadOnlyCollection* type is found in the *System.Collections.ObjectModel* namespace. After displaying the elements of the read-only collection, the code attempts to modify an element. Since the collection is read-only, a compile error occurs at this line:

```
using System;
using System.Collections.Generic;
using System.Collections.ObjectModel;


namespace Donis.CSharpBook{
    public class Starter{
        public static void Main(){
            int [] zArray={1,2,3,4};
            zArray[1]=10;
```

```
        ReadOnlyCollection<int> roArray=Array.AsReadOnly(zArray);
        foreach(int number in roArray) {
            Console.WriteLine(number);
        }
        roArray[1]=2;   // compile error
    }
  }
}
```

Array.Clone Method

In the following code, the *CommissionedEmployee* type inherits from the *Employee* type. An array of commissioned employees is defined and then cloned with the *Clone* method. The clone type is an array of *Employees*. Because *Clone* returns an object array, which is unspecific, you should cast to a specific array type. The cast from *System.Object* is not type-safe, and an incorrect cast would cause an exception. Polymorphism is employed in the *foreach* loop to call the *Pay* method of the derived class.

```
using System;
using System.Collections.Generic;


namespace Donis.CSharpBook{
    public class Starter{
        public static void Main(){
            CommissionedEmployee [] salespeople=
                {new CommissionedEmployee("Bob"),
                 new CommissionedEmployee("Ted"),
                 new CommissionedEmployee("Sally")};

            Employee [] employees=
                (Employee [])salespeople.Clone();

            foreach(Employee person in
                    employees) {
                person.Pay();
            }
        }
    }

    public class Employee {
        public Employee(string name) {
            m_Name=name;
        }

        public virtual void Pay() {
            Console.WriteLine("Paying {0}", m_Name);
        }

        private string m_Name;
    }
```

```
public class CommissionedEmployee: Employee {
    public CommissionedEmployee(string name) :
        base(name) {
    }

    public override void Pay() {
        base.Pay();
        Console.WriteLine("Paying commissions");
    }

}

}
```

Array.CreateInstance Method

The following code demonstrates both the *CreateInstance* and *SetValue* methods. *CreateInstance* creates a new array at run time. This requires some degree of reflection, which will be discussed in Chapter 10, "Metadata and Reflection." This code reads the array type, method to call, and initial values for each element from the command line. *CreateInstance* creates a new array using the type name read from the command line. In the *for* loop, *Activator.CreateInstance* creates instances of the element type, where values from the command line are used to initialize the object. In the *foreach* loop, the elements of the array are enumerated while calling the method stipulated in the command-line arguments as the second parameter.

```
using System;
using System.Reflection;

namespace Donis.CSharpBook{
    public class Starter{
        public static void Main(string [] argv){
            Assembly executing=Assembly.GetExecutingAssembly();
            Type t=executing.GetType(argv[0]);
            Array zArray=Array.CreateInstance(
                t, argv.Length-2);
            for(int count=2;count<argv.Length;++count) {
                System.Object obj=Activator.CreateInstance(t, new object[] {
                    argv[count]});
                zArray.SetValue(obj, count-2);
            }
            foreach(object item in zArray) {
                MethodInfo m=t.GetMethod(argv[1]);
                m.Invoke(item, null);
            }
        }
    }

    public class ZClass {
        public ZClass(string info) {
            m_Info="ZClass "+info;
        }

        public void ShowInfo() {
```

```
                Console.WriteLine(m_Info);
        }

        private string m_Info;
    }

    public class YClass {
        public YClass(string info) {
            m_Info="YClass "+info;
        }

        public void ShowInfo() {
            Console.WriteLine(m_Info);
        }

        private string m_Info;
    }

    public class XClass {
        public XClass(string info) {
            m_Info="XClass "+info;
        }

        public void ShowInfo() {
            Console.WriteLine(m_Info);
        }

        private string m_Info;
    }
}
```

A typical command line and results of the application are shown in Figure 5-2.

Figure 5-2   A command line and the results from running the application

Array.FindAll Method

Several *System.Array* methods use predicates, such as the *Exists*, *Find*, *FindAll*, and *FindLastIndex* methods. Predicates are delegates initialized with functions that find matching elements. The predicate function is called for each element of the array. A conditional test is performed in the function to isolate matching elements; *true* or *false* is returned from the predicate indicating that a match has or has not been found, respectively.

This is the syntax of the Predicate delegate:

```
delegate bool Predicate<T>(T obj)
```

Predicate methods are generic methods. The type parameter indicates the element type. The return value is the result of the comparison.

The following code finds all elements equal to three. *MethodA* is the predicate method, which compares each value to three.

```
public static void Main(){
    int [] zArray={1,2,3,1,2,3,1,2,3};
    Predicate<int> match=new Predicate<int>(MethodA<int>);
    int [] answers=Array.FindAll(zArray, match);
    foreach(int answer in answers) {
        Console.WriteLine(answer);
    }
}

public static bool MethodA<T>(T number) where T:IComparable {
    int result=number.CompareTo(3);
    return result==0;
}
```

Array.Resize Method

The *Resize* method resizes a one-dimensional array.

Here is sample code for resizing an array. The elements added to the array are initialized to a default value.

```
using System;

namespace Donis.CSharpBook{
    public class Starter{
        public static void Main(){
            int [] zArray={1,2,3,4};
            Array.Resize<int>(ref zArray, 8);
            foreach(int number in zArray) {
                Console.WriteLine(number);
            }
        }
    }
}
```

System.Array Properties

System.Array has several properties that are useful when working with arrays. Table 5-3 lists the various properties.

Table 5-3   *System.Array* Properties

Description	Syntax
IsFixedSize This property returns *true* if the array is a fixed size. Otherwise, *false* is returned. Always *true* for arrays.	```virtual bool IsFixedSize{ get;}```
IsReadOnly This property returns *true* if the array is read-only. Otherwise, *false* is returned. Always *false* for arrays.	```virtual bool IsReadOnly{ get;}```
IsSynchronized This property returns *true* if the array is thread-safe. Otherwise, *false* is returned. Always *false* for arrays.	```virtual bool IsSynchronized{ get;}```
Length This property returns the number of elements in the array.	```int Length{ get;}```
LongLength This property returns the number of elements in the array as a 64-bit value.	```Long LongLength{ get;}```
Rank This property returns the rank of the array, which is the number of dimensions. For example, a two-dimensional array has a rank of two.	```int Rank{ get;}```
SyncRoot This property returns a synchronization object for the current array. Arrays are not inherently thread-safe. Synchronize access to the array with the synchronization object.	```virtual object SyncRoot{ get;}```

Many of the preceding properties are used in sample code. The *SyncRoot* property is particularly important and not included in previous sample code.

Array.SyncRoot Property

The purpose of the *SyncRoot* object is to synchronize access to an array. Arrays are unsafe data structures. As documented, the *IsSynchronized* property always returns *false* for an array. Accesses to arrays are easily synchronized with the *lock* statement, where the *SyncRoot* object is the parameter.

In the following code, the array is a field in the *Starter* class. The *DisplayForward* and *DisplayReverse* methods list array elements in forward and reverse order correspondingly. The functions are invoked at threads, in which the *SyncLock* property prevents simultaneous access in the concurrent threads.

```
using System;
using System.Threading;

namespace Donis.CSharpBook{
    public class Starter{
```

```
public static void Main(){
    Array.Sort(zArray);
    Thread t1=new Thread(
        new ThreadStart(DisplayForward));
    Thread t2=new Thread(
        new ThreadStart(DisplayReverse));
    t1.Start();
    t2.Start();
}

private static int [] zArray={1,5,4,2,4,2,9,10};
public static void DisplayForward() {
    lock(zArray.SyncRoot) {
        Console.Write("\nForward: ");
        foreach(int number in zArray) {
            Console.Write(number);
        }
    }
}

public static void DisplayReverse() {
    lock(zArray.SyncRoot) {
        Array.Reverse(zArray);
        Console.Write("\nReverse: ");
        foreach(int number in zArray) {
            Console.Write(number);
        }
        Array.Reverse(zArray);
    }
}
}
}
```

Comparable Elements

System.Array methods require elements to be instances of comparable types.

- *Array.IndexOf*
- *Array.LastIndexOf*
- *Array.Sort*
- *Array.Reverse*
- *Array.BinarySearch*

Comparable types implement the *IComparable* interface, which requires the implementation of the *CompareTo* method. The *CompareTo* method returns zero when the current and target instances are equal. If the current instance is less than the target, a negative value is returned. A positive value is returned if the current instance is greater than the target. The preceding methods call *IComparable.CompareTo* to perform the required comparisons to sort, reverse, and otherwise access the array in an ordered manner.

A run-time error occurs in the following code when *Array.Sort* is called. Why? The *XClass* does not implement the *IComparable* interface.

```
using System;

namespace Donis.CSharpBook{
    public class Starter{
        public static void Main(){
            XClass [] objs={new XClass(5), new XClass(10),
                new XClass(1)};
            Array.Sort(objs);
        }
    }

    public class XClass {
        public XClass(int data) {
            propNumber=data;
        }

        private int propNumber;
        public int Number {
            get {
                return propNumber;
            }
        }
    }
}
```

Here is the proper code, where the *XClass* implements the *IComparable* interface. This program runs successfully.

```
using System;

namespace Donis.CSharpBook{
    public class Starter{
        public static void Main(){
            XClass [] objs={new XClass(5), new XClass(10),
                new XClass(1)};
            Array.Sort(objs);
            foreach(XClass obj in objs) {
                Console.WriteLine(obj.Number);
            }
        }
    }

    public class XClass: IComparer {
        public XClass(int data) {
            propNumber=data;
        }

        private int propNumber;
        public int Number {
            get {
                return propNumber;
            }
```

```
        }

        public int CompareTo(object obj) {
            XClass comp=(XClass) obj;
            if(this.Number==comp.Number){
                return 0;
            }
            if(this.Number<comp.Number){
                return -1;
            }
            return 1;
        }
    }
}
```

Many of the methods and properties of *System.Array* are mandated in interfaces that the type implements. The following section lists those interfaces and methods.

ICollection Interface

The *ICollection* interface is one of the interfaces implemented in *System.Array* type; it returns the count of elements and supports synchronization of collections. The members of the *ICollection* interface are as follows:

- *CopyTo method*
- *Count property*
- *IsSynchronized property*
- *SyncRoot property*

ICloneable Interface

System.Array implements the *ICloneable* interface. This is the interface for duplicating an object, such as an array. The only member of this interface is the *Clone* method.

IEnumerable

System.Array type implements the *IEnumerable* interface. *IEnumerable.GetEnumerator* is the sole member of this interface. *GetEnumerator* returns an enumerator object that implements the *IEnumerator* interface. The enumerator provides a consistent interface for enumerating any collection. The benefit is the ability to write a generic algorithm, which requires enumerating the elements of a collection in a consistent manner. For example, the *foreach* statement uses an enumerator object to consistently iterate all collection types.

Chapter 7, "Iterators," will focus more on enumerators.

Here is sample code that enumerates an array using an enumerator object:

```
using System;
using System.Collections;
```

```
namespace Donis.CSharpBook{
    public class Starter{
        public static void Main(){
            int [] numbers={1,2,3,4,5};
            IEnumerator e=numbers.GetEnumerator();
            while(e.MoveNext()) {
                Console.WriteLine(e.Current);
            }
        }
    }
}
```

IList Interface

System.Array type implements the *IList* interface. However, only part of this implementation is publicly available. The private implementation of some *IList* members effectively removes those members from the public interface. These are members contrary to the array paradigm, such as the *RemoveAt* method. Arrays are immutable. You cannot remove elements from the middle of an array.

Table 5-4 lists the *IList* interface and indicates the public versus private implementation in *System.Array*.

Table 5-4   List Members

Member Name	Public or Private
Add	Private
Clear	Public
Contains	Private
IndexOf	Public
Insert	Private
Remove	Private
RemoveAt	Private

Indexers

You can treat instances as arrays by using indexers. Indexers are ideal for types that wrap collections, in which additional functionality is added to the type that augments the collection. Access the object with the indexing operator to get or set the underlying collection. Indexers are a combination of an array and a property. The underlying data of an indexer is often an array or a collection. The indexer defines a *set* and *get* method for the *this* reference. Indexers are considered a default property because the indexer is a nameless property. Internally, the compiler inserts the *get_Item* and *set_Item* method in support of indexers.

Indexers are fairly typical properties. However, there are some exceptions. Here are some of the similarities and differences between indexers and properties:

- Indexers can be overloaded.
- Indexers can be overridden.

- Indexers can be added to interfaces.

- Indexers support the standard access modifiers.

- Indexers cannot be a static member.

- Indexers are nameless and associated with the *this* reference.

- Indexers parameters are indices. Properties do not have indices.

- Indexers in the base class are accessed as base[*indices*], while a similar property is accessed base.*Property*.

  Indexers are also similar to arrays:

- Indexers are accessed using indices.

- Indexers support non-numeric indices. Arrays support only integral indices.

- Indexers use a separate data store, whereas an array is the data store.

- Indexers can perform data validation, which is not possible with an array.

This is the syntax of an indexer:

accessibility modifier type this[*parameters*]

{ *attributes* get {*getbody*} *attributes* set {*setbody*} }

Except for static accessibility, indexers have the same accessibility and modifiers of a normal property. Indexers cannot be static. The parameters are a comma-delimited list of indexes. The list includes the type and name of each parameter. Indexer indices can be nonintegral types, such as string and even *Employee* types.

The following is example code for indexers. The *Names* type is a wrapper of an array of names and ages. The indexer is read-only in this example and provides access to the array field. Per the parameters of the indexer, the indexer manipulates object elements and has a single index. However, the _names array is two-dimensional, which requires two indexes. Flexibility is one of the benefits of indexers versus standard arrays. In the sample code, the parameter of the indexer represents the row, whereas the column is a constant.

```
using System;

namespace Donis.CSharpBook{
    public class Starter{
        public static void Main(){
            Names obj=new Names();
            Console.WriteLine(obj[1]);
        }
    }

    public class Names {
        object [,] _names={
            {"Valerie", 27},
```

```
                {"Ben", 35},
                {"Donis", 29}};

        public object this[int index] {
            get {
                return _names[index,0]+" "+_names[index,1];
            }
        }
    }
}
```

Indexers can be overloaded based on the parameter list. Overloaded indexers should have a varying number of parameters or parameter types. The following code overloads the indexer property twice. The first property is read-only and returns the name and age information. The second overload is a read-write property that sets and gets the age of a person. This property, which uses a string parameter, also demonstrates non-numerical indexes.

```
using System;

namespace Donis.CSharpBook{
    public class Starter{
        public static void Main(){
            Names obj=new Names();
            obj["Donis"]=42;
            Console.WriteLine(obj["Donis"]);
        }
    }

    public class Names {
        object [,] _names={
                {"Valerie", 27},
                {"Ben", 35},
                {"Donis", 29}};

        public object this[int index] {
            get {
                return _names[index,0]+" "+_names[index,1];
            }
        }

        public object this[string sIndex] {

            get {
                int index=FindName(sIndex);
                return _names[index, 1];
            }
            set {
                int index=FindName(sIndex);
                _names[index, 1]=value;
            }
        }

        private int FindName(string sIndex) {
            for(int index=0; index<_names.GetLength(0);
```

```
                ++index) {
            if((string)(_names[index,0])==sIndex) {
                return index;
            }
        }
        throw new Exception("Name not found");
    }
  }
}
```

params Keyword

The *params* keyword is a parameter modifier, which indicates that a parameter is a one-dimensional array of any length. This defines a variable-length parameter list. The *params* modifier can be applied to only one parameter in the parameter list, which must be the final parameter. The *ref* and *out* modifiers cannot be applied to the *params* modified parameter. You have probably used methods of the Microsoft .NET Framework class library (FCL) that have variable-length parameter lists, such as *Console.WriteLine*. *Console.WriteLine* accepts a variable number of arguments. It has a *param* parameter.

Initialize the *params*-modified argument with an implicit or explicit array. This is done at the call site. For implicit initialization, the C# compiler consumes the optional parameters that follow the fixed parameter list. The fixed parameters are the parameters that precede the *params*-modified parameter in the function signature. The optional arguments are consolidated into an array. If there are six optional arguments after the fixed arguments, an array of six elements is created and initialized with the values of the optional arguments. Alternatively, an explicit array can be used. Finally, the *params* argument can be omitted. When omitted, the *params* parameter is assigned an empty array. An empty array is different from a null array. Empty arrays have no elements but are valid instances.

In the following code, *Names* is a static method, where the *params* modifier is applied to the second parameter. Therefore, the *employees* argument is a single-dimensional string array, and the *Names* method offers a variable-length parameter list.

```
public static void Names(string company,
    params string [] employees) {
    Console.WriteLine("{0} employees: ",
        company);
    foreach(string employee in employees) {
        Console.WriteLine("   {0}", employee);
    }
}
```

For a variable-length parameter list, the number of parameters, which includes the parameter array, is set at the called site. The following code shows the *Names* method being called with varying numbers of parameters. In both calls, the first parameter is consumed by the company parameter. The remaining parameters are used to create an array, which is assigned to the *params* parameter. A three-argument array is created for the first method call, whereas the second method creates a six-argument array that is assigned to the *params* parameter.

```
Names("Fabrikam","Fred", "Bob", "Alice");
Names("Contoso", "Sally", "Al", "Julia",
    "Will", "Sarah", "Terri");
```

The following code calls the *Names* method with an explicit array. This is identical to calling the method with three optional arguments.

```
Names("Fabrikam", new string [] {"Fred", "Bob",
        "Alice"});
```

In this statement, the *Names* method is called without a *params* argument. For the omitted parameter, the compiler creates an array with no elements, which is subsequently passed to the method.

```
Names("Fabrikam");
```

Variable-length methods can be overloaded similar to any method. You can even overload a method with a fixed number of parameters with a method with a variable number of parameters. Where there is ambiguity, the method with the fixed number of parameters is preferred and called.

In the following code, the *Names* method is overloaded with three methods. The first two overloads have a variable-length parameter list, whereas the final method has a fixed-length parameter list. In *Main*, the first two calls of the *Names* method are not ambiguous. The final call is ambiguous and can resolve to either the first or third overload. Because the third overload has a fixed-length parameter list, it is called instead of the first overloaded method.

```
using System;

namespace Donis.CSharpBook{
    public class Starter{
        public static void Main(){
            Names("Fabrikam","Fred", "Bob", "Alice");
            Names("Fabrikam",1234, 5678, 9876, 4561);
            Names("Fabrikam","Carter", "Deborah");
        }

        public static void Names(string company,
            params string [] employees) {
            Console.WriteLine("{0} employees: ",
                company);
            foreach(string employee in employees) {
                Console.WriteLine("  {0}", employee);
            }
        }

        public static void Names(string company,
            params int [] emplid) {
```

```
        Console.WriteLine("{0} employees: ",
            company);
        foreach(int employee in emplid) {
            Console.WriteLine("  {0}", employee);
        }
    }

    public static void Names(string company,
        string empl1, string empl2) {
        Console.WriteLine("{0} employees: ",
            company);
        Console.WriteLine("  {0}",empl1);
        Console.WriteLine("  {0}",empl2);
    }
  }
}
```

Array Conversion

You can cast between arrays. Arrays are implicit *System.Array* types. For that reason, regardless of type or the number of dimensions, any array can be cast to *System.Array*. All arrays are compatible with that type.

When casting or converting between arrays, the source and destination array are required to have the same dimensions. In addition, an array of value types is convertible only to arrays of the same dimension and type. Arrays of reference types are somewhat more flexible. Arrays of reference types can be converted to arrays of the same or ascendant type. This is called *array covariance*. Array reference types are covariant, whereas arrays of value types are not.

Arrays can be inserted as function parameters and returns. In these roles, proper conversion is important.

Arrays as Function Returns and Parameters

Arrays provided as function arguments are passed by reference. This is more efficient than caching potentially a large number of elements on the stack. As a reference type, the array state can be changed in the called method. Array parameters are normal parameters and support the regular assortment of modifiers. Of course, the array argument must be convertible to the array parameter.

In the following code, the *ZClass* has two static methods, which both have an array parameter. The *ListArray* method has a *System.Array* parameter, which accepts any array argument. For this reason, the *ListArray* method is called in *Main* with different types of array arguments. The *Total* method limits array arguments to one-dimensional integer arrays.

```
using System;

namespace Donis.CSharpBook{
    public class Starter{
```

```
public static void Main(){
    int [] zArray={10,9,8,7,6,5,4,3,2,1};
    string [] xArray={"a", "b", "c", "d"};
    Console.WriteLine("List Numbers");
    ZClass.ListArray(zArray);
    Console.WriteLine("List Letters");
    ZClass.ListArray(xArray);
    Console.WriteLine("Total Numbers");
    ZClass.Total(zArray);
}
}


public class ZClass {

    public static void ListArray(Array a) {
        foreach(object element in a) {
            Console.WriteLine(element);
        }
    }

    public static void Total(int [] iArray) {
        int total=0;
        foreach(int number in iArray) {
            total+=number;
        }
        Console.WriteLine(total);
    }
}
}
```

Arrays can also be returned from functions, which is one means of returning more than a single value. You can return multiple values as elements of an array. Returning an array gives the calling function a reference to the array, which provides direct access to the array. Arrays are not returned on the stack.

Collections

Arrays are the most popular collection. However, the .NET FCL offers a variety of other collections with different semantics. Collections are abstractions of data algorithms. *ArrayList* is an abstraction of a dynamic array, the *Stack* collection abstracts a stack data structure, the *Queue* collection abstracts queues, the *Hashtable* collection abstracts a lookup table, and so on. Each collection exposes both unique and standard interfaces. The unique interface is specific to the collection type. For example, the *Stack* type has pop and push methods, whereas the *Queue* type has *Dequeue* and *Enqueue* methods. Collections minimally implement the *ICollection*, *IEnumerable*, and *ICloneable* interfaces. (These interfaces were described earlier in this chapter.) The nongeneric collection classes are implemented in the *System.Collections* namespace. Generic collections are reviewed in Chapter 6, "Generics."

Table 5-5 lists the nongeneric collections in the .NET FCL.

Table 5-5   Collection Types

Class Name	Description
ArrayList	Dynamic array
BitArray	Bit array
Hashtable	Lookup table of keys and values
Queue	First-in/first-out (FIFO) collection of elements
SortedList	Sorted list of elements
Stack	Last-in/first-out (LIFO) collection of elements

What follows is a detailed explanation of each collection found in the *Collections* namespace. The explanations are complemented with sample code, which demonstrates the uniqueness of each collection.

ArrayList Collection

An array list is a dynamic array. Although indigenous arrays are static, elements can be added or removed from an *ArrayList* at run time. Elements of the *ArrayList* are not automatically sorted. Similar to single-dimensional arrays, the elements of an *ArrayList* are accessible using the indexing operator and indices.

In addition to the standard collection interfaces, *ArrayList* implements the *IList* interface.

Table 5-6 lists the *ArrayList*-specific methods and properties. The static members of *ArrayList* are thread-safe, whereas instance members are not. The common collection interfaces—*ICollection*, *IEnumerable*, and *ICloneable*—are not discussed in detail. (These interfaces and their members were reviewed earlier in the chapter.)

Table 5-6   ArrayList Members

Member Name	Syntax

Constructors	`ArrayList()`
	`ArrayList(`
	
	`    ICollection sourceCollection)`
	
	`ArrayList(int capacity)`

Adapter This method creates a wrapper for an *IList* collection.	`static ArrayList Adapter(` `    IList list)`
Add This method adds an element to the end of the *ArrayList* collection.	`virtual int Add(object value)`

Table 5-6 ArrayList Members (Continued)

Member Name	Syntax
AddRange This method adds a range of elements to the *ArrayList* collection. The elements are input from an *ICollection* type, such as a regular array.	```virtual void AddRange(
ICollection elements)```
BinarySearch This method performs a binary search for a specific value in a sorted array.	```virtual int BinarySearch(
object value)``` ```virtual int BinarySearch(
object value,
IComparer comparer)``` ```virtual int BinarySearch(
int index,
int count,
object value,
IComparer comparer)```
Capacity This property gets or sets the number of properties allowed in the collection. The default capacity is 16 elements. Capacity is different from the number of elements. The capacity is automatically increased as elements are added. When the number of elements exceeds the current capacity, the capacity doubles. Capacity is for better memory management of elements in the collection.	```virtual int Capacity {
get; set}```
Clear This method removes all the elements of the collection.	```virtual void Clear()```
Contains This method returns *true* if the specified item is found in a collection. If the item is not found, *false* is returned.	```virtual bool Contains(object item)```
Count This property returns the number of elements in the collection.	```virtual int Count{
get; }```
FixedSize This method creates a wrapper for an *ArrayList* or *IList* collection, in which elements cannot be added or removed.	```static ArrayList FixedSize(
ArrayList sourceArray)``` ```static IList FixedSize(
IList sourceList)```
GetRange This method returns a span of elements from the current array. The result is stored in a destination *ArrayList*.	```virtual ArrayList GetRange(
int index, int count)```

Table 5-6 ArrayList Members (Continued)

Member Name	Syntax
IndexOf This method returns the index of the first matching element in the collection.	```virtual int IndexOf(
object value)``` ```virtual int IndexOf(object value,
int startIndex)``` ```virtual int IndexOf(object value,
int startIndex,
int count)```
Insert This method inserts an element into the collection at the specified index.	```virtual void Insert(int index,
object value)```
InsertRange This method inserts multiple elements into the collection at the specified index.	```virtual void InsertRange(
int index,
ICollection sourceCollection)```
IsFixedSize This property returns *true* if the collection is fixed-length. Otherwise, the property returns *false*.	```virtual bool IsFixedSize{
get;}```
IsReadOnly This property returns *true* if the collection is read-only. Otherwise, the property returns *false*.	```virtual bool IsReadOnly{
get;}```
Item This property gets or sets the element at the index.	```virtual object this[int index] {
get;set;}```
LastIndexOf This method returns the index of the last matching element in the collection.	```virtual int LastIndex(
object value)``` ```virtual int LastIndexOf(object value,
int startIndex)``` ```virtual int LastIndexOf(object value,
int startIndex,
int count)```
ReadOnly This method creates a read-only wrapper for an *IList* object.	```static ArrayList ReadOnly(
ArrayList sourceArray)``` ```static IList ReadOnly(
IList sourceList)```
Remove This method removes the first element in the collection that matches the value.	```virtual void Remove(
object value)```

Table 5-6 ArrayList Members (Continued)

Member Name	Syntax
RemoveAt This method removes the element at the index from the collection.	```virtual void RemoveAt(``` ``` int index)```

RemoveRange
 	
This method removes a range of elements from a collection.
	```virtual void RemoveRange(```
	``` int index,```
	``` int count)```

Repeat
 	
This method returns an *ArrayList* with each element initialized to the same value. Count is the number of times to replicate the value.
	```static ArrayList Repeat(```
	``` object value,```
	``` int count)```

Reverse
 	
This method reverses the order of elements in the collection.
	```virtual void Reverse()```
	
	```virtual void Reverse(```
	``` int beginIndex,```
	``` int endingIndex)```

SetRange
 	
This method copies elements from a collection into the same elements in the *ArrayList* collection.
	```virtual void SetRange(```
	``` int index,```
	``` ICollection sourceCollection)```

Sort
 	
This method sorts an *ArrayList*.
	```virtual void Sort()```
	
	```virtual void Sort(```
	``` IComparer comparer}```
	
	```virtual void Sort(int index,```
	``` int count,```
	``` IComparer comparer)```

Synchronized
 	
This method returns a thread-safe wrapper of an *ArrayList* or *IList* object.
	```static ArrayList Synchronized(```
	``` ArrayList sourceArray)```
	
	```static IList Synchronized(```
	``` IList sourceList)```

ToArray
 	
This method copies elements from the current array into a new collection.
	```virtual object [] ToArray()```
	
	```virtual Array ToArray(Type type)```

TrimToSize This method sets the capacity to the number of elements in the collection.	```virtual void TrimToSize()```
IEnumerable members	*GetEnumerator*
ICloneable members	*Clone*
ICollection members	*CopyTo, Count, IsSynchronized*, and *SyncRoot*

The following code uses various *ArrayList* methods and properties. It creates a new *ArrayList*, which is then initialized with command-line parameters. The *Add* method is called to add elements to the *ArrayList*. The *ArrayList* is then sorted and cloned. Then the values at the elements of the cloned *ArrayList* are doubled. Afterward, the cloned *ArrayList* is enumerated and every element is displayed.

```csharp
using System;
using System.Collections;

namespace Donis.CSharpBook{
    public class Starter{
        public static void Main(string [] argv){

            ArrayList al1=new ArrayList();
            foreach(string arg in argv) {
                al1.Add(int.Parse(arg));
            }
            al1.Sort();
            ArrayList al2=(ArrayList)al1.Clone();
            for(int count=0;count<al2.Count;++count) {
                al2[count]=((int)al2[count])*2;
            }
            foreach(int number in al2) {
                Console.WriteLine(number);
            }

        }
    }
}
```

BitArray Collection

The *BitArray* collection is a composite of bit values. Bit values are 1 and 0, where 1 is *true* and 0 *false*. This collection provides an efficient means of storing and retrieving bit values.

Table 5-7 list the *BitArray*-specific methods and properties. The static members of the *BitArray* are thread-safe, whereas instance members are not.

Table 5-7 BitArray Members

Member Name	Syntax

Constructor
 	
 The *BitArray* constructor is overloaded. These are some of the overloaded constructors.
	`BitArray(bool [] bits)`
	
	 `BitArray(int [] bits)`
	
	 `BitArray(int count,`
	 `    bool default)`

And This method performs a bitwise *And* on the current and *BitArray* parameter. The result is placed in the returned *BitArray*.	`BitArray And(BitArray value)`

Table 5-7   BitArray Members (Continued)

Member Name	Syntax
Get This method returns a specific bit in the *BitArray* collection.	`bool Get(int index)`
IsReadOnly This property returns *true* if the collection is read-only. Otherwise, the property returns *false*.	`virtual bool IsReadOnly{` `   get;}`
Item This property gets or sets the bit at the index.	`virtual object this[int index] {` `   get;set;}`
Length This property gets or sets the number of bits in the collection.	`public int Length{` `   get; set; }`
Not This method negates the bits of the *BitArray* collection. The result is placed in the returned *BitArray*.	`BitArray Not()`
Or This method performs a bitwise *Or* on the current and *BitArray* parameter. The result is placed in the returned *BitArray*.	`BitArray Or(BitArray value)`
Set This method sets a specific bit in the collection.	`Void Set(int index, bool value)`
SetAll This method sets all the bits of the collection to *true* or *false*.	`void SetAll(bool value)`
Xor This method performs an exclusive *OR* on the current collection and the *BitArray* parameter.	`BitArray Xor(` `   BitArray value)`
IEnumerable members	*GetEnumerator*
ICloneable members	*Clone*
ICollection members	*CopyTo, Count, IsSynchronized*, and *SyncRoot*

The following code demonstrates the *BitArray* collection. The *Employee* class contains a *BitArray* collection that tracks employee enrollment in various programs, such as the health plan and credit union. This is convenient because enrollment is either *true* or *false* and never maybe. In the *Employee* class, properties are provided to set and get enrollment in various programs.

```
using System;
using System.Collections;

namespace Donis.CSharpBook{
    public class Starter{
        public static void Main(){
            Employee ben=new Employee();
            ben.InProfitSharing=false;
```

```
        ben.InHealthPlan=false;
        Employee valerie=new Employee();
        valerie.InProfitSharing=false;
        Participation("Ben", ben);
        Participation("Valerie", valerie);
    }

    public static void Participation(string name, Employee person) {
        Console.WriteLine(name+":");
        if(person.InProfitSharing) {
            Console.WriteLine("   Participating in"+
                " Profit Sharing");
        }
        if(person.InHealthPlan) {
            Console.WriteLine("   Participating in"+
                " Health Plan");
        }
        if(person.InCreditUnion) {
            Console.WriteLine("   Participating in"+
                " Credit Union");
        }
    }
}

public class Employee {

    public Employee() {
        eflags.SetAll(true);
    }

    private BitArray eflags=new BitArray(3);

    public bool InProfitSharing{
        set {
            eflags.Set(0, value);
        }
        get {
            return eflags.Get(0);
        }
    }

    public bool InHealthPlan{
        set {
            eflags.Set(1, value);
        }
        get {
            return eflags.Get(1);
        }
    }

    public bool InCreditUnion{
        set {
            eflags.Set(2, value);
        }
        get {
```

```
            return eflags.Get(2);
        }
    }
  }
}
```

Hashtable Collection

The *Hashtable* collection is a collection of key/value pairs. Entries in this collection are instances of the *DictionaryEntry* type. *DictionaryEntry* types have a *Key* and *Value* property to get and set keys and values.

In addition to the standard collection interfaces, the *Hashtable* collection implements the *IDictionary*, *ISerializable*, and *IDeserializationCallback* interfaces.

The entries are stored and retrieved in order based on a hash code of the key.

Table 5-8 lists the members of the *Hashtable* collection.

Table 5-8   Hashtable Members

Member Name	Syntax

Constructor
 	
 The *Hashtable* constructor is overloaded. These syntaxes are some of the overloaded constructors.
	`Hashtable()`
	 `Hashtable(int capacity)`
	
	 `Hashtable(int capacity,`
	 `    float loadFactor)`

Add This method adds an element to the collection.	`virtual void Add(object key,` `    object value)`
Contains This method returns *true* if the key is found in the collection. If the key is not present, *false* is returned.	`virtual bool Contains(` `    object key)`
ContainsKey This method returns *true* if the key is found in the collection. If the key is not present, *false* is returned. Identical to the *Contains* method.	`virtual bool ContainsKey(` `    object key)`
ContainsValue This method returns *true* if the value is found in the collection. If the value is not present, *false* is returned.	`virtual bool ContainsValue(` `    object value)`
EqualityComparer	`IEqualityComparer EqualityComparer {` `    get;}.`
GetHash This method returns the hash code for the specified key.	`virtual int GetHash(` `    object key)`

Table 5-8   Hashtable Members (Continued)

Member Name	Syntax

GetObjectData
 	
This is the method implemented to serialize the collection.
	`virtual void GetObjectData(`
	`  SerializationInfo info,`
	`  StreamingContext context)`

IsFixedSize This property returns *true* if the collection is fixed size. Otherwise, *false* is returned.	`virtual bool IsFixedSize{` `  get;}`
IsReadOnly This property returns *true* if the collection is read-only. Otherwise, *false* is returned.	`virtual bool IsReadOnly{` `  get;}`
IsSynchronized This property returns *true* if the collection is synchronized.	`virtual bool IsSynchronized{` `  get;}`
Item This property gets or sets a value related to a key.	`virtual object this[object key]{` `  get; set;}`

KeyEquals
 	
This method compares a key to a value. If equal, *true* is returned. Otherwise, *false* is returned. This method is primarily used to compare two keys.
	`virtual bool KeyEquals(`
	`  object item,`
	`  object key)`

Keys Returns a collection that contains the keys of the *Hashtable*.	`virtual ICollection Keys{` `  get;}`
OnDeserialization This method is called when deserialization is completed.	`virtual void OnDeserialization(` `object sender)`
Remove This method removes an element with the specified key from the collection.	`virtual void Remove(` `  object key)`
Synchronized This method returns a thread-safe wrapper of the collection.	`static Hashtable Synchronized(` `  Hashtable sourceTable)`
Values Returns a collection that has the values of the *Hashtable*.	`virtual ICollection values{` `  get;}`
IEnumerable members	*GetEnumerator*
ICloneable members	*Clone*
ICollection members	*CopyTo*, *Count*, *IsSynchronized*, and *SyncRoot*

*Hashtable.GetEnumerat*or implements *IDictionary.GetEnumerator*, which returns an *IDictionary Enumeator. IDictionaryEnumerator* implements the *IEnumerator* interface. It also adds three properties: *Entry, Key,* and *Value.*

The following code extends the previous sample code for the *BitArray* collection. The program creates a *Hashtable,* in which employee identifiers are the keys. The values associated with the keys are instances of the *Employee* type.

```csharp
using System;
using System.Collections;

namespace Donis.CSharpBook{
    public class Starter{
        public static void Main(){
            Hashtable employees=new Hashtable();
            employees.Add("A100", new Employee(
                "Ben", true, false, true));
            employees.Add("V100", new Employee(
                "Valerie", false, false, true));
            Participation((Employee) employees["A100"]);
            Participation((Employee) employees["V100"]);
        }

        public static void Participation(Employee person) {
            Console.WriteLine(person.Name+":");
            if(person.InProfitSharing) {
                Console.WriteLine("   Participating in"+
                    " Profit Sharing");
            }
            if(person.InHealthPlan) {
                Console.WriteLine("   Participating in"+
                    " Health Plan");
            }
            if(person.InCreditUnion) {
                Console.WriteLine("   Participating in"+
                    " Credit Union");
            }
        }
    }

    public class Employee {

        public Employee(string emplName) {
            propName=emplName;
            eflags.SetAll(true);
        }

        public Employee(string emplName,
                        bool profitSharing,
                        bool healthPlan,
                        bool creditUnion) {
            propName=emplName;
            InProfitSharing=profitSharing;
            InHealthPlan=healthPlan;
```

```
            InCreditUnion=creditUnion;
        }

        private BitArray eflags=new BitArray(3);

        public bool InProfitSharing{
            set {
                eflags.Set(0, value);
            }
            get {
                return eflags.Get(0);
            }
        }

        public bool InHealthPlan{
            set {
                eflags.Set(1, value);
            }
            get {
                return eflags.Get(1);
            }
        }

        public bool InCreditUnion{
            set {
                eflags.Set(2, value);
            }
            get {
                return eflags.Get(2);
            }
        }

        private string propName;
        public string Name {
            get {
                return propName;
            }
        }
    }
}
```

This is sample code of the *IDictionaryEnumerator* enumerator:

```
using System;
using System.Collections;

namespace Donis.CSharpBook{
    public class Starter{
        public static void Main(){
            Hashtable zHash=new Hashtable();
            zHash.Add("one", 1);
            zHash.Add("two", 2);
            zHash.Add("three", 3);
            zHash.Add("four", 4);
            IDictionaryEnumerator e=
```

```
            zHash.GetEnumerator();
        while(e.MoveNext()){
            Console.WriteLine(
                "{0} {1}",
                e.Key, e.Value);
        }
        }
    }
}
```

Queue Collection

Queue collections abstract FIFO data structures. The initial capacity is 32 elements. *Queue* collections are ideal for messaging components.

Table 5-9 lists the member of the *Queue* collection.

Table 5-9   Queue Members

Member Name	Syntax

Constructor	`public Queue()`
	`public Queue(`
	`    ICollection sourceCollection)`
	
	`public Queue(int capacity)`
	
	`public Queue(int capacity,`
	`    float factor)`

Clear This method removes all the elements of the collection.	`virtual void Clear()`
Contains This method returns *true* if the specified value is found in the collection. If the value is not found, *false* is returned.	`virtual bool Contains(object value)`
Dequeue This method removes and returns the first element of the queue.	`virtual object Dequeue()`
Enqueue This method adds an element to the queue.	`virtual void Enqueue(` `    object element)`
Peek This method returns the first element of the queue without removing it.	`virtual object Peek()`
Synchronized This method returns a thread-safe wrapper for a queue object.	`static Queue Synchronized(` `    Queue sourceQueue)`

Table 5-9 Queue Members (Continued)

Member Name	Syntax
ToArray This method creates a new array initialized with the elements of the queue.	`virtual object[] ToArray()`
TrimToSize This method sets the capacity to the number of elements in the collection.	`virtual void TrimToSize()`
IEnumerable members	*GetEnumerator*
ICloneable members	*Clone*
ICollection members	*CopyTo, Count, IsSynchronized,* and *SyncRoot*

This is sample code of the *Queue* collection. Customers are added to the queue and then displayed.

```
using System;
using System.Collections;

namespace Donis.CSharpBook{
    public class Starter{
        public static void Main(){
            Queue waiting=new Queue();
            waiting.Enqueue(new Customer("Bob"));
            waiting.Enqueue(new Customer("Ted"));
            waiting.Enqueue(new Customer("Kim"));
            waiting.Enqueue(new Customer("Sam"));

            while(waiting.Count!= 0) {
                Customer cust=
                    (Customer) waiting.Dequeue();
                Console.WriteLine(cust.Name);
            }
        }

        public class Customer{
            public Customer(string cName) {
                propName=cName;
            }

            private string propName;
            public string Name {
                get {
                    return propName;
                }
            }
        }
    }
}
```

SortedList

The *SortedList* collection is a combination of key/value entries and an *ArrayList* collection, where the collection is sorted by the key. The collection is accessible per the key or an index.

Table 5-10 include the members of the *SortedList* collection.

Table 5-10   SortedList Members

Member Name	Syntax

Constructor
 	
The *SortedList* constructor is overloaded. These are some of the overloaded constructors.
	`SortedList()`
	
	`SortedList(IComparer comparer)`
	
	`SortedList(`
	`    IDictionary sourceCollection)`

Add This method adds an element to the collection.	`virtual void Add(object key,` `    object value)`
Capacity This property gets or sets the capacity of the collection.	`virtual int Capacity{` `    get; set;}`
Clear This method removes all the elements of the collection.	`virtual void Clear()`
Contains This method returns *true* if the specified value is found in the collection. If the value is not found, *false* is returned.	`virtual bool Contains(object value)`
ContainsKey This method returns *true* if the key is found in the collection. If the key is not present, *false* is returned. Identical to the *Contains* method.	`virtual bool ContainsKey(` `    object key)`
ContainsValue This method returns *true* if the value is found in the collection. If the value is not present, *false* is returned.	`virtual bool ContainsValue(` `    object value)`
GetByIndex This method returns the value at the index.	`virtual object GetByIndex(` `    int index)`
GetKey This method returns the key at the specified index.	`virtual object GetKey(` `    int index)`
GetKeyList This method returns all the keys in the collection.	`virtual IList GetKeyList()`
GetValueList This method returns all the values of the *SortedList* in a new collection.	`virtual IList GetValueList()`

Table 5-10   SortedList Members (Continued)

Member Name	Syntax
IndexOfKey This method returns the index of a key found in the collection.	```virtual int IndexOfKey(object key)```
IndexOfValue This method returns the index to the first instance of this value in the collection.	```virtual int IndexOfValue(object value)```
IsFixedSize This property returns *true* if the collection is fixed size. Otherwise, *false* is returned.	```virtual bool IsFixedSize{ get;}```
IsReadOnly This property returns *true* if the collection is read-only. Otherwise, *false* is returned.	```virtual bool IsReadOnly{ get;}```
Item This property gets or sets the value of this key.	```virtual object this[object key] {get; set;}```
Keys This property returns the keys of the *SortedList* collection.	```public virtual ICollection Keys{ get;}```
Remove This method removes an element, which is identified by the key, from the collection.	```virtual void Remove(object key)```
RemoveAt This method removes an element at the specific index.	```virtual void RemoveAt(int index)```
SetByIndex This method set the value of the element at the specified index.	```virtual void SetByIndex(int index, object value)```
Synchronized This method returns a thread-safe wrapper for a queue object.	```static SortedList Synchronized(SortedList sourceList)```
TrimToSize This method trims the capacity to the actual number of elements in the collection.	```virtual void TrimToSize()```
Values This property returns the values of the collection.	```virtual ICollection Values{ get;}```
IEnumerable members	*GetEnumerator*
ICloneable members	*Clone*
ICollection members	*CopyTo, Count, IsSynchronized,* and *SyncRoot*

This following program is an application that tracks auto repair tickets. Each ticket, which is an instance of the *AutoRepairTicket*, is added to a sorted list. The key is the customer name. The value is the actual ticket. After populating the *SortedList* type, the *CustomerReport* method lists the open tickets.

```csharp
using System;
using System.Collections;

namespace Donis.CSharpBook{
    public class Starter{
        public static void Main(){
            SortedList tickets=new SortedList();
            AutoRepairTicket ticket=NewTicket("Ben");
            tickets.Add(ticket.Name, ticket);
            ticket=NewTicket("Donis");
            tickets.Add(ticket.Name, ticket);
            ticket=NewTicket("Adam");
            tickets.Add(ticket.Name, ticket);
            CustomerReport(tickets);
        }

        public static AutoRepairTicket NewTicket(
                string customerName) {
            return new AutoRepairTicket(customerName,
                DateTime.Now);
        }

        public static void CustomerReport(SortedList list) {
            foreach(DictionaryEntry entry in list) {
                int nextTag=((AutoRepairTicket) entry.Value).Tag;
                string nextTime=((AutoRepairTicket)
                    entry.Value).Time.ToShortTimeString();
                Console.WriteLine("Customer: {0} Ticket: {1} Time: {2}",
                    entry.Key, nextTag, nextTime);
            }
        }
    }

    public class AutoRepairTicket{
        public AutoRepairTicket(string customerName,
            DateTime ticketTime) {
            propName=customerName;
            propTime=ticketTime;
            propTag=++count;
        }

        private string propName;
        public string Name {
            get {
                return propName;
            }
        }
```

```
    private DateTime propTime;
    public DateTime Time {
        get {
            return propTime;
        }
    }

    private int propTag;
    public int Tag {
        get {
            return propTag;
        }
    }

    private static int count=1000;
    }
}
```

Stack Collection

Stack collections abstract LIFO data structures in which the initial capacity is 32 elements.

Table 5-11 lists the member of the *Stack* collection.

Table 5-11   Stack Members

Member Name	Syntax
Clear This method removes all the elements of the collection.	`virtual void Clear()`
Contains This method returns *true* if the specified value is found in the collection. If the value is not found, *false* is returned.	`virtual bool Contains(object value)`
Peek The *Peek* method previews the last element on the stack. The element is returned without removal from the stack.	`virtual object Peek()`
Pop This method returns and removes the top element of the stack.	`virtual object Pop()`
Push This method pushes another element on the stack.	`virtual void Push(object obj)`
Synchronized This method returns a thread-safe wrapper for the *Stack* collection.	`static Stack Synchronized(` `    Stack sourceStack)`
ToArray This method returns the *Stack* collection as a regular array.	`virtual object[] ToArray()`

The following code adds numbers to a *Stack* collection. The values of the collection are then enumerated and displayed.

```
using System;
using System.Collections;

namespace Donis.CSharpBook{
    public class Starter{
        public static void Main(){
            Stack numbers=new Stack(
                new int [] {1,2,3,4,5,6});
            int total=numbers.Count;
        for(int count=0;count<total;++count) {
                Console.WriteLine(numbers.Pop());
            }
        }
    }
}
```

Specialized Collections

In addition to the common collections that most developers use, the .NET FCL offers specialized collections. These collections are found in the *System.Collections.Specialized* namespace. Although these collections are used infrequently, they are valuable in certain circumstances.

Table 5-12 lists the specialized collections.

Table 5-12   Specialized Collections

Member Name	Description
BitVector32	This is an array of 32 bits. It is similar to a *BitArray*, but limited to 32 bits. Because of this array's refined use, *BitVector32* structures are more efficient then a *BitArray* collection.
HybridDictionary	This collection is a combination of a *ListDictionary* and *Hashtable*. It operates as a *ListDictionary* when containing a small number of elements. For optimum performance, the collection switches to a *Hashtable* as the elements increased. *ListDictionary* of 10 elements or fewer is recommended.
NameValueCollection	This is a collection of keys and values, in which both the key and value are strings. The collection is accessible via an index or key. A key can refer to multiple values.
OrderedDictionary	Not documented at the time of this book.
StringCollection	This is a collection of strings.
StringDictionary	This is a combination of the *Hashtable* and *StringCollection* collections, in which both the key and value are strings.

Generics

The next chapter is about Generics, which improves upon the performance and other factors related to nongeneric collections. The collections reviewed in this chapter manipulate object types. For this reason, when populating collections with value types, boxing is required. Excessive boxing is both a performance and memory issue. Another problem is type-safeness. You often cast elements that are object types to a specific type. The cast is not type-safe and can cause run-time errors when done incorrectly.

Generics types are classes with type parameters. The type parameter acts as a placeholder for a future type. When a generic type is declared, type arguments are substituted for the type parameters. The type argument is the actual type. At that time, the generic is type-specific, which resolves many of the problems of a nongeneric type. Generic methods, like generic types, have type parameters. However, the type argument can be inferred from the way the method is called.

A complete explanation of generic types and methods follows in Chapter 6.

Chapter 6
Generics

The definition of *generic*, as found in the *Merriam-Webster's Collegiate Dictionary,* is "adj. of a whole genus, kind, class, etc.; general; inclusive." Based on this definition, a person is generic, whereas Donis Marshall is quite specific. A city is generic, whereas Seattle is specific. For developers, a data algorithm is generic, whereas the implementation is specific. A stack is generic, whereas a stack of integers is specific. A spreadsheet is generic, whereas a spreadsheet of strings is specific. To lesser extent, general abstractions can use generic implementation. An arithmetic class is generic, whereas integer calculations are specific.

In .NET, a type is specific, such as a class or structure. A *StackInt* class is a specific type and represents a specialization of the stack pattern, which targets integers. A stack of strings or floats would require additional implementations of the same algorithm, such as *StackString* and *StackFloat.*

Here is an implementation of the *StackInt* class:

```
"using System;

namespace Donis.CSharpBook{
    public class Starter{
        public static void Main(){
            StackInt stack=new StackInt(5);
            stack.Push(10);
            stack.Push(15);
            Console.WriteLine("Pushed 3 values");
            stack.ListItems();
            stack.Pop();
            Console.WriteLine("Popped 1 value");
            stack.ListItems();
        }
    }
```

```
public class StackInt {

    public StackInt(int firstItem) {
        list=new int[1] {firstItem};
        top++;
    }

    public int Pop() {
        if(top!=(-1)) {
            return list[top--]; //was list[--top]
        }
        throw new Exception("Stack empty");
    }

    public void Push(int topitem) {
        ++top;
        if(top==list.Length) {
            int [] temp=new int[top+1];
            Array.Copy(list, temp, top);
            list=temp     ;
        }
        list[top]=topitem;
    }

    public void ListItems () {
        for(int item=0;item<=top;++item) {
            Console.WriteLine(list[item]);
        }
    }

    private int [] list;
    private int top=(-1);
}

}
```

The implementation works, but not without some issues:

- Replicating the algorithm is time-consuming and is the antithesis of code reuse.

- This approach is not maintainable. What if the core algorithm is refashioned for better performance? It requires updating and testing multiple sets of nearly identical source code.

- Specific types are not extensible. As an application matures, the number of implementations could become unwieldy. In a graphics program, as additional geometric shapes are supported, the list of stack classes could expand to include *StackEllipse*, *StackOval*, *StackLine*, *StackTriangle*, *StackCurve*, *StackText*, ad infinitum.

Inheritance polymorphism, which is polymorphism using inheritance and virtual functions, is an alternate solution to type specialty. In a personnel application, *ExemptEmployee*, *HourlyEmployee*, and *TempEmployee* are specific classes that are related through inheritance, where *Employee* is the generic base class. Using it solves some of the aforementioned problems, such as code reuse. This is a potential solution to generic abstraction but not a generic data algorithm. Abstracting the stack algorithm based on inheritance encourages bad design. Is a stack a kind of integer? Is an integer a kind of stack? Neither statement is true. For a stack solution, inheritance polymorphism is a contrived solution at best.

A simple solution is *generic implementation*, which is single implementation for all types—a stack of *anything*, versus a stack of integers. This is the function of collections in the .NET Framework class library (FCL), which are general-purpose containers. All types—value or reference—are derived directly or indirectly from *System.Object*, making it the ubiquitous type. *System.Object* can be *anything*. General-purpose collections are containers of *System.Object* instances. These collections are discussed in Chapter 5, "Arrays and Collections."

In the following code, a stack of integers is implemented using the stack collection class from the .NET FCL. The stack collection is reused as a stack of strings, which demonstrates the amorphous nature of the stack collection class.

```
using System;
using System.Collections;

namespace Donis.CSharpBook{
    public class Starter{

        public static void Main(){
            Console.WriteLine("Integer stack");
            Integers();
            Console.WriteLine("String stack");
            Strings();
        }

        public static void Integers() {
            Stack list=new Stack();
            list.Push(5);
            list.Push(10);
            list.Push(15);
            foreach(int item in list) {
                Console.WriteLine(item);
            }
        }

        public static void Strings() {
            Stack list=new Stack();
            list.Push("a");
            list.Push("b");
            list.Push("c");
            foreach(string item in list) {
                Console.WriteLine(item);
            }
        }

    }
}
```

General-purpose collections (described in the previous chapter) are valuable, but there are some drawbacks. Performance is the first problem. These collections manage instances of *System.Object*. Casting is required to access, remove, and insert items into a collection. For integers, boxing occurs as items are added to the collection. Unboxing happens when items are accessed in the collection. Boxing occurs if a collection contains value types—integers are value types. Frequent boxing can prompt earlier garbage collection, which is especially expensive. The incremental penalty for boxing and unboxing can be substantial for a collection of value types. For a collection of reference types, there is the cost of down-casting, which is lighter. The second problem is type-safeness. Although the *StackInt* type is type-safe, the general-purpose collection of integers is not. The stack collection stores elements in memory as *System.Object*. As a *System.Object* type, the behavior of each element is limited to *ToString*, *GetHashCode*, *Equals*, and *GetType*. Casting is required for expanded behavior. However, you can cast to anything, which is inherently type-unsafe. Incorrect casts cause run-time exceptions. The third problem is clarity. Frequent casting, as required with collection classes, obfuscates the source code. Generics are the solution.

Generics are parameterized types and methods. Each parameter is a placeholder of a yet-unspecified type. The polymorphic behavior of the generic type or method is conveyed through parameters, which is called *parametric* polymorphism. There is a single implementation of the algorithm, which is abstracted through parameters. Many developers were introduced to this concept in C++ as parameterized templates. Other languages also support this feature. However, generics in .NET avoid some of the problems emblematic of parametric polymorphism in these other languages.

Generics address the shortcomings of generic collections. Generics perform better because needless boxing and unboxing are eliminated. At run time, generic types with value type arguments expand to type-specific instances. For example, a generic stack with an integer type parameter becomes an actual stack of integers, which make generics inherently type-safe. Generic types become specific types, which avoids the necessity of casting. Because casting is avoided, clarity is enhanced.

Generic types and methods are not suitable in all circumstances:

- The entry point method cannot be a member of an generic type.
- Unmanaged types cannot be generic.
- Constructors cannot be generic.
- Operator member functions cannot be generic methods.
- Properties cannot be generic.
- Indexers cannot be generic.
- Attributes cannot be generic.

Generic Types

Generics are types with parameters, and parameters are placeholders for future types. Generic types include classes, structures, and interfaces. The essence of the type remains. The persona of a class, even a generic class, remains a class—it is simply a class with type parameters.

Type Parameters

Parameters appear after the class header and are placed in anchor brackets (< and >). The type parameters are accessible to the class declaration, header, body, and constraints. Because collections are typically general-purpose, generics are ideal for implementing collections. .NET provides generic collections for arrays, stacks, queues, and other common data structures. However, there is no predefined spreadsheet collection, which is a collection of rows and columns. Sounds like an opportunity to me.

Here is sample code for a sheet collection:

```
using System;

namespace Donis.CSharpBook{
    public class Starter{
        public static void Main(){
            int count=1;
            Sheet<int> asheet=new Sheet<int>(2);
            for(byte row=1; row<3; ++row) {
                for(byte col=1; col<3; ++col) {
                    asheet[row,col]=count++;
                }
            }
            for(byte row=1; row<3; ++row) {
                for(byte col=1; col<3; ++col) {
                    Console.WriteLine("R{0} C{1}= {2}",
                        row, col, asheet[row,col]);
                }
            }

            Console.WriteLine("Current[{0},{1}] = {2}",
                asheet.R, asheet.C, asheet.Current);
            asheet.MoveDown();
            asheet.MoveRight();
            Console.WriteLine("Current[{0},{1}] = {2}",
                asheet.R, asheet.C, asheet.Current);
        }
    }

    class Sheet<T> {
        public Sheet(byte dimension) {
            if(dimension<0) {
                throw new Exception("Invalid dimensions");
            }
            m_Dimension=dimension;
            m_Sheet=new T[dimension, dimension];
            for(byte row=0; row<dimension; ++row) {
                for(byte col=0; col<dimension; ++col) {
                    m_Sheet[row,col]=default(T);
                }
            }

        }
```

```
public T this[byte row, byte col] {
    get {
        ValidateCell(row, col);
        return m_Sheet[row-1, col-1];
    }
    set {
        m_Sheet[row-1, col-1]=value;
    }
}

public void ValidateCell(byte row, byte col) {
    if((row < 0) || (row > m_Dimension)) {
        throw new Exception("Invalid Row");
    }
    if((col < 0) || (col > m_Dimension)) {
        throw new Exception("Invalid Col");
    }
}


public T Current {
    get {
        return m_Sheet[curRow-1, curCol-1];
    }
    set {
        m_Sheet[curRow-1, curCol-1]=value;
    }
}

public void MoveLeft() {
    curCol=Math.Max((byte) (curCol-1), (byte) 1);
}

public void MoveRight() {
    curCol=Math.Min((byte) (curCol+1), (byte) m_Dimension);
}

public void MoveUp() {
    curRow=Math.Max((byte) (curRow-1), (byte) 1);
}

public void MoveDown() {
    curRow=Math.Min((byte) (curRow+1), (byte) m_Dimension);
}

private byte curRow=1;
public byte R {
    get {
        return curRow;
    }
}

private byte curCol=1;
public byte C {
    get {
        return curCol;
```

```
            }
        }

        private byte m_Dimension;
        private T [,] m_Sheet;
    }
}
```

Sheet is a generic type and collection, with a single parameter. For generics with a single parameter, by convention, *T* is the name of the parameter. (*T* is for type.) In the sheet generic type, the type parameter is used as a function return, field type, and local variable. When the sheet is instantiated, the specific type is specified. This defines a spreadsheet of strings, which has two rows and columns:

```
Sheet<string> asheet=new Sheet<string>(2);
```

Review the constructor of the sheet generic type. Notice the use of the default keyword:

```
for(byte row=0; row<dimension; ++row) {
    for(byte col=0; col<dimension; ++col) {
        m_Sheet[row,col]=default(T);
    }
}
```

The preceding *for* loop initializes the internal collection of the *Sheet* generic type. However, the implementation is not based on a specific type. A generic type implementation has placeholders instead of specific types. The challenge is initializing a nonspecific type, which could be a reference or value type. The default expression returns null for a reference type and bitwise zero for a value type. This is the syntax of the default expression:

zerovalue default(*type*)

The *Sheet* generic type has a single parameter. Generics can have multiple parameters. The type parameter list is contained within the anchor brackets. Parameters in the type parameter list are comma-delimited. If a generic has two parameters, the parameters are normally named *K* and *V*, for key and value. Here is sample code of a generic type that has two parameters:

```
public class ZClass<K, V> {
    static void Method(K key, V data) {

    }
}
```

This code creates an instance of the *ZClass*, which has two parameters:

```
ZClass<string, float> obj=new ZClass<string, float>();
```

Generic types have parameters. Those parameters can themselves be generic types. In the following code, *XClass* is generic and is also inserted as a nested parameter:

```
using System;

namespace Donis.CSharpBook{
```

```
public class Starter{
    public static void Main(){
        ZClass<XParameter<string>, float> obj=
            new ZClass<XParameter<string>, float>();
    }
}

public class XParameter<P> {
    public static void MethodA(P data) {
    }
}

public class ZClass<K, V> {
    public static void MethodB(K key, V data) {
    }
}

}
```

The syntax of nested parameters can be somewhat complicated. What if the type parameter was extrapolated even further? You could have a type parameter that is a generic, which has a type parameter that is also generic, and so on, which could become somewhat labyrinthine. If the declaration is repeated, it would be particularly problematic. An alias is a good solution. Alias the declaration containing a nested parameter and rely on the alias in the code. The following alias is used for this purpose:

```
using ZClass2=ZClass<XParameter<string>, int>;

public class Starter{
    public static void Main(){
        ZClass2 obj=new ZClass2();
    }
}

public class XParameter<P> {
    public static void MethodA(P data) {
    }
}

public class ZClass<K, V> {
    public static void MethodB(K key, V data) {
    }
}
```

This is the syntax of a generic type:

attributes accessibility modifiers **class** *classname* : *baselist*

   <parameterlist> where *parameter:constraintlist*:

   { *class body* };

Constructed Types

Generic types are also called constructed types. There are *open constructed* and *closed constructed* types. An open constructed type has at least one type parameter. The type parameter is a placeholder, which is unbound to a specific type. The implementation of a generic type is an example of an open constructed type. This is an open constructed type:

```
public class ZClass<K, V> {
    static void Method(K key, V data) {

    }
}
```

For a closed constructed type, all type parameters are bound. Bound parameters are called type arguments and are assigned a specific type. Closed constructed types are used in several circumstances: to create an instance of a generic type, inherit a generic type, and more. In the following code, *ZClass<int, decimal>* is a closed constructed type. The first parameter is bound to an integer, whereas the second is a decimal. The type arguments are *int* and *decimal*.

```
ZClass<int, decimal> obj=new ZClass<int, decimal>();
```

Generic Methods

A generic method can declare method-specific generic parameters. These parameters can be used in the method header or body. An open method has type parameters, which are non-specific. A closed method has type arguments, whereas specific types are substituted for type parameters. For a generic method, the type parameters are listed after the function header. The type parameter list is enclosed in anchor brackets, whereas each parameter is delimited with commas.

This is a prototypical generic method:

```
using System;

namespace Donis.CSharpBook{

    public class Starter{
        public static void Main(){
            ZClass.MethodA<int>(20);
        }
    }

    public class ZClass{
        public static void MethodA<T>(T param) {
            Console.WriteLine(param.GetType().ToString());
        }
    }
}
```

When calling a generic method, provide the type arguments as a substitute for type parameters. There is an alternate syntax to calling a generic method, called *type inference*, in which the type argument is inferred from the actual method parameters. The type argument can then be omitted. Basically, the generic method is called similarly to any method. The benefit is ease of use. However, type inference disguises the true nature of the call, which could be relevant when debugging an application.

In the previous code, *ZClass.MethodA* is a generic method. The following statement calls *MethodA* using type inference:

```
ZClass.MethodA(20);
```

This is the syntax of a generic method:

attributes accessibility modifiers returntype methodname <parameterlist>

(*argumentlist*) where *parameter:constraintlist*

{ *method body* }

Overloaded Methods

Generic methods can be overloaded, which creates an interesting dilemma. Is a method ambiguous based on extrapolation alone? In the following code, *MethodA* is overloaded:

```
public void MethodA(T arg) {
}
public void MethodA(U arg) {
}
```

Both functions have a single type parameter. The type parameters are different, but each parameter could be anything, including both parameters being identical. This makes certain renditions of *MethodA* ambiguous. For example, they both could have a single integer parameter. However, the C# compiler is concerned with actual ambiguity and does not highlight, as an error or warning, potential ambiguousness related to overloading generic methods. A compile error is manifested when *MethodA* is called, if ever, in an ambiguous manner. This is a potential land mine for developers of libraries. Test every permutation of type parameters to predict and avoid potential ambiguousness for clients of a library.

In the following code, *MethodA* is called ambiguously. Interestingly, *MethodA* is known to be ambiguous at the generic type instantiation. However, the compiler error occurs on the next statement at the call site.

```
using System;

namespace Donis.CSharpBook{

    public class Starter{
        public static void Main(){
```

```
            ZClass<int, int> obj=new ZClass<int, int>();
            obj.MethodA(5); // ambiguous error
        }
    }

    public class ZClass<T, U> {
        public void MethodA(T arg) {
            Console.WriteLine("ZClass.MethodA(T arg)");
        }

        public void MethodA(U arg) {
            Console.WriteLine("ZClass.MethodA(U arg)");
        }

        public void MethodA() {
            Console.WriteLine("ZClass.MethodA()");
        }
    }
}
```

Generic methods can overload nongeneric methods. If the combination of a generic and non-generic method is ambiguous, the nongeneric method is called. The compiler prefers nongeneric methods over generic methods of the same signature.

The following code contains a generic and nongeneric *MethodA*. When *MethodA* is called with an integer parameter, the call would otherwise be ambiguous. Because the ambiguous methods are generic and nongeneric methods, the nongeneric *MethodA* is simply called. Then *MethodA* is called with a double, which is not ambiguous, and the generic *MethodA* is called appropriately.

```
using System;

namespace Donis.CSharpBook{

    public class Starter{
        public static void Main(){
            ZClass<int> obj1=new ZClass<int>();
            obj1.MethodA(5);
            ZClass<double> obj2=new ZClass<double>();
            obj2.MethodA(5.0);
        }
    }

    public class ZClass<T> {
        public void MethodA(T arg) {
            Console.WriteLine("ZClass.MethodA(T arg)");
        }

        public void MethodA(int arg) {
            Console.WriteLine("ZClass.MethodA(int arg)");
        }

        public void MethodA() {
```

```
                Console.WriteLine("ZClass.MethodA()");
        }
    }
}
```

This Reference for Generic Types

Generic types, similar to any type, have a *this* reference, which is a reference to the current object and the same type of that object. If the object is an *XClass* instance, the *this* reference is also of the *XClass* type. The *this* reference is used implicitly to refer to instance members and explicitly as function returns and parameters. The *this* reference of a generic type is associated with the closed constructed type, which is normally defined at generic type instantiation.

The following code displays the type of a *this* reference. The following is a *this* reference of a generic type, which is *Donis.CSharpBook.ZClass`1[System.Int32]*. From the type, you know that the closed constructed type has a single parameter that is a 32-bit integer.

```
using System;

namespace Donis.CSharpBook{

    public class Starter{
        public static void Main(){
            ZClass<int> obj=new ZClass<int>();
            obj.MethodA();
        }
    }

    class ZClass<T> {
        public T MethodA() {
            T var=default(T);
            Console.WriteLine(this.GetType().ToString());
            return var;
        }
    }
}
```

Constraints

When a generic type is implemented, the deferred specialty of the type parameter is unknown. Managed code has plenty of cool features, but they do not include foretelling the future. Therefore, within the implementation of a generic type, a type parameter could eventually be *anything*. We are assured that the type parameter inherits from *System.Object*–nothing else. .NET guarantees that all types are a derivation of *System.Object*. For this reason, type parameters are implied *System.Object* types and must behave accordingly. This limits type parameters to the public interface of the *System.Object*, which assures type safeness.

In the following code, *ZClass* has a single parameter, which is *T*. My intention is that *T* is an array of some type. *ZClass.MethodA* will enumerate that array while displaying each value. *System.Array* is the underlying type of an array and implements the *IEnumerable* interface. This is the required interface for enumeration and an essential ingredient of a *foreach* loop. Unfortunately, the C# compiler does not know my intention. Regardless of my future intention, *T* is an implied *System.Object*, which does not implement the *IEnumerable* interface. Therefore this code does not compile.

```
class ZClass<T> {

    public void Iterate(T data) {
       foreach(object item in data) {
         Console.WriteLine(item);
       }
    }
}
```

This problem is resolved with a generic constraint. Constraints define the future intention of a type parameter. The following program uses a constraint, which is a *where* clause, to indicate the intention of the *T* parameter. It is intended that the *T* parameter is an *IEnumerable* type. With this understanding, the program compiles and executes successfully:

```
using System;
using System.Collections;

namespace Donis.CSharpBook{

    public class Starter{
        public static void Main(){
            ZClass<int[]> obj=new ZClass<int[]>();
            obj.Iterate(new int[] {1,2,3,4});
        }
    }

    public class ZClass<T> where T: IEnumerable {

        public void Iterate(T data) {
          foreach(object item in data) {
            Console.WriteLine(item);
          }
        }
    }
}
```

There are five types of constraints:

- **Derivation constraints**   state the ascendancy of a type parameter.
- **Interface constraints**   are interfaces that are implemented by the type parameter.
- **Value type constraints**   restrict a type parameter to a value type.
- **Reference type constraints**   restrict a type parameter to a reference type.
- **Constructor constraints**   stipulate that the type parameter has a default or parameterless constructor.

Constraints can be applied to both generic types and methods.

Derivation Constraint

The derivation constraint states the derivation of a type parameter. The type parameter must be derived from that constraint, which is enforced by the C# compiler. This allows the compiler to relax the restriction that access to type parameters is limited to the *System.Object*. The public interface of the constrained type parameter is expanded to include the derivation type. A type can inherit from a single class because multiple inheritance is not available in C#. For this reason, a type parameter can optionally have a single constraint. However, each parameter can have separate derivation constraints, in which each constraint is space-delimited.

Because the constraint is enforced by the compiler, the type parameter can only be used accordingly. This avoids an unsafe usage of the type parameter. The compiler assures that all access to the type parameter is type-safe as defined in the constraint. This is different in C++, in which the compiler performs no such type-checking on type parameters. In C++, you can basically do anything with a type parameter. Errors are uncovered when the parameter template is expanded at compile time, deep in the bowels of the expansion code. This can lead to cryptic error messages that are hard to debug. Anyone that has used the Active Template Library (ATL) and had expansion errors can attest to this. The C# compiler also updates Microsoft IntelliSense per the derivation constraint. A type parameter reflects the IntelliSense of any constraints on that parameter.

ZClass is a generic type and is defined in the following code. It has a *K* and *V* type parameter, each with a separate constraint. Per the constraints, the *K* parameter must be derived from *XClass*, while the *V* parameter should be derived from *YClass*. *Main* has three generic type instantiations. The first two are okay, but the third causes compile errors. The problem is the first type argument. *WClass* is not derived from *XClass*, which is a requirement of the first parameter per the constraint.

```
using System;

namespace Donis.CSharpBook{

    public class Starter{
        public static void Main(){

            // good
            ZClass<XClass, YClass> obj=
                new ZClass<XClass, YClass>();

            // good
            ZClass<XClass, WClass> obj2=
                new ZClass<XClass, WClass>();

            // bad
            ZClass<WClass, YClass> obj3=
                new ZClass<WClass, YClass>();

        }
    }
```

```
public class ZClass<K, V> where K:XClass
                       where V:YClass {

}

public class XClass {

}

public class YClass {
}

public class WClass: YClass {
}
}
```

The following code shows a generic method with a derivation constraint:

```
class ZClass {
  public T MethodA<T>() where T:XClass {
     return default(T);
  }
}
```

Generic types can function as constraints, which include both open and closed constructed types. This is demonstrated in the following code. *XClass* is a nongeneric type. *YClass* is a generic type with a single parameter. *ZClass* is also a generic type, also with a single parameter, where *YClass<XClass>* is the constraint on that parameter. *YClass<XClass>* is a closed constructed type. In *Main*, an instance of the *YClass* is created, where *XClass* is the type parameter. Next, an instance of the *ZClass* is created, and the parameter type is *YClass<XClass>*, which is required by the constraint mentioned earlier. *ZClass.MethodA* is then called, where the *YClass* instance is passed as a parameter.

```
using System;

namespace Donis.CSharpBook{

    public class Starter{
        public static void Main(){
            YClass<XClass> param=new YClass<XClass>();
            ZClass <YClass<XClass>> obj=new ZClass <YClass<XClass>>();
            obj.MethodA(param);
        }
    }

    public class ZClass<T> where T: YClass<XClass> {
        public void MethodA(T obj) {
            Console.WriteLine("ZClass::MethodA");
            obj.MethodB();
        }
    }

    public class YClass<T> {
        public void MethodB() {
```

```
            Console.WriteLine("YClass::MethodB");
        }
    }

    public class XClass {
        public void MethodC() {
            Console.WriteLine("XClass::MethodA");
        }
    }

}
```

A type parameter can be used as a constraint. In this circumstance, one type of parameter is constraining another. You are stating that a parameter is derived from another parameter. In this code, the *T1* parameter must be derived from the eventual *T2* type argument:

```
using System;
using System.Collections;

namespace Donis.CSharpBook{

    public class Starter{
        public static void Main(){
            XClass<YClass, ZClass> obj=new XClass<YClass, ZClass>();
        }
    }

    public class ZClass {
        public void MethodA() {
            Console.WriteLine("YClass::MethodA");
        }
    }

    public class YClass: ZClass {
    }

    public class XClass<T1, T2> where T1:T2 {
        public void MethodB(T1 arg) {

        }
    }

}
```

Nodes are the ideal generic type. You can have nodes of integers, floats, employees, or even football teams. When creating a link list, each node has reference to the next and previous node. The node should reference nodes of the same type. For an employee node, the next and previous node must also be an employee. This relationship between nodes is enforced with a recursive constraint:

```
    public class Node<T> where T:  Node<T> {

        // partial implementation
```

```
    public T Previous {
        get {
            return default(T);
        }
        set {
        }
    }

    public T Next {
        get {
            return default(T);
        }
        set {
        }
    }
}
```

The type parameter cannot exceed the visibility of the constraint. In the following code, *XClass* has internal accessibility and is visible in the current assembly alone. The *T* parameter is public and is visible outside the current assembly. The accessibility of the *T* parameter exceeds *XClass*. For this reason, it is an error to use *XClass* as a constraint on the type parameter.

```
public class ZClass<T> where T: XClass{
}

internal class XClass {
}
```

In addition, value types cannot be used as constraints, which is a good introduction to a limitation with generics. Look at the following code, which will not compile. Why not?

```
public class Arithmetic<T> {
    public T Cubed (T number) {
        return number*number*number;
    }
}
```

As with any parameter, the *T* parameter is an inferred *System.Object* type. *System.Object* does not have an operator *. Therefore, "*number*number*number*" will not compile. An integer constraint should resolve the problem, which would confirm that the type parameter is an integer. Integers have an operator *. However, value types and primitives are not valid constraints. The following code will not compile:

```
class Arithmetic<T> where T: System.Int32 {
    public T Cubed (T number) {
        return number*number*number;
    }
}
```

The inability to use standard operators with value types is a major limitation to generics. The workaround is implementing named operators, such as *Add*, *Multiply*, and *Divide*, as members of the generic type.

In addition to value types, there are other restrictions on constraints. The following types cannot be used as constraints:

- Sealed classes
- Open constructed types
- Primitive types
- *System.Array*
- *System.Delegate*
- *System.Enum*
- *System.ValueType*

Interface Constraints

Interfaces can also be constraints, which requires that the type argument implement the interface. Although a type parameter can have at most one derivation constraint, it can have multiple interface constraints. This is logical because a class can inherit a single base class but can implement many interfaces. The syntax for an interface constraint is identical to a derivation constraint. Class and interface constraints can be combined in a list of constraints. However, a class constraint should precede interface constraints in the list.

Interface and derivation constraints share many of the same rules and restrictions, such as the visibility of the interface constraint exceeding that of the type parameter.

In the following code, the find capability has been added to the *Sheet* collection. The *Find* method returns an array of cells that contain a certain value. A comparison is made between the cell and value, where both are the type indicated in the type argument. Types that implement the *IComparable* interface support comparisons. If a comparison is equal, *IComparable* .*CompareTo* returns 0. To support this behavior, an interface constraint for *IComparable* is added to the type parameter. This is a partial implementation of the *Sheet* collection that shows *Find* and related methods. (Some of the code shown previously is omitted.)

```
using System;

namespace Donis.CSharpBook{
    public class Starter{
        public static void Main(){
            Sheet<int> asheet=new Sheet<int>(5);
            for(byte row=1; row<6; ++row) {
                for(byte col=1; col<6; ++col) {
                    asheet[row,col]=row*col;
                }
            }

            Cell [] found=asheet.Find(6);
            foreach(Cell answer in found) {
```

```
                    Console.WriteLine("R{0} C{1}",
                        answer.row, answer.col);
            }
        }
    }

    public struct Cell {
        public byte row;
        public byte col;
    }

    public class Sheet<T> where T: IComparable {
            ...

        public Cell[] Find(T searchValue) {
            int total=Count(searchValue);
            int counter=0;
            Cell [] cells=new Cell[total];
            for(byte row=1; row<=m_Dimension; ++row) {
                for(byte col=1; col<=m_Dimension; ++col) {
                    if(m_Sheet[row-1,col-1].CompareTo(searchValue)==0) {
                        cells[counter].row=row;
                        cells[counter].col=col;
                        ++counter;
                    }
                }
            }
            return cells;
        }

        public int Count(T searchValue) {
            int counter=0;
            for(byte row=1; row<=m_Dimension; ++row) {
                for(byte col=1; col<=m_Dimension; ++col) {
                    if(m_Sheet[row-1,col-1].CompareTo(searchValue)==0) {
                        ++counter;
                    }
                }
            }
            return counter;
        }
            ...
    }
}
```

This code works, but there is a subtle problem. The *IComparable* interface manipulates objects, which causes boxing and unboxing when working with value types. This could become expensive in a large collection of value types. In the preceding code, the type argument is an integer, which is a value type. This causes boxing with the *IComparable* interface. Generic interfaces obfuscate this problem. .NET Framework 2.0 includes several general-purpose generic interfaces for developers. This is the class header updated for the *IComparable* generic interface:

```
public class Sheet<T> where T: IComparable<T>
```

Value Type Constraint

A value type constraint restricts a type parameter to a value type. Value types are derived from the *System.ValueType* type. Primitives and structures are examples of value types. The exception is the *Nullable* type. The *Nullable* type is a value type, but it is not allowed with a value type constraint. A value type constraint is a constraint using the *struct* keyword.

The following code demonstrates the value type constraint. The commented source line uses a reference type, which would cause compile errors because of the value type constraint.

```
using System;
using System.Collections;

namespace Donis.CSharpBook{

    public class Starter{
        public static void Main(){
            ZClass<int> obj1=new ZClass<int>();
            // ZClass<XClass> obj2=new ZClass<XClass>(); [illegal]
        }
    }

    public class ZClass<T> where T: struct {

        public void Iterate(T data) {
        }
    }

    public class XClass{
    }
}
```

Reference Type Constraint

A reference type constraint restricts a type parameter to a reference type. Reference types are generally user-defined types, including classes, interfaces, delegates, and array types. A reference type constraint uses the *class* keyword.

The following code has a reference type constraint. Although this code is similar to the code presented in the previous section, a reference type constraint is used instead of a value type constraint. For this reason, the illegal line has moved. You cannot use an integer type with a reference type parameter.

```
using System;
using System.Collections;

namespace Donis.CSharpBook{

    public class Starter{
        public static void Main(){
            // ZClass<int> obj1=new ZClass<int>(); [illegal]
            ZClass<XClass> obj2=new ZClass<XClass>();
```

```
            }
    }

    public class ZClass<T> where T: class {

        public void Iterate(T data) {
        }
    }

    public class XClass{
    }
}
```

Default Constructor Constraint

Will this code compile? It looks fairly innocuous:

```
class ZClass<T> {
    public void MethodA() {
        T obj=new T();
    }
}
```

This code does not compile. The problem is the default constructor. Although prevalent, not every type has a default constructor. A default constructor, or a constructor with no arguments, assigns a default state to an object. The default constructor is called with a parameterless new operator. However, because a default constructor is not guaranteed, the new operator is not universally applicable. Therefore, the new operator is disallowed on type parameters.

The solution is the constructor constraint. The derivation constraint does not help with constructors because derived types do not inherit constructors for the base class. Constructor constraints mandate that a type parameter have a default constructor, which is confirmed at compile time. This allows the new operator to be used with the type parameter. The constructor constraint is added to the *where* clause and is a new operator. When combined with other constraints, the default constructor constraint must be the last item in the constraint list. The constructor constraint applies only to the default constructor. You are still prevented from using constructors with arguments.

Here is sample code of the constructor constraint. The constructor constraint is used on the *ZClass*.

```
using System;

namespace Donis.CSharpBook{

    public class Starter{
        public static void Main(){
            ZClass obj=new ZClass();
            obj.MethodA<XClass>();
        }
    }
}
```

```
public class ZClass {
    public void MethodA<T>()
                where T:XClass, new() {
        Console.WriteLine("ZClass.MethodA");
        T obj=new T();
        obj.MethodB();
    }
}

public class XClass{
    public void MethodB() {
        Console.WriteLine("XClass.MethodB");
    }
}
```

Casting

You may need to a cast a generic type. Since generic types are implicit *System.Object* types, they can always be cast to that type. In addition, generic types can be cast to the derivation constraint, which is also a type. The derivation constraint assures that the generic type is a descendant of the constraint. This assures a safe cast. Finally, generics can be cast to any interface even if the interface is not included in an interface constraint. Since there is no restriction on casting to interfaces, it is not type-safe. For that reason, care should be taken to cast to an implemented interface.

In the following code, *ZClass* is a generic type. It has a single type parameter (*T*) that has three constraints: *YClass* type derivation, *IA* interface derivation, and the constructor constraint. An instance of the *T* parameter is created in the method called *Cast*. The instance is then cast in succession to the *YClass*, *IA*, and *IB* interface. The first two casts work as expected. The third cast fails spectacularly. The type parameter is not related to *IB*. However, the compiler does not notice. Therefore, an exception is raised at run time, which is the worst possible time and underscores the type-unsafe nature of interface cast of generic types.

```
public class ZClass<T> where T:YClass, IA, new() {
    static public void Cast() {
        T obj=new T();
        ((YClass) obj).MethodA();
        ((IA) obj).MethodA();
        ((IB) obj).MethodB();      // kaboom
    }
}

public class YClass : IA {
    public void MethodA() {
        Console.WriteLine("YClass.MethodA");
    }
}
```

Generic type parameters cannot be assigned a null or zero. There is no assurance that a type parameter is either a reference or value type, which prevents safely assigning a null or zero value to a type parameter. However, you can test a type parameter against null but not zero. If the comparison succeeds, the type parameter is a reference type. Otherwise, the type parameter is a value type.

Inheritance

Generic and nongeneric classes can inherit a generic type. In addition, a generic type can be the base class to a generic or nongeneric type. Some basic rules apply. For example, the derived class cannot be a closed constructed type. Table 6-1 lists all the possible permutations.

Table 6-1   Inheritance Table for Generic Types

Base Class	Derived Class	Comments
Generic (open)	Generic (open)	Permitted when the derived class consumes the type parameters of the base class
Generic (open)	Generic (closed)	Not permitted
Generic (open)	Nongeneric	Permitted
Generic (closed)	Generic (open)	Permitted
Generic (closed)	Generic (closed)	Not permitted
Generic (closed)	Nongeneric	Not permitted
Nongeneric	Generic (closed)	Permitted
Nongeneric	Generic (open)	Not permitted

This sample code shows some of the permitted and not permitted combinations:

```
public class ZClass<T> {
}

public class XClass<T> : ZClass<T> {
}

public class BClass<Y> {
}

public class AClass<Z> : BClass<int> {
}

public class YClass: ZClass<int> {
}

/*
public class AClass<Z> : BClass<Y> {     [ illegal ]
}

public class YClass: ZClass<T> {         [ illegal ]
}
*/
```

When inheriting an open constructed type, the constraints of the base class must be repeated in the derived type. Furthermore, the derived type can provide additional constraints on type parameters declared at the base type. This is not applicable to closed constructed types because closed constructed types do not have type parameters or constraints.

Here is sample code combining inheritance of generic types and constraints:

```csharp
public class ZClass<T> where T: IComparable {
}

public class YClass<T> : ZClass<T> where T: IComparable {
}

public class XClass<T> : ZClass<T> where T: IComparable, IDisposable {
}

public class BClass<Y> where Y: IEnumerable {
}

public class AClass<Z> : BClass<int[]> where Z:IDisposable {
}
```

Overriding Methods

Methods that have a type parameter can be overridden, regardless of where the type parameter is declared. These methods can also override other methods. Table 6-2 lists the various combinations of overriding generic and nongeneric methods. If a base class is nongeneric or closed, overriding methods cannot have type parameters. Conversely, if the base class is open, overriding methods can employ type parameters.

Table 6-2   Combination of Overriding Generic Methods

Base Method	Derived Method	Comments
Nongeneric	Generic (open)	Permitted
Nongeneric	Generic (closed)	Permitted
Generic (open)	Nongeneric	Not permitted
Generic (open)	Generic (open)	Permitted; must use the same type parameters
Generic (open)	Generic (closed)	Not permitted
Generic (closed)	Nongeneric	Permitted
Generic (closed)	Generic (closed)	Permitted
Generic (closed)	Generic (open)	Not permitted

Here is some example code:

```csharp
using System;

namespace Donis.CSharpBook{

    public class Starter{
```

```
        public static void Main(){
        }
    }

    public class ZClass<T> {
        public virtual void MethodA(T arg) {
        }
    }

    public class YClass<T>   : ZClass<T>{
        public override void MethodA(T arg) {
        }
//      public override void MethodA(int arg) { [ illegal ]
//      }

    }

    public class XClass<X>   : ZClass<int>{
        public override void MethodA(int arg) {
        }
//      public override void MethodA(X arg) {   [ illegal ]
//      }

    }

    public class WClass: ZClass<int> {
        public override void MethodA(int arg) {
        }
    }
}
```

When a generic method overrides another generic method, it inherits the constraints of that method. The overriding method cannot change the inherited constraints.

The following code correctly overrides a generic method:

```
    public class ZClass {
        public virtual void MethodA<T>(T arg)
            where T: new() {
        }
    }

    public class YClass : ZClass {
        public override void MethodA<T>(T arg) {
            T obj=new T();
        }
    }
```

Nested Types

You can nest a generic type inside a nongeneric type. Conversely, a nongeneric type can be nested in a generic type. More intriguing is nesting generic types inside of generic types. The nested generic type can consume the type parameters of the surrounding type. A type parameter of the surrounding type cannot be redefined as a new type parameter in the nested type. However, the nested generic type can declare entirely new type parameters.

This is sample code of nested generic types:

```
using System;

namespace Donis.CSharpBook{
    public class Starter{
        public static void Main(){
            ZClass<int>.Nested<double> obj=
                new ZClass<int>.Nested<double>();
            obj.MethodA(10, 12.34);
        }
    }

    public class ZClass<T> {
        public void MethodA(T arg) {

        }

        public class Nested<S> {
            public void MethodA(T arg1, S arg2) {
                Console.WriteLine("arg1: {0}",
                    arg1.GetType().ToString());
                Console.WriteLine("arg2: {0}",
                    arg2.GetType().ToString());
            }
        }
    }
}
```

Static Members

Generic types can have static members. If present, a closed constructed type owns a set of any static members. Therefore, there are possibly multiple instances of the static members—one for each closed constructed type. Static members are not referable from the open constructed type. Static members are usually accessed through the class name. With generic types, static members are accessible using the closed constructed type notation. Static constructors, which are called implicitly, initialize the static fields in the context of the current closed constructed type.

This is the constructed type notation:

classname<argumentlist>.staticmember

classname is the name of the generic type; *argumentlist* is a comma-delimited list of type arguments; *staticmember* is the name of the static member.

Static members are frequently used as counters. The following code counts the instances of generic types. There are several generic type instantiations—each using a closed constructed type. The static count is specific to each closed constructed type. The count counts the number of instances of a closed constructed type.

```
using System;

namespace Donis.CSharpBook{
    public class Starter{
        public static void Main(){
            ZClass<int> obj1=new ZClass<int>();
            ZClass<double> obj2=new ZClass<double>();
            ZClass<double> obj3=new ZClass<double>();
            ZClass<int>.Count(obj1);
            ZClass<double>.Count(obj2);
        }
    }

    public class ZClass<T> {

        public ZClass() {
            ++counter;
        }

        public static void Count(ZClass<T> _this) {
            Console.WriteLine("{0} : {1}",
                _this.GetType().ToString(),
                counter.ToString());
        }

        private static int counter=0;
    }

}
```

Several articles describing generics bemoan the extra cost of static fields in generic types. This is a misplaced concern. A generic type often supplants the explicit implementation of separate classes: *StackCircle*, *StackTriangle*, and so on. As separate classes, static members would also be replicated. Alternatively, a general-purpose collection would have a single set of static members but incur other costs, such as boxing and unboxing. From every perspective, the overhead from extra sets of static members from generic types is comparable to or better than any alternate solution.

Operator Functions

You can implement operator functions for generic types. Operator member functions are static members. Therefore, the rules of static members also apply to operator member functions. An operator member function cannot be a generic method. However, the operator member function can use type parameters of the generic type.

An *operator+* has been added to the *Sheet* generic type. It adds two *Sheet* collections. The results of the calculations are placed in a third sheet. Only integral sheets can be added.

Because type parameters cannot be constrained by a value type, a helper function called *Add* is provided:

```
public abstract class AddClass<T> {
    public abstract T Add(T op1, T op2);
}

public class Sheet<T> : AddClass<int> where T: IComparable{
    public Sheet(byte dimension) {
        if(dimension<0) {
            throw new Exception("Invalid dimensions");
        }
        m_Dimension=dimension;
        m_Sheet=new T[dimension, dimension];
        for(byte row=1; row<=dimension; ++row) {
            for(byte col=1; col<=dimension; ++col) {
                m_Sheet[row-1,col-1]=default(T);
            }
        }

    }

    public static Sheet<int> operator+(Sheet<int> sheet1,
        Sheet<T> sheet2)
            {
        byte dimension=Math.Max(sheet1.m_Dimension,
            sheet2.m_Dimension);
      Sheet<int> total=new Sheet<int>(dimension);

        for(byte row=1; row<=dimension; ++row) {
            for(byte col=1; col<=dimension; ++col) {
                total[(byte) row,(byte)col]=
                    sheet1.Add(sheet1[(byte) row,(byte)col],(int)
                    (object) (sheet2[(byte) row,(byte)col]));
            }
        }
        return total;
    }

    public override int Add(int op1, int op2) {
        return op1+op2;
    }
...
```

This is the signature of the *operator+* function in the *Sheet* generic type:

```
public static Sheet<int> operator+(Sheet<int> sheet1,
    Sheet<T> sheet2)
```

An *operator+* is a binary operator with two operands. Notice that one operand is a closed constructed type, whereas the other is an open constructed type. Why? The *operator+* requires that one of the operands be the containing class, which is the open constructed type, so there is a chance of adding incompatible sheets. This explains the cast:

```
(int) (object) (sheet2[(byte) row,(byte)col])
```

sheet2 is the right-hand parameter of the *operator+* function. The unknown type in *sheet2* is being cast back to an integer. If the type is incompatible, an exception is raised at that moment. Exception handling could mitigate this problem. However, to keep the code simple, the problem is left unresolved. This code is meant as demonstration only.

Serialization

Serialization persists the state of an object to a stream. Serializing the instance of a generic type is similar to a regular type. This book does not provide a detailed overview of serialization. This section presents targeted information on serializing generic types.

Serialization is done mostly with the *SerializationInfo* object. For generic types, there are additional overloads of the *SerializationInfo.AddValue* and *SerializationInfo.GetValue* methods for object types. This requires casting to and from object types.

For serialization, the generic type must be adorned with the *Serializable* attribute.

The *GetObjectData* method implements the serialization of an object. This includes serializing both the metadata and instance data of the type. *GetObjectData* has a *SerializationInfo* and *StreamingContext* parameter. The *SerializationInfo.AddValue* method is called to serialize generic type content:

```
public void GetObjectData(SerializationInfo info,
    StreamingContext ctx) {
    info.AddValue("fielda", fielda, typeof(T));
}
```

To deserialize, add a two-argument constructor to the generic type. The arguments are a *SerializationInfo* and *StreamingContext* parameter. Call the *SerializationInfo.GetValue* method to rehydrate the instance:

```
private ZClass(SerializationInfo info,
    StreamingContext ctx) {
    fielda=(T) info.GetValue("fielda", typeof(T));
}
```

Objects can be serialized in different formats, which is accomplished with formatters, such as the *BinaryFormatter* type. The *SoapFormatter* type cannot be used with generic types. Serialization also requires creating an appropriate stream, such as a *FileStream*. The stream is where the instance is serialized or deserialized. Call *BinaryFormatter.Serialize* to serialize a generic type instance. Conversely, call *BinaryFormatter.Deserialize* to deserialize.

The following program accepts a command-line argument. The *Set* command instructs the program to serialize an instance of the *ZClass* generic type to a file. A *Get* command asks the program to deserialize the *ZClass* generic type.

```
using System;
using System.Runtime.Serialization;
```

```csharp
using System.Runtime.Serialization.Formatters.Binary;
using System.IO;

namespace Donis.CSharpBook{

    public class Starter{
        public static void Main(string [] args){
            BinaryFormatter binary=new BinaryFormatter();
            FileStream file=
                new FileStream("data.bin", FileMode.OpenOrCreate);

            if(args[0].ToLower()=="set") {
                ZClass<int> obj=new ZClass<int>(5);
                binary.Serialize(file, obj);
                return;
            }

            if(args[0].ToLower()=="get") {
                ZClass<int> obj=(ZClass<int>)
                    binary.Deserialize(file);
                Console.WriteLine(obj.GetValue());
                return;
            }

        }
    }

    [Serializable] public class ZClass<T> {

        public ZClass(T init) {
            fielda=init;
        }

        public void GetObjectData(SerializationInfo info,
            StreamingContext ctx) {
            info.AddValue("fielda", fielda, typeof(T));
        }

        private ZClass(SerializationInfo info,
            StreamingContext ctx) {
            fielda=(T) info.GetValue("fielda", typeof(T));
        }

        public void SetValue(T data) {
            fielda=data;
        }

        public T GetValue() {
            return fielda;
        }

        private T fielda=default(T);
    }

}
```

Generics Internals

Generics are economical and expeditious, especially when compared with past implementations of parametric polymorphism. The disparity is found in the compile-time and run-time semantics of code expansion in generics. This section focuses on improvement in this area as compared with parameterized types in C++, which has a widely-recognized implementation of parametric polymorphism.

Although an inspection of parameterized templates in C++ might uncover cursory similarities with generics, there are considerable differences between them. These differences make generics more efficient and better-performing than parameterized templates. The exact implementation of templates is specific to each C++ compiler. However, the concepts of parameterized templates are similar in all implementations.

The major difference between generics and parameterized templates is that the latter is purely compile-time based. Instances of parameterized templates expand into separate classes and are inlined at compile time. The Standard Template Library (STL) of C++ offers a stack collection. If ellipse, rectangle, triangle, and curve instances of the stack are defined, the stack template expands into separate classes—one for each type. The expansion occurs at compile time. What happens when two stacks of circles are defined separately? Is there a consolidation of the code? The answer is no, which can lead to significant code bloating.

The compile-time expansion has some shortcomings. This makes the parameterized templates specific to C++. In .NET, generic types expand at run time and are not language-specific. Therefore, generics are available to any managed language. The *Sheet* generic type presented in this chapter is usable in Microsoft Visual Basic .NET. With C++, the particulars of the template, such as the parameterized types, are lost at compile time and not available for later inspection. Managed code, including generics, undergoes two compilations. The first compilation, administered by the language compiler, emits metadata and Microsoft intermediate language (MSIL) code specific to generic types. Because the specifics of the generic type are preserved, it is available for later inspection, such as reflection. There are new metadata and MSIL instructions that target generic types. The second compilation, performed by the just-in-time compiler (jitter), performs the code expansion. The jitter is part of the Common Language Runtime (CLR).

Figure 6-1 shows the MSIL-specific code for a generic type.

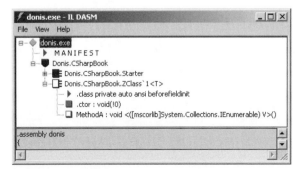

Figure 6-1   MSIL view of a generic type

The CLR performs an intelligent expansion of generic types, unlike C++, which blindly expands parameterized types. Intelligent expansion is conducted differently for value type versus reference type arguments.

When a generic type with a value argument is defined, it is expanded into a class at run time, where the specific type is substituted for the parameter throughout the class. The resulting class is cached in memory. Future instances of the generic type with the same type argument reference the existing class. In this circumstance, there is code sharing between the separate generic type instantiations. Additional class expansion is prevented and unnecessary code bloating is avoided.

If the type argument is a reference type, the CLR conducts intelligent expansion differently. The run time creates a specialized class for the reference type, where *System.Object* is substituted for the parameter. The new class is cached in memory. Future instances of the generic type with any reference type parameter references this same class. Generic type instantiations that have a reference type parameter share the same code.

Look at the following code. How many specialized classes are created at run time?

```
Sheet<int> asheet=new Sheet<int>(2);
Sheet<double> bsheet=new Sheet<double>(5);
Sheet<XClass> csheet=new Sheet<XClass>(2);
Sheet<YClass> dsheet=new Sheet<YClass>(5);
Sheet<int> esheet=new Sheet<int>(3);
```

The preceding code results in three specialized classes. The *Sheet<int>* instantiations share a class. *Sheet<double>* is a separate class. *Sheet<XClass>* and *Sheet<YClass>* also share a class.

Generic Collections

As discussed in the previous chapter, the .NET Framework Class Library includes general-purpose collection classes for commonplace data algorithms, such as a stack, queue, dynamic array, and dictionary. These collections are object-based, which affects performance, hinders type-safeness, and potentially consumes the available memory. The .NET FCL includes parameterized versions of most of the collections.

The parameterized data algorithms are found in the *System.Collections.Generic* namespace. Generic interfaces are also included in the namespace. Table 6-3 lists some of the types and interfaces members of this namespace.

Table 6-3   Generic Types and Interfaces

Description	Type
Dynamic array	*List<T>*
LIFO list	*Stack<T>*
FIFO list	*Queue<T>*
Collection of key/value pairs	*Dictionary<K,V>*

Table 6-3   Generic Types and Interfaces (Continued)

Description	Type
Compares a current and other object	*IComparable<T>*
Compares two objects	*IComparer<T>*
Returns an enumerator	*IEnumerable<T>*
Defines an enumerator	*IEnumerator<T>*

Enumerators

The next chapter pertains to enumerators, a topic that is a natural extension of this chapter. Enumerators are typically used to iterate collections, which have been the focus of the last two chapters. Enumerators are implemented and typically exposed from an enumerable object. Enumerable objects implement the *IEnumerable* interface. The *IEnumerable.GetEnumerator* method returns an enumerator object.

The *foreach* statement is the most visible expression of enumeration in a C# program. The target of the *foreach* statement is not any object—it has to be an enumerable object.

The next chapter documents the enumerator pattern, including how to implement an enumerator and enumerable object.

Chapter 7
Iterators

Stacks, queues, dictionaries, dynamic arrays, normal arrays, and various other collections were introduced in previous chapters. Collections are assemblages of related types. There could be a dynamic array of Employee types, which would include *HourlyEmployee*, *ExemptEmployee*, and *CommissionedEmployee* instances. There could be a queue of bank requests, such as *DepositTransaction*, *WithdrawalTransaction*, and *InterestTransaction* types. Inheritance relates these types at compile time, whereas polymorphism binds them at run time. Collections are also assemblages of similar items. Enumerating the elements of a collection is a recurrent and valuable behavior. Enumeration iterates the items in a collection. A report that lists new employees would need to enumerate the employee collection. Bank statements require enumerating transactions of a particular bank client.

Enumeration is a valuable tool to almost every developer, encouraging some standardization. Enumerable nongeneric types implement the *IEnumerator* and *IEnumerable* interfaces, whereas generic types implement the *IEnumerator<T>* and *IEnumerable<T>* generic interfaces. *IEnumerable* interfaces return unique enumerator objects to clients. An enumerator object implements the *IEnumerator* interface, which defines the behavior of enumeration. Collections are enumerable objects, which implement one of the *IEnumerable* interfaces and adhere to the enumeration pattern.

Collections are usually enumerated in a loop. Most collections offer collection-specific interfaces to enumerate elements. The *ArrayList* type has indexes. The *Stack* has the *Pop* method. *Hashtables* have the *Keys* and *Values* properties. Collections also offer a standardized approach to enumeration with the *IEnumerator* interface. Loops are often harbingers of subtle bugs. The *foreach* statement is a compiler-generated loop that uses *IEnumerator* objects to iterate error-free enumerable collections. This reduces the code required to iterate a collection and makes developer code more robust.

The following is a straightforward *foreach* loop. The *colors* array is an array of strings. Arrays are collections and are therefore enumerable. Instead of writing a *for* loop, with indexes and a counter to manage, the *foreach* loop keeps everything simple. No indexes. No counters. The *foreach* loop automatically enumerates each element of the collection.

```
string [] colors={"red", "green", "blue"};
foreach(string color in colors) {
    Console.WriteLine(color);
}
```

Here is another example of a *foreach* loop. This code manipulates a *Stack* collection—a more complex structure than a simple array. However, stacks are also collections, meaning that the *foreach* statement is available.

```
Stack<int> collection=new Stack<int>();
collection.Push(10);
collection.Push(15);
collection.Push(20);
foreach(int number in collection) {
    Console.WriteLine(number);
}
```

Implementing the *IEnumerator* interface in an enumerable object can be challenging—especially for complex data structures. Iterators have been introduced for this reason. Iterators provide a standardized implementation of the enumerator pattern and prevent individual developers from re-creating the same wheel.

Enumerable Objects

Enumerable objects implement the *IEnumerable* interface. The *GetEnumerator* method is the only member of this interface. It returns an enumerator, which is used to enumerate non-generic collections.

This is the *IEnumerable* interface:

```
public interface IEnumerable {
    IEnumerator GetEnumerator();
}
```

Each invocation of the *GetEnumerator* method returns a unique enumerator. The enumerator is a state machine that minimally maintains a snapshot of the target collection and a cursor. The cursor points to the current item of the collection. The snapshot is a static copy of the collection. What happens if a collection is modified while being enumerated? An exception occurs. You could lock the collection during enumeration, but it might cause substantial performance degradation. As a best practice, an enumerator should capture the collection as a snapshot. This isolates the enumerator from changes to the original collection. In addition, the snapshot collection is read-only. The *GetEnumerator* method should be thread-safe, guaranteeing that a unique enumerator is returned, which references an isolated collection regardless of the thread context.

Enumerators

Enumerators are part of the enumeration pattern and normally implemented as a nested class within the collection type. The primary benefit of nested classes is access to the private members of the outer class. This access allows you to avoid breaking the rules of encapsulation to allow the enumerator class to access the data store of the collection. The data store is undoubtedly a private member of the collection class.

Enumerators implement the *IEnumerator* interface, which has three members. This is the *IEnumerator* interface:

```
public interface IEnumerator {
    object Current {get;}
    bool MoveNext();
    void Reset();
}
```

The *Current* property returns the current element of the collection. *MoveNext* moves the *Current* property to the next element. If the iteration has completed, *MoveNext* returns *false*. Otherwise, *MoveNext* returns *true*. Notice that there is not a *MovePrevious* method; enumeration is forward only. The *Reset* method returns the enumeration to the beginning of the collection.

The enumerator is the state machine representing the enumeration. Part of the state machine is the cursor, which is the collection index or locator. The cursor is not necessarily an integral value, but normally it is. For a link list, the cursor may be a node, which is an object. When the enumerator is created, the cursor initially points before the first element of the collection. Do not access the *Current* property while the cursor is in this initial state. Call *MoveNext* first, which positions the cursor at the first element of the collection.

The following is a typical constructor of an enumerator. In this example, the constructor makes a snapshot of the collection. For reasons of simplicity, the collection is a basic array. The cursor is then set to –1, which is before the first element of the collection.

```
public Enumerator(object [] items) {
   elements=new object[items.Length];
   Array.Copy(items, elements, items.Length);
   cursor=-1;
}
```

The *MoveNext* method increments the value of the cursor. This action moves the *Current* property to the next element of the collection. If the list has been fully iterated, *MoveNext* returns *false*. Collections are not circular, where *MoveNext* might cycle through a collection. Circular collections are not within the enumerator pattern. The *Current* property is not valid after the collection has been fully enumerated. For this reason, do not use the *Current* property after *MoveNext* returns *false*.

Here is one possible implementation of the *MoveNext* method:

```
public bool MoveNext() {
    ++cursor;
    if(cursor>(elements.Length-1)) {
        return false;
    }
    return true;
}
```

The *Reset* method resets the enumeration. The cursor is updated to point to before the collection again. Resetting the cursor also automatically resets the *Current* property.

Here is a *Reset* method:

```
public void Reset() {
    cursor=-1;
}
```

With the cursor as a reference to the current item, the *Current* property provides access to the current element of the collection. The *Current* property must be read-only. Implement the *get* method of the property but not the *set* method. The implementation should check for fence-post errors. If the index is before or after the collection, the appropriate exception should be thrown.

Here is an implementation of the *Current* property:

```
public object Current {
    get {
        if(cursor>(elements.Length-1)) {
            throw new InvalidOperationException(
                "Enumeration already finished");
        }
        if(cursor == -1) {
            throw new InvalidOperationException(
                "Enumeration not started");
        }
        return elements[cursor];
    }
}
```

Enumerator states   Enumerators can be in one of four possible states. Table 7-1 lists the enumerator states.

Table 7-1   Enumerator States

State	Description
Before	This is the state of the enumerator before enumeration has started or after it has been reset. The first call to *MoveNext* changes the state from *Before* to *Running*.
Running	This is the state when *MoveNext* is calculating the next element (*Current*) of the iteration. When *MoveNext* returns *true*, the next element has been enumerated, and the state changes to *Suspended*. If *MoveNext* returns *false*, the state changes to *After*. At that time, the *Current* property is no longer available.
Suspended	The state of the enumerator between enumerations. Calling *MoveNext* changes the state from *Suspended* to *Running* while calculating the next *Current* property.
After	This is the state after enumeration has completed. *Reset* returns the enumeration to *Before*, and enumeration can be restarted.

Enumerator Example

Sample code for an enumerator class and client are provided as follows. This is also the complete listing for some of the partial code presented earlier in this segment. The *SimpleCollection* is a thin wrapper for a basic array. Actually, it is somewhat redundant because arrays are already fully functional collections, including exposing an enumerator. However, this simple example is ideal for demonstrating the enumerator pattern.

The enumerator pattern recommends isolation of the underlying collection. In this code, the enumerator is created as a nested class, in which a snapshot of the collection is made in the constructor. The isolated collection is created from a copy of the array. In addition, the *Current* property is read-only, which prevents changes to the collection data.

In *Main*, an instance of the *SimpleCollection* is created. It is initialized with an integer array. The collection is then iterated using the *IEnumerator* interface.

```
using System;
using System.Collections;

namespace Donis.CSharpBook{

    public class Starter{

        public static void Main(){
            SimpleCollection simple=new SimpleCollection(
                new object[] {1,2,3,4,5,6,7});

            IEnumerator enumerator=simple.GetEnumerator();
            while(enumerator.MoveNext()) {
                Console.WriteLine(enumerator.Current);
            }
        }
    }
```

```csharp
public class SimpleCollection: IEnumerable {

    public SimpleCollection(object [] array) {
        items=array;
    }

    public IEnumerator GetEnumerator() {
        return new Enumerator(items);
    }

    private class Enumerator: IEnumerator {

        public Enumerator(object [] items) {
            elements=new object[items.Length];
            Array.Copy(items, elements, items.Length);
            cursor=-1;
        }

        public bool MoveNext() {
            ++cursor;
            if(cursor>(elements.Length-1)) {
                return false;
            }
            return true;
        }


        public void Reset() {
            cursor=-1;
        }

        public object Current {
            get {
                if(cursor>(elements.Length-1)) {
                    throw new InvalidOperationException(
                        "Enumeration already finished");
                }
                if(cursor == -1) {
                    throw new InvalidOperationException(
                        "Enumeration not started");
                }
                return elements[cursor];
            }
        }

        private int cursor;
        private object [] elements=null;
    }


    private object [] items=null;
    }
}
```

As mentioned, the *SimpleCollection* class makes a copy of the collection in the enumerator. This isolates the collection from contamination caused by modifications. This is the recommended approach for volatile collections. *SimpleCollection* is volatile because the elements of the underlying collection can be modified. If the collection is static, a copy may not be necessary. Isolation protects a collection against changes. If the collection is static, this is not an issue, and isolation is not required.

Enumerator Example (Static Collection)

Here is the *SimpleCollection* class rewritten for a static collection. The underlying collection is read-only, which makes it static. When the enumerator is created, the *this* reference of the enumerable object is passed to the constructor. Future and unique enumerators share this reference to access the same collection—maybe simultaneously. The state machine encapsulates the back reference and a cursor. The back reference is the *this* reference to the outer object. With the back reference, the enumerator gains access to members of the outer class, including the collection, which allows the enumerator to iterate the collection directly.

```
public class SimpleCollection: IEnumerable {

    public SimpleCollection(object [] array) {
        items=array;
    }

    public IEnumerator GetEnumerator() {
        return new Enumerator(this);
    }

    private class Enumerator: IEnumerator {

        public Enumerator(SimpleCollection obj) {
            oThis=obj;
            cursor=-1;
        }

        public bool MoveNext() {
            ++cursor;
            if(cursor>(oThis.items.Length-1)) {
                return false;
            }
            return true;
        }


        public void Reset() {
            cursor=-1;
        }

        public object Current {
            get {
                if(cursor>(oThis.items.Length-1)) {
                    throw new InvalidOperationException(
```

```
                        "Enumeration already finished");
                }
                if(cursor == -1) {
                    throw new InvalidOperationException(
                        "Enumeration not started");
                }
                return oThis.items[cursor];
            }
        }

        private int cursor;
        private SimpleCollection oThis;
    }


    private object [] items=null;
}
```

Collections that have inconstant changes are not ideal for either of the enumerator models presented: contentious or static. Copying the collection per each enumerator is costly when changes are infrequent. The static model is inappropriate because the collection may indeed change, albeit not regularly. A versioned collection is the solution and combines traits of the contentious and static models for implementing enumerators.

Enumerator Example (Versioned Collection)

The following code contains an implementation for a versioned collection. A private field called *version* has been added to the collection class. An indexer has been added to allow clients to modify the collection. The version is incremented whenever the collection is modified. A version number has also been added to the enumerator, which is the nested class. In the constructor, the version is initialized to the version of the outer collection. When the *Current* property is accessed, the version number inside the enumerator is compared to that of the collection. If unequal, the collection has been modified since the enumerator was created and an exception is raised. This is the implementation model of the collections in the .NET Framework class library (FCL), such as the *ArrayList*, *Stack*, *Queue*, and other collection classes.

The *Main* method is changed to test the versioning. The collection is modified in the method after the enumerator has been obtained. After the modification, the *Current* property is used, which causes the expected exception:

```
using System;
using System.Collections;

namespace Donis.CSharpBook{

    public class Starter{

        public static void Main(){
            SimpleCollection simple=new SimpleCollection(
                new object[] {1,2,3,4,5,6,7});
```

```
            IEnumerator enumerator=simple.GetEnumerator();
            enumerator.MoveNext();
            Console.WriteLine(enumerator.Current);
            enumerator.MoveNext();
            simple[4]=10;
            Console.WriteLine(enumerator.Current);   // Exception raised
            enumerator.MoveNext();
        }
    }

    public class SimpleCollection: IEnumerable {

        public SimpleCollection(object [] array) {
            items=array;
            version=1;
        }

        public object this[int index] {
            get {
                return items[index];
            }
            set {
                ++version;
                items[index]=value;
            }
        }

        public IEnumerator GetEnumerator() {
            return new Enumerator(this);
        }

        private class Enumerator: IEnumerator {

            public Enumerator(SimpleCollection obj) {
                oThis=obj;
                cursor=-1;
                version=oThis.version;
            }

            public bool MoveNext() {
                ++cursor;
                if(cursor>(oThis.items.Length-1)) {
                    return false;
                }
                return true;
            }


            public void Reset() {
                cursor=-1;
            }

            public object Current {
                get {
                    if(oThis.version != version) {
```

```
                    throw new InvalidOperationException(
                        "Collection was modified");
                }

                if(cursor>(oThis.items.Length-1)) {
                    throw new InvalidOperationException(
                        "Enumeration already finished");
                }
                if(cursor == -1) {
                    throw new InvalidOperationException(
                        "Enumeration not started");
                }
                return oThis.items[cursor];
            }
        }

        private int version;
        private int cursor;
        private SimpleCollection oThis;
    }


    private object [] items=null;
    private int version;
    }
}
```

IEnumerator Problem

Several techniques to implement the enumerator pattern have been shown. The varied strategies share common problems. Enumerators, which implement the *IEnumerator* interface,
manipulate *System.Object* types. This is the heart of the problem.

- There is a performance penalty from boxing and unboxing value types.

- Alternatively, there is a performance cost to downcasting to reference types.

- Frequent boxing stresses the managed heap.

- Casting to and from *System.Object* is required, which is not type-safe.

These problems were identified in the previous chapter. The solution was generic types. That
is the solution here also. The .NET Framework offers generic versions of the *IEnumerable* and
IEnumerator interfaces.

Generic Enumerators

Nongeneric enumerable objects and enumerators are oblique. There is a lack of type specialty,
which leads to performance problems and other issues. You can implement enumerable
objects and enumerators using generic interfaces, which avoid some of the problems mentioned earlier. Implement the *IEnumerable<T>* interface for generic enumerable objects. For

generic enumerator objects, implement the *IEnumerator<T>* interface. Both *IEnumerable<T>* and *IEnumerator<T>* are generic interfaces found in the .NET FCL in the *System.Collections .Generic* namespace. *IEnumerable<T>* and *IEnumerator<T>* inherit their nongeneric counterparts *IEnumerable* and *IEnumerator*, respectively. This means that generic enumerable objects and enumerators are available generically or nongenerically.

IEnumerable<T> Interface

Generic enumerable objects implement the *IEnumerable<T>* interface. This is the *IEnumerable<T>* interface:

```
public interface IEnumerable<T> : IEnumerable {
    IEnumerator<T> GetEnumerator();
}
```

As shown, *IEnumerable<T>* inherits *IEnumerable*, which is the nongeneric version of the same interface. This includes a nongeneric version of the *GetEnumerator* method. Enumerators inheriting *IEnumerable<T>* must therefore implement a generic and nongeneric *GetEnumerator* method. The two *GetEnumerator* methods differ in return type only. As you know, the return type alone is insufficient for overloading a method. To prevent ambiguousness, one of the *GetEnumerator* methods must have explicit interface member implementation.

This is sample code of the *GetEnumerator* methods for a generic enumerable object. (The nongeneric version of *GetEnumerator* is implemented explicitly.)

```
public IEnumerator<T> GetEnumerator() {
    return new Enumerator<T>(this);
}

IEnumerator IEnumerable.GetEnumerator() {
    return new Enumerator<T>(this);
}
```

The generic version of *GetEnumerator* naturally returns a generic enumerator, which implements the *IEnumerator<T> interface*.

IEnumerator<T> Interface

Generic enumerators implement the *IEnumerator<T>* interface, shown here:

```
public interface IEnumerator<T>: IDisposable, IEnumerator {
    T Current {get;}
}
```

Current is a read-only property and is the only direct member of the *IEnumerator<T>* generic interface. The remaining members are inherited from the *IDisposable* and *IEnumerator* interfaces. The *IDisposable* interface defines generic enumerators as disposable. This requires implementing the *IDisposable.Dispose* method. The *IEnumerator* interface adds the nongeneric enumerator interface. The *MoveNext* and *Reset* methods do not require a generic implementation and are therefore not defined in the generic portion of the interface. A second *Current* property, a nongeneric version, is inherited from the *IEnumerable* interface. Therefore, *IEnumerator* has overloaded *Current* properties, where both should be implemented in the enumerator.

This is sample code of a generic and nongeneric implementation of the *Current* property. The nongeneric *Current* property delegates to the generic version.

```
public __T Current {
    get {
        if(oThis.version != version) {
            throw new InvalidOperationException(
                "Collection was modified");
        }

        if(cursor>(oThis.items.Length-1)) {
            throw new InvalidOperationException(
                "Enumeration already finished");
        }
        if(cursor == -1) {
            throw new InvalidOperationException(
                "Enumeration not started");
        }
        return oThis.items[cursor];
    }
}

object IEnumerator.Current {
    get {
        return Current;
    }
}
```

The *Dispose* method supports deterministic garbage collection. This method is called explicitly to clean up for an object. In this circumstance, the method is called to clean up resources assigned to an enumerator. *Dispose* methods of enumerators are most frequently called by iterators, which is the next topic of this chapter. In the *Dispose* method, set the state of the enumeration to *After* and perform any necessary cleanup. Some enumerators track the state using a flag (an enumeration type), where the flag is updated in the *Dispose* method and elsewhere in the enumerator. The code presented earlier does not employ a state flag. If the cursor is beyond the collection, the *After* state is assumed. Conversely, a cursor of −1 indicates the *Before* state. Based on these assumptions, this is one implementation of a *Dispose* method for an enumerator:

```
public void Dispose() {
    cursor=oThis.items.Length+1;
}
```

Generic Enumerator Example (Versioned Collection)

Earlier in the chapter, a version collection model of enumeration was presented. Here is the versioned collection example redone with generic interfaces. The following code also completes some of the partial code presented earlier in this section. In *Main*, the collection is enumerated in a generic and nongeneric manner. In the second *foreach* loop, the simple collection is cast to the nongeneric *IEnumerable* interface. This instructs the *foreach* statement to call the nongeneric *GetEnumerator* method, which returns a nongeneric enumerator. The nongeneric enumerator is then used to iterate the simple collection.

Here is the sample code:

```csharp
using System;
using System.Collections;
using System.Collections.Generic;

namespace Donis.CSharpBook{

    public class Starter{

        public static void Main(){
            SimpleCollection<int> simple=
                new SimpleCollection<int>(
                new int [] {1,2,3,4,5,6,7});

            foreach(int number in simple) {
                Console.WriteLine(number);
            }

            foreach(int number in
                (IEnumerable) simple) {
                Console.WriteLine(number);
            }
        }
    }

    public class SimpleCollection<T>: IEnumerable<T> {

        public SimpleCollection(T[] array) {
            items=array;
            version=1;
        }

        public T this[int index] {
            get {
                return items[index];
            }
            set {
                ++version;
                items[index]=value;
            }
        }
```

```csharp
        public IEnumerator<T> GetEnumerator() {
            Console.WriteLine(
                "IEnumerator<T> GetEnumerator()");
            return new Enumerator<T>(this);
        }

        IEnumerator IEnumerable.GetEnumerator() {
            Console.WriteLine(
                "IEnumerator GetEnumerator()");
            return new Enumerator<T>(this);
        }

        private class Enumerator<__T>: IEnumerator<__T>

        {

            public Enumerator(SimpleCollection<__T> obj) {
                oThis=obj;
                cursor=-1;
                version=oThis.version;
            }

            public __T Current {
                get {
                    if(oThis.version != version) {
                        throw new InvalidOperationException(
                            "Collection was modified");
                    }

                    if(cursor>(oThis.items.Length-1)) {
                        throw new InvalidOperationException(
                            "Enumeration already finished");
                    }
                    if(cursor == -1) {
                        throw new InvalidOperationException(
                            "Enumeration not started");
                    }
                    return oThis.items[cursor];
                }
            }

            public void Dispose() {
                cursor=oThis.items.Length+1;
            }

            public bool MoveNext() {
                ++cursor;
                if(cursor>(oThis.items.Length-1)) {
                    return false;
                }
                return true;
            }
```

```
        public void Reset() {
            cursor=-1;
        }

        object IEnumerator.Current {
            get {
                return Current;
            }
        }

        private int version;
        private int cursor;
        private SimpleCollection<__T> oThis;
    }


    private T [] items=null;
    private int version;
    }
}
```

Iterators

Iterators implement the enumerator pattern. This chapter has demonstrated different implementation strategies for enumerators. The chosen implementation depends on the answer to
relevant questions. Should the enumerator be implemented as a nested class? Should a version collection be used? Should the implementation be generic or nongeneric? Having every
developer answer these questions and author a proprietary enumerator is not a productive
use of their collective mental prowess. Almost assuredly, the various implementations of the
enumerator pattern are within an acceptable delta in performance and memory requirements.
Anyway, a certain number of developers simply visit the MSDN Web site, from which they
copy and paste the enumerator implementation. Therefore, the various implementations are
undoubtedly quite similar. Iterators standardize the enumerator pattern for developers.

When implementing enumerators ourselves, the real challenge is complex enumerations. As
shown, forward iterations are usually straightforward. Reverse iterations are more complex,
however. Coding an enumerator to iterate a sparse collection, nodal list, or binary tree can also
be daunting. What about enumerating a temporary collection? This often requires maintaining multiple enumerators, such as a forward and reverse enumerator. Does this sound like
fun? Actually, I would gladly pass the baton to the compiler.

.NET 2.0 introduced the iterator, which is a compiler-manifested enumerator. When the enumerable object calls *GetEnumerator*, either directly or indirectly, the compiler generates and
returns an appropriate iterator object. Optionally, the iterator can be a combined enumerable
and enumerator object. You are not completely excluded from the process. Developers can
affect the enumeration in an iterator block. The essential ingredient of an iterator block is the
yield statement.

Yield Statement

The following code demonstrates one of the obvious benefits of the *yield* statement and an iterator block: brevity. The previous sample code of a generic enumerator required more than 50 lines of code. The following example implements a similar enumerator using the *yield* statement, which requires three lines of code:

```
public IEnumerator<T> GetEnumerator() {
    foreach(T item in items) {
        yield return item;
    }
}
```

In the previous code, the C# compiler implements the enumerator. You are still coding the *IEnumerable* interface. Optionally, the compiler can implement both the enumerable and enumerator object in the iterator. If the iterator block returns *IEnumerable*, the compiler responds by creating an enumerable and enumerator object. Iterator blocks are explained soon. This removes even having to implement the *GetEnumerator* method.

```
public IEnumerable<T> MethodA() {
    foreach(T item in items) {
        yield return item;
    }
}
```

For clients, iterators are similar to enumerators. Clients call *GetEnumerator* or other iterator methods to obtain an iterator object. You then use the *IEnumerator* or *IEnumerator<T>* interface to enumerate the collection. There is one big difference between iterators and enumerators: Iterators do not implement the *Reset* method. Calling the *Reset* method on an iterator causes an exception.

The pivotal statement of an iterator is *yield*. This is the syntax of the *yield* statement:

yield return *expression*;

yield break;

The *yield return* statements iterate the next element of a collection. The statement expression is assigned to the *Current* property. Enumerators start in the *Before* state. The initial *MoveNext* method calls the first *yield* statement. After the *Current* property is set, the enumerator is suspended. The next *MoveNext* calls the next *yield*. This pattern continues until the enumeration is finished. The iterator block is not called anew for each *MoveNext*. Between *yield* statements of the same iterator block, enumeration is suspended. The iterator is a state machine that maintains the state of the enumeration between calls to the *MoveNext* method.

The *yield break* statements finish an enumeration, which ultimately changes the enumerator state to after. The *Dispose* method is then called to clean up the enumerator. This is sample code of the *yield break* statement. The *yield break* statement stops the enumeration after the fourth element.

```
public IEnumerator<T> GetEnumerator() {
    int count=0;
    foreach(T item in items) {
        ++count;
        yield return item;
        if(count==4) {
            yield break;
        }
    }
}
```

Iterator Blocks

Iterator blocks contain the logic to enumerate a collection. This includes one or more *yield* statements. Methods, properties, and operator functions can be iterator blocks. Iterator blocks are not executed continuously and are sometimes suspended. The function is suspended between successive *yield* statements, which are controlled by the *MoveNext* method. As mentioned, the iterator block maintains the state machine of the enumerator between iterations.

There are restrictions on iterator blocks. For example, iterator blocks cannot have a *return* statement. Only *yield return* statements are allowed:

```
public IEnumerator<T> GetEnumerator() {
    foreach(T item in items) {
        yield return item;
        return;  // not allowed
    }
}
```

There are several other restrictions on iterator blocks:

- Iterator blocks can be contained only in method, operator, or property functions.

- Iterator blocks cannot be in anonymous methods.

- Iterator blocks cannot be contained in a *try* with a *catch* handler.

- Iterator blocks cannot be placed in a *finally* block.

Functions with iterators or iterator methods also have certain restrictions:

- Iterator methods must return a generic or nongeneric *IEnumerable* or *IEnumerator* interface.

- Iterator methods cannot have *ref* parameters.

- Iterator methods cannot have *out* parameters.

- Iterator methods cannot be unsafe.

When an iterator block is exited, the *Dispose* method of the enumerator is called. Internally, the iterator creates the enumerator in a *using* block. This provides an opportunity to clean up for the enumerator when the enumeration is completed.

Iterator Internals

Iterators are implemented as nested classes, which are created by the C# compiler. The nested class maintains the state of the current enumeration. It persists the enumeration state between *yield* statements. Iterators are created by the language compiler, not by the Common Language Runtime (CLR). Neither Microsoft intermediate language (MSIL) nor metadata has changed to especially accommodate iterators. The nested class for an enumerator is a normal class, which is created for a method that contains an iterator block. If three methods within a class have enumerator blocks, the compiler adds three nested classes to that class.

This is how the nested class is named:

<membername>uniqueid<T>

<membername>uniqueid

If the iterator method returns either the *IEnumerator<T>* or *IEnumerable<T>* interfaces, the name of the nested class has the *<T>* suffix.

In this code, *ZClass* has multiple iterator methods:

```
public class ZClass {

    public IEnumerator GetEnumerator() {
       int [] array=new int [] {1,2,3,4};
       int count=0;
        for(count=0;count<4;++count){
            yield return array[count];
        }
    }
    public IEnumerator MethodA() {
        int [] array=new int [] {1,2,3,4};
        int count=0;
        for(count=0;count<4;++count){
            yield return array[count];
        }
    }

    public IEnumerable<T> MethodB<T>() {
        T local=default(T);
        yield return local;
    }

}
```

The compiler adds three nested classes, one for each enumerator method, to the *ZClass* type. The various nested classes represent the state machine for different enumerators. Figure 7-1 shows *ZClass* and the nested classes.

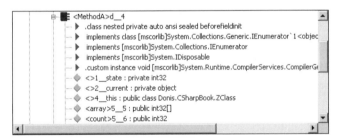

```
☐··◆ internals.exe
   ··▶ M A N I F E S T
 ☐··▮ Donis.CSharpBook
   ☐··▤ Donis.CSharpBook.Starter
   ☐··▤ Donis.CSharpBook.ZClass
      ····▶ .class public auto ansi beforefieldinit
      ☐··▤ <GetEnumerator>d__0
      ☐··▤ <MethodA>d__4
      ☐··▭ <MethodB>d__8`1<T>
      ····▮ .ctor : void()
      ····▮ GetEnumerator : class [mscorlib]System.Collections.IEnumerator()
      ····▮ MethodA : class [mscorlib]System.Collections.IEnumerator()
      ····▭ MethodB : class [mscorlib]System.Collections.Generic.IEnumerable`1<!!T> <T>()
   ☐··▤ <PrivateImplementationDetails>{58DB5763-6927-4528-9E01-306AF12018E2}
```

Figure 7-1   A view of the *ZClass* type, which includes the nested enumerator classes

The nested enumerator class has several private fields. The local variables of the iterator method are lifted to fields of the nested class. The fields maintain the state of these local variables throughout the enumeration. The nested class also has three special purpose fields. The state of the enumeration, such as running or after, is in the <>1__state field. The <>2__current field is the result of the last iteration. It is the current item. The <4>__field is a back pointer to the outer class. If the iterator method is static, the back pointer is not initialized; it is initialized only for instance methods. Combined, the lifted and specialty fields are the state of the enumeration.

Figure 7-2 shows the fields of a typical nested class for an enumerator.

```
☐··▤ <MethodA>d__4                                                    ▲
   ····▶ .class nested private auto ansi sealed beforefieldinit
   ····▶ implements class [mscorlib]System.Collections.Generic.IEnumerator`1<objec
   ····▶ implements [mscorlib]System.Collections.IEnumerator
   ····▶ implements [mscorlib]System.IDisposable
   ····▶ .custom instance void [mscorlib]System.Runtime.CompilerServices.CompilerGe
   ····◆ <>1__state : private int32
   ····◆ <>2__current : private object
   ····◆ <>4__this : public class Donis.CSharpBook.ZClass
   ····◆ <array>5__5 : public int32[]
   ····◆ <count>5__6 : public int32                                     ▼
```

Figure 7-2   A view of a nested class and fields

Iterator Examples

This section presents several examples of iterators to demonstrate the flexibility of iterators and provide techniques for using them.

Dual iteration   The first example iterates two collections simultaneously:

```
using System;
using System.Collections.Generic;
```

```
namespace Donis.CSharpBook{
    public class Starter{
        public static void Main(){
            ZClass obj=new ZClass();
            foreach(int item in obj) {
                Console.Write(item);
             }
        }
    }

    public class ZClass {

        private int [] list1=new int [] {0,2,4,6,8};
        private int [] list2=new int [] {1,3,5,7,9};

        public IEnumerator<int> GetEnumerator() {
            for(int index=0; index<4; ++index) {
                yield return list1[index];
                yield return list2[index];
            }
        }

    }
}
```

The preceding code alternates between yielding *list1* and *list2*. As the iteration moves between collections, the even and odd numbers are intermixed. The result is 0123456789. *ZClass* does not inherit the *IEnumerable* interface. However, it adheres to the enumerator pattern by implementing the *GetEnumerator* method. This is sufficient for defining enumerable objects. The following examples implement the iteration pattern but not explicitly the interfaces.

Reverse iteration   The following example iterates a collection forward and reverse. Two iterators are exposed for this reason. *GetEnumerator* exposes the standard forward iterator. The reverse iterator is implemented in the *Reverse* property. Because the property returns *IEnumerable*, the *Reverse* property is both an enumerable and enumerator object. When an iterator method returns *IEnumerable*, the nested class generated by the compiler is implemented as both an enumerable and enumerator object. In *Main*, there are two *foreach* loops: The first *foreach* loop uses the forward iterator, whereas the reverse iterator is requested in the second loop:

```
using System;
using System.Collections.Generic;

namespace Donis.CSharpBook{
    public class Starter{
        public static void Main(){
            Console.WriteLine("Forward List");
            ZClass obj=new ZClass();
            foreach(int item in obj) {
                Console.Write(item);
            }
```

```
            Console.WriteLine("\nReverse List");
            foreach(int item in obj.Reverse) {
                Console.Write(item);
            }
        }
    }

    public class ZClass {

        private int [] list1=new int [] {0,2,4,6,8};

        public IEnumerator<int> GetEnumerator() {
            for(int index=0; index<5; ++index) {
                yield return list1[index];
            }
        }

        public IEnumerable<int> Reverse {
            get {
                for(int index=4; index>=0; --index) {
                    yield return list1[index];
                }
            }
        }

    }
}
```

Temporary collections   Temporary collections are calculated at run time and are useful in a variety of circumstances. The list of prime numbers, the records of a file, and fields in a dataset are examples of collections that can be calculated. Temporary collections can be populated lazily. You can read a flat file or dataset on demand at run time to hydrate a temporary collection.

The following code enumerates days from the current date until the end of the month, which is calculated using *DateTime* structure. The method *ToEndOfMonth* is enumerable by virtue of returning the *IEnumerable* interface and possessing a *yield* statement. Each repeat of the *while* loop extrapolates the next day until the end of the month is reached. The *yield* statement iterates the days as they are calculated.

```
using System;
using System.Collections;

namespace Donis.CSharpBook{
    public class Starter{
        public static void Main(){
            foreach(string day in ToEndOfMonth()) {
                Console.WriteLine(day);
            }
        }

        public static IEnumerable ToEndOfMonth() {
            DateTime date=DateTime.Now;
```

```
            int currMonth=date.Month;
            while(currMonth==date.Month) {
                string temp=currMonth.ToString()+
                    "/"+date.Day.ToString();
                date=date.AddDays(1);
                yield return temp;
            }
        }
    }
}
```

Complex iteration   Link lists are complex data structures. Iterators are particularly useful when iterating complex data structures, such as a link list. Each item in the list is considered a node. Nodes maintain a reference to the previous and next node. From any node, you can walk the link list either forward or backward. For several reasons, the iteration is more complex. First, data structure must be iterated forward and backward during the same iteration. Second, fence posts are not as definable. Fence posts in arrays, stacks, queues, and other sequenced containers are easily found, which helps avoid fence post error exceptions. Finally, the iteration can start from any node in the link list, not necessarily just the beginning or end of the list.

Below is a partial listing of the *Node* class. The key code is in the *GetEnumerator* method. In the first *while* loop, the link list is iterating in reverse–from the current node to the beginning of list. This is accomplished by walking the *prevNode* member of the node class. The current node is enumerated next. Finally, the second *while* loop iterates the link list going forward from the current note to the end of the list. The *nextNode* members are walked.

```
public class Node<T> {

    public Node(Node<T> node, T data) {
        m_Info=data;
        if(node==null) {
           if(firstNode != null) {
                Node<T> temp=firstNode;
                this.nextNode=temp;
                temp.prevNode=this;
                firstNode=this;
                return;
           }
           prevNode=null;
           nextNode=null;
           firstNode=this;
           return;
        }

        this.prevNode=node;
        this.nextNode=node.nextNode;
        node.nextNode=this;
        if(node.nextNode==null) {
            lastNode=null;
        }
    }
```

```
public void AddNode(T data) {
    this.nextNode=new Node<T>(this, data);
}

public IEnumerator<T> GetEnumerator () {
    Node<T> temp=prevNode;
  while(temp!=null) {
        yield return temp.m_Info;
        temp=temp.prevNode;
    }
    yield return m_Info;
    temp=nextNode;
     while(temp!=null) {
        yield return temp.m_Info;
        temp=temp.nextNode;
    }
}

private T m_Info;
private static Node<T> lastNode=null;
private static Node<T> firstNode=null;
private Node<T> prevNode=null;
private Node<T> nextNode=null;

}
```

Delegates and Events

The next chapter pertains to delegates and events, which are related topics. Function pointers are prevalent in unmanaged programming languages and helpful in streamlining algorithms. As function pointers, functions can be treated as local variables, function parameters, or even function returns—which adds considerable flexibility in the way functions are managed and called. Because pointers are simply pointers into raw memory, function pointers can be unsafe. .NET offers a type-safe version of function pointers called delegates. Delegates provide the same flexibility as function pointers but in a type-safe manner.

Delegates are frequently used as callbacks, in which a function is called upon something happening. The Event model promotes an effective paradigm for callbacks, where there are publishers and subscribers. Publishers expose something that happens—better known as an event. Subscribers subscribe to an event with a delegate. The delegates of the subscriber are called when the event occurs.

Part III
More C# Language

Chapter 8
Delegates and Events

Function pointers are indirect references to functions and support calling functions through variables. With function pointers, you can pass a function as a parameter to a function or as a return type. Function pointers are an important ingredient of many programming languages, including C, C++, and Microsoft Visual Basic. Function pointers can make applications more flexible, extensible, and scalable. Function pointers have been the source of many application bugs, however, because function pointers point to raw bytes of memory. Function pointers are not type-safe, and calling an incompatible method through a function pointer is an infrequent error. .NET has delegates that are essentially type-safe function pointers. Unlike function pointers in other languages, particularly C and C++, delegates are type-safe, object-oriented, and secure. This reduces common problems associated with using function pointers.

A *delegate* is an abstraction of one or more function pointers. Delegates are derived from *System.MulticastDelegate*, which is a reference type. *System.MulticastDelegate* is derived from *System.Delegate*. The delegate classes offer a public interface for initializing, adding, removing, and invoking delegates. An instance of a delegate is an object that abstracts the semantics of a function pointer. The object encapsulates a function pointer and a target object. When a delegate is invoked, the delegate calls the function on that object.

Delegates have a signature and a return type. A function pointer dropped into the delegate must have a compatible signature, which makes the function pointer type-safe. The return type should also match. Delegate covariance, which is discussed later in the chapter, provides some flexibility with the signature. You assign function pointers to delegates based on signature, not type. Regardless of the object or type that binds the function, it is assignable to a delegate of the same signature.

Functions called with a delegate are given the security context of the caller, which prevents a delegate from performing a task not available to a lower-privilege caller. Delegates can be initialized with pointers to functions that are implemented anywhere. The only limitation is the signature. Callers need to be careful when invoking delegates containing function pointers to unknown sources, where there could be unexpected implementation. Use code access security to protect delegates.

Delegates are useful as general function pointers, callbacks, events, and threads. As a general function pointer, a delegate can be a method parameter, function return, class member, or local variable. Callbacks are valuable in many scenarios, including promoting peer-to-peer relationships, in which objects swap function pointers to send bilateral messages. Events support a publisher/subscriber model. The publisher notifies subscribers of events, whereas the subscriber registers functions to be called when the event occurs. Finally, a delegate is a path of execution for a thread, which is an asynchronous function call. This chapter focuses on general function pointers, callbacks, and events. Threads are discussed only in this context.

Many .NET applications are event-driven. Event-driven architecture is common in the .NET environment with Microsoft Windows Forms, ASP.NET, and XML Web Service applications. The lifetime of an event-driven application is spent waiting for events to handle, such as a paint event for Windows Forms, a page load event in an ASP.NET application, or a session event in an XML Web Service application. Although procedural applications execute linearly, event-driven code runs disjointedly. The sequence of code in an event-driven application is determined at run time from the user interface and other input sources. Poorly designed or implemented procedural code is commonly referred to as spaghetti code. Poorly implemented code for an event-driven application is called ravioli code and it can literally run in circles. The randomness of an event-driven application makes poorly written code harder to maintain and debug.

Events are the most practical application of delegates. Events mark an occurrence as defined by an application. For proper application design, events in an application should mirror events in the problem domain. Events represent a wide variety of actions and include predefined and custom events. Predefined events include button click, page load, timer, unhandled exception, and so on. Custom events include events for monitoring hardware devices, starting and stopping communications, overdrawing a checking account, setting alarms, and so on.

The event model includes subscribers and publishers: A publisher is an object or type that exposes an event; a subscriber registers for an event with a delegate. The delegate contains the response to the event. When an event is raised, publishers invoke the delegates of any subscribers. The Observer pattern, which includes the event patterns, documents the best practices of an event-driven environment. Use the following link to view the Observer pattern on the Microsoft Developer Network (MSDN): *http://msdn.microsoft.com/library/default .asp?url=/library/en-us/dnbda/html/observerpattern.asp.*

Delegates

The common blueprint for using delegates includes steps to define, create, and invoke a delegate.

1.   Define a classification of a delegate using the delegate keyword:

```
public delegate int DelegateClass(string info);
```

2. Create an instance of a delegate using the new keyword. In the constructor, initialize the delegate with a function pointer. You can also create and initialize a delegate implicitly without the new keyword:

```
DelegateClass obj=new DelegateClass(MethodA);
DelegateClass obj2=MethodA; // implicit
```

3. Invoke the delegate with the call operator "( )". The call operator is convenient, but makes it harder to discern a delegate invocation from a regular function call. Alternatively, invoke the delegate with the *Invoke* method, which clearly distinguishes invoking a delegate from a normal function call:

```
obj("1");
obj.Invoke("2"); // Alternative.
```

4. As with any object, when the delegate is no longer needed, set the delegate to null:

```
obj=null;
```

The complete list of the example application follows:

```
using System;

namespace Donis.CSharpBook{

 public delegate int DelegateClass(string info);

     public class Steps{

         public static void Main(){
             DelegateClass obj=new DelegateClass(MethodA);
             DelegateClass obj2=MethodA; // implicit
             obj("1");
             obj.Invoke("2"); // Alternative
             obj=null;
             obj2=null;
         }

         public static int MethodA(string info) {
             Console.WriteLine("Steps.MethodA");
             return int.Parse(info);
         }
     }
}
```

Define a Delegate

The delegate keyword is for defining new delegates. The delegate statement looks like a function signature. Rather, it defines a new delegate type. Function pointers matching the delegate signature and return type can be stored into the delegate. Therefore, only functions with similar signatures can be called through the delegate. This code defines a new delegate, which internally becomes a class named *DelegateClass*:

```
public delegate int DelegateClass(string info);
```

This is the syntax for defining a new delegate class:

accessibility delegate *return delegatename(parameterslist)*

Accessibility is limited to the valid accessibility of classes, such as public or private. The remainder of the syntax defines the signature and return type of the delegate. *delegatename* is the name of the delegate classification.

Because defining a delegate creates a new class, delegates can be defined anywhere a class is appropriate. A delegate can be defined in a namespace as a namespace member and within a class as a nested class, but not as a class field or a local variable within a method.

Create a Delegate

As a class, use the new keyword to create an instance of a delegate. As mentioned, delegates are derived from the *System.MulticastDelegate* reference type. Multicast delegates are repositories of zero or more function pointers. The list of pointers in a multicast delegate is called the invocation list. When a delegate hosts multiple function pointers, the functions are called on a first-in, first-out (FIFO) basis.

The delegate constructor is not overloaded and has a single parameter, which is the target method. For an instance method, use the *object.method* format. If static, use the *class.method* format. If the method and delegate are contained in the same class, neither the object nor class name is required. The following code initializes a delegate in a variety of ways:

```
using System;

namespace Donis.CSharpBook{

    public delegate void DelegateClass();

    public class Constructors{

    public static void Main(){
        DelegateClass del1=new
            DelegateClass(Constructors.MethodA);
        DelegateClass del2=new DelegateClass(MethodA);

        ZClass obj=new ZClass();
        DelegateClass del3=new DelegateClass(obj.MethodB);
    }

    public static void MethodA() {
    }
}
```

```
    public class ZClass {

        public void MethodB() {
        }
    }
}
```

You can assign a function pointer directly to a delegate and omit the new operator, which is called delegate inference. Delegate inference infers a delegate signature from the function pointer, creates a new delegate, initializes the source delegate with the function pointer in the constructor, and assigns the source delegate to the target delegate. The source delegate and the target delegate should have compatible signatures. Although the code is more concise, the intent is not as obvious. Here is the previous code, changed for delegate inference:

```
DelegateClass del1=Constructors.MethodA;
DelegateClass del2=MethodA;

ZClass obj=new ZClass();
DelegateClass del3=obj.MethodB;
```

The signatures of delegates are not entirely rigid. Through contravariance and covariance, there is some flexibility. The signature of the function pointer does not have to match the delegate signature exactly.

Contravariance and Covariance

When are delegates compatible or similar? The parameters of the function pointer can be derivations of the parameters indicated in the delegate signature—this is called *contravariance*. Because the delegate parameters refine that of the function pointer, any input from the target method is acceptable to the delegate. Conversely, the return type of the delegate must be a derivation of the return type of the function pointer. The return of the function pointer can refine the return of the delegate. Therefore, any return from the delegate is compatible with that of the function pointer—this is called *covariance*. Contravariance and covariance expand the set of methods assignable to a delegate while maintaining type-safeness. Here is an example of both contravariance and covariance:

```
using System;

namespace Donis.CSharpBook{
    delegate ZClass DelegateClass(BClass obj);
    public class Starter{
        public static void Main(){
            DelegateClass del=MethodA;
        }

        public static YClass MethodA(AClass obj) {
            return null;
        }
    }
```

```
public class ZClass {
}

public class YClass: ZClass {
}

public class AClass {
}

public class BClass: AClass {
}
}
```

In the preceding code, this is the signature of the delegate:

```
delegate ZClass DelegateClass(BClass obj);
```

This is the signature of the function pointer:

```
public static YClass MethodA(AClass obj)
```

The signature of the delegate and function pointer are not exactly the same. This is okay because the parameter of the delegate (*BClass*) refines the parameter of the function (*AClass*), which is contravariance. In addition, the return type of the function (*YClass*) refines the return type of the delegate (*ZClass*). This is covariance.

Invoking a Delegate

Delegates are invoked through the call operator or the *Invoke* method. The C# compiler translates the call operator into an invocation of the *Invoke* method, which has the same signature as the delegate and calls the function pointers contained in the delegate. The parameters of the delegate become the parameters and input to the function calls. If the delegate contains a function pointer, the return from that function becomes the return of the delegate. When multiple function pointers are stored in the delegate, the return of the last function becomes the return of the delegate.

Arrays of Delegates

Arrays of delegates can be the impetus of elegant solutions that would otherwise be unavailable. Creating an array of delegates is the same as creating an array of any type. Selecting from a set of tasks at run time is an example of when an array of delegates is essential to an elegant solution. The switch statement is one solution, in which each case of the switch statement is assigned to a task. Suppose that there are about three lines of code associated with each task. In the next revision of the application, 30 additional tasks are added, which results in an additional 90 lines of code. This solution provides linear growth and is not particularly scalable. With an array of delegates, regardless of the number of tasks, the solution is one line of code. Now and in the future, this solution remains one line of code. This solution is more scalable than the switch statement approach. In the following code, an array of delegates facilitates invoking a task from a menu of choices:

```csharp
using System;

namespace Donis.CSharpBook{

    public delegate void Task();

    public class Starter{

        public static void Main(){
            // array of delegates
            Task [] tasks={MethodA, MethodB, MethodC};
            string resp;
            do {
                Console.WriteLine("TaskA - 1");
                Console.WriteLine("TaskB - 2");
                Console.WriteLine("TaskC - 3");
                Console.WriteLine("Exit - x");
                resp=Console.ReadLine();
                if(resp.ToUpper()=="X") {
                    break;
                }
                try {
                    int choice=int.Parse(resp)-1;
                    // as promised, one line of code to invoke
                    // the correct method.
                    tasks[choice]();
                }
                catch {
                    Console.WriteLine("Invalid choice");
                }
            } while(true);
        }

        public static void MethodA() {
            Console.WriteLine("Doing TaskA");
        }

        public static void MethodB() {
            Console.WriteLine("Doing TaskB");
        }

        public static void MethodC() {
            Console.WriteLine("Doing TaskC");
        }
    }
}
```

System.MulticastDelegate Class

Delegates default to multicast delegates, which inherit from the *System.MulticastDelegate* class. A multicast delegate is similar to a basket. Multiple function pointers or delegates can be dropped into the basket. The list of delegates is stored in an invocation list, which can even include multiple instances of the same delegate. When you execute the contents of the basket, the function pointers of the delegates are called FIFO. Multicast delegates are useful for invoking a chain of functions.

Combining delegates   Multiple delegates are combined using the *Combine* method, the plus operator (+), or the += assignment operator. *Combine* is a static method. In C#, the *Combine* method is called with two delegate parameters or an array of delegates. The method returns a reference to the combined delegate.

The following code combines two delegates separately wrapping functions *MethodA* and *MethodB*. When the *Combine* delegate is invoked, *MethodA* is run first and *MethodB* second. This is the order in which the function pointers are added to the multicast delegate. Both the *Combine* method and the += assignment operators are shown, with the *Combine* statement commented to avoid duplication.

```
using System;

namespace Donis.CSharpBook{
 public delegate void DelegateClass();
    public class Starter{
        public static void Main(){
            DelegateClass del=MethodA;
            del+=MethodB;
            // del=(DelegateClass) DelegateClass.Combine(
            // new DelegateClass [] {MethodA, MethodB});
            del();
        }
        public static void MethodA() {
            Console.WriteLine("MethodA...");
        }

        public static void MethodB() {
            Console.WriteLine("MethodB...");
        }
    }
}
```

Removing delegates   To remove delegates from a multicast delegate, use the *Remove* method, the minus operator (-), or the -= assignment operator. *Remove* is a static method that accepts the source delegate as the first parameter and the delegate to remove as the second parameter. Be careful not to inadvertently remove all delegates from a multicast delegate, which causes a run-time error when invoked. The following code removes *MethodB* from a multicast delegate. When the delegate is invoked, *MethodA* is invoked, but not *MethodB*. The three methodologies are shown, with the *Combine* statement and operator minus commented to avoid duplication.

```
using System;

namespace Donis.CSharpBook{

    public delegate void DelegateClass();
```

```
public class Starter{
public static void Main(){
    DelegateClass del=MethodA;
    del+=MethodB;
    del+=MethodC;
    del=del-MethodB;

    // del=(DelegateClass) DelegateClass.Remove(del,
        (DelegateClass) MethodB);
    // del-=MethodB;
    del();
}
public static void MethodA() {
    Console.WriteLine("MethodA...");
}

public static void MethodB() {
    Console.WriteLine("MethodB...");
}

public static void MethodC() {
    Console.WriteLine("MethodC...");
}
    }
}
```

Invocation List

Multicast delegates maintain an invocation list, which has an entry for each delegate of the multicast delegate. Entries are added to the invocation list in the same order in which delegates are added. *GetInvocationList* returns the invocation list as an array of delegates.

This is the syntax of the *GetInvocationList* method:

delegate [] *GetInvocationList*()

This code retrieves the list of delegates in a multicast delegate, in which each delegate is a wrapper of a function. The name of each function is displayed. The *Delegate.Method* property returns a *MethodInfo type*, which encapsulates the function abstracted by the delegate.

```
using System;

namespace Donis.CSharpBook{
    public delegate void DelegateClass();
    public class Starter{
        public static void Main(){
            DelegateClass del=(DelegateClass)
            DelegateClass.Combine(new DelegateClass []
                { MethodA, MethodB, MethodA, MethodB } );
            del();
            foreach(DelegateClass item in
                del.GetInvocationList()) {
            Console.WriteLine(item.Method.Name+
                " in invocation list.");
        }
```

```
        }
    public static void MethodA() {
        Console.WriteLine("MethodA...");
    }

    public static void MethodB() {
        Console.WriteLine("MethodB...");
    }
  }
}
```

The delegate signature can contain reference parameters. When invoked, the reference is passed to the called functions. Reference parameters are a way for functions on an invocation list to share state. Value parameters are not shareable across the functions. Because the invocation list is called in sequence, beginning with the first delegate and function, each successive entry in the chain can view changes in the reference parameter. The next item in the chain can view those changes and possibly change the state again. In this way, when the multicast delegate is invoked, the state information is propagated along the invocation list. Furthermore, functions in invocation lists that have the same target object or class share the state of the object or class. The following code uses the reference parameter of a multicast delegate as a counter. The delegate has a value and reference parameter. The value parameter is lost between function calls in the invocation list. However, the reference parameter persists.

```
using System;

namespace Donis.CSharpBook{

    public delegate void DelegateClass(int valCount,
        ref int refCount);

    public class Counter{
        public static void Main(){
            DelegateClass del=(DelegateClass) AddOne+
                (DelegateClass) AddTwo+ (DelegateClass) AddOne;
            int valCount=0;
            int refCount=0;
            del(valCount, ref refCount);
            Console.WriteLine("Value count = {0}",
                valCount); // 0
            Console.WriteLine("Reference count = {0}",
                refCount); // 4
        }

        public static void AddOne(int valCount,
                ref int refCount){
            ++valCount;
            ++refCount;
        }

        public static void AddTwo(int valCount,
                ref int refCount) {
```

```
            valCount+=2;
            refCount+=2;
        }
    }
}
```

You can access the invocation list to execute each delegate and function therein directly. There are two reasons to invoke the invocation list directly. First, invoke the delegates explicitly to obtain the return of each delegate. When the invocation list is invoked implicitly, only the return of the last function is garnered. Second, invoke the invocation list directly in special circumstances (for example, to modify how exceptions are handled in a multicast delegate, which is described later).

The following code uses the invocation list to calculate a factorial. The *Incrementer* method increments a number, which is a reference parameter. The incremented value is returned from the method. Five delegates are created and initialized with the *Increment* method and combined into a multicast delegate. The *foreach* loop iterates the invocation list, multiplying the results of each function to calculate a factorial.

```
using System;

namespace Donis.CSharpBook{

    public delegate int IncrementDelegate(
        ref short refCount);

    public class Factorial{
        public static void Main(){

            IncrementDelegate [] values=
                { Incrementer, Incrementer,
                Incrementer, Incrementer,
                Incrementer};
            IncrementDelegate del=(IncrementDelegate)
            IncrementDelegate.Combine(
                values);
            long result=1;
            short count=1;
            foreach(IncrementDelegate number
                    in del.GetInvocationList()) {
                result=result*number(ref count);
            }
            Console.WriteLine("{0} factorial is {1}",
            del.GetInvocationList().Length,
                result);
        }

        public static int Incrementer(
                ref short refCount){
            return refCount++;
        }
    }

}
```

Methods and properties   Several members of delegate object, such as *GetInvocationList*, have already been introduced. Table 8-1 is a list of some of the public properties and methods of the *MulticastDelegate* type. Some of the members are inherited from *System.Delegate*.

Table 8-1   Delegate Members

Member	Description
BeginInvoke	Invokes a delegate asynchronously.
Combine	Combines delegates into a multicast delegate. This is a static method.
CreateDelegate	Defines a delegate at run time. This is a static method.
DynamicInvoke	Dynamically invokes a delegate that was created at run time.
EndInvoke	Requests the results of a delegate that was executed asynchronously.
Invoke	Executes a delegate, which calls all functions contained in the delegate.
Method	This is a property that returns the *MethodInfo* type of the last function in the invocation list. *MethodInfo* provides a description of a function.
Remove	Removes a delegate from a multicast delegate. This is a static method.
RemoveAll	Removes the invocation list of a delegate from the invocation list of another delegate. The result is returned. This is a static method.
Target	This is a property that returns the instance of the last function in the invocation list. For static functions, *Target* is null.

Generics and Delegates

A delegate can contain closed generic methods, whereas open generic methods cannot be added to a delegate. Some permutation of the generic method must be compatible with the signature of the delegate. Otherwise, the generic cannot be added to the invocation list. If the generic method contains actual parameters, the type is inferred. However, the return type cannot be inferred and must be specified.

In addition, the delegate itself can be generic and closed when the delegate is created. Functions added to a generic delegate need to match the signature of the closed generic delegate.

This is an example of a normal delegate initialized with a generic method:

```
using System;


namespace Donis.CSharpBook{
    public delegate void DelegateClass(int data);
    public class Starter{
        public static void Main(){
            DelegateClass del1=MethodA<int>;
            del1(5);
            DelegateClass del2=MethodA;
            del1(10); // inferred
        }
```

```
    public static void MethodA <T>(T data) {
        Console.WriteLine("MethodA ({0})", data);
    }
    }
}
```

This is an example of a generic delegate being initialized with a normal method:

```
using System;

namespace Donis.CSharpBook{
    public delegate void DelegateClass<T>(T data);
    public class Starter{
        public static void Main(){
            DelegateClass <string> del=MethodA;
            del("data");
        }

        public static void MethodA(string data) {
            Console.WriteLine("MethodA ({0})", data);
        }
    }
}
```

Asynchronous Invocation

Delegates are invoked synchronously via the *Invoke* method or call operator. Delegates can also be invoked asynchronously on a separate worker thread. A delegate performing a time-consuming task might improve application performance by running on a separate thread. This is especially true for Windows Forms applications, in which responsiveness of the user interface is a concern. The user interface could freeze for an extended period time while a synchronous delegate is performing an extended task. Other types of operations benefit from asynchronous delegates: network services, methods dependent on hardware devices, timed routines, and more. Synchronous solutions are simpler. However, this often falls short of the sophistication required for a professional application. Developers must be concerned with thread synchronization in asynchronous executions, which undoubtedly adds complexity. There is much more to writing robust multithread applications then simply spawning threads.

When a delegate is defined, the C# compiler adds several methods for invoking function pointers. The *Invoke* method is for synchronous invocation, while the *BeginInvoke* and *End-Invoke* methods are included for asynchronous invocation. The default for the call operator is synchronous execution.

BeginInvoke Method

BeginInvoke is callable on single-cast delegates alone. A single-cast delegate is a multicast delegate that contains a single function pointer. *BeginInvoke* adds the operation to a queue, where it is then serviced by a separate thread from a Common Language Runtime (CLR) managed thread pool. Therefore, functions on the invocation list run on a different thread from the caller of the delegate. The thread pool for asynchronous execution has a maximum of 25 threads per processor.

This is the syntax of the *BeginInvoke* method:

IAsyncResult BeginInvoke(*arguments*, AsyncCallback callback, object AsynState)

BeginInvoke begins with the parameters of the delegate signature. If the delegate signature names four arguments, those are the first four parameters of *BeginInvoke*. The next parameter is the completion routine. This routine is called back when the asynchronous call has completed. The final parameter is a state object. The completion routine and state objects are optional and either can be set to null. The return is an *IAsyncResult* object, which maintains the state of the object. *IAsyncResult* has four properties, which are listed in Table 8-2.

Table 8-2   *IAsyncResult* Properties

Property	Description
AsyncState	The state object that has information on the asynchronous operation.
AsyncWaitHandle	Use the *WaitHandle* to block until the asynchronous operation is completed.
CompleteSynchronously	Indicates that the operation completed synchronously.
IsCompleted	Indicates that the asynchronous operation has completed.

The following code highlights the *IAsyncResult* and delegate state object:

```
using System;
using System.Threading;

namespace Donis.CSharpBook{
    public delegate void DelegateClass();

    public class Starter{

        public static void Main(){
            DelegateClass del=MethodA;
            DelegateStateBag state=new DelegateStateBag();
            IAsyncResult ar=del.BeginInvoke(Callback, state);
            if(ar.IsCompleted==true) {
                Console.WriteLine("MethodA completed");
            }
            else {
                Console.WriteLine("MethodA not completed");
            }
            ar.AsyncWaitHandle.WaitOne();

            // doing something else

            Thread.Sleep(100);
            lock(state) {
```

```
            Console.WriteLine("Back in Main");
            Console.WriteLine(state.message);
        }
    }

    public static void Callback(IAsyncResult ar) {
        DelegateStateBag state=
            (DelegateStateBag) ar.AsyncState;
        lock(state) {
            Console.WriteLine("Callback running");
                ((DelegateStateBag) ar.AsyncState).message=
                "State object modified in callback.";
        }
    }

    public static void MethodA() {
        Console.WriteLine("MethodA running...");
        Thread.Sleep(200);
    }
}

class DelegateStateBag {
    public string message;
}
}
```

This is the result of the application:

```
MethodA not completed
MethodA running...
Callback running
Back in Main
State object modified in callback.
```

Interestingly, the *not completed* message is received before *MethodA* has even started. This confirms that *BeginInvoke* does not directly invoke the function in the delegate. Rather, it adds a request to the thread pool queue, which is eventually handled. There is a *Thread .Sleep* statement near the end of the *Main* method. If removed, a race condition would exist between *Main* and the completion routine called *Callback*. What is the source of the race condition? Note the *WaitHandle.WaitOne* command in *Main*, which blocks *Main* until the asynchronous operation is complete. As the completion routine, *Callback* also waits for the asynchronous operation to finish. When the asynchronous operation finishes, the *Main* and *Callback* routines *both* resume, and the race begins. *Callback* needs to update the state object before *Main* displays the contents of the state object. The *Thread.Sleep* statement is a primitive way of removing the race condition and allowing the *Callback* routine to lock the shared state object first.

EndInvoke Method

EndInvoke provides that the result of an asynchronous operation is callable in the completion routine or the thread of the delegate caller. *EndInvoke* has the same signature as the delegate without the value parameters and has an additional final parameter, which is an *IAsyncResult* object. To obtain the signature of the *EndInvoke* method, remove the value parameters from the delegate signature and add an *IAsyncResult* parameter. The *IAsyncResult* parameter is the same *IAsyncResult* object that is returned from *BeginInvoke*. The return type of *EndInvoke* is identical to the return of the delegate.

This is the syntax of the *EndInvoke* method:

returntype EndInvoke(*ref_out_arguments*, IAsyncResult ar)

Calling *EndInvoke* before functions of the asynchronous delegate has finished executing blocks the caller until the operation is completed. For each *BeginInvoke*, there should be a complementing *EndInvoke* to confirm the results of the operation, detect an exception, and to allow the CLR to properly clean up the delegate. Calling the *EndInvoke* method more than once on the same delegate yields undefined results and should be avoided.

Here is sample code for the *EndInvoke* method:

```
using System;
using System.Threading;

namespace Donis.CSharpBook{
    public delegate int DelegateClass(out DateTime start,
        out DateTime stop);

    public class Starter{

        public static void Main(){
            DelegateClass del=MethodA;
            DateTime start;
            DateTime stop;
            IAsyncResult ar=del.BeginInvoke(out start, out stop,
                null, null);

            ar.AsyncWaitHandle.WaitOne();

            // doing something else

            int elapse=del.EndInvoke(out start, out stop, ar);
            Console.WriteLine("Start time: {0}",
            start.ToLongTimeString());
            Console.WriteLine("Stop time: {0}",
            stop.ToLongTimeString());
            Console.WriteLine("Elapse time: {0} seconds",
                elapse);
        }


        public static int MethodA(out DateTime start,
                out DateTime stop) {
            start=DateTime.Now;
            Thread.Sleep(5000);
```

```
            stop=DateTime.Now;
            return (stop-start).Seconds;
        }
    }
}
```

Asynchronous Delegate Diagram

The preceding text explains how to invoke a delegate asynchronously and to obtain the results. Figure 8-1 diagrams the relationship and sequence of operations. This includes the delegate, the *BeginInvoke* method, the *EndInvoke* method, and the delegate completion routine.

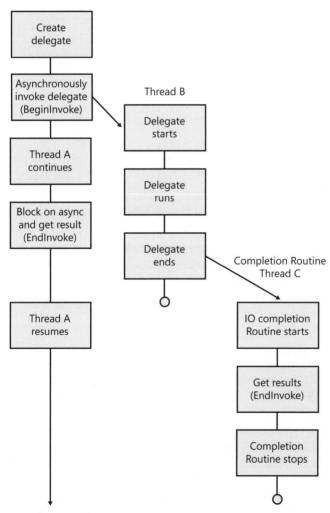

Figure 8-1   Asynchronous processing of a delegate

Delegate Internals

Delegates may appear to be magical to developers because so much is hidden. The magician is the C# compiler. This section explains the magic of the compiler. Why should you care? Understanding how delegate are implemented internally should help in the how, where, and when to use delegates.

The C# compiler builds a class from the definition of a delegate. The class shares the name of the delegate and has four methods: a constructor, *Invoke*, *BeginInvoke*, and *EndInvoke*. Importantly, the delegate class is derived from *System.MulticastDelegate*. This is a typical definition of a delegate:

```
public delegate int ADelegate(int arg1, ref int arg2);
```

As viewed in ildasm, C# creates the *ADelegate* class from this delegate. (See Figure 8-2.)

Figure 8-2   C# manifested delegate class

Members of the delegate class, such as *Invoke* and *BeginInvoke*, were described earlier in this chapter. However, it is comforting to actually see them. It is not magic after all. There may be a slight surprise: The constructor of the delegate has two arguments. The code in this chapter shows the delegate constructor being called with a single parameter. The C# compiler helps us here: It interprets the single parameter as a target object and function pointer, which are the parameters of the two argument constructors. Also notice that the signatures of *Invoke*, *BeginInvoke*, and *EndInvoke* were defined as described earlier in this chapter.

Exceptions

What happens if an unhandled exception is raised in a multicast delegate? If the delegate is invoked inside a protected block of code, the exception is trapped. The invocation list is called until an exception occurs. Functions later in the invocation list do not execute. Let us assume that the invocation list has pointers to *MethodA*, *MethodB*, *MethodC*, and *MethodD*. They were also added to the delegate in that order. If an unhandled exception is raised in *MethodB*, *MethodC* and *MethodD* are not called. The situation might appear to be more complicated if the exception is raised in a delegate that is running asynchronously. In this circumstance, the exception is raised on a different thread. However, the run time will route the exception back to the calling thread, as evidenced in the following code. Therefore, the exception is handled as if the delegate were called synchronously.

```
using System;
using System.Threading;

namespace Donis.CSharpBook{

    public delegate void DelegateClass();

    public class Starter{
        public static void Main(){
            Console.WriteLine("Running on primary thread");
            try {
                DelegateClass del=MethodA;
                IAsyncResult ar=del.BeginInvoke(null, null);
                del.EndInvoke(ar);
            }
            catch(Exception except){
                Console.WriteLine("Running on primary thread");
                Console.WriteLine("Exception caught: "
                    +except.Message);
            }
        }

        public static void MethodA() {
            if(Thread.CurrentThread.IsThreadPoolThread==true) {
                Console.WriteLine(
                    "Running on a thread pool thread");
            }
            else {
                Console.WriteLine("Running on primary thread");
            }
            throw new Exception("failure");
        }
    }
}
```

Anonymous Methods

An anonymous method is a nameless method. Sometimes a function is intended exclusively for a delegate. Without an anonymous method, you would have to define a separate function as part of a class. The function can then be assigned to the delegate. Assigning an anonymous method prevents creating a separate method. This is cleaner and more convenient than a named method. Anonymous methods can substitute for delegates as parameters, return values, and in other situations.

Define an anonymous method with the delegate keyword. This code assigns an anonymous method to a delegate:

```
using System;
using System.Threading;

namespace Donis.CSharpBook{

    public delegate void DelegateClass();
```

```
    public class Starter{
        public static void Main(){
            DelegateClass del= delegate {
                Console.WriteLine("Running anonymous method");
            };
            del();
        }
    }
}
```

In the preceding example, the anonymous method does not have a signature. The signature of the anonymous method is inferred from the delegate signature, which is another example of delegate inference. Despite not having a signature, the return of the anonymous method must match the delegate return. The advantage of an anonymous method without a signature is its compliance with almost any delegate. The disadvantage is that anonymous methods defined without a signature cannot access the parameters of the delegates. This means that the anonymous method cannot utilize the parameters. For this reason, anonymous methods without a signature cannot be employed where delegates have out parameters. Out parameters must be initialized in the called method, which is impossible in an anonymous method. When an anonymous method is called through the delegates, the parameters must still be provided, even if ignored inside the method. Of course, if the delegate has no parameters, none should be provided.

This is the syntax of an anonymous method:

delegate *optional_signature {anonymous method expression}*

The C# compiler performs several tasks to assign an anonymous method without a signature to a delegate:

1. Validates the signature of the delegate—no out parameters

2. Infers the signature of the anonymous method from the delegate

3. Confirms that the return type of the delegate is compatible with the anonymous method

4. Creates a new delegate that is initialized with a function pointer to the anonymous method

Anonymous methods can be assigned a signature, which is appended to the delegate keyword. This restricts the anonymous method to a delegate with a matching signature and return type. Like conventional methods, the parameters are initialized with the parameters from the delegate call. This is an example of an anonymous method with a signature:

```
using System;
using System.Threading;

namespace Donis.CSharpBook{

    public delegate int DelegateClass(out int param);
```

```
public class Starter{
    public static void Main(){
        int var;
        DelegateClass del= delegate(out int inner) {
            inner=12;
            Console.WriteLine("Running anonymous method");
            return inner;
        };
        del(out var);
        Console.WriteLine("Var is {0}", var);
    }
}
}
```

As demonstrated in the preceding code, anonymous methods can be used for delegates. The exception is the -= assignment operator. Because the anonymous method is unnamed, it cannot be used to remove a named method from a multicast delegate. This is the exception to freely substituting delegates with anonymous methods.

Actually, anonymous methods are not nameless. The C# compiler implements the anonymous method as the named method in the containing class. The generated method is both static and private. The wrapper delegate is initialized with this method. The following format is used to name anonymous methods:

<functionname>uniqueid

The function name is the function in which the anonymous method is implemented. The unique identifier is a combination of a letter and number. The method has the same signature as the target delegate.

The wrapper delegate initialized with the anonymous method is also added to the class as a static and private field. This is the format of the wrapper delegate. The identifier is a compiler-generated number, whereas # is a character added to the name of the wrapper delegate.

<>id__CachedAnonymousMethodDelegate#

The following code offers two delegates and anonymous methods:

```
using System;

namespace Donis.CSharpBook{

    public delegate void ADelegate(int param);
    public delegate int BDelegate(int param1, int param2);

    public class Starter{
        public static void Main(){
            ADelegate del= delegate(int param) {
                param=5;
            };
        }
```

```
            public int MethodA() {
                BDelegate del= delegate(int param1, int param2) {
                    return 0;
                };
                return 0;
            }

        }
    }
```

Figure 8-3 is a disassembly of this application program. It shows the wrapper delegates and anonymous methods.

Figure 8-3 Disassembly showing wrapper delegates and anonymous methods

Outer Variables

Anonymous methods can refer to local variables of the containing function and class members within the scope of the method definition. Local variables used in an anonymous method are called outer variables.

The scope of a local variable is closely linked to the method in which the local is declared. When the method ends, local variables are removed from memory. Local variables used in an anonymous method are captured, which extends the lifetime of the variable. The lifetime of a captured or outer variable is of the same as that of the delegate. The outer variable is removed when the delegate is garbage-collected. In the following code, the local variable of *MethodA* is captured in the anonymous method. The lifetime of the local variable would usually end when *MethodA* is exited. However, the delegate is garbage-collected until the end of the program, which extends the lifetime of the local variable for the entire program.

```
using System;

namespace Donis.CSharpBook{
    public delegate void DelegateClass(out int arg);

    public class Starter{

        public static void Main(){

            DelegateClass del=MethodA();
            int var;
            del(out var);
```

```
            Console.WriteLine(var);
        }

        public static DelegateClass MethodA() {
            int local=0;
            return delegate(out int arg) {
                arg=++local;
            };
        }
    }
}
```

Because the lifetime of outer variables is aligned with the delegate, it remains persistent across invocations of the anonymous method. In the following code, the anonymous method is invoked thrice through the delegate. As a local variable, local would be initialized on each call to the method. However, as an outer variable, it is initialized once in *MethodA* and maintains its value across multiple calls to the anonymous method. Therefore, the value displayed is 3.

```
using System;

namespace Donis.CSharpBook{

    public delegate void DelegateClass(out int var);

    public class Starter{

        public static void Main(){

            DelegateClass del=MethodA();
            int var;
            del(out var);
            del(out var);
            del(out var);
            Console.WriteLine(var);
        }

        public static DelegateClass MethodA() {
            int increment=0;
            return delegate(out int var) {
                var=++increment;
            };
        }
    }
}
```

The C# compiler creates a private nested class for anonymous methods that capture local variables, whereas anonymous methods that contain no outer variables are implemented as private static methods. The nested class has a public field for each outer variable used in the anonymous method. The local variable is persisted to this public field. It also contains a named method for the anonymous method. The named method has the same signature as the related delegate. This is the method used to initialize the wrapper delegate. Figure 8-4 illustrates the nested class created for an anonymous method.

Figure 8-4   Disassembly of nested class for an anonymous method that uses outer variables

Locals are fixed variables and are not normally available to garbage collection. Local variables are removed from memory when the applicable method is exited. When a local variable is captured, it becomes a movable variable. Movable variables are placed on the managed heap. As such, outer variables then become available for garbage collection. For this reason, captured variables must be pinned or otherwise fixed before being used with unsafe code.

Generic Anonymous Methods

Anonymous methods can use generic parameters of the class or delegate. However, anonymous methods cannot define new generic parameters and constraints. Here are two examples of anonymous methods using generic parameters:

```
public delegate void ADelegate<T>(T tvalue);

public class ZClass{
    public void MethodA() {
        ADelegate<int> del=delegate(int var) {
        };
    }
}

public class YClass<T>{
    public delegate void BDelegate(T tValue);
    public void MethodA() {
        BDelegate del=delegate(T tValue) {
        };
    }
}
```

Limitations of Anonymous Methods

Although anonymous methods are similar to other methods, they also have some limitations (some have already been mentioned):

- Do not attempt to jump out of an anonymous method.
- Do not use a ref or out outer variable in an anonymous method.

- Do not define new generic parameters or constraints.

- Do not apply attributes to anonymous methods.

- Do not use anonymous method with -= assignment operator.

- Cannot be a member method.

- Cannot be an unsafe method.

Events

An event is an occurrence that an object or class wants to notify someone else about. (The *someone else* is either another object or class.) A button notifies a form object that someone clicked on the button. A timer notifies some other object that a time period has elapsed. An application domain notifies an application of an unhandled event. A Web application notifies an object of an application event. You can create custom events, such as a device notifying a monitoring application that data transmission has started or stopped. This list of events is somewhat eclectic, which underscores that there is no strict definition. Events are literally anything worth notifying someone else about. Public events are exposed as public members of a publisher class, such as a button class. You can also have private and protected events that are used within the realm of the containing or derived class.

Any object or class interested in an event can subscribe. Subscribers register for an event by submitting a delegate. The delegate must be single cast and contain a single function pointer. That function is the subscriber's response to the event. When the event is raised, the publisher calls the function, affording the subscriber an opportunity to respond to the event. For this reason, the function is called an event handler. Events can have multiple subscribers. A device could publish a power-off event in which multiple applications might want to be notified and respond.

What happens when there are no subscribers to a particular event? In other words, *if a tree falls in the woods and no one hears it, does it make a sound?* If the tree is an event, no sound is made. Events that have no subscribers are not raised.

Publishing an Event

Both classes and objects can publish events. Static events are published at classes, whereas objects publish instance events. Multicast delegates underlie events. You must create a delegate for the event or leverage a predefined event. Events are defined with the event keyword. This is the syntax for defining an event:

accessibility event *delegatename eventname*

Events are defined as a field in a class. The accessibility of an event is typically public or protected. Protected events restrict subscribers to child objects. A public event is available to every interested subscriber. Delegate name is the underlying delegate of the event, which defines the signature of the event. Event name is the identity of the event.

```
public delegate void DelegateClass();
public event DelegateClass MyEvent;
```

As a best practice, event handlers should return void and have two arguments. *EventHandler* is a predefined delegate created for this purpose. It is included in the .NET Framework class library (FCL) and prevents you from having to declare a separate delegate for the standard event type. The first parameter is the object that raised the event. The second parameter is an *EventArgs* derived instance, which offers optional data that further explains the event.

Internally, events declared in a class become a field of that class. Delegates used to define the event, which is a multicast delegate, are types used for the field. The C# compiler also inserts methods to add and remove subscribers to the event. The names of the methods are *add_EventName* and *remove_EventName*, respectively. The fourth member added to the class is the event itself. See Figure 8-5 for a disassembly of an event class.

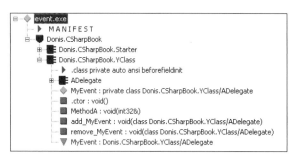

Figure 8-5   Disassembly of the event class

Subscribe

The publisher/subscriber relationship is a *one-to-many* relationship. For each publisher there can be zero or more subscribers. Conversely, a subscriber can subscribe to multiple events. For example, a form can subscribe to a button click and a text change event. Subscribers add a delegate to an event to register for the event. The delegate is a wrapper for the function to be called when the event is raised. Subscribe to an event using the add method or the += assignment operator:

```
using System;

namespace Donis.CSharpBook{
    class Publisher {
        public event EventHandler MyEvent;
    }

    public class Subscriber{

        public static void Handler(object obj, EventArgs args) {
        }
```

```
        public static void Main(){
            Publisher pub=new Publisher();
            pub.MyEvent+=Handler;
            // other processing
        }
    }
}
```

Cancel a subscription to a delegate with the -= assignment operator.

Raising an Event

At the discretion of a publisher, an event is raised and the methods of the subscribers are called back. Raise an event with the call operator "( )". Adding the call operator to the event raises the event. Because a delegate underlies an event, the *Invoke* method inherited from a multicast delegate is another means to raising an event. The signature of both the call operator and the *Invoke* method match the delegate of the event. Any parameters are passed to the called methods of the subscribers. If an event returns a value as defined by the event delegate, the function of the last subscriber sets the return. Do not raise an event for events without subscribers. Events with no subscribers are null, which can be tested. An application that raises an event that has no subscribers will incur an exception because of a null reference. This is the proper way to raise an event:

```
public void SomeMethod() {
        if(anEvent!=null) {
            anEvent(null, null);
        }
}
```

EventArgs

Events sometime provide subscribers with custom information pertaining to the event. The mouse click event provides the *x* and *y* coordinates of the mouse pointer in the *MouseEventArgs* class. The *DataRowChangeEventArgs* class provides the affected row and action of several database-related events, such as the *RowChanged* event. The *PaintEventArgs* class is instantiated in a paint event. It gives developers the clip rectangle and graphics object for the paint event. Custom information about an event is defined in an *EventArgs* derived class. *MouseEventArgs*, *DataRowChangeEventArgs*, *PaintEventArgs*, and other related classes derive from the *EventArgs* class. These classes represent the state information for the event.

The *EventArgs* derived class that contains the state information of the event is typically passed as the second parameter of the event. State information can also be specified in the other parameters of events.

This is code for a bank account. The *NSF* event is raised when the account is overdrawn. The *BankEventArgs* class provides the bank account balance and amount of the transaction that would overdraw the account.

```csharp
using System;

namespace Donis.CSharpBook{

    public class Starter {
        public static void Main(){
            Bank account=new Bank();
            account.NSF+=NSFHandler;
            account.Deposit(500);
            account.Withdrawal(750);
        }

        public static void NSFHandler(object o,
                BankEventArgs e) {
            Console.WriteLine("NSF Transaction");
            Console.WriteLine("Balance: {0}", e.Balance);
            Console.WriteLine("Transaction: {0}",
                e.Transaction);
        }

    }

    public delegate void OverDrawn(object o, BankEventArgs e);
    public class Bank {
        public event OverDrawn NSF; // non sufficient funds

        public decimal Deposit(decimal amountDeposit) {
            propBalance+=amountDeposit;
            return propBalance;
        }

        public decimal Withdrawal(decimal amountWithdrawn) {
            decimal newBalance=propBalance-amountWithdrawn;
            if(newBalance < 0) {
                if(NSF != null) {
                    BankEventArgs args=new BankEventArgs(
                        Balance, amountWithdrawn);
                    NSF(this, args);
                }
                return propBalance;
            }
            return propBalance=newBalance;
        }

        private decimal propBalance=0;
        public decimal Balance {
            get {
                return propBalance;
            }
        }

    }

    public class BankEventArgs: EventArgs {
```

```
        public BankEventArgs(decimal amountBalance,
            decimal amountTransaction) {
          propBalance=amountBalance;
          propTransaction=amountTransaction;
        }

        private decimal propBalance;
        public decimal Balance {
          get {
            return propBalance;
          }
        }

        private decimal propTransaction;
        public decimal Transaction {
          get {
            return propTransaction;
          }
        }
      }
    }
  }
```

Exception Handling

This chapter focused on delegates and events. In the next chapter we will cover the importance and benefits of exception handling.

Chapter 9
Exception Handling

Exception handling is an important ingredient of a robust application and should be included in the application design of every .NET program. Exception handling helps applications identify and respond to exceptional events in a known and robust manner. This enhances the correctness of an application, which naturally improves customer satisfaction. Unfortunately, exception handling is often an afterthought, which leads to poorly implemented solutions for exception handling and a less robust application. Starting with application design, exception handling should be included in all aspects of application planning and development.

What is an exception? Exceptions are exceptional events or error conditions within an application and are categorized as system or application exceptions. System exceptions are raised by the Common Language Runtime (CLR) and include null reference, out of memory, divide by zero, and stack overflow exceptions. Application exceptions, considered custom exceptions, are thrown by the application, not by the CLR. Some exceptional events or error conditions are detectable by application logic, not by the runtime. Application exceptions are useful in those circumstances. As an example, constructors that fail are not always detectable by the CLR. In addition, constructors implicitly return void, which prevents returning an error code. For these reasons, throwing an application exception in the failed constructor is the best solution.

Exceptions should be used only for exceptions. Exception handling is not a substitute for transfer of control or a *goto* statement. Exceptions are expensive when compared with conventional transfer of control. Whenever possible, applications should preempt exceptions and avoid the accompanying costs. Performing data validation, where incorrect values can cause exceptions, is one measure that prevents exceptions. Data validation and, if necessary, return-ing an error code is undoubtedly cheaper than raising an exception.

The overuse of exceptions makes code harder to read and maintain. Errors that frequently occur should not be handled with exception handling, but with error codes or returns. Remember, exceptions should be reserved for exceptional events.

Exception Example

A common exception is *dividing by zero*. Exceptions are generally linked to an action. For dividing by zero, the action is a divisor of zero. Integer division, where the divisor is zero, triggers a divide by zero exception. (However, floating-point division by zero does not cause an exception; instead, infinity is returned.) The following code causes an unhandled divide by zero exception, which terminates the application:

```csharp
using System;

namespace Donis.CSharpBook{
    public class Starter{
        public static void Main(){
            int var1=5, var2=0;
            var1/=var2;    // exception occurs
        }
    }
}
```

Place code that is likely to raise an exception in a *try* block because code in a *try* block is protected from exceptions. Exceptions raised in the *try* block are trapped. The stack is then walked by the CLR, searching for the appropriate exception handler. Code not residing in a *try* block is unprotected from exceptions. In this circumstance, the exception eventually evolves into an unhandled exception. As demonstrated in the previous code, an unhandled exception is apt to abort an application.

In the following code, the divide by zero exception is caught in a *try* block. Trapping, catch-ing, and handling an exception are separate tasks. The *catch* statement consists of a *catch* filter and block. The *DivideByZeroException* filter catches the divide by zero exception. The *catch* block handles the exception, which is to display the stack trace. The proximity of the infraction is included in the stack trace. Execution then continues at the first statement after the *catch* block.

```csharp
using System;

namespace Donis.CSharpBook{
    public class Starter{
        public static void Main(){
            try {
                int var1=5, var2=0;
```

```
                var1/=var2;    // exception occurs
            }
            catch(DivideByZeroException except) {
                Console.WriteLine("Exception "+except.StackTrace);
            }
        }
    }
}
```

Common Exception Model

.NET offers a common exception model. Exception handling is implemented within the CLR and is not specific to a managed language. Each managed language exposes exception handling using language-specific syntax. The uniform exception model contributes to language independence, which is an important tenet of .NET. In addition, exceptions raised in one managed language can be caught in a different managed language. Prior to .NET, there were competing models for error handling: Microsoft Visual Basic 6.0, Win32 SDK, MFC, COM, and more. In a component-driven architecture, this disparity contributed to complexity and potential product instability. In .NET, exception handling between disparate components is consistent, simple, and stable.

As part of the common exception model, .NET advocates structured exception handling, which is essentially the *try* and *catch* statements. C-based and Java developers are probably familiar with structured exception handling. For Visual Basic developers, this is a seismic shift from unstructured exception handling. The unstructured model, such as *on error goto* and *on error resume*, is thankfully now obsolete.

Structured Exception Handling

A structured exception evaluates the stack to determine when code is protected and where an exception is caught and handled. When exceptions occur, the stack is walked in search of an exception handler. When a matching *catch* filter is located, the exception is handled in the exception handler, which is the *catch* block. This sets the scope of the exception on the stack. After the exception is handled, the CLR unwinds the stack to that scope.

Try Statement

Try blocks are observers; they watch for exceptions in protected code. Place code prone to raising exceptions in a *try* block. Do not attempt to protect an entire application in a *try* block—there are more convenient and practical means of accomplishing the same feat, as described later in this chapter.

As mentioned, exceptions are stack-based. The following code contains a fence-post error that happens when the bounds of the array are exceeded. The result is an exception in the unprotected *MethodA* method. *Main* calls *MethodA*, where the scope of *Main* encompasses *MethodA*.

For this reason, the *try* block in *Main* extends protection to *MethodA*. The exception is trapped in *Main*.

```
using System;

namespace Donis.CSharpBook{
    public class Starter{

        public static void Main(){
            try {
                MethodA();
            }-
            catch(Exception except) {
                Console.WriteLine(except.Message);
            }
        }

        public static void MethodA() {
            int [] values={1,2,3,4};
            for(int count=0; count<=values.Length; ++count) {
                Console.WriteLine(values[count]);
            }
        }
    }
}
```

This is the syntax of the *try* statement:

try { *protected*} catch[1](*filter*[1]) { *handler*[1]} catch[n](*filter* [n]) { *handler* [n]} finally {*terminationhandler*}

Try statements must be paired with either a *catch* statement or a *finally* statement. There can be zero or more *catch* statements attached to a *try* statement; there are zero or one *finally* statements. If both *catch* and *finally* are present, the *catch* statement should precede the *finally* statement. The following code has various combinations of *try*, *catch*, and *finally* statements:

```
// try..catch
try {
}
catch(Exception e) {
}

// try..finally
try {
}
finally{
}

// try..catch..finally
try {
}
catch(Exception e) {
}
finally{
}
```

```
// try..catches..finally
try {
}
catch(Exception e) {
}
catch {
}
finally{
}
```

Catch Statement

Catch statements filter and handle exceptions. When an exception is raised, the filter sets which exceptions are handled at that scope in the stack. If the filter matches the exception, the exception is suppressed, and control is transferred to the adjoining *catch* block to be handled. The CLR searches the stack for an appropriate filter. If a matching filter is not found, the exception becomes an unhandled exception.

Exceptions must be derived from *System.Exception*. The *catch* filter defines an exception type and catches exception of that type or any descendants. The exception object contains details of the exception, such as a user-friendly message describing the exception. The exception object caught in the filter is accessible only in the *catch* block. *System.Exception* is the base class of .NET exceptions and the generic filter.

A *System.Exception* filter catches all managed exceptions. Derived classes of *System.Exception* catch more-specific exceptions. In the previous code, the *DivideByZeroException* filter caught integer divide by zero exceptions and nothing else. A *try* block can be appended to multiple catches for catching distinct exceptions. The catches are ordered from specific to generic. The following code has several exception filters, from specific to generic:

```
using System;

namespace Donis.CSharpBook{
    public class Starter{
        public static void Main(){
            try {
                int var1=5, var2=0;
                var1/=var2;
            }
            catch(DivideByZeroException except) {
                Console.WriteLine("Exception "+except.Message);
            }
            catch(System.ArithmeticException except) {
                Console.WriteLine("Exception "+except.Message);
            }
            catch(Exception except) {
                Console.WriteLine("Exception "+except.Message);
            }
        }
    }
}
```

In the preceding code, *DivideByZeroException* is very specific and catches only divide by zero exceptions. *ArithmeticException* is less specific and catches a variety of arithmetic exceptions, including the divide by zero exception. *Exception* catches all managed exceptions, which includes divide by zero and arithmetic exceptions. In the preceding code, the exception is caught at the *DivideByZeroException* catch handler.

The *catch* filter is optional, and the default is *catch all*. Although *System.Exception* catches any managed exceptions, *catch all* catches both managed and unmanaged exceptions. In most circumstances, native exceptions are mapped to managed exceptions, which are thrown in the *RaiseTheException* native function. *RaiseTheException* uses the *RaiseException* API to construct the managed exception. Exceptions not mapping to managed exceptions are outside this normal mechanism. A catch with no *catch* filter is a *catch all*. This code has a *catch all*:

```csharp
using System;

namespace Donis.CSharpBook{
    public class Starter{
        public static void Main(){
            try {
                int var1=5, var2=0;
                var1/=var2;
            }
            catch(DivideByZeroException except) {
                Console.WriteLine("Exception "+except.StackTrace);
            }
            catch {
                // catch remaining managed and unmanaged exceptions
            }
        }
    }
}
```

Propagating Exceptions

Exceptions are not always handled locally where the exception is caught. It is sometimes beneficial to catch an exception and then propagate the exception. *Propagating* an exception is catching and then rethrowing the exception. Rethrowing an exception continues the search along the call stack to find an appropriate handler. Here are some reasons to propagate an exception:

■   There is a centralized handler for the exception. There are several reasons for implementing centralized handlers, including code reuse. Instead of handling an exception in various locations in an application, concentrate code for certain exceptions in a centralized handler. Wherever the exception is raised, the proper response is to record the exception and then delegate to the centralized handler. A central handler can be used to handle all exceptions in a single place.

- Resources required to handle the exception are not available locally. For example, an exception is raised because of an invalid database connection. However, the correct connection string is read from a file not available where the exception occurs. The solution is to propagate the exception to a handler that has access to the file resource.

- Propagate unwanted exceptions caught in the umbrella of the exception filter. This would be useful for catching all *DataException* types with the exception of the *DuplicateNameException*. One solution would be to write 12 individual catches—one for each of the data exceptions except for the *DuplicateNameException* exception. A better solution is to catch the *DataException* type and propagate the *DuplicateNameException* when necessary. This is one *catch* statement versus 12 *catch* statements and eliminates redundant code.

- Catch an exception to gather information or to report on an exception, and then propagate the exception.

To propagate an exception, rethrow the same exception or another exception in the *catch* block. An empty *throw* statement propagates the caught exception. Alternatively, throw a different exception.

Exceptions might propagate through several layers of an application. Ultimately, the exception could percolate to the user interface level. As an exception percolates, the exception becomes less specific. Exceptions from the lower echelon of an application contain detailed information appropriate to the application developer, but probably not relevant to the user. Internal exceptions might contain security and other sensitive information not appropriate for a benign (or malicious) user. Record the facts of the internal exception if logging is preferable. Exceptions that reach the user should present user-relevant information: a user-friendly message, steps to resolve the exception, or even a customer support link.

When an original exception is rethrown, you can preserve the *that* exception in the *InnerException* attribute. Successive *InnerException* attributes form a chain of exceptions from the current exception to the original exception. The *InnerException* can be initialized in the constructor of the new exception. Here is sample code that propagates an exception and sets the inner exception:

```
using System;

namespace Donis.CSharpBook{
    public class Starter{
        public static void Main(){
            try {
                MethodA();
            }
            catch(Exception except) {
                Console.WriteLine(except.Message);
            }
        }
```

```
    public static void MethodA() {
        try {
            MethodB();
        }
        catch(DivideByZeroException inner) {

            // record divide by zero exception in
            //      event log.

            // except is inner exception
            throw new Exception("Math exception",
                inner);
        }
    }

    public static void MethodB() {
        int var1=5, var2=0;
        var1/=var2;
    }
}
}
```

Finally Statement

The *finally* block is the termination handler. When an exception is raised, protected code after the infraction is not executed. What if it is cleanup code? If cleanup code is not executed, resources are left dangling. Termination handlers are the solution. Code that must execute, regardless of an exception occurring, is placed in a termination handler. When an exception is raised, the *finally* blocks within scope are called before the stack is unwound. Note that the termination handler is executed even when there is no occurrence of an exception. Execution simply falls through the *try* block into the attached *finally* block. In the termination handler, you could close a file, release a database connection, or otherwise manage resources.

Here is a typical termination handler:

```
using System;
using System.IO;

namespace Donis.CSharpBook{
    public class FileWriter{
        public static void Main(){
            StreamWriter sw=null;
            try {
                sw=new StreamWriter("date.txt");
                sw.Write(DateTime.Now.ToLongTimeString());
                throw new ApplicationException("exception");
                // dangling code
            }
            finally {
                sw.Close();
```

```
            Console.WriteLine("file closed");
        }
    }
  }
}
```

Exception Information Table

The CLR refers to the Exception Information Table to track protected code in an efficient manner. Because of the Exception Information Table, there is no overhead associated with an exception unless an exception occurs.

An Exception Information Table is constructed for every managed application. The table has an entry for each method in the program. Each entry is an array, where the array elements describe the filters and handlers of that method. Entries in the array represent a *catch* filter, *user-filtered* handler, *catch* handler, or *termination* handler. User-filtered handlers use the *when* clause and are available in Visual Basic .NET, but not in C#.

When an exception occurs, the CLR consults the Exception Information Table. The entry for the method hosting the exception is searched for a filter that matches the exception. If the array is empty or a matching filter is not found, the entry of the outer method is examined next. When the boundary of the application is reached, the exception is considered unhandled.

Nested Try Blocks

Try blocks can be nested. The order of evaluation is more complex with nested *try* blocks. This is the order of execution when an exception occurs:

1. The first step is to find an appropriate *try* block. If an exception is raised outside a protected block, the exception is not trapped and is therefore unhandled.

2. From the *try* block, walk the stack until a matching *catch* filter is found. If a matching filter is not found, the exception is unhandled. This defines the scope of the exception.

3. Before the stack is unwound, *finally* blocks within the scope of the exception are run. The innermost *finally* blocks are executed first.

4. The *catch* block of the filter is executed as the exception handler.

5. Execution continues at the first statement after the *catch* block.

6. *Finally* blocks at scope of exception are executed.

Figure 9-1 diagrams the sequence when an exception is raised in a nested *try* block.

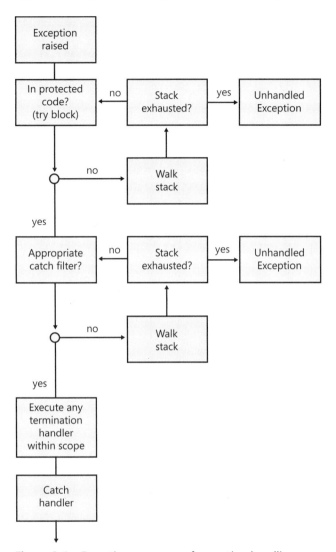

Figure 9-1   Execution sequence of exception handling

The following code has several nested *try* blocks:

```
using System;

namespace Donis.CSharpBook{
    public class Starter{

        public static void Main(){
            try {
```

```
            Console.WriteLine("outer - try");
            try {
                Console.WriteLine("inner - try");
                throw new ApplicationException("exception");
            }
            finally {
                Console.WriteLine("inner - finally");
            }
        }
        catch(Exception except){
            Console.WriteLine("outer - catch");
        }
        finally {
            Console.WriteLine("outer - finally");
        }

    }

  }
}
```

System.Exception

System.Exception is the base exception class. All exceptions in .NET are derived from *System.Exception. System.SystemException* is the base class for system exceptions raised by the CLR, such as *System.Data.DataException* or *System.FormatException. SystemException* is derived directly from *System.Exception. System.SystemException* does not refine *System.Exception.* However, it is an important marker that distinguishes between system and application exception, as demonstrated in the following code:

```
using System;

namespace Donis.CSharpBook{
    public class Starter{
        public static void Main(){
            try {
                int var1=5, var2=0;
                var1/=var2;    // exception occurs
            }
            catch(Exception except) {
                if(except is SystemException) {
                    Console.WriteLine("Exception thrown by runtime");
                }
                else {
                    Console.WriteLine("Exception thrown by application");
                }
            }
        }
    }
}
```

System.Exception Functions

System.Exception has four constructors:

public Exception[1]*()*

public Exception[2]*(string message)*

public Exception[3]*(string message, Exception innerException)*

protected Exception[4]*(Serialization info, StreamingContext context)*

Exception[1] is the default constructor. *Exception*[2] constructor sets the user-friendly message of the exception. *Exception*[3] constructor also sets the inner exception, which is the originating exception. *Exception*[4] deserializes an exception raised remotely.

The *Exception* class has several other helpful functions. Table 9-1 lists the important methods of the class.

Table 9-1   *Exception* Methods

Method Name	Result
GetBaseException	Returns the root exception in a chain of exception objects
GetObjectData	Serializes data of the *Exception* class
GetType	Returns the type of the exception
ToString	Concatenates the name of the exception object with the user-friendly message

The following code calls *GetBaseException* and outputs the error message of the initial exception. If the current exception is the first exception in a chain of exceptions, *GetBaseException* returns null. Alternatively, you can walk *InnerException* properties back to the first exception.

```
using System;

namespace Donis.CSharpBook{
    public class Starter{
        public static void Main(){
            try {
                MethodA();
            }
            catch(Exception except) {
                Exception original=except.GetBaseException();
                Console.WriteLine(original.Message);
            }
        }

        public static void MethodA(){
            try {
                MethodB();
            }
```

```
        catch(Exception except) {
            throw new ApplicationException( "Inner Exception", except);
        }
    }

    public static void MethodB(){
        throw new ApplicationException("Innermost Exception");
    }

    }
}
```

System.Exception Properties

System.Exception has a full complement of attributes providing information on the exception. Table 9-2 describes the properties of the *Exception* class.

Table 9-2   *Exception* Properties

Property	Description	Type	Read/Write
Data	Returns a dictionary collection that provides optional user-defined details of exception.	IDictionary	R
HelpLink	Link to a help file for the exception.	string	R/W
HResult	The HRESULT, which is a 32-bit error code common to COM, assigned to the exception. This is a protected property.	int	R/W
InnerException	When exceptions are propagated, the inner exception represents the previous exception.	Exception	R
Message	User-friendly message describing the exception.	string	R
Source	Name of application or object where exception occurred.	string	R/W
StackTrace	String representation of the call stack when the exception occurred.	string	R
TargetSite	Reference to the method where exception is raised.	MethodBase	R

The *Message* and *InnerException* properties are settable in constructors of the *Exception* class.

The following code uses some of the properties of the *Exception* class. In *Main*, *MethodA* is called, and an exception is raised. The exception is caught and handled in *Main*. In the *catch* block, the exception flag is set to false. Leveraging the *TargetSite* property, *MethodA* is then called again successfully. The *TargetSite* property returns a *MethodBase* type, which can be used to late bind and invoke a method.

```csharp
using System;
using System.Reflection;

namespace Donis.CSharpBook{
    public class Starter{
        public static bool bException=true;
        public static void Main(){
            try {
                MethodA();
            }
            catch(Exception except) {
                Console.WriteLine(except.Message);
                bException=false;
                except.TargetSite.Invoke(null, null);
            }
        }

        public static void MethodA() {
            if(bException) {
                throw new ApplicationException("exception message");
            }
        }
    }
}
```

Application Exceptions

Application exceptions are custom exceptions and are thrown by the application, not by the CLR. Application exceptions are derived from *System.ApplicationException* or *System.Exception*. *System.ApplicationException* adds nothing to *System.Exception*. While *System.SystemException* is a marker for system exceptions, *System.ApplicationException* brands application exceptions. A custom exception derived from *System.Exception* accomplishes the same feat. When several custom exceptions are planned, create a custom base exception class to categorize the exceptions. For convenience and maintainability, deploy application exceptions together in a separate assembly.

Do not create an application exception for an existing exception. Research the available system exceptions to avoid replicating an existing exception.

These are the steps for creating an application exception:

1. Name the application exception. As a best practice, the class name should have the *Exception* suffix, as in *ApplicationException*.

2. Derive the application exception from *System.Exception*.

3. Define constructors that initialize the state of the application exception. This includes initializing members inherited from the base class.

4. Within the application exception, refine *System.Exception* as desired, such as by adding attributes that further delineate this specific exception.

To raise an application exception, use the *throw* statement. You can also throw system exceptions. Thrown exceptions are considered software exceptions. The CLR treats software exceptions as standard exceptions.

throw syntax:

throw *exceptioninstance*[1];

throw[2];

The second syntax is specialized: It is available in the *catch* block, but nowhere else. This version of the *throw* statement rethrows as an exception caught in the *catch* block. However, the best policy is to add additional context to an exception before propagating the exception object. Propagating exceptions is reviewed later in this chapter.

Application exceptions are typically prompted by an exceptional event. What is an exceptional event? A strict definition does not exist. You define the basis of the event using whatever criteria are appropriate. Remember, raising an exception simply for transfer of control or a nonexceptional event is bad policy. In an application, the following could be considered exceptional events where throwing an application exception is warranted:

- Constructor fails to initialize the state of an object.

- A property does not pass validation.

- Null parameters.

- An exceptional value is returned from a function.

ConstructorException is an application exception. Throw this exception when a constructor fails. It refines the *System.Exception* base class with name of the type and time of exception. In addition, the *Message* property is assigned a congruous message. This is the code for the *ConstructorException* class:

```
using System;

namespace Donis.CSharpBook{

    public class ConstructorException: Exception{

        public ConstructorException(object origin)
                : this(origin, null) {
        }

        public ConstructorException(object origin, Exception innerException)
                : base("Exception in constructor", innerException) {
            prop_Typename=origin.GetType().Name;
            prop_Time=DateTime.Now.ToLongDateString()+" "+
                DateTime.Now.ToShortTimeString();
        }
```

```
    protected string prop_Typename=null;
        public string Typename {
            get {
                return prop_Typename;
            }
        }

        protected string prop_Time=null;
        public string Time {
            get {
                return prop_Time;
            }
        }
    }
}
```

This code uses the *ConstructorException* class:

```
using System;

namespace Donis.CSharpBook{
    public class Starter{
        public static void Main(){
            try {
                ZClass obj=new ZClass();
            }
            catch(ConstructorException except) {
                Console.WriteLine(except.Message);
                Console.WriteLine("Typename: "+except.Typename);
                Console.WriteLine("Occured: "+except.Time);
            }
        }
    }

    class ZClass {
        public ZClass() {
            // initialization fails
            throw new ConstructorException(this);
        }
    }
}
```

Exception Translation

In some circumstances, the CLR catches an exception and rethrows a different exception. The inner exception of the translated exception contains the original exception. Invoking a method dynamically using reflection is one such circumstance. Exceptions raised in methods invoked by *MethodInfo.Invoke* are automatically trapped and converted to *TargetInvocation-Exception*. .NET documentation in MSDN will always confirm when exception translation will happen. Here is an example of exception translation:

```
using System;
using System.Reflection;
```

```
namespace Donis.CSharpBook{

    public class ZClass {
        public static void MethodA() {
            Console.WriteLine("ZClass.MethodA");
            throw new Exception("MethodA exception");
        }
    }

    public class Starter{
        public static void Main(){
            try {
                Type zType=typeof(ZClass);
                MethodInfo method=zType.GetMethod("MethodA");
                method.Invoke(null, null);
            }
            catch(Exception except) {
                Console.WriteLine(except.Message);
                Console.WriteLine("original: "+
                    except.InnerException.Message);
            }
        }
    }
}
```

COM Interoperability Exceptions

.NET applications often host COM components or expose managed components to COM clients. These applications must be prepared to handle and possibly throw COM exceptions, respectively. The prevalence of COM components makes COM interoperability an important consideration for managed applications into the foreseeable future.

COM Exceptions

COM components should sandbox exceptions, which protects COM clients from potential language-specific exceptions. COM methods return an HRESULT structure, which is the result code of the method. An HRESULT is a 32-bit structure, where the severity bit is the high-order bit. The severity bit is set if an exception is raised. The Win32 SDK defines constants representing various HRESULT codes. E_NOINTERFACE, E_INVALIDARG, E_OUTOFMEMORY, S_OK, and S_FALSE are common HRESULT codes. E_*codes* are error codes indicating that an exception was raised or some other exceptional event happened. S_*codes* are success codes where no failure occurred.

When managed components call methods on COM objects, the CLR consumes the resulting HRESULT. If the HRESULT represents a known COM error (E_*code*), the CLR maps the HRESULT to a managed exception. For example, E_POINTER maps to the *NullReference-Exception*, which is a managed exception. An error code from an unknown HRESULT is mapped to a *COMException* object. No exception is thrown if the HRESULT is a success code (S_*code*). Table 9-3 shows the common translations of HRESULT to managed exceptions.

Table 9-3   COM Exception Table

COM Exception	Managed Exception
COR_E_OVERFLOW	*OverflowException*
COR_E_THREADSTOP	*ThreadStopException*
E_NOINTERFACE	*InvalidCastException*
E_NOTIMPL	*NotImplementedException*
E_OUTOFMEMORY	*OutOfMemoryException*
E_POINTER	*NullReferenceException*

The *COMException* is derived from *System.Runtime.InteropServices.ExternalException*, which indirectly derives from *System.Exception*. The *COMException* class has additional properties providing the details of the unknown COM exception. The *ErrorCode* property contains the unrecognized HRESULT from the COM method.

COM components implement *Error* objects to provide extended error information to clients. An *Error* object implements the *IErrorInfo* interface. Members of the *IErrorInfo* interface correlate to members of the *COMException* class and are therefore accessible to the managed client. Table 9-4 maps members of the *Error* object to the *COMException* class.

Table 9-4   *IErrorInfo* to *COMException* Mapping

IErrorInfo Member	COMException Member
IErrorInfo::GetDescription	*COMException.Message*
IErrorInfo::GetSource	*COMException.Source*
If IErrorInfo::GetHelpFile is non-zero, *IErrorInfo::GetHelpFile+"#"+IErrorInfo::HelpContext*	*COMException.HelpLink*

The following code is a partial listing from an ATL project that publishes a COM component. The COM component exposes the *CComponentZ::MethodA*. Using the *AtlReportError* API, *CComponentZ::MethodA* builds an *Error* object to return extended error information to the client. The method also returns a custom error code in the HRESULT, which will be unknown to the CLR.

```
// ComponentZ.cpp : Implementation of CComponentZ

#include "stdafx.h"
#include "ComponentZ.h"
#include ".\componentz.h"

// CComponentZ

STDMETHODIMP CComponentZ::MethodA(void) {
    // TODO: Add your implementation code here

    HRESULT hResult=MAKE_HRESULT( 1, FACILITY_NULL, 12 );

    MessageBox(NULL, "COM component", "Hello from", MB_OK);
```

```
    return AtlReportError (GetObjectCLSID(), "My error message", 5,
        "http://error.asp",GUID_NULL, hResult);
}
```

The following code is managed code, in which the ATL component is called from a managed COM client. Because the HRESULT is unknown, the error code appears as a *COMException* exception.

```
using System;
using System.Runtime.InteropServices;

namespace COMClient {
    class Program {
        static void Main(string[] args) {
            try {
                COMLib.CComponentZClass com_object =
                    new COMLib.CComponentZClass();
                com_object.MethodA();
            }
            catch (COMException except){
                Console.WriteLine(except.ErrorCode);
                Console.WriteLine(except.HelpLink);
                Console.WriteLine(except.Message);
            }
            catch (Exception) {

            }
        }
    }
}
```

Generating COM Exceptions

Managed components have an HRESULT property that translates a managed exception to a COM error result. System exceptions are already assigned an appropriate HRESULT. For application exceptions, you should initialize the HRESULT property in the constructor. It is important that managed components that expect COM clients set the HRESULT to a known COM error code.

TypeException is an application exception, which should be thrown when an object is the wrong type. *TypeException* has two overloaded constructors. Both constructors set the *HResult* property of the exception to the E_NOTIMPL error code (0x80004001). The one-argument constructor accepts a type object, which is the required type that was not implemented. The name of the type is added to the error message of the exception. This is the code for the *TypeException* class:

```
using System;

namespace Donis.CSharpBook{

    public class TypeException: Exception{
```

```
        public TypeException()
                : base("object type wrong") {
            HResult=unchecked((int) 0x80004001); // E_NOTIMPL
        }

        public TypeException(Type objectType)
                : base("Argument type wrong: "+objectType.Name
                    +" required"){
            prop_RequiredType=objectType.Name;
            HResult=unchecked((int) 0x80004001); // E_NOTIMPL
        }

        private string prop_RequiredType;
        public string RequiredType {
            get {
                return prop_RequiredType;
            }
        }
    }
}
```

The *Delegator* class uses the *TypeException* class. *Delegator* delegates method calls of *Delegator* *.MethodA* to an external object. For the delegation to be successful, the external object must also implement the *MethodA* method, which is defined in the *ZInterface*. Appropriately, the code in *Delegator.MethodA* confirms that the external object implements the *ZInterface*. If not, the *TypeException* is thrown. Otherwise, *Delegator.MethodA* proceeds with the delegation:

```
using System;

namespace Donis.CSharpBook{
    interface ZInterface {
        void MethodA();
    }

    public class Delegator {
        public Delegator(object obj) {
            externalobject=obj;
        }

        public void MethodA() {
            if(externalobject is ZInterface) {
                ((ZInterface)externalobject).MethodA();
            }
            else {
                throw new TypeException(
                    typeof(ZInterface));
            }
        }

        private object externalobject;
    }
}
```

YClass creates an instance of the *Delegator* class. A *ZClass* object is passed into the *Delegator* constructor as the external object. *ZClass* does not implement *MethodA*. *Delegator.MethodA* is called in *YClass.UseDelegator*. A *TypeException* is thrown because the *ZClass* does not implement the appropriate interface:

```
using System;
using System.Runtime.InteropServices;
using Donis.CSharpBook;

class ZClass {
}

[ClassInterface(ClassInterfaceType.AutoDual)]
public class YClass{
    public void UseDelegator(){
        ZClass obj=new ZClass();
        Delegator del=new Delegator(obj);
        del.MethodA();
    }
}
```

COM clients can access managed code through COM Callable Wrappers (CCWs). The following unmanaged code creates an instance of *YClass* and invokes *YClass.UseDelegator*. As expected, an exception occurs, which translates to E_NOTIMPL in unmanaged code. The COM client checks for this exception and displays the appropriate message.

```
#import "..\yclass.tlb" no_namespace, raw_interfaces_only, named_guids

#include "objbase.h"

void main() {
    CoInitialize(NULL);
    _YClassPtr obj(CLSID_YClass);
    HRESULT hResult=obj->UseDelegator();
    if(hResult==E_NOTIMPL) {
        MessageBox(NULL,"Required interface not implemented",
            "In Managed Component", MB_OK);
    }
    else {
        MessageBox(NULL, "Managed Component", "No error",
            MB_OK);
    }

}
```

Remote Exceptions

Exceptions sometime occur in remote code. An exception that is raised in a different application domain is a remote exception. Remote exceptions include exceptions thrown in a .NET Remoting application or a Web service application. Exceptions that cross application domains must be serialized to maintain the state. System exceptions are serializable. However, you need to make application exceptions serializable.

Follow these steps to serialize an application exception:

1. Adorn the application exception with the *serializable* attribute.

2. Implement a two-argument constructor with a *SerializationInfo* and *StreamingContext* parameter. Deserialize the exception with the *SerializationInfo* parameter, which is a state bag. Retrieve state information of the exception using the *Get* methods of the *SerializationInfo* object. The *StreamingContext* parameter provides additional data about the source or target of the serialization process. In addition, call the same constructor in the base class to allow the base class to deserialize its state.

3. Implement the *GetObjectData* method to serialize the exception. The method also has two parameters: *Serialization* and *StreamingContext*. Use the *Serialization.AddValue* to serialize the state of the exception. Invoke *GetObjectData* on the base class to allow it to serialize itself.

4. For the exception to be available in the client assembly, share the assembly through a global assembly cache or an application configuration file. If the assembly is not shared, the assembly must be copied into the private directory of the client application.

CustomException is an application exception that supports remoting. There is one property, *prop_Time*, which is serialized in *GetObjectData* and deserialized in the two-argument constructor:

```csharp
using System;
using System.Reflection;
using System.Runtime.Serialization;

[assembly:AssemblyVersion("1.1.0.0")]
[assembly:AssemblyCultureAttribute("")]

namespace Donis.CSharpBook{

    [Serializable]
    public class CustomException: Exception{

        public CustomException()
                : base("custom exception", null) {
            prop_Time=DateTime.Now.ToLongDateString()+" "+
                DateTime.Now.ToShortTimeString();
        }

        protected CustomException(SerializationInfo info,
                StreamingContext context) : base(info, context){
            prop_Time=info.GetString("Time");
        }
```

```
public override void GetObjectData( SerializationInfo info,
        StreamingContext context ){
    info.AddValue("Time", prop_Time, typeof(string));
    base.GetObjectData(info,context);
}

protected string prop_Time=null;
public string Time {
    get {
        return prop_Time;
    }
}
    }
  }
}
```

In Microsoft Visual Studio, the assembly attributes, such as *AssemblyVersion*, are found in the *AssemblyInfo.cs* file.

Unhandled Exceptions

Unhandled exceptions are not handled directly in application code; they are handled in a global handler. The global handler reports the exception in an error box that offers the Debug, Send Error Report, and Don't Send buttons. For applications within the realm of a debugger, a potential unhandled exception is handled in the debugger.

What is the life cycle of an exception? Exceptions are initially categorized as first chance exceptions. If the application is attached to a debugger, the debugger is first consulted about the exception. Debuggers typically ignore first chance exceptions, and the exception is forwarded to the application next. When no debugger is present, the first chance exception is immediately sent to the application. If the application does not handle the first chance exception, the exception becomes a high-priority second chance exception. If a debugger is attached, the second chance exception is handled by the debugger. Upon finding a second chance exception, the Visual Studio debugger transfers the user to the location in the source code where the exception happened. If no debugger is present, execution is transferred to a global exception handler, which displays an error dialog box and then terminates the application. Figure 9-2 shows the life cycle of an exception.

Applications can trap unhandled exceptions. The mechanism is different for Windows Forms and for Console applications. For Windows Forms, add a handler to the *Application.ThreadException* event. For Console applications, the handler is added to the *AppDomain.UnhandledException* event. Methods added to the *Application.ThreadException* event chain catch and handle the exception. This is an advantage when compared with *AppDomain.UnhandledException*. Methods added to the *AppDomain.UnhandledException* event can respond to an unhandled exception, but the exception is not caught. Therefore, the exception will resurface after the handlers have completed.

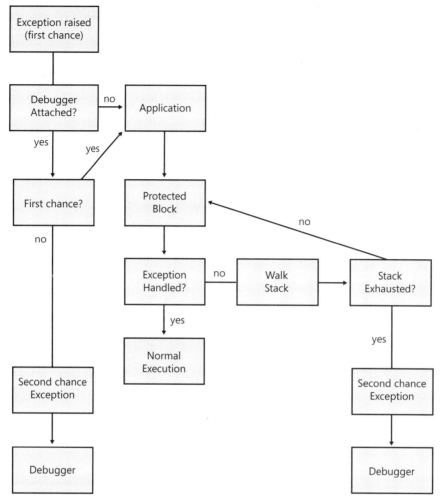

Figure 9-2   Life cycle of an exception

Do not use the unhandled exception handler to catch all exceptions. Proper application design identifies specific exceptions that an application should anticipate. Those exceptions should be caught and handled within the confines of structured exception handling. Reserve the unhandled exception method for unanticipated exceptions.

Application.ThreadException

In a Windows Forms application, the windows procedure raises the *Application.ThreadException* event upon an unhandled exception. Subscribe to the *ThreadException* event to handle the unhandled exception. The subscriber is an exception handler, which prevents the application from being terminated. Do not propagate an exception caught in this manner in the unhandled exception handler. The new exception is unprotected and will likely terminate the application. After the unhandled exception handler completes, execution continues at the next message in the message pump.

Subscribe to the *ThreadException* event with a *ThreadExceptionEventHandler* delegate, which has two parameters. The object parameter is the thread object of the thread that raised the exception. The *ThreadExceptionEventArg* parameter of the *System.Threading* namespace contains the exception that was unhandled. This is the signature of the *ThreadException-EventHandler*:

ThreadExceptionEventHandler syntax:

> void ThreadExceptionEventHandler(object sender,
>
> > ThreadExceptionEventArgs e)

In the following code, the *OnThreadException* handler is added to the *ThreadException* event. The *bthException_Click* method raises an unhandled divide by zero exception. The unhandled exception is then handled in the *OnThreadException* method, which displays an informative message. Run the application in release mode for the expected results. Otherwise, the Visual Studio debugger intercedes the exception.

```
private void btnException_Click(object sender, EventArgs e) {
    int vara = 5, varb = 0;
    vara /= varb;
}

private void Form1_Load(object sender, EventArgs e) {
    Application.ThreadException += new
        System.Threading.ThreadExceptionEventHandler(
            OnThreadException);
}

void OnThreadException(object sender, ThreadExceptionEventArgs e) {
    Thread t = (Thread) sender;
    Exception threadexception = e.Exception;
    string errormessage = "Thread ID: " +
        t.ManagedThreadId.ToString() +
            " [ "+ threadexception.Message + " ]";
    MessageBox.Show(errormessage);
}
```

AppDomain.UnhandledException

When an unhandled exception is manifested in a Console application, the *AppDomain .UnhandledException* is raised. Subscribe to the event to clean up the resources of the application, such as closing files and relinquishing data connections. You might also record the unhandled exception in the event log or another location. It is important to note that the exception is not caught in the *AppDomain.UnhandledException* handler. After the handler finishes, the unhandled exception causes the application to be terminated. The *AppDomain.Unhandled-Exception* event is triggered only in the initial application domain; it is ignored in other application domains.

Subscribe to the *AppDomain.UnhandledException* event with an *UnhandledExceptionEvent-Handler* delegate. The delegate has two parameters. The *object* parameter is the *AppDomain* object of the initial application domain. The *UnhandledExceptionEventArgs* parameter contains the specifics of the unhandled exception. This is the syntax of the *UnhandledExceptionEvent-Handler:*

UnhandledExceptionEventHandler syntax:

    void UnhandledExceptionEventHandler(object sender, UnhandledExceptionEventArgs e)

UnhandledExceptionEventArgs offers the *IsTerminating* and *ExceptionObject* properties. *IsTerminating* is a Boolean property indicating the status of the application. If true, the application is terminating because of the exception. If false, the application survives the exception. In .NET 2.0, this property is always true. Unhandled exceptions on both managed and unmanaged threads terminate an application. This is cleaner than the .NET 1.1 unhandled exception model, where exceptions raised on managed threads were nonfatal. The *Exception* property is an exception object for the unhandled exception. Inexplicably, this property is an object type, not an Exception type. Cast the property to the Exception type to access the details of the exception.

In the following Console application, the *OnUnhandledException* method is added to the *AppDomain.UnhandledException* event. When the subsequent divide by zero exception occurs, the *OnUnhandledException* method is called.

```
using System;

namespace Donis.CSharpBook{
    public class Starter{
        public static void Main(){
            AppDomain.CurrentDomain.UnhandledException+=
                new UnhandledExceptionEventHandler(
                    OnUnhandledException);

            int vara = 5, varb = 0;
            vara /= varb;
        }

        public static void OnUnhandledException(
                object sender, UnhandledExceptionEventArgs e) {
            string application_name=sender.ToString();
            Exception except=(Exception) e.ExceptionObject;
            string errormessage = "Application " +application_name+
                " [ Exception " + except.Message + " ]";
            Console.WriteLine(errormessage);
        }
    }
}
```

Managing Exceptions in Visual Studio

Visual Studio 2005 can configure exceptions for debugging. The Exception Assistant provides helpful information to developers when an unhandled exception is raised. The Exceptions dialog box alters how the Visual Studio debugger handles exceptions.

Exception Assistant

The Exception Assistant appears in Visual Studio when an unhandled exception occurs. It displays a translucent frame that partially obfuscates the application code. The source code that prompted the exception is highlighted and tethered to the Exception Assistant window. The Exception Assistant is shown in Figure 9-3.

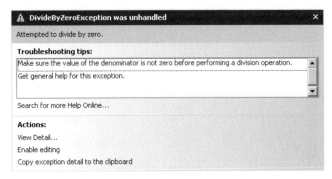

Figure 9-3   The Exception Assistant

The Exception Assistant header identifies the unhandled exception and offers a brief explanation. The Troubleshooting Tips section offers hints to diagnose the exception. Each hint is also a link to further information. The Actions pane specifies two actions:

- New Detail displays the properties of the exception object.

- Copy Exceptional Detail To The Clipboard copies basic information on the exception onto the Clipboard.

The Exception Assistant can be disabled or otherwise configured from the Tools menu. Select the Options menu item. Configure the Exception Assistant in the Debugging pane.

Exceptions Dialog Box

In the Exceptions dialog box, the Visual Studio debugger can be instructed to interrupt on first chance exceptions. Open the Exceptions dialog box from the Debug menu. Choose the Exceptions menu item. Figure 9-4 shows the Exceptions dialog box.

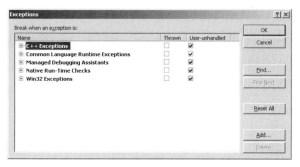

Figure 9-4 The Exceptions dialog box

The Thrown and User-unhandled columns have a series of option boxes that are organized into categories and specific exceptions. Visual Studio debugger interrupts on first chance exceptions for exceptions selected in the Thrown column. For protected code, the debugger intercedes before the exception is caught. In the development phase of an application, it can be instructive to be notified of exceptions that would otherwise be consumed in an exception handler. The second column selects specific user-handled exceptions to break on. The Add button appends application exceptions to the list of available exceptions that are selectable in the dialog box. These exceptions can later be deleted.

Metadata and Reflections

.NET assemblies adhere to the Portable Executable Common Object File Format (PE COFF). PE COFF files have headers and sections, such as a PE and CLR Header. .NET assemblies consist of metadata and MSIL code. Metadata describes the types and other characteristics of the assembly. You can inspect the metadata of an assembly using reflection. Tools, such as ILDASM, browse an assembly using reflection. Reflection also provides support for late binding. The next chapter explores metadata and reflection.

Part IV
Debugging

Chapter 10
Metadata and Reflection

Metadata, which is often described as data about data, formalizes the composition of an assembly. Metadata is the actualization of the state of an assembly. As a reflection of an assembly, metadata includes all information pertaining to the assembly, including a detailed description of each type, the attributes of the assembly, and other particulars of the assembly itself. Metadata is similar to a type library in COM, except that metadata is always persisted in the application that it describes. For this reason, assemblies are often referred to as self-describing. Because metadata is indigenous to the assembly, metadata cannot be lost, and versioning problems are avoided. Metadata is emitted primarily by managed language compilers and consumed by metadata browsers, other .NET tools, and managed applications. The Common Language Runtime (CLR) uses metadata extensively. Just-in-time compilation, code access security, garbage collection, and other services of the CLR rely heavily on metadata. Once emitted, metadata is read-only.

Metadata is important to anyone programming in the managed environment. Assembly inspection, late binding, and advanced concepts such as self-generating code require a non-trivial understanding of metadata. You can interrogate metadata by using reflection. *Reflection* facilitates late binding and other means of leveraging metadata. Most important, mastery of metadata promotes a better understanding of the managed world, which (one hopes) translates into better-written code.

Metadata

Metadata about the overall assembly and modules is called the *manifest*. Some of the macro information assembled in the manifest includes the simple name, version number, external references, module name, and public key of the assembly. A portion of the manifest is created from the assembly attributes found in the AssemblyInfo.cs file of a Microsoft Visual Studio .NET C# project. This is a partial listing of a typical AssemblyInfo.cs file:

```
using System.Reflection;
using System.Runtime.CompilerServices;
using System.Runtime.InteropServices;
```

```
// General Information about an assembly is controlled through the following
// set of attributes. Change these attribute values to modify the information
// associated with an assembly.
[assembly: AssemblyTitle("WindowsApplication4")]
[assembly: AssemblyDescription("")]
[assembly: AssemblyConfiguration("")]
[assembly: AssemblyCompany("")]
[assembly: AssemblyProduct("WindowsApplication4")]
[assembly: AssemblyCopyright("Copyright ©  2005")]
[assembly: AssemblyTrademark("")]
[assembly: AssemblyCulture("")]
```

Metadata also chronicles the microdata of the assembly, such as types, methods, and attributes. Metadata paints a portrait of each type, including the type name, methods of the type, parameters of each method of the type, each field of the type, and further details related to the loading and executing of that type at run time. Types are probably the most important construct in a .NET application, and metadata about types is used throughout the life cycle of a managed application. Here are a couple of examples. At startup, metadata is used to identify the entry point method where the program starts executing. During program execution, when a class is first touched, an EECLASS is built ostensibly from metadata to represent that type to the just-in-time compiler. The EECLASS is an important component of the just-in-time process. The EECLASS is further described in Chapter 13, "Advanced Debugging."

To extend either manifest or type-related metadata, employ attributes. *Attributes* are the adjectives of a managed application and extend the description of an assembly, class, method, field, or other target. Attributes are recorded as metadata and extend the axiomatic metadata of an assembly. In addition, the Microsoft .NET Framework class library (FCL) offers predefined-custom and pseudo-custom attributes. *Obsolete* and *StructLayout* attributes are examples of predefined attributes. *Serializable* is an example of a pseudo-custom attribute. The *Obsolete* attribute marks an entity as deprecated, whereas the *StructLayout* attribute stipulates the memory layout of fields in the context of unmanaged memory. The latter attribute is essential when passing a managed type to an unmanaged function or application programming interface (API). You can augment the predefined attributes with programmer-defined custom attributes, where the limit is only your imagination. Applying a version number to a class, assigning the name of the responsible developer or team to a class, and identifying design documents used to architect an application are some ways to exploit custom attributes.

Metadata persisted to an assembly is organized as a nonhierarchical but relational database of cross-referencing tables. The metadata database has many tables that can—and often do—reference each other. However, no parent-child relationship between tables is ever implied. Each categorization of data is maintained in a separate table, such as the TypeDef and Method-Def tables. Types alone are stored in the TypeDef table. Each record of the TypeDef table represents a type. If there were six types in the assembly, there would be six records or rows in the TypeDef table. Methods of all types are stored in the MethodDef table. Each row of the MethodDef table describes a method. The TypeDef table references the MethodDef table to link types to member methods. The MethodList column of the TypeDef table has record indexes

(RIDs) into the MethodDef table. Extending this model, the MethodDef table has a ParamList column, which is index to the method's parameters found in the Param table.

Metadata tables are assigned unique table identifiers, which are 1-byte unsigned integers. For example, the table identifier for the TypeDef table is 2, whereas 6 identifies the MethodDef table. Metadata tables reserved for the run time are not published and not assigned an external table identifier for the RID. Table 10-1 lists some of the popular metadata tables.

Table 10-1   Metadata Tables

Table Name	Table ID	Table Description
Assembly	0x20	Data related to assembly
Field	0x04	Fields (data member) of types
MethodDef	0x06	Methods (member functions) of types
NestedClass	0x29	Type definitions for nested types
Param	0x08	Method parameters of methods
Property	0x17	Properties of types
TypeDef	0x02	Type definitions of types in current assembly
TypeRef	0x01	Type definitions of types external to this module

Metadata tables are collections of records and columns. A metadata table contains a certain type of data, and each record is an instance of that type. Columns represent specific data on each instance, and each column contains a constant or index. The index references another table or heap where the metadata token is an example of an index. Metadata tokens are used as metadata pointers, allowing tables to cross-reference each other. Metadata tables can be optimized (compressed) or not optimized. For the purpose of this book, it is assumed that metadata is optimized. Metadata that is not optimized requires intermediate tables for ordered access between tables.

Tokens

Metadata tokens cross-reference other metadata tables and heaps. *Tokens* are 4-byte unsigned integers and a combination of the table identifier and RID. As shown in Figure 10-1, the high byte is the table identifier, and the lower 3 bytes are the RID. A token into the Field table might be 04000002. The token refers to the second row of the Field table. The RID is one-based, not zero-based. Because tokens are padded with zeros, the run time might optimize them. Metadata tokens are probably the most public manifestation of metadata. You will repeatedly see metadata tokens over the next few chapters.

Table ID 0	RID 1	2	3

Figure 10-1   Layout of a metadata token

In addition to other tables, metadata tables reference metadata heaps. Records of metadata tables hold fixed-length metadata information. Variable-length data is stored in one of the metadata heaps. Methods signatures are variable length and typical of content found on the String heap.

Metadata Heaps

The four metadata heaps are as follows: String, Userstring, Blob, and GUID.

- The String heap is an array of null-terminated strings. Namespace, type, field, and method names, as well as other identifiers, are stored on the String heap.

- User-defined strings are not placed on the String heap but instead reside on the Userstring heap, which is also an array of null-terminated strings. String literals from your program are cached on this heap.

- The Blob heap is a binary heap and a composite of length prefix data, such as default values, method signatures, and field signatures.

- The GUID heap is an array of globally unique identifiers (GUIDs). Yes, this is obvious. You might remember GUIDs from COM as 16-byte unique identifiers assigned to almost everything—most notably, class identifiers (CLSIDs) are assigned to class factories. What kind of GUID is stored on the GUID heap? The GUID heap contains module version identifiers (MVIDs).

Streams

Physically, metadata tables and heaps are persisted in *streams* as part of an assembly. Six possible streams, including streams for each metadata heap, are available in .NET. There are also two mutually exclusive streams, optimized and nonoptimized, which are reservoirs of metadata tables. Metadata tables are optimized or not optimized. There is no concept of partially optimized metadata tables. If the metadata tables are optimized, the optimized stream is present. Otherwise, the nonoptimized stream is available. Therefore, a managed application has at most five streams. Table 10-2 provides a complete list of the metadata streams.

Table 10-2   Metadata Streams

Name	Description
#~	Optimized or compressed metadata tables
#-	Nonoptimized metadata tables
#Blob	Physical repository of the blob heap
#GUID	Physical repository of the GUID heap
#String	Physical repository the String heap
#US	Physical repository of the Userstring heap

Metadata Validation

Managed execution is largely dependent on metadata. Improperly formed metadata could cause a managed application to fail unceremoniously. An assembly with bad metadata is like a house built on quicksand. Loading a class, just-in-time compilation, code access security, and other run-time operations depend on robust data. Metadata validation tests the correctness of metadata and is enacted preemptively, preventing applications with inferior metadata from being executed. Preventing application crashes manifested by improper metadata enforces code isolation.

Several tests are performed to validate metadata. Here is a short list:

- Cross-references between tables are validated.

- Offsets into metadata heaps are validated.

- Metadata tables must have a valid number of rows. For example, the Assembly table is allowed one row.

- Metadata tables cannot have duplicate rows.

- Several more tests are enacted to certify metadata.

Developers can request metadata validation on demand with the PEVerify and Intermediate Language Disassembler (ILDASM) tools. Both tools are included in the .NET Framework software development kit (SDK).

PEVerify submits an assembly for metadata validation and Microsoft intermediate language (MSIL) verification and then reports the results. (MSIL verification is discussed in Chapter 11, "MSIL Programming.") This is the basic syntax for PEVerify:

PEVerify assemblyname

PEVerify validates the metadata of *assemblyname*. If metadata validation is successful, MSIL verification is applied next. MSIL verification is skipped if the metadata validation fails. If validation fails, execution is not viable. This removes a compelling reason to conduct MSIL verification. PEVerify offers a variety of optional arguments, including the capability to force MSIL verification even when the metadata validation fails.

Table 10-3 lists some of the PEVerify arguments.

Table 10-3   PEVerify Options

Argument	Description
/break=errorcount	Aborts verification when errors exceed *errorcount.*
/clock	Collects data and reports duration of verification and validation tests.
/help	Help information on parameters.

Table 10-3 **PEVerify Options**

Argument	Description
/ignore=errorcode1, errorcode2, errorocoden	Ignores listed error codes.
/il	Conducts MSIL verification. When you use this command, if metadata validation is also required it must be requested explicitly.
/md	Conducts metadata validation. If MSIL verification and metadata validation are jointly desired, MSIL verification should be requested explicitly.
/?	Same as the */help* argument.

The following is a simple Hello World application, which is compiled to hello.exe. It is a minimal application, in which not much can go wrong. PEVerify will confirm this.

```
using System;

class Starter {
  static void Main() {
    Console.WriteLine("Hello, World!");
  }
}
```

The following code shows the result of running PEVerify on Hello.exe with the */il* and */clock* options. Since the *md* command is omitted, metadata verification is skipped.

```
c:\>peverify /il /clock hello.exe

All Classes and Methods in hello.exe Verified.
Timing: Total run      125 msec
        IL Ver.cycle  125 msec
        IL Ver.pure    93 msec
```

The elapsed cycle for validation and pure times is listed. Pure time is the duration of the actual metadata validation, whereas cycle encapsulates the startup and shutdown processes.

ILDASM is a .NET tool that performs validation and can browse and display the metadata of an assembly. ILDASM inspects an assembly using reflection and presents the results in a window, console, or file.

ILDASM Tool

ILDASM, which is a .NET disassembler and metadata browser, is a popular tool for developers. It proffers an internal representation of an assembly, which includes the metadata and MSIL code of an assembly in a variety of formats. ILDASM exercises reflection to inspect an assembly. The core syntax of ILDASM requires only an assembly name, which opens ILDASM and displays the metadata of the assembly:

ildasm *assemblyname*

The following simple application is a basic .NET application that references a library. The simple application has a *ZClass* and *ZStruct* type, whereas the dynamic-link library (DLL) publishes the *YClass* type.

```
using System;

namespace Donis.CSharpBook{

    interface IA {
    }

    struct ZStruct {
    }

    class Starter {

        public static void Main() {
            YClass obj1=new YClass();
            obj1.DisplayCreateTime();
            ZClass obj2=new ZClass();
            obj2.DisplayCreateTime();
        }
    }

    class ZClass: IA {

    public enum Flag {
            aflag,
            bflag
        }

    public event EventHandler AEvent=null;

        public void DisplayCreateTime() {
            Console.WriteLine("ZClass created at "+m_Time);
        }

        private string m_Time=DateTime.Now.ToLongTimeString();
        public string Time {
            get {
                return m_Time;
            }
        }
    }
}
```

Figure 10-2 is a view of Simple.exe from ILDASM. ILDASM displays a hierarchal object graph with an icon for each element of the application.

Some icons are collapsible and expandable, as indicated by a + or − symbol. The Assembly icon expands to show the details of the loaded assembly, the Namespace icon expands to show the members of the namespace, and so on. You can drill down the object graph from the assembly down to the class members. An icon depicts each item category of the graph. Table 10-4 describes each icon for which the action is double-clicking the icon.

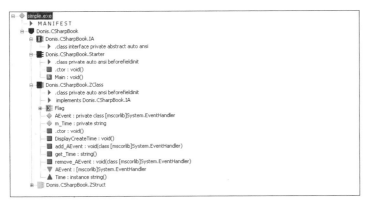

Figure 10-2   Simple.exe displayed in ILDASM

Table 10-4   Elements of ILDASM

Icon Descriptions	Action
Assembly	Shows elements of the assembly
Class	Shows members of a class
Enum	Shows members of enum type
Event	Views metadata and MSIL code of event
Field	Views metadata of field
Interface	Shows members of interface
Manifest	Views attributes of an assembly
Method	Views metadata and MSIL code of method
Namespace	Shows members of the namespace
Property	Views metadata and MSIL code of property
Static Field	Views metadata of static field
Static Method	Views metadata and MSIL code of static method
Value Type	Shows members of a value type

Some elements are displayed twice. For example, a property is presented as itself and separately as *accessor* and *mutator* methods.

ILDASM has a variety of command-line options. Table 10-5 lists these parameters.

Table 10-5   ILDASM Options

ILDASM Option	Description
Out	Renders metadata and MSIL to a text file.
Text	Renders metadata and related MSIL to console.
HTML	Combines with the *out* option to display metadata and MSIL in an HTML format.

Table 10-5   ILDASM Options

ILDASM Option	Description
RTF	Renders metadata and MSIL in Rich Text Format.
Bytes	Shows MSIL code with opcodes and related bytes.
Raweh	Shows label form of *try* and *catch* directives in raw form.
Tokens	Shows metadata tokens.
Source	Shows MSIL interlaced with commented source code; for this command, the source code and debug file must be accessible.
Linenum	Inserts line directives into an output stream that matches source code to MSIL. This command requires the debug file.
Visibility	Disassembles only members with the stated visibility: pub (public), pri (private), fam (family), asm (assembly), FAA (family and assembly), foa (family and assembly), and PSC (private scope).
Pubonly	Disassembles only public elements; short notation for *visibility=pub*.
QuoteAllNames	Brackets all identifiers in single quotes.
NOCA	Excludes custom attributes.
CAVerbal	Displays blob information of custom attributes in symbolic form and not binary.
NOBAR	Do not display progress bar.
UTF8	Renders output file in UTF8 (default ANSI).
UNICODE	Renders output file in UNICODE.
NOIL	Do not disassemble language source code.
Forward	Generates forward references and assemble in the Class Structure Declaration section.
TypeList	Displays list of types.
Headers	Includes DOS, PE, COFF, CLR, and metadata header information.
Item	Disassembles a particular class or method.
Stats	Displays statistical information on file, PE Header, CLR Header, and metadata.
ClassList	Provides a commented list of classes with attributes.
All	Combination of the *Header*, *Bytes*, *Stats*, *ClassLists*, and *Tokens* commands.
Metadata	Displays specific information related to metadata.
Objectfile	Shows metadata of a library file.

The user interface of ILDASM presents the same choices as the command-line options. The following command line is typical. It disassembles simple.exe and outputs the resulting metadata, MSIL, metadata tokens, and source code in the simple.il file.

```
ildasm /out=simple.il /source /tokens simple.exe
```

The source option of the preceding command interlaces source code in between MSIL code. The source code is commented. Associating MSIL to source code is invaluable when debugging.

The tokens generated per the tokens option are also commented. The disassembly created by ILDASM is a valid MSIL program that can be recompiled (which is the reason for the *il* extension, as in client.il). The assembly can be reassembled with the ILASM compiler, which compiles MSIL code. The newly assembled assembly is identical to the original assembly.

Some ILDASM options impede the creation of a full disassembly. When a partial disassembly is requested, ILDASM issues a warning, which prevents you from attempting to use a partial assembly as a full assembly. One limitation is that partial assemblies cannot be reassembled using ILASM. The following command creates a partial assembly:

```
ildasm /out=simple.il /item=Donis.CSharpBook.ZClass simple.exe
```

The preceding command targets only the *ZClass* of the simple.exe assemblies. Because other types are omitted from the disassembly, it is not complete. For this reason, a warning is added to the output file. Following is a partial listing of the output file with the embedded warning:

```
// Microsoft (R) .NET Framework IL Disassembler.  Version 2.0.50601.0
//  Microsoft Corporation. All rights reserved.


// warning : THIS IS A PARTIAL DISASSEMBLY, NOT SUITABLE FOR RE-ASSEMBLING



.class private auto ansi beforefieldinit Donis.CSharpBook.ZClass
       extends [mscorlib]System.Object
       implements Donis.CSharpBook.IA
{
  .field private class [mscorlib]System.EventHandler AEvent
  .field private string m_Time
  .method public hidebysig specialname instance void
```

This is the final example of ILDASM and command-line options. This command profiles the metadata yields counts, validates the metadata, and persists the results to the simple.txt file:

```
ildasm /metadata=csv /metadata=validate /out=simple.txt simple.exe
```

Reflection

An assembly is a piñata stuffed with goodies such as type information, MSIL code, and custom attributes. You use reflection to break open the assembly piñata to examine the contents. Reflection adds important features to .NET, such as metadata inspection, run-time creation of types, late binding, MSIL extraction, self-generating code, and so much more. These features are crucial to solving complex real-world problems that developers face every day.

The *Reflection* namespace is the container of all things related to reflection. *Assembly, Module, LocalVariableInfo, MemberInfo, MethodInfo, FieldInfo,* and *Binder* are some of the important members of the *Reflection* namespace. Reflection exposes several predefined customer attributes, such as *AssemblyVersionAttribute*, *AssemblyKeyFileAttribute*, and *AssemblyDelay-SignAttribute*. The *Reflection* namespace contains other reflection-related namespaces; most notably the *Reflection.Emit* nested namespace. *Reflection.Emit* is a toolbox filled with tools for building assemblies, classes, and methods at run time, including the ability to emit metadata and MSIL code. *Reflection.Emit* is reviewed in Chapter 11.

The central component of reflection is the *Type* object. Its interface can be used to interrogate a reference or value type. This includes browsing methods, fields, parameters, and custom attributes. General information pertaining to the type is also available via reflection, including identifying the hosting assembly. Beyond browsing, *Type* objects support more intrusive operations. You can create instances of classes at run time and perform late binding of methods.

Obtaining a Type Object

The *Object.GetType* method, the *typeof* operator, and various methods of the *Assembly* object return a *Type* object. *GetType* is a member of the *Object* class, which is the ubiquitous base class. Therefore, *GetType* is inherited by .NET types and available to all managed instances. Each instance can call *GetType* to return the related *Type* object. The *typeof* operator extracts a *Type* object directly from a reference or value type. Assembly objects have several members that return one or more *Type* objects. For example, the *Assembly.GetTypes* method enumerates and returns the *Types* of the target assembly.

As a member base class object, *GetType* is accessible to all instances of reference and values types. *GetType* returns the *Type* object of the instance. This is the syntax of the *GetType* method:

```
Type Type.GetType method:
Type GetType()
```

The following code creates instances of a value and a reference type, which are passed individually as object parameters to successive calls to the *DisplayType* method, which homogenizes the objects, where each object loses its distinction. The function extracts the type of the instance and displays the *Type* name. Finally, if the *Type* represents a *ZClass*, the *ZClass.Display* method is called:

```
using System;

namespace Donis.CSharpBook{
    class Starter{

        static void Main() {
            int localvalue=5;
            ZClass objZ=new ZClass();
            DisplayType(localvalue);
            DisplayType(objZ);
        }
```

```
        static void DisplayType(object parameterObject) {
            Type parameterType=parameterObject.GetType();
            string name=parameterType.Name;
            Console.WriteLine("Type is "+name);
            if(name == "ZClass") {
                ((ZClass) parameterObject).Display();
            }
        }

    }

    class ZClass {

        public void Display() {
            Console.WriteLine("ZClass::Display");
        }
    }
}
```

The *typeof* operator returns a *Type* object from a type. The *typeof* operator is evaluated at compile time, whereas the *GetType* method is invoked at run time. For this reason, the *typeof* operator is quicker but less flexible than the *GetType* method:

```
typeof operator:
typeof(type)
```

An assembly is typically the host of multiple types. *Assembly.GetTypes* enumerates the types defined in an assembly. *Assembly.GetType* is overloaded four times. The zero-argument method returns the *Type* object of the *Assembly* and essentially the *GetType* method derived from the *Object* class. The one-argument version, in which the parameter is a string, returns a specific type defined in the assembly. The final two versions of *GetType* are an extension of the one-argument overloaded method. The two-argument method also has a Boolean parameter. When true, the method throws an exception if the type is not located. The three-argument version has a second Boolean parameter that stipulates case sensitivity. If this parameter is false, the case of the type name is significant.

Here are the methods:

```
Assembly.GetTypes method:
Type [] GetTypes()
Assembly.GetType method:
Type GetType()
Type GetType(string typename)
Type GetType(string typename, bool throwError)
Type GetType(string typename, bool throwError, bool ignoreCase)
```

An assembly can be diagrammed through reflection. The result is called the Reflection tree of that assembly. Each element of reflection, such as an *AssemblyInfo*, *Type*, *MethodInfo*, and *ParameterInfo* component, is placed on the tree. *AppDomain* is the root of the tree; *GetAssemblies* expands the tree from the root. The Reflection tree is a logical, not a physical representation.

Assembly, *Type*, and *ParameterInfo* are some of the branches on the Reflection tree. You can explore the Reflection tree while inspecting the metadata of the application by using enumeration. For example, *Assembly.GetCurrentAssembly* returns the current assembly. *Assembly.GetTypes* will enumerate the types defined in the assembly. *Type.GetMethods* will enumerate the methods of each type. This process can continue until the application is fully reflected.

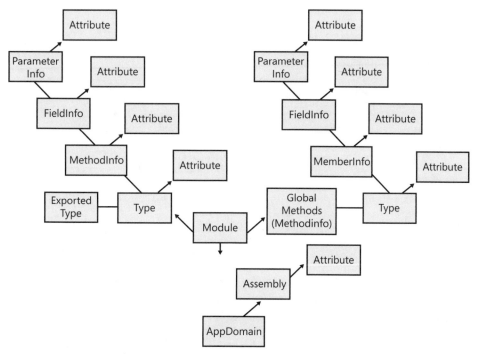

Figure 10-3   Diagram of the Reflection tree

Loading Assemblies

Assemblies near the root of the reflection tree can be loaded at run time using *Assembly.Load* and *Assembly.LoadFrom*. *Assembly.Load* uses the assembly loader to locate and bind to the correct assembly. *Assembly.LoadFrom* consults the assembly resolver to locate an assembly, which uses a combination of the strong name identifier and probing to bind and then load an assembly. The strong name includes the simple name, version, culture, and public key token of the assembly. Probing is the algorithm for locating an assembly. Both *Assembly.Load* and *Assembly.LoadFrom* are static methods that are overloaded several times. This is the core syntax:

```
Assembly.Load method:
static Assembly Assembly Load(string assemblyName)
Assembly.LoadFrom method:
static Assembly Assembly.LoadFrom(string AssemblyFileName)
```

When the chosen assembly isn't found, *Assembly.Load* and *Assembly.LoadFrom* will fail. The Assembly Binding Log Viewer Tool (fuslogvw.exe), included in the .NET Framework SDK, is a useful tool for diagnosing probing failures because it displays information on the binding error.

The following sample code accentuates the difference between *Assembly.Load* and *Assembly.LoadFrom*:

```
using System;
using System.Reflection;

namespace Donis.CSharpBook{
  class Starter{
    static void Main(){
      Assembly library=Assembly.Load("library, Version=2.0.0.0, "+
        "Culture=Neutral, PublicKeyToken=9b184fc90fb9648d");
      Console.WriteLine("Assembly.Load:  {0}", library.FullName);
      library=Assembly.LoadFrom("library.dll");
      Console.WriteLine("Assembly.LoadFrom {0}", library.FullName);
    }
  }
}
```

Assembly.Load and *Assembly.LoadFrom* reference external assemblies. How about referencing the currently executing assembly? *Assembly.GetExecutingAssembly* is a static method and returns a reference to the currently executing assembly. This is valuable for interrogating the metadata or MSIL of the running assembly.

```
Assembly.GetExecutingAssembly method:
static Assembly Assembly.GetExecutingAssembly()
```

Both *Assembly.Load* and *Assembly.LoadFrom* return a reference to an assembly. That assembly can be reflected, code loaded, and then executed. *Assembly.ReflectionOnlyLoad* and *Assembly.ReflectionOnlyLoadFrom* load an assembly only for reflection, so the code cannot be executed later. Although you could reflect a type and iterate all the methods, you could not invoke a method of that type. To confirm the way an *Assembly* is loaded, use the *ReflectionOnly* property. *ReflectionOnly* is a Boolean attribute of an *Assembly* and is true if an *Assembly* is loaded for reflection only. *Assembly.ReflectionOnlyLoad* and *Assembly.ReflectionOnlyLoadFrom* are equivalent to *Assembly.Load* and *Assembly.LoadFrom*, respectively, without the execute capability. *ReflectionOnly* yields performance benefits.

The following program benchmarks the performance of *Assembly.Load* versus *Assembly.ReflectionOnlyLoad*. The *DateTime* function has poor resolution and is inferior for most testing scenarios. Instead, a high-performance timer is needed to obtain added resolution. The *QueryPerformanceCounter* API returns a high-performance counter accurate to a nanosecond. Prior to .NET Framework 2.0, *QueryPerformanceCounter* was available only through interoperability. The *Stopwatch* class, which is a thin wrapper for the *QueryPerformanceCounter* and related APIs, was introduced in .NET Framework 2.0 and found in the *System.Diagnostics* namespace:

```
using System;
using System.Reflection;
using System.Diagnostics;

namespace Donis.CSharpBook{
  class OnlyLoad{
    static void Main() {
      Stopwatch duration=new Stopwatch();
      duration.Reset();
      duration.Start();
      Assembly a=Assembly.Load("library");
      duration.Stop();
      Console.WriteLine(duration.ElapsedTicks.ToString());
      duration.Reset();
      duration.Start();
      a=Assembly.ReflectionOnlyLoad("library");
      duration.Stop();
      Console.WriteLine(duration.ElapsedTicks.ToString());
    }
  }
}
```

Execution time of *Assembly.Load* versus *Assembly.ReflectionOnlyLoad* might vary between different implementations of the CLI and other factors. The program compares ticks, which is an abstraction of time. Running the problem several times indicates that *Assembly.Reflection-OnlyLoad* is about 29 percent faster than *Assembly.Load*. This is only an approximation.

Type.ReflectionOnlyGetType combines the functionality of *Assembly.ReflectionOnlyLoad* and the *typeof* operator. The named assembly is loaded for inspection only, and a *Type* object is returned to the specified type. Because the assembly is opened only for browsing, you cannot create an instance of the type or invoke a method on the type. *ReflectionOnlyGetType* is a static method of the *Type* class and loads a *Type* for inspection only. The method returns a *Type* object:

```
Type.ReflectionOnlyType method:
static Type ReflectionOnlyType(string typeName, bool notFoundException,
  bool ignoreCase)
```

The *typeName* parameter is a combination of the *Assembly* and *Type* names. The *Assembly* and *Type* names are comma-delimited. To raise an exception if the type is not found, set the *notFoundException* parameter to *true*. When false, the *ignoreCase* parameter indicates that the *Type* name is case sensitive:

```
using System;
using System.Reflection;

namespace Donis.CSharpBook{
  class ReflectOnlyType{
```

```
static void Main() {
  Type zType=Type.ReflectionOnlyGetType("Donis.CSharpBook.ClassA,
    Library", false, false);
  Console.WriteLine(zType.Name);
  }
 }
}
```

Browsing Type Information

Inspecting a type begins with the *Type* object. *Reflection* has a straightforward interface for mining the metadata of a type. Inspecting the metadata of a type essentially consists of spanning a series of collections. The *Type* object interface publishes several methods and properties related to reflection.

Type.GetMembers returns the ultimate collection: the collection of all members. All members, whether the member is a method, field, event, or property, are included in the collection. *GetMembers* returns a *MemberInfo* array that contains an item for each member. *GetMember* returns a single *MemberInfo* object for the named member. *MemberInfo.MemberType* is a property of the *MemberInfo.MemberTypes* type, which is a bitwise enumeration distinguishing a member as a method, field, property, event, constructor, or something else. (See Table 10-6.) *MemberInfo* has relatively few properties and operations. Here are some of the more useful. The *MemberInfo.Name* offers the name of the type member. *MemberInfo.MetadataToken*, another property, returns the metadata token of the member. *MemberInfo.ReflectedType* provides the *Type* object from which the *MemberInfo* object was extracted.

Table 10-6 *MemberTypes* **Enumeration**

MemberType	Value
MemberTypes.Constructor	0x01
MermberTypes.Custom	0x40
MemberTypes.Event	0x02
MemberTypes.Field	0x04
MemberTypes.Method	0x08
MemberTypes.NestedType	0x80
MemberTypes.Property	0x10
MemberTypes.TypeInfo	0x20
MemberTypes.All	0xBF

Type.GetMembers creates a basket that contains all the members of the reflected type. You can be somewhat more granular. *Type.GetMethods* or *Type.GetMethod* returns a collection of methods or a specific method. *Type.GetFields* or *Type.GetField* similarly returns a collection of fields or a specific field. Table 10-7 lists the methods that return specific collections where the non-plural method returns a specific member of that collection.

Table 10-7 Type Methods That Return Metadata Collections

Method	Returns	Type of Member
GetConstructors	ConstructorInfo []	Constructor
GetCustomAttributes	Object []	Custom attribute
GetDefaultMembers	MemberInfo []	Default member
GetEvents	EventInfo []	Event
GetFields	FieldInfo []	Field
GetInterfaces	Type []	Implemented interface
GetMembers	MemberInfo []	All members
GetMethods	MethodInfo []	Method
GetNestedTypes	Type []	Nested Type
GetProperties	PropertyInfo []	Property

The *Type.GetMethods* that return *MethodInfo* arrays are overloaded to be called with no parameters or with a single parameter, which is *BindingFlags*:

```
Type.GetMethods method:
MethodInfo [] GetMethods();
MethodInfo[] GetMethods(BindingFlags binding)
```

BindingFlags is a bitwise enumeration that filters the results of a collection. For example, to include private members in a collection stipulates the *BindingFlags.NonPublic* flag. Some *BindingFlags*, such as *InvokeMember*, are not applicable in this context. When stipulating *Binding-Flags*, there are no default flags. If you specify one flag, you must specify every required flag. Each inclusion must be specified explicitly. The zero-argument version of *GetMethods* grants default bindings, which vary depending on the method. At a minimum, most of the methods default to *BindingFlags.Public* and *BindingFlags.Instance*. Notably, the *BindingFlags.Static* flag is not always defaulted and static members are often excluded from a collection. The following code first iterates private instance (nonpublic) members. Afterward, static public members are iterated.

```
using System;
using System.Reflection;

namespace Donis.CSharpBook{
  class DumpType{
    public static void Main() {
      ZClass zObj=new ZClass();
      Type tObj=zObj.GetType();
      MemberInfo [] members=tObj.GetMembers(
        BindingFlags.Instance|
        BindingFlags.NonPublic);
      foreach(MemberInfo member in members) {
        Console.WriteLine(member.Name);
      }
      members=tObj.GetMembers(
        BindingFlags.Public|BindingFlags.Static);
```

```
    Console.WriteLine(" ");
      foreach(MemberInfo member in members) {
         Console.WriteLine(member.Name);
      }
    }
  }

  class ZClass {
    private int vara=5;
    public int PropA {
      get {
        return vara;
      }
    }
    static public void MethodA() {
      Console.WriteLine("ZClass::MethodA called.");
    }
  }
}
```

The following application calls *DumpMethods* to dump the public methods of a class. This code demonstrates various aspects of *Reflection*.

```
using System;
using System.Reflection;

namespace Donis.CSharpBook{
    class DumpType{
        static void Main(string [] argv) {
            targetType=LoadAssembly(argv[0], argv[1]);
            DumpReportHeader();
            DumpMethods();
         }

        static public Type LoadAssembly(string t, string a) {
            return Type.ReflectionOnlyGetType(t+","+a, false, true);
        }

        static void DumpReportHeader() {
            Console.WriteLine("\n{0} type of {1} assembly",
                targetType.Name, targetType.Assembly.GetName().Name);
            Console.WriteLine("\n{0,22}\n", "[ METHODS ]");
        }

        static void DumpMethods() {
            string dashes=new string('-', 50);
            foreach(MethodInfo method in targetType.GetMethods()) {
                Console.WriteLine("{0,12}{1,-12}", " ", method.Name+" "+
                    "<"+method.ReturnParameter.ParameterType.Name+">");
                int count=1;
                foreach(ParameterInfo parameter in method.GetParameters()){
                    Console.WriteLine("{0, 35}{1, -12}",
                        " ", (count++).ToString()+" "+ parameter.Name+
                        " ("+parameter.ParameterType.Name+")");
                }
```

```
                    Console.WriteLine("{0,12}{1}", " ", dashes);
            }
        }

        private static Type targetType;
    }
}
```

In the preceding code, a type name and an assembly name are read from the command line. The type to be dumped is *argv[0]*, while the assembly hosting the type is *argv[1]*. With this information, the *LoadAssembly* method employs *Type.ReflectionOnlyGetType* and loads the type for inspection only. The *DumpMethods* function iterates the methods of the target type, and then iterates the parameters of each method. The name of each method and parameter is displayed. This dumps the members of the *Console* class:

```
dumpmethods System.Console mscorlib.dll
```

Dynamic Invocation

Methods can be dynamically invoked at run time using reflection. The benefits and perils of early binding versus late binding were reviewed in the discussion on delegates earlier in the book.

In dynamic binding, you build a method signature at run time and then invoke the method. This is somewhat later than late binding with delegates. When compared with delegates, dynamic binding is more flexible, but is regrettably slower. At compile time, the method signature must match the delegate at the site of the run-time binding. Dynamic binding removes this limitation, and any method can be invoked at the call site, regardless of the signature. This is more flexible and extensible than run-time binding.

In reflection, there are two approaches to invoking a method dynamically: *MethodInfo.Invoke* and *Type.InvokeMember*, where *MethodInfo.Invoke* is the simplest solution. However, *Type.InvokeMember* is more malleable. The basic syntax of *MethodInvoke* requires only two parameters: an instance of a type and an array of parameters. The method is bound to the instance provided. If the method is static, the instance parameter is null. To avoid an exception at run time, which is never fun, care must be taken to ensure that the instance and parameters given to *MethodInfo.Invoke* match the signature of the function.

This is the *MethodInfo.Invoke* syntax:

```
object Invoke¹(object obj, object [] arguments)
object Invoke² (object obj, BindingFlags flags, Binder binderObj,
    object [] arguments, CultureInfo culture)
```

The second *Invoke* method has several additional parameters. The *obj* parameter is the instance that method is bound. If invoking a static method, the *obj* parameter should be null but is otherwise ignored. *BindingFlags* are next and further describe the Invoke operation, such as *Binding.InvokeMethod*. When no binding flags are specified, the default is *Binding-Flags.DefaultBinding*. *Binderobj* is used to select the appropriate candidate among overloaded methods. *Arguments* is the array of method arguments as defined by the method signature. The *culture* argument sets the culture, which defaults to the culture of the system. Return is the method return or null for a void return.

Alternatively, you can invoke a method dynamically at run time using *Type.InvokeMember*, which is overloaded several times.

This is the *Type.InvokeMember* syntax:

```
object InvokeMember¹(string methodName, BindingFlags flags,
    Binder binderObj, object typeInstance, object [] arguments)
object InvokeMember²(string methodName, BindingFlags flags,
    Binder binderObj, object typeInstance, object [] arguments,
    CultureInfo culture)
object InvokeMember³(string methodName, BindingFlags flags,
    Binder binderObj, object typeInstance, object [] arguments,
    ParameterModifier [] modifiers, CultureInfo culture,
    string [] namedParameters)
```

*InvokeMember*¹ is the core overloaded method, and it has several parameters. The *method-Name* parameter is the name of the method to invoke. The next parameter is *BindingFlags*. *Binderobj* is the binder used to discriminate between overloaded methods. The object to bind the method again is *typeInstance*. *arguments* is the array of method parameters. *InvokeMember*² adds an additional parameter. To set the culture, use the culture parameter. *InvokeMember*³ is the final overload with one additional parameter: *namedParameters*, which is used to specify named parameters.

In the following code, dynamic invocation is demonstrated with *MethodInfo.Invoke* and *Type.InvokeMember*:

```
using System;
using System.Reflection;

namespace Donis.CSharpBook{

    class Starter{

        static void Main(){
            ZClass obj=new ZClass();
            Type tObj=obj.GetType();
            MethodInfo method=tObj.GetMethod("MethodA");

            method.Invoke(obj, null);
            tObj.InvokeMember("MethodA", BindingFlags.InvokeMethod,
                null, obj, null);
        }
    }
    class ZClass {
```

```
      public void MethodA() {
         Console.WriteLine("ZClass.Method invoked");
      }
   }
}
```

Binders

Members such as methods can be overloaded. In reflection, binders determine the specific method to invoke from a list of possible candidates. The default binder selects the best match based on the number and type of arguments. You can provide a custom binder and choose a specific overloaded member. Both *MethodInfo.Invoke* and *Type.InvokeMember* offer a binder argument for this reason.

The *Binder* class is an abstract class; as such, it is implemented through a derived concrete class. *Binder* has abstracted methods to select a field, property, and method from available overloaded candidates. *Binder* is a member of the *Reflection* namespace. Table 10-8 lists the public members of the *Binder* class. Each method included in the table is abstract and must be overridden in any derivation.

Table 10-8   Abstract Methods of the *Binder* Class

Binder Method	Description
BindToField	Selects a field from a set of overloaded fields
BindToMethod	Selects a method from a set of overloaded methods
ChangeType	Coerces the type of an object
ReorderArgumentArray	Resets the argument array; associated with the state parameter of *BindToMethod* member
SelectMethod	Selects a method from candidate methods
SelectProperty	Selects a property from candidate properties

Binder.BindToMethod is called when a method is invoked dynamically. To override the default selection criteria of overloaded methods, create a custom binder class. Inherit the binder class and at least minimally override and implement each abstract method of the base class. How the binder is used determines the methods to fully implement. If the *MethodInfo.Invoke* and *Type.InvokeMember* methods are called with the *BindingFlags.InvokeMethod* flag set, *BindToMethod* will be invoked and should be completely implemented.

The *Binder.BindToMethod* syntax is as follows:

```
public abstract BindToMethod(BindingFlags flags, MethodBase [] match,
   ref object [] args, ParameterModifier [] modifiers, CultureInfo culture,
   string [] names, out object state)
```

The first parameter of *BindToMethod* is *BindingFlags*, which is the usual assortment of binding flags. *match* is a *MethodBase* array with an element for each possible candidate. If there are three candidates, *match* has three elements. At present, *MethodBase*-derived classes are limited to *ConstructorInfo; MethodInfo.args* are the values of method parameters. *Modifiers* is an array of *ParameterModifier* used with parameter signatures of modified types. *Culture* sets the culture. *Names* are the identifiers of methods included as candidates. The *modifiers, culture,* and *names* parameters can be null. The final parameter, *state,* is used with parameter reordering. If this parameter is non-null, *Binder.ReorderArgumentArray* is called after *BindToMethod* and returns the parameters to the original order.

There is no prescription for selecting a method from a set of candidates. You are free to be creative and employ whatever logic seems reasonable. Here is a partially implemented but workable custom *Binder* class. *BindToMethod* is implemented but the other methods are essentially stubbed. This code is somewhat circumscribed and not written for general-purpose application.

```csharp
using System;
using System.Reflection;
using System.Globalization;

class CustomBinder:Binder {
    public override FieldInfo BindToField(BindingFlags bindingAttr,
            FieldInfo[] match, object value, CultureInfo culture) {
        return null;
    }

    public override MethodBase BindToMethod(BindingFlags bindingAttr,
            MethodBase[] match, ref object[] args,
            ParameterModifier[] modifiers, CultureInfo culture,
            string[] names, out object state) {
        Console.WriteLine("Overloaded Method:");
        foreach(MethodInfo method in match) {
            Console.Write("\n {0} (", method.Name);
            foreach(ParameterInfo parameter in
                    method.GetParameters()) {
                Console.Write(" "+parameter.ParameterType.ToString());
            }
            Console.WriteLine(" )");
        }
        Console.WriteLine();
        state=null;
        if(long.Parse(args[0].ToString())>int.MaxValue) {
            return match[0];
        }
        else {
            return match[1];
        }
    }

    public override object ChangeType(object value, Type type,
            CultureInfo culture) {
        return null;
    }
}
```

```csharp
    public override void ReorderArgumentArray(ref object[] args,
            object state){
    }

    public override MethodBase SelectMethod(BindingFlags bindingAttr,
            MethodBase[] match, Type[] types,
            ParameterModifier[] modifiers) {
        return null;
    }

    public override PropertyInfo SelectProperty(BindingFlags bindingAttr,
            PropertyInfo[] match, Type returnType, Type[] indexes,
            ParameterModifier[] modifiers) {
        return null;
    }
}

class ZClass {
    public void MethodA(long argument) {
        Console.WriteLine("Long version: "+argument.ToString());
    }

    public void MethodA(int argument) {
        Console.WriteLine("Int version: "+argument.ToString());
    }

    public void MethodA(int argument, int argument2) {
        Console.WriteLine("ZClass::Method 2 arg");
    }
}

class Starter {
    public static void Main() {
    ZClass obj=new ZClass();
    Type tObj=obj.GetType();
        CustomBinder theBinder=new CustomBinder();
        tObj.InvokeMember("MethodA", BindingFlags.InvokeMethod,
            theBinder, obj, new Object[] {int.MinValue});
        Console.WriteLine();
        tObj.InvokeMember("MethodA", BindingFlags.InvokeMethod, theBinder,
            obj, new Object[] {long.MaxValue});
    }
}
```

In the preceding code, *CustomBinder* inherits from the *Binder* class. As mentioned, *BindTo-Method* is the sole method implemented in the code. This function lists the signatures of each candidate. The appropriate method is then chosen. The first *foreach* loop iterates the candidates while listing the method names. The inner *foreach* loop iterates and lists the parameters of each *MethodInfo* object. This version of *BindToMethod* is written specifically for the one-argument methods of the *ZClass BindToMethod*. The argument value is tested. If the value is within the range of a long, the first method is returned. This method has a long parameter. Otherwise, the second candidate, which has an integer parameter, is returned.

In *Main*, an instance of the *ZClass* and custom binder is created. *ZClass* is a simple class with an overloaded method. *ZClass.MethodA* is overloaded three times. The type object is then extracted from the *ZClass* instance, and *Type.InvokeMember* is called twice with the custom binder. *InvokeMember* is called to dynamically invoke "MethodA", first with an integer parameter and then with a long parameter. This is the output from the application:

```
Overloaded Method:
MethodA ( System.Int64 )

MethodA ( System.Int32 )

Int version: -2147483648

Overloaded Method:

MethodA ( System.Int64 )

MethodA ( System.Int32 )

Long version: 9223372036854775807
```

Type Creation

Until now, the emphasis of this chapter has been on reflecting existing objects. Object instances can also be created dynamically at run time. You can reflect, bind methods, and otherwise treat the dynamic object as a static object. As often with *Reflection*, the primary benefit is added flexibility. What if the type of an instance is not determinable at compile time? With *Reflection*, that decision can be delayed until run time, when the particular class can be chosen by the user, stipulated in a configuration file, or otherwise selected by some intermediary.

The *Activator* class is a member of the *Reflection* namespace and facilitates the creation of objects at run time. *Activator* consists of four static member methods: *CreateInstance* creates an instance of a type; *CreateInstanceFrom* leverages *Assembly.LoadFrom* to reference an assembly and then create an instance of a type found in the assembly; and *CreateComInstanceFrom* and *GetObject* instantiate a COM object and a proxy to a *Remote* object, respectively. To simply create an instance of a .NET type, call *CreateInstance* or *CreateInstanceFrom*. Both *CreateInstance* and *CreateInstanceFrom* are overloaded several times. This is the list of *CreateInstance* methods:

```
Activator.CreateInstance syntax:
static T CreateInstance<T>()
static public ObjectHandle CreateInstance(ActivationContext context)
static object CreateInstance(Type type)
static public ObjectHandle CreateInstance(ActivationContext context, string [] customData)
static ObjectHandle CreateInstance(string assemblyName, string typeName)
static object CreateInstance(Type type, bool ctorPublic)
static object CreateInstance(Type type, object [] ctorArgs)
static ObjectHandle CreateInstance<T, U> (T, U)
static ObjectHandle CreateInstance(string assemblyName, string typeName,
  object [] activationAttributes)
static object CreateInstance(string assemblyName, string TypeName,
```

```
    object [] activationAttributes)
static object CreateInstance(Type type, BindingFlags bindingAttr,
  Binder binder, object [] args, CultureInfo culture)
static object CreateInstance(Type type, object [] args, object [] activationAttributes)
static Object CreateInstance(Type type, BindingFlags bindingAttr, Binder binder,
  object [] args, CultureInfo culture, object [] activationAttributes)
static ObjectHandle CreateInstance(string assemblyName, string typeName,
  bool ignoreCase, BindingFlags bindingAttr, Binder Binder,
  object [] args, CultureInfo culture, object [] activationAttributes,
  Evidence securityInfo)
```

Some *CreateInstance* methods—and all *CreateInstanceFrom* methods—return an *ObjectHandle*, which is usually returned when creating an instance of a type foreign to the current assembly. *ObjectHandle* is found in the *System.Runtime.Remoting* namespace. *ObjectHandle.Unwrap* unwraps the *ObjectHandle* to disclose a proxy to the remoted object. Alternatively, the *AppDomain.CreateInstanceFromAndUnwrap* method creates an instance of the type and returns the object unwrapped with one less step. Of course, this means that an additional step of obtaining an *AppDomain* object is necessary. However, if the *AppDomain* object is handy, *CreateInstanceFromAndUnwrap* is convenient.

The following code creates three instances of the same type. A local and two remote proxies to object instances are constructed:

```
using System;
using System.Reflection;
using System.Runtime.Remoting;

namespace Donis.CSharpBook{

  class ZClass {
    public void MethodA(DateTime dt) {
        Console.WriteLine("MethodA invoked at "+
          dt.ToLongTimeString());
    }
  }

  class Starter{

    static void Main() {
      CreateLocal();
      CreateRemote1();
      CreateRemote2();
    }

    static void CreateLocal() {
      object obj=Activator.CreateInstance(typeof(ZClass));
      ((ZClass) obj).MethodA(DateTime.Now);
    }

    static void CreateRemote1() {
      ObjectHandle hObj=Activator.CreateInstance("library",
        "Donis.CSharpBook.ZClass");
      object obj=hObj.Unwrap();
```

```
      MethodInfo method=obj.GetType().GetMethod("MethodA");
      method.Invoke(obj, new object [1] {DateTime.Now});
    }

    static void CreateRemote2() {
      AppDomain domain=AppDomain.CurrentDomain;
      object obj=domain.CreateInstanceFromAndUnwrap("library.dll",
         "Donis.CSharpBook.ZClass");
      MethodInfo method=obj.GetType().GetMethod("MethodA");
      method.Invoke(obj, new object [1] {DateTime.Now});
    }

  }
}
```

The preceding code presents three vehicles for creating an instance of a type, binding a method to the type, and finally invoking that method dynamically. Dynamically invoking a method through casting is a mechanism not previously demonstrated. (*Method.Invoke* and *Type.InvokeMember* were reviewed earlier.)

The code for engaging a method through casting is listed as follows. Calling a method dynamically through casting has substantial performance gains when compared with *Method-Info.Invoke* or *Type.InvokeMember*. (*MethodInfo.Invoke* and *Type.InvokeMember* were reviewed earlier in this chapter.)

```
((ZClass) obj).MethodA(DateTime.Now);
```

Either directly or indirectly, the *Activator.CreateInstance* and *CreateInstanceFrom* methods return an object. As the preceding code demonstrates, you can cast the generic object to a specific type and invoke the chosen method. This combines late and early binding, which has significant performance benefits when compared with late binding the type and method.

Late Binding Delegates

A *delegate* is a repository of type-safe function pointers. A *single-cast delegate* holds one function pointer, whereas a *multicast delegate* is a basket of one or more delegates. Delegates are type-safe because the signatures of the delegate and function pointer must match. Normally a compile error is generated if there is a mismatch. Unlike *MethodInfo*, a function pointer is discriminatory and bound to a specific object. *MethodInfo* is nondiscriminatory and can be associated with *any* affiliated object. This is the reason why *MethodInfo.Invoke* and *Type.InvokeMember* methods have an object parameter to associate an instance with the target method. This section assumes a fundamental understanding of delegates. If you would like a review, take a look at Chapter 8, "Delegates and Events." The following code is typical of delegates:

```
using System;
using System.Reflection;

namespace Donis.CSharpBook{
  delegate void XDelegate(int arga, int argb);
```

```
class ZClass {
  public void MethodA(int arga, int argb) {
    Console.WriteLine("ZClass.MethodA called: {0} {1}", arga, argb);
  }
}

class Starter{
  static void Main(){
    ZClass obj=new ZClass();
    XDelegate delObj=new XDelegate(obj.MethodA);
    delObj.Invoke(1,2);
    delObj(3,4);
  }
}
```

In this code, *XDelegate* is the delegate type. *MethodA* is then added to the delegate and invoked. First, invoke using the *Delegate.Invoke* method. Second, invoke the function through the delegate using the C# syntax. At compile time, *XDelegate* expands into a class derived from a *Delegate* type. The *Invoke* method is the most important member implemented and added to the class interface of the derived type. The signature of *Invoke* matches the signature of the delegate. Therefore, *XDelegate.Invoke* has two integer parameters and enforces type safeness of related function pointers.

The preceding code assumes the delegate signature is known at compile time. What if the signature of the delegate is not known at compile time? Because a delegate is an implied class that is similar to any class, you can create an instance of a delegate at run time, bind a method to the delegate, and invoke the method. Instead of invoking a member method, a function pointer is bound and executed against the delegate. The *Delegate.CreateDelegate* and *Delegate.DynamicInvoke* methods provide this behavior. Late binding is not as type-safe as compile-time type checking. (This also pertains to late binding of delegates.) Care must be taken to avoid run-time exceptions. As always, the seminal benefit of late binding is additional flexibility, but performance might suffer.

CreateDelegate constructs a new delegate at run time and then assigns a function pointer to the newly invented delegate. *CreateDelegate* is an overloaded method where the essential parameters are the delegate type and method identity. The *delegateType* is the type of delegate being created. Method is the initial function pointer being assigned to the delegate. The signature of the method represented by a *MethodInfo* object should match that of the delegate type. These are the overloaded methods:

The *Delegate.CreateDelegate* syntax is as follows:

```
static Delegate CreateDelegate(Type type, MethodInfo method)
static Delegate CreateDelegate(Type type, MethodInfo method, bool thrownOnBindFailure)
static Delegate CreateDelegate(Type type, object firstArgument, MethodInfo method)
static Delegate CreateDelegate(Type type, object target, string method)
static Delegate CreateDelegate(Type type, Type target, string method)
```

```
static Delegate CreateDelegate(Type type, object firstArgument, MethodInfo method, bool
throwOnBindFailure)
static Delegate CreateDelegate(Type type, object target, string method,
  bool ignoreCase)
static DelegateCreateDelegate(Type type, object firstArgument, Type target, string method)
static Delegate CreateDelegate(Type type, Type target, string method, bool ignoreCase)
static Delegate CreateDelegate(Type type, object target, string method, bool ignoreCase,
bool throwOnBindFailure)
static Delegate.CreateDelegate(Type type, object firstArgument, Type target, string method,
bool ignoreCase)
static Delegate.CreateDelegate(Type type, Type target, string method, bool ignoreCase, bool
throwOnBindFailure)
static Delegate.CreateDelegate(Type type, object firstArgument, Type target, string method,
bool ignoreCase, bool throwOnBindFailure)
```

After creating a delegate at run time, call *DynamicInvoke* to invoke any function pointers assigned to the delegate. The dynamically created delegate is deprived of the *Invoke* method and language-specific operations. Subsequently, you cannot call the *Invoke* method on a delegate returned from *CreateDelegate*. This is the major difference between compile-time and run-time instances of delegates. An array of function arguments is the only parameter of *DynamicInvoke*.

This is the *DynamicInvoke* syntax:

```
object DynamicInvoke(object [] args)
```

CreateDelegate and *DynamicInvoke* are demonstrated in the following code:

```
using System;
using System.Reflection;

namespace Donis.CSharpBook{
  delegate void theDelegate(int arga, int argb);

  class ZClass {
    public void MethodA(int arga, int argb) {
      Console.WriteLine("ZClass.MethodA called: {0} {1}", arga, argb);
    }
  }

  class Starter{
    static void Main(){
      Type tObj=typeof(System.MulticastDelegate);
      ZClass obj=new ZClass();
      Delegate del=Delegate.CreateDelegate(typeof(theDelegate), obj,
        "MethodA");
      del.DynamicInvoke(new object [] {1,2});
    }
  }
}
```

Function Call Performance

Several ways to invoke a method have been presented in this chapter—from a simple method call to the more complex dynamic invocation. Performance is an important criterion when evaluating competing methodologies. For example, a simple call bound at compile time should be quicker than a method bound at run time. Depending on the application, the differentiation might be material. Losing a few nanoseconds occasionally might not be conspicuous in a user interface–driven application. However, a few lost nanoseconds in a server application multiplied by thousands of users can pose a real problem.

Reflection and Generics

In .NET Framework 2.0, *Reflection* is extended to accommodate open and closed generic types and methods. Predictably, the *Type* class is the focal point of changes to accommodate generic types. For generic methods, *MethodInfo* has been enhanced to reflect generic methods. (Generics were introduced in Chapter 6.) Open types are generic types with unbound type parameters, whereas closed types have bound type parameters. With *Reflection*, you can browse bound and unbound parameters, create instances of generic types, and invoke generic methods at run time.

IsGeneric and IsGenericTypeDefinition

With *Reflection*, you can query the state of a generic type of method. Is this a generic type or method? If confirmed, is the generic type or method open or closed? *Type.IsGeneric* is a Boolean property that confirms the presence of a generic type; *Type.IsGenericTypeDefinition*, another Boolean property, indicates whether the generic is open or closed. For methods, the *MethodInfo.IsGenericMethod* property confirms that a method is a generic method, whereas the *MethodInfo.IsGenericTypeDefinition* property indicates whether the generic method is open or closed. This program demonstrates the four properties:

```
using System;
using System.Reflection;

public class ZClass<T, V> {
    public T membera;
}

public class XClass {
    public void MethodA<T>() {
    }
}

namespace Donis.CSharpBook{

    class Starter{
```

```
static void Main(){
    Type [] types={typeof(ZClass<,>), typeof(ZClass<int,int>)};
    bool [,] bresp= { {types[0].IsGenericType,
                       types[0].IsGenericTypeDefinition},
                      {types[1].IsGenericType,
                       types[1].IsGenericTypeDefinition}};
    Console.WriteLine("Is ZClass<,> a generic type? "+bresp[0,0]);
    Console.WriteLine("Is ZClass<,> open? "
        +bresp[0,1]);
    Console.WriteLine("Is ZClass<int,int> a generic type? "
        +bresp[1,0]);
    Console.WriteLine("Is ZClass<int,int> open? "+bresp[1,1]);

    Type tObj=typeof(XClass);
    MethodInfo method=tObj.GetMethod("MethodA");
    bool [] bMethod={method.IsGenericMethod,
                     method.IsGenericMethodDefinition};
    Console.WriteLine("Is XClass.MethodA<T> a generic method? "
        +bMethod[0]);
    Console.WriteLine("Is XClass.MethodA<T> open? "+bMethod[1]);
    }
  }
}
```

typeof

The *typeof* operator is used in the preceding code to extract the *Type* object of an open or constructed type. The *Type* object has a single parameter, which is a string and identifies the generic type. Connote an open type using empty parameters. For example, *ZClass<T>* would be *ZClass<>*. Multiple generic type parameters are indicated with n-1 commas. For the *typeof* operator, *ZClass<,>* is compatible with *ZClass<K,V>*. Indicate a closed type by including the actual parameter types, such as *ZClass<int, int>*. In addition to the *typeof* operator, *Type.GetType* and *Type.GetGenericTypeDefinition* methods return *Type* objects representing generic types.

GetType

Type.GetType is available in two flavors: an instance and a static method. *Type.GetType* is an instance method and returns the open type used to construct the object. The method has no parameters. The *Type.GetType* static method is overloaded to return a *Type* object for either an open or a closed type. The pivotal parameter of the static *GetType* method is a string naming the generic type. To specify an open type, the string is the name of the generic with the number of parameters affixed. The suffix is preceded with a "`". For example, "NamespaceA .XClass`2" would represent *XClass<K,V>*. *XClass* has two type parameters. For a closed type, you need to add the bound type parameters. After the number of type parameters, list the bound type parameters. The bound type parameters are contained in square brackets.

"NamespaceB.ZClass`3[System.Int32, System.Int32, System.Decimal]" identifies *ZClass <int, int, decimal>*. This is the general format:

```
Open type: GenericType`NumberofParameters
Closed Type: GenericType`NumofParameters[parameter list]
```

The following sample code demonstrates both the instance and static *GetType* methods:

```csharp
using System;

namespace Donis.CSharpBook {

    class ZClass<K,V> {
        public void FunctionA(K argk, V argv) {
        }
    }

    class XClass<T> {
        public void FunctionB(T argt) {
        }
    }

    class Starter {

        public static void Main() {
            ZClass<int, decimal> obj=new ZClass<int, decimal>();
            Type typeClosed=obj.GetType();
            Console.WriteLine(typeClosed.ToString());

            Type typeOpen=Type.GetType("Donis.CSharpBook.XClass`1");
            Console.WriteLine(typeOpen.ToString());
            Type typeClosed2=Type.GetType(
                "Donis.CSharpBook.ZClass`2[System.Int32, System.Decimal]");
            Console.WriteLine(typeClosed2.ToString());
        }
    }
}
```

GetGenericTypeDefinition

Closed types are constructed from open types. *Type.GetGenericTypeDefinition* returns the *Type* object of the open type used to construct a closed type.

This is the *Type.GetGenericTypeDefinition* syntax:

```csharp
Type GetGenericTypeDefinition()
```

The following code highlights the *GetGenericTypeDefinition* method:

```csharp
using System;

namespace Donis.CSharpBook {
```

```
class ZClass<K,V> {
    public void FunctionA(K argk, V argv) {
    }
}

class Starter {

    public static void Main() {
        ZClass<int, decimal> obj=new ZClass<int, decimal>();
        ZClass<string, float> obj2=new ZClass<string, float>();

        Type closedType=obj.GetType();
        Type openType=closedType.GetGenericTypeDefinition();

        Type closedType2=obj2.GetType();
        Type openType2=closedType2.GetGenericTypeDefinition();

        Console.WriteLine(openType.ToString());
        Console.WriteLine(openType2.ToString());
    }
}
}
```

The preceding code displays identical strings. Why? The open type of *ZClass<int, decimal>* and *ZClass<string, float>* is the same, which is *ZClass<K, V>*.

Type.GetMethod and *MethodInfo.GetGenericMethodDefinition* are comparable to *Type.GetType* and *Type.GetGenericTypeDefinition*, respectively, but pertain to generic methods.

GetGenericArguments

You can now extract a *Type* object for a generic type and a *MethodInfo* object for a generic method. Determining the number of unbound or bound parameters is a natural next step. If bound, the type of each parameter would be useful. *GetGenericArguments* is the universal method for enumerating parameters of generic type or method. *GetGenericArguments* enumerates unbound and bound parameters.

This is the *Type.GetGenericArguments* syntax:

```
Type [] GetGenericArguments()
MethodInfo.GetGenericArguments syntax:
Type [] GetGenericArguments()
```

The following code demonstrates both *Type.GetGenericArguments* and *MethodInfo.GetGeneric-Arguments*:

```
using System;

namespace Donis.CSharpBook {

    class ZClass<K,V> {
        public void FunctionA(K argk, V argv) {
```

```
        }
    }

    class Starter {

        public static void Main() {
            ZClass<int, decimal> obj=new ZClass<int, decimal>();
            ZClass<string, float> obj2=new ZClass<string, float>();

            Type closedType=obj.GetType();
            Type openType=closedType.GetGenericTypeDefinition();

            Type closedType2=obj2.GetType();
            Type openType2=closedType2.GetGenericTypeDefinition();

            Console.WriteLine(openType.ToString());
            Console.WriteLine(openType2.ToString());
        }
    }
}
```

Creating Generic Types

Generic types can be created at run time using *Reflection*. First, extract the open type of the generic. This chapter has shown several ways to accomplish this, including using *GetType* and *GetGenericTypeDefinition*. Next, bind the type arguments of the open type. The result will be a bound (closed) type. Finally, create an instance of the bound type in the customary manner. (*Activator.CreateInstance* works well.)

The *Type.MakeGenericType* method binds type parameters to an open type of a generic. *MakeGenericType* has a single parameter, which is an array of *Type* objects. Each element of the array matches a specific type to a generic parameter. If the generic has three parameters, the array passed to *MakeGenericType* will have three elements—each representing a bound parameter.

This is the prototype of the *MakeGenericType* method:

```
Type.MakeGenericType syntax:
void MakeGenericType(Type [] genericArguments)
```

Generic methods, like nongeneric methods, can be invoked dynamically at run time. *MethodInfo.MakeGenericType* binds parameters to generic types, similar to *Type.MakeGenericType*. The benefits and pitfalls of dynamic invocation are similar to nongeneric methods. After binding parameters to a generic method, the method can be invoked using *Reflection*. The following code creates a generic type and then invokes a generic method at run time:

```
using System;
using System.Reflection;


namespace Donis.CSharpBook{
```

```
public class GenericZ <K, V, Z>
    where K: new()
    where V: new() {

    public void MethodA<A>(A argument1, Z argument2) {
        Console.WriteLine("MethodA invoked");
    }

    private K field1=new K();
    private V field2=new V();
}

class Starter{

    static void Main(){
        Type genericType=typeof(GenericZ<,,>);
        Type [] parameters={typeof(int),typeof(float),
            typeof(int)};
        Type closedType=genericType.MakeGenericType(parameters);
        MethodInfo openMethod=closedType.GetMethod("MethodA");
        object newObject = Activator.CreateInstance(closedType);
        parameters=new Type [] {typeof(int)};
        MethodInfo closedMethod=
            openMethod.MakeGenericMethod(parameters);
        object[] methodargs={2, 10};
        closedMethod.Invoke(newObject, methodargs);
    }
}
}
```

Reflection Security

Some reflection operations, such as accessing protected and private members, require *ReflectionPermission* security permission. *ReflectionPermission* is typically granted to local and intranet applications, but not to Internet applications. Set the appropriate *ReflectionPermission* flag to grant or deny specific reflection operations.

Table 10-9 lists the *ReflectionPermission* flags.

Table 10-9   *ReflectionPermission* Flags

Flag	Description
MemberAccess	Reflection of nonvisible members granted.
NoFlags	Reflection denied to nonvisible types.
ReflectionEmit	*System.Reflection.Emit* operations granted.
TypeInformation	This flag is now deprecated.
AllFlags	Combines *TypeInformation*, *MemberAccess*, and *ReflectionEmit* flags.

Attributes

Attributes extend the description of some elements of an assembly. Attributes fulfill the role of adjectives in .NET and annotate assemblies, classes, methods, parameters, and other elements of an assembly. Attributes are commonplace in .NET and fulfill many roles: They delineate serialization, stipulate import linkage, set class layout, indicate conditional compilation, mark a method as deprecated, and much more.

Attributes extend the metadata of the targeted element. An instance of the attribute is stored alongside the metadata and sometimes the MSIL code of the constituent. This is demonstrated in the following code and in Figure 10-4. The *Conditional* attribute marks a method for conditional compilation. Use this attribute to flag one or more symbols. If the symbol is defined, the target method and call sites are included in the compiled applications. If not defined, the method and any invocation are ignored.

```
#define LOG

using System;
using System.IO;
using System.Diagnostics;

namespace Donis.CSharpBook{

  class Starter{
    static void Main(){
      LogInfo(new StreamWriter(@"c:\logfile.txt"));
    }

    [Conditional("LOG")]
    private static void LogInfo(StreamWriter sr) {
        // write information to log file
    }
  }
}
```

This is the MSIL code of the *LogInfo* method as displayed in ILDASM. Notice the custom directive that defines the *Conditional* attribute. It is integrated into the MSIL code of the method (see Figure 10-4).

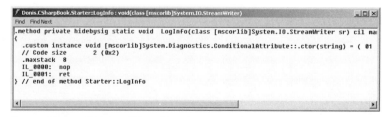

Figure 10-4 The *Conditional* attribute in MSIL code

Attributes are available in different flavors: predefined custom attributes, programmer-defined custom attributes, and pseudo-custom attributes.

Predefined Attributes

Predefined custom attributes, which are defined in the .NET FCL, are the most prevalent custom attributes. There is an encyclopedic list of predefined custom attributes fulfilling a variety of responsibilities in .NET. A short list of predefined custom attributes includes *Assembly-Version*, *Debuggable*, *FileIOPermission*, *Flags*, *Obsolete*, and *Serializable*. The following code uses the *Obsolete* attribute to flag a method as deprecated:

```
[Obsolete("Deprecated Method", false)]
public static void MethodA() {
  Console.WriteLine("Starter.MethodA");
}
```

Combining Attributes

An entity can be assigned multiple attributes. In certain circumstances, even the same attribute can be applied multiple times. There are two ways to combine attributes: They can be grouped together or listed separately. Here, the attributes are applied separately:

```
[Obsolete("Deprecated Method", false)]
[FileIOPermission(SecurityAction.Demand,
      Unrestricted=true)]
   public static void MethodA() {
   Console.WriteLine("Starter.MethodA");
}
```

In the following code, two attributes are combined and applied to a method:

```
[Obsolete("Deprecated Method", false),
 FileIOPermission(SecurityAction.Demand,
      Unrestricted=true)]
   public static void MethodA() {
   Console.WriteLine("Starter.MethodA");
}
```

Programmer-defined Custom Attributes

You can also create programmer-defined custom attributes to personally extend metadata of an application. There are few limitations to a programmer-defined custom attribute: Your attributes can be applied to any entity, except another programmer-defined custom attribute, and can be designed for almost any purpose.

Pseudo-custom Attributes

Pseudo-custom attributes are interpreted by the run time and modify the metadata of the assembly. Unlike predefined or custom attributes, pseudo-custom attributes do not extend metadata. Examples of pseudo-custom attributes include *DllImport*, *MarshalAs*, and *Serializable*.

Anatomy of an Attribute

What exactly is an attribute? Attributes are derived from the *System.Attribute* class, which is the common template of all attributes. *System.Attribute* is an abstract class defining the intrinsic services of an attribute. Manage compilers and the run time often accord special treatment to attributes. For example, the *ObsoleteAttribute* causes the compiler to generate error or warning messages when a deprecated member is used.

This is the syntax of an attribute:

```
[target type: attribute name(positional parameter¹, positional parameterⁿ, named parameter¹=
value, named parameterⁿ=value)] target
```

The target type designates the type of the target and must be included in the defined attribute usages. Attribute target is optional and usually inferred correctly if not omitted.

Here is a list of the valid target types:

- field
- event
- method
- *Param*
- *Property*
- *Return*
- *Type*

The attribute name is the class name of the attribute. By convention, attribute names have an *Attribute* suffix. *OneWayAttribute* is representative of an attribute name. You can also use the alias of an attribute, which omits the *Attribute* suffix. The alias for *OneWayAttribute* is *OneWay*.

Attributes accept zero or more positional parameters. If present, position parameters are not optional and must be listed in a declared sequence. In addition, an attribute can offer any number of named parameters, which must follow positional parameters and are optional. Named parameters are not ordered and can be presented in any sequence.

The following code applies the *UIPermissionAttribute* to the *Starter* class:

```
[type: UIPermissionAttribute(SecurityAction.Demand,
   Clipboard=UIPermissionClipboard.OwnClipboard)]
class Starter{
  static void Main(){

  }
}
```

This is the same attribute expressed somewhat more succinctly:

```
[UIPermission(SecurityAction.Demand)]
class Starter{
  static void Main(){

  }
}
```

Creating a Custom Attribute

You can create custom attributes for personal consumption or to be published in a library for others. There are definitive procedures to creating a programmer-defined custom attribute. Here are the steps to follow:

1. Select an appropriate name for the custom attribute. As mentioned, attribute names should conclude with the *Attribute* suffix.

2. Define an attribute class that derives from *System.Attribute*.

3. Set potential targets with the *AttributeUsage* attribute.

4. Implement class constructors, which determine the positional parameters.

5. Implement write-accessible properties, which define the named parameters.

6. Implement other members of the attribute class.

ClassVersionAttribute is a programmer-defined custom attribute that can apply a version number to types. It illuminates the steps to creating a custom attribute. The attribute assigns a target and current version number to a type. The target version is the version number of the type that the attribute adorns. The current version number is the version applied to the most recent version of the type. When the target type of the attribute is the most recent version, the target and current version are identical. In addition, the *ClassVersionAttribute* can request that future instances of the target type be replaced with the current type.

The first and most important task of creating a programmer-defined attribute is selecting a fabulous name. Alas, *ClassVersionAttribute* is a mundane but descriptive name. As an attribute, *ClassVersionAttribute* must inherit *System.Attribute*. *AttributeUsageAttribute* sets the potential target of the attributes. *AttributeTargets* is the only positional parameter of the *AttributeUsage-Attribute* and is a bitwise enumeration. *AttributeUsageAttribute* has three named parameters: *AllowMultiple*, *Inherited*, and *ValidOn*. *AllowMultiple* is a Boolean flag. When true, the attribute can be applied multiple times to the same target. The default is false. *Inherited* is another Boolean flag. If true, which is the default, the attribute is inheritable from base classes. *ValidOn* is an *AttributeTargets* enumeration. This is an alternate method of setting the potential target of the attribute.

Here is a list of the available *AttributeTargets* flags:

- *All*
- *Assembly*
- *Class*
- *Constructor*
- *Delegate*
- *Enum*
- *Event*
- *Field*
- *GenericParameter*
- *Interface*
- *Method*
- *Module*
- *Parameter*
- *Property*
- *ReturnValue*
- *Struct*

This is the start of the *ClassVersionAttribute* class:

```
[AttributeUsage(AttributeTargets.Class|AttributeTargets.Struct,
    Inherited=false)]
  public class ClassVersionAttribute: System.Attribute {
}
```

Instance constructors of an attribute provide the positional parameters for the attribute. Attributes are created at compile time, upon reflection, and when applied at run time. When attributes are created, the selected constructor runs. The positional arguments should match the signature of a constructor in the attribute. Overloading the constructor allows different sets of positional parameters. Positional and named parameters are restricted to certain types. The following is a list of available attribute parameter types.

- *bool*
- *byte*
- *char*
- *double*

- *float*

- *int*

- *long*

- *sbyte*

- *short*

- *string*

- *uint*

- *ulong*

- *ushort*

ClassVersionAttribute has two overloaded constructors. The first constructor accepts the target version; the second constructor accepts the target and current version number:

```
public ClassVersionAttribute(string target)
  :this(target, target) {
 }

public ClassVersionAttribute(string target,
    string current) {
  m_TargetVersion=target;
  m_CurrentVersion=current;
}
```

Define named parameters as write-only or read-write instance properties of the derived attribute class. You can duplicate positional parameters as named parameters for additional flexibility. *ClassVersionAttributes* offers a *UseCurrentVersion* and *CurrentName* named parameter. *UseCurrentVersion* is a Boolean value. If true, instances of the current type should be substituted for the target type. *CurrentName* names the type of the current version. This is how the named parameters are described in the *ClassVersionAttribute* class:

```
private bool m_UseCurrentVersion=false;
public bool UseCurrentVersion {
  set {
     if(m_TargetVersion != m_CurrentVersion) {
       m_UseCurrentVersion=value;
     }
  }
  get {
    return m_UseCurrentVersion;
  }
}

private string m_CurrentName;
public string CurrentName {
  set {
    m_CurrentName=value;
  }
```

```
    get {
      return m_CurrentName;
    }
  }
}
```

For completeness, read-only properties are added to the *ClassVersionAttribute* class for the target and current version. Here is the completed *ClassVersionAttribute* class:

```csharp
using System;

namespace Donis.CSharpBook{
  [AttributeUsage(AttributeTargets.Class|AttributeTargets.Struct,
    Inherited=false)]
  public class ClassVersionAttribute: System.Attribute {

    public ClassVersionAttribute(string target)
      :this(target, target) {
     }

    public ClassVersionAttribute(string target,
        string current) {
      m_TargetVersion=target;
      m_CurrentVersion=current;
    }

    private bool m_UseCurrentVersion=false;
    public bool UseCurrentVersion {
      set {
         if(m_TargetVersion != m_CurrentVersion) {
           m_UseCurrentVersion=value;
         }
      }
      get {
        return m_UseCurrentVersion;
      }
    }

    private string m_CurrentName;
    public string CurrentName {
      set {
        m_CurrentName=value;
      }
      get {
        return m_CurrentName;
      }
    }

    private string m_TargetVersion;
    public string TargetVersion {
      get {
        return m_TargetVersion;
      }
    }
```

```
    private string m_CurrentVersion;
    public string CurrentVersion {
      get {
        return m_CurrentVersion;
      }
    }
  }
}
```

The *ClassVersionAttribute* class is compiled and published in a DLL. The following application minimally uses the *ClassVersionAttribute*:

```
using System;
namespace Donis.CSharpBook{
  class Starter{
    static void Main(){

    }
  }

  [ClassVersion("1.1.2.1", UseCurrentVersion=false)]
  class ZClass {
  }
}
```

Attributes and Reflection

Programmer-defined custom attributes are valuable as information. However, the real fun and power is in associating a behavior with an attribute. You can read custom attributes with *Reflection* using the *Attribute.GetCustomAttribute* and *Type.GetCustomAttributes* methods. Both methods return an instance or instances of an attribute. You can downcast the attribute instance to a specific attribute type and leverage the intricacies of the attribute to implement the appropriate behavior.

Type.GetCustomAttributes returns attributes applied to a type. *GetCustomAttributes* is also available with other metadata elements, including *Assembly.GetCustomerAttributes*, *MemberInfo.GetCustomAttributes*, and *ParameterInfo.GetCustomerAttributes*. *GetCustomAttributes* has a single Boolean parameter. If true, the inheritance hierarchy of the type is evaluated for additional attributes.

This is the *Type.GetCustomAttributes* method:

```
object [] GetCustomAttributes(bool inherit)
object [] GetCustomAttribute(type AttributeType, bool inherit)
```

Attribute.GetCustomAttribute, which is a static method, creates and returns an instance of a specific attribute. When a specific attribute is desired, *GetCustomAttribute* is invaluable and more efficient than *GetCustomAttributes*. *GetCustomAttribute* assumes that the attribute is assigned only once to the target. *GetCustomAttribute* is overloaded for each potential target, with one notable exception: *GetCustomAttribute* is not overloaded for a type target, which is inexplicable. *Type.GetCustomAttributes* is the sole option for enumerating attributes of a *Type*. *GetCustomAttribute* is overloaded for two and three arguments. The two-argument versions have the target and attribute type as parameters. The three-argument version has an additional parameter, which is the inherit parameter. If the inherit parameter is true, the ascendants of the target class are also searched for the attribute.

This is the *Attribute.GetCustomAttribute* method:

```
static Attribute GetCustomAttribute (Assembly targetAssembly, type attributeType)
static Attribute GetCustomAttribute(MemberInfo targetMember, type attributeType)
static Attribute GetCustomAttribute(Module targetModule, type attributeType)
static Attribute GetCustomAttribute(ParameterInfo targetParameter, type attributeType)
```

This following sample code uses *GetCustomAttribute*:

```
using System;
using System.Reflection;

namespace Donis.CSharpBook{

  class Starter{

    static void Main(){
      Type tObj=typeof(Starter);
      MethodInfo method=tObj.GetMethod("AMethod");
      Attribute attrib=Attribute.GetCustomAttribute(
        method, typeof(ObsoleteAttribute));
      ObsoleteAttribute obsolete=(ObsoleteAttribute) attrib;
      Console.WriteLine("Obsolete Message: "+obsolete.Message);
    }

    [Obsolete("Deprecated function.", false)]
    public void AMethod() {
    }
  }
}
```

The following is sample code of *GetCustomAttributes*. The application inspects the *ClassVersionAttribute* attribute with the *GetCustomAttributes* method and acts upon the results. The application contains two versions of *ZClass* and both are applied to the *ClassVersionAttribute*. Each version of *ZClass* shares a common interface: *IZClass*. The *ClassVersionAttribute* of *Donis.CSharpBook.ZClass* lists *ANamespace.ZClass* as the current version or most recent version. Also, *UseCurrentVersion* is assigned *true* to indicate that the newer version should replace instances of *Donis.CSharpBook.ZClass*. The function *CreateZClass* accepts a *ZClass* as defined by the *IZClass* interface. Within the *foreach* loop, *GetCustomAttributes* enumerates the attributes of the *ZClass*. If the attribute is a *ClassVersionAttribute*, the attribute is saved and the *foreach* loop is exited. Next, the properties of the attribute are examined. If *UseCurrentVersion* is true and a current version is named, an instance of the new version is created and returned from the method. Otherwise, the target version is returned.

```csharp
using System;
using System.Reflection;

interface IZClass {
  void AMethod();
}

namespace Donis.CSharpBook{
  class Starter{
    static void Main(){
      IZClass obj=CreateZClass(typeof(ZClass));
      obj.AMethod();
    }

    private static IZClass CreateZClass(Type tObj) {
      ClassVersionAttribute classversion=null;
      foreach(Attribute attrib in tObj.GetCustomAttributes(false)) {
        if(attrib.ToString()==
          typeof(ClassVersionAttribute).ToString()) {
          classversion=(ClassVersionAttribute) attrib;
        }
        else {
          return null;
        }
      }
      if(classversion.UseCurrentVersion &&
          (classversion.CurrentName != null)) {
        AppDomain currDomain=AppDomain.CurrentDomain;
        return (IZClass) currDomain.CreateInstanceFromAndUnwrap(
          "client.exe", classversion.CurrentName);
      }
      else {
        return (IZClass) Activator.CreateInstance(tObj);
      }
    }
  }

  [ClassVersion("1.1.2.1", "2.0.0.0", UseCurrentVersion=true,
    CurrentName="Donis.CSharpBook.ANamespace.ZClass")]
  public class ZClass: IZClass {
  public void AMethod() {
      Console.WriteLine("AMethod: old version");
    }
  }
```

```
namespace ANamespace {
  [ClassVersion("2.0.0.0", UseCurrentVersion=false)]
  public class ZClass: IZClass {
    public void AMethod() {
      Console.WriteLine("AMethod: new version");
    }
  }
}
}
```

MSIL

Metadata and the ability to inspect metadata using *Reflection* were the topics of this chapter. .NET assemblies consist of metadata and MSIL, in which understanding MSIL is equally important to a developer. (MSIL is the topic of Chapter 11.) Understanding MSIL is important for writing, maintaining, and, later, debugging a C# application. *Reflection* can be used with MSIL code. You can inspect MSIL code at run time, create self-generating code, and otherwise manipulate MSIL using *Reflection*.

Chapter 11
MSIL Programming

Microsoft intermediate language (MSIL) is the programming language of the Common Language Runtime (CLR) and the Common Instruction Language (CIL) for managed code. A managed application undergoes two compilations. The first compilation is from source code to MSIL and is performed by the language compiler. The second compilation occurs at run time, when the MSIL is compiled to native code. The CLR orchestrates the second compilation as part of process execution. The CLR is blind to the original source code. From the perspective of the CLR, managed applications are simply MSIL code and metadata. For this reason, .NET is considered language-agnostic, or independent. The process execution of a managed application is identical regardless of the source language, such as C# or Microsoft Visual Basic .NET.

MSIL promotes the concept of compile-once-and-run-anywhere in the .NET environment. Just-in-time (JIT) compilers, otherwise known as *jitters,* compile assemblies into native binary that targets a specific platform. You can write an application or component once and then deploy the application to Microsoft Windows, Linux, and other environments in which a compliant .NET platform is available. Prior to .NET, vendors maintained different versions of their product, which is costly and time-consuming. Another advantage to compile-once-and-run anywhere is the ability to assemble applications from components deployed on disparate hardware and platforms. This was one of the objectives of component technologies such as Component Object Model (COM) and Common Object Request Broker Architecture (CORBA), but it was never truly realized. .NET makes this a reality. If platform-agnostic code is a design goal for an application, best practices must be adopted to insulate the program from platform-specific code. This includes avoiding or isolating interoperability and calls to native application programming interfaces (APIs).

MSIL is a full-featured, object-oriented programming (OOP) language. However, there are some differences when compared with C# programming. For example, global functions are allowed in MSIL, but not supported in the C# language. Despite being a lower-level language, MSIL has expanded language elements. It encompasses the constituents common to most object-oriented languages: classes, structures, inheritance, transfer-of-control statements, an assortment of arithmetic operators, and much more. Indeed, you can write .NET applications directly in MSIL.

This is a book on C# programming. In that context, why is understanding MSIL important? An understanding of MSIL code advances a deeper comprehension of C# programming and .NET in general. It isn't just magic. MSIL removes much of the mystery and helps C# developers better maintain, debug, and write efficient code.

Managed applications, particularly production applications purchased from third-party vendors, are sometimes deployed without the original source code. How is an application maintained without the source code? For a managed application, as part of the assembly, the MSIL code is always available. The exception is when the assembly is obfuscated. Several tools, including Intermediate Language Disassembler (ILDASM), can disassemble an assembly and provide the MSIL code. With the MSIL code, a developer can essentially read the application. You can even modify the code as MSIL and reassemble the application. This is called roundtripping. Of course, this assumes that the developer is erudite in MSIL programming.

In a native application, debugging without a debug file (.pdb) is a challenge (which is an understatement). Debugging a native application without symbol files invariably meant interpreting assembly code. That was the challenge. More than a visceral understanding of assembly programming is needed to debug without symbol files. MSIL can be viewed as the assembly code of the CLR. Debugging a managed application without the germane symbol files requires more than a superficial understanding of MSIL. However, when compared to the tedious task of reading assembly, MSIL is a leisure cruise.

MSIL is instructive in managed programming. Learning MSIL programming is learning C# programming. What algorithms are truly efficient? When has boxing occurred? Which source code routines expand the footprint of the application? These secrets can be found in understanding MSIL code.

Inline MSIL is mentioned in numerous programming blogs, but is not currently available. I am an advocate of inline MSIL for C#. MSIL is more than an abstraction of higher-level source code. There are unique features in MSIL code that are not exposed in C#. In addition, C# is a code generator that emits MSIL code. In rare circumstances, the MSIL may not be as ideal for your specific application. For these reasons, I favor inline MSIL. However, the problem with inline MSIL is maintaining safe code. Inline MSIL is inherently unsafe and could lead to abuse. If a safe implementation of inline MSIL is not possible, it should not be added to the language.

As mentioned, managed applications incur two compilations. First the language compiler and then the run time (jitter) compiles the application. You can compile MSIL code directly into an assembly with the MSIL compiler Intermediate Language Assembler (ILASM). Conversely, you can disassemble an assembly by engaging the MSIL disassembler (ILDASM).

This chapter is an overview of MSIL programming, not a comprehensive narrative on MSIL. The intention is to convey enough information on the language to aid in the interpretation, maintenance, and debugging of C# applications. For an authoritative explanation of MSIL, I recommend *Inside Microsoft .NET IL Assembler*, written by Serge Lidin (Microsoft Press, 2002). Serge is one of the original architects of the ILASM compiler, the ILDASM disassembler, and other tools included in the .NET Framework. Alternatively, consult the European Computer Manufacturers Association (ECMA) documents pertaining to CIL, which are available online at *http://www.ecma-international.org/publications/standards/Ecma-335.htm*.

"Hello World" Application

An example is a great place to begin an exploration of MSIL code programming. Following is a variation of the universally known Hello World application. It displays "Hello *Name*", where *Name* is read from the memory of a local variable.

```
// Hello World Application

.assembly extern mscorlib {}
.assembly hello {}

/* Starter class with entry point method */

.namespace Donis.CSharpBook {
 .class Starter {
    .method static public void Main() cil managed {
        .maxstack 2
        .entrypoint
        .locals init (string name)
        ldstr "Donis"
        stloc.0
        ldstr "Hello, {0}!"
        ldloc name
        call void [mscorlib] System.Console::WriteLine(
        string, object)
        ret
        }
    }
}
```

This is the command line that compiles the MSIL code to create a hello executable:

```
ilasm /exe /debug hello.il
```

The *exe* option indicates that the target is a console application, which is also the default. The *dll* option specifies a library target. The *debug* option asks the compiler to generate a debug file (pdb) for the application. A debug file is useful for a variety of reasons, including viewing source code in a debugger or disassembler.

The application begins with comments and three declaratives:

```
// Hello World Application
.assembly extern mscorlib{}
.assembly hello{}
/* Starter class with entry point method */
.namespace Donis.CSharpBook {
```

MSIL supports C++ style comments—both single and multiline comments. The first declarative is an external reference to the mscorlib library. Mscorlib.dll contains the core of the .NET Framework class library (FCL), which includes the *System.Console* class. The assembly directive describes the executing assembly, in which the simple name of the assembly is *hello*. Notice that the simple name does not include the extension. The third directive defines a namespace.

The next two lines define a class and a method. This class directive introduces a public class named *Starter*, which implicitly inherits the *System.Object* class. The method directive defines *Main* as a member method. *Main* is a managed, public, and static function:

```
.class Starter {
 .method static public void Main() cil managed {
```

The *Main* method starts with three directives. The *.maxstack* directive sets the size of the evaluation stack to two slots. The *.entrypoint* directive designates *Main* as the entry point of the application. By convention, *Main* is always the entry point of a C# executable. In MSIL, the entry point method is whatever method contains the *.entrypoint* directive, which could be a method other than *Main*. Finally, the *.local* directive declares a local string variable called *name*.

```
.maxstack 2
.entrypoint
.locals init (string name)
```

Table 11-1 describes the MSIL code of the *Main* method.

Table 11-1   Hello World MSIL Code

Instruction	Description
ldstr "Donis"	Load the string *"Donis"* onto the evaluation stack.
stloc.0	Store *"Donis"* from the evaluation stack into the first local variable, which is called *name*.
ldstr "Hello, {0}!"	Load the *"Hello"* string prefix onto the evaluation stack.

Table 11-1   Hello World MSIL Code

Instruction	Description
ldloc name	Load the local variable onto the evaluation stack. (Local variables are referenced by index or by name.)
call void [mscorlib] System.Console::WriteLine(string, object)	Call the *Console::WriteLine* method, which consumes the two items on the evaluation stack as parameters from right to left. "Hello *name*" is displayed.
ret	Return from the method.

Evaluation Stack

The evaluation stack, which is mentioned often in the description of the Hello World application, is the pivotal structure of MSIL applications. It is the bridge between your application and memory locations. It is similar to the conventional stack frame, but there are salient differences. The evaluation stack is the viewer of the application, and you can use it to view function parameters, local variables, temporary objects, and much more. Traditionally, function parameters and local variables are placed on the stack. In .NET, this information is stored in separate repositories, in which memory is reserved for function parameters and local variables. You cannot access these repositories directly. Accessing parameters or local variables requires moving the data from memory to slots on the evaluation stack using a *load* command. Conversely, you update a local variable or parameter with content on the evaluation stack using a *store* command. Slots on the evaluation stack are either 4 or 8 bytes.

Figure 11-1 shows the relationship between the evaluation stack and the repositories for function parameters and local variables.

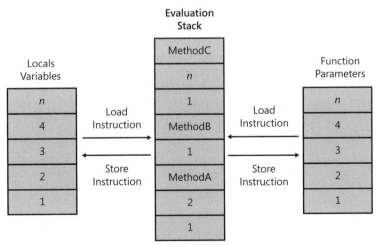

Figure 11-1   A depiction of the evaluation stack, function parameters, and local variables

The evaluation stack is a *stack* and thereby a last in/first out (LIFO) instrument. When a function starts, the evaluation stack is empty. As the function runs, items are pushed and popped from the evaluation stack. Before the function exits, except for a return value, the evaluation stack must once again be empty. The *jmp* and *tail* instructions are exceptions to this rule. If the evaluation stack is not empty at exit, the run time raises an *InvalidProgramException* exception.

The *.maxstack* directive limits the number of items permitted simultaneously on the stack. The directive is optional. If the directive is not present, eight slots are reserved on the evaluation stack. The *.maxstack* directive is a confirmation that an application is performing as expected. Extra items on the evaluation stack are an indication of potential logic problems in an application or a security violation. In either circumstance, this is a violation worthy of a notification.

MSIL in Depth

Here are some basic facts about MSIL programming. The content of an MSIL program is case sensitive. MSIL is also a freeform language. Statements can span multiple lines of code, in which lines can be broken at the white space. Statements are not terminated with a semicolon. Comments are the same as in the C# language. Double slashes (//) are used for single-line comments, and "/* *comment* */" is used for multiline comments. Code labels are colon-terminated and reference the next instruction. Code labels must be unique within the scope in which it is defined.

In addition to the evaluation stack, the other important elements of a MSIL application are directives and the actual MSIL source code. Directives are dot-prefixed and are the declarations of the MSIL program. Source code is the executable content and control flow of the application.

Directives

There are several categories of directives. Assembly, class, and method directives are the most prominent. Assembly directives contain information that the compiler emits to the manifest, which is metadata pertaining to the overall assembly. Class directives define classes and the members of the class. This information is also emitted as standard metadata, which is data about types. Method directives define the particulars of a method, such as any local variables and the size of the evaluation stack.

Assembly Directives

Table 11-2 lists common assembly directives.

Table 11-2 Assembly Directives

Directive	Description
.assembly	The .assembly directive defines the simple name of the assembly. The simple name does not include the extension. Assembly probing will uncover the correct extension. Adding the extension will cause normal probing to fail and manifest a binding exception when the assembly is referenced.
	This is the syntax of the .assembly directive:
	.assembly name {block}
	The assembly block contains additional directives that further describe the assembly. These directives are optional. You need to provide only enough directives to uniquely identify the assembly. This is an assembly block with additional details:
	.assembly Hello {
	.ver 1:0:0:0
	.locale "en.US"
	}
	These are some of the directives available in the assembly block:
	.ver—The four-part version number of the assembly
	.publickey—The 8-byte public key token of the public/private key pair used to encrypt the hash of the assembly
	.locale—The language and culture of the assembly
	.custom—Custom attributes of the assembly
.assembly extern	The .assembly extern directive references an external assembly. The public types and methods of the referenced assembly are available to the current assembly.
	This is the syntax of the .assembly extern directive:
	.assembly extern name as aliasname {block}
	The as clause is optional and for referencing assemblies that are similarly named but a different version, public key, or culture.
	Add the .ver, .publickey, .locale, and .custom directives to the assembly extern block to refine the identification of that assembly.
	Because of the importance of mscorlib.dll, the ILASM compiler automatically adds an external reference to that library. Therefore, assembly extern mscorlib is purely informative.
.file	The .file directive adds a file to the manifest of the assembly. This is useful for associating documents, such as a readme file, with an assembly.
	This is the syntax of the .file directive:
	.file nometadata file name .hash = (bytes) .entrypoint
	The file name is the sole required element of the declaration. Nometadata is the primary option and stipulates that the file is unmanaged.
	`.file nometadata documentation.txt`

Table 11-2   Assembly Directives

Directive	Description
.subsystem	The .subsystem directive indicates the subsystem used by the application, such as the graphical user interface (GUI) or console subsystem. This is distinct from the target type of the application, which is an executable, library, module, or so on. The ILASM compiler inserts this directive based on options specified when the application is compiled. You can also explicitly add this directive. This is the syntax of the .subsystem directive: .subsystem *number* *Number* is a 32-bit integer in which: 2 is a GUI application. 3 is a console application.
.corflags	The .corflags directive sets the run-time flag in the CLI header. This defaults to 1, which stipulates an IL-only assembly. The corflags tool, introduced in .NET 2.0, allows the configuration of this flag. This is the syntax of the .corflags directive: .corflags *flag* The flag is a 32-bit integer.

.stackreserve	The .stackreserve directive sets the stack size. The default size is 0x00100000. The following code calls *MethodA* iteratively. Without the .stackreserve directive, which defaults to 0x00100000, the *MethodA* method is called iteratively more than 110,000 times before exhausting the stack. Set the stack size to 0x0001000 using the .stackreserve directive. Now *MethodA* is called only about 21,000 times before quitting. Although the results may vary on your actual computer, the relative values are consistent.
	
	`.assembly iterative {}`
	`.imagebase 0x00800000`
	`.stackreserve 0x00001000`
	
	`.namespace Donis.CSharpBook {`
	`    .class Starter {`
	`        .method static public void Main() il managed {`
	`            .entrypoint`
	`            ldc.i4.0`
	`            call void Donis.CSharpBook.Starter::`
	`                MethodA(int32)`
	`            ret`
	`        }`
	
	`        .method static public void MethodA(int32)`
	`                il managed {`
	`            ldarg.0`
	`            ldc.i4.1`
	`            add`

Table 11-2 Assembly Directives

Directive	Description

.stackreserve (cont.)	```
	        dup
	        call void [mscorlib]
	            System.Console::WriteLine(int32)
	        call void Donis.CSharpBook.Starter::
	            MethodA(int32)
	        ret
	      }
	    }
	  }
	``

.imagebase	The *.imagebase* directive sets the base address where the application is loaded. The default is 0x00400000. The load address of the application image and stack size is confirmable using the dumpbin tool. For example: dumpbin /headers iterative.exe >iterative.txt

Class Directives

Table 11-3 describes the important class directives.

Table 11-3 Class Directives

Directive	Description
.class header *{members}*	The *.class header* directive introduces a new reference type, value type, or interface into an assembly. The syntax of the *.class header* directive is as follows: *attributes classname* extends *basetype* implements *interfaces* There are a variety of attributes. This is a short list of the common attributes: ■ *abstract*—The type is abstract, and instances cannot be created. ■ *ansi* and *unicode*—Strings can be marshaled as ANSI or UNICODE. ■ *auto*—The memory layout of fields is controlled by the CLR. ■ *beforefieldinit*—Static methods are callable before the type is initialized. ■ *private* and *public*—Sets the visibility of the class outside of assembly. ■ *sealed*—The class cannot be inherited. ■ *serializable*—The contents of the class can be serialized. If the type inherits from another type, use the extends option. .NET supports only single class inheritance. The extends option is optional. If not present, the type inherits implicitly from *System.Object* or *System.ValueType*. The implements option lists the interfaces implemented by the type. The implements clause is optional and there are no default interfaces. The list of interfaces is comma-delimited. In the *members* block, members are declared with the appropriate directive: *.method*, *.field*, *.property*, and so on.

Table 11-3   Class Directives

Directive	Description
.custom constructorsig-nature	The .custom directive adds a custom attribute to the type.
.method	The .method directive defines a method. C# does not support global methods. Therefore, the .method directive is always included within a type.

The .method directive defines a method. C# does not support global methods. Therefore, the .method directive is always included within a type.

This is the syntax of the .method directive:

.method attributes callingconv return methodname arguments implat-tributes { methodbody }

The method attributes are varied, including the accessibility attributes: public, private, family, and others. The default is private. Static methods have the static attribute, whereas instance methods possess the instance attribute. The default is an instance method.

Here are additional attributes:

- final—The method cannot be overridden.
- virtual—The method is virtual.
- hidebysig—Hides the base class interface of this method. This flag is used only by the source language compiler.
- newslot—Creates a new entry in the vtable for this method, which prevents overriding a method of the same name in a base class. For example, this option is used with the add_Event and remove_Event methods of an event.
- abstract—The method has no implementation and is assumed to be implemented in a descendant.
- specialname—The method is special, such as get_Property and set_Property methods. These methods are treated in a special way by tools.
- rtspecialname—The method has a special name, such as a construc-tor. These methods are treated in a special way by the CLR.

The calling convention pertains mostly to native code, in which a variety of calling conventions are supported: fastcall, cdecl, and others.

The implementation attributes include the following:

- cil—The method contains MSIL code.
- native—The method contains platform-specific code.
- runtime—The implementation of the method is provided by the CLR. When defining delegates, the delegate class and methods are generated by the run time.
- managed—The implementation is managed.

Table 11-3   Class Directives

Directive	Description
.method (cont.)	Here is the declaration of a C# method:
| | ```
virtual public int MethodA(int param1, int param2)
``` |
| | This is the MSIL code for that same method: |
| | ```
.method public hidebysig newslot virtual

instance int32 MethodA(int32 param1,

    int32 param2) cil managed
``` |
.field	The *.field* directive defines a new field, which contains state for a class or instance.
	The syntax of the *.field* directive is as follows:
	.field *attributes type fieldname fieldinit* at *datalabel*
	The accessibility attributes are the same as described with methods. Fields can be assigned the *static* attribute but not the *instance* attribute. The default is an *instance* field.
	This is a list of other common field attributes:
	■ *initonly*—Defines a *readonly* field.
	■ *specialname*—The field is special.
	■ *rtspecialname*—The field has a special name.
	The *fieldinit* and *datalabel* options are optional.
	This is a field defined in a C# class:
| | ```
private readonly int fielda=10;
``` |
| | This is the same field translated to MSIL code. The compiler adds a no-argument constructor, where *fielda* is initialized to 10. |
| | ```
.field private initonly int32 fielda
``` |
.property	The *.property* directive introduces a property member to a class. It also declares the *get* and *set* methods associated with the property.
	This is the syntax of the *.property* directive:
	.property *attributes return propertyname parameters default* {*propertyblock*}
	The attributes of a property can be *specialname* or *rtspecialname*. The *return* is the return type of the property. The composition of *propertyname* and *parameters* is the signature of the property. The *default* option sets the default value of the property.
	Within the *property* block, the *.get* directive declares the signature of the *get* method, whereas the *.set* directive declares the *set* method. The *.propertybody* includes only the method declarations. The *get* and *set* methods are actually implemented at the class level, not within the property.

Table 11-3   Class Directives

Directive	Description
.property (cont.)	This is a property defined and implemented in a C# application:

```
public int propa {
 get {
 return 0;
 }
}
```

This is the same property in MSIL code:

```
.property instance int32 propa()
{
 .get instance int32
 Donis.CSharpBook.Starter::get_propa()
}
```

| *.event* | The *.event* directive defines a new event in a class. |

This is the syntax of the *.event* directive:

.event *classref eventname* { *eventbody* }

Classref is the underlying type of the event, such as *EventHandler*.

The *.eventbody* directive encapsulates the *.addon* and *.removeon* directives. The *.addon* directive declares the method used to add subscribers. The *.removeon* directive declares the method for removing subscribers. The *add* and *remove* methods are implemented in the class and not the event.

This is the C# code that declares an event:

```
public event EventHandler EventA;
```

Here is the MSIL code for that same event:

```
.event [mscorlib]System.EventHandler EventA
{
 .addon instance void
 Donis.CSharpBook.Starter::add_EventA(
 class [mscorlib]System.EventHandler)
 .removeon instance void
 Donis.CSharpBook.Starter::remove_EventA(
 class [mscorlib]System.EventHandler)
}
```

Method Directives

The *.method* directive adds a method to a class. MSIL allows for global methods. Global methods break the rules of encapsulation and other tenets of OOP. For this reason, C# does not support global methods. MSIL generated from the C# compiler (csc) uses the *.method* directive solely to define member methods. The *method* block contains further directives and the implementation code (MSIL).

Table 11-4 lists the directives that are frequently included in the *method* block.

Table 11-4   Directives Included in the Method Block

Directive	Description
.locals	The *.locals* directive declares local variables that are accessible using a symbolic name or index. Local variables form a zero-based array.
	This is the syntax of the *.locals* directive:
	.locals^1 (*[index]local1, [index] local2, [index] localn*)
	.locals^2 init (*[index]local1, [index] local2, [index] localn*)
	The *.locals*^{1} directive defines one or more local variables. Explicit indexes can be set for each local variable. By default, the local variables are indexed sequentially starting at zero.
	The *.locals*^{2} directive adds the *init* keyword, which requests that local variables be initialized to a zero-based value before the method executes. The *init* keyword is required to pass code verification. Therefore, the C# compiler only emits the *.locals*^{2} directive.
	Local variables do not have to be declared at the beginning of a method, and they can appear more than once in a method—each time declaring different local variables.
.maxstack	The *.maxstack* directive sets the number of slots available on the evaluation stack. Without this directive, the default is eight slots, which is the number of items that can be placed on the evaluation stack simultaneously.
	This is the syntax of the *.maxstack* directive:
	.maxstack *slots*
.entrypoint	The *.entrypoint* directive designates a method as the entry point method of the application. This directive can appear anywhere in the method, but best practice places the *.entrypoint* directive at the start of the method.
	In C#, the entry point method is *Main*. In MSIL, any *static* method can be accorded this status.

The following program defines *MSILFunc* as the entry point method. The *.entrypoint* directive is found at the end of this method. The *.locals* directive defines two locals and assigns explicit indexes. Essentially, the normal indexes are reversed. The instruction *stloc.0* will update the second local variable. *MSILFunc* refers to the local variables both as symbolic names and indexes. The *MSILFunc* method returns *void*. In MSIL code, the *ret* instruction is required even when a function returns nothing. In C#, the return is optional for methods returning *void*. The method displays the values of 10 and then 5.

```
.assembly extern mscorlib {}
.assembly application {}

.namespace Donis.CSharpBook {

    .class Starter {
```

```
        .method static public void MSILFunc() il managed {
           .locals init ([1] int32 locala, [0] int32 localb)
           ldc.i4.5
           stloc.0
           ldc.i4 10
           stloc.1
           ldloc locala
           call void [mscorlib] System.Console::WriteLine(int32)
           ldloc localb
           call void [mscorlib] System.Console::WriteLine(int32)
           .entrypoint
           ret
           }
      }
}
```

MSIL Instructions

MSIL includes a full complement of instructions, many of which were demonstrated in previous examples. Each instruction is also assigned an opcode, which is commonly 1 or 2 bytes. 2-byte opcodes are always padded with a 0xFE byte in the high-order byte. Opcodes are often followed with operands. Opcodes, which provide an alternate means of defining MSIL instructions, are used primarily when emitting code dynamically at run time. The *ILGenerator* *.Emit* method records instructions using opcodes, which is in the *System.Reflection.Emit* namespace.

The byte option of ILDASM adds opcodes to the disassembly. The following is a partial listing of the hello.exe disassembly, which includes just the *Main* method. As ascertained from the disassembly, the opcode for *ldstr* is 72, the opcode for *stloc* is 0A, and the opcode for *call* is 28.

```
.method public static void Main() cil managed
{
    .entrypoint
    .maxstack 2
    .locals init (string V_0)
    IL_0000: /* 72 | (70)000001 */ ldstr "Donis"
    IL_0005: /* 0A | */ stloc.0
    IL_0006: /* 72 | (70)00000D */ ldstr "Hello, {0}!"
    IL_000b: /* FE0C | 0000 */ ldloc V_0
    IL_000f: /* 28 | (0A)000001 */ call void
    [mscorlib]System.Console::WriteLine(string, object)
    IL_0014: /* 2A | */ ret
}
```

Short Form   Some MSIL instructions have normal and short-form syntax. The short forms of the instruction have a .s suffix. The short form of the *ldloc* instruction is *ldloc.s*. The short form of the *br* instruction is *br.s*. Normal instructions have 4-byte operands, and short-form instructions are limited to 1-byte operands.

When used injudiciously, the short-form syntax can cause unexpected results:

```
.assembly extern mscorlib {}
.assembly application {}
```

```
.namespace Donis.CSharpBook {

 .class Starter {
 .method static public void Main() il managed {
 .entrypoint
 ldc.i4.s 50000
 call void [mscorlib] System.Console::WriteLine(int32)
 ret
 }
 }
}
```

In the preceding application, a constant of 50000 is placed on the evaluation stack. However, the *ldc* instruction is in the short form. It is difficult to fit 50000 into a single byte, so the constant overflows the byte. For this reason, the application incorrectly displays *80*.

The next section of the book reviews the categories of MSIL instructions, such as branch, arithmetic, call, and array groups of instructions. Because of the prevalence of the evaluation stack, load and store instructions are the most frequently used of all MSIL instructions. That is a good place to start.

Load and Store Methods   Load and store instructions transfer data between the evaluation stack and memory. Load commands push memory, such as a local variable, to the evaluation stack. Store commands move data from the evaluation stack to memory. Information placed on the evaluation stack is then consumed by method parameters, arithmetic operations, and other MSIL instructions. Data not otherwise consumed should be removed from the evaluation stack before the current method returns. The pop instruction is the best command to remove extraneous data from the evaluation stack. Data needed for an instruction should be placed on the evaluation stack immediately prior to the execution of that instruction. If not, an *InvalidProgramException* is triggered. Method returns are also placed on the evaluation stack.

Table 11-5 lists the basic load instructions.

Table 11-5   Load Instructions

Instruction	Description
ldc	The *ldc* instruction posts a constant to the evaluation stack, which can be an integral or floating-point value.
	This is the syntax of the *ldc* instruction:
	ldc[1].*type value*
	ldc[2].i4.*number*
	ldc[3].i4.s *number*
	The *ldc*[1] instruction loads a constant of the specified type onto the evaluation stack.
	The *ldc*[2] instruction is more efficient and transfers an integral value of –1 and between 0 and 8 to the evaluation stack. The special format for –1 is *ldc.i4.m1*.

Table 11-5   Load Instructions

Instruction	Description
ldloc	The *ldloc* instruction copies the value of a local variable to the evaluation stack.
	This is the syntax of the *ldloc* instruction:
	ldloc^1 *index*
	ldloc^2.s *index*
	ldloc^3 *name*
	ldloc^4.s *name*
	ldloc^5.n
	The *ldloc^1* and *ldloc^2* instructions use an index to identify a local variable, which is then loaded on the evaluation stack. The *ldloc^3* and *ldloc^4* instructions identify the local variable with the symbolic name. The short form of *ldloc* efficiently loads local variables from 4 to 255. The *ldloc^5* instruction is optimized to load local variables from 0 to 3.
ldarg	The *ldarg* instruction places a method argument on the evaluation stack.
	This is the syntax of the *ldarg* instruction, which is identical to the *ldloc* instruction:
	ldarg^1 *index*
	ldarg^2.s *index*
	ldarg^3 *name*
	ldarg^4.s *name*
	ldarg^5.n
ldnull	The *ldnull* instruction places a null on the evaluation stack. This instruction has no operands.

Table 11-6 lists the basic store instructions.

Table 11-6   Store Instructions

Instruction	Description
stloc	The *stloc* instruction transfers a value from the evaluation stack to a local variable. The value is then removed from the evaluation stack.
	This is the syntax of the *stloc* instruction, which is the same as the *ldloc* instruction:
	stloc *index*
	stloc.s *index*
	stloc *name*
	stloc.s *name*
	stloc.*n*

Table 11-6   Store Instructions

Instruction	Description
starg	The *starg* instruction moves a value from the evaluation stack to a method argument. The value is then popped from the evaluation stack.
	This is the syntax of the *starg* instruction:
	starg *num*
	starg.s *num*
	The short form of the *starg* instruction is efficient for the first 256 arguments.

Complex Tasks

Until now, the focus has been on individual instructions. Most programs consist of complex tasks, such as creating a new class, creating an array, or executing a *for* loop. Complex tasks consist of multiple instructions.

Managing Types

Classes contain static and instance members. The static members are accessible through the class name, whereas instance members are bound to an object. The *WriteLine* method is a static method. As demonstrated, *WriteLine* is called directly on the *Console* class (for example, *System.Console::WriteLine*). Instance members require an object. The *newobj* instruction creates an instance of a class and then invokes the constructor to initialize the object. It also deposits a reference to the object onto the evaluation stack. This reference can be used to call a member method or access a field. Such an action consumes the reference and removes it from the evaluation stack. Several actions require several references. The *dup* instruction is convenient for duplicating a reference or whatever is on the top of the evaluation stack.

This is the syntax of the *newobj* instruction:

newobj *instance* instruction:

new *ctorsignature*

Constructors are specially named methods. The name of a constructor is *ctor*, and a constructor is declared with the *.ctor* directive. By convention in C#, constructors return *void*, which is enforced by the C# compiler. In MSIL code, a constructor can return a value. Static constructors are named *cctor* and are declared with the identically named directive. The static constructor is called when the class or instance is first accessed.

The *.field* directive adds a field to the class. The *ldfld* and *ldsfld* instructions load an instance and static field onto the evaluation stack, respectively. Conversely, the *stfld* and *stsfld* instructions store data on the evaluation stack into a field. The *stfld* and *stsfld* instructions consume a reference to the related object. The load and store instructions have a single operand, which is the field signature.

The following program creates a class that contains an instance and static field in which the instance and static constructors initialize the fields. The *AddField* and *SubtractField* methods return the total and difference of the fields. An instance of the object is created in the *Main* method. The resulting reference is duplicated with the *dup* instruction. Why? Both the *AddField* and *SubtractField* methods are called, which require two references:

```
.assembly extern mscorlib {}
.assembly application {}

.namespace Donis.CSharpBook {

    .class Starter {

        .method static public void Main() il managed {
        .entrypoint
        .locals (int32 temp)
        newobj instance void Donis.CSharpBook.ZClass::.ctor()
        dup
        call instance int32 Donis.CSharpBook.ZClass::AddFields()
        stloc.0
        ldstr "The total is {0}"
        ldloc.0
        box int32
        call void [mscorlib] System.Console::WriteLine(string, object)
        call instance int32 Donis.CSharpBook.ZClass::SubtractFields()
        stloc.0
        ldstr "The difference is {0}"
        ldloc.0
        box int32
        call void [mscorlib] System.Console::WriteLine(string, object)
        ret
    }
}

    .class ZClass {

        .method private hidebysig specialname rtspecialname
        static void .cctor() cil managed {
        ldstr "In static constructor"
        call void [mscorlib] System.Console::WriteLine(string)
        ldc.i4.s 10
        stsfld int32 Donis.CSharpBook.ZClass::fielda
        ret
    }

    .method public hidebysig specialname rtspecialname
            instance void .ctor() cil managed {
        ldstr "In constructor"
        call void [mscorlib] System.Console::WriteLine(string)
        ldarg.0
```

```
        ldc.i4.s 5
        stfld int32 Donis.CSharpBook.ZClass::fieldb
        ret
    }

    .method public int32 AddFields() cil managed {
        ldsfld int32 Donis.CSharpBook.ZClass::fielda
        ldarg.0
        ldfld int32 Donis.CSharpBook.ZClass::fieldb
        add
        ret
    }


    .method public int32 SubtractFields() cil managed {
        ldsfld int32 Donis.CSharpBook.ZClass::fielda
        ldarg.0
        ldfld int32 Donis.CSharpBook.ZClass::fieldb
        sub
        ret
    }

    .field static private int32 fielda
    .field private int32 fieldb

    }
}
```

Boxing   The previous code uses the *box* instruction.

```
ldstr "The total is {0}"
ldloc.0
box int32
call void [mscorlib] System.Console::WriteLine(string, object)
```

The *box* instruction prevents an exception. The *Console::WriteLine* method has two parameters, which are both reference types. However, the top of the evaluation stack has a value type and a reference type. The assignment of a value to a reference type is the problem. The memory models are inconsistent. The *box* instruction removes the value type from the evaluation stack, creates an object on the managed heap that boxes the value type, and places a reference to the newly created object back on the evaluation stack. Now that the value type has been replaced with a reference type, *Console::WriteLine* is called successfully. The *unbox* instruction works in reverse. It unboxes a reference that is on the evaluation stack. This instruction unboxes the reference type to the specified value type. The reference is replaced on the evaluation stack with the unboxed value.

This is the syntax of the *box* and *unbox* instructions:

box *valuetype*

unbox *valuetype*

Inheritance   In previous examples in this chapter, no class has directly inherited from another class. The classes implicitly inherited *System.Object*. Most classes can be inherited explicitly, including *System.Object*, by using the *extends* keyword. The child class will inherit most members of the base class, except constructors. In the base class, methods that are expected to be overridden in the child should be prefixed with the keyword *virtual*. The *callvirt* instruction calls a function overridden in a child. A child instance should be on the evaluation stack. Here is sample code of inheritance in MSIL code:

```
.assembly extern mscorlib {}
.assembly application {}

.namespace Donis.CSharpBook {

    .class Starter {

        .method static public void Main() il managed {
            .entrypoint
            newobj instance void Donis.CSharpBook.XClass::.ctor()
            dup
            call instance void Donis.CSharpBook.ZClass::MethodA()
            callvirt instance void Donis.CSharpBook.XClass::MethodC()
            ret
        }
    }

    .class abstract ZClass {

        .method public instance void MethodA() il managed {
            ldstr "ZClass::MethodA"
            call void [mscorlib] System.Console::WriteLine(string)
            ret
        }

        .method public virtual instance void MethodC() il managed {
            ldstr "ZClass::MethodC"
            call void [mscorlib] System.Console::WriteLine(string)
            ret
        }
    }

    .class XClass {

        .method public specialname rtspecialname
                instance void .ctor() cil managed {
            ret
        }

        .method public instance void MethodB() il managed {
            ldstr "XClass::MethodB"
            call void [mscorlib] System.Console::WriteLine(string)
            ret
        }
```

```
    .method public virtual instance void MethodC() il managed {
        ldstr "XClass::MethodC"
        call void [mscorlib] System.Console::WriteLine(string)
        ret
    }
  }
}
```

Did you notice the following statement in the preceding code?

```
call instance void Donis.CSharpBook.ZClass::MethodA()
```

This statement is interesting. Before this instruction is executed, there is a reference to an *XClass* object on the evaluation stack. *XClass* has inherited *MethodA* from the *ZClass*. *XClass* does not override or hide the interface of *MethodA* in the base class. Therefore, the implementation of *MethodA* resides solely in the base class. Therefore, you must call the base function on the derived reference to successfully invoke the method.

Interfaces   Classes are permitted to inherit from one class but can implement multiple interfaces. There is no interface directive; instead, add the *interface* keyword to the details of the class directive. The *interface* keyword enforces the semantics of an interface type on the class. Member methods must be public, abstract, and virtual. Fields are not allowed in an interface class. In addition, constructors and destructors are not permitted. The ILASM compiler enforces these and other rules. A class identifies interfaces to implement with the *implements* keyword. The class must implement all the members of the interface to prevent run-time errors. This code demonstrates an interface and the implementation of an interface:

```
.assembly extern mscorlib {}
.assembly application {}

.namespace Donis.CSharpBook {

    .class interface public abstract IA {
        .method public abstract virtual instance void MethodA() il managed {
        }
    }

    .class Starter{
        .method static public void Main() il managed {
            .entrypoint
            newobj instance void Donis.CSharpBook.ZClass::.ctor()
            callvirt instance void Donis.CSharpBook.ZClass::MethodA()

            ret
        }
    }

    .class ZClass implements Donis.CSharpBook.IA {
        .method public specialname rtspecialname
                instance void .ctor() cil managed {
            ret
        }
```

```
        .method public virtual instance void MethodA() il managed {
            ldstr "ZClass:MethodA"
            call void [mscorlib] System.Console::WriteLine(string)
            ret
        }
    }
}
```

MethodA is defined as part of *interface IA* and is an abstract function. In C#, abstract functions do not have a function body. In MSIL code, however, abstract methods have a body, but the body cannot contain an implementation. An abstract method has a body but no code.

Structures   As discussed, interfaces are defined with the class directive. Structures are similarly defined. To define a structure, declare a type with the class directive and add the *value* keyword to the class detail. The semantics of a structure are then enforced by the MSIL compiler. For example, a structure does not have a default constructor or destructor, a structure is sealed, and so on. The *value* keyword is implemented by the ILASM compiler as an explicit inheritance of *System.ValueType*. You could drop the *value* keyword and inherit the *System. ValueType* directly. The compiler also adds keywords required for a structure, such as the *sealed* keyword.

As a value type, structures are defined as local variables with the *.locals* directive. Value types are stored on the stack, not on the managed heap. Accessing a member, such as calling a member method, requires binding to the address of the structure. This entails loading the address of the structure onto the evaluation stack before accessing a member. The *ldloc* instruction would load the structure on the evaluation stack. We need the address of the structure. To load the address of a local variable, use the *ldloca* instruction. (The "a" variation of an MSIL instruction refers to an address.)

Call the constructor of a structure explicitly with the *call* instruction, not the *newobj* instruction. Structures are not created on the heap. When the constructor is called directly, the type is simply initialized.

This code creates and initializes a structure:

```
.assembly extern mscorlib {}
.assembly application {}

.namespace Donis.CSharpBook {

    .class Starter {
        .method static public void Main() il managed {
            .entrypoint
            .locals init (valuetype Donis.CSharpBook.ZStruct obj)
            ldloca.s obj
            ldc.i4.s 10
            call instance void Donis.CSharpBook.ZStruct::.ctor(int32)
            ldloca.s obj
```

```
        ldfld int32 Donis.CSharpBook.ZStruct::fielda
        call void [mscorlib]System.Console::WriteLine(int32)
        ret
    }
}

.class value ZStruct {

    .method public specialname rtspecialname
            instance void .ctor(int32) cil managed {
        ldarg.0
        ldarg.1
        stfld int32 Donis.CSharpBook.ZStruct::fielda
        ret
    }

    .field public int32 fielda
}
}
```

Branching

The branch instruction is available in various permutations, but in all circumstances it is essentially a *goto* statement. The target of a branch instruction is a label. Most branch instructions are conditional and based on a comparative expression or a Boolean condition. For an unconditional *goto*, use the *br* instruction. Loop and other transfer-of-control statements in C# are implemented as some combination of branch instructions.

A conditional branch can be made with the *brtrue* and *brfalse* statements. The *brtrue* instruction branches on a true condition, whereas the *brfalse* branches on a false condition. These instructions consume a Boolean value, which should be on the evaluation stack.

Compare instructions perform a comparison on the top two values of the evaluation stack. The two values are replaced on the evaluation stack with the result of the comparison, which is either *true* or *false*. The comparison should be between related types.

Table 11-7 lists the compare instructions. In the table, assume that t2 is top value on the evaluation stack, and t1 is the second value. t2 is the last item placed on the evaluation stack and the next to be removed.

Table 11-7   Compare Instructions

Instruction	Comparison
ceq	t1 equal to t2
cgt	t1 greater than t2
clt	t1 less than t2
cgt.un and *clt.un*	Unsigned or unordered version of the comparison operations

This sample code shows unconditional and conditional branching. It also contains an example of a comparison instruction:

```
.assembly extern mscorlib {}
.assembly application {}

.namespace Donis.CSharpBook {

    .class Starter {

        .method static public void Main() il managed {
            .entrypoint
            ldc.i4.3
            ldc.i4.1
            cgt
            brtrue greater
            ldstr "{0} is less than or equal {1}"
            br end
greater:    ldstr "{0} is greater than {1}"
end:        ldc.i4.3
            box int32
            ldc.i4.m1
            box int32
            call void [mscorlib] System.Console::WriteLine(
                string, object, object)
            ret
        }
    }
}
```

As a convenience, branch and compare instructions are combinable. The combined instruction compares the top two values of the evaluation stack and branches on the result. These are called comparative branching instructions. Instead of requiring two instructions to perform the test, only one is needed.

Table 11-8 lists comparative branching instructions.

Table 11-8   Comparative Branching

Instruction	Description
Beq	Branch on equal
Bne	Branch on not equal
Bge	Branch on greater than or equal
Bgt	Branch on greater than
Ble	Branch on less than or equal
Blt	Branch on less than
bgt.un, *blt.un*, and *bne.un*	The unsigned version of these instructions

Here is an example of a *for* loop in MSIL code. The loop increments the count from zero to five. The current count is displayed in iterations of the loop:

```
.assembly extern mscorlib {}
.assembly application {}

.namespace Donis.CSharpBook {

    .class Starter {

        .method static public void Main() il managed {
            .entrypoint
            .locals (int32 count)
            ldc.i4.0
            stloc.0
            br.s loop
for:        ldloc count
            ldc.i4.1
            add
            dup
            stloc count
            call void [mscorlib] System.Console::WriteLine(int32)
loop:       ldloc count
            ldc.i4.5
            clt
            brtrue.s for
            ret
        }
    }
}
```

The sample code uses the short form of the branch instruction. Be careful when branching in the short form. As with all short-form instructions, the operand is limited to a single byte. The short form of branch instructions cannot jump to a label further than 1 byte away. The distance from the branch site to the label must be describable in a single byte. If not, the application might branch to the wrong location.

Calling Methods

There are a variety of ways to call methods. So far, only the *call* and *callvirt* methods have been shown in sample code. Some instructions or actions, such as *newobj*, call a method implicitly. The *newobj* instruction calls a constructor, whereas the *static* constructor is called implicitly on the first access to the class or object.

The *call* methods have the same general syntax:

call*suffix* returntype [*assembly*] *signature*

The *returntype* is placed on the evaluation stack; *assembly* is the location of the method. If in the current assembly, the *assembly* element can be ignored. The complete signature of the method is represented by *signature*.

Table 11-9 lists the call instructions in MSIL.

Table 11-9 Call Instructions

Instruction	Description
call	Intended for calling nonvirtual methods. However, the instruction can be applied to virtual methods. The invocation is still interpreted as a nonvirtual call.
callvirt	Calls a virtual method. For nonvirtual methods, a nonvirtual call is conducted.

calli	Calls a function indirectly through a function pointer. Place each function parameter and then the function pointer on the evaluation stack. The *calli* syntax is slightly different from other call instructions. It does not include the target assembly or method name in the syntax. Use the *ldftn* instruction to place a function pointer on the stack for a particular method.
	
	This sample code includes both the *calli* and *ldftn* instructions:
	
	<pre>.assembly extern mscorlib {}
	.assembly application {}
	
	.namespace Donis.CSharpBook {
	
	  .class Starter {
	
	    .method static public void Main() il managed {
	      .entrypoint
	      ldstr "Donis"
	      ldftn void
	Donis.CSharpBook.Starter::Name(string)
	      calli void(string)
	      ret
	    }
	
	    .method static public void Name(string)
	      il managed {
	      ldstr "Hello, {0}!"
	      ldarg.0
	      call void [mscorlib]
	      System.Console::WriteLine(string, object)
	      ret
	    }
	  }
	}</pre>

jmp	Jumps from the current method to the target method and transfers the arguments. The caller and callee must have matching signatures. Code after the *jmp* site in the calling function is abandoned.

Table 11-9   Call Instructions

Instruction	Description
jmp (cont.)	Here is sample code of the *jmp* instruction:

```
.assembly extern mscorlib {}
.assembly application {}
.namespace Donis.CSharpBook {
    .class Starter {
        .method static public void Main() il managed {
            .entrypoint
            ldstr "Aloha!"
            call void
Donis.CSharpBook.Starter::MethodA(string)
            ret
        }
        .method static public void
          MethodA(string) il managed {
          ldstr "Before jump"
          call void [mscorlib]
          System.Console::WriteLine(string)
          ldstr "In MethodA: {0}"
          ldarg.0
          call void [mscorlib]
          System.Console::WriteLine(string, object)
          jmp void
Donis.CSharpBook.Starter::MethodB(string)
          ldstr "After jump"
          call void [mscorlib]
          System.Console::WriteLine(string)
          ret
        }
        .method static public void
            MethodB(string) il managed {
          ldstr "In MethodB: {0}"
          ldarg.0
          call void [mscorlib]
          System.Console::WriteLine(string, object)
          ret
        }
    }
}
```

This program jumps from *MethodA* to *MethodB*. In *MethodA*, the instruction after the *jmp* instruction is orphaned. Therefore, the message *"After jump"* is not displayed. *MethodB* returns directly to *Main*, not *MethodA*.

| *tail* | The *tail* command is a prefix instruction and similar to the *jmp* command. However, the arguments must be loaded explicitly on the evaluation stack and the method signatures can be different. Otherwise, the functions are operationally equivalent. |

This is the syntax of the *tail* instruction:

tail.

callsuffix returntype [assembly] signature

Arrays

An array is a collection of related types, and there are several ways to declare an array in MSIL. Regardless, the underlying type of any array is *System.Array*. Exploiting the array reference, you can call the methods and access the properties of *System.Array*.

Table 11-10 lists different syntaxes for defining an array.

Table 11-10   Syntax for Defining Arrays

Array Syntax	Description
type [] *arrayname*	Declares a one-dimensional array of an undetermined size.
type [,] *arrayname*	Declares a two-dimensional array of an undetermined size.
type [n] *arrayname*	Declares an array of *n*-size.
type [m,n] *arrayname*	Declares an array in which the size is *m*-columns and *n*-rows.
type [][] *arrayname*	Declares a jagged array of undetermined size.
type [m][] *arrayname*	Declares a jagged array of *m* arrays.

The *newarr* instruction initializes a one-dimensional array. In addition, the instruction pushes a reference to the array onto the evaluation stack. You might want to use the array for some time. Move the array reference from the evaluation stack to memory, such as a local variable, to extend to the array. The *newarr* instruction requires the number of elements, which should be stored on the evaluation stack.

The syntax is as follows:

newarr *type*

Elements of an array can be accessed with the *ldelem* or *stelem* instructions. The *ldelem* instruction loads an element of an array onto the evaluation stack; the *stelem* instruction stores a value from the evaluation stack into an element of an array. Both instructions have variations that depend on the type of data being manipulated. The variations of *ldelem* are *ldelem.i1*, *ldelem.i2*, *ldelem.i4*, *ldelem.i8*, *ldelem.u1*, *ldelem.u2*, *ldelem.u4*, *ldelem.u8*, *ldelem.r4*, *ldelem.r8*, *ldelem.i*, and *ldelem.ref*. The permutations of the *stelem* instruction are *stelem.i1*, *stelemi2*, *stelem.i4*, *stelem.i8*, *stelem.r4*, *stelem.r8*, *stelem.i*, and *stelem.ref*. The *ldelem* instruction requires, in order, the array reference and the element index. The *stelem* instruction requires the array reference, element index, and the new value.

In the following code, an array of three strings is created. Each element is initialized to a different color. The array elements are then displayed in a loop.

```
.assembly extern mscorlib {}
.assembly application {}
```

```
.namespace Donis.CSharpBook {

    .class starter {

        .method static public void Main() il managed {
            .locals init (string [] names, int32 count)
            .entrypoint
            ldc.i4.3
            newarr string
            stloc names
            ldloc names
            ldc.i4.0
            ldstr "Aqua"
            stelem.ref
            ldloc names
            ldc.i4.1
            ldstr "Violet"
            stelem.ref
            ldloc names
            ldc.i4.2
            ldstr "Orange"
            stelem.ref
            ldc.i4.0
            stloc count
loop:       ldloc names
            ldloc count
            ldelem.ref
            call void [mscorlib] System.Console::WriteLine(string)
            ldloc count
            ldc.i4.1
            add
            dup
            stloc count
            ldc.i4.3
            blt loop
            ret
        }
    }
}
```

Arithmetic Instructions

MSIL supports the standard arithmetic instructions. The operands of the arithmetic operation are retrieved from the evaluation stack and replaced with the result. For example, the *add* instruction has two operands, which are removed for the evaluation stack and replaced with the summation.

Table 11-11 lists the common arithmetic instructions. The final column is the number of operands consumed from the evaluation stack during the instruction.

Table 11-11   **Arithmetic Instructions**

Instruction	Description	Operands
add	Addition	2
sub	Subtraction	2
mul	Multiplication	2
div	Division	2
rem	Remainder	2
neg	Negate	1

Conversion Operations

It is often necessary to convert between types. The *conv* instruction casts between primitive types. The instruction has a single operand, which is the target of the cast. Conversions can cause overflows when the memory size of the source is larger than the target. For example, this could happen when casting from a 64-bit integer to a 32-bit integer. The high-order bits are trimmed when an overflow occurs, which changes the normal results. It's important to note that the overflow is ignored, and subtle bugs are possible. The *conv.ovf* instruction prevents an overflow from going undetected. When an overflow occurs, the modified instruction raises an overflow exception.

The following code contains an ostentatious overflow condition. The conversion raises the overflow exception. This code is not protected from exceptions, and the application is terminated.

```
.assembly extern mscorlib {}
.assembly application {}

.namespace Donis.CSharpBook {

    .class Starter {

        .method static public void Main() il managed {
            .entrypoint
            ldc.i8 4000000000
            conv.ovf.i4
            pop
            ret
        }
    }
}
```

Exception Handling

Exception handling is implemented in the CLR. Each managed language exposes exception handling in a language-specific manner. In C#, there are the *try*, *catch*, *throw*, and *finally* keywords. The language compiler, such as *csc*, compiles code for exception handling into language-agnostic MSIL code. For the details of exception handling in C#, read Chapter 9, "Exception Handling."

There are two strategies for implementing exception handling in MSIL code: as exception clauses or as scoped exceptions.

Exception clauses are implemented after the core MSIL code of a method in the exception-handling section. An exception clause consists of a protected block, an exception identification, and an exception handler. Execution must fall into a protected block naturally. Also, you cannot jump into a protected block. To exit the protected block or handler, use the *leave* instruction. Of course, when an exception is raised, execution is transferred away from the protected block. Do not attempt to exit a protected block or exception handler with a branch statement.

Exception clauses have a handler. There are four types of handlers, and each is assigned a unique code. Table 11-12 lists the four handlers.

Table 11-12   Exception Clauses

Code	Description
0	This clause defines an exception handler.
1	This clause defines an exception filter. The filter determines when the handler should be run. The exception filter ends at an *endfilter* instruction.
2	This clause defines a finally handler. The finally handler is called whether an exception is raised or not. Cleanup code that must be executed regardless should reside in the finally handler. The finally handler ends at an *endfinally* instruction.
4	This clause defines a fault handler. This is similar to a finally handler, except that this clause is called only when an exception is raised. The fault handler ends at the *endfault* instruction.

This is the syntax of the try clause:

.try $label^1$ to $label^2$ exceptiontype handler $label^3$ to $label^4$

$label^1$ and $label^2$ define the protected code, whereas $label^3$ and $label^4$ set the scope of the handler. The exception type specifies the type of handler as catch, filter, finally, or fault handler.

In the previous example, an overflow exception is thrown and not caught. The following code catches the overflow exception:

```
.assembly extern mscorlib {}
.assembly application {}

.namespace Donis.CSharpBook {

    .class Starter {

        .method static public void Main() il managed {
            .entrypoint
```

```
start:          ldc.i8 4000000000
                conv.ovf.i4
                pop
                leave done
stop:           callvirt instance string [mscorlib]
 System.Exception::get_Message()
                call void [mscorlib] System.Console::WriteLine(string)
                leave done
done:           ret
                .try start to stop catch [mscorlib] System.Exception
 handler stop to done
        }
    }
}
```

Scoped exceptions are similar to exception handling in C#, in which there is a try and catch block. Scoped exceptions do not employ exception clauses at the end of the method.

This is the conversion exception code written for scoped exceptions:

```
.assembly extern mscorlib {}
.assembly application {}

.namespace Donis.CSharpBook {

    .class Starter {

        .method static public void Main() il managed {
            .entrypoint
            .try {
                ldc.i8 4000000000
                conv.ovf.i4
                pop
                leave done
            }
            catch [mscorlib] System.Exception {
                callvirt instance string
                [mscorlib] System.Exception::get_Message()
                call void
 [mscorlib] System.Console::WriteLine(string)
                leave done
            }
done:           ret
        }
    }
}
```

Miscellaneous Operations

This chapter includes several tables that explain categories of MSIL instructions. However, some MSIL instructions appearing in the sample code of this chapter have not been included in any table. Other instructions have not appeared in the body of code or in a table but are valuable nonetheless. Table 11-13 details some of these miscellaneous MSIL instructions.

Table 11-13   **Miscellaneous MSIL Instructions**

Instruction	Description
and	Bitwise *and*.
break	Insert a debugger breakpoint.
castclass	Cast an instance to a different type.
dup	Duplicate the top slot of the evaluation stack.
dop	Nonoperational instruction (a blank instruction).
or	Bitwise *or*.
pop	Remove the top element of the evaluation stack.
rethrow	Propagate an exception.
throw	Throw an application exception.

Process Execution

How and when is MSIL code compiled to native binary? The MSIL code is compiled into binary at run time. Only methods that are called are compiled into binary. This is part of a larger procedure called process execution. Most of the information in this section is obtained from the Shared Source CLI, which is an open source implementation of the Common Language Infrastructure (CLI). The Shared Source CLI is often referred to as Rotor. For more information on Rotor, visit this page: *msdn.microsoft.com/net/sscli*. This section explains method compilation in the examination of how the entry point method is executed.

Process execution begins when a managed application is launched. At that time, the CLR is bootstrapped into the application. The CLR is bootstrapped as the mscoree.dll library. This library starts the process of loading the CLR into the memory of the application. *_CorExeMain* is the starting point in mscoree.dll. Every managed application includes a reference to mscoree.dll and *_CorExeMain*. You can confirm this with the dumpbin.exe tool. Execute the following command line on any managed application for confirmation:

```
dumpbin /imports application.exe
```

Figure 11-2 shows the result of the *dumpbin* command.

Managed applications have an embedded stub. The stub fools the Windows environment into loading a managed application. The stub temporarily masks the managed application as a native Windows application. The stub calls *_CorExeMain* in moscoree.dll. *_CorExeMain* then delegates to *_CorExeMain2* in mscorwks.

_CorExeMain2 eventually calls *SystemDomain::ExecuteMainMethod*. As the name implies, *ExecuteMainMethod* is responsible for locating and executing the entry point method. The entry point method is a member of a class. The first step in executing the method is locating that class. During process execution, classes are represented as EECLASS structures internally. *ExecuteMainMethod* calls *ClassLoader::LoadTypeHandleFromToken* to obtain an instance of the EECLASS for the class that has the entry point method. *LoadTypeHandleFromToken* is provided the metadata token for the class and returns an instance of an EECLASS as an *out* parameter. In a managed application, only classes that are touched have a representative EECLASS structure. The important members of the EECLASS are a pointer to the parent class, a list of fields, and a pointer to a method table.

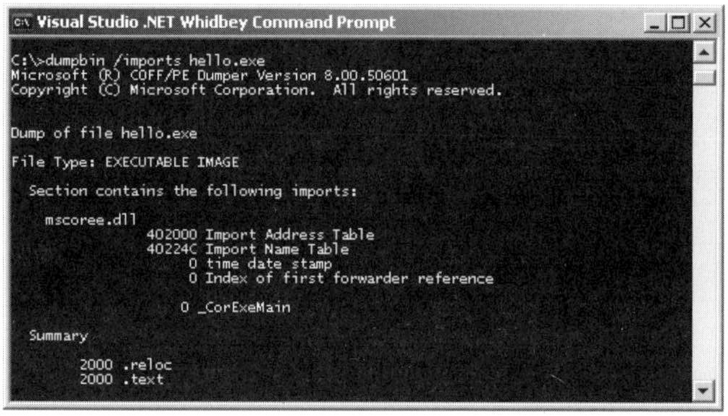

Figure 11-2   The dumpbin command with the imports option

The method table contains an entry for each function in the class. The entries are called method descriptors. The method descriptor is subdivided into parts. The first part is *m_CodeOrIL*. Before a method is jitted, *m_CodeOrIL* contains the relative virtual address to the MSIL code of the method. The second part is a stub containing a thunk to the JIT compiler. The first time the method is called, the jitter is invoked through the stub. The jitter used the IL RVA part to locate and then compile the implementation of the method into binary. The resulting native binary is cached in memory. In addition, the stub and *m_CodeOrIL* parts are updated to reference the virtual address of the native binary. This is an optimization and prevents additional jitting of the same method. Future calls to the function simply invoke the native binary.

Roundtripping

Roundtripping is disassembling an application, modifying the code through the disassembly, and then reassembling the application. This provides a mechanism for maintaining or otherwise updating an application without the original source code.

The following C# application simply totals two numbers, where the project name is "Add". The result is displayed in the console window.

```
using System;

namespace Donis.CSharpBook{
    public class Starter{
        public static void Main(string [] args){
            if(args.Length<2) {
                Console.WriteLine("Not enough parameters.");
                Console.WriteLine("Program exiting...");
                return;
            }
```

```
try {
    byte value1=byte.Parse(args[0]);
    byte value2=byte.Parse(args[1]);
    byte total=(byte) (value1+value2);
    Console.WriteLine("{0} + {1} = {2}",
        value1, value2, total);
}
catch(Exception e) {
    Console.WriteLine(e.Message);
}
    }
  }
}
```

Let us assume that the above program was purchased from a third-party vendor for quintillion dollars. Of course, the source code was not included with the application–even for quintillion dollars. Almost immediately, a bug is discovered in the application. When the program is executed, the total is sometimes incorrect. Look at the following example:

```
c:\ >add 200 150
200 + 150 = 94
```

The result should not be 350, not 94. How is this problem fixed without the source code? Roundtripping is the answer. This begins by disassembling the application. For convenience, the ILDASM disassembler is used:

```
ildasm /out=newadd.il add.exe
```

Open *newall.il* in a text editor. In examining the MSIL code, we can easily find the culprit. The *addition* instruction adds two byte variables. The result is cached in another byte variable. This is an unsafe action that occasionally causes an overflow in the total. Instead of notifying the application of the overflow event, the value is cycled. This is the reason for the errant value. Add the *ovf* suffix to the *conv* instruction to correct the problem. The exception is now raised when the overflow occurs.

You can use roundtripping to add features not otherwise available directly in C#. C# supports general exception handling but not exception filters. When an exception is raised, the exception filter determines whether the exception handler executes. If the exception filter evaluates to one, the handler runs. If zero, the handler is skipped.

Here is a partial listing of the disassembled program. It is modified to throw an exception when the additional overflows the total. An exception filter has also been added to the exception handling. Changes in the code are highlighted:

```
IL_0035: ldelem.ref
IL_0036: call uint8 [mscorlib]System.Byte::Parse(string)
IL_003b: stloc.1
IL_003c: ldloc.0
IL_003d: ldloc.1
IL_003e: add
IL_003f: conv.ovf.u1
```

```
IL_0040: stloc.2
IL_0041: ldstr "{0} + {1} = {2}"
IL_0046: ldloc.0
IL_0047: box [mscorlib]System.Byte
IL_004c: ldloc.1
IL_004d: box [mscorlib]System.Byte
IL_0052: ldloc.2
IL_0053: box [mscorlib]System.Byte
IL_0058: call void [mscorlib]System.Console::WriteLine(string,
object,
object,
object)
IL_005d: nop
IL_005e: nop
IL_005f: leave.s IL_0072

} // end .try
filter
{
pop
ldc.i4.1
endfilter
}
// catch [mscorlib]System.Exception
{
IL_0061: stloc.3
IL_0062: nop
IL_0063: ldloc.3
```

Because the filter returns one, the exception is always handled. The ILASM compiler can reassemble the application, which completes the roundtrip. Here is the command:

```
ilasm newadd.il
```

Run and test the *newadd* application. The changed program is more robust. Roundtripping has been a success!

Debugging with Visual Studio 2005

The first two chapters of Part IV, "Debugging," review the metadata and MSIL code of an assembly. The next two chapters focus on debuggers. There is a variety of debuggers available for managed code. Chapter 12 starts with Visual Studio 2005.

The Visual Studio 2005 debugger has two primary advantages. First, Visual Studio uses a familiar graphic user interface. Second, the debugger is integrated with other aspects of the programming environment. You can develop, test, debug, and return to developing an application within a single product. This is very convenient.

The debugger in Visual Studio 2005 has a plethora of rapid application development (RAD) tools for debugging, including a multitude of debug windows, a specialized toolbar, the ability to open dumps, and much more. The next chapter explores these tools and how to debug an application with Visual Studio 2005.

Chapter 12
Debugging with Visual Studio 2005

Microsoft Visual Studio is a popular development environment that has an effective debugger to help developers quickly diagnose and correct application problems. The Visual Studio debugger is a multipurpose tool that includes an assortment of tools, features, and windows to help developers quickly ascertain and correct problems. Use the Visual Studio debugger to inspect the values of variables, view the call stack, determine thread status, dump memory, set various types of breakpoints, and much more. Visual Studio 2005 introduces new features such as visualizers, tracepoints, crash dumps (opening directly), and the Exception Assistant. One benefit of the Visual Studio debugger is the familiar user interface. Developers experienced with the Visual Studio environment should be comfortable with the look and feel of the debugger.

Visual Studio debugging is extensible. Developers can customize many aspects of the debugger, including extending many of the types related to debugging. For example, developers can create user-defined visualizers and trace listeners. Visual Studio debugging is adaptable to specific problems, objectives, and goals.

In a debugging session, developers control how an application executes. A developer can start, interrupt, or stop a debugging session. These are the controls explained in Table 12-1.

Table 12-1   Control of a Debugging Session

Control	Description
Start Execution	From the Debug menu, there are various commands to start a debugging session. If you use the Start Debugging, Step Into, or Step Over menu command, the application is in running mode. Alternatively, the Start Without Debugging menu command starts an application without attaching the Visual Studio debugger.
	You can also start a debugging session with the Run To Cursor command. In the source editor, position the cursor on the target source code. Open the shortcut menu and select the Run To Cursor menu command. This command starts an application in debug mode, but breaks when a breakpoint or the cursor is reached. If neither occurs, the application runs uninterrupted.

Table 12-1   Control of a Debugging Session *(Continued)*

Control	Description
Break Execution	You can break into an application running in a debug session, which is most commonly accomplished by setting breakpoints. Developers can forcibly break into an application using the Break All menu command from the Debug menu. The command interrupts all applications currently being debugged by the Visual Studio debugger. After breaking into the application, the user is transferred to the source code being executed when the break occurred. If source code is not available, the user is transferred to the disassembly. When execution is interrupted, the application is in break mode.
Stop Execution	Developers can choose to end a debugging session. From the Debug menu, select the Stop Debugging command to end a debugging session.
	You can terminate an attached process in the Processes window. In that window, select the process and choose the Terminate Process menu command from the context menu.
	A debug session can be stopped and restarted again. On the Debug menu, the Restart menu command restarts a debugging session.

Applications in a debugging session are either in a running mode or a break mode. In running mode, an application is executing. In break mode, an application is interrupted, which is when a developer commonly diagnoses an application. Certain features are applicable only in break mode, such as the Threads and Call Stack windows. While debugging, an application can transition between running and break modes. The following actions can transfer an application from running to break mode:

- A breakpoint is hit.
- A tracepoint is hit.
- The cursor is hit with a Run To Cursor command.
- The Break All command is executed.
- An unhandled exception is raised.
- Stepping through an application.

You can transition from break mode to running mode by starting execution again, which is defined in Table 12-1.

Debugging Overview

Debugging techniques vary between project types. For example, the strategy for debugging a Microsoft Windows application is different from debugging a class library. This section provides an overview of debugging strategies for basic project types.

Debugging Windows Forms Projects

Of the project types, managing a debugging session for a Windows Forms project is probably the easiest. Initiate a debugging session to begin debugging a Windows Forms application.

Start a debugging session of a Windows Forms project with a start execution action, such as the Start Debugging menu command. When the execution starts, the Visual Studio debugger is attached to the application.

Set breakpoints before or during the debugging session. Windows Forms applications are event driven, and breakpoints can be placed in event handlers. Breakpoints can also be added to functions called from event handlers. When the breakpoint is hit, the debugging session is transferred to break mode. To run between breakpoints, use the Start Debugging menu command.

Attaching to a Running Process

You can attach the debugger to processes running outside of Visual Studio. At that time, a debug session is initiated. There are several reasons to attach to a process:

- When a problem occurs in an application, you can immediately debug the situation. Attach the debugger and diagnose the problem.

- You can debug a class library project in the context of a running process.

- You can debug a production application. If you attach to an application that is not a debug build, an error message box is displayed. You can then proceed into a debugging session. However, source code, symbols, and other ingredients of a normal debugging session might not be available. Care must be taken when debugging a production application. Some actions can interfere with the normal execution of the program. For example, breakpoints can interrupt execution of the application and strand users.

Open the Attach To Process window to attach to a process. (From the Debug menu, choose the Attach To Process menu command.) Figure 12-1 shows the Attach To Process window. The Debug menu is not available when no solution is open. In that circumstance, choose the Attach To Process menu command from the Tools menu.

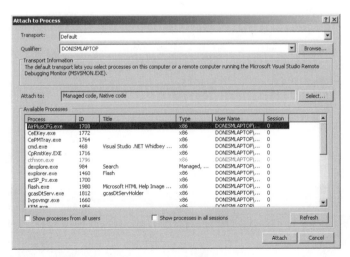

Figure 12-1   Attach To Process window

A list of processes is presented in the Attach To Process window. To attach to a specific process, select a process from the Available Processes list and then click the Attach button. If not a debug build, an error message box is displayed. The debugger can be attached to multiple processes. All the attached processes are dimmed in the process list. However, you can actively debug only a single process, which defaults to the last process attached. You can change a current process by using the Debug Location toolbar and the Process drop-down list, which is shown in Figure 12-2. You can also select the Debug Location toolbar from the Toolbars submenu on the View menu.

Figure 12-2   Debug Location toolbar

The Attach To Process window has several options. Transport is the transport used to connect to a target device or remote machine. Default connects to a local machine or remote machine using the Microsoft Visual Studio Remote Debugging Monitor (msvsmon.exe). The Qualifier window is the name of the target machine. The Attach To choice selects the target type as managed, native, script, or T-SQL. The default is managed. The Show Processes For All Users option lists processes from all users of the current logon session. For Terminal Service clients remotely connected to a machine, Show Processes In All Sessions displays the processes of the remote machine session. The process list is not static. As new processes start up and existing processes finish, the list of running processes changes. The Refresh button updates the list box to reflect any changes in the process list.

After attaching to an application, interrupt the application with a breakpoint. You can then use debugging techniques and the various debugging windows to debug the application. To set a breakpoint, open the source code of the application and insert a breakpoint. When execution hits the breakpoint, the application is interrupted. Alternatively, use the BreakAll menu command on the Debug menu.

Terminate the debugging session to detach the debugger from the running process. For example, the Stop Debugging menu command on the Debug menu terminates a debugging session and detaches from a running process. The running process will continue to execute.

Debugging Console Application Projects

Debugging a Console project is similar to debugging a Windows application, with some notable differences:

- Console applications typically output to the Console window, but debug messages are normally displayed in the Output window. Displaying messages in separate windows has both advantages and disadvantages. Clarity in isolation of debug messages is the primary advantage. Parsing debug and normal messages in separate windows helps track both. Conversely, the advantage of a single window for all output is convenience. The developer need not toggle between the Console and Output windows. With the *TraceSource* type, you have the option of displaying trace messages in several locations, including the Console window, Output window, or both windows simultaneously.

■ Console applications often require command-line arguments. Open Project properties from the Project menu. From the Debug window, enter the command-line arguments as part of the Startup Options. Be sure to refresh the command-line arguments as needed.

■ In a debugging session, the results of a short running console application are only briefly displayed before the console window is closed. Therefore, the results may be difficult to view. Freeze the window by inserting a *Console.ReadLine* statement. Alternatively, after debugging the application, execute in release mode to persist the Console window. In that case, Press Any Key To Continue is displayed.

Debugging Class Library Projects

A class library project creates a dynamic-link library (DLL), which does not execute directly. This makes the proposition of debugging more challenging. The DLL must run within the context of another application. The execution of the host application precedes the DLL. The host loads the DLL when needed.

You can specify the host application in the debug settings for the project. In the Debug pane of the Project properties window, select the Start External Program option as the Start action and enter the name of the hosting application. At the start of the debugging session, the specified host is executed and the DLL is loaded as needed. You can then debug the class library project.

If the host application and class library projects are in the same solution, setting the external program is not necessary. Simply set the host application to the startup project. Start a debugging session normally and debug both the host and class library projects.

When the host application is already running, attach the debugger to that process in the Attach To Process window. This process will initiate a debug session in which the class library project can then be debugged.

Debugging Setup

The Visual Studio debugger is fully configurable. Debugging sessions can be tailored to a developer or to the specific requirements of an application. For convenience, debug settings are saved in a configuration. Debug and Release are the default configurations and represent the most commonly used settings. The Debug configuration contains the project options for creating debug builds of an application. The Release configuration contains the options for release builds. Prior to changing project settings, it is good policy to confirm the active configuration. This avoids inadvertently changing the wrong configuration.

Debug and Release Configurations

As mentioned, the default configurations are Debug and Release. There are literally dozens of project options set in the predefined Debug and Release configurations. You can view and set debug configurations from Project properties in Solution Explorer. Open Project properties using the project context menu.

The important settings of the Debug configuration are as follows:

- The *DEBUG* and *TRACE* constants—which control the behavior of the *TraceSource*, *Debug*, and *Trace* types—are defined.

- The Debug Info option is set to *full*. This option requests the creation of a symbol file (*pdb*) whenever a project is built.

- The output path is *bin\debug*.

- The Optimize Code option is set to *false*, which disables code optimization.

The settings of the Release configuration are as follows:

- The *DEBUG* constant is not defined; however, the *TRACE* constant is defined.

- The Debug Info option is set to *pdb-only*.

- The output path is *bin\release*.

- The Optimize Code option is set to *true*, which enables code optimization.

Configuration Manager

Use the Configuration Manager to view, edit, and create configurations of project settings. To open the Configuration Manager, choose the Configuration Manager menu command from the Build Menu. Figure 12-3 shows the Configuration Manager. The Configuration Manager lists the current configuration of each project in the solution.

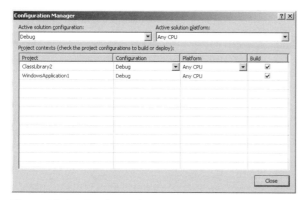

Figure 12-3   Configuration Manager

In the Configuration Manager, the Active Solution Configuration drop-down list selects a common configuration for every project. You can also create a new configuration from the drop-down list. In addition, you can rename or remove an existing configuration. The Active Solution Platform drop-down list selects the current platform.

Each row of the Configuration Manager represents a project. The project list has several columns of information:

- **Project**   This column shows the name of each project.
- **Configuration**   This column selects the current configuration of each project.
- **Platform**   This column selects the target platform of each project.
- **Build**   This column is an option box, which includes or excludes projects in builds of the solution.

Debug Settings

The Visual Studio environment, solution, and project maintain separate debug settings:

- Debug settings of the Visual Studio environment are set in the Options dialog box. (From the Tools menu, choose the Options menu command.)
- Debug settings of a project are set in the Project properties dialog box, which is opened by using the Project properties menu command on the Project menu.
- Debug settings of a solution are set in the Solution properties window. Open this window from the context menu of the solution in Solution Explorer.

Visual Studio Environment Debug Settings

Debug settings for the Visual Studio product affect all projects. You can configure Edit And Continue, just-in-time (JIT) debugging, native debugging options, symbol servers, and general debugging options for the environment.

General window   The general debugging options are an assortment of miscellaneous options. Each option can be enabled or disabled. Figure 12-4 shows the General window for setting these options.

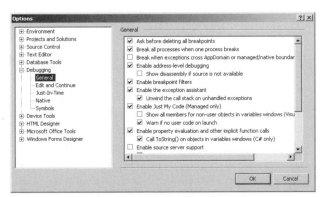

Figure 12-4   The General window for setting general debugging options

Each option is described in Table 12-2.

Table 12-2   General Debugging Options

Option	Description	Default
Ask Before Deleting All Breakpoints	This option requests confirmation with the Delete All Breakpoints command.	Enabled
Break All Processes When One Process Breaks	This option interrupts all processes being debugged when a break occurs.	Enabled
Break When Exceptions Cross AppDomain Or Managed/Native Boundaries (Managed Only)	This option asks the Common Language Runtime (CLR) to catch exceptions that cross an application domain or cross between managed and native code.	Disabled
Enable Address-Level Debugging	This option allows certain operations at the address level, such as setting breakpoints on instruction addresses.	Enabled
Show Disassembly If Source Is Not Available	This option requests that the disassembly window be displayed when user source code is not available.	Disabled
Enable Breakpoint Filters	This option lets developers set filters on breakpoints, which can limit the scope of a breakpoint to a thread, process, or machine.	Enabled
Enable The Exception Assistant	This option automatically displays the Exception Assistant when an exception is raised while debugging.	Enabled
Unwind The Call Stack On Unhandled Exceptions	This option allows the user to unwind the call stack on a first chance exception, in which code changes can be made including repairing the source of the exception.	Enabled
Enable Just My Code (Managed Only)	This option allows the debugger to step into user code. Other code, such as system code, is skipped.	Enabled
Warn If No User Code On Launch	This option displays a warning when debugging is initiated if no user code is available.	Enabled
Enable Property Evaluation And Other Implicit Function Calls	This option evaluates the result of properties and other implicit function calls in Watch and Variables windows.	Enabled
Call ToString() On Objects In Variables Windows (C# Only)	This option calls *ToString* implicitly on objects displayed in variables windows.	Enabled
Enable Source Server Support	This option requests that Visual Studio get source course from the source code server (srcsrv.dll).	Disabled
Print Source Server Diagnostics Messages To The Output Window	This option displays messages from the source server in the Output window.	Disabled

Table 12-2   General Debugging Options *(Continued)*

Option	Description	Default
Highlight Entire Source Line For Breakpoints And Current Statement	This option highlights an entire line of source code to emphasize the current breakpoint or statement.	Disabled
Require Source Files To Exactly Match The Original Version	This option asks the Visual Studio debugger to verify that the current source file matches the version built with the application.	Enabled
Redirect All Output Window Text To The Immediate Window	This option redirects messages from the Output window to the Immediate window.	Disabled
Show Raw Structure Of Objects In Variables Windows	This option disables debugger customizations, such as the *DebuggerDisplay* attribute.	Disabled
Suppress JIT optimizations On Module Load (Managed Only)	This option disables JIT optimizations, which can make code easier to debug.	Enabled
Warn If No Symbols On Launch (Native Only)	This option displays a warning when no symbol information is available.	Enabled

Edit And Continue window   Edit And Continue permits changes to the source code while debugging. The changes are applied immediately without having to rebuild and restart the application. Edit And Continue is automatically enabled when breaking and then stepping through an application.

Most changes within a method are supported, such as deleting a line of code. However, Edit And Continue supports few changes that are made outside of a method. For example, deleting class members is not allowed. The following changes are not supported in Edit And Continue:

- Modifying an active statement.

- Surrounding an active statement with a *foreach*, *using*, or *lock* block.

- If the active statement is in the current stack frame, you cannot surround the active statement with a *catch* or *finally* block. You also cannot add a nested exception handler beneath six levels.

- If the active statement is not in the current stack frame, you cannot surround the active statement with a *try*, *catch*, or *finally* block. In addition, you cannot add a nested exception handler beneath six levels. Finally, you cannot change the code in the *try* block that contains the active statement.

- Adding a new member.

- Adding or changing a global symbol.

- Changing the signature of a member.

- Editing an anonymous method or a function containing a anonymous method.

- Changing, adding, or deleting an attribute.

- Changing or deleting a local variable.

- Modifying a method that contains a yield return or yield break statement.

- Changing, adding, or deleting a using directive.

- Modifying a constructor that contains a local variable that is initialized in an anonymous method.

Edit And Continue is not available in the following environments:

- Mixed-mode debugging

- SQL debugging

- Unhandled exceptions, unless the Unwind The Call Stack On Unhandled Exceptions general debugging option is enabled

- Attached application debugging

- 64-bit application debugging

- After a failed rebuild of the current application

In the Edit And Continue window, the Edit And Continue feature can be enabled or disabled. Figure 12-5 shows the Edit And Continue window. The remaining settings pertain to native code.

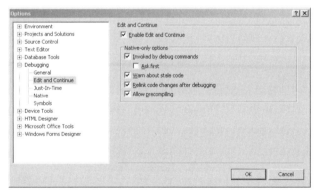

Figure 12-5   Edit And Continue debug settings

Just-In-Time Debugging window   The JIT debugger is attached to a running application when the program fails. Register Visual Studio as the JIT debugger in the Just-In-Time Debugging window. (See Figure 12-6.) Visual Studio can be the JIT debugger for Managed code, Native code, and Scripting. JIT debugging is discussed in the next chapter, "Advanced Debugging."

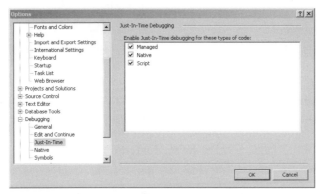

Figure 12-6   Just-In-Time Debugging window

Native window   The Native window has two debugging options. Enable the Load DLL Exports option to load the export tables for DLLs. This is beneficial when the debug symbols are not available. For example, you can set breakpoints on functions exported from the library even though symbols are not available. The Enable RPC Debugging option enables stepping into Component Object Model (COM) remote procedure calls. Both options are disabled by default.

Symbols window   Visual Studio can be configured to consult a symbol server and download the correct debugging symbols for the environment. Developers can use the Microsoft public symbol server or a local symbol server. Identify symbol servers and downstream paths in the Symbols window, which is shown in Figure 12-7. In the Symbol File Locations list box, symbol server paths can be entered or removed. Enter downstream servers in the Cache Symbols From Symbol Servers To This Directory Value.

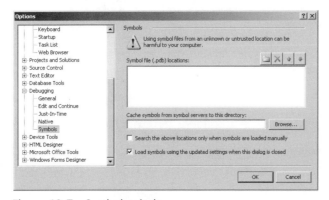

Figure 12-7   Symbols window

Symbols can be loaded manually in the Modules window, as shown in Figure 12-8. Open the Modules window from the Debug menu and the Windows submenu. The Modules window lists the modules loaded in the current application. This window is applicable in break mode, not running mode. Each row of the window has the name of the module, path to the module, whether the module is optimized, source code availability, symbol status, and fully qualified path to the symbol file. The Symbol Status column indicates whether the symbols are loaded or skipped. Symbols are automatically skipped for optimized code. For skipped symbols, you can manually load the symbols for a specific module using the context menu. The Load Symbols menu command loads the symbols for the selected module. The Load Symbols and Symbol File columns are then updated. The Symbol Status column shows whether the symbols are successfully loaded for the module. The Symbol File column displays the path to the loaded symbol file. If the symbol file cannot be found for the specified module, you are prompted with the Find Symbols dialog box, as shown in Figure 12-9. From there, you can browse to the relevant symbol file.

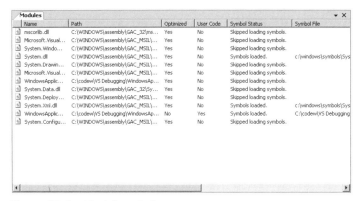

Figure 12-8   Modules window

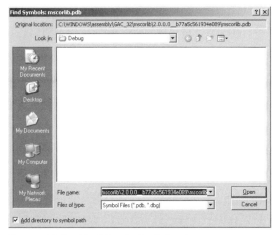

Figure 12-9   Find Symbols dialog box

From a module's context menu, the Symbol Load Information menu command displays general information about the symbols for the module. There is also a Symbol Setting menu command, which opens the Symbol debug window. You can configure symbols in this window.

Debug Settings for a Solution

Debug settings for a solution are set in the Solution property pages. The only settings available are Debug Source Files settings. (The Debug Source Files window is shown in Figure 12-10.) In this window, you can designate the directories that include and exclude source files.

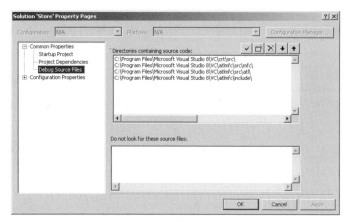

Figure 12-10   Debug Source Files window

Debug Settings for a Project

Debug settings for a project set the startup action, command-line arguments, and other debug options. Figure 12-11 shows the Debug pane of the Project Property pages.

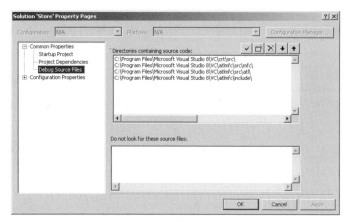

Figure 12-11   Debug pane of the Project Property pages

The Start Action option box indicates the startup action for debugging, which determines the application to launch when starting a debugging session. Here are the options:

- The Start Project option, which is the default, starts the application of the startup project.

- The Start External Program option is typically selected to debug class library projects. Specify the hosting application that loads the DLL of the class library project. You can then debug into the class library.

- The Start Browser With URL option is useful for debugging Web applications. Browse to a URL that is controlled by the Web application. The Web application is then loaded via the Web server, which provides an opportunity to debug the Web application.

The Start Options option box contains the following miscellaneous settings:

- Enter command-line arguments for the application in the Command Line Arguments text box.

- The Working Directory text box sets the working directory of the application. This is the default path for directory- and file-related tasks.

- The Use Remote Machine option names a remote machine, where the target application resides.

The Enable Debuggers option box indicates the kind of code that can be debugged:

- The Enable Unmanaged Code Debugging option enables mixed-mode debugging. Developers can debug between managed and unmanaged code.

- The Enable SQL Server Debugging option allows developers to debug CLR assemblies running within Microsoft SQL Server 2005.

- The Enable The Visual Studio Hosting Process option activates the Visual Studio hosting process, which is a new feature in Visual Studio 2005.

Visual Studio Debugging User Interface

The user interface in Visual Studio 2005 has new debugging features, which include data tips and visualizers. These enhancements improve developers' debugging experience. Other features, such as tracepoints, represent improvements of existing features. Tracepoints are a new style of breakpoints.

Data Tips

While you are debugging, a data tip is displayed when the cursor is paused over a variable. Previously, data tips were helpful when viewing simple types, such as integers and other value types. However, the details of a complex type were not visible in a data tip. In Visual Studio 2005, data tips are improved and can display the fields of a complex type. The complex type is at first collapsed in the data tip. Expansion displays the type members and values in the data tip.

Visualizers

Visualizers display the underlying HTML, XML, or text associated with a data tip. For example, the improved data tip can display the composition of a dataset, which is a complex type. A dataset is more than the composition of all its members. Datasets are an abstraction of an XML data source. The ability to view the underlying data while debugging is invaluable. Imagine programmatically parsing XML data and receiving incorrect results. You need to know if the problem is in the XML or the program logic. The XML Visualizer provides a convenient way to view the source XML data.

Data tips now have an optional menu that displays available visualizers. When a data tip detects values that are compatible with a visualizer, the visualizer menu is automatically displayed.

In the following code, *myxml* is a field that contains XML. The XML defines an array of books.

```
private string myxml = "<books><book><title>" +
    "The Gourmet Microwave</title>" +
    "<price>19.95</price>" +
    "</book><book><title>Sushi, Anyone?</title>" +
    "<price>49.99</price></book></books>";
```

The following code changes the content of the *myxml* field:

```
 string newbook="<book><title>" +
    "Donis's Great Adventure</title>" +
    "<price>9.95</price>" +
    "</book>";

myxml=myxml.Insert(5, newbook);
```

A string that contains XML, which describes another book, is added to the *myxml* string. A data tip can easily display the modified *myxml* string. Viewing *myxml* as XML provides additional clarification and important information. Move the cursor over the *myxml* variable, and a data tip appears. The modified string is displayed. From the data tip menu, select XML Visualizer. The XML Visualizer opens, as shown in Figure 12-12. The Visualizer uncovers a problem, which is that the underlying XML is not well-formed. Why not? The additional book was inserted at the wrong location in the *myxml* string, which is not detected from a simple data tip. However, the problem is caught by the Visualizer.

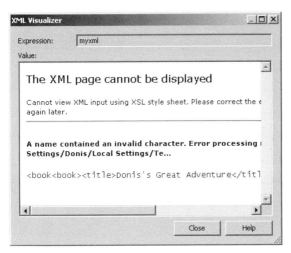

Figure 12-12   XML Visualizer uncovers a problem

The following code is modified to insert the book at the correct location in the *myxml* string. Now the XML Visualizer correctly displays the XML of the string. (See Figure 12-13.) You have just found and successfully resolved a bug!

```
myxml=myxml.Insert(7, newbook);
```

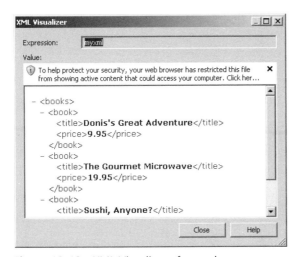

Figure 12-13   XML Visualizer of myxml

Visualizers are extensible; developers can create user-defined visualizers. The DataSet Visualizer is an example of a custom visualizer. It will display the data behind a dataset, which is very helpful. The following code displays rows in a dataset. A breakpoint is placed on the highlighted line.

```
DataSet ds = new DataSet();
ds.ReadXml(@"C:\Xml\titles.xml");
DataRowCollection rows = ds.Tables[0].Rows;
```

```
foreach (DataRow row in rows)
{
    lblData.Items.Add(row[0].ToString());
}
```

The cursor is placed over the *ds* variable, which is an instance of a dataset. A data tip appears, which has several rows. There is a Visualizer menu on the row of the DataSet type. Choose the DataSet Visualizer from the menu. The dataset is then displayed in DataSet Visualizer window, with the results shown in Figure 12-14. From here, you can choose the data table to view, sort the data columns, and make basic changes to the fields.

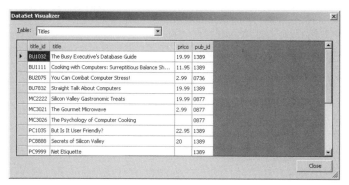

Figure 12-14   Dataset Visualizer

Breakpoints

Breakpoints are stop signs in code where execution is interrupted. When a breakpoint is hit, the application enters the break mode. You can then debug the application with a variety of Visual Studio debugger commands. There are different kinds of breakpoints. A normal breakpoint appears as a red circle to the left of the target.

The F9 function key is the breakpoint command that sets a simple breakpoint on the selected line of source code. F9 is a toggle, which sets or clears a breakpoint. In addition, clicking in the leftmost dimmed column sets or clears a breakpoint. The Continue menu command (F5) on the Debug menu resumes an application. The application runs until another breakpoint is hit, the application is otherwise interrupted, or the debug session ends. Other commands, such as Run To Cursor, also resume execution.

You can add new breakpoints from the Debug menu and the New Breakpoint submenu. Break At Function adds a function breakpoint. New Data Breakpoint sets a breakpoint that breaks when a variable has changed. This option is not available in C# or Microsoft Visual Basic .NET.

Function Breakpoints

Function breakpoints break on the first line of a function and can be set at compile time or run time.

Set a function breakpoint from the New Breakpoint submenu. Choose the Break at Function command. Figure 12-15 shows the New Breakpoint dialog box. The shortcut key is Ctrl+B. In this example, a breakpoint is set on the first line of the *WClass.MethodA* function. As a short-cut, select the name of the target function first and open the New Breakpoint dialog box. The function name will automatically appear in the New Breakpoint dialog box. If you're breaking on an ambiguous or overloaded name, the Choose Breakpoints dialog box opens. For example, in the sample code, *MethodA* is ambiguous. There are several instances of *MethodA* in the application. In Figure 12-16, the New Breakpoint dialog box sets a breakpoint on *MethodA*. Figure 12-17 displays the Choose Breakpoints dialog box that subsequently appears, in which the user can select a specific location to set the breakpoint. To avoid ambiguity, you can enter the class name (*Classname.Methodname*) or the method signature.

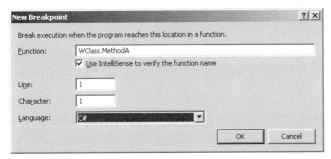

Figure 12-15   New Breakpoint dialog box

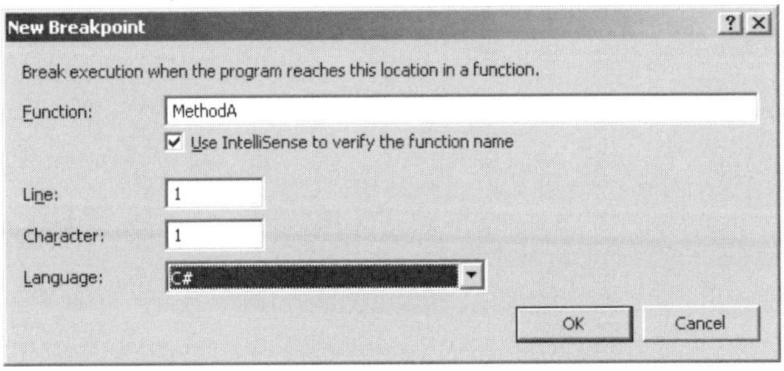

Figure 12-16   Setting a breakpoint on MethodA

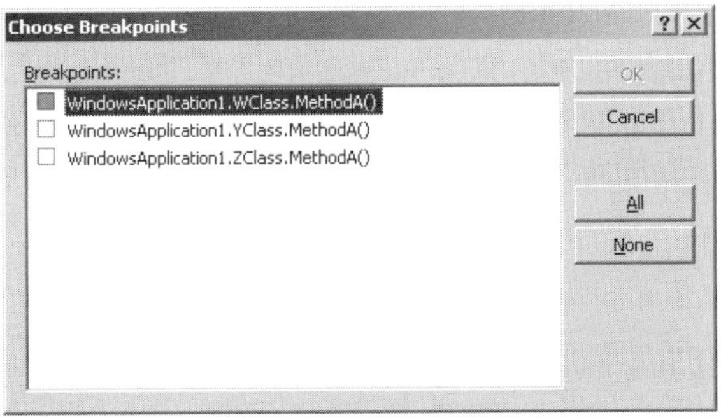

Figure 12-17   Choose Breakpoints dialog box

The Use IntelliSense To Verify The Function Name option of the New Breakpoint dialog box requests the Choose Breakpoint dialog box whenever a user enters an ambiguous or over-loaded function name. With this option, users are notified of invalid function names. With the option disabled, there is no notification, and the New Breakpoint dialog box simply closes without setting the breakpoint.

You can also set breakpoints in the Call Stack window, which is available on the Debug menu within the Windows submenu. A function breakpoint on the call stack breaks upon re-entering that method as the stack unwinds. For example, *MethodA* calls *MethodB*. *MethodB* then calls *MethodC*. A breakpoint is then set on *MethodA* in the Call Stack window. When *MethodB* returns and the related stack frame is removed, the application is interrupted on re-entering *MethodA*. The Call Stack window is available in break mode. Set a breakpoint for a specific method using the context menu or the F9 breakpoint keyboard shortcut. A breakpoint set on *MethodA* in the call stack is exhibited in Figure 12-18.

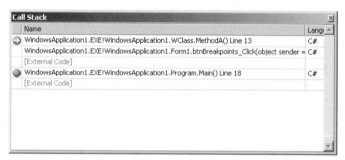

Figure 12-18   Breakpoint in the Call Stack window

Breakpoints Window

Developers can manage breakpoints in the Breakpoints window (opened from the Debug menu and the Windows submenu). Figure 12-19 shows the Breakpoints window.

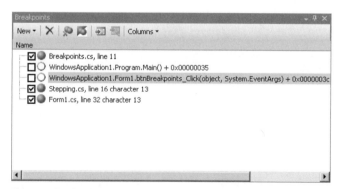

Figure 12-19   Breakpoints window

In the Breakpoints window, breakpoints are shown on separate rows. The first column of each row is the enabled/disabled options box. If a breakpoint is enabled, the option box is checked. Uncheck the column to disable the breakpoint. The next column provides the description and location of the breakpoint. The Condition column shows any conditions set on the breakpoint. The final column shows the hit count. In that column, Break Always means that the program is interrupted every time the breakpoint is hit.

The context menu has several valuable options that affect the selected breakpoint. The first menu command is Delete, which removes the breakpoint. The Go To Source Code menu command redirects to the breakpoint in the source code. The Go To Disassembly menu command redirects to the disassembly at the breakpoint. For this command, the application must be in break mode. The remaining commands of the context menu customize the selected breakpoint and are explained in the following sections.

Location   This command changes the location of a breakpoint. You are presented with the Address Breakpoint or File Breakpoint dialog box (shown in Figures 12-20 and 12-21). The Address Breakpoint dialog box is displayed for memory breakpoints, such as a breakpoint set on the call stack. The File breakpoint dialog box is displayed for line breakpoints in source code.

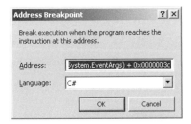

Figure 12-20   Address Breakpoint Dialog Box

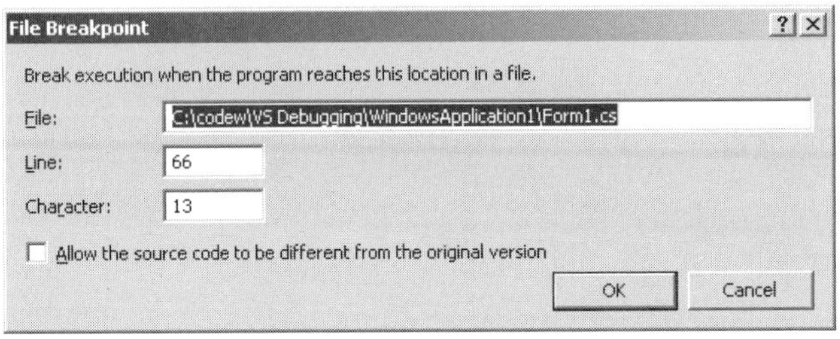

Figure 12-21   File Breakpoint Dialog Box

Condition   This command sets additional criteria for honoring a breakpoint. The condition can be a Boolean expression. If true, the breakpoint is honored. Otherwise, the breakpoint is ignored. The condition can also be based on changes to a value. If the value is changed, the breakpoint is honored.

Look at the following sample code. The breakpoint is set on the dimmed line. We want to honor the breakpoint only when *ivalue* contains an even value.

```
int[] numbers ={1,2,3,4,5,6,7,8,9,10,
    11,12,13,14,15,165,17,18,18,20};
int total = 0;
```

```
foreach (int ivalue in numbers)
{
    total += ivalue;
}
```

The Breakpoint Condition dialog box, shown in Figure 12-22, sets the condition to break on even values.

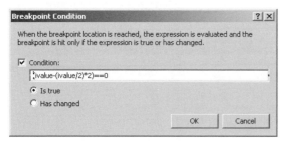

Figure 12-22   Conditional Breakpoint dialog box

Hit Count   This command honors a breakpoint based on the hit count. Table 12-3 lists the hit count options.

Table 12-3   Hit Count Options

Option	Description
Break Always	This option always honors the breakpoint.
Break When The Hit Count Is Equal To	This option honors the breakpoint when that instance of the breakpoint occurs. For example, interrupt on the fourth occasion of a specific breakpoint.
Break When The Hit Count Is A Multiple Of	This option honors the breakpoint as a multiple of a value, for example, every third instance of the breakpoint.
Break When The Hit Count Is Greater Than Or Equal To	This option honors the breakpoint starting at a certain instance; for example, honor the breakpoint at the third and every successive instance.

The Breakpoint Hit Count dialog box, shown in Figure 12-23, honors every third instance of the selected breakpoint.

Figure 12-23   Breakpoint Hit Count dialog box

Filter   This command sets the affinity of a breakpoint to a machine, thread, or process. The breakpoint interrupts only in the context of the stated filter. Table 12-4 lists the available contexts.

Table 12-4   Filter Contexts

Context	Description
MachineName	This context is the name of the machine. Breakpoint is honored if the process is running on that machine.
ProcessId	This context is the process identifier. Breakpoint is honored if code is executing in the specified process.
ProcessName	This context is the process name. Functionally equivalent to the *ProcessId* context.
ThreadId	This context is the thread identifier. Breakpoint is honored if code is executing on a specific thread.
ThreadName	This context is the thread name. Functionally equivalent to the *ThreadId* context.

The following code creates two threads that asynchronously execute the same method (*MethodA*). The threads are named *FirstThread* and *SecondThread*. A breakpoint is set on the highlighted line in *MethodA*. As a standard breakpoint, both threads are interrupted—probably alternating between the threads.

```
private void btnFilter_Click(object sender, EventArgs e)
{
    Thread t1=new Thread(new
        ThreadStart(MethodA));
    t1.Name="FirstThread";
    t1.IsBackground=false;
    Thread t2=new Thread(new
        ThreadStart(MethodA));
    t2.Name="SecondThread";
    t2.IsBackground = false;
    t1.Start();
    t2.Start();
}

public void MethodA()
{
    while (true)
    {
        Thread.Sleep(3000);
    }
}
```

To break on the first thread alone, open the Breakpoint Filter dialog box, shown in Figure 12-24. Specify *FirstThread* as the thread name. Future instances of the breakpoint interrupt the first thread, but not the second thread. You can confirm the results in the Threads window.

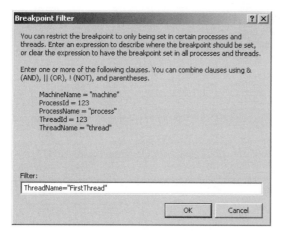

Figure 12-24   Breakpoint Filter dialog box

When Hit   This command creates a tracepoint (discussed in the next section).

The Breakpoints window toolbar, shown in Figure 12-25, offers several shortcuts. The controls on the toolbar are New, Delete, Delete All Breakpoints, Disable All Breakpoints, Go To Source Code, Go To Disassembly, and Columns. The New drop-down list inserts a new function or data breakpoint. Data breakpoints are not available in managed code. The Columns button customizes the content of the Breakpoints window, in which developers can add or remove columns of information.

Figure 12-25   Breakpoints window toolbar

Tracepoints

Tracepoints assign an operation to a breakpoint. You can assign source code or a macro to a breakpoint. When the breakpoint is hit, the source code or macro is executed. Before tracepoints, this process required two steps: setting a breakpoint and inserting temporary code into source file. When the breakpoint was no longer needed, the developer had to remember to remove the temporary code.

There are two methods for setting a tracepoint. You can open the context menu on the source line in which the tracepoint should be inserted. Select the Breakpoint submenu and the Insert Tracepoint menu command. Alternatively, you can open the context menu on a source line that already contains a breakpoint. From the Breakpoint submenu, choose the When Hit menu command. Either approach opens the When Breakpoint Is Hit dialog box, in which a tracepoint is defined. (See Figure 12-26.)

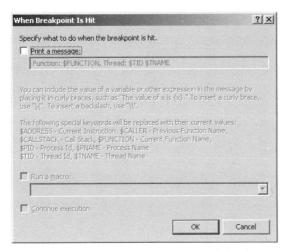

Figure 12-26   When Breakpoint Is Hit dialog box

In the Print A Message edit box, enter a display string for the output window. Expressions are entered within curly braces: {*expression*}. Special keywords can be used, such as *$ADDRESS*, *$TID*, and *$FUNCTION*. In the Run A Macro edit box, enter the name of a macro. This macro is run when the breakpoint is hit. The Continue Execution option sets a soft breakpoint. When the breakpoint is hit, soft breakpoints do not interrupt the application; they execute the designated code or macro. Soft breakpoints appear as diamonds in the source code editor.

The statement in the following When Breakpoint Is Hit dialog box (shown in Figure 12-27) adds two local variables and displays the results in the output window.

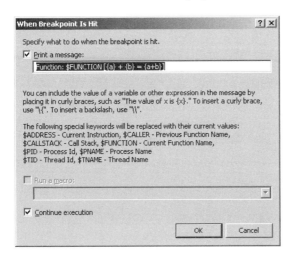

Figure 12-27   Print a message selected in the When Breakpoint Is Hit dialog box

From the preceding tracepoint, the following code is displayed in the Output window:

```
Function: WindowsApplication1.WClass.MethodA() [5 + 10 = 15]
```

Table 12-5 lists the special keywords that can be used in the *Print a message* statement.

Table 12-5   Tracepoint Keywords

Keyword	Description
$ADDRESS	This keyword returns the address of the current instruction.
$CALLER	This keyword returns the name of the previous function on the call stack, which is the calling function.
$CALLSTACK	This keyword returns the call stack.
$FUNCTION	This keyword returns the name of the current function.
$PID	This keyword returns the process identifier of the current process.
$PNAME	This keyword returns the name of the current process.
$TID	This keyword returns the thread identifier of the current thread.
$TNAME	This keyword returns the name of the current thread.

Breakpoint Symbols

Breakpoints are annotated with icons in both the source code and the Breakpoints window. Each category of breakpoint has a different symbol, as described in Table 12-6.

Table 12-6   Breakpoint Symbols

Symbol	Description
Filled circle	This icon signifies a normal breakpoint, such as a function or location breakpoint.
Diamond	This icon signifies a tracepoint that has the *Continue execution* option enabled.
Filled circle with a plus +	This icon signifies a filter breakpoint. Filter breakpoints include the Condition, Hit Count, and Filter breakpoints.
Hollowed circle	This icon signifies a disabled breakpoint.

Code Stepping

Stepping through source code is the most common action in a debugging session. Step commands execute an application in source line increments. With each step, execution continues incrementally. Between steps, expressions can be evaluated, variables updated, functions called, and scope changed. Debug windows are updated at each step to reflect any changes that occurred during the partial execution. This sometimes requires refreshing. Extensive monitoring and expressions in debug windows can precipitously hurt performance.

Step Commands

There are several step commands, described as follows:

- **Step Into**   This command steps to the next source line. If that is a function call, the debugger steps into the function. You can then step through that function. For nested function calls, the Step Into command steps into the innermost functions first.

- **Step Over**   This command steps to the next source line. However, it will not step into a function call. The function call is treated as a single line of source code.

- **Step Out**   This command executes the remainder of the current function. Execution is then interrupted at the first source line after the call site.

- **Set The Next Statement**   This command lets developers change the next statement, which is useful for skipping one or more lines of source code. In the source editor, the current line is highlighted with a yellow arrow. This is the next statement to execute. When the cursor hovers over the yellow arrow, it changes into an arrow itself. You can then drag the current source line up or down. The next step selected must be within the scope of the current source line. For example, dragging the next step to another function is illegal. This command is not available during JIT debugging. It is also not available when debugging a *StackOverflowException* or *ThreadAbortException* exception.

Set The Next Statement Walkthrough

This walkthrough demonstrates the *Next Statement* command. In the sample application, variables *locala* and *localb* are initialized in *MethodA*. They are then incremented. The *SwitchValues* method is called to swap the values of the local variables. The parameters are passed by reference. After the method call, *locala* is 11 and *localb* is 6. This is the code:

```
public void MethodA()
{
    int locala = 5, localb = 10;
    ++locala;
    ++localb;
    SwitchValues(ref locala, ref localb);
    MessageBox.Show(locala.ToString());
    MessageBox.Show(localb.ToString());
}

public void SwitchValues(ref int param1,
    ref int param2)
{
    int temp = param1;
    param1 = param2;
    param2 = temp;
}
```

These are the steps of the walkthrough that uses the previous code:

1. Set a breakpoint on the source line where *locala* is incremented. When the breakpoint is hit, the current line is marked with a yellow arrow. The breakpoint and the current source line are initially at the same location, as shown in Figure 12-28.

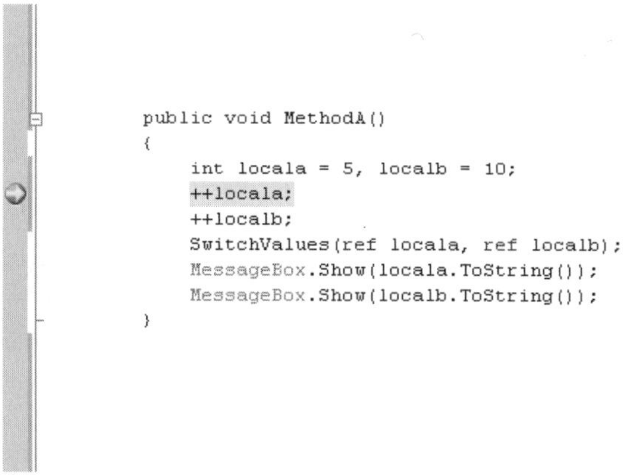

```
public void MethodA()
{
    int locala = 5, localb = 10;
    ++locala;
    ++localb;
    SwitchValues(ref locala, ref localb);
    MessageBox.Show(locala.ToString());
    MessageBox.Show(localb.ToString());
}
```

Figure 12-28   Breakpoint and current line

2. Drag the yellow highlight for the current line down to the first *MessageBox.Show* statement, which jumps past the statements that increment the local variables and the *SwitchValues* method call. Therefore, the values are neither incremented nor swapped. Figure 12-29 shows the repositioned current line.

```
public void MethodA()
{
    int locala = 5, localb = 10;
    ++locala;
    ++localb;
    SwitchValues(ref locala, ref localb);
    MessageBox.Show(locala.ToString());
    MessageBox.Show(localb.ToString());
}
```

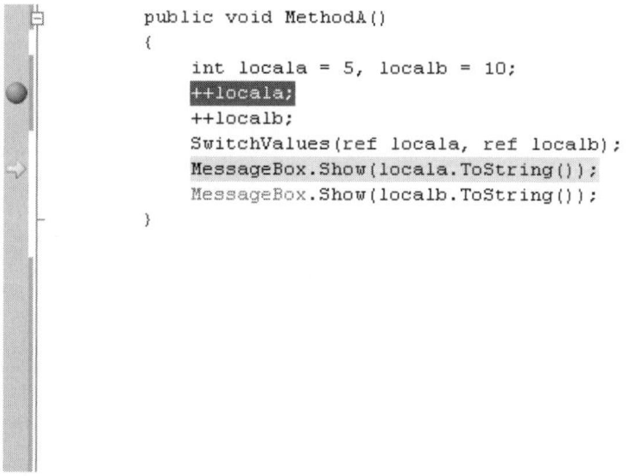

Figure 12-29   Repositioned current line

3. Continue execution, and the values for *locala* and *localb* are displayed. The *locala* variable is 5, whereas *localb* is 10. Otherwise, the values would have been 11 and 6, respectively.

Debug Toolbar

The Debug toolbar contains shortcuts to several debugging commands, including the step commands. (See Figure 12-30.) Some of the buttons and commands are enabled only in break mode.

Figure 12-30   Debug toolbar

The first set of buttons on the toolbar includes the Start Debugging, Break All, Stop Debugging, and Restart buttons. The next set of buttons includes the Show Next Statement, Step Into, Step Over, and Step Out buttons. The Show Next Statement button redirects to the next statement in the code editor. This statement is highlighted with a yellow arrow. Next is the Hexadecimal button, which changes the values in the debug windows from decimal to hexadecimal. The final button is a drop-down list that displays a menu of debug commands.

Debug Windows

To assist in debugging, Visual Studio 2005 offers a myriad of debug windows, described in the following sections.

Breakpoints Window

Manage breakpoints in the Breakpoints window. In this window, you can insert, delete, and disable breakpoints. (The Breakpoints window was shown and discussed in detail earlier in this chapter.)

Output Window

This window contains messages from various sources in Visual Studio. The Output window is also available from the View menu. The Output window is displayed in Figure 12-31.

Figure 12-31   Output window

The Output window has a toolbar, which has several buttons. Output From is the first button on the toolbar. It filters the message sources, such a Build and Debug messages. The next three buttons locate build errors in the code editor: Find Message in Code, Go to Previous Message, and Go to Next Message. The next button, Clear All, erases the content of the Output window. The Toggle Word Wrap button toggles word wrap in the Output window.

Script Explorer Window

ASP.NET Web applications have client- and server-side code. Client-side code is written in either JavaScript or VBScript. In the Script Explorer window, developers can debug client-side scripts, including setting breakpoints. The window lists script files and their scripts. The Script Explorer window is shown in Figure 12-32. In the sample Script Explorer window, the scripts of the *default.aspx* page are listed. The anonymous scripts are usually scripts associated with for server-side controls, such as validation controls.

Figure 12-32   Script Explorer window

To use the Script Explorer window, you must enable Script debugging in Microsoft Internet Explorer. The Disable Script Debugging (Internet Explorer) option is enabled by default in Internet Explorer. This option must be disabled to allow script debugging. Open the Tools menu and select the Internet Options menu command. On the Advanced tab, disable the Disable Script Debugging (Internet Explorer) option.

Watch Window

You can watch variables and expressions in a Watch window. The Watch, Locals, Auto, and QuickWatch windows are considered variables windows—they have the same general user interface and functionality. The variables windows are disabled in running mode; you must be in break mode to use them. A Watch window, like other variables windows, has three columns. The Name column has the variable name or expression to evaluate. The Value column displays the variable value or result of the expression. The Type column is the data type of the variable or expression. There are four Watch windows for grouping related values.

Variable values can be modified directly in a Watch window. Changed values are highlighted in red. This is an exceptional way to test applications with values that stress the program. You can also test how the application handles errant conditions.

You can add variables and expressions in a Watch window directly. The QuickWatch dialog box is an expedited means of inspecting a value or expression and optionally adding that item to a permanent Watch window. The QuickWatch dialog box has an Add Watch button. If desired, you can enter new expressions in the Expression text box. The QuickWatch window is available on the Debug menu. Shortcuts for QuickWatch are Ctrl+Alt+Q or Shift+F9. Before opening the QuickWatch window, select the target variable in the source editor.

Expressions   Debugger expressions are expressions entered in the Watch, Quickwatch, Breakpoints, or Immediate window. These expressions are evaluated by the Managed Expression Evaluator of the Visual Studio debugger. Use debugger expressions to calculate values or to call methods. IntelliSense is available when entering debugger expressions in a debug window or visualizer. The added flexibility of doing more than examining static data is invaluable.

Debugger expressions are evaluated similarly to regular expressions. There are some unique idiosyncrasies of the Managed Expression Evaluation.

- It ignores access modifiers.
- All members, regardless of accessibility, are available.
- Expressions are evaluated in an implicitly unsecure context.
- Checked blocks are ignored and evaluated as unchecked.
- Anonymous methods are not supported in debugger expressions.

Expressions can contain constants, function calls, and identifiers within scope, such as locals, parameters, and fields. Most operators, such as +, -, ==, !=, ++, --, and / are available. You can even use the *typeof* and *sizeof* operators. The *this* reference is supported. In addition, simple casts are allowed.

Expressions are evaluated between every step command. Refresh the expression to view any updates. Beware of side effects, which can alter the state or execution of the programming unknowingly. For example, calling a function in an expression that changes the state or outcome of the application may cause adverse side effects.

Expression walkthrough   The following steps list a walkthrough of expressions. A breakpoint is set on the *Form_Load* event in the Expressions application. Run the application until the breakpoint is hit.

1. Open a Watch window from the Debug menu. The *Form_Load* method has a sender and an *e* parameter. (You can view their values in the Watch window.) This Watch window, including the two parameters, is shown in Figure 12-33.

Figure 12-33   Watch window with two parameters

2. The Sample application has a *ZClass*, which is relatively simple:

```
class ZClass
{
    private int fielda = 5;
     private int fieldb = 10;

    public int MethodA()
    {
        int locala = 5;
        locala = 12;
        return fielda + fieldb;
    }
}
```

3. A breakpoint is set on the highlighted line in *MethodA*. When the breakpoint is hit, add *fielda*, *fieldb*, *locala*, and *localb* to the Watch window. Click the Test button to hit the breakpoint. The *localb* variable is not declared in the function. For that reason, it is displayed with an exclamation symbol. Enter the *++fielda* expression. Figure 12-34 shows the new Watch window.

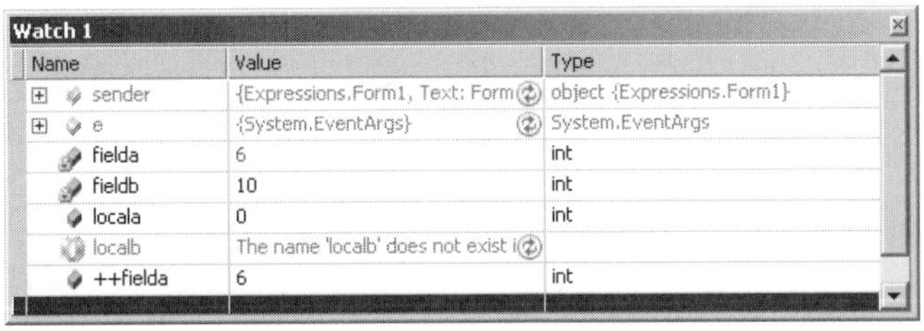

Figure 12-34 Watch window with locala, localb, fielda, and fieldb values

4. Step two individual statements. (Press F10 twice.) Click the Refresh button to update the value of the *++fielda* expression. (The Refresh button is the green swirling button to the right of the field.)

5. The *DumpType* class has a static method, which dumps the methods and parameters of a type. The *DumpType.GetReflection* method returns a string that contains the methods of a type. This function is not called elsewhere in the program. It is created purely for debugging reasons. Enter the *DumpType.GetReflection* in the expression..Pass the type of the current object as the sole parameter. (See Figure 12-35.) You view the returning value of *GetReflection* with the Text Visualizer. The results are shown in Figure 12-36.

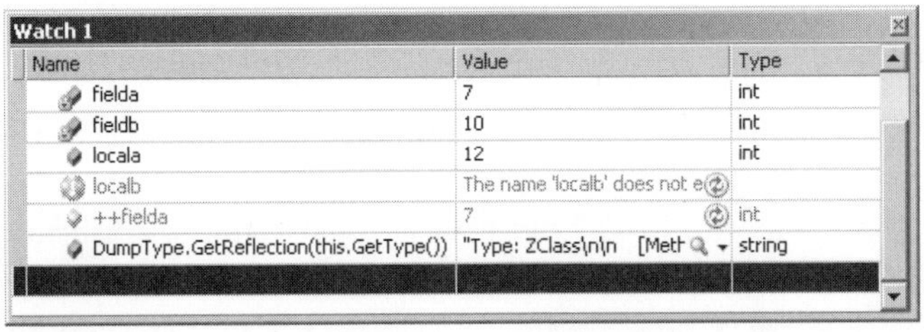

Figure 12-35 DumpType.GetReflection expression in the Watch window

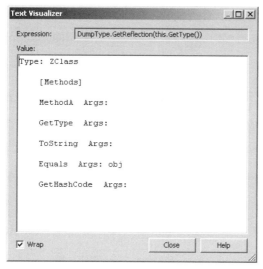

Figure 12-36 Results in the Text Visualizer

Autos Window

The Autos window lists the values from the current and preceding line of code, which includes this reference. The items of the Autos window are populated by the Visual Studio debugger, not the developer. You can change the values in the window, which are then highlighted in red. Figure 12-37 shows the Autos window.

Figure 12-37 Autos window

Locals Window

The Locals window lists the local variables that are currently in scope. Otherwise, the functionality is identical to the Autos window.

Immediate Window

The Immediate window is the command-line version of the Visual Studio debugger. You can enter print values, evaluate expressions, perform menu commands, execute statements, and more. This can be done without having to change the application. Command windows are either in immediate or command mode. Command mode is preferred for executing one or more Visual Studio commands. These are menu and other commands.

For evaluating expressions, inspecting values, and otherwise debugging an application, immediate mode is preferred. The default is the command mode. When in immediate mode, switch to command mode temporarily by prefixing commands with a greater than (>) symbol. From the Immediate window, the *cmd* command switches to command mode in the Command window. Switch back to immediate mode and the Immediate window with the *immed* command.

You can navigate the Immediate window with arrows. Table 12-7 shows the various ways to navigate the window.

Table 12-7   Navigating the Immediate Window

Keystroke	Description
Up arrow on command line	Previous command.
Down arrow on command line	Next command.
Ctrl+Up Arrow or Up arrow in Command window	Up window.
Ctrl+Down Arrow or Down arrow in Command window	Down window.
Esc	Transfer focus to code editor. If not at the last command in the Immediate window, Esc is required.

There are limitations to the tasks that can be performed in the Immediate window. For example, you cannot declare new variables, define a label, or create an instance of an object. Special commands such as the *K* command are not available in managed-only code. Therefore, special commands for the Immediate window are not explored here. In addition, the Immediate window does not accept *goto*, *return*, and *loop* statements, or any statement requiring transfer of control.

Commands can have arguments and options. For example, the *FindinFiles* command has both. IntelliSense will present the options, which are preceded with a forward slash. You must type a forward slash for IntelliSense to display the available options. The following code is an example of the *Edit.FindinFiles* command. If the command is represented by a window in the user interface, consult that window for an understanding of options and arguments. In the window, edit text boxes are usually interpreted as arguments, and everything else becomes an option. Figure 12-38 shows the Find In Files dialog box, which has one text box and several options. The text box is the single argument of the *FindinFiles* command. You can use as many options as needed. The defaults are defined in the window. In the example, the *FindinFiles* command is used with two options: The first option requests a case-sensitive search, and the second option directs the command to search all files in the root directory. This command has a single argument, which is the search text.

```
>Edit.FindinFiles /case /lookin:"c:\*" donis
```

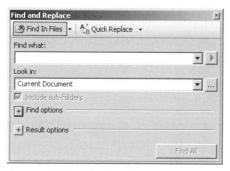

Figure 12-38   Find in Files window

Aliases are short forms of debugging commands. They are a convenience and never required. Table 12-8 lists some useful aliases.

Table 12-8   Command Aliases

Alias	Command
?	Debug.Print
bl	Debug.Breakpoints
callstack	Debug.CallStack
cls	Debug.ClearAll
cmd	View.CommandWindow
du	Dump Unicode
g	Debug.Start
immed	Tools.ImmediateMode
K	Debug.ListCallStack
locals	Debug.Locals
memory1	Debug.Memory1
memory2	Debug.Memory2
P	Debug.StepOver
pr	Debug.StepOut
print	File.Print
q	Debug.StopDebugging
rtc	Debug.RunToCursor
saveall	File.SaveAll
T	Step.Into
threads	Debug.Threads
~	Debug.ListThreads
~*k	Debug.ListCallStack /AllThreads

Developers might want to create user-defined aliases for frequently performed tasks. The *alias* command defines a new alias. The following command defines two new aliases. The *pripro* alias replaces all instances of the private with the protected keyword in the current source file. The *propri* alias performs the reverse operation.

```
>alias pripro edit.replace /all private protected
>alias propri edit.replace /all protected private
```

Call Stack Window

The Call Stack window shows the functions currently on the stack. The current function is highlighted with a yellow arrow. By default, the window has two columns: the name of the function and the source language. The Name column combines several fields: the module name, function name, parameter information, line number, and byte offset. Parameter information includes parameter type, parameter name, and parameter values. Use the context menu to customize the display. Except for the function name, everything is optional. Figure 12-39 shows the Call Stack window, which is available only in break mode.

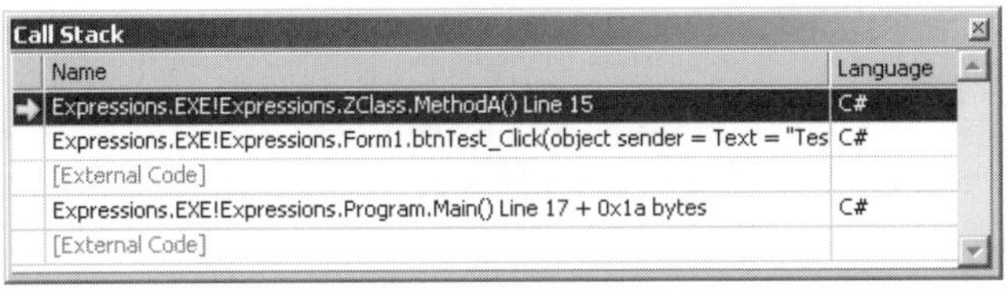

Figure 12-39 Call Stack window

The call stack does not include external code. In some circumstances, information on external functions in the call stack can be helpful. To view external code, disable the Enable Just My Code (Managed Only) option in the Options dialog box of the Tools menu under the Debugging settings in the General node. Figure 12-40 shows the Call Stack window with this option disabled. For clarity, extraneous information is removed from the Name column. You can now trace the call stack into *System* functions to obtain what may be invaluable information.

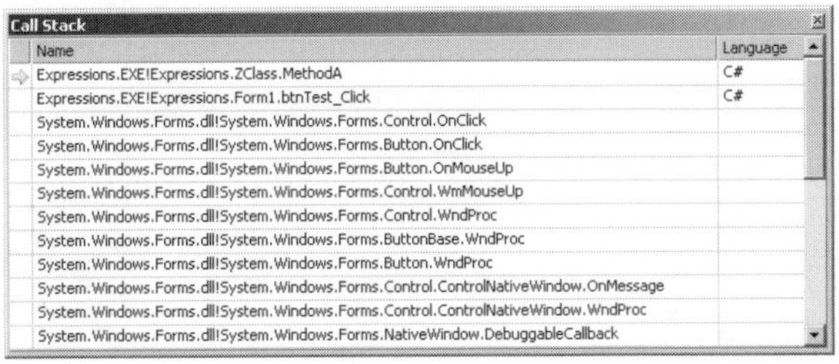

Figure 12-40 Call Stack window with Enable Just My Code disabled

Each row of the call stack represents a function and a stack frame. Some variables windows are based on the current stack frame. For example, the Autos and Locals windows are from the current stack frame. However, you might want to view similar information about the other stack frame. To switch stack frames, position the cursor on the target frame. Open the context menu in the call stack and choose the Switch To Frame menu command. A curved green arrow appears next to the updated current stack frame. Variable windows are updated according to the change.

Another option on the Call Stack context menu is the Include Calls From/To Other Threads menu command. This command follows the call stack through thread calls. For example, this is helpful when tracing the call stack from an XML Web Service into an ASP.NET application.

Function breakpoints and tracepoints are settable in the Call Stack window. You can use shortcut keys, such as F9, or you can use the context menu.

Threads Window

The Threads window presents the active threads of the current process. This window is available only in break mode. A thread is a single path of execution in a process. Threads own assets, such as local variables, thread context, and thread local storage.

The Thread application is provided to create threads. You can assign a name and priority to each new thread. Each thread executes the sample *MethodA* function. When you run the Thread application in a debugging session, thread T1, T2, and T3 are created of varying priorities. Then the *BreakAll* command is issued from the Debug menu. Figure 12-41 shows the Threads window for the application at that moment.

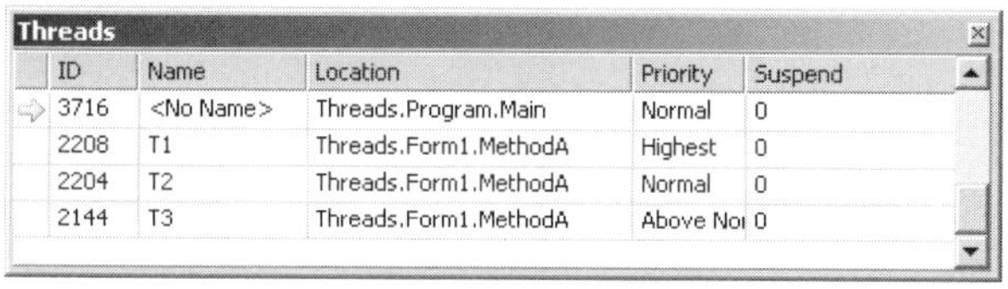

Figure 12-41   Threads window

The columns of the Threads window are Thread Identifier, Thread Name, Method Location, Thread Priority, and Suspend Count. From the context menu, suspend a thread with the Freeze menu command. Suspended threads are assigned a double-bar icon. Choose the Thaw menu command to resume the thread. Forcibly suspending a thread can affect the normal operation of an application. The Switch To Thread menu command of the context menu changes the current thread. You can also double-click the target thread to switch the current thread. Some windows are based on the current thread, such as the Call Stack. These windows are updated when the current thread is changed.

Modules Window

The Modules window lists the modules, executables, and DLLs, which are loaded into the application. There is considerable information presented on each module, as described in Table 12-9.

Table 12-9   Modules Window Columns

Column	Description
Name	This column is the name of the module.
Path	This column presents the fully qualified path to the module.
Optimized	This column indicates whether the module is optimized during JIT compilation. The current module being debugged is likely not optimized. Debug versions of modules are generally not optimized.
User Code	This column indicates whether user code is available for a particular module.
Symbol Status	This column indicates whether symbols are loaded for this module. It also indicates if exports are only loaded.
Symbol File	When loaded, this column displays the fully qualified path and name of the symbol file.
Order	This column lists the load order of modules.
Version	This column provides the version number of the module.
Timestamp	This column is the timestamp when the module was created.
Address	This column is the start and end load address of the module.
Process	This column is the process identifier of the application that hosts the module.

From the context menu, you can request additional information on the symbol file. You can also visit Symbol settings in Project options, where symbols are managed.

Processes Window

The Processes window enumerates the processes being debugged by the Visual Studio debugger, including attached processes. Table 12-10 describes each column of the window.

Table 12-10   Processes Window Columns

Column	Description
Name	This column is the name of the process.
ID	This column is the process identifier of the process.
Path	This column is the path to the executable.
Title	This column contains the title of application. For a Windows Forms application, this is the content of the title bar.
State	This column shows the state of the application, such as the break or running state.
Debugging	This column indicates the type of debugging, such as managed or native debugging.
Transport	This column is the transport to the application. The default is no authentication.
Transport Qualifier	This column is the machine name.

Memory Window

The Memory window dumps the memory of the current process. (See Figure 12-42.)
Other windows format memory for specific purposes. For example, the Locals window
displays the memory of local variables alone. The Memory window provides an unfiltered
and raw presentation of process memory. Four memory windows provide the opportunity
to maintain different views of the process. Memory windows are available in break
mode and only if the Enable Address-Level Debugging Option is enabled. Set this option
within Debug settings in the General node. Open from the Tools menu and the Options
command.

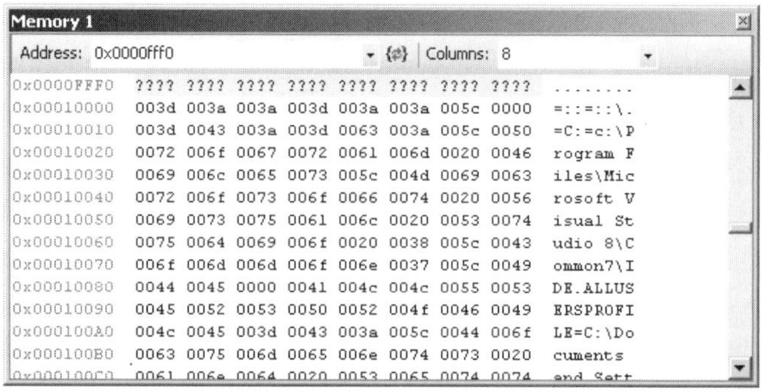

Figure 12-42   Memory window

Enter a memory address in the Address edit box. You can enter a memory address directly
or by using a drag-and-drop operation. The Memory window displays rows of data at
memory addresses. Column 1 of the Memory window is the starting address of a row of
data. The final column is the text translation. The memory dump is in the intervening
columns.

The Memory window can be formatted using the context menu. You can change the size
of the data columns to 1-, 2-, 4-, or 8-byte columns. The display can also be changed to
32- or 64-bit data presentation. The text translation can be formatted as ANSI, Unicode, or
hidden.

Disassembly Window

The Disassembly window shows the native assembly of the application, which is the native
code generated by JIT compilation. By default, if available, the source code is displayed
also. Each assembly instruction is displayed in several columns: the instruction address,
mnemonic, and parameters. (See Figure 12-43.) Use the context menu to change the format of
the Disassembly window.

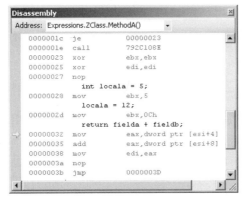

Figure 12-43   Disassembly window

Registers Window

The Registers window displays the state of the registers. Assembly-level programming typi-cally relies heavily on registers. For this reason, the Disassembly and Registers windows are often used together. The Registers window is shown in Figure 12-44. Use the context menu to change the format of the display.

```
Registers
  ESI = 013B7C8C EDI = 00000000 EIP = 00DD1602 ESP = 03C6E4F4
  EBP = 03C6E538 EFL = 00000246

  013B7C90 = 00000005
```

Figure 12-44   Registers window

Table 12-11 describes the common registers.

Table 12-11   Registers

Register	Description
EAX	This register is a general-purpose register. It is commonly used as the destination of a math operation.
EBX	This register is a general-purpose register.
ECX	This register is a general-purpose register and is commonly used for counting.
EDX	This register is a general-purpose register.
EIP	This register contains the next instruction pointer.
ESP	This register contains the pointer to the top of the stack.
ESI	This register is the source index. The *ESI* and *EDI* registers are frequently used in string operations.

Table 12-11 Registers *(Continued)*

Register	Description
EDI	This register is the destination index. The *ESI* and *EDI* registers are frequently used in string operations.
EBP	This register contains the base pointer of the current stack frame.

Tracing

Tracing instruments an application through trace messages sent during program execution. Trace messages are used for a variety of reasons. They can confirm the execution sequence of a program, which is useful for assuring that program flow is correct (often the cause of bugs). Trace messages can display the state of the application at different stages. You can track the state of objects, local variables, or other data throughout the lifetime of an application. Finally, trace messages are used to track events, such as start, stop, and user-defined events. Tracing replaces the old technique of monitoring an application via *Console.WriteLine* statements.

In the Microsoft .NET Framework 2.0, *TraceSource* is the preferred type for tracing. It replaces the *Debug* and *Trace* classes, which remain available as legacy types. The *TraceSource* class is in the *System.Diagnostics* namespace. To enable tracing, the *TRACE* symbol must be defined in the application. In the source code, this is accomplished with the *#define* statement. Alternatively, define the symbol while compiling the program. The */d* compiler option defines a symbol:

```
csc /d:TRACE test.cs
```

Table 12-12 explains the important members of the *TraceSource* class.

Table 12-12 TraceSource Methods

Level	Description
Constructors	*TraceSource(string name)*
Both constructors assign a name to the *TraceSource* object. The two-argument constructor also sets a default severity level for all trace messages originating from this instance.	*TraceSource(string name, SourceLevels defaultLevel)*
Close	*void Close()*
This method closes all the trace listeners in the *Listeners* collection.	
Flush	*void Flush()*
This method flushes the trace listeners in the *Listeners* collection. This ensures that cached messages are reported.	

Table 12-12   TraceSource Methods *(Continued)*

Level	Description
TraceData This method creates a trace message consisting of event type, a trace identifier, and any trace data. The event type is the severity level.	*[ConditionalAttribute("TRACE")]* *public void TraceData(* *TraceEventType eventType,* *int id,* *Object data)* *[ConditionalAttribute("TRACE")]* *public void TraceData(* *TraceEventType eventType,* *int id,* *Object [] data)*
TraceEvent This method creates a trace message consisting of an event type and message, which is written to the *Listeners* collection. The first overload—the method without the message parameter—creates a blank trace message.	*[ConditionalAttribute("TRACE")]* *public void TraceEvent(* *TraceEventType eventType,* *int id)* *[ConditionalAttribute("TRACE")]* *public void TraceEvent(* *TraceEventType eventType,* *int id,* *string message)* *[ConditionalAttribute("TRACE")]* *public void TraceEvent(* *TraceEventType eventType,* *int id,* *object [] data)*
TraceInformation This method creates an informational message, which is written to the *Listeners* collection.	*[ConditionalAttribute("TRACE")]* *public void TraceInformation(* *string message)* *[ConditionalAttribute("TRACE")]* *public void TraceInformation(* *string format,* *params Object[] args)*
TraceTransfer This method creates transfer messages, which are written to the *Listeners* collection.	*[ConditionalAttribute("TRACE")]* *public void TraceTransfer(* *int id,* *string message,* *Guid relatedActivityID)*

The *TraceSource* type also has several valuable properties. Table 12-13 lists the properties.

Table 12-13   TraceSource Properties

Property	Type
Attributes	*StringDictionary*
This property gets the custom switch attributes that are defined in the application configuration file.	
Listeners	*TraceListenerCollection*
This property gets an array of listeners. Listeners are the targets of trace messages.	
Name	*string*
This property gets the name of the *TraceSource* object. This name is most likely used with the *SourceFilter* property of a listener.	
Switch	*SourceSwitch*
This property gets or sets the trace switch associated with this *TraceSource* object. This filters the trace messages sent from the *TraceSource* object.	

Tracing is based on criteria including severity levels, switches, listeners, and listener filters. This determines when, where, and how trace messages are reported. *TraceSource* instances create trace messages. Severity levels are assigned to trace messages, which set the message importance. Switches filter trace messages based on their severity levels. Listeners receive trace messages. Finally, listener filters control the trace messages reported from a listener. Tracing is configurable either programmatically or using an application configuration file. The application configuration file is recommended. With the application configuration file, tracing is controlled, enabled, or disabled without recompiling the program. For a production application, this is essential. To introduce tracing concepts, the programmatic approach is presented first.

Trace messages are set to severity levels. The trace levels determine the importance or urgency of a message. Some trace messages are activity related, such as the start and stop time of an application. Informational trace messages are used to stub methods and check program flow. Tracing the value of an invalid parameter, which results in an exception, should be higher priority. *TraceEventType* enumeration defines the trace levels. Table 12-14 enumerates the trace levels. The levels are listed in order of highest to lowest priority.

Table 12-14   Trace Levels

Level	Description
TraceEventType.Critical	This error level is reserved for conditions that destabilize an application or are fatal.
TraceEventType.Error	This error level is reserved for conditions that destabilize an application but are recoverable.

Table 12-14   Trace Levels *(Continued)*

Level	Description
TraceEventType.Warning	This error level is reserved for noncritical conditions.
TraceEventType.Information	This error level is reserved for general information that might aid in the diagnosing of an error condition.
TraceEventType.Verbose	This error level is reserved for general information not necessarily associated with an error condition.
TraceEventType activities	See Table 12-14.

Some trace levels are related to activities, which are linked to events. The activity traces are grouped at the same trace level, which is the lowest trace level, beneath the Verbose level. Table 12-15 shows the list of activity traces.

Table 12-15   Activity Traces

Activity	Description
TraceEventType.Start	This activity indicates that an operation is starting.
TraceEventType.Stop	This activity indicates that an operation is stopping.
TraceEventType.Suspend	This activity indicates that an operation is suspending.
TraceEventType.Resume	This activity indicates that an operation is resuming.
TraceEventType.Transfer	This activity indicates a change of correlation identity.

Switches filter trace messages based on trace levels, which determine which messages a *TraceSource* sends. With switches, developers can selectively enable or disable certain trace messages. If an application is crashing, you might decide to enable critical and error trace messages. When algorithms are performing incorrectly, you might want to enable general and activity traces. Avoiding unnecessary tracing improves performance. Tracing can generate a voluminous amount of information. A filter reduces the volume of trace messages, which conserves resources. Switch filters are defined in the *SourceSwitch* class. The *SourceSwitch* class has the *Level* property, which is a *SourceLevels* type. *SourceLevels* is the enumeration that defines the trace messages that are filtered. This is a bitwise flag, and the various *SourceLevels* can be combined. The source levels are detailed in Table 12-16.

Table 12-16   Source Level

Filter	Description
SourceLevels.ActivityTracing	This level forwards activity trace messages. Other messages are filtered.
SourceLevels.All	This level forwards all trace messages.
SourceLevels.Critical	This level forwards only critical trace messages.
SourceLevels.Error	This level sends error and critical trace messages. Other trace levels are filtered.
SourceLevels.Information	This level filters verbose and activity trace messages. Other trace messages are sent.
SourceLevels.Off	This level filters all trace messages.

Table 12-16   Source Level *(Continued)*

Filter	Description
SourceLevels.Verbose	This level filters activity trace messages. All other messages are sent.
SourceLevels.Warning	This level filters all trace messages except for *Critical, Error,* and *Warning events.*

To set the filter, assign an instance of *SourceSwitch* to the *TraceSource.Switch* property. The *SourceSwitch* has two constructors:

public SourceSwitch(string name)

public SourceSwitch(string name, string defaultLevel)

SourceSwitch also has several useful properties, which are listed in Table 12-17.

Table 12-17   SourceSwitch Properties

Property	Type
Attributes	*StringDictionary*
This property gets the custom attributes that are defined in the application configuration file.	
Description	*string*
This property gets a general description of the switch. It defaults to an empty string.	
DisplayName	*string*
This property gets the name of the switch.	
Level	*SourceLevels*
This property gets or sets the level of the switch.	

The following code creates an instance of *TraceSource* and *TraceSwitch*. The switch is then assigned to the *TraceSource*.

```
TraceSource ts=new TraceSource("sample");
SourceSwitch sw=new SourceSwitch("switch");
sw.Level=SourceLevels.All;
ts.Switch=sw;
```

The event type of trace messages and the switch source level combine to determine which messages are sent. The following code sends trace messages in each event type: critical, error, information, and so on. The switch level, which is case sensitive, is read from the command line and determines which messages are recognized. A console listener is used in the application, which displays the unfiltered trace messages in a console window. This is an excellent program for understanding the combination of trace event types and switch levels.

```
#define TRACE
using System;
using System.Diagnostics;
```

```
namespace Donis.CSharpBook{
    public class Starter{
        public static void Main(string [] argv){
            TraceSource ts=new TraceSource("sample");
            SourceSwitch sw=new SourceSwitch("switch");

            sw.Level=(SourceLevels)Enum.Parse(
                typeof(SourceLevels), argv[0]);
            ts.Switch=sw;
            ConsoleTraceListener console=
                new ConsoleTraceListener();
            ts.Listeners.Add(console);
            ts.TraceEvent(TraceEventType.Start, 0,
                "Activity trace messages on");
            ts.TraceEvent(TraceEventType.Verbose, 0,
                "Verbose trace messages on");
            ts.TraceEvent(TraceEventType.Information, 0,
                "Information trace messages on");
            ts.TraceEvent(TraceEventType.Warning, 0,
                "Warning trace messages on");
            ts.TraceEvent(TraceEventType.Error, 0,
                "Error trace messages on");
            ts.TraceEvent(TraceEventType.Critical, 0,
                "Critical trace messages on");

            ts.Flush();
            ts.Close();

        }
    }
}
```

Trace messages can be sent to a variety of targets, including the console window, a text file, and a XML file. Trace targets are called *listeners*. A *TraceSource* type maintains an array of listeners called the *Listeners* collection. By default, the *Listeners* collection has a single element, the *DefaultTraceListener*, which displays trace messages in the Output window of Visual Studio. When the *Listeners* collection contains more than one listener, trace messages are sent to multiple targets. If the collection contains a *ConsoleTraceListener* and the *XMLWriterTraceListener*, trace messages are displayed in the console window and saved into an XML file. Trace listeners receive trace messages sent from a trace source, which is filtered by the trace switch.

Table 12-18 reviews the available predefined listeners.

Table 12-18   Trace Listeners

Listeners	Description
TextWriterTraceListener	This listener forwards trace messages to instances of stream-related classes, such as a *TextWriter* class.
EventLogTraceListener	This listener forwards trace messages to an event log.
DefaultTraceListener	This listener forwards trace messages to the Output window. This is the default listener and initially the only member included in the *Listeners* collection.

Table 12-18   Trace Listeners *(Continued)*

Listeners	Description
ConsoleTraceListener	This listener forwards trace messages to a standard output or error stream.
DelimitedListTraceListener	Similar to the *TextWriterTraceListener* class, this listener forwards messages to an instance of a stream-related class. However, the messages are separated with user-defined delimiters.
XmlWriterTraceListener	This listener saves traces messages as XML-encoded text.

Trace listeners inherit the *TraceListener* base class, which provides the core functionality of a listener. Most of the methods of the *TraceListener* mirror those of the *TraceSource*, *Trace*, and *Debug* types. *TraceSource*, *Trace*, and *Debug* forward messages to listeners by invoking identically named trace operations in listeners. All the listeners have a default constructor. Some listeners have multiargument constructors, in which the listener is assigned a name or a destination is defined. For example, the following code creates a new *TextWriterTraceListener*. It is named *samplelistener* and writes to the test.txt file.

```
TextWriterTraceListener file=new
    TextWriterTraceListener("samplelistener", "test.txt");
```

Table 12-19 details the properties of the *TraceListener* class.

Table 12-19   TraceListener Properties

Property	Type
Attributes	*StringDictionary*
This property gets the custom attributes that are defined in the application configuration file.	
Filter	*TraceFilter*
This property gets and sets the filter of the listener.	
IndentLevel	*int*
This property gets and sets the level of indentation.	
IndentSize	*int*
This property gets and sets the amount of indentation per indentation level.	
IsThreadSafe	*bool*
This property indicates whether the listener is thread-safe.	
Name	*string*
This property gets and sets the name of the listener.	
NeedIndent	*bool*
This is a protected property, which enables or disables indentation.	
TraceOutputOptions	*TraceOptions*
This property gets and sets an enumeration that controls the output options of the listener.	

The values of the *TraceOption* enumeration are described in Table 12-20. These values are bitwise, which allows multiple options to be combined.

Table 12-20   TraceOptions Values

Value	Description
TraceOptions.CallStack	This option includes the call stack in each trace message. This information is found at the *Environment.StackTrace* property.
TraceOptions.DateTime	This option includes the date and time in each trace message.
TraceOptions.LogicalOperationStack	This option includes the logical operation stack in each trace message. This information is found at the *CorrelationManager.LogicalOperationStack* property.
TraceOptions.None	This option excludes all options. The trace message will contain no optional data.
TraceOptions.ProcessId	This option includes the current process identifier in each trace message. This information is found at the *Process.Id* property.
TraceOptions.ThreadId	This option includes the current thread identifier in each trace message. This information is found at the *Thread.MangedThreadId* property.
TraceOptions.TimeStamp	This option includes a timestamp in the each trace message. This information is returned from the *Stopwatch.GetTimeStamp* method.

The listeners of a *TraceSource* type are managed at the *TraceSource.Listeners* property. The *Listeners* property is a *TraceListenerCollection* type, which implements the *IList*, *ICollection*, and *IEnumerable* interfaces. You can add a listener with the *Add* method. The *TraceListenerCollection* type also implements the *AddRange* method. Call this method to add multiple listeners to the *Listeners* collection. The *AddRange* method is overloaded to accept an array of listeners or a *TraceListenerCollection* type as the sole parameter. The following code adds a *ConsoleTraceListener* to a *Listeners* collection:

```
ConsoleTraceListener console=
    new ConsoleTraceListener();
ts.Listeners.Add(console);
```

Trace messages can be filtered at the collection. Listener filters are perfect for identifying important messages in a flood of trace messages. You can focus on a particular problem. Listener filters and trace switch are both filters. The trace switch filters messages from the *TraceSource* object. Those messages are forwarded to a listener, in which the listener filter further refines the set of trace messages. There are two types of listener filters: *SourceFilter* and *EventTypeFilter*. *SourceFilter* focuses the listener on a specific source. For example, when tracing messages from several classes, you use *SourceFilter* to limit trace messages to a specific class. *EventTypeFilter* further refines trace messages based on priority. The priority of *Event-TypeFilter* is usually a subset of the source switch filter.

This is the constructor of the *SourceFilter* type:

SourceFilter constructor syntax:

public SourceFilter(string source)

The only parameter is the name of the source. The listener will output only messages from the specific source. If the name is invalid, the filter is ignored.

This is the constructor of the *EventTypeFilter* type:

EventTypeFilter constructor syntax:

public EventTypeFilter(SourceLevels level)

The *SourceLevels* parameter states the priority of allowed trace messages. Other trace messages are ignored.

The following code demonstrates the *SourceFilter* type. The *EventTypeFilter* is included in a later example. Three *TraceSource* instances are defined in the code. A *ConsoleTraceListener* is also defined, which displays trace messages in the console window. The *ConsoleTraceListener* .*Filter* is then updated to display trace messages from only the second source. Later, the *SourceFilter* is changed to limit trace messages to the first source.

```
#define TRACE

using System;
using System.Diagnostics;

namespace Donis.CSharpBook{
    public class Starter{

        public static void Main() {
            TraceSource ts1=new TraceSource("ts1");
            TraceSource ts2=new TraceSource("ts2");
            TraceSource ts3=new TraceSource("ts3");
            SourceSwitch sw=new SourceSwitch("sw",
                "Information");
            ts1.Switch=sw;
            ts2.Switch=sw;
            ts3.Switch=sw;
            ConsoleTraceListener cs=new ConsoleTraceListener();
            ts1.Listeners.Add(cs);
            ts2.Listeners.Add(cs);
            ts3.Listeners.Add(cs);

            // Include only the ts2 source

            Console.WriteLine("Filters t1 and t3 messages");
            ts1.Listeners[1].Filter=new SourceFilter("ts2");
            ts1.TraceInformation("ts1:trace");
            ts2.TraceInformation("ts2:trace");
            ts3.TraceInformation("ts3:trace");
```

```
        // Include only the ts1 source

        Console.WriteLine("\nFilters t2 and t3 messages");
        ts1.Listeners[1].Filter=new SourceFilter("ts1");
        ts1.TraceInformation("ts1:trace");
        ts2.TraceInformation("ts2:trace");
        ts3.TraceInformation("ts3:trace");

        ts1.Flush();
        ts2.Flush();
        ts3.Flush();

        ts1.Close();
        ts2.Close();
        ts3.Close();
    }
  }
}
```

Tracing Example

The following example code declares a *ZClass* and *YClass*; both classes contain a *TraceSource* instance. It is a best practice to maintain separate *TraceSource* instances for individual classes, which affords individualized management of tracing at the class level. For example, you could filter trace messages for specific classes. Expose *TraceSource* as a static member of the class, which is initialized in the static constructor. Functions of the class leverage the static *TraceSource* to send trace messages. If using the disposable pattern, clean up the *TraceSource* object in the *Dispose* method.

```
public class ZClass: IDisposable {

    static ZClass() {
        ts=new TraceSource("ZTrace");
        ts.Switch=new SourceSwitch("sw1", "Information");
        ts.Listeners.Add(new ConsoleTraceListener());
        TextWriterTraceListener file=new
            TextWriterTraceListener("samplelistener", "test.txt");
        file.Filter = new EventTypeFilter(SourceLevels.Critical);
        file.TraceOutputOptions=TraceOptions.DateTime;
        ts.Listeners.Add(file);
    }

    static private TraceSource ts;

    // partial listing

    public void Dispose() {
        ts.Flush();
        ts.Close();
    }

}
```

The following code is a complete listing of the sample code used in this section. *Main* also has a trace source, which sends trace messages to listeners for the Output and Console windows. Both the *ZClass* and *YClass* have separate trace sources. The methods of the *ZClass* and *YClass* use their respective *TraceSource* instances to send trace messages. To demonstrate both techniques, the *TraceEvent* and *TraceData* methods are called. The hash codes of the objects are used as the trace identifier, which identifies trace messages by class type and instance. This is sometimes useful. The trace source of the *ZClass* sends trace messages to listeners for the Output window, Console window, and a text file. The switch of that trace source forwards all trace messages. However, the filter for the *Console* listener restricts output to error type messages. The *YClass* trace source sends trace messages of error priority to listeners for the Output and Console windows. The switch limits the trace messages to informational messages.

```csharp
#define TRACE

using System;
using System.Diagnostics;

namespace Donis.CSharpBook{
    public class Starter{
        public static void Main(){

            TraceSource ts=
                new TraceSource("StarterTrace");
            ts.Switch=new SourceSwitch("sw3");
            ts.Switch.Level=SourceLevels.ActivityTracing;
            ts.Listeners.Add(new ConsoleTraceListener());
            ts.TraceEvent(TraceEventType.Start,
                0, "Starting");

            ZClass obj1=new ZClass();
            obj1.MethodA();
            obj1.MethodB(1,2,3);

            YClass obj2=new YClass();
            obj2.MethodC();

            ZClass obj3=new ZClass();
            obj1.MethodA();
            obj1.MethodB(4,5,6);


            ts.TraceEvent(TraceEventType.Stop,
                0, "Stopping");

            obj1.Dispose();
            obj2.Dispose();

        }
    }

    public class ZClass: IDisposable {

        static ZClass() {
```

```
            ts=new TraceSource("ZTrace");
            ts.Switch=new SourceSwitch("sw1", "All");
            ts.Listeners.Add(new ConsoleTraceListener());
            TextWriterTraceListener file=new
                TextWriterTraceListener("samplelistener", "test.txt");
            file.Filter = new EventTypeFilter(SourceLevels.Critical);
            file.TraceOutputOptions=TraceOptions.DateTime;
            ts.Listeners.Add(file);
        }

        static private TraceSource ts;


        public void MethodA() {
            ts.TraceEvent(TraceEventType.Error,
                GetHashCode(), "ZClass.MethodA");
        }

        public void MethodB(int parama, int paramb,
                int paramc) {
            ts.TraceData(TraceEventType.Critical,
                GetHashCode(), "ZClass.MethodB", parama,
                paramb, paramc);
        }

        public void Dispose() {
            ts.Flush();
            ts.Close();
        }

    }

    public class YClass: IDisposable {

        static YClass() {
            ts=new TraceSource("YTrace");
            ts.Switch=new SourceSwitch("sw2", "Information");
            ts.Listeners.Add(new ConsoleTraceListener());
            ts.Listeners[1].IndentSize=4;
            ts.Listeners[1].IndentLevel=2;
        }

        static private TraceSource ts;

        public void MethodC() {
            ts.TraceEvent(TraceEventType.Error,
                GetHashCode(), "YClass.MethodC");
        }

        public void Dispose() {
            ts.Flush();
            ts.Close();
        }

    }
}
```

Configuration File

Trace switches, listeners, and listener filters are configurable in an application configuration file. Actually, this is the best practice and is preferable to programmatic configuration. Developers can update the specifics of tracing without recompiling the application. The application configuration file has the same name as the target assembly plus a *.config* extension. For example, the application configuration file for hello.exe is hello.exe.config. The application configuration file should be in the same directory as the assembly. For a software system, you can configure multiple applications with a publisher policy file, which is deployed in the global assembly cache. Visit this link for a "how to" on publisher policy files: *msdn2.microsoft.com/en-us/library/dz32563a*. You can configure tracing in both the configuration file and programmatically. Where there is overlap, programmatic configuration takes precedent.

In the configuration file, the tracing is placed within the *system.diagnostics* element. For the complete explanation of the *system.diagnostics* element, open this link: *msdn2.microsoft.com/en-us/library/1txedc80*.

```xml
<?xml version="1.0" encoding="utf-8" ?>
<configuration>
    <system.diagnostics>
    </system.diagnostics>
</configuration>
```

Sources element   Define the trace sources within the *sources* element. A specific trace source is declared in a *source* element. The important attributes of the *source* element are *name* and *switchName*. The *name* attribute is the name of the trace source, and *switchName* names the switch assigned to the trace source. Here is an example:

```xml
<sources>
    <source name="ZTrace" switchName="sw1">
    </source>
</sources>
```

Listeners element   The listeners of a particular source are listed within the *source* elements. The *listeners* element encapsulates the listeners of a trace source. Individual listeners are added to the *Listeners* collection with the *add* element. The key attributes of the add element are *type*, *name*, *traceOutputOptions*, and *initializeData*. The *type* attribute is the kind of listener. The *name* attribute is the name assigned to the listener. The *initializeData* attribute is additional data used to create the listener, such as the target file name. The *traceOutputOtions* attribute adds optional data to trace messages of the listener, such as a timestamp. Here are example elements:

```xml
<sources>
    <source name="ZTrace" switchName="sw1">
        <listeners>
            <add initializeData="data.txt"
                type="System.Diagnostics.TextWriterTraceListener"
                name="tListener" />
            <add name="cListener" />
        </listeners>
    </source>
</sources>
```

sharedListeners element   The *listeners* element assigns a listener to a specific trace source. You can also share listeners. Listeners are shared between trace sources in the *sharedListeners* element. A shared listener is added with an *add* element. Shared listeners are added to a specific trace source as a regular listener. However, the *add* element need only have the *name* attribute, which identifies the shared listener:

```
 <system.diagnostics>
    <sharedListeners>
        <add type="System.Diagnostics.ConsoleTraceListener"
            name="cListener"
            traceOutputOptions="None" />
    </sharedListeners>
</switches>
```

Switches element   Switches are defined within the *switches* elements. An individual switch is added with an *add* element. The basic attributes are *name* and *value*. The *name* attribute is the name of the switch, and the *value* attribute is the filter for the trace message. Here is an example:

```
    <system.diagnostics>
        <switches>
            <add name="sw1" value="Critical" />
            <add name="sw2" value="Information" />
        </switches>
    </system.diagnostics>
</configuration>
```

Tracing Example with a Configuration File

The programmatic example of tracing has been rewritten to leverage an application file. The following code is the new source code for the application. The switch and collection code is removed from the source code and placed in the configuration file.

```
#define TRACE

using System;
using System.Diagnostics;

namespace Donis.CSharpBook{
    public class Starter{
        public static void Main(){

            TraceSource ts=
                new TraceSource("StarterTrace");
            ts.TraceEvent(TraceEventType.Start,
                0, "Starting");

            ZClass obj1=new ZClass();
            obj1.MethodA();
            obj1.MethodB(1,2,3);

            YClass obj2=new YClass();
            obj2.MethodC();
```

```
                  ZClass obj3=new ZClass();
                  obj1.MethodA();
                  obj1.MethodB(4,5,6);


                  ts.TraceEvent(TraceEventType.Stop,
                      0, "Stopping");

                  obj1.Dispose();
                  obj2.Dispose();

            }
      }

      public class ZClass: IDisposable {

          static ZClass() {
              ts=new TraceSource("ZTrace");
          }

          static private TraceSource ts;


          public void MethodA() {
              ts.TraceEvent(TraceEventType.Error,
                  GetHashCode(), "ZClass.MethodA");
          }

          public void MethodB(int parama, int paramb,
                  int paramc) {
              ts.TraceData(TraceEventType.Critical,
                  GetHashCode(), "ZClass.MethodB", parama,
                  paramb, paramc);
          }

          public void Dispose() {
              ts.Flush();
              ts.Close();
          }

      }

      public class YClass: IDisposable {

          static YClass() {
              ts=new TraceSource("YTrace");
          }

          static private TraceSource ts;

          public void MethodC() {
              ts.TraceEvent(TraceEventType.Error,
                  GetHashCode(), "YClass.MethodC");
          }
```

```
    public void Dispose() {
        ts.Flush();
        ts.Close();
    }

  }
}
```

The following application configuration file sets up tracing for the application. There are some differences from the first example. For example, the three trace sources share the same *Console* listener. The *YTrace* trace source also has an *XML* listener. Otherwise, the results are virtually the same as the earlier code.

```xml
<?xml version="1.0" encoding="utf-8" ?>
<configuration>
    <system.diagnostics>
        <sources>
            <source name="StarterTrace" switchName="sw3">
                <listeners>
                    <add name="cListener" />
                </listeners>
            </source>
            <source name="ZTrace" switchName="sw1">
                <listeners>
                    <add initializeData="data.txt"
                        type="System.Diagnostics.TextWriterTraceListener"
                        name="tListener" />
                    <add name="cListener" />
                </listeners>
            </source>
            <source name="YTrace" switchName="sw2">
                <listeners>
                    <add name="cListener" />
                    <add name="xListener" />
                </listeners>
            </source>
        </sources>
        <sharedListeners>
            <add initializeData="data.xml" type="System.Diagnostics.XmlWriterTraceListener"
                name="xListener" traceOutputOptions="DateTime" />
            <add type="System.Diagnostics.ConsoleTraceListener" name="cListener"
                traceOutputOptions="DateTime" />
        </sharedListeners>
        <switches>
            <add name="sw1" value="Information" />
            <add name="sw2" value="All" />
            <add name="sw3" value="ActivityTracing" />
        </switches>
    </system.diagnostics>
</configuration>
```

DebuggerDisplayAttribute

The *DebuggerDisplayAttribute* type controls how values are displayed in a debugger window. This attribute is valid for assembly, class, struct, enum, indexer, property, field, and delegate constructs. You cannot use *DebuggerDisplayAttribute* on methods. When this attribute is used as an assembly-level attribute, the *Target* property must be assigned the name of the applicable type. The *DebuggerDisplayAttribute* type is also found in the *System.Diagnostics* namespace.

The *DebuggerDisplayAttribute* type has a one-argument constructor. The single argument, which is a string, is the display value of the type in the debug window. The value can contain an expression. Expressions must be enclosed in curly braces: {*expression*}. Constants, static members, and instance members are valid in the expression. Prefix static members with the class name. The expression cannot contain pointers, aliases, or local variables.

The *DebuggerDisplayAttribute* type is inheritable. A derived class inherits the attribute from the base class. However, the derived class can redefined *DebuggerDisplayAttribute* as desired.

Figure 12-45 shows the values in a debug window for the *ZClass* and *YClass* instances without *DebuggerDisplayAttribute*.

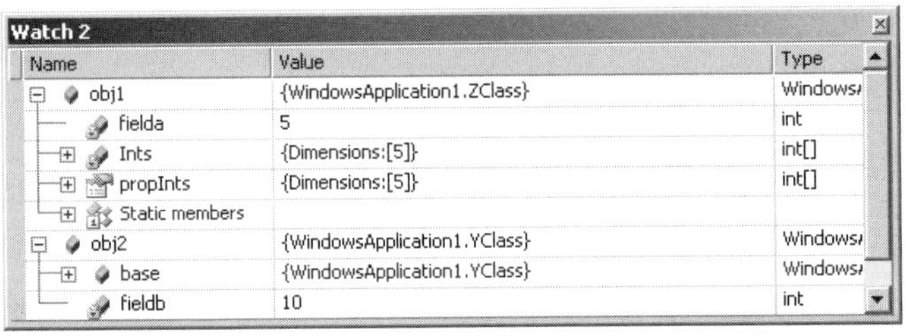

Figure 12-45   View of the ZClass and YClass instances before applying DebuggerDisplayAttribute

The following code decorates the *ZClass* and *YClass* with the *DebuggerDisplayAttribute* type. The *ZClass* is assigned the value *NewName*, which is overridden in the derived class. In addition, *ZClass.fielda* is adorned with the attribute, which contains an expression in this circumstance.

```
[DebuggerDisplay("NewName")]
class ZClass
{
    public static int test = 1;
    public virtual void MethodA()
    {
        int vara=5, varb=10;
        Console.WriteLine("{0} {1}", vara,
```

```
            varb);
    }

    public void MethodB()
    {
        Console.WriteLine("ZClass.MethodB");
        Console.WriteLine("ZClass.fielda {0}",
            fielda);
    }

    [DebuggerDisplay("fielda = {fielda}")]
    private int fielda = 5;
}

[DebuggerDisplay("DerivedName")]
class YClass : ZClass
{
    public override void MethodA()
    {
        Console.WriteLine("YClass.MethodA");
        Console.WriteLine("Fieldb: {0}", fieldb);
    }

    private int fieldb = 10;
}
```

Figure 12-46 shows the results of using the *DebuggerDisplayAttribute* type with the *ZClass* and *YClass*.

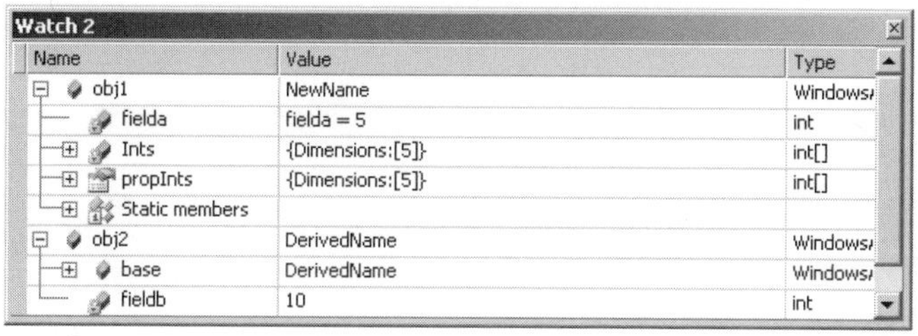

Figure 12-46   View of ZClass and YClass types in the debugger window after applying the DebuggerDisplayAttribute type

DebuggerBrowsableAttribute

Another debugger attribute is the *DebuggerBrowsableAttribute* type, which determines how a member is displayed in the debugger window. This attribute is valid for properties, indexers, and fields.

DebuggerBrowsableAttribute has one constructor, which is a one-argument constructor. The parameter is the *DebuggableBrowsableState* enumeration. Table 12-21 lists the elements of the enumeration.

Table 12-21   DebuggableBrowserState Values

Value	Description
Never	This element hides the member in the debugger window.
Collapsed	This element displays the member, which is collapsed initially. This is the default.
RootHidden	If the element is an array or collection, this element hides the root member but displays the child elements. For example, when applied to a property that is an integer array, the integer elements are displayed instead of the array itself.

Figure 12-47 shows the values for the *ZClass* and *YClass* types without the *DebuggerBrowsableAttribute* type.

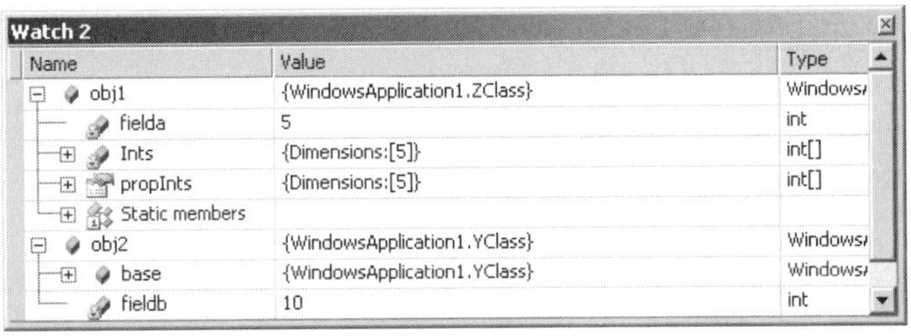

Figure 12-47   View of ZClass and YClass types before applying the DebuggerBrowsableAttribute type

The following code shows the *ZClass* and *YClass* types decorated with *DebuggerBrowsableAttribute*. In the *ZClass*, the array related to the *propInts* property is displayed. In the *YClass* type, *fieldb* is hidden.

```
class ZClass
{
    public static int test = 1;
    public virtual void MethodA()
    {
        int vara=5, varb=10;
        Console.WriteLine("{0} {1}", vara,
            varb);
    }

    public void MethodB()
    {
        Console.WriteLine("ZClass.MethodB");
        Console.WriteLine("ZClass.fielda {0}",
            fielda);
    }

    private int[] Ints ={ 1, 2, 3, 4, 5 };
    [DebuggerBrowsable(DebuggerBrowsableState.RootHidden)]
    public int[] propInts
    {
```

```
        get
        {
            return Ints;
        }
    }

    private int fielda = 5;
}

class YClass : ZClass
{
    public override void MethodA()
    {
        Console.WriteLine("YClass.MethodA");
        Console.WriteLine("Fieldb: {0}", fieldb);
    }

    [DebuggerBrowsable(DebuggerBrowsableState.Never)]
    private int fieldb = 10;
}
```

Figure 12-48 shows the results of using the *DebuggerBrowsableAttribute* type on the *ZClass* and *YClass*.

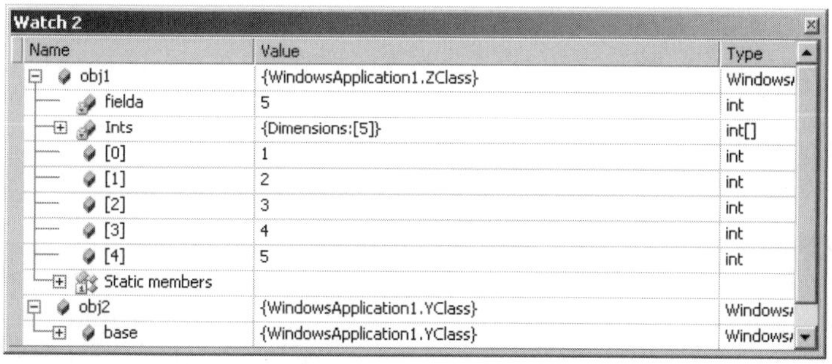

Figure 12-48   View of ZClass and YClass types after applying DebuggerBrowsableAttribute

DebuggerTypeProxyAttribute

The *DebuggerTypeProxyAttribute* type names a type as a proxy for another type. The type proxy is displayed instead of the type in debugger windows. The attribute type is *DebuggerTypeProxyAttribute*. This attribute is valid for assembly, class, and struct constructs. When used at the assembly level, the target name property must be assigned the name of the target type.

The proxy type must have a one-argument constructor that accepts an instance of the target type. For this reason, it is recommended that the proxy type be nested within the target type. This provides the proxy type constructor easy access to the instance of the surrounding object. Only public members of the proxy are visible in the debugger window.

The *DebuggerTypeProxyAttribute* type is useful for hiding sensitive data within a type. In the following code, *XClass* has a password field. This field should not be exposed during live debugging because passwords represent sensitive data. The *DebuggerTypeProxyAttribute* type in the sample code names *XClassDebug* as the proxy. *XClassDebug* hides the password field and displays an appropriate value, which is *"Not Available"*.

This is the code for the *XClass* and the nested *XClassDebug* class, which is the proxy class:

```
[DebuggerTypeProxy(typeof(XClassDebug))]
public class XClass
{
    public XClass(string _password)
    {
        password=_password;
    }
    private string password;
    internal class XClassDebug
    {
        public XClassDebug(XClass obj)
        {
        }

        public string password = "Not Available";
    }
}
```

Dump Files

Visual Studio 2005 can open and interpret dump files from managed, native, or mixed-mode applications. A dump is a snapshot of an application's memory that lets a developer debug an application at a convenient location and time, which is particularly beneficial for debugging production applications. Dumps created on a production machine can then be debugged on another machine, without interfering with the production machine. Several tools are available for creating a dump, including Windbg, Dr. Watson, Autodump+ (ADPlus), and Visual Studio. Visual Studio can create dumps while debugging native applications, such as Microsoft Visual C++ applications. This feature is not available in managed projects. Dump files and other advanced debugging topics are discussed in the next chapter, "Advanced Debugging."

In Visual Studio, dump files are opened as projects. Choose the Open Solution/Project menu command from the Open submenu of the File menu. Dump files have the *.dmp* extension. After opening the file, start a debug session to examine the dump file. The Debug Start menu command (F5) on the Debug menu starts a debug session. When debugging a dump, a break-point is hit almost immediately. You can then debug and diagnose the dump using the various debug windows. Figures 12-49 and 12-50 show the Call Stack and Modules debug windows, which provide different views of the dump.

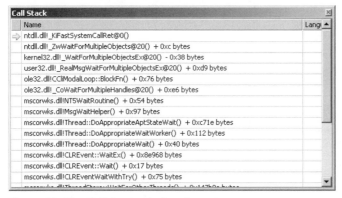

Figure 12-49   Call Stack window for a dump

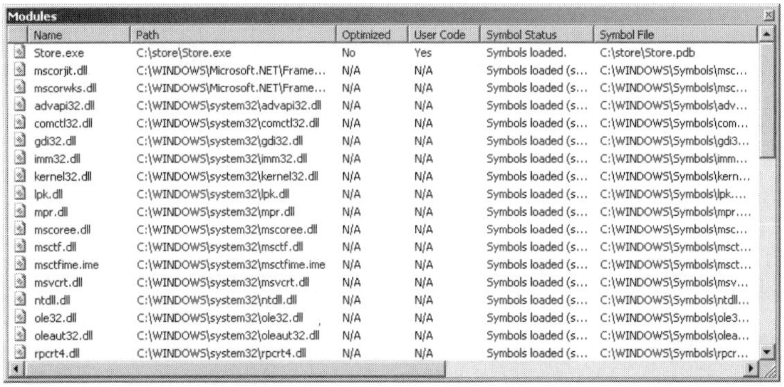

Figure 12-50   Modules window for a dump

The Debug windows of Visual Studio can provide a native perspective of an unmanaged application. This is helpful with dumps of managed applications, but a managed view is also sometimes merited. Load the Son of Strike debugger extension (*SOS.DLL*) for a managed perspective of a dump. Load Son of Strike with the *.load sos* command in the Immediate window. You can then issue various Son of Strike commands, which are prefixed with an exclamation point. In Figure 12-51, Son of Strike is loaded. Afterward, the DumpHeap command is invoked. Output is shown in the Immediate window. Some Son of Strike commands are thread-specific. Set the thread context in the Thread window before issuing one of those commands.

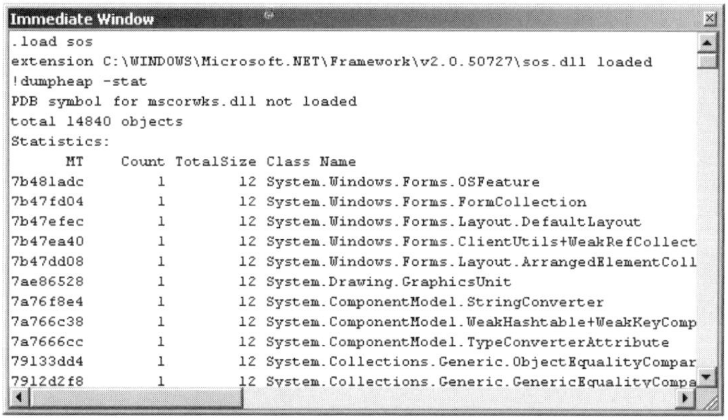

```
Immediate Window                                          ⊕          ×
.load sos
extension C:\WINDOWS\Microsoft.NET\Framework\v2.0.50727\sos.dll loaded
!dumpheap -stat
PDB symbol for mscorwks.dll not loaded
total 14840 objects
Statistics:
      MT       Count TotalSize  Class Name
7b481adc          1         12  System.Windows.Forms.OSFeature
7b47fd04          1         12  System.Windows.Forms.FormCollection
7b47efec          1         12  System.Windows.Forms.Layout.DefaultLayout
7b47ea40          1         12  System.Windows.Forms.ClientUtils+WeakRefCollect
7b47dd08          1         12  System.Windows.Forms.Layout.ArrangedElementColl
7ae86528          1         12  System.Drawing.GraphicsUnit
7a76f8e4          1         12  System.ComponentModel.StringConverter
7a766c38          1         12  System.ComponentModel.WeakHashtable+WeakKeyComp
7a7666cc          1         12  System.ComponentModel.TypeConverterAttribute
79133dd4          1         12  System.Collections.Generic.ObjectEqualityCompar
7912d2f8          1         12  System.Collections.Generic.GenericEqualityCompa
```

Figure 12-51   Son of Strike in the Immediate window

Advanced Debugging

A variety of tools are available for advanced debugging. Many of these tools are downloaded from the Debugging Tools for Windows Web site. Windbg, the latest version of Son of Strike (*SOS.DLL*), and Auto-Dump Plus are three of the most valuable tools received from the download.

Windbg is a native and kernel debugger, which is commonly used by software support engineers to diagnose problems. It supports live and postmortem debugging. Live debugging is performed by attaching the debugger to a running process. Postmortem analysis is conducted via dump files. This includes examining memory, evaluating call stacks, setting breakpoints, viewing threads, and much more. *SOS.DLL* is a debugger extension that publishes commands for managed debugging. Son of Strike can be used in Windbg and Visual Studio 2005, as shown earlier in this chapter.

Mdg is the new managed debugger. As the dedicated managed debugger, it offers features that are found neither in Visual Studio debugger nor in Windbg products.

Chapter 13
Advanced Debugging

Successful debugging is about asking the correct questions. Many (but not all) of those questions can be answered with the Microsoft Visual Studio Debugger. Some questions require advanced debugging techniques and tools. What are the outstanding synchronization objects? How much native versus managed memory has been allocated? What is the size of each generation and the large object heap? These and other advanced questions are not answerable in the Visual Studio Debugger, but may be essential to quickly resolving a debugging problem.

This chapter provides general techniques for debugging managed applications. Some of these techniques are also helpful in debugging Web applications. For guidance on debugging ASP.NET applications, refer to *http://msdn.microsoft.com/library/default.asp?url=/library/en-us/dnbda/html/DBGch01.asp.*

Advanced debugging tools and services are available from a variety of sources, including the Microsoft Windows operating environment, the Microsoft .NET Framework, Visual Studio .NET, and the Debugging Tools for Windows Web site at Microsoft.com. Performance Monitor, Task Manager, and Dr. Watson are distributed with the Windows environment. The .NET Framework has the Son of Strike (SOS) debugger extension (SOS.dll), DbgClr, CorDbg, and other debugger tools. Visual Studio offers Spy++, Dependency Walker, OLE Viewer, and much more. Advanced debugging tools can be downloaded from the Debugging Tools for Windows Web site at *www.microsoft.com/whdc/devtools/debugging.* This Web site is updated periodically.

You should download the current tools regularly. The Windows Debugger (WinDbg) and ADPlus script are the most frequently used tools from this Web site.

WinDbg is the primary focus of this chapter. However, it is not intended as a replacement for the Visual Studio Debugger. The first rule of debugging is to look for simple solutions first. The Visual Studio Debugger is ideal for basic debugging: It is convenient, it has a familiar user interface, and superior documentation is available. Visual Studio is a pen hammer, whereas WinDbg is a sledge hammer. If a problem occurs, diagnose the problem first with Visual Studio before attempting a complete reclamation with WinDbg. Find uninitialized variables or parameters, errant loop counters, logic errors, and code coverage problems with the Visual Studio Debugger. These are likely problems in an erroneous application.

The goal of debugging is to resolve abnormal error conditions. Program hangs, crashes, memory leaks, and unhandled exceptions are possible error conditions. Some abnormal conditions are not exceptional events. These primarily include logic errors. For example, a program that reports incorrect results has a bug. It may not be as intrusive as an exception, but it is a bug nonetheless.

Debugging is conducted in three phases: discovery, analysis, and testing. The *discovery phase* is the process of gathering data related to the problem. In this stage, you capture the state of the application or environment when the error condition occurred. The *analysis* (or *debugging*) *phase* is when the abnormal condition is diagnosed. The *testing phase* validates the analysis phase. This is an iterative process. Based on the results of the testing phase, further discovery, analysis, and testing could be mandated.

Debugging is an integral part of the life cycle of an application. Debugging a production application is a challenge when compared with debugging in the development environment. First, the constraints are different. The priority for debugging a production application is restarting the application, not exhaustive analysis. With a high-traffic retail Web site, the primary concern of the client might be lost revenue. Second, the production machine might lack debugging resources, such as symbols, source code, and debugging tools. Third, re-creating the abnormal condition could be problematic. Load factors, memory stress, and other conditions are hard to replicate on a developer machine. Finally, the production application may be offsite—in a locked server closet or another otherwise inconvenient location. This might necessitate remote debugging, which could entail setup and possible trust issues.

Debugging can be invasive or noninvasive. Noninvasive debugging is the preference for debugging production applications that are running. The advantages of noninvasive debugging are that the debuggee is not altered or shut down during the debugging process. Invasive debugging provides additional data and flexibility, but should be limited to the development environment.

You can debug live applications or perform postmortem analysis. Live debugging is debugging an active and running application, and it often involves breakpoints. Breakpoints are set where the live application should be interrupted. Starting at the breakpoint, the developer can step through the application to verify program logic, monitor local variables, inspect the heap, watch the call stack, and more. Live debugging usually entails user interaction, which is not always possible. The antithesis to live debugging is postmortem analysis. Postmortem analysis is performed against static data, such as a dump or log file. You can create a dump or log file once and then debug as often as needed. Using a static file is often simpler than live debugging, where the state is constantly evolving. Postmortem analysis also has disadvantages. It is harder to pose future-tense questions with postmortem analysis. What is the call stack after a future operation is performed? What is the effect of further executing a *for* loop? What is the impact of changing the value of a local variable? Deriving answers to these questions from a dump or log file is indeed difficult.

Production and beta applications are typically release builds, whereas alpha and proof of concepts are often debug builds. Release builds are optimized but harder to debug. Conversely, debug builds are not optimized and run slightly slower. In .NET 1.1, release builds might have incomplete tracking information from the inlining of methods. The missing stack frames could lead to unreliable stack traces in debuggers. This optimization is not performed on .NET 2.0 applications. In addition, there is code optimization, which is a compilation of several performance-improving techniques, including inserting jumps, reducing the lifetime of local references, reordering instructions efficiently, and so on.

This chapter presents different versions of the Store application. Each version demonstrates a different aspect of advanced debugging. The Store applications can be found in the companion Web content.

DebuggableAttribute Attribute

Just-in-time (JIT) optimizations are defined in the *DebuggableAttribute* custom attribute. When compiled in debug mode, this attribute is added to the metadata of the application with any optimizations disabled. The *DebuggableAttribute* attribute contains the *IsJITOptimizerDisabled* and *IsJITTrackingEnabled* properties, which indicate the status of JIT optimizations.

These optimizations can make debugging a production application difficult. Fortunately, you can create an application initialization file that disables the optimization of a release product. The initialization file must be in the same directory as the application, have the same root name of the application, and have the .ini extension. For myapp.exe, the filename would be myapp.ini. The initialization file has two entries. The *GenerateTrackingInfo* entry enables or disables generating complete tracking information. This entry is redundant in .NET 2.0, where tracking information is always generated. The *AllowOptimize* entry controls code optimization. In the initialization file, 1 is true and 0 is false. The following is an initialization file that disables both JIT optimizations:

```
[.NET Framework Debugging Control]
GenerateTrackingInfo=1
AllowOptimize=0
```

This is a partial listing of assembly code generated by the JIT compiler with optimizations enabled:

```
00e40a0b 8b45b8          mov     eax,[ebp-0x48]
00e40a0e 8b8854010000    mov     ecx,[eax+0x154]
00e40a14 8b15086c3902    mov     edx,[02396c08] ("Transaction cancelled")
00e40a1a 8b01            mov     eax,[ecx]
00e40a1c ff9068010000    call    dword ptr [eax+0x168]
00e40a22 83c301          add     ebx,0x1
00e40a25 3b5ddc          cmp     ebx,[ebp-0x24]
00e40a28 0f8c58fdffff    jl      00e40786
00e40a2e 8d65f4          lea     esp,[ebp-0xc]
00e40a31 5b              pop     ebx
00e40a32 5e              pop     esi
00e40a33 5f              pop     edi
00e40a34 5d              pop     ebp
00e40a35 c20400          ret     0x4
00e40a38 e8713f2579      call    mscorwks!JIT_RngChkFail (7a0949ae)
00e40a3d cc              int     3
```

The following assembly originated from the same Microsoft intermediate language (MSIL) code as the preceding assembly code. For this assembly, the JIT optimizations are disabled. I will not torment you with the intricacies of assembly code. However, compare the before and after code—and note the differences. Obviously, disabling optimizations made a considerable difference in the assembly code generated.

```
01050aba 90              nop
01050abb eb17            jmp     01050ad4
01050abd 8b45c0          mov     eax,[ebp-0x40]
01050ac0 8b8854010000    mov     ecx,[eax+0x154]
01050ac6 8b15086c3902    mov     edx,[02396c08] ("Transaction cancelled")
01050acc 8b01            mov     eax,[ecx]
01050ace ff9068010000    call    dword ptr [eax+0x168]
01050ad4 ff45d4          inc     dword ptr [ebp-0x2c]
01050ad7 8b45d4          mov     eax,[ebp-0x2c]
01050ada 3b45d8          cmp     eax,[ebp-0x28]
01050add 0f8c1efdffff    jl      01050801
01050ae3 90              nop
01050ae4 8d65f4          lea     esp,[ebp-0xc]
01050ae7 5b              pop     ebx
01050ae8 5e              pop     esi
01050ae9 5f              pop     edi
01050aea 5d              pop     ebp
01050aeb c20400          ret     0x4
```

Other differences can exist between release and debug products. Debug methods are likely to be omitted from the release version. Trace methods are probably included in the release build, but that is not guaranteed. These and other dissimilarities sometimes amount to relevant differences between a release and debug version of a product. For that reason, an abnormal condition in a production application may mysteriously disappear in a debug version. The opposite also applies. Errors in a debug version might disappear in the release product. Make sure that *Debug* and *Trace* methods cause no side effects. This will eliminate most cross-build problems. It's important to always extensively test both the debug and release versions of products. After exhaustive unit testing of the debug build, submit the release build to identical tests.

Debuggers

There are several useful tools and debuggers available to managed developers. The following list is a compilation of some of these tools. (This list does not include third-party tools.)

- **Visual Studio Debugger**   Most Windows developers have some experience with this tool. Consult this debugger first to diagnose a problem. It is included with the installation of Visual Studio .NET.

- **Managed Debugger (MDbg)**   This tool is a console debugger that is dedicated to the advanced debugging of managed code, so it has a wide variety of commands and options specific to managed code that are not available in other debuggers. You download the code for MDbg at the Microsoft downloads site: *www.microsoft.com/downloads*. It is described as the CLR Managed Debugger (mdbg) Sample. There is a GUI extension available for MDbg that can also be downloaded. It provides a user-friendly veneer to MDbg.

- **CLR Debugger (DbgClr)**   This tool is a managed debugger and a scaled-down version of the Visual Studio Debugger. It has the familiar Visual Studio interface, but with only debugging capabilities. This tool provides some debugging preparedness for production machines in which Visual Studio might not be installed. DbgClr does not support remote or mixed-mode debugging. It is distributed with the .NET Framework.

- **Performance Monitor**   Performance Monitor instruments a live application. It can plot a host of data points onto a variety of graphs and reports. Alternatively, results can be logged in text files for later examination. Performance Monitor is included with the Windows operating system.

- **Windows Console Debugger (CDB)**   CDB is both a kernel- and user-mode debugger. To debug managed applications, load the SOS debugger extension (SOS.dll). Download CDB from the Debugging Tools for Windows Web site at Microsoft.com.

- **Windows Debugger (WinDbg)**   WinDbg is also a kernel- and user-mode debugger. It offers a user interface to many of the command-line instructions available in CDB and NTSD. The command-line instructions of WinDbg and CDB are similar. Load SOS to debug managed applications. WinDbg is probably the most popular of the advanced debugging tools. Download WinDbg from the Debugging Tools for Windows Web site at Microsoft.com.

- **Dr. Watson**   Dr. Watson is a JIT debugger that creates logs or dump files when an abnormal condition occurs in an application. Dr. Watson is available on production machines on which other debuggers may not be available. It is convenient and is the one debugging tool everyone should have. This tool is distributed with the Windows operating environment.

- **ADPlus (ADPlus.vbs)**   This service is a Visual Basic script that automates common CDB tasks, such as creating dumps. This is another tool downloaded from the Debugging Tools for Windows Web site at Microsoft.com.

■ **Son of Strike (SOS.dll)**   This tool is a debugger extension that exposes commands for debugging managed applications. This tool is distributed with the .NET Framework and downloadable from the Debugging Tools for Windows Web site at Microsoft.com. Several versions of the SOS.dll are available. The version of the SOS.dll included in the clr10 subdirectory of Debugging Tools For Windows is not compatible with some examples in this chapter.

Some of these tools are available from multiple sources. For example, SOS is found in the .NET Framework, distributed with Visual Studio .NET, and downloaded at the Debugging Tools for Windows Web site at Microsoft.com. When a tool is available from various sources, the most recent version is downloadable from the Debugging Tools for Windows Web site at Microsoft.com.

Just-In-Time (JIT) Debugging

JIT debugging attaches a registered debugger to an application when an unhandled exception is raised or otherwise crashes. The JIT debugger for these events can be set in the registry. You can inspect the registry using the Regedit tool. In this text, HKLM is shorthand for HKEY_LOCAL_MACHINE.

For managed code, the following key manages JIT debugging:

HKLM\Software\Microsoft\.NETFramework

The *DbgJITDebugLaunchSetting* value at this key sets the behavior of the just-in-time dialog box. There are three possible values. A value of zero requests that the Microsoft Error Reporting dialog box is displayed for JIT debugging. In the Microsoft Error Reporting dialog box, click the Don't Send button to launch the JIT debugging dialog box. Both the Microsoft Error Reporting and the JIT debugging dialog boxes are shown in Figures 13-1 and 13-2. A value of 1 causes the Microsoft Error Reporting dialog box to be suppressed. A value of 2 forces the JIT debugging dialog box to be displayed when JIT debugging occurs. However, the Microsoft Error Reporting dialog box is not shown. The default value for *DbgJITDebugLaunchSetting* is zero. In addition to the DbgJITDebugLaunchSetting value, you can name the managed JIT debugger in the Dbg-ManagedDebugger value. Figure 13-3 has the managed debugging key and values.

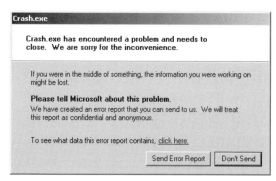

Figure 13-1   Microsoft Error Report dialog box

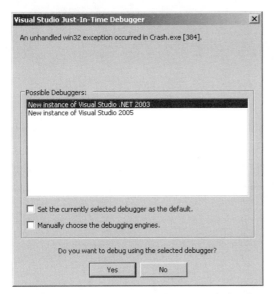

Figure 13-2   Just-in-Time Debugging dialog box

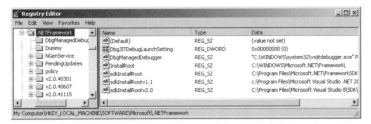

Figure 13-3   View of the .NETFramework key and DbgManagedDebugger value

For unmanaged code, you configure JIT debugging at the following registry key:

HKLM\Software\Microsoft\Windows NT\CurrentVersion\AeDebug

The *Auto* value of this key controls the Just-in-Time Debugging dialog box. *Zero* causes the Microsoft Error Reporting dialog box to be displayed. If the Debug button is clicked on the Microsoft Error Reporting dialog box, the Just-in-Time Debugging dialog box is displayed next. A value of 1 displays the Just-in-Time Debugging dialog box directly. The Debugger value of the *AeDebug* registry key holds the name of the JIT unmanaged debugger.

Visual Studio .NET is named as the default managed and unmanaged debugger when the product is installed. If that changes, you can reappoint Visual Studio .NET as the default debugger from the Tools menu and the Options dialog box. Choose the Just-In-Time section in the Debugging pane. From that window, choose the types of code for which Visual Studio .NET should be the JIT debugger.

Figure 13-4 shows the JIT debugging selections.

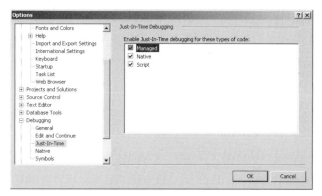

Figure 13-4   Just-In-Time pane

You can install other debuggers as the default JIT debugger. The I startup option of the WinDbg or Dr. Watson tools installs either as the default unmanaged debugger. You can also manually change the registry to make these tools the default managed or unmanaged JIT debuggers:

- WinDbg –I
- Drwtsn32 –I

Managed Debugger

MDbg supports user-mode debugging of managed applications and does not support mixed-mode debugging. Because MDbg is dedicated to managed code, it has an expanded repertoire of debugging commands specific to managed code. As mentioned previously, it is a console debugger. MDbg supersedes the Runtime Debugger (CorDbg), which is the previous managed debugger. CorDbg remains available and continues to be distributed with Visual Studio .NET and the .NET Framework.

Conveniently, MDbg and CorDbg share many of the same commands. However, MDbg commands are different from those of WinDbg and SOS. For developers who switch between these tools frequently, leveraging the benefits of each, the nonstandardization of the public interface of these tools is sometimes frustrating. For example, here are three distinct commands to display a call stack. In WinDbg, you have the k commands, such as *k*, *kb*, and *kp*. SOS offers the *!clrstack* command. MDbg has the most original name for a stack trace command, which is the *w* (*w* for *where*) command.

The following walkthrough demonstrates and highlights many of the unique features of MDbg. As mentioned, Store.exe is the demonstration application provided for walkthroughs in this chapter. In this application, you record sales as transactions. To add a transaction, enter the number of transactions in the *# of Transactions* text box and then click the Add Transactions button. The default number of transactions is 1. The Transaction dialog box appears next, in which you select the items sold in this transaction. After accepting, the new transaction is added to the list of transactions, and the display is updated. The Store application is modified minimally to facilitate some of the walkthroughs. Each walkthrough has its own version of the Store application. The generic Store application is shown in Figure 13-5.

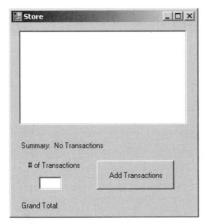

Figure 13-5   The user interface of the Store application

MDbg Walkthrough

The ability to create instances of new objects or invoke managed functions is one of the coolest features included in MDbg. You can seed an application with classes and functions that are used during debugging sessions exclusively. They are never actually called in the application during normal operation, but are instead called only from the debugger. A *Debug* class has been added to the Store application for this purpose. *Debug.Reset* is a static method and the sole member of the *Debug* class. The *Reset* method resets the Store application. The *Debug* class and *Reset* method are a normal class and method. There are no hooks in them especially for the debugger. This is the *Debug* class:

```
public class Debug
{
    public static void Reset()
    {
        Form1.formItems.Clear();
        Form1.formListBox.Items.Clear();
        Form1.formMessage.Text = "Grand Total:";
        Form1.formSummary.Text = "Summary: No Transactions";
        Console.WriteLine("Application reset.");
    }
}
```

These are the steps of the walkthrough:

1. Start the demonstration by running the Store application and adding multiple transactions.

2.   Start MDbg.

3.   Display the active processes by using the *pro(cessnum)* command. The command lists the process identifier, executable, and domain of each process. The Store application is included in the list.

```
  mdbg> pro
Active processes on current machine:
(PID: 3636) C:\codew\debugging\memory\bin\Release\Store.vshost.exe
        (ID: 1) Store.vshost.exe
(PID: 3812) C:\Program Files\Microsoft Visual Studio 8\Common7\IDE\devenv.exe
        (ID: 1) DefaultDomain
(PID: 2812) C:\store\Store.exe
        (ID: 1) Store.exe
```

4.   The *a(ttach)* command attaches MDbg to a running application. The prompt will change to indicate that you are debugging an application. As part of attaching to the program, the debugger interrupts the application.

```
mdbg> a 2812
[p#:0, t#:0] mdbg>
```

5.   How is the *Reset* method described in the debugger? That would help in calling that method. The *x* command displays functions in a module. Without parameters, the *x* command lists the modules in the application. List the modules:

```
[p#:0, t#:0] mdbg> x
:0      mscorlib.dll#0  (no symbols loaded)
:1      Store.exe#0
:2      System.Windows.Forms.dll#0  (no symbols loaded)
:3      System.dll#0  (no symbols loaded)
:4      System.Drawing.dll#0  (no symbols loaded)
:5      System.Configuration.dll#0  (no symbols loaded)
:6      System.Xml.dll#0  (no symbols loaded)
```

6.   Module ":1" is Store.exe. With that information, the functions in that module can be listed using the *x* command again, this time with the ":1" parameter:

```
[p#:0, t#:0] mdbg> x :1
~0. Store.Transaction.Dispose(disposing)
~1. Store.Transaction.InitializeComponent()
~2. Store.Transaction..ctor()
~3. Store.Transaction.btnAdd_Click(sender,e)
~4. Store.Transaction.chkComputer_CheckedChanged(sender,e)
~5. Store.Transaction.chkLaptop_CheckedChanged(sender,e)
~6. Store.Transaction.chkPrinter_CheckedChanged(sender,e)
~7. Store.Transaction.chkSoftware_CheckedChanged(sender,e)
~8. Store.Transaction.get_newItem()
~9. Store.Transaction.btnCancel_Click(sender,e)
~10. Store.Form1.Dispose(disposing)
~11. Store.Form1.InitializeComponent()
~12. Store.Form1..ctor()
~13. Store.Form1.get_formItems()
~14. Store.Form1.get_formMessage()
~15. Store.Form1.get_formSummary()
```

```
~16. Store.Form1.get_formListBox()
~17. Store.Form1.btnTransaction_Click(sender,e)
~18. Store.Form1.btnBad_Click(sender,e)
~19. Store.Form1..cctor()
~20. Store.Properties.Resources..ctor()
~21. Store.Properties.Resources.get_ResourceManager()
~22. Store.Properties.Resources.get_Culture()
~23. Store.Properties.Resources.set_Culture(value)
~24. Store.Program.Main()
~25. Store.Properties.Settings.get_Default()
~26. Store.Properties.Settings..ctor()
~27. Store.Properties.Settings..cctor()
~28. Store.Item..ctor()
~29. Store.Item.get_Products()
~30. Store.Item.set_Products(value)
~31. Store.Item.get_ItemId()
~32. Store.Item.Dispose()
~33. Store.Item..cctor()
~34. Store.Debug.Reset()
~35. Store.Debug..ctor()
```

7. The *Store.Debug.Reset* method is found at the bottom of the list. *Store* is the namespace, *Debug* is the class, and *Reset* is the method. The next time a transaction is added, we want to call this method to reset the application. The button-click handler for adding transactions is *Store.Form1.btnTransaction_Click*, which is also found in the preceding list. Set a breakpoint on this method and resume the Store application. The *b(reakpoint)* command sets breakpoints, and the *g(o)* command resumes an interrupted application:

```
[p#:0, t#:0] mdbg> b Store.Form1.btnTransaction_Click
Breakpoint #1 bound (Store.Form1::btnTransaction_Click(+0))
[p#:0, t#:0] mdbg> g
```

8. Click the Add Transaction button in the Store application. The breakpoint is hit, and the MDbg debugger interrupts the application. The source line where the program is interrupted is displayed. We no longer need this breakpoint. The *b* command without parameters lists all breakpoints, whereas the *del(ete)* command removes a breakpoint:

```
STOP: Breakpoint 1 Hit
64:            {
[p#:0, t#:0] mdbg> b
Current breakpoints:
Breakpoint #1 bound (Store.Form1::btnTransaction_Click(+0))
[p#:0, t#:0] mdbg> del 1
```

9. The *newo(bj)* command creates new instances of classes. However, *Reset* is a static method and does not require an instance. The method is called directly on the class. Invoke the method with the *f(unceval)* command:

```
[p#:0, t#:0] mdbg> f Store.Debug.Reset
STOP EvalComplete
```

10. Resume the Store application with the *g* command, and the application should be reinitialized.

Here is a second demonstration of the MDbg debugger. This walkthrough highlights exception management. When a second-chance exception is raised in an attached application, MDbg does not intercede. Interesting, this is contrary to the behavior of most debuggers. Second-chance exceptions are catastrophic. The exception will terminate the application or prompt JIT debugging. If you want the debugger to intercede, you can request that MDbg catch second-chance exceptions.

1. Restart the Store application.

2. Attach MDbg to the application and resume the program.

3. Click the Bad Action button. As advertised, a bad action occurs, which is an unhandled exception. The Just-in-Time Debugging dialog box will most likely appear where the application can be terminated. Terminate the application. The Bad Action button is not particularly creative in manifesting an exception. The method has filler code but eventually raises a divide-by-zero exception:

    ```
    private void btnBad_Click(object sender, EventArgs e)
    {
        int a = 5, b = 0;
        ++a;
        a /= 2;
        a /= b;
    }
    ```

4. Restart the Store application.

5. Attach the MDbg debugger.

6. Ask the MDbg debugger to catch all second-chance exceptions with the *ca*(*tch*) *ex*(*ception*) command:

    ```
    [p#:0, t#:0] mdbg> ca ex
    ```

7. Resume the application and then click the Bad Action button. This time, the exception is trapped in MDbg, and execution transfers to the debugger. In the debugger, the exception type and the properties of the current exception object are dumped, providing important information on the exception. The source code at the infraction is also displayed and shows the divide-by-zero operation. You now have plenty of information to debug the problem.

    ```
    [p#:0, t#:0] mdbg> g
    STOP: Exception thrown
    Exception=System.DivideByZeroException
            _className=<null>
            _exceptionMethod=<null>
            _exceptionMethodString=<null>
            _message="Attempted to divide by zero."
            _data=<null>
            _innerException=<null>
            _helpURL=<null>
            _stackTrace=array [24]
            _stackTraceString=<null>
    ```

```
            _remoteStackTraceString=<null>
            _remoteStackIndex=0
            _dynamicMethods=<null>
            _HResult=-2147352558
            _source=<null>
            _xptrs=1240048
            _xcode=-1073741676
134:                a /= b;
```

MDbg Commands

MDbg has a full complement of commands for debugging managed applications. Some of the commands were demonstrated in the previous walkthroughs. Table 13-1 lists the MDbg commands.

Table 13-1   MDbg Commands

Command	Description
? and *h(elp)*	These are the help commands and display the MDbg commands with a brief description.
ap(process)	This command switches to another managed process, which is currently being debugged. Without parameters, the command displays the attached processes. MDbg can simultaneously debug multiple applications.
a(ttach)	This command attaches the MDbg debugger to a managed process. Without parameters, the command lists the available managed processes.
b(reakpoint)	This command sets a specific breakpoint or displays all the breakpoints.
ca(tch)	This command stipulates which events to catch. It can also display the events.
conf(ig)	This command sets a particular configuration or displays the configuration options.
del(ete)	This command deletes a breakpoint.
de(tach)	This command detaches the debugger from the current debugged application.
d(own)	This command moves the stack frame down.
echo	This command echoes text to the display.
ex(it) and *q(uit)*	These commands exit the debugger.
fo(reach)	This command executes an action on all threads.
f(unceval)	This command calls a method.
g(o)	This command resumes execution of a debugged application.
ig(nore)	This command displays or stipulates which events to ignore. This command complements the *ca(tch)* command.
int(ercept)	This command intercepts exception at the specified stack frame.
k(ill)	This command kills an active process.
l(ist)	This command lists loaded modules, *AppDomains*, or assemblies.
lo(ad)	This command loads an MDbg extension.
mo(de)	This command sets a specific MDbg option or displays all the options.

Table 13-1   **MDbg Commands** *(Continued)*

Command	Description
newo(bj)	This command creates an instance of a type.
n(ext)	This commands steps over the next instruction.
o(ut)	This command steps out of a function.
pa(th)	This command sets or displays the source path.
p(rint)	This command displays the values of the local or debug variables.
proc(essenum)	This command enumerates the available managed processes.
re(sume)	This command resumes a suspended thread.
r(un)	This command runs a program with the MDbg debugger immediately attached.
set	This command sets a local or debug variable to a new value.
setip	This command moves the instruction pointer within the current function.
sh(ow)	This command shows the source code at the current instruction.
s(tep)	This command steps into a function.
su(spend)	This command suspends a running thread.
sy(mbol)	This command sets or displays the symbol path.
t(hread)	This command switches to a specified thread or display all threads.
U(p)	This command moves up the stack frame.
uwgc(handle)	This command displays the object specified by the GC handle.
when	This command executes a command based on a debugger event.
w(here)	This command displays a stack trace.
x	This command displays the functions in a module or lists all the modules.
Ctrl+C	This keystroke interrupts a running application.
Ctrl+Break	This keystroke terminates the running application and exits the debugger.

WinDbg

WinDbg is both a kernel- and user-mode debugger. It is pronounced Windbag, Win"d-b-g," or, more intuitively, WinDebug. For many developers, WinDbg is the center of the advanced debugging universe. It has been available for some time and has evolved to encompass an impressive array of commands. Some of these commands are admittedly bewildering but always interesting. I have taught the .NET Advanced Debugging Workshop at Microsoft for years, which includes coverage of WinDbg. I still learn something new and amazing about WinDbg almost every month.

The focus of this book is C# and managed code. This is not the ideal place to troll the depths of WinDbg. It would be fun, but probably not entirely relevant. However, some basic WinDbg commands are helpful even when debugging managed applications. Although WinDbg offers a basic user interface, most developers operate from the command line. For this reason, we will use the user interface in a limited manner.

WinDbg Basic Commands

When WinDbg is launched, the debugger can be attached to an application using command-line arguments. This requires the process identifier of the debuggee. *Tlist* is a utility installed with Debugging Tools for Windows to lists the process identifier of active processes.

The following is sample output from the *Tlist* utility. Applications are listed in execution sequence. The first column is the process identifier, the second column is the program, and the final column contains a description, if available.

```
C:\store>tlist
   0 System Process
   4 System
 784 smss.exe
 844 csrss.exe
 872 winlogon.exe
 916 services.exe
 928 lsass.exe
 736 KHALMNPR.exe        KHALHPP_MainWindow
1052 gcasDtServ.exe      GIANT AntiSpyware Data Service
1444 DVDRAMSV.exe
1488 inetinfo.exe
1524 mdm.exe
1748 sqlservr.exe
1828 nvsvc32.exe         NVSVCPMMWindowClass
1440 wscntfy.exe
2380 iPodService.exe
2620 alg.exe
3384 iTunes.exe          iTunes
3648 WINWORD.EXE         MarshallChap14_0830 - Microsoft Word
2892 cmd.exe             Visual Studio .NET Whidbey Command Prompt - tlist
2572 Store.exe           Store
2696 tlist.exe
```

The *–p* argument attaches WinDbg to an application based on the process identifier:

```
windbg -p 2572
```

You can also attach to a running process simply with the application name:

```
windbg -pn store.exe
```

Alternatively, WinDbg can be started without being attached to anything. You can later attach to an application using the File menu of the WinDbg user interface. From the File menu, select the *Attach to a Process* command. Choose the debuggee from the list of available processes. The *Open Executable* command on the same menu starts an application and immediately attaches the debugger. This is convenient if the application is not already running.

When using WinDbg, some essential commands are helpful. Most of the WinDbg commands are case insensitive, but there are exceptions. Table 13-2 lists the basic commands.

Table 13-2   Basic WinDbg Commands

Command	Description
g(o)	This command resumes execution of the debugged application.
Ctrl+Break	This keystroke interrupts the running application.
q(uit)	This command quits the debugger.
?	This command displays help documentation.

Now that the basic commands have been presented, we can discuss the more interesting commands.

Displaying the active threads and changing thread context are frequent requests for any debugger. In WinDbg, the tilde (~) command is for thread manipulation.

- The ~ command without parameters lists the threads. Thread identifier, status, and address of the thread environment block include some of the information reported. If the thread context is elsewhere, the current thread is highlighted with the pound (#) prefix.

- The ~n command displays information on the specified thread, where n is the thread number. Thread priority, status, priority class, and other thread-relevant information is presented.

- The ~ns command changes the thread context to the thread that is indicated. The WinDbg prompt is updated to reflect the new thread context. When the context is changed, the context record of the new thread is displayed, which includes the register values.

The following demonstration lists the threads, displays information pertaining to Thread 2, and then selects Thread 3 as the current thread:

```
0:001> ~
   0  Id: a1c.9c0 Suspend: 1 Teb: 7ffde000 Unfrozen
.  1  Id: a1c.804 Suspend: 1 Teb: 7ffdd000 Unfrozen
   2  Id: a1c.ea0 Suspend: 1 Teb: 7ffdc000 Unfrozen
   3  Id: a1c.de0 Suspend: 1 Teb: 7ffdb000 Unfrozen
#  4  Id: a1c.c04 Suspend: 1 Teb: 7ffda000 Unfrozen
0:001> ~2
   2  Id: a1c.ea0 Suspend: 1 Teb: 7ffdc000 Unfrozen
      Start: mscorwks!Thread::intermediateThreadProc (79ee80cf)
      Priority: 2  Priority class: 32
0:001> ~3s
eax=4ec62ef0 ebx=0103fe7c ecx=0000d9c7 edx=7c90eb94 esi=00000000 edi=7ffdf000
eip=7c90eb94 esp=0103fe54 ebp=0103fef0 iopl=0         nv up ei pl zr na po nc
cs=001b  ss=0023  ds=0023  es=0023  fs=003b  gs=0000             efl=00000246
ntdll!KiFastSystemCallRet:
7c90eb94 c3                  ret
```

Stack Trace Commands

Stack traces are invaluable when debugging. Even for managed code, viewing the unmanaged call stack can be informative. As demonstrated later in this chapter, many of the answers and hints to abnormal conditions in managed code are found in the unmanaged world.

In WinDbg, variations of the *k* command present varied permutations of a stack trace. Optionally, you can follow a stack trace command with a number, which indicates the depth of the call stack.

Table 13-3 explains the common stack trace commands.

Table 13-3   Stack Trace Commands

Command	Description
k	This command lists the methods on the call stack. In addition, the child frame pointer and the return address of the calling method are listed in columns. No parameters are displayed.
kb	This command lists the call stack and the first three parameters of the methods.
kp	This command lists the call stack and the entire parameter list of the methods.
kn	This command lists the call stack with the frame number for each method. You can use the frame information to move between frames on the call stack using the frame directive.

The following is the call stack from a thread in the Store application. Three parameters are displayed because the *kb* command is used.

```
0:003> kb
ChildEBP RetAddr  Args to Child
0103fe50 7c90e9ab 7c8094f2 00000002 0103fe7c ntdll!KiFastSystemCallRet
0103fe54 7c8094f2 00000002 0103fe7c 00000001 ntdll!ZwWaitForMultipleObjects+0xc
0103fef0 77d495f9 00000002 0103ff18 00000000 KERNEL32!WaitForMultipleObjectsEx+0x12c
0103ff4c 77d496a8 00000001 0103ffac ffffffff USER32!RealMsgWaitForMultipleObjectsEx+0x13e
0103ff68 4ec95846 00000001 0103ffac 00000000 USER32!MsgWaitForMultipleObjects+0x1f
0103ffb4 7c80b50b 00000000 00000000 0012e0d0 gdiplus!BackgroundThreadProc+0x59
0103ffec 00000000 4ec957ed 00000000 00000000 KERNEL32!BaseThreadStart+0x37
```

What if you want the stack trace of every thread? Each thread could be selected and a *k* command submitted. However, that approach becomes tedious if there are dozens of threads. The solution is '~*'. Commands prefixed with '~*' are applied to all threads of the application. This command performs a stack trace on every thread:

```
~* k
```

Display Memory Commands

Displaying memory is another important tool of debugging. The *d* command is the fundamental display memory command. There is a bounty of variants to the *d* command for dumping different types and quantities of memory. Display commands list rows and columns of data. Rows begin with a memory address. This is the starting address for the contiguous bytes displayed on that row. The memory is organized in row order. By default, bytes are organized in two-byte columns. Certain display commands add byte translation at the end of every row. This is a typical display of memory:

```
0:003> d 0103fe50
0103fe50  cc 33 66 00 ab e9 90 7c-f2 94 80 7c 02 00 00 00  .3f....|...|....
0103fe60  7c fe 03 01 01 00 00 00-00 00 00 00 00 00 00 00  |...............
```

```
0103fe70  00 00 00 00 02 00 00 00-00 00 00 00 94 06 00 00   ...............
0103fe80  8c 06 00 00 cc 99 99 00-cc 99 cc 00 cc 99 ff 00   ...............
0103fe90  cc cc 00 00 cc cc 33 00-cc cc 66 00 14 00 00 00   ......3...f.....
0103fea0  01 00 00 00 00 00 00 00-00 00 00 00 10 00 00 00   ...............
0103feb0  cc ff 66 00 cc ff 99 00-cc ff cc 00 00 b0 fd 7f   ..f.............
0103fec0  00 c0 fd 7f ff 00 33 00-00 00 00 00 7c fe 03 01   ......3.....|...
```

This is the syntax of a display command:

dL address1 address2

The second letter (*L*) of the display command varies based on the actual display command, such as *dc*, *dd*, and *du*. The second letter is also case sensitive. *address1* is the beginning address, whereas *address2* is the ending address. Memory is displayed from *address1* to *address2*. Omit the ending address, and a default number of bytes are displayed. If neither the beginning nor the ending memory address is provided, the command displays from the current address forward.

Table 13-4 lists some of the commands that display memory.

Table 13-4   Common Display Memory Commands

Command	Description
d	This command repeats the previous display command and defaults to the *db* command.
da	This command displays the ASCII interpretation of the memory.
dc	This command displays the data in four-byte columns.
dd	This command is the same as *dc*, except the byte translation is omitted at the end of each row.
du	This command displays the Unicode interpretation of the memory.

The following command has four-byte columns of memory, three columns per row, and a starting address. The */c* option controls the number of columns displayed:

```
0:003> dd /c 3 0103fe50
0103fe50  006633cc 7c90e9ab 7c8094f2
0103fe5c  00000002 0103fe7c 00000001
0103fe68  00000000 00000000 00000000
0103fe74  00000002 00000000 00000694
0103fe80  0000068c 009999cc 00cc99cc
0103fe8c  00ff99cc 0000cccc 0033cccc
0103fe98  0066cccc 00000014 00000001
0103fea4  00000000 00000000 00000010
0103feb0  0066ffcc 0099ffcc 00ccffcc
0103febc  7ffdb000 7ffdc000 003300ff
0103fec8  00000000 0103fe7c
```

Breakpoints Memory Commands

Debugging requires being a detective, and breakpoints are important investigative tools. Breakpoints interrupt a program based on certain conditions, such as memory address, location, or event. Setting effective breakpoints is an art, which is obtained with experience.

Naturally, WinDbg offers several breakpoint commands, as detailed in Table 13-5.

Table 13-5 Common Display Memory Commands

Command	Description
bp	This is the standard breakpoint command. The program is interrupted when execution reaches the specified location.
	This is an abbreviated syntax for the *bp* command:
	bp *location options*
	The /1 option is useful for defining one-off breakpoints. This type of breakpoint is automatically removed after being hit. Therefore, the breakpoint is reached only once.
ba	This command is break on access to a memory address.
	This is the abbreviated syntax for the *ba* command:
	ba *options size address*
	options specifies the action to break on:
	■ *e* – execute
	■ *r* – read/write
	■ *w* – write
	■ *i* – input/output
	size is the width of the memory address.
bc	This command clears a breakpoint. You can clear multiple breakpoints in a space- or comma-delimited list. Alternatively, specify a range with a hyphen.
bl	This command lists the available breakpoints. Multiple breakpoints can be specified as described for the *bc* command.

The following is a demonstration of the breakpoint command. The *sxe* command is the set exception command. This command requests that the debugger interrupt on an exception or other event. In this example, the *sxe* command asks the debugger to interrupt when the *mscorwks* module is loaded, which is where the Common Language Runtime (CLR) is found. For a compound statement, use a semicolon. In the following command, the *sxe* and *g* commands are combined into a compound statement.

The following command breaks when the *mscorwks* module is loaded (the application is then resumed):

```
0:000> sxe ld mscorwks;g
ModLoad: 77dd0000 77e6b000   C:\WINDOWS\system32\ADVAPI32.dll
ModLoad: 77e70000 77f01000   C:\WINDOWS\system32\RPCRT4.dll
ModLoad: 77f60000 77fd6000   C:\WINDOWS\system32\SHLWAPI.dll
ModLoad: 77f10000 77f56000   C:\WINDOWS\system32\GDI32.dll
ModLoad: 77d40000 77dd0000   C:\WINDOWS\system32\USER32.dll
ModLoad: 77c10000 77c68000   C:\WINDOWS\system32\msvcrt.dll
ModLoad: 76390000 763ad000   C:\WINDOWS\system32\IMM32.DLL
ModLoad: 629c0000 629c9000   C:\WINDOWS\system32\LPK.DLL
ModLoad: 74d90000 74dfb000   C:\WINDOWS\system32\USP10.dll
ModLoad: 79e70000 7a3cf000   C:\WINDOWS\Microsoft.NET\Framework\v2.0.50727\mscorwks.dll
```

```
eax=00000000 ebx=00000000 ecx=009f0000 edx=7c90eb94 esi=00000000 edi=00000000
eip=7c90eb94 esp=0012f1c0 ebp=0012f2b4 iopl=0         nv up ei ng nz ac po nc
cs=001b  ss=0023  ds=0023  es=0023  fs=003b  gs=0000             efl=00000296
ntdll!KiFastSystemCallRet:
7c90eb94 c3              ret
```

The following command sets a breakpoint on the *ExecuteMainMethod* method:

```
0:000> bp mscorwks!SystemDomain::ExecuteMainMethod;g
ModLoad: 78130000 781ca000   C:\WINDOWS\Microsoft.NET\Framework\v2.0.50727\MSVCR80.dll
ModLoad: 7c9c0000 7d1d4000   C:\WINDOWS\system32\shell32.dll
ModLoad: 773d0000 774d2000   C:\WINDOWS\WinSxS\x86_Microsoft.Windows.Common-
Controls_6595b64144ccf1df_6.0.2600.2180_x-ww_a84f1ff9\comctl32.dll
ModLoad: 5d090000 5d127000   C:\WINDOWS\system32\comctl32.dll
ModLoad: 60340000 60348000   C:\WINDOWS\Microsoft.NET\Framework\v2.0.50727\culture.dll
ModLoad: 790c0000 79baa000   C:\WINDOWS\assembly\NativeImages_v2.0.50727_32\mscorlib\cee6ddb
471db1c489d9b4c39549861b5\mscorlib.ni.dll
Breakpoint 0 hit
eax=0012ff38 ebx=00000002 ecx=00000000 edx=ffffffff esi=00000000 edi=00000000
eip=79efb428 esp=0012ff1c ebp=0012ff68 iopl=0         nv up ei pl nz na pe nc
cs=001b  ss=0023  ds=0023  es=0023  fs=003b  gs=0000             efl=00000202
mscorwks!SystemDomain::ExecuteMainMethod:
79efb428 55              push    ebp
```

After the breakpoint is hit, the *kb* command performs a stack trace. You see *ExecuteMain-Method* in the call stack:

```
0:000> kb
ChildEBP RetAddr  Args to Child
0012ff18 79efb3cb 00400000 00000000 b4ebfe93 mscorwks!SystemDomain::ExecuteMainMethod
0012ff68 79ef8bc8 00400000 b4ebfe4b 00080000 mscorwks!ExecuteEXE+0x59
0012ffb0 790122f6 00d9fa9c 79e70000 0012fff0 mscorwks!_CorExeMain+0x11b
0012ffc0 7c816d4f 00080000 00d9fa9c 7ffd8000 mscoree!_CorExeMain+0x2c
0012fff0 00000000 790122c2 00000000 78746341 KERNEL32!BaseProcessStart+0x23
```

Step Commands

After reaching a breakpoint, it is common to step through an application and evaluate the results. There are also plenty of other reasons and opportunities to step through an application. The best means of stepping through an application is by using the Debugging toolbar. (Choose the View menu and the Toolbar option to display the Debugging toolbar.)

Figure 13-6 shows the Step buttons on the Debugging toolbar: the Step In, Step Over, Step Out, and Run to Cursor buttons.

Figure 13-6   Step buttons on the Debugging toolbar

WinDbg Directives   WinDbg commands affect the application currently being debugged. The commands display, modify, or otherwise affect or inspect the debuggee. Conversely, WinDbg directives alter the debugging session. For example, the *.load* directive loads a debugging extension dynamic-link library (DLL). The *.logopen* directive opens a log file and echoes any subsequent activity to this file.

There are several WinDbg directions. Table 13-6 includes some of the available directives. Directives are prefixed with a dot (.).

Table 13-6   WinDbg Directives

Command	Description
.load dllname	This command loads a debugger extension DLL. Extension commands are exposed as the exported functions of the DLL. Developers of managed code routinely load the SOS (SOS.dll) debugger extension. Commands from debugger extensions are prefixed with an exclamation point (!).
.unload dllname	This command unloads a debugger extension.
.chain	This command lists the debugger extensions that are presently available.
.reload	This command reloads symbols and is usually requested after the symbol path has been updated. Normally, symbols are retrieved as needed. The */f* option forces the immediate load of all symbols.
.logopen filename	This command opens a log file and echoes any subsequent activity to this file.
.logclose	This command closes the log file.
.kill	This command terminates the current debuggee and ends the debugging session.
.frame n	This command shifts the stack to the designated frame number or displays the current local context.
.srcpath	This command sets or displays the source code path.
.dump options filename	This command creates a user- or kernel-mode dump, which is used for postmortem analysis. *.dump filename* creates a minidump. The following command creates a minidump with full memory and handle information: *.dump /mfh filename* This command creates a full dump. The full dump command is available only in kernel-mode operations of WinDbg (which is not discussed in this chapter): *.dump /f*

Son of Strike (SOS)

SOS is a debugger extension for debugging managed code and is used in collaboration with the unmanaged debugger to diagnose abnormal conditions. Expect that some problems cannot be isolated with SOS alone. It is the collaboration between the unmanaged debugger and SOS that is powerful. Problems in managed applications are diagnosable without SOS, but that requires your interpretation of complex commands and internal structures. With SOS, that challenge is avoided, allowing developers to concentrate on the problem— debugging the application.

Any of the following statements loads the SOS extension DLL. To load a particular version of SOS, provide a fully qualified directory path. When live debugging, the current version of WinDbg automatically loads SOS. However, it is not automatically loaded for postmortem analysis.

.load sos

.load sos.dll

.load c:\path\sos.dll

SOS Walkthrough Part I

This walkthrough is an introduction to SOS. Details from previous walkthroughs and demonstration are omitted for brevity. Some of the listings have also been abbreviated for clarity.

1. Start the Store application. Open the Transaction dialog box, as shown in Figure 13-7. For this debugging session, do not complete or close this dialog box.

Figure 13-7　Store application and the Transaction dialog box

2. Launch the WinDbg debugger and then attach it to the Store application.

3. SOS has a *!threads* command, which lists the managed threads of the application. Use the *!threads* command. This is the abbreviated result:

```
0:004> !threads
ThreadCount: 2
UnstartedThread: 0
BackgroundThread: 1
PendingThread: 0
DeadThread: 0
Hosted Runtime: no
```

	ID	OSID	ThreadOBJ	State	PreEmptive GC	GC Alloc Context	Domain	Lock Count
0	1	424	001501f8	6020	Enabled	013da5dc:013dadb8	001483a8	0
2	2	c24	00153e40	b220	Enabled	00000000:00000000	001483a8	0

4. Change to Thread 0, which is a managed thread.

```
0:004> ~0s
eax=790ff90c ebx=01392b50 ecx=013a7704 edx=0000ce7d esi=00000000 edi=013da5b8
eip=7c90eb94 esp=0012edb4 ebp=0012ee4c iopl=0         nv up ei pl zr na po nc
cs=001b  ss=0023  ds=0023  es=0023  fs=003b  gs=0000         efl=00000246
ntdll!KiFastSystemCallRet:
7c90eb94 c3              ret
```

5. Enter the *!clrstack* command to show a stack trace of the current thread. The *p* option requests that the parameters be displayed.

```
0:000> !clrstack -p
OS Thread Id: 0x424 (0)
ESP       EIP
0012edc0 7c90eb94 [InlinedCallFrame: 0012edc0] System.Windows.Forms.UnsafeNativeMethod
s.WaitMessage()
0012edbc 7b094838 System.Windows.Forms.Application+ComponentManager.System.Windows.For
ms.UnsafeNativeMethods.IMsoComponentManager.FPushMessageLoop(Int32, Int32, Int32)
    PARAMETERS:
        this = 0x013a76ac
        dwComponentID = <no data>
        reason = 0x00000004
        pvLoopData = 0x00000000

0012eef8 7b22e03e System.Windows.Forms.Form.ShowDialog(System.Windows.Forms.IWin32Window)
    PARAMETERS:
        this = 0x013b4494
        owner = <no data>
```

6. The *ShowDialog* method appears in the stack trace, where the parameters are also shown. The *this* reference is the first parameter of the method. Use the *dumpobj* command to dump the *this* reference, which confirms that the *Store.Transaction* form is displayed.

```
0:000> !dumpobj 0x013b4494
Name: Store.Transaction
MethodTable: 00d453a4
EEClass: 00db3034
Size: 372(0x174) bytes
 (C:\store\Store.exe)
Fields:
      MT     Field   Offset                 Type VT     Attr     Value Name
790fa098  4000184        4        System.Object  0 instance 00000000 __identity
7a765ca4  40008bc        8 ...ponentModel.ISite  0 instance 00000000 site
7a762e84  40008bd        c ....EventHandlerList  0 instance 013b6964 events
790fa098  40008bb      108        System.Object  0   static 00000000 EventDisposed
7b4777e4  40010fa       10 ...ntrolNativeWindow  0 instance 013b55c4 window
7b4754b4  40010fb       14 ...ows.Forms.Control  0 instance 00000000 parent
7b4754b4  40010fc       18 ...ows.Forms.Control  0 instance 00000000 reflectParent
7b478924  40010fd       1c ...orms.CreateParams  0 instance 013b560c createParams
790fe920  40010fe       34        System.Int32  0 instance      346 x
790fe920  40010ff       38        System.Int32  0 instance       22 y
790fe920  4001100       3c        System.Int32  0 instance      266 width
```

SOS Commands

Table 13-7 is an overview of some of the SOS commands. For a complete listing, see the help command.

Table 13-7   Son of Strike Commands

Command	Description
!ClrStack	This command displays the call stack of the current thread.
	Here are some of the options:
	■ The *-l* option includes the local variables in the output.
	■ The *-p* option includes the parameters in the output.
	■ The *-a* option combines both the *-l* and *-p* options.
!DumpHeap	This command first displays the objects that are on the managed heap. It then displays statistics about the type of objects on the managed heap.
	Here are some of the options:
	■ The *–stat* option displays the type of objects alone.
	■ The *–min* option excludes objects less than the minimum address from the report.
	■ The *–max* option excludes objects greater than the maximum address from the report.
	■ The *–mt* option lists only objects of the provided method table address.
	■ The *startaddress* option is the starting address of the report; for example: *!DumpHeap 7b471e40*.
	■ The *endaddress* option is the ending address of the report; for example: *!DumpHeap 7b471e40 7b471e88*.
!DumpIL mdaddress	This command dumps the MSIL of the method associated with the method descriptor.
!DumpMT mtaddress	This command dumps information about the method table. The *–md* option lists information on the method descriptors in the method table, such as the function names and method descriptor addresses.
!DumpObj objaddress	This command dumps information on the specific object.
!DumpStackObjects option	This command lists value types and references that are on stack of the current thread. The only option is *-verify*.
!EEHeap options	This command dumps information on Generation 0, 1, 2, and the managed heap. The *–loader* option lists the private heaps of each *AppDomain*, module, and heap associated with the JIT compiler.
!EEVersion	This command displays information of the run-time environment, such as the version number.
!FinalizeQueue option	This command lists the objects on the finalization queue. For additional information on *SyncBlocks* and *RuntimeCallableWrappers*, use the *–detail* option.

Table 13-7   Son of Strike Commands (Continued)

Command	Description
!GCroot -options objaddress	This command lists instances that hold references to the specified object. The *–nostacks* option excludes references held on the stack.
!IP2MD jitaddress	This command displays the method descriptor of a jitted method.
!Name2EE program target	If *target* is a type, the command dumps the method table of that type. If *target* is a method name, the method descriptor of that method is dumped.
!Syncblk	This command lists the indexes of the sync block table.
!Threads	This command lists the managed threads.
!Token2EE token	For this command, the token must be an entry of the *typedef* or *methoddef* table. If it is a *typedef* token, the method table address and other information about the token are displayed. If it is a *methoddef* token, the corresponding method descriptor is displayed.
!Help command	This command displays detailed help on SOS commands. Without the *command* option, an overview of all the commands is displayed.

SOS Walkthrough Part II

Now that a few more commands have been introduced, an additional walkthrough is helpful. The following walkthrough dumps the source code, MSIL, and assembly code of the *btnTransaction_Click* button handler, which is informative.

1. Start the walkthrough by running the Store application and attach WinDbg to the application.

2. Dump information about the *btnTransaction_Click* method with the *!name2ee* command. Notice that the method has not been jitted yet, which means that the method has not been invoked before. A function is jitted when it is first invoked.

```
0:004> !name2ee store.exe Store.Form1.btnTransaction_Click
Module: 00d40c14 (Store.exe)
Token: 0x06000004
MethodDesc: 00d43968
Name: Store.Form1.btnTransaction_Click(System.Object, System.EventArgs)
Not JITTED yet. Use !bpmd -md 00d43968 to break on run.
0:004> !u 00d43968
Not jitted yet
```

3. Continue the Store application using the g(o) command and click the Add Transactions button. Interrupt the program in the debugger with Ctrl+Break. Dump information on *Store.Form1.btnTransaction_Click* again. This time, the method is shown as jitted, and the virtual address of the cached native binary is displayed:

```
0:004> !name2ee store.exe Store.Form1.btnTransaction_Click
Module: 00d40c14 (Store.exe)
Token: 0x06000004
MethodDesc: 00d43968
Name: Store.Form1.btnTransaction_Click(System.Object, System.EventArgs)
JITTED Code Address: 00de07c0
```

4. The *!u* command displays the assembly code of a jitted method. Use this command for the *btnTransaction_Click* method:

```
0:004> !u 00d43968
Normal JIT generated code
Store.Form1.btnTransaction_Click(System.Object, System.EventArgs)
Begin 00de07c0, size 3e9
00de07c0 55                    push     ebp
00de07c1 8bec                  mov      ebp,esp
00de07c3 57                    push     edi
00de07c4 56                    push     esi
00de07c5 53                    push     ebx
00de07c6 83ec50                sub      esp,0x50
00de07c9 33c0                  xor      eax,eax
00de07cb 8945d0                mov      [ebp-0x30],eax
00de07ce 8945c4                mov      [ebp-0x3c],eax
00de07d1 33c0                  xor      eax,eax
00de07d3 8945e8                mov      [ebp-0x18],eax
00de07d6 894dc0                mov      [ebp-0x40],ecx
00de07d9 8955dc                mov      [ebp-0x24],edx
00de07dc 833dc80dd40000        cmp      dword ptr [00d40dc8],0x0
```

5. Challenge two is to list the MSIL code for the *btnTransaction_Click* method. The *dumpil* command shows the MSIL code of the method:

```
0:004> !dumpil 00d43968
ilAddr = 0040247c
IL_0000: nop
.try
{
  IL_0001: nop
  IL_0002: ldarg.0
  IL_0003: ldfld Store.Form1::txtNumber
  IL_0008: callvirt System.Windows.Forms.Control::get_Text
  IL_000d: call System.Int32::Parse
  IL_0012: stloc.0
  IL_0013: nop
  IL_0014: leave.s IL_001d
} // end .try
.catch
{
  IL_0016: pop
  IL_0017: nop
  IL_0018: ldc.i4.1
  IL_0019: stloc.0
  IL_001a: nop
  IL_001b: leave.s IL_001d
} // end .catch
```

6. The final task is to display the source code. Set the source code path in WinDbg. From the File menu, choose the Source File Path command and then enter the source code path. Enter the *lsf* command to set *form1.cs* as the source code file. List the source with the *ls* command. For the walkthrough, lines 10 to 50 are displayed:

```
0:004> lsf form1.cs
0:004> ls 10, 40
    22:
    23:          private void btnTransaction_Click(object sender, EventArgs e)
```

```
24:            {
25:                int numofTransactions;
26:                try
27:                {
28:                    numofTransactions= int.Parse(txtNumber.Text);
29:                }
30:                catch
31:                {
32:                    numofTransactions = 1;
33:                }
34:                for (int count = 0; count < numofTransactions; ++count)
35:                {
36:                    int itemTotal=0;
```

Dumps

Dumps are used for postmortem analysis, which is sometimes the most effective means of debugging an application. When a program intermittently crashes, postmortem analysis may be the sole option to resolve the problem. You can capture a dump when the crash occurs, which is then used to diagnose the problem. Production applications are not ideal for live debugging. How do you perform live debugging on an active Web server? Convenience is another advantage to postmortem analysis. You remove the dump to a developer machine that hosts an assortment of debugging tools and resources. In this environment, diagnosing the problem is much easier.

Postmortem analysis is usually conducted by scrutinizing a dump, which is a memory snapshot of an application. There are full dumps and minidumps. A minidump is only a snapshot of the application memory. Full dumps also include other modules in the memory snapshot—even system modules. The benefit of a full dump is convenience, and symbols are more easily aligned. The disadvantage is that full dumps tend to be large. Not all minidumps are equivalent—some minidumps contain more information than others. Check the documentation for the command or tool that creates a minidump to confirm what the minidump includes.

Remember that memory dumps are static. The debugging paradigm is different from performing live debugging. You cannot step through the application, threads cannot be restarted, and so on.

As documented earlier, the *.dump* directive in WinDbg creates dump files. Dump files can also be created with ADPlus and Dr. Watson tools.

ADPlus

The ADPlus tool is downloaded from the Debugging Tools for Windows Web site at Microsoft.com. It is a Microsoft VBScript that automates the CDB debugger. Use ADPlus to debug applications that hang or crash. The utility creates dump and log files for postmortem analysis. Unique names are assigned to these files to avoid overriding previously generated files. ADPlus operates in either the crash or hang mode.

In crash mode, ADPlus attaches *cdb* to the target processes. It is attached invasively. You run ADPlus before the application crashes. At that time, a minidump and log file are created. ADPlus will also write an entry into the Event Log. A crash is interpreted as the application ending from an unhandled exception or other abnormal condition. To detach prematurely before a crash, open the minimized CDB console window and press Ctrl+C. This is the syntax of running ADPlus in the crash mode. Multiple processes can be attached to simultaneously. All instances of the named processes are attached.

adplus −crash −pn *processname*[1] −pn *processname*[2] −pn *processname*[n]

Alternatively, the process identifier can be used to identify the target processes:

adplus −crash −p *pid*[1] −p *pid*[2] −p *pid*[n]

In hang mode, run ADPlus after the hang occurs, which attaches CDB to the target application noninvasively. The debuggee is resumed after the dump is created. This is the syntax to start ADPlus in the hang mode:

adplus −hang −pn *processname*[1] −pn *processname*[2] −pn *processname*[n]

adplus −hang −p *pid*[1] −p *pid*[2] −p *pid*[n]

There are three other options worth mentioning:

- **O(utput) option**   This option sets the output directory for dump and log files.
- **Q(uiet) option**   This option suppresses alerts related to ADPlus.
- **N(otify) option**   This option notifies a user that an application has crashed.

ADPlus Walkthrough   The Store application for this walkthrough has an error and unexpectedly crashes. ADPlus is used to create a dump when the application crashes. The dump is then opened in WinDbg, and the problem is isolated:

1. Start the Store application.

2. Click the Hang button. As expected, this procedure hangs the application.

3. Run ADPlus in hang mode to attach the CDB debugger to the Store application. Get the correct process identifier from the *tlist* utility:

   ```
   c:\store>adplus -hang -p 3520 -o c:\dumps
   Attaching the debugger to: STORE.EXE
                           (Process ID: 3520)
   ```

4. Start WinDbg and open the dump. From the File menu, choose the Open Crash Dump command. Find and open the dump.

5. Load the Son of Strike extension. Change to Thread 0 and request a managed stack trace. The following is a partial listing of the call stack. It shows correctly that the *btnHang_Click* handler was the last method entered. This provides a starting point in uncovering the culprit that caused the hang.

   ```
   0:000> .load sos
   0:000> !clrstack
   OS Thread Id: 0xae8 (0)
   ESP        EIP
   ```

```
0012f030 00de0906 Store.Form1.btnHang_Click(System.Object, System.EventArgs)
0012f044 7b070a8b System.Windows.Forms.Control.OnClick(System.EventArgs)
0012f054 7b114cd9 System.Windows.Forms.Button.OnClick(System.EventArgs)
0012f060 7b114ddf System.Windows.Forms.Button.OnMouseUp(System.Windows.Forms.MouseEventArgs)
0012f084 7b0dfeea System.Windows.Forms.Control.WmMouseUp(System.Windows.Forms.Message
ByRef, System.Windows.Forms.MouseButtons, Int32)
0012f0d0 7b082bbf System.Windows.Forms.Control.WndProc(System.Windows.Forms.Message ByRef)
0012f0d4 7b09149e [InlinedCallFrame: 0012f0d4]
0012f170 7b0913bb System.Windows.Forms.Button.WndProc(System.Windows.Forms.Message ByRef)
0012f178 7b08a70d System.Windows.Forms.Control+ControlNativeWindow.OnMessage(System.Wi
ndows.Forms.Message ByRef)
0012f17c 7b08a6e6 System.Windows.Forms.Control+ControlNativeWindow.WndProc(System.Windows
.Forms.Message ByRef)
0012f190 7b08a535 System.Windows.Forms.NativeWindow.Callback(IntPtr, Int32, IntPtr, IntPtr)
0012f324 003420d4 [NDirectMethodFrameStandalone: 0012f324] System.Windows.Forms.Unsafe
NativeMethods.DispatchMessageW(MSG ByRef)
0012f334 7b094682 System.Windows.Forms.Application+ComponentManager.System.Windows.For
ms.UnsafeNativeMethods.IMsoComponentManager.FPushMessageLoop(Int32, Int32, Int32)
0012f3d4 7b094249 System.Windows.Forms.Application+ThreadContext.RunMessageLoopInner(I
nt32, System.Windows.Forms.ApplicationContext)
0012f440 7b094087 System.Windows.Forms.Application+ThreadContext.RunMessageLoop(Int32,
 System.Windows.Forms.ApplicationContext)
0012f470 7b0d66ea System.Windows.Forms.Application.Run(System.Windows.Forms.Form)
0012f480 00de00a8 Store.Program.Main()
0012f69c 79e80b8b [GCFrame: 0012f69c]
```

Dr. Watson

Dr. Watson (drwtsn32.exe) also creates dumps. This product is installed with the operating system. On nondeveloper machines, Dr. Watson is the only JIT debugger present. Dr. Watson attaches to a failing application to create a log file and optionally a dump file.

Figure 13-8 shows the main window of Dr. Watson. In this window, you configure Dr. Watson for JIT debugging.

Figure 13-8   Main window of Dr. Watson

The following list describes the configurable items in the Dr. Watson window:

- **Log File Path**   The path for the log files created by the Dr. Watson.
- **Crash Dump**   The path and name of the dump file.
- **Wave File**   The path to whatever musical accompaniment you deem appropriate for an application failure. *Flight of the Valkyrie* might be appropriate.
- **Number of Instructions**   The number of instructions to disassemble around the instruction pointer.
- **Number of Errors to Save**   The maximum number of errors to save in the log file.
- **Crash Dump Type**   The type of dump request: full, mini, or NT-compatible.
- **Dump Symbol Table**   Dump the name and address of every symbol into the log file.
- **Dump All Thread Contexts**   Include the thread context, register values, and other context data in the log file.
- **Append To Existing Log File**   Add the next log entry from a program failure to the current log file. If not selected, a new log file is created for each failure.
- **Visual Notification**   Display a dialog box to notify of program failure and just-in time debugging.
- **Sound Notification**   Play the *Flight of the Valkyrie* or whatever WAV file is specified.
- **Create Crash Dump File**   When a program fails, create a dump file.

Dr. Watson Walkthrough   Following is a walkthrough of Dr. Watson, which is the only walkthrough that does not use the Store application. The walkthrough uses the Crash application. The Crash application fails immediately after the application is launched.

1. Make sure that Dr. Watson is installed as the native debugger.

   ```
   C:\>drwtsn32 -i
   ```

2. Configure Dr. Watson to create a minidump file, set the dump file path and name, and then request notification. Accept all other defaults.

3. Run the Crash program. This program should immediately hang, which will prompt notification from Dr. Watson.

4. Confirm that the dump and log file are created. Inspect the log file, which includes general information, system information, task list, module list, thread context, stack trace, symbol table, and a variety of raw dumps:

   ```
   Microsoft (R) DrWtsn32
   Copyright (C) 1985-2001 Microsoft Corp. All rights reserved.

   Application exception occurred:
           App: C:\codew\Crash\Debug\Crash.exe (pid=4004)
   ```

```
            When: 9/5/2005 @ 08:19:29.796
            Exception number: 80000007
()


*----> System Information <----*
        Computer Name: DONISMLAPTOP
        User Name: Donis
        Terminal Session Id: 0
        Number of Processors: 2
        Processor Type: x86 Family 15 Model 2 Stepping 9
        Windows Version: 5.1
        Current Build: 2600
        Service Pack: 2
        Current Type: Multiprocessor Free
        Registered Organization:
        Registered Owner: Donis


*----> Task List <----*
   0 System Process
   4 System
 788 smss.exe
 908 csrss.exe
 932 winlogon.exe
 976 services.exe
 988 lsass.exe
1152 svchost.exe
1220 svchost.exe


*----> Module List <----*
(0000000000400000 - 000000000041a000: C:\codew\Crash\Debug\Crash.exe
(0000000010200000 -
0000000010320000: C:\WINDOWS\WinSxS\x86_Microsoft.VC80.DebugCRT_1fc8b3b9a1e18e3b_8.0.
50727.7_x-ww_ec5d0b23\MSVCR80D.dll
(00000000629c0000 - 00000000629c9000: C:\WINDOWS\system32\LPK.DLL
(0000000074d90000 - 0000000074dfb000: C:\WINDOWS\system32\USP10.dll
(0000000076390000 - 00000000763ad000: C:\WINDOWS\system32\IMM32.DLL
(0000000077b40000 - 0000000077b62000: C:\WINDOWS\system32\Apphelp.dll
(0000000077c00000 - 0000000077c08000: C:\WINDOWS\system32\VERSION.dll
(0000000077c10000 - 0000000077c68000: C:\WINDOWS\system32\msvcrt.dll
(0000000077d40000 - 0000000077dd0000: C:\WINDOWS\system32\USER32.dll


*----> State Dump for Thread Id 0xb5c <----*

eax=00390000 ebx=0012f6fc ecx=00001000 edx=7c90eb94 esi=0000007c edi=00000000
eip=7c90eb94 esp=0012f6e0 ebp=0012f9e8 iopl=0          nv up ei pl nz na pe nc
cs=001b  ss=0023  ds=0023  es=0023  fs=003b  gs=0000              efl=00000202


*----> Stack Back Trace <----*
ChildEBP RetAddr  Args to Child
0012f9e8 102116d1 0012fa5c 00000002 00000000 ntdll!KiFastSystemCallRet
0012fa0c 004119a2 c0000005 0012fa5c 1021c2b4 MSVCR80D!XcptFilter+0x61
0012fa18 1021c2b4 00000000 00000000 00000000 Crash!__tmainCRTStartup+0x1f2
0012ffb8 0041179d 0012fff0 7c816d4f 023dd680 MSVCR80D!seh_longjmp_unwind4+0x2e
0012ffc0 7c816d4f 023dd680 7c90e1fe 7ffdd000 Crash!wmainCRTStartup+0xd
```

Memory Management

Traditionally, memory-related issues have been the impetus to a vast majority of bugs. Win32 processes, including managed applications that run in the Windows environment, own several assets. Of those assets, virtual memory is one of the most important. Win32 processes normally own four gigabytes of virtual memory, where the operating system resides in the upper two gigabytes. The upper two gigabytes are shared and protected. There is no reason to load the operating system for each instance of a Win32 process. The lower two gigabytes are private memory in which the application code, heaps, static data area, stack, and other aspects of the application are loaded. This memory is private and protected from access by other processes. Virtual Memory Manager (VMM), which is the kernel-level component of the NT Executive, guards private memory from incidental or deliberate external modifications.

The managed heap is created in the private memory of a managed application. There are several families of APIs that allocate memory from the available virtual memory, including the Heap APIs such as *HeapCreate*, *HeapAlloc*, and *HeapFree*. The Memory Mapped family of APIs include *CreateFileMapping*, *MapViewOfFile*, *UnmapViewOfFile*, and related functions. The Virtual APIs include *VirtualAlloc*, *VirtualFree*, and others. Internally, the Heap and Memory Mapped File APIs decompose to Virtual APIs.

Initially, the garbage collector (GC) calls *VirtualAlloc* with the *MEM_RESERVE* flag and reserves a block of memory. It then requests memory from the reserved area with successive calls to *VirtualAlloc*, but with the *MEM_COMMIT* flag. When committing memory, the first parameter of *VirtualAlloc* is the base address to a block of committed memory. The GC keeps the ending address of the previous memory allocation. With that information, it can calculate the base address of the next block of committed memory, which is stacked upon the previous allocation. This is a quick and efficient method of allocating memory. *VirtualAlloc* can be called with a null first parameter, which requires the VMM search for an appropriate location to commit memory, which is expensive. This is the syntax of *VirtualAlloc*:

LPVOID *VirtualAlloc*(LPVOID lpAddress, SIZE_T dwSize,

DWORD *flAllocation*Type, DWORD flProtect)

The following is a stack trace and shows *VirtualAlloc* being called in a managed program. The first argument (0x00b54000) is the location of the allocation. This is where the memory is being committed.

```
0:000> kb
ChildEBP RetAddr  Args to Child
0012e674 79e74391 00b54000 00001000 00001000 KERNEL32!VirtualAlloc
0012e6b4 79e74360 00b54000 00001000 00001000 mscorwks!EEVirtualAlloc+0x104
0012e6c8 79e74348 7a38b1b0 00b54000 00001000 mscorwks!CExecutionEngine::ClrVirtualAlloc+0x15
0012e6e0 79e8b7a4 00b54000 00001000 00001000 mscorwks!ClrVirtualAlloc+0x1b
0012e718 79e9f940 000000a8 00000001 00010000 mscorwks!UnlockedLoaderHeap::GetMoreCommittedPa
ges+0x90
```

```
0012e750 79e7f89f 000000a4 00000004 0012e794 mscorwks!UnlockedLoaderHeap::UnlockedAllocAlign
edMem_NoThrow+0x6c
0012e764 79e7f853 000000a4 00000004 0012e794 mscorwks!UnlockedLoaderHeap::UnlockedAllocAlign
edMem+0x15
0012e7a4 79e85010 0012e7d0 000000a4 00000004 mscorwks!LoaderHeap::RealAllocAlignedMem+0x40
0012e7f0 79e84eca 7a389bec 00000094 00000000 mscorwks!Stub::NewStub+0xc1
0012e834 79e8733c 7a389bec 00000000 00000000 mscorwks!StubLinker::Link+0x59
```

Reference Tree

The GC does not perform reference counting. Some memory models maintain a reference count on each memory object. When the count drops to zero, the object is immediately removed from memory. Overhead attributed to reference counting, especially for objects that are never reclaimable, is considerable. There are two benefits to the reference counting model. First, the cost of garbage collection is distributed across the life of the application. Second, it is proactive. Memory is reclaimed prior to being needed.

In managed code, a reference tree is erected when garbage collection is initiated, which avoids expensive reference counting. References no longer in the tree are assumed collectable and the memory for those objects is reclaimed. Memory is then consolidated and outstanding references are updated. This phase of memory management prevents fragmentation of the managed heap. The model described ignores finalization for the moment. The tree is not cached between garbage collection cycles. Rebuilding the tree is one reason why garbage collection is expensive. However, garbage collection is performed only when needed, which is a considerable efficiency.

An object is rooted when another object holds a reference to it. Conversely, root objects are not referenced by another object, including static, global, and local objects. C# does not support global objects. The root objects are the base of the object tree. The branches of the tree emerge from the root objects, as shown in Figure 13-8.

Memory Walkthrough

In this tutorial, the Store application is explored again. Three transactions are added and the root reference of each transaction is displayed.

1. Start the Store application and add three transactions.

2. Attach to the Store application with WinDbg.

3. Transactions are instances of the *Item* class. Display information on the *Item* class using the *!name2ee* command:

```
0:004> !name2ee store.exe Store.Item
Module: 00d40c14 (Store.exe)
Token: 0x02000002
MethodTable: 00d442dc
EEClass: 00db21c4
Name: Store.Item
```

4. With the *MethodTable* address, you can list the address of each transaction item. This is information is obtained with the *dumpheap* command:

```
0:004> !dumpheap -mt 00d442dc
 Address        MT      Size
013a03b8 00d442dc       20
013b409c 00d442dc       20
013bca10 00d442dc       20
total 3 objects
Statistics:
      MT    Count TotalSize Class Name
00d442dc       3        60 Store.Item
Total 3 objects
```

5. Check the root of each object using the *!gcroot* command. This is a partial listing from the first *Item* object:

```
0:004> !gcroot 013a03b8
Note: Roots found on stacks may be false positives. Run "!help gcroot" for
more info.
ebx:Root:01392b60(System.Windows.Forms.Application+ThreadContext)->
01392214(Store.Form1)->
01392454(System.Collections.Generic.List`1[[Store.Item, Store]])->
013d5f2c(System.Object[])->
013a03b8(Store.Item)
Scan Thread 0 OSTHread ee4
Scan Thread 2 OSTHread c48
DOMAIN(001483A8):HANDLE(WeakLn):9f1088:Root:013a074c(System.Windows.Forms.NativeMethod
s+WndProc)->
0139ec94(System.Windows.Forms.Control+ControlNativeWindow)->
0139ebc4(System.Windows.Forms.CheckBox)->
0139d6f8(Store.Transaction)->
013a03b8(Store.Item)
```

6. Are you curious about composition of the *Item* object? The items objects are shown as 20 bytes. What do those 20 bytes contain? Here is the source code for the *Item* class:

```
public class Item: IDisposable
{
    public Item()
    {
        ++nextPropId;
        propItemId = nextPropId;
    }

    public enum eProducts
    {
        Computer = 1,
        Laptop = 2,
        Printer = 4,
        Software = 8
    };

    private eProducts propProducts=0;
```

```
public eProducts Products
{
    get
    {
        return propProducts;
    }
    set
    {
        propProducts = value;
    }
}

static private int nextPropId=0;
private int propItemId;
public int ItemId
{
    get
    {
        return propItemId;
    }
}

public void Dispose()
{
    --nextPropId;
}

private float[] buffer = new float[100];
}
```

That was easy because the source code was available. What if the source code is not available? This is the normal case on a production machine. The *!dumpclass* command dumps the class. It uses the *EEClass* address, which is provided with *!name2ee* command. Actually, *!dumpclass* provides information that may be more valuable than the source code. You also receive state information. In the following listing, we are told that the static count is 3, which is the correct value at this moment.

```
0:004> !dumpclass 00db21c4
Class Name: Store.Item
mdToken: 02000002 (C:\store\Store.exe)
Parent Class: 790fa034
Module: 00d40c14
Method Table: 00d442dc
Vtable Slots: 5
Total Method Slots: 9
Class Attributes: 100001
NumInstanceFields: 3
NumStaticFields: 1
      MT     Field    Offset            Type   VT     Attr     Value Name
00d44224   4000001         8   System.Int32    0 instance           propProducts
790fe920   4000003         c   System.Int32    0 instance           propItemId
79129180   4000004         4 System.Single[]   0 instance           buffer
790fe920   4000002        24   System.Int32    0   static         3 nextPropId
```

Generations

The managed heap is organized into three generations and a large object heap. Generations are numbered 0, 1, and 2. New objects are placed in a generation or large object heap. Younger and smaller objects are found in the earlier generations, whereas older and larger objects are found in the later generations and the large object heap. This is efficiency by proximity. Objects that are apt to message other objects are kept close together in memory. This decreases page faults, which are costly, and the amount of physical memory required at any time.

Garbage collection in .NET is often described as nondeterministic, which means that memory recovery cannot be predicted. Garbage collection occurs when memory commits exceed the memory reserved for a particular generation. Because only a portion of the managed heap is being collected, this is more efficient. When an application starts, objects are allocated on Generation 0 first. Eventually, the memory available to Generation 0 is exceeded, which triggers garbage collection. If enough memory is reclaimed during garbage collection, the pending allocation is performed on Generation 0. If enough memory cannot be reclaimed, Generation 0 objects are promoted to Generation 1. This continues until Generation 0 and 1 are replete with objects. At that time, Generation 0 and 1 objects are promoted to Generation 1 and 2, respectively. By design, the older and larger objects tend to migrate toward the higher generations, whereas younger and smaller object are found in lower generations.

Memory on the managed heap is allocated top-down. The new objects are at the higher addresses. Generation 0 is at a higher address than Generation 1. 256 kilobytes, 2 megabytes, and 10 megabytes are reserved for Generation 0, 1, and 2, respectively. These thresholds may be adjusted. The GC changes these thresholds based on the pattern of allocations in the managed application.

As the name implies, the large object heap hosts large objects. Objects greater than 85 kilobytes (KB) in size are considered large objects. Instead of promoting these objects from one generation to another, which is costly, large objects are immediately placed on the large object heap at allocation.

Generations Walkthrough

This time the Store application has an Add Transactions button and an Add Large Transactions button. The Add Large Transactions button adds large transactions, which are instances of the *LargeItem* class. The *LargeItem* class inherits from the *Item* class and adds additional fields, such as the *largeStuff* field. The *largeStuff* field is greater than 85 KB and qualifies as a large object. The objective of this walkthrough is to determine the generation of each *Item*, *LargeItem* and *largeStuff* instance.

1.   Start the Store application. Add three regular transactions and four large transactions.

2.   Launch WinDbg and attach to the Store application.

3. There should be three instances of the *Item* class in memory. Retrieve the method table address of the *Item* class with the *!name2ee* command. Then dump the *Items* instances using the *!dumpheap −mt* command:

```
0:004> !name2ee Store.exe Store.Item
Module: 00d40c14 (Store.exe)
Token: 0x02000005
MethodTable: 00d4431c
EEClass: 00db22f4
Name: Store.Item
0:004> !dumpheap -mt 00d4431c
Address      MT      Size
013a8bd0 00d4431c      20
013aabb0 00d4431c      20
013aadd8 00d4431c      20
013adffc 00d4431c      20
013b513c 00d4431c      20
013c1a4c 00d4431c      20
total 6 objects
Statistics:
      MT    Count TotalSize Class Name
00d4431c        6       120 Store.Item
Total 6 objects
```

4. Unexpectedly, there are six instances, not three. Has a bug been uncovered?! This issue will be explored further later.

5. Use the *!name2ee* command to obtain the method table address of the *LargeItem*. Dump the *LargeItem* objects. As expected, there are four objects:

```
0:004> !dumpheap -mt 00d460a8
Address      MT      Size
013ab03c 00d460a8    5016
013ae5a4 00d460a8    5016
013be020 00d460a8    5016
013ca900 00d460a8    5016
total 4 objects
Statistics:
      MT    Count TotalSize Class Name
00d460a8        4     20064 Store.LargeItem
Total 4 objects
```

6. There should be four *largeStuff* fields—one for each *LargeItem* object. The easiest way to locate them by using is the *!dumpheap −stat* command. The objects are sorted by size, with the larger objects at the bottom of the list:

```
0:004> !dumpheap -stat
total 16356 objects
Statistics:
      MT    Count TotalSize Class Name
7b481adc        1        12 System.Windows.Forms.OSFeature
7b47fd04        1        12 System.Windows.Forms.FormCollection
7b47efec        1        12 System.Windows.Forms.Layout.DefaultLayout
7ae86e80      134      5896 System.Drawing.BufferedGraphics
790f8230      374      5984 System.WeakReference
```

```
79124ec4      41       8136 System.Collections.Hashtable+bucket[]
790fd688     341       8184 System.Version
79116738     250       9000 System.Collections.Hashtable+HashtableEnumerator
79124d8c       5      10596 System.Byte[]
79110f78     523      12552 System.Collections.Stack
7ae868e8    1049      12588 System.Drawing.KnownColor
00d460a8       4      20064 Store.LargeItem
7b47e850     522      33408 System.Windows.Forms.Internal.DeviceContext
7910acbc    2104      42080 System.SafeGCHandle
79124ba8     642      57496 System.Object[]
00152760      14      77744      Free
790fa860    7067     407316 System.String
00e80838       4   16000128 System.Single[,]
```

7. The last item in the report is a two-dimensional array of *Single* types. This is the *largeStuff* field. There are four instances shown. The first column of the command is the method table address. Dump the *largeStuff* instances using the *!dumpheap –mt* command:

```
0:004> !dumpheap -mt 00e80838
Address      MT      Size
02396da8 00e80838  4000032
027676c8 00e80838  4000032
02b37fe8 00e80838  4000032
02f08918 00e80838  4000032
total 4 objects
Statistics:
      MT    Count TotalSize Class Name
00e80838        4  16000128 System.Single[,]
Total 4 objects
```

8. Finally, list the memory range for Generations 0, 1, and 2 and the large object heap. This is accomplished with the *!eeheap –gc* command:

```
0:004> !eeheap -gc
Number of GC Heaps: 1
generation 0 starts at 0x013d2488
generation 1 starts at 0x013af93c
generation 2 starts at 0x01391000
ephemeral segment allocation context: none
 segment    begin allocated      size
0016bf58 7a74179c  7a76248c 0x00020cf0(134384)
001687e0 7b45baa0  7b471f0c 0x0001646c(91244)
00154b20 790d6314  790f575c 0x0001f448(128072)
01390000 01391000  013ff3ac 0x0006e3ac(451500)
Large object heap starts at 0x02391000
 segment    begin allocated      size
02390000 02391000  032d9248 0x00f48248(16024136)
Total Size  0x100cb98(16829336)
-------------------------------
GC Heap Size  0x100cb98(16829336)
```

Based on the addresses of the *Item*, *LargeItem*, and *largeStuff* instances, Table 13-8 maps each object to the managed heap. None of the instances resides in Generation 0.

Table 13-8   Item, LargeItem, and largeStuff Instances

Item	Address
No objects	N/A
Generation 0 Starts	*0x013d2488*
LargeItem[4]	*0x013ca900*
Item[6]	*0x013c1a4c*
LargeItem[3]	*0x013be020*
Item[5]	*0x013b513c*
Generation 1 Starts	*0x013af93c*
LargeItem[2]	*0x013ae5a4*
LargeItem[1]	*0x013ab03c*
LargeItem[2]	*013ae5a4*
Item[3]	*0x013aadd8*
Item[2]	*0x013aabb0*
Item[1]	*0x013a8bd0*
Generation 2 Starts	*0x01391000*
largeStuff[4]	*02f08918*
largeStuff[3]	*02b37fe8*
largeStuff[2]	*027676c8*
largeStuff[1]	*02396da8*
largeStuff[2]	*027676c8*
Large object heap	*0x02391000*

It is time to diagnose the earlier bug. Actually, there is no bug. The issue is nondeterministic collection. In the Store application, each transactions is initially an *Item* object. A *LargeItem* object is then initialized with the *Item* transaction. At that point, the *Item* object is no longer required, but the memory is not reclaimed. Therefore, there is a shadow item in memory for every *LargeItem*, which is the reason for the extra *Item* instances. At the next garbage collection, those items will be removed from memory. For demonstration purposes, there is a version of the Store application that forces garbage collection. It has a Collect Memory button that calls *GC.Collect* and removes the extra *Item* instances. When using this Store application, dump the *Item* instances before and after clicking the Collect Memory button to confirm that *GC.Collect* is reclaiming the extra objects. In general, calling *GC.Collect* is not recommended because it is an expensive operation.

Finalization

The finalization process has been ignored until now. It plays a vital role in garbage collection. Finalization also affects the performance and effectiveness of garbage collection. In C#, finalization is linked to class destructors. For C++ programmers, .NET presents an entirely different methodology for destructors.

Object.Finalize is the universal destructor in .NET. In C#, *Finalize* calls the class destructor. Destructors are called deterministically in C++. However, CLR calls destructors nondeterministically during garbage collection. Do not invoke destructors directly. Destructors are called as part of the garbage-collection process and are not called in a guaranteed sequence. In addition, you should clean up for only unmanaged resources in the destructor. For deterministic garbage collection, implement the *IDisposable* interface.

Destructors add processing overhead to an object. The overhead is incurred even before object is collected. The GC adds references for objects with destructors to the Finalization queue when the object is created. Thus, the extra overhead starts at the beginning of the object's lifetime.

Objects that have destructors but no outstanding references require at least two garbage collections to be reclaimed. During the first garbage-collection cycle, references to reclaimable objects are transferred from the *Finalization* queue to the *FReachable* queue, which is serviced by a dedicated thread. These objects are added to the list of objects already waiting on the *FReachable* queue to have their destructors called. The *Finalization* thread is responsible for invoking destructors on objects and then removing that object from the *FReachable* queue. When that happens, the object can be reclaimed and removed from memory during the next garbage collection.

The *!finalizequeue* command reports on objects waiting to have their destructors called. These are the objects on the *FReachable* queue.

Performance Monitor

The Performance Monitor has several counters that are helpful when debugging managed applications. Table 13-9 itemizes some of the more useful memory-related counters.

Table 13-9   Performance Monitor Counters

Name	Description
#GC Handles	The number of GC handles to external resources, such as windows and files.
# Bytes in All Heaps	Total number bytes allocated for Generation 0, 1, 2, and the large object heap.
# Induced GC	The peak number of times garbage collection was induced because of *GC.Collect*.
# of Pinned Objects	The number of pinned objects discovered during the last garbage collection.
# of Sinks Blocks in Use	A count of syncblock entries. (The syncblock is discussed in the section on debugging threads.)
#Gen 0 Collections	The number of times that Generation 0 has been garbage collected.
#Gen 1 Collections	The number of times that Generation 1 has been garbage collected.
#Gen 2 Collections	The number of times that Generation 2 has been garbage collected.

Table 13-9   Performance Monitor Counters *(Continued)*

Name	Description
# Total Committed Bytes	The total number of virtual memory committed by the GC.
# Total Reserve Bytes	The total number of virtual memory reserved by the GC.
Gen 0 Heap Size	Maximum number of allocated bytes for Generation 0.
Gen 1 Heap Size	Maximum number of allocated bytes for Generation 1.
Gen 2 Heap Size	Maximum number of allocated bytes for Generation 2.
Large Object Heap Size	Number of bytes currently allocated for the large object heap.
%Time in GC	The percentage of time spent in garbage collection, which is updated at each garbage collection cycle.
Allocated Bytes/Sec	The number of bytes allocated per second, which is updated at each garbage collection cycle.
Finalization Survivors	The number of object that survived garbage collection and waiting for destructors to be called.
Gen 0 Heap Size	The maximum number bytes allocated for Generation 0.
Gen 0 Promoted Bytes/Sec	The number of bytes per second promoted from Generation 0 to 1.
Gen 1 Heap Size	The current number of bytes in Generation 1.
Gen 1 Promoted Bytes/Sec	The number of bytes per second promoted from Generation 1 to 2.
Gen 2 Heap Size	The current number of bytes in Generation 2.
Promoted Finalization-Memory from Gen 0	The number of bytes promoted to Generation 1 because of pending finalizers.
Promoted Finalization-Memory from Gen 1	The number of bytes promoted to Generation 2 because of pending finalizers.
Promoted Memory from Gen 0	Total bytes for objects that were promoted to Generation 1. This does not include the objects waiting on pending finalizers.
Promoted Memory from Gen 1	Total bytes for objects that were promoted to Generation 2. This does not include the objects waiting on pending finalizers.

Threads

Multithread applications have multiple threads. Each thread represents a path of execution and owns resources, such as stack, thread local storage, local variables, and thread environment block. Proper use of threads can enhance the performance of an application, whereas poor implementation can hinder performance.

Creating threads is not difficult. Managing threads is the real challenge. Thread synchronization, which is the management of threads, entails several activities, including preventing race conditions and controlling access to resources. Threads are like children that require corralling.

Improperly implemented threads can lead to a high utilization or low utilization condition. High utilization is characterized by one or more threads consuming at or near 100-percent

CPU utilization. Other threads are starved for time, which makes the application appear to hang or behave incorrectly. Low utilization is the reverse. The process and contained threads are receiving minimal or no CPU usage.

There are two primary reasons for high utilization:

- Threads in tight loop that usurp all CPU resources
- Active high-priority threads that prevent lower-priority threads from receiving attention from the CPU

There is an assortment of reasons for low utilization:

- Threads waiting for resources that never become available. Threads in that state are suspended indefinitely and receive little CPU time.
- Threads mutually blocked on each other. This deadlock suspends both threads indefinitely, and both receive little CPU time.
- A low-priority thread in a sea of high priority threads has little opportunity to sail. It is accorded minimal CPU time.
- Threads with an erroneously high suspend counts are not resumed when planned. For this reason, the thread continues to receive no CPU time.

The previous items highlight some of the reasons for high and low utilization. There are plenty more. However, high and low utilization are not the only issues. Multithreaded and simultaneous access to non-thread-safe resources is another cause for application failures. Actually, the list of potential transgressions from multithreading is almost endless. Threading is fertile ground for debugging.

For brevity, this section focuses on monitors and mutexes. Synchronization problems from semaphores, events, and reader-writer locks are not discussed. Monitors synchronize access to a single resource. The resource could be an object, data structure, or even an algorithm—anything that requires singular access. Monitors are limited to synchronizing threads within the same process. A mutex also synchronizes access to a single resource. However, mutexes have additional power and flexibility. For example, mutexes can synchronize threads across processes.

Monitors are the most frequently used synchronization device. For that reason, the CLR tracks monitors for efficient access. Instances of objects have an additional field called the syncblock index, which is an index into the syncblock table where monitors are tracked. The syncblock index of an object defaults to zero. When an object is assigned to a monitor, the syncblock index is updated to point to an entry in the syncblock table. Otherwise, the syncblock index remains 0. In .NET 2.0, a syncblock entry is not created for every object associated with a monitor. If the monitor is not already associated with a syncblock, a thinlock is created instead. The command *!syncblk −all* lists the outstanding syncblocks, *!dumpheap -thinlock* reports the thinlocks.

Markers for thread synchronization can be found on the call stack. Finding *AwareLock.Enter*, *WaitHandle.WaitAll*, and *WaitForMultipleObjects* in the call stack are indications of thread synchronization activity.

- **AwareLock.Enter** This method is called when an object is bound to a monitor. If the following breakpoint is hit, that thread is entering a monitor:

```
bp mscorwks!AwareLock::Enter
```

- **WaitHandle.WaitAll** Except for monitors, most synchronization objects in .NET are derived from the *WaitHandle* class. Look for method calls from this class on the managed call stack, including *WaitOne* and *WaitAll*, as a sign of pending synchronization.

- **WaitForMultipleObjects** Most waits on synchronization objects, managed or unmanaged, dissolve in a *WaitForMultipleObjects* API, which is the workhorse of thread synchronization. This is the syntax of the *WaitForMultipleObjects* API:

DWORD *WaitForMultipleObjects*(DWORD nCount, const HANDLE*

lphandles, BOOL bWaitAll, DWORD dwMilliseconds)

Threads Commands

The first step for debugging threads in WinDbg and SOS is to use the thread commands. In WinDbg, the tilde (~) is the thread command; in SOS, the command is *!threads*.

This is sample output from the WinDbg thread command:

```
0:000> ~
. 0  Id: f7c.f80 Suspend: 1 Teb: 7ffdd000 Unfrozen
   1  Id: f7c.f9c Suspend: 1 Teb: 7ffdc000 Unfrozen
   2  Id: f7c.fa0 Suspend: 1 Teb: 7ffdb000 Unfrozen
   3  Id: f7c.fa4 Suspend: 1 Teb: 7ffda000 Unfrozen
   4  Id: f7c.de0 Suspend: 1 Teb: 7ffd9000 Unfrozen
```

Listed in order, the columns are thread number, process identifier, thread identifier, suspend count, address of thread environment block, and status of the thread.

Here is output from the SOS threads command:

```
0:000> !threads
ThreadCount: 4
UnstartedThread: 1
BackgroundThread: 1
PendingThread: 0
DeadThread: 0
Hosted Runtime: no
                              PreEmptive   GC Alloc        Lock
        ID OSID ThreadOBJ    State    GC      Context      Domain   Count APT Exception
   0     1 f80  001501f8     6020 Disabled 013c2cf0:013c32bc 001483a8    0 STA
   2     2 fa0  00153e40     b220 Enabled  00000000:00000000 001483a8    0 MTA (Finalizer)
   4     3 de0  0018b898     b020 Disabled 013b4cdc:013b52bc 001483a8    2 MTA
XXXX     4 0    0018e750     9400 Enabled  00000000:00000000 001483a8    0 Ukn
```

The information on managed threads includes the following:

- **ID** Unmanaged thread number
- **OSID** Managed thread number
- **ThreadObject** Address of related thread object
- **State** State of the thread
- **Preemptive GC** Whether a thread can be preempted for garbage collection
- **AppDomain** Address of the *AppDomain* that hosts the thread
- **Lock Count** Lock count
- **APT** Apartment model

Threads Walkthrough

Multithread capabilities have been added to the Store application. Two buttons have been added. The Enumerate button writes the transactions to the forward.txt file. The Reverse Enumerate button writes the transactions, in reverse order, to the reverse.txt file. Each button handler creates and starts a thread to accomplish the reporting tasks.

1. Close all instances of the Store application.

2. Start the Store program and add three transactions. Click the Enumerate button to write the transactions to the forward.txt file. Close the Store program and open the forward.txt file, which is found to be empty. It should contain three transactions!

3. Try again. Reopen the Store application and add three transactions. However, upon clicking the Enumerate button an unhandled exception occurs. What is the problem? You need to investigate.

4. Start the Store application yet again. Retrieve the process identifier using the *tlist* command. However, notice that there are two Store applications running. Apparently a previous version is still running in the background. This kind of problem is typical of a hung thread, which keeps an application alive after the user closes the main window.

5. Use ADPlus to obtain a dump of the earlier Store application. This is the command:

   ```
   adplus -hang -o c:\dumps -p 2696
   ```

6. Open the resulting dump file in WinDbg.

7. Load the SOS debugger extension and list out the managed threads. For readability, some of the columns have been removed from this listing:

   ```
   0:000> .load sos
   0:000> !threads
   ThreadCount: 3
   UnstartedThread: 0
   BackgroundThread: 2
   PendingThread: 0
   DeadThread: 0
   Hosted Runtime: no
   ```

	ID	OSID	ThreadOBJ	State	PreEmptive GC	GC Alloc Context	Domain	Lock Count
0	1	a90	001501f8	2016220	Enabled	013dbe2c:013dc990	001483a8	0
2	2	9c8	00153e40	b220	Enabled	00000000:00000000	001483a8	0
4	3	3e0	00190718	b020	Disabled	013d63b0:013d6990	001483a8	2

Thread 4 seems to be the culprit. It is the only thread with a positive lock count. What is the thread waiting for? This question is answered with the *!dumpheap –thinlock* command:

```
0:000> !dumpheap -thinlock
 Address       MT    Size
01392440 00d443e8     24       ThinLock owner 3 (00199a78) Recursive 0
01392468 790fa098     12       ThinLock owner 3 (00199a78) Recursive 0
```

From the preceding listing, both thinlocks are owned by Thread 4. The address of the Thread 4 object is 0x00199a78, which could be nested locks. Dump the method tables of the thinlocks to uncover what Thread 4 is waiting for:

```
0:000> !dumpmt 00d443e8
EEClass: 79126bb0
Module: 790c2000
Name: System.Collections.Generic.List`1[[Store.Item, Store]]
mdToken: 02000287  (C:\WINDOWS\assembly\GAC_32\mscorlib\2.0.0.0__b77a5c561934e089\mscorlib.dll)
BaseSize: 0x18
ComponentSize: 0x0
Number of IFaces in IFaceMap: 6
Slots in VTable: 30
0:000> !dumpmt 790fa098
EEClass: 790fa034
Module: 790c2000
Name: System.Object
mdToken: 02000002  (C:\WINDOWS\assembly\GAC_32\mscorlib\2.0.0.0__b77a5c561934e089\mscorlib.dll)
BaseSize: 0xc
ComponentSize: 0x0
Number of IFaces in IFaceMap: 0
Slots in VTable: 14
```

What is known? When the program hung, Thread 4 had outstanding locks on an *Item* and *Object* instance. No other thread is holding a lock, which narrows the problem to Thread 4. Here is the source code for Thread 4:

```
private void Forward()
{
    lock (items)
    {
        lock (syncObj)
        {
            StreamWriter sw = new StreamWriter("forward.txt");
            IEnumerator<Item> enumerator = items.GetEnumerator();
            while (true)
            {

            }

            while (true)
```

```
        {
            if (enumerator.MoveNext())
            {
                Item current = enumerator.Current;
                string message = current.ItemId + " Product Mask: "
                    + ((int)current.Products).ToString();
                sw.WriteLine(message);
            }
            else
            {
                break;
            }
        }
        sw.Close();
    }
  }
}
```

Review the code—I hope that the problem is obvious. The lock statement is a shortcut to call-ing the *Monitor.Enter* method. After acquiring the locks, the program enters an infinite loop, which was shown previously. Because execution never continues past the loop where the locks are released, the locks are still being held. Remove the extraneous *while(true)* loop and retry the program. Before recompiling the application, you have to kill the hung process. The forward.txt file should be created and contain transactions.

Threads Walkthrough 2

The Store application appears to be working, but not in all circumstances. Delete the for-ward.txt and reverse.txt files. End any current sessions of the Store application. Start a new session of the Store application and add a couple of transactions.

1. Click the Reverse Enumerate button followed by the Enumerate button. Close the applica-tion and check for the forward.txt and reverse.txt files. Neither file is created. Why not?

2. Restart the Store application. Add two new transactions. Click the Reverse Enumerate button followed by the Enumerate button.

3. Start WinDbg and attach to the Store application.

4. List the available threads with the *!threads* command. Threads 4 and 5 have a positive lock count. Both threads are waiting for something:

```
0:006> !threads
ThreadCount: 4
UnstartedThread: 0
BackgroundThread: 1
PendingThread: 0
DeadThread: 0
Hosted Runtime: no
                                        PreEmptive   GC Alloc               Lock
      ID OSID ThreadOBJ    State     GC      Context           Domain    Count
   0   1  e54 001501f8      6020 Enabled  013e7afc:013e7b68 001483a8       0
   2   2  d84 00153e40      b220 Enabled  00000000:00000000 001483a8       0
   4   3  2e0 00191f60    200b020 Enabled  013d9bec:013dbb68 001483a8       1
   5   4  ccc 00190b98    200b020 Enabled  013dfb9c:013e1b68 001483a8       1
```

The *!syncblk* command reports the syncblock entries. Thread 5 is using an *Item* instance as a monitor. Thread 4 is using an *Object* instance as a monitor. This confirms Threads 4 and 5 as the potential source of the problem. The other threads are not using monitors:

```
0:006> !syncblk
Index SyncBlock MonitorHeld Recursion Owning Thread Info  SyncBlock Owner
    2 00174854           3         1 00190b98   ccc   5   01392440
System.Collections.Generic.List`1[[Store.Item, Store]]
   21 001747f4           3         1 00191f60   2e0   4   01392468 System.Object
-----------------------------
Total            44
CCW               0
RCW               0
ComClassFactory   0
Free              0
```

5. Perform a stack trace on Threads 4 and 5. Notice the inclusion of the *AwareLock::Enter* method, which is a marker of thread synchronization. Also note that the top of the call stack is populated with *WaitForMultipleObjects* methods, which means the thread is currently blocked on something:

```
0:004> kb
ChildEBP RetAddr  Args to Child
0358f4a0 7c90e9ab 7c8094f2 00000001 0358f4cc ntdll!KiFastSystemCallRet
0358f4a4 7c8094f2 00000001 0358f4cc 00000001 ntdll!ZwWaitForMultipleObjects+0xc
0358f540 79f4aa60 00000001 00174868 00000000 KERNEL32!WaitForMultipleObjectsEx+0x12c
0358f5a8 79f16d92 00000001 00174868 00000000 mscorwks!WaitForMultipleObjectsEx_SO_TOLE
RANT+0x6f
0358f5c8 79f16d03 00000001 00174868 00000000 mscorwks!Thread::DoAppropriateAptStateWai
t+0x3c
0358f64c 79f16b9e 00000001 00174868 00000000 mscorwks!Thread::DoAppropriateWaitWorker+
0x144
0358f69c 79f4a9d9 00000001 00174868 00000000 mscorwks!Thread::DoAppropriateWait+0x40
0358f6f8 79ebc06e ffffffff 00000001 00000000 mscorwks!CLREvent::WaitEx+0xf7
0358f708 7a0fd093 ffffffff 00000001 00000000 mscorwks!CLREvent::Wait+0x17
0358f794 7a0fd28f 00191f60 ffffffff 00191f60 mscorwks!AwareLock::EnterEpilog+0x94
0358f7b0 79f0fe6a 8a20e59b 0358f888 01392214 mscorwks!AwareLock::Enter+0x61
```

6. Look at the parameters for *WaitForMultiple* objects. Thread 4 is waiting for a single synchronization object, which is the first parameter. The second parameter is an address, which is a pointer to an array of handles. Dump that parameter to find the handle to the synchronization object:

```
0:004> dd 00174868
00174868  00000658 0000000d 00000000 00000000
00174878  00000000 00000000 00000000 00000000
00174888  00000000 00000000 00000000 80000023
```

7. The handle to the synchronization object is 0x00000658. Use the *!handle* command to obtain more information on that handle. It is an event handle:

```
0:004> !handle 00000658
Handle 658
  Type          Event
```

8. Repeat steps 1 through 7 for Thread 5. The result should be similar.

The problem has been isolated to Threads 4 and 5. Threads 4 and 5 are started in the Forward and Reverse handlers. Here is the source code for these methods. Both methods have nested locks. However, the locks in the *Forward* and *Reverse* methods are in reverse order, which is causing a deadlock.

```
private void Forward()
{
    lock (items)
    {
        lock (syncObj)
        {
            StreamWriter sw = new StreamWriter("forward.txt");
            IEnumerator<Item> enumerator = items.GetEnumerator();

            while (true)
            {
                // other code
            }
            sw.Close();
        }
    }
}

Object syncObj= new Object();

private void Reverse()
{
    lock (syncObj)
    {
        Thread.Sleep(5000);
        lock (items)
        {
            StreamWriter sw = new StreamWriter("reverse.txt");
            items.Reverse();
            IEnumerator<Item> enumerator = items.GetEnumerator();
            while (true)
            {
                // other code
            }
            items.Reverse();
            sw.Close();
        }
    }
}
```

9. Reverse the order of the locks in either method, which resolves the problem. Restart the Store application and test.

Exceptions

Have you ever been presented with a memory exception? See Figure 13-9. Of course, I am sure this exception occurred while you were using an application that *someone else* wrote. As a kind gesture, you volunteered to help diagnose the problem and make an unstable application robust.

Figure 13-9 Typical dialog box that reports an exception

Managed exceptions start life as native exceptions. To raise an exception, the CLR calls *mscorwks!RaiseTheException. RaiseTheException* then calls *RaiseException*, which is a system-level API. *RaiseException* assigns all managed exceptions the E0434F4D exception code. Because all managed exceptions are raised with this same exception code, it is difficult to distinguish between managed exceptions. Fortunately, the first parameter of the *RaiseThe-Exception* function call is the managed exception object. You can dump that object to ascertain the specific exception objection.

Exception Walkthrough

The Exception application is modified to raise an exception when the Add Transactions button is clicked. The object of this walkthrough is to determine the type of exception.

1. Start the Store application. Open WinDbg and attach to that program.

2. Set a breakpoint on the *RaiseException* API and resume the application:

    ```
    0:004> bp Kernel32!RaiseException; g
    ```

3. Click the Add Transaction button. The exception is raised and the breakpoint is hit in WinDbg. Display the call stack.

4. Use the *!dumpobj* command to dump the first parameter of *RaiseTheException*, which is the managed exception object. You now have the details of the exception, including the exception type.

There are two other ways to trap managed exceptions.

■ **sxe clr**   This command breaks on all unhandled managed exceptions. You can then perform a back trace for the details of the exception, which exist on the call stack. This is an alternative to breaking on *RaiseTheException* API.

■ **!soe *exceptiontype***   This is the *Stop On Exception* command and an SOS command. A breakpoint is set on the type of exception specified. Before issuing the command, switch to the thread on which the exception is expected.

Symbols

Until now, it is has been assumed that debug symbol files have aligned perfectly. Admittedly, that is a major assumption. However, the advent of symbol stores and servers makes me optimistic that your symbols are aligning without the obligatory drama. Having the correct debug symbols files for the environment and application make the debugging experience infinitely easier. With symbol files, function names, parameter names, local variables, source code line, and data to resolve, frame pointer omissions (FPOs) are available. Without symbol files, little of this valuable information is available, which makes your debugging quest much more difficult.

Debug symbol files are versioned. Different versions of debug symbol files are available for separate Windows environments. Windows 98, Windows 2000, Windows XP, and other Windows operating environments do not have identical symbols. Service packs may also have different symbols. Because of the large assortment of symbol combinations, obtaining the correct symbols for an environment becomes a trial-and-error process—which is further complicated when performing postmortem analysis. The dump may have originated on another machine that has a different operating system, which requires having the symbols for the environment on the source machine available on your machine. Things are getting complicated very quickly. A more direct approach is needed, and the solutions are symbol servers and symbol stores.

Symbol servers orchestrate the downloading of required symbols from a symbol store. The symbol server assumes the responsibility of finding the correct symbols; a symbol store is a repository of related debug symbol files. Symbol servers consult with the symbol store to download the correct versions of the debug symbol files. Microsoft publishes a public symbol store for developers, which can be accessed here:

http://msdl.microsoft.com/download/symbols

You can download symbols directly instead of using symbol servers. However, the approaches are not mutually exclusive. Symbol packages for different Windows environments are downloadable from this location:

http://www.microsoft.com/whdc/devtools/debugging/symbolpkg.mspx

Symsrv Symbol Server

Symsrv.dll is the symbol server distributed with Debugging Tools for Windows, and it must be installed in the same directory as the debugger. Symsrv contacts the listed symbol stores and downloads debug symbol files into a downstream directory. Files can be transferred over http and https.

This is the generic syntax to download debug symbol files with a symbol server:

Symsrv*ServerDLL*DownstreamStore*SymbolStore*

The following command leverages the symsrv.dll symbol server. The symbol server is instructed to contact the Microsoft Public Symbol Store to download missing or correct versions of symbol files. The symbols are transferred to *c:* symbols, which is the downstream store:

Symsrv*Symsrv*c:\symbols*http://msdl.microsoft.com/download/symbols*

Because symsrv.dll is the most prevalent symbol server, an abbreviated syntax is available that is specific for that server:

srv*DownstreamStore*SymbolStore

The following command uses the abbreviated syntax and is identical to the previous expanded command that used the symsrv.dll symbol server:

srv*c:\symbols**http://msdl.microsoft.com/download/symbols*

As shown in the following syntax, symbol servers can have multiple downstream servers. If the symbol file is not in $DownstreamStore^1$, it is downloaded from $DownstreamStore^2$. Furthermore, if the file is not in $DownstreamStore^2$, $DownstreamStore^3$ is contacted. If the file is found there, it is downloaded from $DownstreamStore^3$ into $DownstreamStore^2$ and then $DownstreamStore^2$ into $DownstreamStore^1$. This pattern continues until the debug symbol is found or the symbol stores are exhausted.

srv*$DownstreamStore^1$*$DownstreamStore^2$* $DownstreamStore^n$*SymbolStore

WinDbg and Visual Studio .NET read the _NT_SYMBOL_PATH environment variable for the default path for the symbol server. Use the System tool in Control Panel to create or modify the _NT_SYMBOL_PATH environment variable.

Application Symbols

The Microsoft Public Symbol Store downloads the symbols for the environment. You also need the symbols for your application. Symbol files are not always distributed with release versions of a product, so a production server might not have the required symbol files. It is imperative that the debug symbol files for the release product be maintained somewhere, such as a private symbol store, for debugging if needed.

Visual Studio .NET creates a symbol file (PDB) for both debug and release versions of the product. It is important to retain the symbol files for each version of the debug and release product. Because clients may have older versions of your product, the debug symbol files for those versions must also be retained and available.

WinDbg

In WinDbg, the symbol path can be set via the user interface or the command line. From the user interface, select the Symbol File Path menu item from the File menu. From the command line, the *.sympath* directive can display or set the symbol path. When the symbol path is changed, the *.reload* directive resynchronizes and potentially downloads additional symbol files.

The *!sym noisy* command helps diagnose errors in loading debug symbol files. This command displays detailed information on each symbol that should be downloaded, which is helpful for resolving symbol problems. The *!sym quiet* command, which is the default, suppresses the extra binding data.

Memory Management

Memory management was introduced in this chapter. Concepts such as root objects, reference trees, generations, and finalization queues were reviewed. The next chapter expands the conversation to include the disposable pattern, weak references, unsafe pointers, and other topics related to memory management.

Understanding the managed paradigm to memory management is particularly important to C- and C++-based programmers. C programmers are accustomed to managing their own memory with minimal assistance from the environment. For them, memory management in .NET represents a different mindset, which includes adopting new best practices for allocating, managing, and releasing memory. Some C developers perceive the managed memory model as confining, when actually it is liberating.

Although the CLR provides memory management, developers have some sway in the process, which includes pinned pointer, memory stress, forcing garbage collection, and allocation patterns. These topics are introduced in the next chapter.

Part V
Advanced Concepts

Chapter 14
Memory Management

Memory management is an essential aspect of every program except the most trivial of applications. There are different classifications of memory. Registers, static data area (SDA), stack, thread local storage, heap, virtual, and file storage are some of the categories of memory. Registers hold data that require quick and efficient memory access. Critical system information, such as the instruction and stack pointer, are stored in registers. Static and global values are automatically stored in the SDA. Stacks are thread-specific and hold the context information (stack frames) of current functions. Local variables, parameters, return values, the instruction pointer of the calling function, and other function-related information is placed on the stack. Thread local storage (TLS) is also thread-specific storage. The TLS table is 64 slots of 32-bit values that contain thread-specific data. TLS slots frequently hold pointers to blocks of data that belong to the thread. A heap is memory allocated at run time from the virtual memory of an application and controlled by the heap manager. An application can have more than one heap. Large objects are commonly placed on the heap, whereas small objects are located on the stack. Virtual memory is raw memory that developers directly manipulate at run time with minimal assistance from the environment. Virtual memory is ideal for collections of disparate-sized data stored in noncontiguous memory addresses, such as a link list.

Developers of managed applications can directly affect the stack and managed heap. The other forms of memory, such as registers and virtual memory, are largely unavailable except through interoperability. Value type instances, local values, are created on the stack. Instances of reference types, objects, are created on the managed heap. Lifetimes of local values are confined by scope. When a local value loses scope, it is removed from the stack. For example, the local variables and parameters of a function are removed from memory when the function is exited. The lifetime of an object, which resides on the managed heap, is controlled by the garbage collector (GC), which is an element of the Common Language Runtime (CLR). The GC periodically performs garbage collection to cleanse memory of unused objects.

The policies and best practices of the GC and garbage collection are the primary focus of this chapter. Although garbage collection is not language-specific, the tradition of C-based developers, as related to memory management, is somewhat different from other developers—particularly Microsoft Visual Basic and Java developers. The memory model employed in Visual Basic and Java is cosmetically similar to the managed environment. However, the memory model of previous C-based languages is dissimilar to this environment. These differences make this chapter especially important.

Developers in C-based languages are accustomed to deterministic garbage collection, in which developers explicitly set the lifetime of an object. The *malloc/free* and *new/delete* statement combinations create and destroy objects that reside on a heap. Managing the memory of a heap required programmer discipline, which proved insufficient for guaranteeing consistently robust code. Memory leaks and other problems were common. These leaks could eventually destabilize the application and cause complete application failure. Instead of each developer individually struggling with these issues, the managed environment has the GC, which is omnipresent and controls the lifetime of objects located on the managed heap.

The GC offers nondeterministic garbage collection. Developers explicitly allocate memory for objects. However, the GC determines when garbage collection is performed and unused objects are vanquished from memory.

When memory for an object is allocated at run time, the GC returns a reference to that object. The new operator requests that an instance of a type (an object) is placed on the managed heap. A reference is an indirect pointer to that object. This indirection helps the GC transparently manage the managed heap, including the relocation of pointers when necessary.

In .NET, unused objects are eventually removed from memory. When is an object unused? Reference counting is not performed in the managed environment. Reference counting was common to Component Object Model (COM) components. When the reference count became zero, the related COM component was considered no longer relevant and removed from memory. There were many problems in this model. First, this required careful synchronization of the *AddRef* and *Release* methods. Breakdown of synchronization could sometimes cause memory leakage and exceptions. Second, reference counting was expensive. Reference counting was applied to collectable and noncollectable components. Finally, programs incurred the overhead of reference counting, even when there was no memory stress on the application. For this reason, reference counting was deservedly abandoned for a more efficient model that addresses the memory concerns of modern applications. When there is memory stress in the managed environment, garbage collection occurs, and an object graph is built. Objects not on the graph become candidates for collection.

Unmanaged Resources

Objects that incorporate unmanaged resources have a managed and unmanaged context, which affects memory management and garbage collection.

For example, the unmanaged resource of a managed object might consume copious amount of unmanaged memory. This cannot be ignored. Managed and unmanaged memories are allocated from the same pool of virtual memory. Corrective action must be taken when the pool is drained, regardless of the source. Developers can compensate for unmanaged resources in .NET Framework 2.0 and take corrective action to prevent out of memory occurrences. You can no longer hide an unmanaged elephant behind a managed object. A managed wrapper class for a bitmap is one example. The wrapper class is relatively small, and the memory associated with the managed object is trivial. However, the bitmap is the elephant. A bitmap requires large amounts of memory, which cannot be ignored. If ignored, creating several managed bitmaps could unexpectedly cause your application to be trampled by a stampede of elephants.

The availability of an unmanaged resource can be discrete. When consumed in a managed application, discrete resources must be tracked to prevent overconsumption. The overconsumption of unmanaged resources can have an adverse affect on the managed application, including the potential of resource contention or raising an exception. For example, a device can support three simultaneous connections. What happens when the fourth connection is requested? In the managed environment, you should be able to handle this scenario gracefully.

The lifetime of an unmanaged resource is a separate consideration apart from the lifetime of the managed object that hosts that resource. Equating the lifetimes can delay the release of sensitive resources. This delay can result in resource contention, poor user responsiveness, or application failure. For example, the *FileStream* class is a wrapper for a native resource: a physical file. The *FileStream* instance, which is a managed component, is collected nondeterministically. Therefore, the lapse between when the file is no longer needed and the managed component is collected could be substantial. This could prevent access to the file from within and outside your application. When the file is no longer required, the ability to release the file deterministically is imperative. You need the ability to say "Close the file *now*." The *Disposable* pattern provides this ability to managed developers and separates the lifetime of managed components and unmanaged resources.

Garbage Collection Overview

This section is an overview of garbage collection. A detailed explanation of the mechanics of garbage collection is presented in Chapter 13, "Advanced Debugging," and not repeated here. Two assumptions guide the implementation of garbage collection in the managed environment. The first assumption is that objects are more likely to communicate with other objects of a similar size. The second assumption is that smaller objects are short-lived objects, whereas larger objects are long-lived objects. For these reasons, the GC attempts to organize objects based on size and age.

In the managed environment, garbage collection is nondeterministic. With the exception of the *GC.Collect* method, which is discouraged, developers cannot explicitly initiate garbage collection. The managed heap is partitioned into generations, which are Generations 0, 1, and 2. The initial sizes of the generations are about 256 kilobytes, 2 megabytes, and 10 megabytes, respectively. As the application executes, the GC fine-tunes the thresholds based on the pattern of memory allocations. Garbage collection is prompted when the threshold for Generation 0 is exceeded. At that time, nonrooted objects are removed from memory. Objects that survive garbage collection are promoted from Generation 0 to 1. Generation 0 is now empty. The generations are then compacted and references updated. If during garbage collection Generation 0 and 1 exceed their thresholds, both are collected. Surviving objects are promoted from Generation 0 to 1 and from Generation 1 to 2. Afterward, Generation 0 is empty again, generations are compacted, and references are updated. In fewer instances, all three generations will exceed thresholds and require collection. The later generations contain larger objects, which live longer. Because the short-lived objects reside primarily on Generation 0, most garbage collection is focused in this generation. Generations allow the garbage collection to implement a partial cleanup of the managed heap at a substantial performance benefit.

Objects larger than 85 kilobytes are considered large objects and are treated differently from other objects. Large objects are placed on the large object heap, not on a generation. Large objects are generally long-lived components. Placing large objects on the large object heap eliminates the need to promote these objects between generations, thereby conserving resources and reducing the number of overall collection cycles. The large object heap is collected with Generation 2, so large objects are collected only during a full garbage-collection cycle.

When garbage collection is performed, the GC builds an object graph to determine which objects are not rooted and can be discarded. The object graph is a graph of live objects. First the GC populates the object graph with root references. The root references of an application are global, static, and local references. Local references include references that are locals and function parameters. The GC then adds to the graph those objects reachable from a root reference. An embedded object of a local is an example of an object reachable from a root reference. Of course, the embedded object could contain other objects. The GC extrapolates all the reachable objects to compose the branches of the object graph. Objects can appear once in the object graph, which avoids circular references and other problems. Objects not in the graph are not rooted and are considered candidates for garbage collection.

Objects that are not rooted can hold outstanding references to other objects. In this circumstance, the entire branch is disconnected from a rooted object and can be collected. (See Figure 14-1.)

The Rooted application demonstrates how nonrooted objects are collected. In the application, the *Branch* class contains the *Leaf* class, which contains the *Leaf2* class. The *Branch* class is used as a field in the *Form1* class. When an instance of the *Branch* class is created, it is rooted through the *Form* class. *Leaf* and *Leaf2* instances are rooted through the *Branch* instances. (See Figure 14-2.)

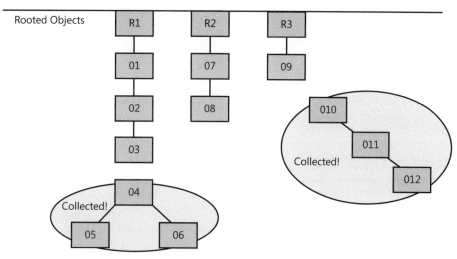

Figure 14-1   Object graph with nonrooted objects

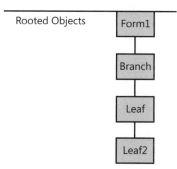

Figure 14-2   Object graph of the Rooted application

In the following code, a modal message box is displayed in the finalizer. This is done for demonstration purposes only and generally considered bad practice.

```
public class Branch
{
    ~Branch()
    {
        MessageBox.Show("Branch d'tor");
    }
    public Leaf e= new Leaf();
}


public class Leaf
{
    ~Leaf()
    {
```

```
        MessageBox.Show("Leaf d'tor");
    }
    public Leaf2 e2= new Leaf2();
}


public class Leaf2
{

    ~Leaf2()
    {
        MessageBox.Show("Leaf2 d'tor");
    }
}
```

The user interface of the Rooted application allows users to create the *Branch*, which includes *Leaf* instances. (See Figure 14-3.) You can then set the *Branch* or any specific *Leaf* to *null*, which interrupts the path to the root object. That nullified object is collectable. Objects that are rooted through the nullified object are also now collectable. For example, if the *Leaf* instance is set to null, the *Branch* instance is not collectable; it is before the *Leaf* reference in the object graph. However, *Leaf2* object is immediately a candidate for collection. After setting the *Branch* or *Leaf* objects to *null*, garbage collection can occur. If it doesn't occur, click the Collect Memory button to force garbage collection.

Figure 14-3   Rooted application

As mentioned, garbage collection occurs when the memory threshold of Generation 0 is exceeded. Other events, which are described in the following list, can prompt garbage collection:

■ When the threshold of Generation 0 is exceeded, garbage collection is triggered. Certain activities, such as frequent allocations, can accelerate garbage collection cycles.

■ Garbage collection is conducted when the extents of memory pressure are reached. The *GC.AddMemoryPressure* method applies pressure to the managed heap for an unmanaged resource.

■ The limit of an unmanaged resource is reached. *HandleCollector* sets limits for unmanaged resources.

- Garbage collection can be forced with the *GC.Collect* method. This behavior is not recommended because forcing garbage collection is expensive. Nonetheless, this is sometimes necessary.

- Garbage collection also occurs when overall system memory is low.

Certain suppositions are made for garbage collection in the managed environment. For example, small objects are generally short-lived. Coding contrary to these assumptions can be costly. Although it makes for an interesting theoretical experiment, this is not recommended for production applications. Defining a basket of short-lived but larger objects is an example of coding against assumptions of managed garbage collection, which would force frequent and full collections. Full collections are particularly expensive. Defining a collection of near-large objects—objects that are slightly less than 85 kilobytes—is another example. These objects would apply immediate memory pressure. Because they are probably long-lived, you have the overhead of eventually promoting the near-large objects to Generation 2. It would be more efficient to pad the objects with a buffer, forcing them into large object status, in which the objects are directly placed onto the large object heap. You must remain cognizant of the underlying principal of garbage collection. Implement policies that enhance, not exasperate, garbage collection in the managed environment.

One such policy is to limit boxing. Constant boxing of value types can cause garbage collection more often. Boxing creates a copy of the value type on the managed heap. Most value types are small. For this reason, the resulting object placed on the managed heap could be larger than the original value. This is yet another reason that boxing is inefficient and should be avoided when possible. This is particularly a problem with collection types. The best solution is to use generic types.

This introduction to garbage collection omits the topic of finalization, which is discussed in complete detail later in this chapter.

GC Flavors

There are two flavors of the garbage collection: Workstation GC is optimized for a workstation or single-processor system, whereas Server GC is fine-tuned for a server machine that has multiple processors. Workstation GC is the default; Server GC is never the default—even with a multiprocessor system. Server GC can be enabled in the application configuration file. If your application is hosted by a server application, that application might select the Server GC.

Workstation GC can have concurrent garbage collection enabled or disabled. *Concurrent* is a single thread concurrently servicing the user interface and garbage collection. The thread simultaneously responds to events of the user interface while also conducting garbage collection responsibilities. The alternative is noncurrent. When garbage collection is performed, other responsibilities, such as servicing the user interface, are deferred.

Workstation GC with Concurrent Garbage Collection

Workstation GC with concurrent garbage collection is the default. It is ideal for desktop applications, in which the user interface must remain responsive. When garbage collection occurs, it will not subjugate the user interface. Concurrent applies only to full garbage collection, which is the collection of Generation 2. When Generation 2 is collected, Generation 0 and 1 are also collected. Partial garbage collection of Generation 0 or 1 is an expeditious activity. The potential impact on the user interface is minimal, and concurrent garbage collection is not merited.

The following are the garbage collection steps for Workstation GC with concurrent processing:

1.   Garbage collection is triggered.

2.   All managed threads are paused.

3.   Perform garbage collection. If garbage collection is completed, proceed to step 5.

4.   Interrupt garbage collection. Resume threads for a short time to respond to user interface requests. Return to step 3.

5.   Resume threads.

Threads are suspended at a secure point. The CLR maintains a table of secure points for use during garbage collection. If a thread is suspended at an nonsecure point, the thread is hijacked until a secure point is reached or the current function returns.

Workstation GC Without Concurrent Garbage Collection

Workstation GC without concurrent garbage collection is selected when Server GC is chosen on a single-processor machine. With this option, priority is placed on garbage collection in lieu of the user interface.

Here are the garbage collection steps for Workstation GC without concurrent processing:

1.   Garbage collection is triggered.

2.   All managed threads are paused.

3.   Garbage collection is conducted.

4.   Managed threads resume.

Server GC

Server GC is designed for multiprocessor machines that are commonly deployed as servers, such as Web, application, and database servers. In the server environment, emphasis is on throughput and not the user interfaces. The Server GC is fine-tuned for scalability. For optimum scalability, garbage collection is not handled on a single thread. The Server GC allocates a separate managed heap and thread for every processor. Garbage collection is not conducted on the thread that requests the allocation.

Here are the garbage collection steps with Server GC:

1. A GC thread performs an allocation.

2. Garbage collection is triggered.

3. Managed threads are suspended.

4. Garbage collection is performed.

5. Managed threads are resumed.

Configuring GC Flavor

Workstation GC with concurrent garbage collection can be enabled or disabled in an application configuration file. Because concurrent is the default, the configuration file is used primarily to disable concurrent garbage collection. This is set in the *gcConcurrent* tag, as shown in the following code:

```
<configuration>
    <runtime>
        <gcConcurrent enabled="false"/>
    </runtime>
</configuration>
```

Server GC is also stipulated in the application configuration file. Remember, Server GC is never the default—even in a multiprocessor environment. Select the Server GC using the *gcServer* tag, which is exhibited in the following code:

```
<configuration>
    <runtime>
        <gcServer enabled="true"/>
    </runtime>
</configuration>
```

You can also use the .NET Framework Configuration Tool (mscorcfg.msc) to select the appropriate GC. This tool is installed in the Administrative Tools of the Control Panel. Open the .NET Framework Configuration tool and select the Applications icon, which is presented in the left pane. Click the Add An Application To Configure link in the Applications window. From the Configure An Application dialog box, browse and select the target application. The application window will appear. In that window, click the View The Application's Properties link. The application's Properties dialog box will appear. From the two options, you can select the appropriate Garbage Collection mode in this window. Figure 14-4 shows the application properties dialog box and the garbage collection options.

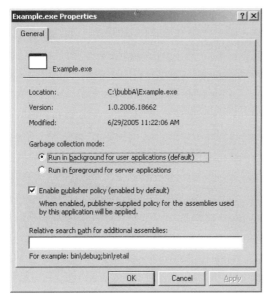

Figure 14-4   Application properties in the .NET Framework Configuration tool

Finalizers

Resources of an object are cleaned up in a *Finalize* method. Before an object is removed from memory, the *Finalize* method is called to release collateral resources. As a group, *Finalize* methods are called finalizers. Every object inherits the *Finalize* method from the *System.Object* type. This is the syntax of the *Finalize* method:

Object.Finalize syntax:

protected virtual void Finalize( )

Finalizers are not called programmatically; they are called automatically during the garbage collection cycle. Garbage collection is nondeterministic, which means that the finalizer may not be called immediately. This means that unmanaged resources, such as files, database connections, and devices, might not be released in a timely manner. This delay in relinquishing resources can have adverse side effects on this and possibly other applications.

Instead of a *Finalize* method, C# has a destructor. Coding a *Finalize* method explicitly causes a compiler error. Destructor methods are preceded with a tilde and share the name of the class.

Destructor syntax:

~Classname( )

The destructor syntax has the following limitations:

- Destructors do not have modifiers.

- Destructors are protected and virtual by default.

- Destructors have no parameters.

- Destructors cannot be overloaded.

- Destructors do not have a return type. The implied return type of a destructor is void.

The C# compiler converts destructors to *Finalize* methods. Here is a simple destructor:

```
~ZClass() {
    --propCount;
}
```

The C# compiler emits a *Finalize* method for the *ZClass*. The *Finalize* method supplants the destructor in Microsoft intermediate language (MSIL) code. Figure 14-5 shows the *ZClass*. Notice the *Finalize* method and the absence of the *Destructor* method.

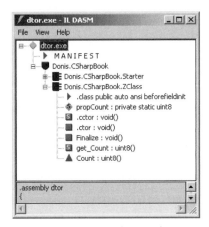

Figure 14-5   View of the ZClass

The C# compiler generated the following MSIL code for the *ZClass* destructor (for clarity, extraneous code has been removed from the listing):

```
.method family hidebysig virtual instance void
        Finalize() cil managed
{
  .maxstack  2
  .try
  {
    IL_0001:  ldsfld      uint8 Donis.CSharpBook.ZClass::propCount
    IL_0006:  ldc.i4.1
    IL_0007:  sub
    IL_0008:  conv.u1
```

```
    IL_0009:  stsfld     uint8 Donis.CSharpBook.ZClass::propCount
    IL_000f:  leave.s    IL_0019

  }
  finally
  {
    IL_0011:  ldarg.0
    IL_0012:  call       instance void [mscorlib]System.Object::Finalize()
    IL_0018:  endfinally
  }
  IL_0019:  nop
  IL_001a:  ret
}
```

The *Finalize* method provided by the C# compiler contains a termination handler. The try block contains the code of the destructor. In this circumstance, the count is decremented. The termination handler calls the *Finalize* method of the base class. Because the call is in a termination handler, the finalizer of the base class is called even if an unhandled exception is raised in the destructor. This means that calls to the *Finalize* method propagate through the class hierarchy even when an exception is raised. This also means that developers should never attempt to directly call the destructor of the base class. The manifested *Finalize* method automatically assumes this responsibility.

The following code defines a class hierarchy, in which each class in the hierarchy has a destructor. This demonstrates that the destructors are called bottom-up automatically. The destructor in the *XClass* throws an unhandled exception. Despite the error condition, the base destructors are called anyway. This confirms that the *Finalize* method of the base class is called in a termination handler:

```csharp
using System;

namespace Donis.CSharpBook{
    public class Starter{
        public static void Main(){
            XClass obj=new XClass();
        }
    }

    public class ZClass{

        ~ZClass() {
            Console.WriteLine("ZClass d'tor");
        }

    }

    public class YClass: ZClass{

        ~YClass() {
            Console.WriteLine("YClass d'tor");
        }

    }
```

```
public class XClass: YClass{

    ~XClass() {
        Console.WriteLine("XClass d'tor");
        throw new Exception("D'tor exception");
    }

}

}
```

Many have lamented the decision to associate finalizers with destructors. C++ developers are familiar with destructors. They are an integral part of the C++ language. This familiarity creates a level of expectation, which is only partially honored in C#. There are credible differences between C++ and C# destructors, including the following:

- C++ destructors can be called deterministically, whereas C# destructors are called nondeterministically.

- C++ destructors can be virtual or nonvirtual, whereas C# destructors are implicitly virtual.

- C++ destructors execute on the same thread that created the object, whereas C# destructors execute on a dedicated finalizer thread.

- C++ destructors cannot be suppressed at run time, whereas C# destructors can be suppressed.

For the remainder of this chapter, C# destructors are referred to as finalizers to distinguish between C# and C++ destructors.

As mentioned, finalizers are called nondeterministically. In code, you cannot call them directly. When are finalizers called?

- During the garbage collection process
- When the *AppDomain* of an object is unloaded
- When the *GC.Collect* method is called
- When the CLR is shutting down

Knowing the specific reason for finalization can be helpful. For example, if finalization is part of normal garbage collection, you might choose to recycle the object. However, if the application domain is being unloaded, recycling a dead object would be pointless. You can confirm that finalization is initiated by an application unload or a CLR shutdown. The *AppDomain* *.IsFinalizingForUnload* method, which is an instance method, returns *true* if the application domain is unloading and finalization has begun on objects in that domain. Otherwise, the method returns *false*. The *Environment.HasShutdownStarted* property is a static property that returns *true* if the CLR is shutting down or the application domain is unloading. Otherwise, the property returns *false*.

The Recycle application recycles an instance of the *ZClass* type. When the object is being final-ized, the *Environment.HasShutdownStarted* property is checked. If *false*, the reference to the object is re-established, which ends finalization. This resurrects the object (more about resur-rection later). If the property is *true*, the object is not recycled. There is no reason to recycle an object if the current application domain is unloading or the CLR is shutting down. This is the *ZClass* type from the Recycle application:

```
public class ZClass
{
    public ZClass()
    {
        ++propCount;
        _count = propCount;
    }

    ~ZClass()
    {
        ++propCount;
        ++_count;
        AppDomain current = AppDomain.CurrentDomain;
        if (!Environment.HasShutdownStarted)
        {
            Form1.obj = this;
            GC.ReRegisterForFinalize(this);
        }
    }

    private static int propCount = 0;
    private int _count;
    public int Count
    {
        get
        {
            return _count;
        }
    }
}
```

At application shutdown, finalizers have a limited amount of time to complete their tasks. This prevents an indefinite shutdown. Each *Finalize* method has two seconds to complete. If the time allotment is exceeded, that finalizer is terminated. The remaining finalizers then con-tinue to execute. As a group, the *Finalize* methods have 40 seconds to complete all finalization chores. When this time limit is exceeded, the remaining finalizers are skipped. Forty seconds is nearly an eternity in processing time and should be sufficient to complete even the most extensive housecleaning of an application.

In the following application, you can adjust the duration of the finalizer and view the results. A number between 1 and 10 provides the best comparative results. Specify the value as a command-line argument:

```
using System;
using System.Threading;
```

```
namespace Donis.CSharpBook{
    public class Starter{
        public static void Main(string [] args){
            Shutdown.ZTime=int.Parse(args[0]);
            ZClass [] obj=new ZClass[500];
            for(int count=0;count<500;++count) {
                obj[count]=new ZClass();
            }
        }
    }

    public class Shutdown {
        static public int ZTime=0;
    }

    public class ZClass{

        public ZClass() {
            ++globalcount;
            localcount=globalcount;
        }

        private int localcount=0;
        private static int globalcount=0;

        ~ZClass() {
            for(int i=0; i< Shutdown.ZTime; ++i) {
                Thread.Sleep(50);
            }
            Console.WriteLine(localcount+" "+
                "ZClass d'tor");
        }

    }
}
```

Finalizer Thread

The finalizer thread calls finalizers on objects waiting in the *FReachable* queue. After the finalizer is called, the object is removed from the *FReachable* queue and deleted from memory during the next garbage collection cycle. The finalizer thread executes the finalizer asynchronously. There is one finalizer thread that services all finalizers of the application, which creates a potential bottleneck. For this reason, finalizers should be short and simple. A long finalizer can delay the finalization of the remaining objects on the *FReachable* queue. In addition, this extends the lifetime of objects pending finalization and increases memory pressure on the managed heap. This causes more garbage collection, which is always expensive.

Finalizer Considerations

When implementing finalizers, there are several considerations. These considerations should help developers implement finalizers correctly. Some of these considerations emphasize that finalizers should be avoided whenever possible. For example, you should never implement an empty finalizer. In the C++ language, an empty destructor is harmless. In C#, an empty destructor (finalizer) is costly, as explained in this section.

Finalizers are expensive   As mentioned, finalizers are expensive. At least two garbage collection cycles are required to collect a finalizable object that is not rooted. During the first garbage collection, the finalizable object is moved from the *Finalizable* queue to the *FReachable* queue. After the finalizer has been called, the memory of the object is reclaimed in a future garbage collection. The lifetime of objects referenced by the finalizable object are equally extended. They must wait for the finalizable object to be reclaimed before being released themselves. Additional object retention increases memory pressure, which causes additional garbage collection. Needless garbage collection is particularly expensive. The finalizable objects are promoted to later generations, which make a full garbage collection more likely. Full garbage collection is much more expensive than collecting only Generation 0. Actually, the extra expense of defining a finalizable object starts at its allocation. When a finalizable object is created, a reference to the object must be added to the *Finalizable* queue. Objects without finalizers avoid this additional expense.

Finalizers are not guaranteed   Finalizers are not always called. Some of the reasons why a finalizer might not be called have already been mentioned. One such reason is the shutdown of the CLR by a host application. At that time, finalizers must run in an allotted amount of time. You can also programmatically suppress a finalizer with the *GC.SuppressFinalize* method. An asynchronous exception, such as a thread abort exception, can cause a finalizer not to run.

Multithreading   Finalizable objects are multithreaded. Object code and the finalizer execute on different threads. For this reason, certain activities should be avoided in the finalizer. Most notably, never access thread-local storage associated with the object in the finalizer. Because the thread context has changed, using thread local storage in the finalizer is inappropriate.

The TLS sample application contains the following code that uses thread local storage. This is a Windows Forms application. A reference to a *StreamWriter* object is placed into the TLS table for each thread. Various threads accessing the same *TMonitor* object will own a different *StreamWriter* reference in the TLS table. Therefore, each thread will write status messages to a different file. In the sample application, two threads are accessing a *TMonitor* instance. In the destructor of the *TMonitor* type, a *StreamWriter* is retrieved from TLS and closed. Which *StreamWriter* is closed? Is this the *StreamWriter* of the first or second thread? The answer is *neither*. The destructor is running on the finalizer thread, which is unrelated to the other threads. This thread has no *StreamWriter* reference, and an error is reported. In Microsoft Visual Studio 2005, *Console.WriteLine* in a Windows Forms application displays in the Output window:

```
class TMonitor
{
    public void WriteFile()
    {
```

```
    StreamWriter sw = Thread.GetData(Form1.Slot)
        as StreamWriter;
    if (sw == null)
    {
        sw = new StreamWriter(string.Format(
            @"C:\{0}File.txt",
            Thread.CurrentThread.Name),
            true);
        Thread.SetData(Form1.Slot, sw);
    }
    sw.WriteLine(DateTime.Now.ToLongTimeString());
}

~TMonitor()
{
    StreamWriter sw = Thread.GetData(Form1.Slot)
        as StreamWriter;
    if (sw != null)
    {
        sw.Close();
    }
    else
    {
        Console.WriteLine("Error in destructor");
    }
}
}
}
```

The preceding application is for demonstration purposes only. In a finalizer, you should not reference other managed objects.

One finalizer thread   There is a single finalizer thread that services the *FReachable* queue. It calls pending finalizers of finalizable objects. The finalizer thread is different from other threads that might be accessing the object methods. Do not change the context of the finalization thread. *This is not your thread.* Changing the context of the finalization thread can have an adverse effect on the finalization process.

Finalizers and virtual functions   Do not call virtual functions from finalizers. This can cause unexpected behavior such as inadvertent leaks and resources not being cleaned up. If overridden, there is no assurance that the derived class will provide the appropriate implementation. This is especially true for classes published in a class library, in which the developer of the derived class may have limited knowledge of the base class.

Look at the following sample code:

```
using System;

namespace Donis.CSharpBook{
    public class Starter{
        public static void Main(){
            YClass obj=new YClass();
        }
    }
```

```
public class ZClass {

    protected virtual void CloseResource() {
        Console.WriteLine("Closing ZClass resource.");
    }

    ~ZClass() {
        CloseResource();
    }
}


public class YClass: ZClass {

    protected override void CloseResource() {
        Console.WriteLine("Closing YClass resource.");
    }

    ~YClass() {
        CloseResource();
    }

    }
}
```

In the preceding code, the finalizer in the *ZClass* calls the *CloseResource* method, which is a virtual method. *YClass* is derived from *ZClass* and overrides the *CloseResource* method. An instance of the derived class is created in the *Main* method. At garbage collection, the following messages are displayed:

```
Closing YClass resource.
Closing YClass resource.
```

Yes, *CloseResource* of the derived class is called twice, which creates a couple of problems. First, an exception could be raised on the second attempt to close the resource. Second, the *ZClass* resource is not removed and leaks.

Order of finalization   Garbage collection is not performed in a guaranteed sequence. For this reason, do not access another managed object in the finalizer. There is no assurance that the other managed object has not been collected and removed from memory.

In the following code, the *ZClass* has a *StreamWriter* field. In the finalizer, the *StreamWriter* is closed. Normally, this is perfectly acceptable behavior, but not in a finalizer. When the application exits, an exception is raised in the finalizer. The *StreamWriter* object was collected before the current object. Therefore, an exception is raised when an instance method of the *StreamWriter* class is called in the finalizer.

```
public class ZClass
{
    public ZClass()
    {
```

```
        sw = new StreamWriter("test.txt");
    }

    ~ZClass()
    {
        sw.Close();
    }

    private StreamWriter sw;
}
```

Resurrection   Zombies do exist. Yikes! Like any object, finalizable objects are created on the managed heap. When there are no outstanding references to the object, a finalizable object is submitted for garbage collection. At that time, the object is dead. However, the object is resurrected to be placed in the *FReachable* queue. After the finalizer is called, the object is removed from the *FReachable* queue. It is removed from memory during the next garbage collection. At that time, the object is dead again.

You can intentionally, or more likely inadvertently, resurrect an object permanently during the finalization process. At that time, the object is resurrected without the finalizer attached. Therefore, the resurrected object is not completely returned to the live status. The object is a zombie. Zombies pose a distinct problem because of their dangling finalizers. Because the finalizer is not called, proper cleanup is not performed when the zombie is later collected. The result could be a memory leak, a resource not being released, or other related problems. You can manually reconnect the finalizer with the *GC.ReRegisterForFinalize* method. Afterward, the object is normal and is no longer a zombie.

Another problem with resurrection is that the original finalizer has executed. This could render the object unusable because needed resources might have been relinquished.

During finalization, a common cause of accidental resurrection is the creation of a new reference to the current object. At that moment, the object is resurrected. Despite being resurrected, the finalizer of the object runs to completion. In the following code, the current object is directly referenced in the finalizer. An indirect reference is more likely. Referencing another managed object in a finalizer can have a domino effect and should be avoided. That object might access another managed object, which might reference another object and so on until someone references the current object. *Voilà*—resurrection has occurred. This is a compelling reason to avoid referencing managed objects in a destructor.

```
using System;
using System.IO;

namespace Donis.CSharpBook{

    public class Starter{

        public static void Main(){
            obj=new ZClass();
            obj.TimeStamp();
```

```
        obj=null;
        GC.Collect();
        GC.WaitForPendingFinalizers();
        obj.TimeStamp();
    }

    public static ZClass obj;
}

public class ZClass {

    public ZClass() {
        sw=new StreamWriter("test.txt");
    }

    public void TimeStamp() {
        sw.WriteLine(DateTime.Now.ToLongTimeString());
    }

    ~ZClass() {
        Starter.obj=this;
        sw.Close();
        sw=null;
    }

    static private StreamWriter sw;
}
}
```

The first statement in the *ZClass* destructor resurrects the object. It assigns the object reference to a static field of the *Starter* class. Because there is again an outstanding reference, the object is resurrected. The underlying file of the *StreamWriter* instance is then closed. In *Main*, an instance of the *ZClass* is created. The instance is assigned to a static field of the *Starter* class. Afterward, the reference is assigned *null*, and garbage collection is forced. This kills and then resurrects the object. The next call on the object raises an exception because the underlying file has been closed in the previous finalization.

The following code corrects the problem and successfully resurrects the object. The first statement confirms whether the CLR is shutting down. If true, the managed application is exiting. In that circumstance, there is no reason to resurrect the object while the application domain is being unloaded. At that time, static objects are submitted to garbage collection. For that reason, the static object (*sw*) is accessible only when the application domain is not being unloaded. In the *if* block, the object is resurrected and the finalizer is reattached.

```
~ZClass() {
    if(Environment.HasShutdownStarted==false) {
        Starter.obj=this;
        sw.Close();
        sw=null;
        GC.ReRegisterForFinalize(this);
    }
}
```

The *TimeStamp* method of the previous code must also be updated. The finalizer sets the *sw* object, which is a *StreamWriter* instance, to *null*. This is checked in the revised *TimeStamp* method. If *null*, the *sw* reference is reinitialized. The file resource is then available again for writing:

```
public void TimeStamp() {
    if(sw==null) {
        sw=new StreamWriter("test.txt",true);
    }
    sw.WriteLine(DateTime.Now.ToLongTimeString());
    sw.Flush();
}
```

This is the entire code of the revised application:

```
using System;
using System.IO;

namespace Donis.CSharpBook{

    public class Starter{

        public static void Main(){
            obj=new ZClass();
            obj.TimeStamp();
            obj=null;
            GC.Collect();
            GC.WaitForPendingFinalizers();
            obj.TimeStamp();
        }

        public static ZClass obj;
    }

    public class ZClass {

        public ZClass() {
            sw=new StreamWriter("test.txt", true);
        }

        public void TimeStamp() {
            if(sw==null) {
                sw=new StreamWriter("test.txt",true);
            }
            sw.WriteLine(DateTime.Now.ToLongTimeString());
            sw.Flush();
        }

        ~ZClass() {
            if(Environment.HasShutdownStarted==false) {
                Starter.obj=this;
                sw.Close();
                sw=null;
```

```
                    GC.ReRegisterForFinalize(this);
            }
        }

        static private StreamWriter sw;

    }
}
```

Finalizers and reentrancy   A finalizer is reentrant. The best example of this is complete resurrection, in which the finalizer is reattached. In that circumstance, the finalizer is called at least twice. When a finalizer is called more than once, resurrection is the likely culprit. Redundant calls on a finalizer should not cause a logic error or an exception.

Deep object graph   A deep object graph can make garbage collection more expensive. Roots and branches of the object graph can be anchored with a finalizable object. As mentioned, the lifetime of a finalizable object is extended to encompass at least two garbage collections. All objects, even nonfinalizable objects, along the path of the finalizable object have their lives similarly extended. Therefore, one finalizable object can keep several other objects from being garbage collected. Deeper graphs by definition have longer branches and can extend the problem.

Finalizer race condition   The finalizer can execute at the same time as other functions of the finalizable object. Because the finalizer executes on a dedicated thread, other functions of the finalizable object could be running when finalization starts. This can cause a race condition to occur between normal operations and the finalization. Standard thread-synchronization techniques can protect against a finalization race condition.

In the following code, *MethodA* is called on a *ZClass* instance. *MethodA* has a built-in delay. Shortly thereafter, the object is set to *null* and collected. The finalizer then runs simultaneously with *MethodA*. The race has begun! The results are usually unpredictable.

```
public class Starter{

    public static void Main(){
        Thread t=new Thread(
            new ThreadStart(MethodA));
        obj=new ZClass();
        t.Start();
        obj=null;
        GC.Collect();
    }

    private static void MethodA() {
        obj.MethodB();
    }

    private static ZClass obj;
}

public class ZClass {
```

```
    public void MethodB() {
        Console.WriteLine("ZClass.MethodB Started");
        Thread.Sleep(1500);
        Console.WriteLine("ZClass.MethodB Finished");
    }

    ~ZClass() {
        Console.WriteLine("ZClass.~ZClass Started");
        // D'tor operation
        Console.WriteLine("ZClass.~ZClass Finished");
    }
}
```

Constructors   An exception in the constructor does not deter the object from being finalized. The finalizer is called regardless of the success of the constructor, which can create an interesting dilemma in which an object that is unsuccessfully constructed is still finalized. Cleanup of a partially constructed object can pose risks.

The following code demonstrates the problems that can occur when an exception is raised in a constructor. The exception is caught by the exception handler in *Main*. At that time, the object exists but is not correctly initialized. Despite the earlier exception in the constructor, the finalizer is called as the application exits.

```
using System;

namespace Donis.CSharpBook{
    public class Starter{
        public static void Main(){
            try {
                ZClass obj=new ZClass();
            }
            catch {
            }
        }
    }

    public class ZClass {

        public ZClass() {
            Console.WriteLine("ZClass c'tor");
            throw new Exception("Error");
        }

        ~ZClass() {
            Console.WriteLine("ZClass d'tor");
        }
    }
}
```

The following code resolves the problem of a partially constructed finalizable object. If the constructor does not complete successfully, *GC.SuppressFinalize* prevents the finalizer from being called later. In addition, a flag is maintained that indicates the state of the object.

The *bPartial* flag is set to *true* if the constructor fails, which is checked in instance methods. If the flag is *true*, the methods raise an exception because the object might not be stable.

```csharp
using System;

namespace Donis.CSharpBook{
    public class Starter{
        public static void Main(){
            try {
                ZClass obj=null;
                obj=new ZClass();
                if(obj!=null){
                    obj.MethodA();
                }
            }
            catch(Exception ex) {
                Console.WriteLine(ex.Message);
            }
        }
    }

    public class ZClass {

        public ZClass() {
            try {
                Console.WriteLine("ZClass c'tor");
                throw new Exception("Error");
            }
            catch {
                GC.SuppressFinalize(this);
                bPartial=true;
            }
        }

public void MethodA() {
            if(bPartial) {
                throw new Exception("Partial construction error");
            }
            Console.WriteLine("ZClass.MethodA");
        }

        ~ZClass() {
            Console.WriteLine("ZClass d'tor");
        }

        private bool bPartial=false;

    }
}
```

Console and finalization You can safely use the *Console* class in a finalizer. The *Console* class is exempted from the rule about not using managed classes in finalizers. It is especially written for use during finalization.

IDisposable.Dispose

The *Dispose* method is an alternative to a finalizer. Contrary to finalizers, *Dispose* methods are deterministic and can freely access managed types. Finalizers are nondeterministic, which delays invocation. This can prevent resources from being released in a timely manner and create resource contention. For example, an unreleased file handle can block or cause errors in other threads waiting on that handle. *Dispose* methods are deterministic and sometimes referred to as explicit garbage collection. You can call the *Dispose* method to release an expendable resource, such as immediately closing a file handle. Accessing managed objects in a finalizer is unadvisable. Garbage collection is undeterminable, and that object may no longer exist. This requirement greatly limits the scope and functionality of a finalizer. The *Dispose* method does not necessarily have these limitations because garbage collection may not be occurring.

The *Dispose* method is defined in the *IDisposable* interface of the *System* namespace. Disposable objects should inherit and implement the *IDisposable* interface, in which the *Dispose* method is the only member. You then call the *Dispose* method as a normal method to start deterministic garbage collection. Although possible, you should not implement the *Dispose* method separate of the *IDisposable* interface. The *IDisposable* interface is an important marker that confirms the presence of a disposable object. There are statements and behaviors, such as the *using* statement, that require this marker.

The following code demonstrates a simple implementation of the *Dispose* method:

```
public class Starter{
    public static void Main(){
        ZClass disposableobject=new ZClass();
        disposableobject.Dispose();
        disposableobject=null;
    }
}

public class ZClass: IDisposable {
    public ZClass() {
        // Allocate resources
    }

    public void Dispose() {
        // Release resources
    }
}
```

In the preceding code, the *Dispose* method is not guaranteed to run. Raising an exception prior to the *Dispose* method call could cause the method to be skipped and result in resource leakage. To protect against this possibility, place the *Dispose* method call in a *finally* block. This assures that the *Dispose* method is called whether or not an exception is raised in the *try* block. This is an updated version of the previous code, in which the *Dispose* method is placed in a *finally* block:

```
public static void Main(){
    ZClass disposableobject=null;
```

```
    try {
        disposableobject=new ZClass();
    }
    finally {
        disposableobject.Dispose();
        disposableobject=null;
    }
}
```

The *using* block is the short form of the preceding code. A new object is defined in the *using* statement. When the *using* block exits, the *Dispose* method is called automatically on the declared object of the *using* statement:

```
public static void Main(){
    using(ZClass disposableobject=
            new ZClass())
    {
        // use object
    }
}
```

The C# compile substitutes a *try* and a *finally* block for the *using* statement and block. This is some of the MSIL code emitted for the *using* block:

```
IL_0006:  stloc.0
.try
{
  IL_0007:  nop
  IL_0008:  nop
  IL_0009:  leave.s     IL_001b
}  // end .try
finally
{
  // partial listing…

  IL_0014:  callvirt    instance void [mscorlib]System.IDisposable::Dispose()
  IL_0019:  nop
  IL_001a:  endfinally
}  // end handler
```

Multiple objects of the same type can be declared in the *using* statement. Delimit the objects with commas. All objects declared in the statement are accessible in the *using* block. When the *using* block exits, the *Dispose* method is called on each of the declared objects from the *using* statement. In the following code, two objects of the same type are declared in the *using* statement:

```
using System;

namespace Donis.CSharpBook{

    public class Starter{
        public static void Main(){
            using(ZClass obj1=new ZClass(),
```

```
                        obj2=new ZClass()) {
            }
        }
    }

    public class ZClass: IDisposable {
        public void Dispose() {
            Console.WriteLine("ZClass.Dispose");
        }
    }

}
```

You can also declare objects of different types for a *using* block—simply stack multiple *using* statements. In the following code, three objects are scoped to the *using* block. One object is the *XClass* type, whereas two objects are *ZClass* types. All three are disposed at the end of the *using* block.

```
using System;

namespace Donis.CSharpBook{
    public class Starter{
        public static void Main(){
            using(XClass obj3=new XClass())
            using(ZClass obj1=new ZClass(),
                            obj2=new ZClass()) {
            }
        }
    }

    public class ZClass: IDisposable {
        public void Dispose() {
            Console.WriteLine("ZClass.Dispose");
        }
    }

    public class XClass: IDisposable {
        public void Dispose() {
            Console.WriteLine("XClass.Dispose");
        }
    }

}
```

Class can contain both a *Dispose* method and a finalizer. You can relinquish both managed and unmanaged resources in the *Dispose* method, whereas the finalizer can clean up only the unmanaged resources. When a *Dispose* method is not called as planned, the finalizer is an effective safety net. Finalizers are called automatically and cannot be forgotten. If not called earlier, finalizers of disposable objects are called at CLR shutdown. Finalization should not be performed on a disposed object. A second iteration of cleanup could have unexpected results. For this reason, developers typically suppress the finalizer in the *Dispose* method. The *GC.SuppressFinalize* method is called in the *Dispose* method to suppress the finalizer. Performance is improved because future finalization of the object is eliminated.

In the following code, the *ZClass* has both a *Dispose* and finalizer method. Note that *GC.SuppressFinalize* is invoked in the *Dispose* method.

```
using System;

namespace Donis.CSharpBook{
    public class Starter{
        public static void Main(){
            using(ZClass obj1=new ZClass()) {
            }
        }
    }

    public class ZClass: IDisposable {
        public void Dispose() {
            Console.WriteLine("Disposing resources");
            GC.SuppressFinalize(this);
        }

        ~ZClass() {
            Console.WriteLine("ZClass.ctor");
            // Cleanup unmanaged resources
        }
    }
}
```

This section reviewed the simple implementation of the *Dispose* method, which is sufficient for sealed classes. However, inheritable classes require the more complex *Disposable* pattern.

Thread Local Storage Example

Earlier in this chapter, an unworkable Thread Local Storage application was presented. The following code shows the corrected version that uses the *Dispose* method. For the *TMonitor* class, the *Dispose* method is called from each thread that is using the class.

```
class TMonitor: IDisposable
{
    public void WriteFile()
    {
        StreamWriter sw = Thread.GetData(Form1.Slot)
            as StreamWriter;
        if (sw == null)
        {
            sw = new StreamWriter(string.Format(
                @"C:\{0}File.txt",
                Thread.CurrentThread.Name),
                true);
            Thread.SetData(Form1.Slot, sw);
        }
        sw.WriteLine(DateTime.Now.ToLongTimeString());
    }
```

```
    public void Dispose()
    {
        StreamWriter sw = Thread.GetData(Form1.Slot)
            as StreamWriter;
        Thread.SetData(Form1.Slot, null);
        if (sw != null)
        {
            sw.Close();
            MessageBox.Show("sw closed");
        }
    }
}
```

Disposable Pattern

The *Disposable* pattern provides a template for implementing the *Dispose* method and finalizer in a base and derived class. The *Disposable* pattern, shown in the following code, should be implemented if the base class does not presently possess resources:

```
using System;
using System.Threading;

namespace Donis.CSharpBook{

    public class Base: IDisposable {

        public void Dispose() {
            Dispose(true);
            GC.SuppressFinalize(this);
        }

        protected virtual void Dispose(bool disposing) {
            if (disposing) {
                // Release managed resources
            }
            // Release unmanaged resources
        }

        ~Base() {
            Dispose (false);
        }
    }

    public class Derived: Base {
        protected override void Dispose(bool disposing) {
            if (disposing) {
                // Release managed resources.
            }
            // Release unmanaged resources
            base.Dispose(disposing);
        }
    }
}
```

We will focus first on the base class, which implements the *IDisposable* interface and contains two *Dispose* methods.

The one-argument *Dispose* method, which is a protected method, has a single argument. The disposing argument indicates whether the method is being called during deterministic or nondeterministic garbage collection. If called during nondeterministic garbage collection, the disposing argument is set to *false*. Otherwise, the argument is true. When the argument is *false*, only unmanaged releases are releasable in the method. When *true*, both managed and unmanaged resources can be released.

Both the no-argument *Dispose* method and the finalizer delegate to the one-argument *Dispose* method. The no-argument *Dispose* method is public and called explicitly for deterministic garbage collection. This *Dispose* method delegates to the one-argument destructor with the disposing flag set to *true*. It also suppresses finalization of this object in future garbage collection. The finalizer delegates to the one-argument destructor with the disposing flag set to *false*. This limits cleanup to unmanaged resources, which is appropriate during normal garbage collection.

The no-argument *Dispose* method is not a virtual method, whereas the one-argument *Dispose* method is virtual. The no-argument *Dispose* method should not be overridden in the derived class. This method should always delegate to the most derived one-argument *Dispose* method. Any other behavior would seriously break the disposable pattern.

In the derived class, override the one-argument *Dispose* method to clean up managed and unmanaged resources of the derived class. Do not override or hide the no-argument *Dispose* method of the base class. Finally, the one-argument *Dispose* method in the derived class should call the same method in the base class, affording that class the opportunity to release its resources.

In the derived class, do not implement a finalizer. The base class implementation of the finalize method will correctly call the most derived dispose method. Disposal then propagates from the most derived class to all ascendants. Therefore, resource cleanup is performed in the correct order.

Disposable Pattern Considerations

There are several factors to consider when implementing a simple dispose or the more complex *Disposable* pattern. This section lists many of the factors that should be considered when implementing a *Dispose* method.

Redundant Dispose Method

In the following code, the *Dispose* method is called twice. Calling the *Dispose* method multiple times should be secure. Set a flag the first time *Dispose* is called. Check the flag in future invocations to confirm that the object is disposed. If the object is disposed, do not dispose it again.

Alternatively, you might be able to confirm the disposability of an object from the state of the object. It is a good practice to confirm the disposed status at the beginning of other member methods. If the object is disposed, revive the object and execute the method or throw the *ObjectDisposedException*.

```
public static void Main(){
    using(ZClass disposableobject=
            new ZClass())
    {
        disposableobject.Dispose();
    }
}
```

The following code demonstrates a resilient *Dispose* method, which can be called multiple times. The *ReverseReader* type is a thin wrapper for a *StreamReader*. It inverts information read from the *StreamReader*. *ReserveReader* contains a *StreamReader* field. It is initialized in the class constructor and closed in the *Dispose* method. If the *StreamReader* is null, the object is presumed disposed. This is checked in the *Dispose* method. If the object is already disposed, the *Dispose* method simply returns. When the object is disposed, the other *ReverseReader* method throws the *ObjectDisposedException* exception. After the using block, a second *Dispose* method is called, which proves to be harmless. A second call to the *ReadLine* method is commented. If uncommented, an exception would be raised.

```
using System;
using System.IO;

namespace Donis.CSharpBook{
    public class Starter{

        public static void Main(){
            using(ReverseReader input=new
                    ReverseReader("text.txt")) {
                string result=input.ReadLine();
                while(result!=null) {
                    Console.WriteLine(result);
                    result=input.ReadLine();
                }
                input.Dispose();
                // input.ReadLine();
            }
        }

    }

    public class ReverseReader:IDisposable {

        public ReverseReader(string filename) {
            file=new StreamReader(filename);
        }

        public string ReadLine() {
            if(file==null) {
```

```
            throw new ObjectDisposedException(
                "ReadLine object");
        }
        if(file.Peek()<0) {
            return null;
        }
        string temp=file.ReadLine();
        char [] tempArray=temp.ToCharArray();
        Array.Reverse(tempArray);
        return new string(tempArray);
    }

    public void Dispose() {
        if(file==null) {
            return;
        }
        else {
            file.Close();
            file=null;
        }
    }

    private StreamReader file=null;
}
```

Close Method

Instead of the *Dispose* method, some classes expose another method for deterministic cleanup. Although this should not be done as a general practice, the exception is when another method is more intuitive than the *Dispose* method. For example, the *FileStream* class exposes the *Close* method. (*Close* is the traditional term for releasing a file.) The alternative method should delegate to the *Dispose* method. Do not implement the disposable routine more than once. Both the *Dispose* and alternative methods are available to the clients for deterministic garbage collection. The correct implementation is demonstrated with the *StreamWriter.Close* method, as shown in the following code. *StreamWriter.Close* delegates to *TextWriter.Dispose* for deterministic garbage collection. *TextWriter.Dispose* is inherited by the *StreamWriter* class. The *Close* method suppresses the finalizer, which is standard behavior of a deterministic method. Both the *Close* and *Dispose* method are available on the *StreamWriter* class. You should clearly document any alternate method for deterministic garbage collection.

```
.method public hidebysig virtual instance void
        Close() cil managed
{
  // Code size       14 (0xe)
  .maxstack  8
  IL_0000:  ldarg.0
  IL_0001:  ldc.i4.1
  IL_0002:  callvirt    instance void System.IO.TextWriter::Dispose(bool)
  IL_0007:  ldarg.0
  IL_0008:  call        void System.GC::SuppressFinalize(object)
  IL_000d:  ret
} // end of method StreamWriter::Close
```

Thread-Safe Dispose Method

The *Dispose* method is not implicitly thread-safe. As a public method, *Dispose* is callable for multiple threads simultaneously. Thread synchronization is required for thread-safeness. The *lock* statement, as demonstrated in the following code, is the convenient means of supporting simultaneous access to the *Dispose* method.

```
public class ZClass: IDisposable {

    public void Dispose() {
        lock(this) {
        }
    }
}
```

Reusable Objects

The *Disposable* pattern accommodates reusable objects. Unless the object is nondisposed, it can be recycled. Do not recycle an object implicitly. Automatically recycling an object on the assignment operator or a function call is not recommended. Expose a method that explicitly recycles the object. There is no convention for naming this method. However, an *Open* method is always a good choice. This method should have the dual purpose of initializing instances created with a default constructor. Recyclable objects should also expose a property that confirms the status of the object as alive or disposed.

The following code is a revision of the *ReverseReader* class, which was presented earlier in this chapter. This version is recyclable. It has a default and one-argument constructor. The one-argument constructor delegates to the *Open* method. You can call the *Open* method to initialize or recycle a *ReverseReader* instance. The *Active* property returns the status of the object. If *true*, the object is active.

```
public class ReverseReader:IDisposable {

    public ReverseReader() {
    }

    public ReverseReader(string filename) {
        Open(filename);
    }

    public bool Open(string filename) {
        if(file!=null) {
            return false;
        }
        file=new StreamReader(filename);
        return true;
    }

    public string ReadLine() {
        if(file==null) {
```

```
            throw new ObjectDisposedException(
                "ReadLine object");
        }
        if(file.Peek()<0) {
            return null;
        }
        string temp=file.ReadLine();
        char [] tempArray=temp.ToCharArray();
        Array.Reverse(tempArray);
        return new string(tempArray);
    }

    public void Dispose() {
        if(file==null) {
            return;
        }
        else {
            file.Close();
            file=null;
        }
    }

    public void Close() {
        Dispose();
    }

    private StreamReader file=null;

    public bool Active {
        get {
            return !(file==null);
        }
    }
}
}
```

Disposing Inner Objects

A disposable class should dispose the disposable fields contained in the type. Call the *Dispose* method of those fields in the *Dispose* method of the class. After disposing, set the disposable fields to *null*. Of course, the inner objects dispose the disposable objects they contain. In this way, the *Dispose* method is transitive.

The proper disposal of inner objects is shown in the following code:

```
public class ZClass: IDisposable{

    public ZClass() {
        inner=new YClass();
    }

    public void Dispose() {
        Console.WriteLine("ZClass.Dispose");
        inner.Dispose();
```

```
            inner=null;
        }

        private YClass inner=null;

    }

public class YClass: IDisposable{
    public void Dispose() {
        Console.WriteLine("YClass.Dispose");
    }
}
```

An object should not dispose any object not fully within its control, which can cause some unwanted side affects. In the following code, the *_inner* field is initialized with a property. The *_inner* field is a disposable type. Two instances of the containing class are created. One is created before the *using* block, and the other is created in the *using* statement. The *_inner* field of both objects is initialized to the same instance. Therefore, neither object has full control of the object. When the *using* block is exited, the inner object is disposed in the second object. However, the other object remains active. When the remaining active object attempts to access the inner object, an exception is raised.

```
using System;

namespace Donis.CSharpBook{
    public class Starter{
        public static void Main(){
            ZClass obj1=new ZClass();
            obj1.Inner=new YClass();
            using(ZClass obj2=new ZClass()) {
                obj2.Inner=obj1.Inner;
            }
            obj1.MethodA();   // exception
            obj1.Dispose();
            obj1=null;
        }
    }

    class ZClass: IDisposable{

        public ZClass() {
        }

        public void Dispose() {
            Console.WriteLine("ZClass.Dispose");
            _inner.Dispose();
        }

        public void MethodA() {
            Console.WriteLine("ZClass.MethodA");
            _inner.MethodA();
        }
```

```
        public YClass Inner {
            set {
                _inner=value;
            }
            get {
                return _inner;
            }
        }

        private YClass _inner=null;
    }

    class YClass: IDisposable{
        public void Dispose() {
            Console.WriteLine("YClass.Dispose");
            disposed=true;
        }

        public void MethodA() {
            if(disposed) {
                throw new ObjectDisposedException(
                    "YClass disposed");
            }
            Console.WriteLine("YClass.MethodA");
        }

        private bool disposed=false;

    }
}
```

Weak Reference

Weak references are one of my favorite features of the .NET Framework. A weak reference accords an object less persistence than a strong reference. A strong reference is a conventional reference and created with the *new* operator. As long as there is a strong reference pointing to the object, the object persists in memory. If not, the object becomes a candidate for removal and is collected in a future garbage collection. Conversely, a weak reference to an object is insufficient to retain that object in memory. A weak reference can be collected as memory is needed. You must confirm that weakly referenced objects have not been collected before use.

Weak references are not ideal for objects that contain information that is expensive to rehydrate. Information read from a persistent source such as a file or data store is preferred. You can simply reread the file or request the dataset again. Rehydrating a dataset can be light or heavy based on several factors, including the location of the dataset.

The central type for establishing weak references is, appropriately, the *WeakReference* type. These are the steps for creating and using a weak reference:

A weak reference usually starts life as a strong reference:

```
XNames objTemp = new XNames();
```

Create a *WeakReference* type. In the constructor, initialize the weak reference with the strong reference. Afterward, set the strong reference to *null.* An outstanding strong reference prevents the weak reference from controlling the lifetime of the object:

```
XNames objTemp = new XNames();
weaknames=new WeakReference(objTemp);
objTemp = null;
```

Before using the object, request a strong reference to the object from the weak reference. *WeakReference.Target* returns a strong reference to the weak object. If *WeakReference.Target* is *null,* the object has been collected and is no longer in memory. In this circumstance, the object needs to be rehydrated:

```
if (weaknames.Target == null)
{
    // do something
}
```

The following class reads a list of names from a file:

```
class XNames
{
    public XNames()
    {
        StreamReader sr=new StreamReader("names.txt");
        string temp = sr.ReadToEnd();
        _Names = temp.Split('\n');
    }
    private string [] _Names;

    public IEnumerator<string> GetEnumerator()
    {
        foreach(string name in _Names)
        {
            yield return name;
        }
    }
}
```

The preceding code is from the Weak application. It uses the *XNames* class to display the names from a file in a list box. The Weak application is shown in Figure 14-6.

In the Weak application, a weak reference is created and initiated with an instance of the *XNames* class. The code in the Fill List button enumerates the names of the *XNames* instance to populate the list box. Before using the instance, the status of the instance must be confirmed. Is it collected or not? The Apply Pressure button applies memory pressure to the application that eventually forces the weakly referenced object to be collected. When this occurs, the content in the list box is removed. You must then refill the list box using the Fill List button.

Figure 14-6 Weak application

This is the code from the form class of the Weak application that pertains to weak references:

```
public partial class Form1 : Form
{
    public Form1()
    {
        InitializeComponent();
    }
    private void btnFill_Click(object sender, EventArgs e)
    {
        if (weaknames.Target == null)
        {
            DialogResult result=MessageBox.Show(
                "Rehydrate?",
                "Names removed from memory.",
                MessageBoxButtons.YesNo);
            if (result == DialogResult.No)
            {
                return;
            }
            else
            {
                weaknames.Target = new XNames();
            }
        }
        foreach(string name in (XNames)weaknames.Target)
        {
            lblNames.Items.Add(name);
        }
    }

    private WeakReference weaknames;

    private void Form1_Load(object sender, EventArgs e)
    {
        XNames objTemp = new XNames();
        weaknames=new WeakReference(objTemp);
        objTemp = null;
    }
```

```
    private void btnApply_Click(object sender, EventArgs e)
    {
        objs.Add(new ZClass());
        if (weaknames.Target == null)
        {
            lblNames.Items.Clear();
        }
    }

    List<ZClass> objs = new List<ZClass>();
}

internal class ZClass
{
    public long[] array = new long[7500];
}
```

Weak Reference Internals

Weak references are tracked in short weak reference and long weak reference tables. Weak references are not created on the managed heap, but are entries in the short weak reference or long weak reference tables. Both tables are initially empty.

Each entry in the short weak reference table is a reference to a managed object on the heap. When garbage collection occurs, objects referenced in the short weak reference table that are not strongly rooted are collectable. The related slot in the table is set to *null*. References to finalizable objects that are being collected are moved from the finalization to the *FReachable* queue.

Entries in the long weak reference table are evaluated next. Long weak references are weak references that track an object through finalization. This allows the resurrection of a weakly referenced object. Objects referenced in the long weak reference table that are not strongly rooted are collectable.

Weak Reference Class

Table 14-1 lists the important members of the *WeakReference* class.

Table 14-1   *WeakReference* Class

Member Name	Description
WeakReference(object target)	The one-argument constructor initializes the weak reference with the target object.
WeakReference(object target, bool trackResurrection)	The two-argument constructor initializes the weak reference with the target object. If *trackResurrection* is *true*, the object is also tracked through finalization.
IsAlive	This is a property and gets whether or not the target object has been collected.
Target	This is an object property and gets or sets the object being referenced.

Critical Finalization Objects

Conditions can prevent a finalizer from running, and critical cleanup code might not execute. Resource leakage and other problems can occur when critical finalization code is abandoned. .NET Framework 2.0 introduces critical finalizable objects to ensure that critical finalizers run. The CLR is more diligent about executing finalizers in critical finalizer objects. Conditions that can prevent a normal finalizer from running, such as a forcible thread abort or an unload of the application domain, do not affect a critical finalizer. This is especially an issue in environments that host the CLR, such as Microsoft SQL Server 2005. A CLR host can asynchronously interrupt a managed application, which can strand important finalizers.

During garbage collection, critical finalizers run after the normal finalizers.

Critical finalizer objects are derived from the *CriticalFinalizerObject*, which is located in the *System.Runtime* namespace. The finalizer runs uninterrupted in a Constrained Execution Region (CER).

Constrained Execution Region

CER is a region of reliable code that is guaranteed to run. Even an asynchronous exception will not prevent the region from executing to completion. Within the CER, developers are constrained to certain actions. This is a shortlist of some of the actions that should be avoided in a CER:

- Boxing
- Unsafe code
- Locks
- Serialization
- Calling unreliable code
- Actions likely to cause an asynchronous exception

In a CER, the CLR delays an asynchronous exception until the region is exited. The CLR performs a variety of checks and does some preparation to ensure that code in the CER runs uninterrupted.

The *RuntimeHelpers.PrepareConstrainedRegions* static method places a subsequent catch, finally, or fault handler in a constrained region. The *RuntimeHelpers* class is in the *System .Runtime.CompilerServices* namespace. The *PrepareConstrainRegions* method call should immediately precede the *try* statement. The code in the *try* block is not reliable and can be interrupted. However, the related handler is within the CER and is uninterruptible.

Developers must make reliability assurances for code in a constrained region. The CLR does not strictly enforce the reliability constraints within the CER. Instead, the CLR relies on developer commitment, which is a reliability contract. Reliability contracts state the level of compliance for a method, class, or assembly. Set a reliability contract with the *ReliabilityContractAttribute*. This attribute is found in the *System.Runtime.ConstrainedExecution* namespace. The *Reliability-ContractAttribute* constructor has two parameters. The first parameter is the *Consistency-Guarantee* property, which indicates the potential scope of corruption if an asynchronous exception occurs during execution. For example, *Consistency.MayCorruptAppDomain* means that an asynchronous exception can leave the application domain in an unreliable state. The second parameter is the *Cer* property, which is a completion guarantee for code in a CER region. *Cer.Success* is the highest guarantee and promises that the code will successfully complete when running in a CER, assuming valid input.

Here is an example of a CER region:

```
[ReliabilityContract(Consistency.WillNotCorruptState,
        Cer.Success)]
class ZClass {

    void MethodA() {
        RuntimeHelpers.PrepareConstrainedRegions();
        try {
        }
        finally {
            // CER Region
        }
    }

}
```

Stephen Toub authored a detailed and informative article on CERs called "Keep Your Code Running with the Reliability Features of the .NET Framework." It can be found at the following link: *http://msdn.microsoft.com/msdnmag/issues/05/10/reliability/default.aspx*

Safe Handles

As a convenience, partial implementation of the *CriticalFinalizerObject* type is found in the *System.Runtime.InteropServices* namespace. The implementation creates a critical finalizer, which contains a CER. *CriticalHandle*, *SafeHandle*, *SafeHandleMinusOneIsInvalid*, and *SafeHandleZeroOrMinusOneIsInvalid* are derived from *CriticalFinalizerObject* and are adequate for most purposes. These classes are found in the *Microsoft.Win32.SafeHandles* namespace. *SafeHandle* implements reference counting, whereas *CriticalHandle* does not support reference counting. Both classes are essentially safe wrappers for kernel handles and ensure that kernel handles are properly closed in the future. The classes are abstract and require minimal implementation in the derived type. The .NET Framework class library (FCL) provides a complete implementation of the *CriticalHandle* and *SafeHandle* classes in the *Microsoft.Win32.SafeHandles* namespace. *SafeWaitHandle* is one implementation. It is a wrapper for a wait handle and indirectly extends the *SafeHandle* class.

In the following code, the *PipeHandle* class is a safe wrapper for a pipe handle. It also exposes the *CreatePipe* and the *CloseHandle* application programming interfaces (APIs) using interoperability. Because the method is called in a CER, a reliability contract is placed on the *CloseHandle* method. *PipeHandle* derives from the *SafeHandleMinusOneIsInvalid* class for the behavior of a critical finalizer object. The finalizer of the base class automatically calls the *ReleaseHandle* method. The *ReleaseHandle* of the derived type, *PipeHandle*, also has a reliability contract.

In the *AnonymousPipe* constructor, two *PipeHandle* instances are initialized, which are a read and write handle. The handle values are also displayed. The *PipeHandle* and *AnonymousPipe* classes are included in the Pipe application found on the companion CD-ROM. In the sample code, the application domain hosting the *PipeHandle* instances can be forcibly unloaded. Because the instances are critical finalizer objects, their destructors are called despite the unloading of the application domain:

```
public sealed class PipeHandle :
    SafeHandleMinusOneIsInvalid
{

    private PipeHandle()
        : base(true)
    {

    }

    [ReliabilityContract(Consistency.WillNotCorruptState,
            Cer.Success)]
    protected override bool ReleaseHandle()
    {
        return CloseHandle(handle);
    }

    [DllImport("kernel32.dll")]
    extern public static bool CreatePipe(
        out PipeHandle hReadPipe,
        out PipeHandle hWritePipe,
        IntPtr securityAttributes,
        int nSize);

    [ReliabilityContract(Consistency.WillNotCorruptState,
            Cer.Success)]
    [DllImport("kernel32.dll")]
    public static extern bool CloseHandle(IntPtr handle);

}

public class AnonymousPipe
{

    public AnonymousPipe()
    {

        PipeHandle.CreatePipe(out readHandle, out writeHandle,
            IntPtr.Zero, 10);
        MessageBox.Show((readHandle.DangerousGetHandle())
            .ToInt32().ToString());
```

```
        MessageBox.Show((writeHandle.DangerousGetHandle())
            .ToInt32().ToString());
    }

    private PipeHandle readHandle = null;
    private PipeHandle writeHandle = null;
}
```

Managing Unmanaged Resources

Managed code often relies on unmanaged resources. The unmanaged resource is typically accessible through a managed wrapper. The MyDevice program is an unmanaged application that emulates a hardware device. *DeviceWrapper* is a managed wrapper for the *MyDevice* unmanaged resource. This is the code for the *DeviceWrapper* class:

```
public sealed class MyDevice
{
    static private int count = 0;

    public MyDevice()
    {
        obj = new MyDeviceLib.DeviceClass();
        ++count;
    }

    private MyDeviceLib.DeviceClass obj;

    public void Open()
    {
        obj.OpenDevice();
    }

    public void Close()
    {
        obj.CloseDevice();
    }

    public void Start()
    {
        obj.StartCommunicating();
    }

    public void Stop()
    {
        obj.StopCommunicating();
    }

    ~MyDevice()
    {
        // resource released
        --count;
    }
}
```

Memory Pressure

The wrapper for an unhandled resource can hide the true memory cost of an object. Incorrect accounting of unhandled memory in the managed environment can cause unexpected out of memory exceptions.

.NET 2.0 introduces memory pressure, which accounts for unmanaged memory in the managed environment. This prevents a wrapper to an unmanaged resource from hiding an elephant in the closet. Memory pressure forces garbage collection sooner, which collects unused instances of the wrapper class. The wrapper releases the unmanaged resource to reduce the memory pressure on both managed and unmanaged memory.

The *GC.AddMemoryPressure* method adds artificial memory pressure on the managed heap for an unmanaged resource, whereas the *GC.RemoveMemoryPressure* method removes memory pressure. Both methods should be integrated into the wrapper class of the unmanaged resource. Call *AddMemoryPressure* and *RemoveMemoryPressure* in the constructor and *Dispose* method, respectively. Each instance of the *MyDevice* unmanaged resource allocates 40,000 bytes of memory on the unmanaged heap. In the following code, the constructor and destructor for the *MyDevice* wrapper now account for the unmanaged memory:

```
public MyDevice()
{
    GC.AddMemoryPressure(40000);
    obj = new MyDeviceLib.DeviceClass();
    ++count;
}

~MyDevice()
{
    GC.RemoveMemoryPressure(40000);
    // resource released
    --count;
}
```

Handles

Some native resources are available in limited quantities. Exhausting the resource can hang the application, crash the environment, or cause other adverse reactions. The availability of a limited resource should be tracked. When the resource is exhausted, corrective action should occur. Some limited kernel resources, such as a window, are assigned handles. The *HandleCollector* class is introduced in .NET Framework 2.0 to manage handles to limited kernel resources. Despite the name, the *HandleCollector* class is not limited to tracking kernel handles. You can use the *HandleCollector* class to manage any resource that has limited availability. The *HandleCollector* class is found in the *System.Runtime.InteropServices* namespace.

The *HandleCollector* class has a three-argument constructor that configures the important properties of the type. The arguments are the name: initial threshold and maximum threshold. The initial threshold sets the minimal requirement for starting garbage collection. The maximum threshold sets the limit where garbage collection is forced. When the availability is exceeded, garbage collection is triggered. Hopefully, this will collect managed wrappers that are holding unmanaged resources and replenish native resources. Using the constructor, create a static instance of the *HandleCollector* in the managed wrapper of the unmanaged resource. In the constructor, call *HandleCollector.Add*. In the finalizer, call *HandleCollector.Remove*.

The following code shows the *MyDevice* class revised for the *HandleCollector* class. The *MyDevice* unmanaged resource supports an initial threshold of three simultaneous connections and a maximum of five. You can test the effectiveness of the wrapper in the *UseResource* application by clicking the Connect button and monitoring the message boxes.

```
public sealed class MyDevice
{
    static private HandleCollector track=
        new HandleCollector("devices", 3,5);

    static private int count = 0;

    public MyDevice()
    {
        GC.AddMemoryPressure(40000);
        track.Add();
        obj = new MyDeviceLib.DeviceClass();
        ++count;
        MessageBox.Show("Device count: " + count.ToString());
    }

    private MyDeviceLib.DeviceClass obj;
    public void Open()
    {
        obj.OpenDevice();
    }

    public void Close()
    {
        obj.CloseDevice();
    }

    public void Start()
    {
        obj.StartCommunicating();
    }

    public void Stop()
    {
        obj.StopCommunicating();
    }

    ~MyDevice()
    {
        GC.RemoveMemoryPressure(40000);
```

```
            track.Remove();
            // resource released
            --count;
        }
    }
```

GC Class

Developers use the *GC* class as an interface to the GC in .NET. You can manipulate and monitor garbage collection with the *GC* class. Some GC commands affect the normal operation of the garbage collection. Garbage collection usefully performs best without developer interference. Table 14-2 lists the static members of the *GC* class.

Table 14-2   GC Class

Member Name	Description
MaxGeneration	This property is an integer property and gets the maximum number of generations.
AddMemoryPressure	This method forces the GC to recognize memory allocations for unmanaged resources.
Collect	This method forces garbage collection on a specific generation. There are two overloads of the method. The no-argument *Collect* performs garbage collection for all the generations. The one-argument *Collect* has a parameter that specifies the oldest generation to be collected.
CollectionCount	This method returns the number of garbage collection cycles for the specified generation.
GetGeneration	This method returns the generation of the specified object.
GetTotalMemory	This method returns the total number of bytes thought to be allocated for the managed heap. You can wait on garbage collection and finalization by setting the Boolean parameter to *true*.
KeepAlive	This method keeps alive the specified object from the beginning of the current routine to where the *KeepAlive* method is called.
RemoveMemoryPressure	This method removes some of the memory pressure set aside for unmanaged resources.
ReRegisterForFinalize	This method reattaches a finalizer to a resurrected object.
SuppressFinalize	This method suppresses future finalization of the specified object.
WaitForPendingFinalizers	This method suspends the current thread until the *Finalization* queue is empty.

Nonsecure Code

The final chapter, which is the next chapter, pertains to unsafe code, which is an ominous name. What developer wants to purposely write unsafe code? In .NET, unsafe code really means potentially unsafe code, which is code or memory that exists outside the normal controls of the CLR. For this reason, developers should approach unsafe code with caution.

Developers have access to raw pointers in C#, which are called pinned pointers. They are C++-style pointers. You can use pointer operators, such as * and &, with these pointers. Pointers should be avoided because they interrupt the normal operation of the GC. However, not secure pointers are sometimes necessary. For example, porting algorithms that rely heavily on pointers is one situation in which not secure pointers are beneficial.

Managed developers must sometime call unmanaged routines. Although the breadth of the .NET FCL is expanding quickly, there is considerable system behavior that still resides outside its realm. In addition, many third-party routines are not managed—particularly legacy applications. Finally, some code will never be managed for performance or other reasons. Interoperability allows managed developers to build bridges back to managed code. You can call unmanaged code from a managed routine. Conversely, you can call managed code from unmanaged routines.

Chapter 15
Unsafe Code

Unsafe code can access unmanaged memory, which is outside the realm of the Common Language Runtime (CLR). Conversely, safe code is limited to accessing the managed heap. The managed heap is controlled by the CLR under the auspices of the garbage collector (GC). Code that addresses the managed heap is intrinsically safer. The CLR automatically releases unused objects, performs type verification, and conducts other checks on managed memory. Developers can focus on core application development instead of administrative tasks such as memory management. For this reason, safe code improves user productivity and satisfaction.

Pointers to unmanaged memory are available in unsafe code. Like unmanaged memory, pointers are also outside the realm of the CLR. Pointers point to a fixed location in unmanaged memory, whereas reference types point to a moveable location in managed memory. The CLR manages reference types, which includes controlling the lifetime of objects and calling cleanup code. Developers do not delete memory allocated for reference types and are not overly involved in the intricacies of memory management. In C and C++ application development, developers were preoccupied with memory management. Despite this, improper management of pointers is a primary contributor to unsafe code in the unmanaged environment, including memory leaks, access of invalid memory, deletion of pointers, and fence post errors. Abstracting the nuances of pointer management and manipulation with reference types has made managed code considerably safer. However, when needed, you can exempt yourself from secure code and access pointers directly.

When is unsafe code appropriate? Not often. Unsafe code is provided within C# as the exception, not the rule. There are specific circumstances in which unsafe code is recommended:

- Unmanaged code often relies heavily on pointers. When porting this sort of code to C#, unsafe code is a possible solution. Most nontrivial C and C++ programmers heavily leverage pointers.

- Implementing a software algorithm, in which pointers are integral to the design, might necessitate unsafe code.

- Calling an unmanaged function might require function pointers.

- Pointers might be required when working with binary memory resident data structures.

- Unmanaged pointers might improve performance and efficiencies in certain circumstances.

Code in an unmanaged module is also considered unsafe. Code in an unmanaged module is shielded from the CLR. Therefore, no code verification, stack tracing, or other checking is performed on the unmanaged code, which makes the code less safe.

Developers sometimes need to call unmanaged code from managed applications. Although the Microsoft .NET Framework class library (FCL) contains most of the code needed for .NET application development, the FCL umbrella does not encompass everything. You might need to call functions (APIs) in operating system libraries for behavior outside the FCL. In addition, proprietary and vendor software might not be available as managed code. Alternatively, you can call managed code from an unmanaged module, such as during a callback. Managed code might also be exposed to unmanaged clients.

Platform invocation services (PInvoke) is the bridge between managed and unmanaged execution. The bridge is bidirectional. From managed code, PInvoke is responsible for locating, loading, and executing a function in an unmanaged module. Marshaling is the primary concern of cross-platform calls and the responsibility of the Interop marshaler. Marshaling converts parameters and return types between unmanaged and managed acceptable formats. Fortunately, marshaling is not always required, which avoids unnecessary overhead. Certain types, such as blittable types, do not require transformation and are the same in managed and unmanaged memory.

You can also build bridges between managed code and COM components, which contain unmanaged code. The Runtime Callable Wrapper (RCW) helps managed code call COM components. The COM Callable Wrapper (CCW) portrays a managed component as a COM component. This makes the managed component indirectly accessible to COM clients. COM components are also available via PInvoke. However, the CCW and RCW are more convenient and are the recommended solutions in most scenarios. COM interoperability is not a topic for this book. *COM Programming with Microsoft .NET*, by John Paul Mueller and Julian Templeman (Microsoft Press, 2003), is an excellent resource for additional information on COM interoperability and .NET.

Unsafe code is also not trusted code. Code access security does not extend to unsafe code. Type verification, which helps prevent buffer overrun attacks, is not performed. Code verification is not performed. Therefore, the reliability of the code is undetermined. These are some of the reasons why unsafe code is not trusted. Because it is not trusted, elevated permissions are required to call unsafe code from managed code. Applications that rely on unsafe code might not execute successfully in every deployment situation and should be thoroughly tested in all potential scenarios. Managed code requires the *SecurityPermission.UnmanagedCode* permission to call unsafe code. The *SuppressUnmanagedCodeSecurityAttribute* attribute disables the stack walk that confirms the *SecurityPermission.UnmanagedCode* permission in callers. This attribute is a free pass for other managed code to call unsafe code. It is a convenient option, but also dangerous.

Managed applications that include unsafe code must be compiled with the unsafe option. The C# compiler option is simply */unsafe*. In Microsoft Visual Studio 2005, this option is found in the project properties. The project properties are accessible from Solution Explorer. Open the context menu on the project name and choose the Properties menu item. In the Build window, choose the *Allow unsafe code* option, as shown in Figure 15-1.

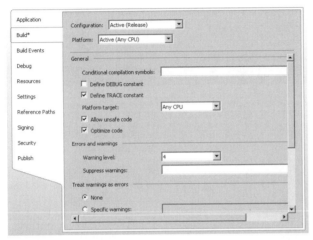

Figure 15-1   The Build window with the unsafe compiler option

Unsafe Keyword

The *unsafe* keyword sets the perimeter of an unsafe context and prevents the inadvertent placement of unsafe code. Code within the unsafe context can be unsafe, which allows unmanaged pointers to be declared and used in expressions. The *unsafe* keyword can be applied to a class, struct, interface, or delegate. When it is applied to a type, all the members of that type are also considered unsafe. You can also apply the *unsafe* keyword to specific members of a type. If applied to a function member, the entire function operates in the unsafe context.

In the following code, the *ZStruct* contains two fields that are pointers. Each is annotated with the *unsafe* keyword.

```
public struct ZStruct {
    public unsafe int *fielda;
    public unsafe double *fieldb;
}
```

In this example, *ZStruct* is marked as unsafe. The unsafe context extends to the entire struct, which includes the two fields. Both fields are unsafe.

```
public unsafe struct ZStruct {
    public int *fielda;
    public double *fieldb;
}
```

You can also create an unsafe block using the *unsafe* statement. All code encapsulated by the block is in the unsafe context. The following code has an *unsafe* block and method. Within the *unsafe* block in the *Main* method, *MethodA* is called and passed an *int* pointer as a parameter. *MethodA* is an unsafe method. It assigns the *int* pointer to a byte pointer, which now points to the lower byte of the *int* value. The value at that lower byte is returned from *MethodA*. For an *int* value of 296, *MethodA* returns 40.

```
public static void Main(){
    int number=296;
    byte b;
    unsafe {
        b=MethodA(&number);
    }
    Console.WriteLine(b);
}

public unsafe static byte MethodA(int *pI) {
    byte *temp=(byte*) pI;

    return *temp;
}
```

The unsafe status of a base class is not inherited by a derived class. Unless explicitly designated as unsafe, a derived class is safe. In an unsafe context, the derived class can use unsafe members of the base class that are accessible.

In the following code, a compile error occurs in the derived type. The *fieldb* member of *YClass* requires an unsafe context, which is not inherited from the *ZClass* base class. Add the *unsafe* keyword explicitly to *fieldb*, and the code will compile successfully.

```
public unsafe class ZClass {
    protected int *fielda;
}

public class YClass: ZClass {
    protected int *fieldb;  // compile error
}
```

Pointers

Unsafe code is mostly about direct access to pointers, which point to a fixed location in memory. Because the location is fixed, the pointer is reliable and can be used for dereferencing, pointer math, and other traditional pointer type manipulation. Pointers are outside the control of the GC. The developer is responsible for managing the lifetime of the pointer, if necessary.

C# does not automatically expose pointers. Exposing a pointer requires an unsafe context. In C#, pointers are usually abstracted using references. The reference abstracts a pointer to memory on the managed heap. That reference and related memory is managed by the GC and subject to relocation. A moveable pointer underlies a reference, which is why references are not available for direct pointer manipulation. Pointer manipulation on a moveable address would yield unreliable results.

This is the syntax for declaring a pointer:

unmanagedtype* identifier;

unmanagedtype* identifier=initializer;

You can declare multiple pointers in a single statement using comma delimiters. Notice that the syntax is slightly different from C or C++ languages:

```
int *pA, pB, pC;  // C++:  int *pA, *pB, *pC;
```

The unmanaged types (a subset of managed types) are *sbyte, byte, short, ushort, int, uint, long, ulong, char, float, double, decimal, bool*, and *enum*. Some managed types, such as *string*, are not included in this list. You can create pointers to user-defined structs, assuming that they contain all unmanaged types as fields. Pointer types do not inherit from *System.Object*, so they cannot be cast to or from *System.Object*.

Void pointers are allowed but dangerous. This is a typeless pointer that can emulate any other pointer type. Any pointer type can be implicitly cast to a void pointer. This unpredictability makes void pointers extraordinarily unsafe. Except for void pointers, pointers are moderately type-safe. Although you cannot implicitly cast between different pointer types, explicitly casting between most pointer types is always allowed. As expected, the following code would cause a compiler error because of the pointer mismatch. This assignment could be forced with an explicit cast to another pointer type. In that circumstance, the developer assumes responsibility for the safeness of the pointer assignment.

```
int val=5;
float* pA=&val;
```

You can initialize a pointer with the address of a value or with another pointer. In the following code, both methods of initializing a pointer are shown:

```
public unsafe static void Main() {
    int ival=5;
    int *p1=&ival;  // dereference
    int *p2=p1;     // pointer to pointer
}
```

In the preceding code, the asterisk (*) is used to declare a pointer. The ampersand (&) is used to dereference a value. Table 15-1 describes the various symbols that are used with pointers.

Table 15-1   Pointer Symbols

Symbol	Description
Pointer declaration (*)	For pointers, the asterisk symbol has two purposes. The first is to declare new pointer variables. `int *pA;`

Pointer dereference (*)	The second purpose of the asterisk is to dereference a pointer. Pointers point to an address in memory. Dereferencing a pointer returns the value at that address in memory.
	
	`int val=5;`
	`int *pA=&val;`
	`Console.WriteLine(*pA); // displays 5`
	
	You cannot dereference a void pointer.

Address of (&)	The ampersand symbol returns the memory location of a variable, which is a fixed value. The following code returns the memory address of an *int*. It is used to initialize an *int* pointer. `int *pA=&val;`

Member access (->)	Arrow notation dereferences members of a type found at a memory location. For example, you can access members of a struct using arrow notation and a pointer. In the following code, *ZStruct* is a struct, and *fielda* is a member of that type.
	
	`ZStruct obj=new ZStruct(5);`
	`ZStruct *pObj=&obj;`
	`int val1=pObj->fielda;`
	
	Alternatively, you can deference the pointer and access a member using dot syntax (.).
	
	`int val2=(*pObj).fielda;   // dot syntax`

Pointer element ([])	A pointer element is an offset from the memory address of a pointer. For example, *p[2]* is an offset of two. Offsets are incremented by the size of the pointer type. If *p* is an *int* pointer, *p[2]* is an increment of eight bytes. In the following code, assume that *ZStruct* has two *int* fields in contiguous memory: *fielda* and *fieldb*.
	
	`ZStruct obj=new ZStruct(5);`
	`int *pA=&obj.fielda;`
	`Console.WriteLine(pA[1]) // fieldb`

Table 15-1   Pointer Symbols *(Continued)*

Symbol	Description

Pointer to a pointer (**)	A pointer to a pointer points to a location in memory that contains the address of a pointer. Although rarely useful, you can extend the chain of pointers even further (***, ****, and so on). You can dereference a pointer to a pointer with a double asterisk (**). Alternatively, you can dereference a pointer to a pointer using individual asterisks in separate steps.
	
	`int val=5;`
	`int *pA=&val;`
	`int **ppA=&pA;`
	`// Address stored in ppA, which is pA.`
	`Console.WriteLine((int)ppA);`
	`// Address stored in pA.`
	`Console.WriteLine((int)*ppA);`
	`// value at address stored in pA (5).`
	`Console.WriteLine((int)**ppA);`

Pointer addition (+)	Pointer addition adds the size of the pointer type to the memory location.
	
	`ZStruct obj=new ZStruct(5);`
	`int *pA=&obj.fielda;`
	`pA=pA+2; // Add eight to pointer`

Pointer subtraction (-)	Pointer subtraction subtracts from the pointer the size of the pointer type.
	
	`ZStruct obj=new ZStruct(5);`
	`int *pA=&obj.fielda;`
	`pA=pA-3; // Subtract twelve from pointer`

Pointer increment (++)	Pointer increment increments the pointer by the size of the pointer type.
	
	`ZStruct obj=new ZStruct(5);`
	`int *pA=&obj.fielda;`
	`++pA; // increment pointer by four`

Pointer decrement (--)	Pointer decrement decrements the pointer by the size of the pointer type.
	
	`ZStruct obj=new ZStruct(5);`
	`int *pA=&obj.fielda;`
	`--pA; // decrement pointer by four`

Relational symbols	The relational operators, such as < > >= <= != ==, can be used to compare pointers. The comparison is based on memory location and not pointer type. In the following code, *pA* and *pB* are compared, even though *pA* and *pB* are pointers of different types.
	
	`ZStruct obj=new ZStruct(5);`
	`int *pA=&obj.fielda;`
	`int val=5;`
	`int *pB=&val;`
	`if(pA==pB) {`
	`}`

Pointer Parameters and Return

A pointer is a legitimate variable. As such, a pointer can be used as a variable in most circumstances, including as a parameter or return type. When used as a return type, ensure that the lifetime of the pointer is the same as or exceeds that of the target. For example, do not return a pointer to a local variable from a function—the local variable loses scope outside of the function and the pointer is then invalid.

In the following code, a pointer is used as both a parameter and return type. *MethodA* accepts a pointer as a parameter. It then returns the same pointer. After the method call, both *pB* and *pA* point to the same location in memory. They are aliases. Therefore, *Console.WriteLine* displays the same number when the values at the pointers are displayed.

```
using System;

namespace Donis.CSharpBook{
    public class Starter{
        public unsafe static void Main() {
            int val=5;
            int *pA=&val;
            int *pB;
            pB=MethodA(pA);
            Console.WriteLine("*pA = {0} | *pB = {0}",
                *pA, *pB);
        }

        public unsafe static int *MethodA(int *pArg) {
            *pArg+=15;
            return pArg;
        }
    }

}
```

The *ref* or *out* modifiers can be applied to pointer parameters. Without the modifiers, the memory location is *passed by pointer*. The pointer itself is *passed by value* on the stack. In the function, you can dereference the pointer and change values at the memory location. These changes will persist even after the function exits. However, changes to the pointer itself are discarded when the function exists. With the *ref* or *out* modifier, a pointer parameter is *passed by reference*. In the function, the pointer can be changed directly. Those changes continue to persist even after the function exits.

In the following code, both *MethodA* and *MethodB* have a pointer as a parameter. *MethodA* passes the pointer by value, whereas *MethodB* passes the pointer by reference. In both methods, the pointer is changed. The change is discarded when *MethodA* exists. When *MethodB* exits, the change persists.

```
using System;

namespace Donis.CSharpBook{
    public class Starter{

        public unsafe static void Main() {
            int val=5;
            int *pA=&val;
            Console.WriteLine("Original: {0}", (int) pA);
            MethodA(pA);
            Console.WriteLine("MethodA:  {0}", (int) pA);
            MethodB(ref pA);
            Console.WriteLine("MethodB:  {0}", (int) pA);
        }

        public unsafe static void MethodA(int *pArg) {
            ++pArg;
        }

        public unsafe static void MethodB(ref int *pArg) {
            ++pArg;
        }

    }

}
```

Fixed

What is wrong with the following code?

```
int [] numbers={1,2,3,4,5,6};
int *pI=numbers;
```

The problem is that the *numbers* variable is an array, which is a reference type. The code will not compile. References are moveable types and cannot be converted to pointers. Because objects are moveable, you cannot obtain a reliable pointer. Conversely, structs are value types and are placed on the stack and outside of the control of the GC. Struct values have a fixed address and are easily converted into pointers. In the preceding code, if the type were changed from an array to a struct, it would compile successfully. With the *fixed* statement, you pin the location of a moveable type—at least temporarily. Pinning memory for an extended period of time can interfere with efficient garbage collection.

Here is the code revised with the *fixed* statement. This code compiles successfully.

```
int [] numbers={1,2,3,4,5,6};
fixed(int *pI=numbers) {
    // do something
}
```

The *fixed* statement pins memory for the span of a block. In the block, the memory is unmovable and is exempt from garbage collection. You can access the pinned memory using the pointer declared or initialized in the *fixed* statement, which is a read-only pointer. When the fixed block exits, the memory is unpinned. Multiple pointers can be declared in the *fixed* statement. The pointers are delimited with commas, and only the first pointer is prefixed with the asterisk (*):

```
int [] n1={1,2,3,4};
int [] n2={5,6,7,8};
int [] n3={9,10,11,12};
fixed(int *p1=n1, p2=n2, p3=n3) {
}
```

This is a more complete example of using the *fixed* statement:

```
using System;

namespace Donis.CSharpBook{
    public class Starter{

        private static int [] numbers={5,10,15,20,25,30};

        public unsafe static void Main(){
            int count=0;
            Console.WriteLine(" Pointer    Value\n");
            fixed(int *pI=numbers) {
                foreach(int a in numbers){
                    Console.WriteLine("{0} : {1}",
                        (int)(pI+count), *((int*)pI+count));
                    ++count;
                }
            }
        }
    }
}
```

In the following code, *ZClass* is a class and a moveable type. The *fixed* statement makes the *ZClass* object fixed in memory. A pointer to the integer member is then obtained.

```
public class Starter{
    public unsafe static void Main() {
        ZClass obj=new ZClass();
        fixed(int *pA=&obj.fielda) {
        }
    }
}

public class ZClass {
    public int fielda=5;
}
```

stackalloc

The *stackalloc* command allocates memory dynamically on the stack instead of the heap. The lifetime of the allocation is the duration of the current function, which provides another option for allocating memory at run time. The *stackalloc* command must be used within an unsafe context. It can be used to initialize only local variables. The CLR will detect buffer overruns caused by the *stackalloc* command.

Here is the syntax for *stackalloc*:

type * stackalloc *type[expression]*

The *stackalloc* command returns an unmanaged type. The expression should evaluate to an integral value, which is the number of elements to be allocated. The base pointer of the memory allocation is returned. This memory is fixed and not available for garbage collection. It is automatically released at the end of the function. These are the particulars of the *stackalloc* command.

The following code allocates 26 characters on the stack. The subsequent *for* loop assigns alphabetic characters to each element. The final loop displays each character.

```
using System;

namespace Donis.CSharpBook{
    public unsafe class Starter{
        public static void Main(){
            char* pChar=stackalloc char[26];
            char* _pChar=pChar;
            for(int count=0;count<26;++count) {
                (*_pChar)=(char)(((int)('A'))+count);
                ++_pChar;
            }
            for(int count=0;count<26;++count) {
                Console.Write(pChar[count]);
            }
        }
    }
}
```

Platform Invoke

You can call unmanaged functions from managed code using platform invoke (PInvoke). Managed and unmanaged memory might be laid out differently, which might require marshaling of parameters or the return type. In .NET, marshaling is the responsibility of the Interop marshaler.

Interop Marshaler

The Interop marshaler is responsible for transferring data between managed and unmanaged memory. It automatically transfers data that is similarly represented in managed and unmanaged environments. For example, integers are identically formatted in both environments and automatically marshaled between managed and unmanaged environments. Types that are the same in both environments are called *blittable* types. *Nonblittable* types, such as strings, are managed types without an equivalent unmanaged type and must be marshaled. The Interop marshaler assigns a default unmanaged type for many nonblittable types. In addition, developers can explicitly marshal nonblittable types to specific unmanaged types with the *MarshalAsAttribute* type.

DllImport

The *DllImportAttribute* imports a function exported from an unmanaged library, and the unmanaged library must export a function. *DllImportAttribute* is in the *System.Runtime .InteropServices* namespace. *DllImportAttribute* has several options that configure the managed environment to import the function. The library is dynamically loaded, and the function pointer is initialized at run time. Because the attribute is evaluated at run time, most configuration errors are not found at compile time; they are found later.

This is the syntax of the *DllImportAttribute*:

[DllImport(*options*)] *accessibility* static extern *returntype* functionname(*parameters*)

Options are used to configure the import. The name of the library is the only required option. The name of the library should include the fully qualified path if it is not found in the path environment variable. Accessibility is the visibility of the function, such as public or protected. Imported functions must be static and extern. The remainder is the managed signature of the function.

The following code imports three functions to display the vertical and horizontal size of the screen. *GetDC*, *GetDeviceCaps*, and *ReleaseHandle* are Microsoft Win32 APIs. The imported functions are configured and exposed in the API class, which is a static class.

```
using System;
using System.Runtime.InteropServices;

namespace Donis.CSharpBook{
    public class Starter{
        public static void Main(){
            IntPtr hDC=API.GetDC(IntPtr.Zero);
            int v=API.GetDeviceCaps(hDC, API.HORZRES);
            Console.WriteLine("Vertical size of window {0}mm.", v);
            int h=API.GetDeviceCaps(hDC, API.HORZRES);
            Console.WriteLine("Horizontal size of window {0}mm.", h);
            int resp=API.ReleaseDC(IntPtr.Zero, hDC);
            if(resp!=1) {
                Console.WriteLine("Error releasing hdc");
            }
        }
    }

    public static class API {
        [DllImport("user32.dll")] public static extern
```

```
        IntPtr GetDC(IntPtr hWnd);

        [DllImport("user32.dll")] public static extern
        int ReleaseDC(IntPtr hWnd, IntPtr hDC);

        [DllImport("gdi32.dll")]public static extern
        int GetDeviceCaps(IntPtr hDC, int nIndex);

        public const int HORZSIZE=4;   // horizontal size in pixels
        public const int VERTSIZE=6;   // vertical size in pixels
        public const int HORZRES=8;    // horizontal size in millimeters
        public const int VERTRES=10;   // vertical size in millimeters
    }
}
```

In the preceding code, the name of the library was the option used. There are several other options, which are described in the following sections.

EntryPoint   This option explicitly names the imported function. Without this option, the name is implied from the managed function signature. When the imported name is ambiguous, the *EntryPoint* option is necessary. You can then specify a different name for the entry point and the managed function.

In the following code, *MessageBox* is being imported. However, the managed name for the function is *ShowMessage*.

```
using System;
using System.Runtime.InteropServices;

namespace Donis.CSharpBook{
    public class Starter{
        public static void Main() {
            string caption="Visual C# 2005";
            string text="Hello, world!";
            API.ShowMessage(0, text, caption, 0);
        }
    }

    public class API {
        [DllImport("user32.dll", EntryPoint="MessageBox")]
        public static extern int ShowMessage(int hWnd,
            string text, string caption, uint type);
    }
}
```

CallingConvention   This option sets the calling convention of the function. The default calling convention is Winapi, which maps to the standard calling convention in the Win32 environment. The calling convention is set with the *CallingConvention* enumeration. Table 15-2 lists the members of the enumeration.

Table 15-2 *CallingConvention* Enumeration

Member	Description
Cdecl	The caller removes the parameters from the stack, which is the calling convention for functions that have a variable-length argument list.
FastCall	This calling convention is not supported.
StdCall	The called method removes the parameters from the stack. This calling convention is commonly used for APIs and is the default for calling unmanaged functions with Platform invoke.
ThisCall	The first parameter of the function is the *this* pointer followed by the conventional parameters. The *this* pointer is cached in the ECX register and used to access instance members of an unmanaged class.
WinApi	Default calling convention of the current platform. For Win32 environment, this is the *StdCall* calling convention. For Windows CE .NET, *CDecl* is the default.

The following code imports the *printf* function, which is found in the C Runtime Library. The *printf* function accepts a variable number of parameters and supports the *CDecl* calling convention.

```
using System;
using System.Runtime.InteropServices;

namespace Donis.CSharpBook{
    public class Starter{
        public static void Main() {
            int val1=5, val2=10;
            API.printf("%d+%d=%d", val1, val2, val1+val2);
        }
    }

    public class API {
        [DllImport("msvcrt.dll", CharSet=CharSet.Ansi,
            CallingConvention=CallingConvention.Cdecl)]
        public static extern int printf(string formatspecifier,
            int lhs, int rhs, int total);
    }

}
```

ExactSpelling   This option stipulates that the exact spelling of the function name is used to resolve the symbol. Names are not always what they seem. For example, the function names of many Win32 APIs are actually macros that map to the *real* API, which is an A or W suffixed method. The A version is the ANSI version, whereas the W (wide) version is the Unicode version of the function. The ANSI versus Unicode extrapolation pertains mostly to Win32 APIs that have string parameters. For example, the supposed *CreateWindow* API is a macro that maps to either the *CreateWindowW* or *CreateWindowA* API. For the *DllImportAttribute*, the version selected is determined in the *CharSet* option. If *ExactSpelling* is false, the function name is treated as the actual name and not translated. The default is false.

The following code imports the *GetModuleHandleW* function specifically. *ExactSpelling* is true to prevent mapping to another name.

```
using System;
using System.Runtime.InteropServices;

namespace Donis.CSharpBook{
    public class Starter{
        public static void Main() {
            int hProcess=API.GetModuleHandleW(null);
        }
    }

    public class API {
        [DllImport("kernel32.dll", ExactSpelling=true)]
        public static extern int GetModuleHandleW(string filename);
    }

}
```

PreserveSig   This option preserves the signature of the method when resolving the symbol. COM functions usually return an *HRESULT*, which is the error status of the call. The real return is the parameter decorated with the *[out, retval]* Interface Definition Language (IDL) attribute. In managed code, the *HRESULT* is consumed and the *[out,retval]* parameter is the return. To resolve a COM function, that managed signature cannot be preserved; it should be mapped to a COM signature. Conversely, the signature of non-COM functions should be preserved. *PreserveSig* defaults to true.

The following code demonstrates the *PreserveSig* option with a fictitious COM function:

```
public class API {
    [DllImport("ole32.dll", PreserveSig=false)]
    public static extern int SomeFunction();
}
```

The signature is not preserved and would become the following:

```
HRESULT SomeFunction([out, retval] int param)
```

SetLastError   This option requests that the CLR cache the error code of the named Win32 API. Most Win32 APIs return false if the function fails. False is minimally descriptive, so developers can call *GetLastError* for an integer error code. *GetLastError* must be called immediately after the failed API; if not, the next API might reset the error code. In managed code, call *Marshal.GetLastWin32Error* to retrieve the error code. The *Marshal* type is in the *System.Runtime .InteropServices* namespace. *SetLastError* defaults to false.

In the following code, *CreateDirectory* and *FormatMessage* are imported in the API class. *CreateDirectory* creates a file directory; *FormatMessage* converts a Win32 error code into a user-friendly message. For *CreateDirectory*, the *SetLastError* option is set to *true*. In *Main*,

CreateDirectory is called with an invalid path. The "c*" drive is probably an incorrect drive on most computers. The resulting error code is stored in the *resp* variable, which is then converted into a message in the *FormatMessage* API. *FormatMessage* returns the user-friendly messages as an *out* parameter.

```csharp
using System;
using System.Text;
using System.Runtime.InteropServices;

namespace Donis.CSharpBook{
    public class Starter{
        public static void Main() {
            bool resp=API.CreateDirectory(@"c*:\file.txt",
                IntPtr.Zero);
            if(resp==false) {
                StringBuilder message;
                int errorcode=Marshal.GetLastWin32Error();
                API.FormatMessage(
                    API.FORMAT_MESSAGE_ALLOCATE_BUFFER |
                    API.FORMAT_MESSAGE_FROM_SYSTEM |
                    API.FORMAT_MESSAGE_IGNORE_INSERTS,
                    IntPtr.Zero, errorcode,
                    0, out message, 0, IntPtr.Zero);
                Console.WriteLine(message);
            }
        }
    }

    public class API {
        [DllImport("kernel32.dll", SetLastError=true)]
        public static extern bool CreateDirectory(
            string lpPathName, IntPtr lpSecurityAttributes);

        [DllImport("kernel32.dll", SetLastError=false)]
        public static extern System.Int32 FormatMessage(
            System.Int32 dwFlags,
            IntPtr lpSource,
            System.Int32 dwMessageId,
            System.Int32 dwLanguageId,
            out StringBuilder lpBuffer,
            System.Int32 nSize,
            IntPtr va_list);

        public const int FORMAT_MESSAGE_ALLOCATE_BUFFER=256;
        public const int FORMAT_MESSAGE_IGNORE_INSERTS=512;
        public const int FORMAT_MESSAGE_FROM_STRING=1024;
        public const int FORMAT_MESSAGE_FROM_HMODULE=2048;
        public const int FORMAT_MESSAGE_FROM_SYSTEM=4096;
        public const int FORMAT_MESSAGE_ARGUMENT_ARRAY=8192;
        public const int FORMAT_MESSAGE_MAX_WIDTH_MASK=255;
    }
}
```

CharSet

This option indicates the proper interpretation of strings in unmanaged memory, which can affect the *ExactSpelling* option. *CharSet* is also an enumeration with three members. The default is *CharSet.Ansi*. Table 15-3 lists the members of the *CharSet* enumeration.

Table 15-3 *CharSet* Enumeration

Value	Description
CharSet.Ansi	Strings should be marshaled as ANSI.
CharSet.Unicode	Strings should be marshaled as Unicode.
CharSet.Auto	The appropriate conversion is decided at run time depending on the current platform.

The following code marshals string for unmanaged memory as ANSI. The *ExactSpelling* option defaults to false, and the *GetModuleHandleA* API is called.

```
using System;
using System.Runtime.InteropServices;

namespace Donis.CSharpBook{
    public class Starter{
        public static void Main() {
            int hProcess=API.GetModuleHandle(null);
        }
    }

    public class API {
        [DllImport("kernel32.dll", CharSet=CharSet.Ansi)]
        public static extern int GetModuleHandle(string filename);
    }

}
```

BestFitMapping   This option affects the Unicode-to-ANSI mapping of text characters passed from managed to unmanaged functions running in the Windows 98 or Windows Me environment. If true, best fit mapping is enabled. When there is not a direct character match, the Unicode character is mapped to the closest match in the ANSI code page. If no match is available, the Unicode character is mapped to a "?" character. The default is true.

ThrowOnUnmappableChar   The *ThrowOnUnmappableChar* option can request an exception when an unmappable character is found in the Unicode-to-ANSI translation for Windows 98 and Windows Me. If true, an exception is raised when a Unicode character cannot be mapped to ANSI, and the character is converted to a "?" character. If false, no exception is raised. See the *BestFitMapping* option for additional details on Unicode-to-ANSI mapping.

Blittable Types

Blittable types are identically represented in managed and unmanaged memory. Therefore, no conversion is necessary from the Interop marshaler when marshaling between managed and unmanaged environments. Because conversion can be expensive, blittable types are more efficient than nonblittable types. For this reason, when possible, parameters and return types should be blittable types, which include *System.Byte*, *System.SByte*, *System.Int16*, *System.UInt16*, *System.Int32*, *System.UInt32*, *System.Int64*, *System.IntPtr*, *System.UIntPtr*, *System.Single*, and *System.Double*. Vectors of blittable types are also considered blittable. Formatted value types that contain only blittable types are also considered blittable.

Nonblittable types have different representation in managed and unmanaged memory. Some nonblittable types are automatically converted by the Interop marshaler, whereas others require explicit marshaling. Strings and user-defined classes are examples of nonblittable types. A managed string can be marshaled as a variety of unmanaged strings: *LPSTR*, *LPTSTR*, *LPWSTR*, and so on. Classes are nonblittable unless formatted. A formatted class marshaled as a formatted value type is blittable.

Formatted Type

A formatted type is a user-defined type in which the memory layout of the members is explicitly specified. Formatted types are prefixed with the *StructLayoutAttribute*, which sets the layout of the members as described in the *LayoutKind* enumeration. Table 15-4 lists the members of the *LayoutKind* enumeration.

Table 15-4   *LayoutKind* Enumeration

Value	Description
LayoutKind.Auto	The CLR sets the location of members in unmanaged memory. The type cannot be exposed to unmanaged code.
LayoutKind.Sequential	Members are stored in contiguous (sequential) and textual order in unmanaged memory. If desired, set packing with the *StructLayout-Attribute.Pack* option.
LayoutKind.Explicit	This value allows the developer to stipulate the order of the fields in memory using *FieldOffsetAttribute*. This value is useful for representing a C or C++ union type in unmanaged code.

In the following code, the API class contains the *GetWindowRect* unmanaged API. This function returns the location of the client area in the screen. The parameters of *GetWindowRect* are a window handle and a pointer to a *Rect* structure, which is also defined in the API class. The *Rect* structure, which is initialized inside the function, is a formatted value type and is blittable. By default, value types are passed by value. To pass by pointer, the *out* modifier is assigned to the *Rect* parameter.

```
public class API
{
    [DllImport("user32.dll")]
```

```
    public static extern bool GetWindowRect(
        IntPtr hwnd,
        out Rect windowRect);

    [StructLayout(LayoutKind.Sequential)]
    public struct Rect
    {
        public int left;
        public int top;
        public int right;
        public int bottom;
    }
}
```

Here is the code that uses the *GetWindowRect* API and the *Rect* structure:

```
API.Rect client = new API.Rect();
API.GetWindowRect(this.Handle, out client);
string temp=string.Format("Left {0} : Top {1} : "+
    "Right {2} : Bottom {3}", client.left,
    client.top, client.right, client.bottom);
MessageBox.Show(temp);
```

The following code is a version of the API class that defines a *Rect* class instead of a structure. Because the *Rect* class has the *StructLayout* attribute, it is a formatted type. Classes are passed by reference by default. The *out* modifier required for a structure is not necessary for a class.

```
class API2
{
    [DllImport("user32.dll")]
    public static extern bool GetWindowRect(
        IntPtr hwnd,
        Rect windowRect);

    [StructLayout(LayoutKind.Sequential)]
    public class Rect
    {
        public int left;
        public int top;
        public int right;
        public int bottom;
    }
}
```

This is the code to call the *GetWindowRect* API using the *Rect* class:

```
API2.Rect client = new API2.Rect();
API2.GetWindowRect(this.Handle, client);
string temp = string.Format("Left {0} : Top {1} : " +
    "Right {2} : Bottom {3}", client.left,
    client.top, client.right, client.bottom);
MessageBox.Show(temp);
```

Unions are fairly common in C and C++ code. A *union* is a type in which the members share the same memory location. This preserves memory by overlaying data in shared memory. C# does not offer a union type. In managed code, emulate a union in unmanaged memory with the *LayoutKind.Explicit* option of *StructLayoutAttribute*. Set each field of the union to the same offset, as shown in the following code:

```
[StructLayout(LayoutKind.Explicit)]
struct ZStruct {
    [FieldOffset(0)] int fielda;
    [FieldOffset(0)] short fieldb;
    [FieldOffset(0)] bool fieldc;
}
```

Directional Attributes

Directional attributes explicitly control the direction of marshaling. Parameters can be assigned *InAttribute*, *OutAttribute*, or both attributes to affect marshaling. This is equivalent to *[in]*, *[out]*, and *[in,out]* of the IDL. *InAttribute* and *OutAttribute* are also represented by keywords in C#. Table 15-5 lists the attributes and related keywords.

Table 15-5   Directional Attributes and C# Keywords

Keyword	Attribute	IDL
Not available	*InAttribute*	*[in]*
Ref	*InAttribute and OutAttribute*	*[in,out]*
Out	*OutAttribute*	*[out]*

The default directional attribute depends on the type of parameter and any modifiers.

StringBuilder

Strings are immutable and dynamically sized. An unmanaged API might require a fixed-length and modifiable string. In addition, some unmanaged APIs initialize the string with memory allocated at run time. A string type should not be used in these circumstances. Instead, use the *StringBuilder* class, which is found in the *System.Text* namespace. *StringBuilders* are fixed-length and not immutable. Furthermore, you can initialize the *StringBuilder* with memory created in the unmanaged API.

In the following code, the *GetWindowText* unmanaged API is imported twice. (This code, which is from the *GetWindowText* application, is included on the CD-ROM for this book.) *GetWindowText* retrieves the text from the specified window. For an overlapped window, this is text from the title bar. The second parameter of *GetWindowText* is a string, which is initialized with the window text during the function call. The first version of *GetWindowText* in the *API* class has a string parameter, whereas the version in the *API2* class has a *StringBuilder* parameter. The *GetWindowText* application is a Windows Forms application that has two buttons. The first button calls *API.GetWindowText*. The second button calls *API2.GetWindowText*.

Because of the string parameter in *API.GetWindowText*, an exception is raised because the API attempts to change that parameter. The second button invokes *API2.GetWindowText* successfully.

```
public class API
{
    [DllImport("user32.dll")]
    public static extern int GetWindowText(
        IntPtr hWnd, ref string lpString, int nMaxCount);
}

public class API2
{
    [DllImport("user32.dll")]
    public static extern int GetWindowText(
        IntPtr hWnd, StringBuilder lpString, int nMaxCount);
}
```

This is the code from the button-click handlers of the form:

```
private void btnGetText_Click(object sender, EventArgs e)
{
    string windowtext=null;
    API.GetWindowText(this.Handle, ref windowtext,
        10);
    MessageBox.Show(windowtext);
}

private void btnGetText2_Click(object sender, EventArgs e)
{
    StringBuilder windowtext=new StringBuilder();
    API2.GetWindowText(this.Handle, windowtext,
        25);
    MessageBox.Show(windowtext.ToString());
}
```

Unmanaged Callbacks

Some unmanaged APIs accept a callback as a parameter, which is a function pointer. The API invokes the function pointer to call a function in the managed caller. Callbacks are typically used for iteration. For example, the *EnumWindows* unmanaged API uses a callback to iterate top-level window handles.

.NET abstracts function pointers with delegates, which are type-safe and have a specific signature. In the managed signature, substitute a delegate for the callback parameter of the unmanaged signature.

These are the steps to implement a callback for an unmanaged function:

1. Find the unmanaged signature of the callback function.

2. Define a matching managed signature for the callback function.

3.   Implement a function to be used as the callback. The function should contain the response to the callback.

4.   Create a delegate, which is initialized with the callback function.

5.   Invoke the unmanaged API using the delegate for the callback parameter.

The following code imports the *EnumWindows* unmanaged API. The first parameter of *Enum-Windows* is a callback. *EnumWindows* enumerates top-level windows. The callback function is called at each iteration and is given the current window handle. In this code, *APICallback* is a delegate and provides a managed signature for the callback.

```
class API
{
    [DllImport("user32.dll")]
    public static extern bool EnumWindows(
        APICallback lpEnumFunc,
        System.Int32 lParam);

    public delegate bool APICallback(int hWnd, int lParam);
}
```

EnumWindows is called in the click handler of a Windows Forms application, where *GetWindow-Handle* is the callback function. *GetWindowHandle* is called for each iterated window handle. The function adds each window handle to a list box:

```
private void btnHandle_Click(object sender, EventArgs e)
{
    API.EnumWindows(new API.APICallback(GetWindowHandle), 0);
}

bool GetWindowHandle(int hWnd, int lParam)
{
    string temp = string.Format("{0:0000000}", hWnd);
    listBox1.Items.Add(temp);
    return true;
}
```

Explicit Marshaling

Explicit marshaling is sometimes required to convert nonblittable parameters and fields, and returns types to proper unmanaged types. Marshaling is invaluable for strings, which have several possible representations in unmanaged memory. Strings default to *LPSTR*. Use the *MarshalAsAttribute* to explicitly marshal a managed type as a specific unmanaged type. The *UnmanagedType* enumeration defines the unmanaged types available to the *MarshalAsAttribute*. Table 15-6 lists the members of the *UnmanagedType* enumeration.

Table 15-6   *UnmanagedType* **Enumeration**

Member	Description
AnsiBStr	Length-prefixed ANSI string
AsAny	Dynamic type for which the type of the value is set at run time
Bool	Four-byte Boolean value
BStr	Length-prefixed Unicode string
ByValArray	Marshals an array by value; *SizeConst* sets the number of elements
ByValTStr	Inline fixed-length character array that is a member of a structure
Currency	COM currency type
CustomMarshaler	A custom marshaler to be used with *MarshalAsAttribute.MarshalType* or *MarshalAsAttribute.MarshalTypeRef*
Error	*HRESULT*
FunctionPtr	C-style function pointer
I1	One-byte integer
I2	Two-byte integer
I4	Four-byte integer
I8	Eight-byte integer
IDispatch	*IDispatch* pointer for COM
Interface	COM interface pointer
IUnknown	*IUnknown* interface pointer
LPArray	Pointer to the first element of an unmanaged array
LPStr	Null-terminated ANSI string
LPStruct	Pointer to an unmanaged structure
LPTStr	Platform-dependent string
LPWStr	Unicode string
R4	Four-byte floating point number
R8	Eight-byte floating point number
SafeArray	Safe array in which the type, rank, and bounds are defined
Struct	Marshals formatted value and reference types
SysInt	Platform-dependent integer (32 bits in Win32 environment)
SysUInt	Platform-dependent unsigned integer (32 bits in Win32 environment)
TBStr	Length-prefixed, platform-dependent string
U1	One-byte unsigned integer
U2	Two-byte unsigned integer
U4	Four-byte unsigned integer
U8	Eight-byte unsigned integer
VariantBool	Two-byte *VARIANT_BOOL* type
VBByRefStr	Microsoft Visual Basic–specific

GetVersionEx is imported in the following code. The function is called in *Main* to obtain information on the current operating system. *GetVersionEx* has a single parameter, which is a pointer to an *OSVERSIONINFO* structure. The last field in the structure is *szCSDVersion*, which is a universally unique identifier (UUID). A UUID is a 128-byte array. The *MarshalAs* attribute marshals the field as a 128-character array. Each character is one byte long.

```
using System;
using System.Runtime.InteropServices;

namespace Donis.CSharpBook{

    public class Starter{
        public static void Main() {
            API.OSVERSIONINFO info=new API.OSVERSIONINFO();
            info.dwOSVersionInfoSize=Marshal.SizeOf(info);
            bool resp=API.GetVersionEx(ref info);
            if(resp==false) {
                Console.WriteLine("GetVersion failed");
            }
            Console.WriteLine("{0}.{1}.{2}",
                info.dwMajorVersion,
                info.dwMinorVersion,
                info.dwBuildNumber);
        }
    }


    public class API {

        [DllImport("kernel32.dll")] public static extern
        bool GetVersionEx(ref OSVERSIONINFO lpVersionInfo);

    [StructLayout(LayoutKind.Sequential)]
        public struct OSVERSIONINFO {
            public System.Int32 dwOSVersionInfoSize;
            public System.Int32 dwMajorVersion;
            public System.Int32 dwMinorVersion;
            public System.Int32 dwBuildNumber;
            public System.Int32 dwPlatformId;
            [MarshalAs( UnmanagedType.ByValTStr, SizeConst=128 )]
                public String szCSDVersion;

        }

    }
}
```

Fixed-Size Buffers

In the previous code, the *MarshalAs* attribute defined a fixed-size field of 128 characters or bytes. As an alternative to the *MarshalAs* attribute, C# 2.0 introduces fixed-size buffers using the *fixed* keyword. The primary purpose of this keyword is to embed aggregate types, such as an array, in a struct. Fixed-size buffers are accepted in structs but not in classes.

There are several rules for using fixed-size buffers:

- Fixed-size buffers are available only in unsafe context.

- Fixed-size buffers can represent only one-dimensional arrays (vectors).

- The array must have a specific length.

- Fixed-size buffers are allowed only in struct types.

- Fixed-sized buffers are limited to *bool, byte, char, short, int, long, sbyte, ushort, uint, ulong, float,* or *double* types.

This is the syntax of the fixed-sized buffer:

attributes accessibility modifier fixed *type identifier* [*expression*]

The following code rewrites the *OSVERSIONINFO* structure that used the *MarshalAs* attribute. This version uses the fixed keyword for the *szCSDVersion* field.

```
public class API {
[StructLayout(LayoutKind.Sequential)]
    unsafe public struct OSVERSIONINFO {
        public System.Int32 dwOSVersionInfoSize;
        public System.Int32 dwMajorVersion;
        public System.Int32 dwMinorVersion;
        public System.Int32 dwBuildNumber;
        public System.Int32 dwPlatformId;
        public fixed char szCSDVersion[128];
    }
}
```

Summary

Although pointers are not normally available in C#, developers can choose to use pointers at their discretion. Pointers are available in the context of unsafe code, which requires the *unsafe* keyword. You can create pointers to unmanaged types, such as the *int, float,* and *char* types. In addition, unsafe code must be compiled with the unsafe compiler option.

You cannot create pointers to moveable memory. Managed memory is moveable and managed by the garbage collector (GC). The fixed statement pins managed memory within a block. Pinned memory is fixed. While pinned, memory is not accessible to the GC.

The *DllImportAttribute*, which describes an unmanaged function that is exported from a library, has various options to configure the importing of a function. The Interop marshaler marshals parameters and returns values between managed and unmanaged memory during the function call. Blittable types do not require conversion. Nonblittable types require conversion to unmanaged memory. Developers can explicitly marshal nonblittable types using the *MarshalAs* attribute.

Appendix
Operator Overloading

Developers add operator overloading to user-defined types to describe how that type works with common operators. A feature of built-in types is the automatic support of most operators. Built-in types, such as *int*, *float*, and long-value types, behave intuitively with mathematical, logical, and conditional operators. As expected, the plus, minus, and multiply operators implicitly perform addition, subtraction, and multiplication when applied to these types. This intrinsic knowledge of operators makes using built-in types convenient. You might want to use user-defined types as conveniently. Unfortunately, the C# compiler cannot interpret user-defined classes in the context of most of the standard operators. For example, how does the compiler interpret *zclass+zclass*? The compiler cannot perform this interpretation without help from the class developer. This assistance is offered through *operator overloading*, which describes an operator in the context of a particular type. Overload several operators in a user-defined type to provide the same transparency found in most built-in types for operators.

User-defined types that represent numerical systems or perform mathematical operations benefit the most from operator overloading. A fraction, complex number, summation, hexa-decimal numerical system, and other similar types that have well-established behavior are improved with operator overloading.

You can also describe type conversion of user-defined types using operator overloading. Conversion operators can convert or cast a user-defined type to another type, which can be a built-in type or another user-defined type. With some exceptions, you can cast from one built-in type to another built-in type. For example, you can implicitly cast from a short to a long value. You can also cast explicitly from a long to a short value. However, what does it mean to cast a *ZClass* instance to an *int* value? This is another situation in which developer input is essential. Developers overload conversion operators to instruct the compiler in the conver-sions of user-defined types.

Operator overloading should be intuitive and is never required. Do not stray from the under-lying intent of the operator. For example, the plus operator should perform some type of addi-tion. *System.String* overloads the *operator+* to concatenate strings. Concatenation and addition are similar concepts. If the implementation of the *operator+* within the string type truncated characters, that would be nonintuitive and more confusing than helpful. Operator overloading can be overused and is not appropriate in all circumstances. The *operator+* is a reasonable addition to a string class. However, an *operator-*, although available, would be nonsensical. Remember, the overloaded operator must be intuitive to everyone, not just to you. Confirm with peers your perception of intuitive behavior. An alternative to operator overloading is simply implementing a named method: *Add* method instead of an *operator+* and *Subtract* method instead of overloading the *operator-*. There is the added benefit that named methods are called overtly, whereas operator functions are called tacitly.

Mathematical and Logical Operators

Mathematical and logical operators can be unary or binary operators, and most binary and unary operators can be overloaded in a user-defined type. The sole ternary operator, which is the conditional operator, cannot be overloaded. This is the complete description of mathematical and logical operators that cannot be overloaded in a user-defined type:

- Dot operator (*identifier.member*)
- Call operator (*methodname()*)
- Assignment operators (=, +=, /=, %=, and so on)
- Conditional operators (*&&*, ||, and ?:)
- Check and unchecked operators
- *new* operator
- *typeof* operator
- *as* and *is* operators
- Array operator (*[]*)
- Pointer operators

The compound assignment operators, such as += and /=, are implicitly overloaded using the individual operators. For example, the += and /= operators are implicitly overloaded by overloading the + and / operators.

In addition, developers cannot use operator overloading to define new operators. For example, you could not define a ^^ operator, which does not otherwise exist.

There are some notable differences between usage in the C++ and C# languages. In C++, you can overload the *assignment*, *new*, and *array* operators. This is not allowed in C#. This may be an issue when porting code from C++ to C#. Instead of overloading the *assignment* operator, implement the *ICloneable* interface. The garbage collector (GC) is responsible for managing dynamic memory. For that reason, the *new* operator cannot be overloaded in managed code.

The *array* operator is commonly overloaded in C++ to create a secure array, where fence post errors are usually checked. Fencepost errors are automatically detected by the CLR, which eliminates one of the primary reasons to overload the *array* operator.

Overloading an operator redefines the behavior of that operator in an expression. However, you cannot change the syntax, precedence, or associativity of an operator with operator overloading. Overloading an operator does not change the core principles of using the operator. Assume that the division operator is overloaded in a user-defined type. The syntax for employing the division operator remains *obj1/obj2*. Precedence is also preserved. In *obj1+obj2/obj3-obj4*, the division operation is performed before a plus or minus operator, but after the increment or decrement operator. Multiple division operations, as in *obj1/obj2+obj3/obj4* are evaluated from left to right, which maintains the normal associativity.

Implementation

Overloaded operators are implemented as static and public functions. Other modifiers, such as virtual and sealed, are not allowed. The unary operator has a single operand, whereas the binary operator has two operands. Parameters of an overloaded operator cannot be *ref* or *out*.

Here is the syntax for overloading a unary or binary operator method:

public static *type* operator *unary*(*classtype operand*)

public static *type* operator *binary*(*type lhsoperand, type rhsoperand*)

For a unary operator method, the operand is the same type as the containing class. For a binary operator method, at least one of the parameters must be the containing type. This allows the type to appear as *lhs*, *rhs*, or both *lhs* and *rhs* in the expression. In the *obj+5* expression, the object instance is passed as the *lhs* operand to the *operator+* method. The object instance is passed as the *rhs* operand in the *5+obj* expression. The return type is any value type but not void.

The following is an example of the implementation and use of an overloaded operator. The *ZClass* is a simple class and wrapper for two integer fields. The *operator+* method is overloaded to add two *ZClass* instances. Because the *operator+* method is part of the class, it has access to the private members of that class. This is convenient when accessing parameters of that type within the operator method. In this code, the *operator+* is called implicitly in the expression: *obj1+obj2*. You cannot call an operator function explicitly.

```
using System;

namespace Donis.CSharpBook{
    public class Starter{
        public static void Main(){
            ZClass obj1=new ZClass(5,10);
            ZClass obj2=new ZClass(15,20);
            ZClass obj3=obj1+obj2;
```

```
                    Console.WriteLine(obj3.Total);
            }
    }

    class ZClass {

        public ZClass(int _fielda, int _fieldb) {
            fielda=_fielda;
            fieldb=_fieldb;
        }

        public static ZClass operator+(ZClass lhs, ZClass rhs) {
            return new ZClass(lhs.fielda+rhs.fielda,
                lhs.fieldb+rhs.fieldb);
        }

        public int Total {
            get {
                return fielda+fieldb;
            }
        }

        protected int fielda, fieldb;
    }
}
```

Operator methods are available in a derived class. At least one operand of the operator function remains the base type. However, you can freely substitute the derived instance with the base type operand and access the base type members. The return type can also be a base type, which might pose problems. As a return, assigning a base instance to a derived type causes a run-time error. In addition, the derived type can replace operator methods of the base class. Simply implement the operator function again in the derived class. The implementation in the derived class overloads the base operator method.

In the following code, *YClass* derives from the *ZClass* class and inherits *operator+*, *fielda*, and *fieldb*. (*ZClass.operator+* was shown in the previous code.) *YClass* also implements an *operator-* function. In Main, both the *operator+* and *operator-* functions are used. The *operator+* on the *YClass* returns a *ZClass* instance, which is the base type. You cannot explicitly cast this result to a *YClass* without raising a run-time exception.

```
namespace Donis.CSharpBook{
    public class Starter{
        public static void Main(){
            YClass obj1=new YClass(5,10);
            YClass obj2=new YClass(15,20);
            ZClass obj3=obj1+obj2;
            Console.WriteLine(obj3.Total);
            YClass obj4=obj1-obj2;
            Console.WriteLine(obj4.Total);
        }
    }
```

```
// Partial listing

public class YClass:ZClass {

    public YClass(int _fielda, int _fieldb)
        :base(_fielda, _fieldb) {
    }

    public static YClass operator-(YClass lhs, YClass rhs) {
        return new YClass(lhs.fielda-rhs.fielda,
            lhs.fieldb-rhs.fieldb);
    }
  }
}
```

You can overload an operator member function. The general rules of overloading apply, and each overloaded operator member function must have a unique signature. Implicit conversion of operands to other types can limit the necessity for some operator overloading. Operators are typically overloaded to use the containing type as an *lhs* or *rhs*.

In the following code, the *operator+* is overloaded three times:

```
public static ZClass operator+(ZClass lhs, ZClass rhs) {
    return new ZClass(lhs.fielda+rhs.fielda,
        lhs.fieldb+rhs.fieldb);
}

public static ZClass operator+(ZClass lhs, int rhs) {
    return new ZClass(lhs.fielda+rhs,
        lhs.fieldb+rhs);
}


public static ZClass operator+(int lhs, ZClass rhs) {
    return new ZClass(lhs+rhs.fielda,
        lhs+rhs.fieldb);
}
```

All three operator member functions are used in the following code:

```
obj3=obj1+obj2;
obj1=obj1+10;
obj2=20+obj2;
```

Operator overloading is not stipulated in the Common Language Specification (CLS) and therefore not guaranteed in all managed languages. It is good practice to implement a parallel named method for each operator member function. The named method should call the operator member function as demonstrated in the following code:

```
public class ZClass {

    public ZClass(int _fielda, int _fieldb) {
        fielda=_fielda;
```

```
            fieldb=_fieldb;
        }

        public static ZClass operator+(ZClass lhs, ZClass rhs) {
            return new ZClass(lhs.fielda+rhs.fielda,
                lhs.fieldb+rhs.fieldb);
        }

        public ZClass Add(ZClass rhs) {
            return this+rhs;
        }

        public int Total {
            get {
                return fielda+fieldb;
            }
        }
    }

        protected int fielda, fieldb;
}
```

The semantics of overloading certain mathematical and logical operators are unique. Special rules must be followed when overloading these operators in a type.

Increment and Decrement Operators

The *Increment* (++) and *Decrement* (–) operators have special semantics. These are unary operators, where the operand and return type must be the containing class or a derivative. To maintain the underlying behavior, the *Increment* and *Decrement* operator should return a modified instance of the current object, which is the operand. You can (but should not) return an entirely new instance. Remember, overloaded operators should preserve the underlying meaning of the operator. Finally, overloading the *Increment* or *Decrement* operator revises both the prefix and postfix usage of the operator.

Here is sample code showing an overloading of both the *Increment* and *Decrement* operators:

```
public class ZClass {

    public ZClass(int _fielda, int _fieldb) {
        fielda=_fielda;
        fieldb=_fieldb;
    }

    public static ZClass operator++(ZClass curr) {
        ++curr.fielda;
        ++curr.fieldb;
        return curr;
    }


    public static ZClass operator--(ZClass curr) {
        --curr.fielda;
```

```
        --curr.fieldb;
        return curr;
    }

    public int Total {
        get {
            return fielda+fieldb;
        }
    }

    public int fielda, fieldb;
}
```

LeftShift and RightShift Operators

The *LeftShift* and *RightShift* operators normally perform a binary shift. Both are binary operators. When overloading these operators, the first operand must be the same type as the containing class. The second operand must be an *int*, which is the amount of the shift. The return type can be anything except void. The *LeftShift* and *RightShift* operators are not paired operator methods. You can implement them independently of each other. However, I would recommend implementing both because the methods are logically related:

```
using System;

namespace Donis.CSharpBook{
    public class Starter{
        public static void Main(){
            ZClass obj1=new ZClass(5,10);
            ZClass obj2=obj1<<2;
            Console.WriteLine(obj2.Total);
        }
    }

    public class ZClass {

        public ZClass(int _fielda, int _fieldb) {
            fielda=_fielda;
            fieldb=_fieldb;
        }


        public static ZClass operator<<(ZClass curr, int shift) {
            int newa=curr.fielda<<shift;
            int newb=curr.fieldb<<shift;
            return new ZClass(newa, newb);
        }


        public static ZClass operator>>(ZClass curr, int shift) {
            int newa=curr.fielda>>shift;
            int newb=curr.fieldb>>shift;
            return new ZClass(newa, newb);
        }
```

```
                public int Total {
                    get {
                        return fielda+fieldb;
                    }
                }

                public int fielda, fieldb;
        }
}
```

Operator True and Operator False

True and false are logical operators and are used in conditional expressions and sometimes in assignments. They are paired operator methods, which require both functions of the pair to be implemented. If either the *operator true* or *operator false* method is overloaded, both must be implemented. Both operators are unary operators, in which the current object is the operand. The operand must be the containing class type or a derivative, and the return type should be *bool*. Add *operator true* and *operator false* methods to classes that have a false or true representation. This representation is typically interpreted from the state of the object. When an object is used as a Boolean expression, the *operator true* method is called. The *operator false* method is called in other circumstances, such as an *&&* expression. Operator overloading and the *&&* operator are discussed later in this appendix.

This is sample code of an *operator true* and *operator false*. The *operator true* is used in the *Main* method at the *if* statement.

```
using System;

namespace Donis.CSharpBook{
    public class Starter{
        public static void Main(){
            ZClass obj1=new ZClass(5,5);
            if(obj1) {
                Console.WriteLine("obj1 is true");
            }
            else {
                Console.WriteLine("obj1 is false");
            }
        }
    }

    public class ZClass {

        public ZClass(int _fielda, int _fieldb) {
            fielda=_fielda;
            fieldb=_fieldb;
        }

        public static bool operator true(ZClass curr) {
            Console.WriteLine("ZClass.operator true");
            return curr.fielda==curr.fieldb;
        }
```

```
    public static bool operator false(ZClass curr) {

        Console.WriteLine("ZClass.operator false");
        return curr.fielda!=curr.fieldb;
    }

    public int Total {
        get {
            return fielda+fieldb;
        }
    }

    protected int fielda, fieldb;
    }
}
```

Paired Operators

In addition to *operator true* and *operator false*, the relational operators are paired operators. Paired operators enforce a practical guideline—which is that related operators should be overloaded to maintain consistency. For example, because they are logically related, you should overload both the *operator==* and *operator!=* methods. This is the complete list of paired relational operators, which are discussed in the following sections:

- *operator==* and *operator!=*
- *operator<=* and *operator>=*
- *operator<* and *operator>*
- *operator|* and *operator&*

Operator== and Operator!=

The overloaded *operator==* method should delegate to the *Equals* method, which ensures that the *operator==* and the *Equals* method exhibit consistent behavior. If not, the definition of equality for an instance will vary based on circumstances, which would be minimally confusing. The *operator==* and *operator!=* methods are paired methods. When overloading these operators, you must also implement the *Equals* method in the same class. The *Equals* method is inherited from *System.Object*:

```
using System;

namespace Donis.CSharpBook{
    public class Starter{
        public static void Main(){
            ZClass obj1=new ZClass(5,10);
            ZClass obj2=new ZClass(5,10);
            ZClass obj3=new ZClass(5,15);
            if(obj1==obj2) {
                Console.WriteLine("obj1 and obj2 are equal.");
            }
```

```
        else {
            Console.WriteLine("obj1 and obj2 are not equal.");
        }
        if(obj1==obj3) {
            Console.WriteLine("obj1 and obj3 are equal.");
        }
        else {
            Console.WriteLine("obj1 and obj3 are not equal.");
        }
    }
}

public class ZClass {

    public ZClass(int _fielda, int _fieldb) {
        fielda=_fielda;
        fieldb=_fieldb;
    }

    public static ZClass operator+(ZClass lhs, ZClass rhs) {
        return new ZClass(lhs.fielda+rhs.fielda,
            lhs.fieldb+rhs.fieldb);
    }

    public static bool operator==(ZClass lhs, ZClass rhs) {
        return lhs.Equals(rhs);
    }

    public static bool operator!=(ZClass lhs, ZClass rhs) {
        return !lhs.Equals(rhs);
    }

    public override bool Equals(object o) {
        return this.GetHashCode()==o.GetHashCode();
    }

    public override int GetHashCode(){
        return fielda+fieldb;
    }

    public int Total {
        get {
            return fielda+fieldb;
        }
    }

    protected int fielda, fieldb;
    }
}
```

Operator|| and Operator&&

Actually, *operator||* and *operator&&* cannot be overloaded directly. These are the logical *and* and *or* operators, respectively. Instead, *operator|*, *operator&*, *operator true*, and *operator false* combine to overload *operator||* and *operator&&*. The bitwise operators are normally *operator|* and *operator&*. If a user-defined type is used in an *&&* or *||* expression, the four mentioned operator functions must be overloaded in that type.

Because of short-circuiting, an *&&* or *||* expression is sometimes partially evaluated. If the *lhs* of an *&&* expression is false, the entire expression is false. This means the *rhs* can be ignored. For *||* expressions, the entire expression is true if the *lhs* is true. When that occurs, the *rhs* of the *||* expression can be ignored. Potential short-circuiting complicates the overloading of the *&&* and *||* operators. Several steps are required to evaluate the *&&* or *||* operators for a user-defined type.

Following are the steps for evaluating the *&&* operator, where the expression is *lhs && rhs*. (Let us assume that *lhs* and *rhs* are the same type as the containing class.)

1. The overloaded operator false method is called. If the method returns *true*, the expression short-circuits because the first part of the *&&* expression is confirmed to be false.

2. If short-circuiting, the expression evaluates to *type.operator true(lhs)*.

3. If the expression does not short-circuit, the overloaded *operator&* is called: *result=type.operator&(lhs, rhs)*.

4. Finally, *type.operator true(result)* is called. This method returns the final result of the *lhs && rhs* expression when short-circuiting does not occur.

Following are the steps for evaluating the *||* operator, where the expression is *lhs || rhs*:

1. The overloaded *operator true* method is called. If the method returns *true*, the expression short-circuits. The expression short-circuits because the first part of the *||* expression is confirmed to be true.

2. If short-circuiting, the expression evaluates to *type.operator true(lhs)*.

3. If the expression does not short-circuit, the overloaded operator *|* is called: *result=type.operator|(lhs, rhs)*.

4. Finally, *type.operator true(result)* is called. This method returns the final result of the *lhs || rhs* expression when short-circuiting does not occur.

For the *operator&* and *operator|* methods, the operand and return must be the same type.

In the following code, *ZClass* is overloaded to support the *&&* and *||* expression. All four required methods are implemented: *operator true*, *operator false*, *operator&*, and *operator|*. The overloaded methods of the *ZClass* type display messages for auditing program flow. In *Main*, *ZClass* instances are used in a *||* expression. Because the *operator true* is hard-coded to return *false*, the expression will never short-circuit.

```
using System;

namespace Donis.CSharpBook{
    public class Starter{
```

```
public static void Main(){
    ZClass obj1=new ZClass(5,10);
    obj1.name="obj1";
    ZClass obj2=new ZClass(15,20);
    obj2.name="obj2";
    if(obj1 || obj2) {
        Console.WriteLine("expression evaluated to true");
    }
}

class ZClass {

    public ZClass(int _fielda, int _fieldb) {
        fielda=_fielda;
        fieldb=_fieldb;
    }

    public static ZClass operator &(ZClass obj1,ZClass obj2) {
        Console.WriteLine("operator &");
        ZClass result= new ZClass(obj1.fielda&obj2.fielda,
                                  obj1.fieldb&obj2.fieldb);
        result.name="result";
        return result;
    }

    public static ZClass operator |(ZClass obj1,ZClass obj2) {
        Console.WriteLine("operator |");
        ZClass result= new ZClass(obj1.fielda|obj2.fielda,
                                  obj1.fieldb|obj2.fieldb);
        result.name="result";
        return result;
    }

    public static bool operator true(ZClass obj) {
        Console.WriteLine("operator true({0})",obj.name);
        return false;
    }

    public static bool operator false(ZClass obj) {
        Console.WriteLine("operator false({0})",obj.name);
        return true;
    }

    public int Total {
        get {
            return fielda+fieldb;
        }
    }

    public string name;
    protected int fielda, fieldb;
    }
  }
}
```

Conversion Operators

Implementing conversion operators facilitates the implicit or explicit casting of user-defined types to built-in types or even other user-defined types. Developers implement a conversion operator to explain to the compiler how to interpret a user-defined type in the context of another type. Like mathematical and logical operators, the primary reason for implementing conversion operators is convenience. It is never required. You could as easily expose *ToType* methods, such as *ToInt*, *ToFloat*, or *ToDecimal*.

An implicit cast is considered a secure cast, whereas explicit casting is required for casting that is not secure. For built-in types, a secure cast is available when there is no potential loss of precision or accuracy. When there is potential loss of precision or accuracy, an explicit cast is required. For example, an *int* can be assigned to long implicitly. Eight bytes are reserved for a long value and four bytes are reserved for an *int* value. The *int* value will be promoted to a long. The promotion occurs silently—no warning or notice. The reverse, in which a long is assigned to an *int*, requires an explicit cast. This is exhibited in the following code:

```
int a=5;
long b=10;
b=a;        // implicit cast
a=(int) b;  // explicit cast
```

C# does not support conversion constructors. A conversion constructor is a one-argument constructor used to create an instance of a type from a different type. Conversion constructors are supported in C++ but are not allowed in C#. Conversion constructors were convenient— too convenient. Conversion constructors were sometimes called transparently when a compiler error for mismatched types was more appropriate.

You cannot overload the cast operator directly. Instead, overload the cast operator selectively with conversion operator methods. This is the syntax of a conversion operator:

public static implicit operator *returntype*(*classtype* obj)

public static explicit operator *returntype*(*type* obj)

For the conversion operator syntax, there are many similarities when compared with mathematical and relational operators. Conversion operators must be public and static. Other modifiers, such as virtual and sealed, are syntax errors. Conversion operators that are implicit do not require casting, whereas explicit conversion operators require casting for use. I recommend explicit casting in all circumstances. Implicit casting allows the conversion function to be called transparently and sometimes inadvertently, which may cause undetected side effects. With explicit casting, developers affirmatively state their intentions through casting. Either the return or operand of the conversion operator must be the same as the containing type. If converting to the containing type, the return type should be the containing class. Notice that the return type is after the operator keyword, not before. When converting from the containing type, the operand should be the same type as the containing class.

Here is sample code of implicit and explicit conversion methods. The *ZClass* has two conversion operators. The first conversion operator converts *ZClass* to an int. The second conversion operator converts a *YClass* to a *ZClass*.

```csharp
using System;

namespace Donis.CSharpBook{
    public class Starter{
        public static void Main(){
            ZClass obj1=new ZClass(5,10);
            int ival=obj1;
            YClass obj2=new YClass(5);
            // ZClass obj3=obj2;  [ error ]
            ZClass obj3=(ZClass) obj2;
        }
    }

    public class ZClass {

        public ZClass(int _fielda, int _fieldb) {
            fielda=_fielda;
            fieldb=_fieldb;
        }

        public static implicit operator int(ZClass curr) {
            return curr.fielda+curr.fieldb;
        }

        public static explicit operator ZClass(YClass curr) {
            return new ZClass(curr.field/2, curr.field/2);
        }

        public int fielda, fieldb;
    }

    public class YClass {

        public YClass(int _field) {
            propField=_field;
        }

        private int propField;
        public int field {
            get {
                return propField;
            }
            set {
                propField=value;
            }
        }
    }

}
```

Conversion operators are often overloaded to provide the illusion of a user-defined type, which can support a variety of casts. In the following code, the conversion operator is over-loaded several times to allow the conversion of *ZClass* instances to a variety of types:

```
using System;

namespace Donis.CSharpBook{

    public class ZClass {

        public ZClass(int _fielda, int _fieldb) {
            fielda=_fielda;
            fieldb=_fieldb;
        }

        public static explicit operator int(ZClass curr) {
            return curr.fielda+curr.fieldb;
        }

        public static explicit operator float(ZClass curr) {
            return (float) (curr.fielda+curr.fieldb);

        }

        public static explicit operator short(ZClass curr) {
            return (short) (curr.fielda+curr.fieldb);

        }

        // and so on

        public int fielda, fieldb;
    }
}
```

Operator String

The *operator string* operator is a special conversion operator that converts a user-defined type to a string. This appears to overlap with the *ToString* method, which is inherited from *System.Object*. Actually, every type is also automatically provided an operator string method, which simply calls the polymorphic *ToString* method. Look at the following code. If a class has both a *ToString* and operator string method, which method is called in the *Console.WriteLine*?

```
using System;

namespace Donis.CSharpBook{
    public class Starter{
        public static void Main(){
            ZClass obj=new ZClass();
            Console.WriteLine(obj);
        }
    }
}
```

```
public class ZClass {

    public static implicit operator string(ZClass curr) {
        return "Zlass.operator string";
    }

    public override string ToString() {
        return "ZClass.ToString";
    }

}
}
```

The preceding program displays *ZClass.operator string*. The *operator string* is called for the *Console.WriteLine* operand. Why? Unlike the default *operator string*, the custom *operator string* does not call *ToString*. In most circumstances, calling *ToString* in the *operator string* is the best practice, which eliminates the necessity of implementing a custom *operator string*. The default operator string already has this behavior. You simply override the *ToString* method with the proper string representation of the type. Inconsistencies and confusion can occur when the operator string and *ToString* have disparate implementations.

Practical Example

Until now, simple examples have been provided to demonstrate operator overloading and conversion operators. The following code contains a more practical example. Summation notation iterates and totals an expression in a specified range. Figure A-1 offers three examples of summation notation.

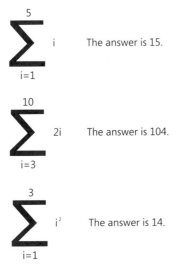

$\sum_{i=1}^{5} i$ The answer is 15.

$\sum_{i=3}^{10} 2i$ The answer is 104.

$\sum_{i=1}^{3} i^2$ The answer is 14.

Figure A-1   Examples of summation notation

Summation is not a predefined type in C#. The following class defines the *Summation* type. It contains several methods:

- The *Summation* class has three constructors. The two- and three-argument constructors delegate to the four-argument constructor and set unspecified parameters a default value.

- The *Calculate* method calculates the result of the summation.

- The class has two *operator+* methods, which allow instances of the class to be either *lhs* or *rhs* in the binary expression. Each *operator+* method extends the iteration by adding to the stop value of the summation. A new instance with an updated number of iterations is returned.

- The *operator++* method extends the number of iterations by one. The current object is then returned.

- The class has an operator *int* conversion constructor. This method converts a *Summation* object into an *int* value, which is the result of the operation.

- There are two string functions: *ToString* returns the result of the operation; *ToNotation-String* displays summation notation and shows the parameters of the operation.

Here is the code for the class:

```
public class Summation {

    public Summation(int _start, int _stop) :
            this(_start, _stop, 1, 1) {
    }

    public Summation(int _start, int _stop,
        int _product) :
            this(_start, _stop, _product, 1) {
    }

    public Summation(int _start, int _stop,
        int _product, int _power) {
        start=_start;
        stop=_stop;
        product=_product;
        power=_power;
        Calculate();
    }

    private void Calculate() {
        propResult=0;
        int temp;
        for(int count=start;count <= stop;
                ++count) {
```

```
            temp=(int)Math.Pow(count, power);
            temp=temp*product;
            propResult+=temp;
        }
    }

    public static Summation operator+(Summation sum, int val) {
        return new Summation(sum.start, sum.stop+val,
            sum.product, sum.power);
    }

    public static Summation operator+(int val, Summation sum) {
        return new Summation(sum.start, sum.stop+val,
            sum.product, sum.power);
    }

    public static Summation operator++(Summation sum) {
        ++sum.stop;
        sum.Calculate();
        return sum;
    }

    public static explicit operator int(Summation sum) {
        return sum.propResult;
    }

    private int propResult;
    public int Result {
        get {
            return propResult;
        }
    }

    public override string ToString() {
        return propResult.ToString();
    }

    public string ToNotationString() {
      string line1="\n  "+stop.ToString();
       string line2="\n\neeeee";
       string line4="\nee    "+
            (product==1?"":product.ToString())+"i";
       string line3="\ne"+new string(' ',line4.Length-2);
       line3+=(power==1?"":power.ToString());
       string line5="\ne";
       string line6="\neeeee";
       string line7="\n\n i="+start.ToString();
       return line1+line2+line3+line4+line5+line6+line7;
    }

    private int start;
    private int stop;
    private int product;
    private int power;
}
```

The following code tests the *Summation* type. The ingredients of the summation are read from the command line. In order, provide the start, stop, product, and power for the summation as command-line arguments. The number of iterations is between the start and stop value. In *Main*, the summation notation is displayed followed by the result. The number of iterations is then increased using the *operator++*. The new results are then displayed:

```
public static void Main(string [] argv){
    Summation sum=
        new Summation(int.Parse(argv[0]),
                      int.Parse(argv[1]),
                      int.Parse(argv[2]),
                      int.Parse(argv[3]));
    Console.WriteLine();
    Console.WriteLine(sum.ToNotationString());
    Console.WriteLine("\n[Result = {0}]",
        sum.Result);

    ++sum;
    int isum=(int)sum;
    Console.WriteLine();
    Console.WriteLine(sum.ToNotationString());
    Console.WriteLine("\n\n[Result = {0}]", isum);
}
}
```

Operator Overloading Internals

Internally, Microsoft intermediate language (MSIL) does not understand operator methods. For that reason, the C# compiler converts operator methods into normal functions. Figure A-2 presents a view of the *Summation* class from the previous section. Although there are no operator methods, there are replacement functions such as *op_Addition* and *op_Explicit*.

Figure A-2   View of the Summation class

Table A-1 lists the replacement methods for mathematical and logical operators.

Table A-1   Replacement Methods for Mathematical and Logical Operators

Operator	Replacement Method
operator+	op_Addition
operator-	op_Subtraction
operator*	op_Multiply
operator++	op_Increment
operator--	op_Decrement
operator/	op_Division
operator%	op_Modulus
operator&	op_BitwiseAnd
operator|	op_BitwiseOr
operator^	op_ExclusiveOr
operator false	op_False
operator true	op_True
operator>>	op_RightShift
operator<<	op_LeftShift
operator!	op_LogicalNot
operator~	op_OnesComplement

Table A-2 lists the replacement methods for relational operators.

Table A-2   Replacement Methods for Relational Operators

Operator	Replacement Method
operator>	op_GreaterThan
operator<	op_LessThan
operator>=	op_GreaterThanOrEqual
operator<=	op_LessThanOrEqual
operator==	op_Equality
operator!=	op_Inequality

Conversion operators are implemented as *op_Explicit* and *op_Implicit* methods. The methods are overloaded for every combination of explicit or implicit conversion operator provided in the contained type. The following class has two explicit operators and one implicit conversion operator:

```
public class ZClass{

    public static explicit operator int(ZClass obj) {
        return 0;
    }
```

```
public static explicit operator float(ZClass obj) {
    return (float) 0;

}
public static implicit operator double(ZClass obj) {
    return 0;
}
}
```

Figure A-3 is an internal view of the application. There are two overloaded *op_Explicit* methods and a single *op_Implicit* method.

Figure A-3   View of *ZClass*

Index

Donis Marshall

Donis Marshall is currently one of the few trainers endorsed by Microsoft Global Learning Services to conduct Microsoft technology classes for Microsoft employees. In this capacity, Mr. Marshall travels internationally, delivering dozens of classes to Microsoft developers and engineers in the United States, Europe, and Asia. His repertoire includes classes on Advanced .NET UMD Debugging, Advanced .NET Debugging workshops, .NET Design and Architecture, Visual Basic .NET Programming, .NET Interoperability and Security, .NET Web Services, and ASP.NET. He also teaches .NET classes at Autodesk, NCCI, and NASA.

Donis Marshall is a nationally recognized teacher of computer technology to developers and scientists. As founder and lead instructor for The Training Alliance, he taught advanced technical classes for many Fortune 500 clients. He also managed a staff of technical instructors as Director of Advanced Technical Learning Services at Productivity Point International, a national franchiser of training services.

Mr. Marshall is President of DebugNow (*www.debugnow*). DebugNow offers an assortment of innovative tools for support engineers and developers to debug and monitor Win32 and .NET applications.

As a contractor, Donis Marshall has written thousands of lines of code for various entities.

Donis Marshall recommends

www.debugnow.com

**the portal of choice for debugging Windows applications
with powerful, easy-to-use debugging tools and services**

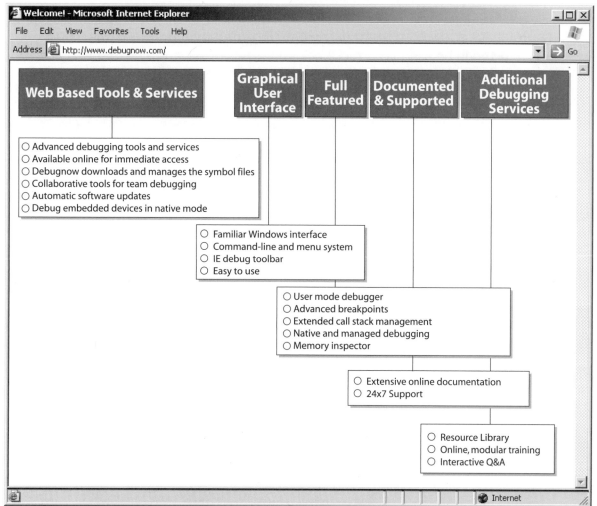

See how **debugnow.com** can increase productivity, improve support services,
and enhance application development in your environment.

Check us out @ www.debugnow.com. Fully available March 2006.

Or register for our mailing list for future announcements.
Contact us at: www.Debugnow.com or customerservice@debugnow.com.

What do you think of this book?
We want to hear from you!

Do you have a few minutes to participate in a brief online survey? Microsoft is interested in hearing your feedback about this publication so that we can continually improve our books and learning resources for you.

To participate in our survey, please visit:

www.microsoft.com/learning/booksurvey

And enter this book's ISBN, 0-7356-2181-0. As a thank-you to survey participants in the United States and Canada, each month we'll randomly select five respondents to win one of five $100 gift certificates from a leading online merchant.* At the conclusion of the survey, you can enter the drawing by providing your e-mail address, which will be used for prize notification *only*.

Thanks in advance for your input. Your opinion counts!

Sincerely,

Microsoft Learning

Learn More. Go Further.